Life Histories of North American
Shore Birds

by Arthur Cleveland Bent

in two parts - Part II

Dover Publications, Inc.,   New York

ADVERTISEMENT

The scientific publications of the National Museum include two series, known, respectively, as *Proceedings* and *Bulletin*.

The *Proceedings*, begun in 1878, is intended primarily as a medium for the publication of original papers, based on the collections of the National Museum, that set forth newly acquired facts in biology, anthropology, and geology, with descriptions of new forms and revisions of limited groups. Copies of each paper, in pamphlet form, are distributed as published to libraries and scientific organizations and to specialists and others interested in the different subjects. The dates at which these separate papers are published are recorded in the table of contents of each of the volumes.

The *Bulletin*, the first of which was issued in 1875, consists of a series of separate publications comprising monographs of large zoological groups and other general systematic treatises (occasionally in several volumes), faunal works, reports of expeditions, catalogues of type-specimens, special collections, and other material of similar nature. The majority of the volumes are octavo in size, but a quarto size has been adopted in a few instances in which large plates were regarded as indispensable. In the *Bulletin* series appear volumes under the heading *Contributions from the United States National Herbarium*, in octavo form, published by the National Museum since 1902, which contain papers relating to the botanical collections of the Museum.

The present work forms No. 146 of the *Bulletin* series.

ALEXANDER WETMORE,

Assistant Secretary, Smithsonian Institution.

WASHINGTON, D. C., *December 11, 1928.*

This new Dover edition, first published in 1962, is an unabridged and unaltered republication of the work first published by the United States Government Printing Office. Part I was originally published in 1927 as Smithsonian Institution United States National Museum *Bulletin 142;* Part II was originally published in 1929 as Smithsonian Institution United States National Museum *Bulletin 146.*

International Standard Book Number: 0-486-20934-2
Library of Congress Catalog Card Number: 62-51562

Manufactured in the United States of America
Dover Publications, Inc.
180 Varick Street
New York, N. Y. 10014

TABLE OF CONTENTS

INTRODUCTION

This is the eighth in a series of bulletins of the United States National Museum on the life histories of North American birds. Previous numbers have been issued as follows:

107. Life Histories of North American Diving Birds, August 1, 1919.

113. Life Histories of North American Gulls and Terns, August 27, 1921.

121. Life Histories of North American Petrels, Pelicans and their Allies, October 19, 1922.

126. Life Histories of North American Wild Fowl, May 25, 1923.

130. Life Histories of North American Wild Fowl, June 27, 1925.

135. Life Histories of North American Marsh Birds, March 11, 1927.

142. Life Histories of North American Shore Birds, December 31, 1927.

The same general plan has been followed, as explained in previous bulletins, and the same sources of information have been utilized. The classification and nomenclature adopted by the American Ornithologists' Union, in its latest check list and its supplements, have been followed, mainly, with such few changes as, in the author's opinion, will be, or should be, made to bring the work up to date and in line with recent advances in the science.

The main ranges are as accurately outlined as limited space will permit; the normal migrations are given in sufficient detail to indicate the usual movements of the species; no attempt has been made to give all the records, for economy in space, and no pretence at complete perfection is claimed. Many published records, often repeated, have been investigated and discarded; many apparently doubtful records have been verified; some published records, impossible to either verify or disprove, have been accepted if the evidence seemed to warrant it.

The egg dates are the condensed results of a mass of records taken from the data in a large number of the best egg collections in the country, as well as from contributed field notes and from a few published sources. They indicate the dates on which eggs have been actually found in various parts of the country, showing the earliest and latest dates and the limits between which half the dates fall, the height of the season.

The plumages are described in only enough detail to enable the reader to trace the sequence of molts and plumages from birth to maturity and to recognize the birds in the different stages and at the different seasons. No attempt has been made to fully describe adult plumages; this has been already well done in the many manuals. The names of colors, when in quotation marks, are taken from Ridgway's Color Standards and Nomenclature (1912) and the terms used to describe the shapes of eggs are taken from his Nomenclature of Colors (1886 edition). The heavy-faced type in the measurements of eggs indicate the four extremes of measurements.

Many of those who contributed material for former volumes have rendered a similar service in this case. In addition to those whose contributions have been acknowledged previously, our thanks are due to the following new contributors: Photographs, notes, or data have been contributed by E. G. Alexander, C. M. Beal, W. W. Bennett, A. D. Boyle, W. J. Brown, M. H. Burroughs, J. J. Carroll, N. W. Cayley, Ralph Chislett, W. M. Congreve, S. J. Darcus, H. G. Deignare, Jonathan Dwight, F. F. Gander, T. S. Gillin, W. E. Glegg, S. P. Gordon, Frank Grasett, R. W. Harding, L. L. Haskin, E. A. Hyer, T. A. James, F. Kermode, H. M. Laing, Carl Lien, G. H. Lings, Julian Lyder, S. H. Lyman, M. J. Magee, Miss M. E. McLellan, F. C. Pellett, R. T. Peterson, H. H. Pittman, C. A. Proctor, J. C. Salyer, A. W. Schorger, Althea R. Sherman, L. W. Smith, E. L. Sumner, jr., Malcolm Taylor, jr., R. M. Thorburn, C. H. Townsend, Josselyn Van Tyne, Stanton Warburton, jr., Alexander Wetmore, F. N. Wilson, L. R. Wolfe.

Receipt of material from over 275 contributors has been acknowledged in previous volumes.

Through the courtesy of the Biological Survey, the services of Frederick C. Lincoln were again secured to compile the distribution paragraphs. With the matchless reference files of the Biological Survey at his disposal and with some advice and help from Dr. Harry C. Oberholser, his many hours of careful and thorough work have produced results far more satisfactory than could have been attained by the author, who claims no credit and assumes no responsibility for this part of the work.

Dr. Charles W. Townsend has contributed the life histories of two species; the Rev. Francis C. R. Jourdain has furnished valuable notes for two, has written nine new life histories and two of his have been transferred from the previous volume; and Dr. Winsor M. Tyler has contributed two life histories. The author is much indebted to Dr. Charles W. Richmond for many hours of careful and sympathetic work in reading the proof and correcting errors in this and all previous volumes; his expert knowledge has been of great value.

As most of the shore birds are known to us mainly, or entirely, as migrants, it has seemed desirable to describe their migrations quite fully. As it is a well-known fact that many, if not all, immature and nonbreeding shore birds remain far south of their breeding ranges all summer, it has not seemed necessary to mention this in each case. Nor did it seem necessary to say that only one brood is raised in a season, as this is a nearly universal rule with all water birds.

The manuscript for this volume was completed in April, 1928. Contributions received since then will be acknowledged later. Only information of great importance could be added. When this volume appears, contributions of photographs or notes relating to the Raptores should be sent to

THE AUTHOR.

LIFE HISTORIES OF NORTH AMERICAN SHORE BIRDS

ORDER LIMICOLAE (PART 2)

By Arthur Cleveland Bent
Of Taunton, Massachusetts

Family SCOLOPACIDAE, Snipes and Sandpipers

TRINGA SOLITARIA SOLITARIA Wilson

SOLITARY SANDPIPER

HABITS

This dainty " woodland tattler " is associated in my mind with some secluded, shady woodland pool in early autumn, where the summer drought has exposed broad muddy shores and where the brightly tinted leaves of the swamp maple float lightly on the still water. Here the solitary wader may be seen, gracefully poised on some fallen log, nodding serenely, or walking gracefully over the mud or in the shallow water. Seldom disturbed by man, it hardly seems to heed his presence; it may raise its wings, displaying their pretty linings, or it may flit lightly away to the other side of the pool, with a few sharp notes of protest and a flash of white in its tail. I have often seen it in other places where one would not expect to find shore birds, such as the muddy banks of a sluggish stream, somewhat polluted with sewage, which flows back of my garden in the center of the city, or some barnyard mud puddle, reeking with the filth of cattle; perhaps it is attracted to such unsavory places by the swarms of flies that it finds there.

Spring.—The solitary sandpiper arrives in the United States during the latter part of March, but it makes slow progress northward, for it does not reach New England until May. We generally see it singly, in pairs, or in small numbers, but according to William Brewster (1925) it sometimes occurs in favorable localities, near Umbagog Lake, Maine, in large numbers; he writes:

According to an entry in my journal I saw them there literally in " swarms " on May 20, 1880, when, as we advanced by way of the river in a boat, they were

1

ceaselessly rising and flitting on ahead, uttering their *peet-weet* calls, and also making a faint yet noticeable rustling sound with their wings. Thus driven they sometimes alighted, one after another, on some muddy point, until as many as seven assembled within the space of a few square feet. Nevertheless, they were for the most part paired, and the mated birds almost invariably kept together, and apart from all the rest when on wing.

The migration in the interior seems to be at least two or three weeks earlier. E. W. Hadeler tells me that in Lake County, Ohio, one is almost sure to find it, on the river where the sewer empties into it, between April 22 and May 18. Many must pass through the inland States in April, for Edward S. Thomas has recorded it in Ohio as early as March 30 and calls the average date of arrival April 15. A. G. Lawrence has recorded it in southern Manitoba as early as April 29 and it reaches its northernmost breeding grounds in Mackenzie and Alaska soon after the middle of May.

Courtship.—Dr. John B. May has sent me the following notes on a courtship display of this species which he saw in New Hampshire:

Paddling down river one day, probably between the 8th and 15th of June, I saw several pairs of solitary and spotted sandpipers where the muddy banks were exposed, near a swamp where bitterns breed. Both species were apparently courting, making considerable noise and showing their white feathers in display. Every little while one of the solitary sandpipers would fly up slowly into the air, only rising a few feet, and rising slowly with rapidly beating or quivering wings, giving a twittering whistle and spreading the tail so that the outer white feathers were very conspicuous. Then it would drop back to the mud again near where it rose. The time taken in rising a few feet would have carried it some distance with its ordinary flight.

Nesting.—The nesting habits of this sandpiper long remained a mystery or were misunderstood. In looking over the literature on the subject I came across no less than seven published records of nests found on the ground and said to be positively identified as this species. These were all published prior to the discovery of the now well-known habit of nesting in the deserted nests of passerine birds. Not a single one of these records seems to be substantiated by an available specimen of the parent bird. The solitary sandpiper may occasionally nest on the ground, but it is yet to be proven.

To Evan Thomson belongs the credit for making the interesting discovery of the tree-nesting habit. This historic incident is described by J. Fletcher Street (1923) as follows:

Mr. Thomson many years ago took up a quarter section of land under the Canadian homestead act, built himself a log cabin at the edge of a muskeg, and commenced the arduous task of clearing the land. Living alone in this wilderness without neighbors and possessing a keen love for nature and a particular interest in the abundant wild life about him, he came to devote his spare moments to the study of birds, counting as his immediate associates such hermit species as the great-horned owl, long-eared owl, saw-whet owl, goshawk, and a large host of water fowl and waders. Seated one day before his cabin he noticed a bird fly to a low tamarack and enter a nest. It was ostensibly one of the waders, and great was his surprise upon examining the nest to find it the structure of a robin. It contained four beautiful eggs, greenish white in ground color and heavily spotted and blotched with reddish brown. Thus, on June 16, 1903, the first authentic eggs of the solitary sandpiper were taken but it was not until a year later that the identity of the bird was definitely established. It was indeed interesting, 20 years later, to be shown the cabin and to view the original tree from which the eggs were collected. Subsequent to the finding of this nest many others have been located, the bird evidencing no particular choice of nest in which to deposit its eggs, the list including those of the bronzed grackle, Brewer's blackbird, cedar waxwing, kingbird, robin, and Canada jay. These have been found at an elevation as low as 4 feet and as high as 40 and in locations contiguous to water and as far away as 200 yards.

Walter Raine (1904), for whom Mr. Thomson was collecting eggs at the time, was the first to publish the important news, but he waited a year until another nest was found and the parent bird shot. The following year, 1904, Mr. Thomson found two more nests and shot the parent bird from the last one. Mr. Raine (1904) then published a full account of all three nests, each of which contained four eggs. The first nest, taken June 16, 1903, was " an old nest of the American robin, built 15 feet up in a tamarack tree, that was growing in the middle of a large muskeg, dotted with tamaracks." The second was found on June 9, 1904, an old " nest of a bronzed grackle, built in a low tree." The third set was taken on June 24, 1904, and the parent bird was shot, as she flew from " the nest of a cedar waxwing, which was built in a small spruce tree growing in a swamp, the nest being about 5 feet from the water." Since then numerous other nests have been found in similar situations. A. D. Henderson (1923) reported a nest found in 1914, about a " dozen feet up in a poplar tree," and on June 7, 1922, a set of eggs was taken for him, with the parent, by a young friend:

The nest was in a white birch tree, growing at the edge of the timber, on the shore of a small lake, and about 150 yards from his home. A brood of young robins had been raised in it last season, he told me. It was about 18 feet from the ground and a typical robin's nest, of grass and mud. The inside lining of grass was gone and the eggs lay in the bare mud cup, no material being added by the sandpiper, which I identified as the eastern form of the bird.

Mr. Henderson and Richard C. Harlow took a set of four fresh eggs on May 30, 1923, near Belvedere, Alberta, from an old robin's nest 10 feet up in a scrubby spruce, 30 feet high, on the muskeg border of a swampy lake. A nest found by Messrs. Street (1923) and Stuart, near Red Lodge, Alberta, on May 29, 1923, was also an old robin's nest only 4 feet from the ground in an 8-foot spruce, in a muskeg surrounded by spruces and tamaracks.

Mr. Henderson tells me that he thinks he now understands the nesting habits of this species more thoroughly, for he has found five sets of eggs this season, 1927. He says:

The principal breeding place seems to be around small lakes or ponds in muskegs; and the bird they are chiefly associated with is the rusty blackbird, which also breeds among the same surroundings, and whose nests are as suitable for the solitary sandpiper as are those of the robin. A few breed around lakes and sloughs, away from the muskegs, but the main body is in the muskeg country associated with the rusty blackbird.

Eggs.—The solitary sandpiper lays almost invariably four eggs; I believe there is only one set of five recorded. They are ovate pyriform in shape, with a slight gloss, and the shell is very fragile. There are two distinct types of ground color, green and buff. These two types are well illustrated by the Rev. F. C. R. Jourdain (1907) in an excellent colored plate. In the green type the ground colors vary from " pale glaucous green," or " pale turtle green," to greenish white; and in the buff type, from "cream buff" to "cartridge buff." They are rather thickly spotted and blotched with irregular markings, usually more thickly about the larger end, where the spots are sometimes confluent. The underlying spots and blotches in various shades of "purple drab" and "heliotrope gray" are often quite conspicuous. Over these the eggs are boldly marked with dark rich browns, "claret brown," "liver brown," "bay" and "chocolate," or even darker colors where the pigment is thickest. One beautiful egg, figured by Mr. Jourdain (1907), has a "pale glaucous green" ground color, with only two blotches of very dark brown near the larger end, heavily splashed elsewhere with "pallid purple drab," and sparingly peppered with light brown. The measurements of 68 eggs average 36 by 25.5 millimeters; the eggs showing the four extremes measure **38.5** by **27**, **33.7** by 23.8 and 36.1 by **23.6** millimeters.

Plumages.—I have never seen this species in natal down, but Ora W. Knight (1908) says that " the downy young are a general grayish buff above with darker suffusions on the back; a darker line through each eye from bill to nape; darkish crown line; below white with slight dusky suffusion on flanks."

Young birds in juvenal plumage are grayish brown above, lighter and more olivaceous than in adults, and thickly spotted with white or buffy white; the sides of the head and neck are grayish, indistinctly streaked with dusky on the neck. A partial postjuvenal molt occurs in the fall producing a first winter plumage, in which young birds may be distinguished by retained juvenal wing coverts. Young birds are also more profusely spotted on the upper parts and less distinctly streaked on the neck and breast than adults. At the first prenuptial molt, the following spring, the young bird becomes practically adult.

Adults have a partial prenuptial molt, between February and May, involving the body plumage, the tail and some scapulars, wing coverts, and tertials. The complete postnuptial molt begins in July with the change of the body plumage and may last through September, but the primaries are not molted until the winter months, December to February. The winter plumage is similar to the nuptial, but the upper parts are grayer and less distinctly spotted; the neck and chest are only very indistinctly streaked with grayish.

Food.—Dr. Elliott Coues (1874) has described the feeding habits of solitary sandpipers so well that I can not do better than to quote his words, as follows:

They differ from most of their relatives in their choice of feeding grounds or of places where they usually alight to rest while migrating; a difference accompanied, I suppose, by a corresponding modification in diet. Their favorite resorts are the margins of small, stagnant pools, fringed with rank grass and weeds; the miry, tide-water ditches that intersect marshes; and the soft, oozy depressions in low meadows and water savannas. They frequent also the interior of woods not too thick and collect there about the rain puddles, the water of which is delayed in sinking by the matted layer of decaying leaves that covers the ground. After heavy rains I have seen them running about like grass plovers on open, level commons, covered only with short turf. They also have a fancy, shared by few birds except the titlarks, for the pools of liquid manure usually found in some out of the way place upon the thrifty farmer's premises. They find abundant food in all these places, aquatic insects of all sorts, and especially their curious larvae, worms, grubs, and perhaps the smallest sorts of molluscs; with all these they also take into their gizzards a quantity of sand and gravel, to help along the grinding process. With food to be had in such plenty with little labor the birds become, particularly in the fall, extremely fat.

Edward H. Forbush (1912) says:

In the fall, on its return from the north, it has a habit of wading into the water in stagnant ditches or ponds, where it advances one foot at a time, and by rapidly moving the forward foot stirs up the vegetation at the bottom ever so slightly. This motion is so swift and delicate that the leg seems to be merely trembling, as if the bird were chilled by contact with the water, but it is done with intent to disturb insects among the algae at the bottom without roiling the water, and the eager bird, leaning forward, plunges in its bill and head, sometimes to the eyes, and catches the alarmed water insects as they dart away. I have watched this carefully with a glass while lying in the grass only 10 or 12 feet from the bird. It is easy by stirring the bottom slightly with a stick to cause a similar movement of the water insects, but I never could agitate it so delicately as to avoid clouding the water with sediment from the bottom.

Giraud (1844) says that " on the wing it is very active, and is sometimes seen darting after winged insects, which it is expert in catching." Other observers have noted in its food various insects and their larvae, dragon-fly nymphs, water-scavenger beetles, water boatmen, grasshoppers, caterpillars, spiders, worms, small crustaceans, and small frogs.

Behavior.—The solitary sandpiper is always light, graceful, and dainty in all its movements. In spite of the unsavory places in which it often feeds, its trim figure is always neat and clean. In flight it is light and airy as it flits away for a short distance, only to alight again and lift its prettily lined wings high above its back before folding them. It flies higher than the spotted sandpiper and more swiftly, often in a zigzag manner, a trick probably learned by dodging branches in the woods, and the wings are raised well above the body on the upward stroke.

Walter H. Rich (1907) says:

There is scarcely another bird which flies with so little apparent effort. His strokes are slow and regular, a short sailing between each motion, but he moves very fast. Let him be alarmed and he will quicken his speed until he seems only a black streak in the air, and as he rises to top the surrounding trees it needs good and quick work with the gun to stop him.

It frequently indulges in a peculiar tilting and nodding habit, similar to that of the spotted sandpiper, but it is more deliberate and not so pronounced; it seems to be more of a bow than a tip-up more like the bobbing of the yellowlegs. It moves about rather sluggishly, wading in shallow water or even standing motionless, where its colors blend into its dark background and make it difficult to see. If it wades beyond its depth, it swims readily and can even dive to escape its enemies. John T. Nichols says in his notes:

In feeding it frequently lowers the head with a drilling motion, especially when immersing its bill in the water, apparently probing in the mud at such times, whereas as a rule our tattlers feed by snatching. It frequently stops to scratch its head with one foot. When bathing it ducks and splashes and sits in the water soaking, and at the conclusion of the bath, trips out onto the mud, raises the wings once or twice, and preens itself thoroughly. I have seen a solitary, alighted in a pool on the marsh, preening its feathers without dipping its bill in the water, and am not aware whether it has this bill-dipping habit common with some of its relatives.

Harrison F. Lewis has sent me the following notes on the rather peculiar behavior of a solitary sandpiper which he watched for some time:

The sandpiper, which was well aware that I was watching it, stepped slowly out onto the open surface of the mud of the bog, and, standing there with its left side toward me, repeated several times the following curious actions. It spread its wings about halfway, holding them stiffly in the plane of its back, neither raised nor lowered, so that the dark markings on its axillards were slightly visible. At the same time it drew its head as far backward and its tail as far forward over its back as possible, and slowly lowered its breast until it almost seemed to touch the mud. After remaining rigid in this position for 10 to 15 seconds, it would suddenly relax and become its normal self, only to repeat the entire procedure almost immediately. I could think of no purpose for these actions, unless they were an attempt at concealment by making the bird's outlines and colors as unlike as possible to those normally to be expected in a sandpiper. Although it did not conceal itself from me by this means, it made itself appear extremely unlike a bird.

Solitary sandpipers are usually very tame and unsuspicious, often to the verge of stupidity, as the following incident, related by Doctor Coues (1874) well illustrates:

Once coming up to a fence that went past a little pool, and peeping through the slats, I saw eight tattlers of this species wading about in the shallow water, searching for food. I pulled trigger on one; the others set up a simultaneous outcry, and I expected them, of course, to fly off, but they presently quieted down and began feeding again. Without moving from my place, I fired three times more, killing a single bird at each discharge; still no effect upon the survivors, except as before. Then I climbed over the fence, and stood in full view of the four remaining birds; they merely flapped to the further side of the pool, and stood still looking at me, nodding away, as if agreed that the whole thing was very singular. I stood and deliberately loaded and fired three times more, taking one bird each time; and it was only as I was ramming another charge, that the sole surviving bird concluded to make off, which he did, I will add in justice to his wits, in a great hurry.

Mr. Brewster (1925) says:

Not less confiding than sluggish, they will usually allow a man to approach in the open to within less than a dozen yards, and sometimes he may almost lay his hands on young and inexperienced birds, while several of these may continue to gaze at him with obviously serene unconcern immediately after he has discharged his gun directly over their heads. There are times, however, especially in calm weather, when the report of a gun, or the sound of one's paddle striking against the side of a boat, will instantly startle all the solitary sandpipers within 20 rods, causing them to rise on wing with loud outcries, and to fly off singly, in various directions, to more or less distant places. In summer and autumn they invariably act thus independently of one another when flushed, and also when engaged in feeding, although by no means averse to assembling rather numerously where food is especially plentiful or easily obtained.

Voice.—Mr. Nichols has described this very satisfactorily, in his notes, as follows:

The ordinary notes of the solitary sandpiper are very close to those of the spotted, but probably always differentiable. They are sharper, cleaner cut, less variable. The full-flight note is a sharp piping *peep weep weep*, more often three than two syllabled when a bird is definitely leaving a locality, or by wandering birds which ordinarily fly high. In birds flushed on, or making longer or shorter flights to different parts of the same marsh where they were living, the same note was usually double *peep weep*, rarely single.

A quite dissimilar call, less frequently heard, is a fine *pit pit pit*, or *chi tit*. This may have no significance other than being a reduction of the preceding, when the bird is less definitely on the wing, but seems to depend on their being another individual fairly close by. There is likely homology between it and the short flocking call of the lesser yellowlegs, and if correctly determined, a certain analogy thereto is also established, perhaps as much as possible with this non-social species. Of similar quality was a peculiar *kikikiki* from one of two birds in company which came to decoys nicely, as they went on past my rig without alighting.

A third kind of note, isolated *pips*, suggesting the call of the water thrush, is expressive of excitement when a bird is on the ground, as when just alighted.

Field marks.—The field characters are also well described by Mr. Nichols, as follows:

In flight the under surface of the solitary sandpiper's wings appears blackish. Birds on the ground not infrequently raise the wings over the back, displaying this mark to advantage. Its tail, spread when about to alight, appears white with a contrasting dark center. When traveling in the air its flight is either swift and darting or else resembles that of a yellowlegs, a little jerkier. When about to alight it usually drops down abruptly, much as the Wilson's snipe does; and when flying only a few yards it has a peculiar jerky flight with wings partially spread. On the ground it looks much like a yellowlegs, but is darker, smaller, and stands relatively lower. Its legs are olive green; very rarely an individual in spring has quite yellow legs.

Fall.—The fall migration of the solitary sandpiper is a general southward movement all across the continent, performed in a leisurely manner. The earliest birds, probably adults, reach New England in July; and late birds, probably young, linger through October. Mr. Brewster (1925) says:

On August 2, 1873, I saw fully 100 along the Androscoggin River between the lake and Errol Dam, and almost as many more, a few hours later, while going up the Magalloway River some 7 or 8 miles. At that date in almost any year there is, throughout the whole Umbagog region, almost no muddy shore of pond, lake, river, lagoon, or brook, whether open to the sun or densely shaded by overhanging foliage, which is not frequented by one or more solitary sandpipers. Hence we may safely assume that in the region at large they are regularly present in far greater numbers during August than at any other time of year.

When with us in the fall they are more likely to be seen on open meadows or salt marshes than they are in the spring, often in company with lesser yellowlegs. Mr. Nichols writes to me:

In the first half of August, 1919, this species was unusually plentiful, living on the bay marsh at Mastic, Long Island, with maximum numbers August 9 to 10. The birds frequented the larger bits of flooded dead marsh that yellowlegs love and were also found in smaller, less open, pools more overshadowed by grass. On August 16 and 17 two birds were also repeatedly found feeding on patches of weed matted at the surface of an adjacent creek, exceedingly tame. The presence of these solitary sandpipers on a coastal marsh may have been due to conditions of high-water level prevailing at the time, flooding the muddy borders of inland pools where they are ordinarily to be looked for.

Capt. Savile G. Reid (1884) says that in Bermuda "they generally come with the other species in August. They soon betake themselves to the wooded swamps, where they may be found singly or in pairs throughout the autumn."

On the Pacific coast both races of the solitary sandpiper occur regularly on the fall migration, but the western race is undoubtedly much commoner and is supposed by some to be the only race found west of the Rocky Mountains. The migration occurs mainly in August and early September. J. A. Munro tells me that he gets both forms regularly at Okanagan Landing, British Columbia.

Winter.—A few birds may spend the winter in the West Indies, but the main winter home of the species is in South America. The distribution of the two forms in winter is not well understood and probably both races are more or less mixed. W. H. Hudson (1920) writes:

I was once pleased and much amused to discover in a small, sequestered pool in a wood, well sheltered from sight by trees and aquatic plants, a solitary sandpiper living in company with a blue bittern. The bittern patiently watched for small fishes and when not fishing dozed on a low branch overhanging the water, while its companion ran briskly along the margin snatching up minute insects from the water. When disturbed they rose together, the bittern with its harsh, grating scream, the sandpiper daintily piping its fine, bright notes— a wonderful contrast! Every time I visited the pool afterwards I found these two hermits, one so sedate in manner the other so lively, living peacefully together.

DISTRIBUTION

Range.—North America chiefly east of the Rocky Mountains to South America.

Breeding range.—The only unquestioned eggs of the solitary sandpiper that have been collected have come from Alberta where it is known to breed from the northern part south as far as Stony Plain and Red Lodge. A pair of adult birds with young also were collected in 1921, 30 miles below Fort Simpson, Mackenzie (Williams, 1922), while the same observer found them common in the vicinity of Fort Norman, Mackenzie, as late as August 14.

It has been reported breeding as far south as Iowa (Keokuk and Winneshiek Counties); Ohio (Columbus); and Pennsylvania (Pocono Mountain and Beaver); and east to New Hampshire (Isle of Shoals, Franconia, and Appledore; Maine (Penobscot and Aroostook Counties); and Quebec (Lake Mistassinni and Godbout). The circumstances attendant upon each of these and intermediate cases are such as to cause doubts concerning their authenticity, although it seems probable that the species did (and possibly still does) breed somewhere in eastern North America.

Winter range.—The solitary sandpipers wintering in South America have been determined subspecifically only on a few occasions, so it should be understood that the following outline includes both *solitaria* and *cinnamomea*. Specimens collected in Colombia by Chapman and Todd all prove to be *solitaria*, while Chapman obtained both races in Ecuador.

The winter range of the species extends north to Vera Cruz (Playa Vicente); rarely Florida (probably Pensacola, probably

Waukeenah, Sevenoaks, and Safety Harbor); rarely Georgia (Chatham County); probably the Bahama Islands (Inagua); Jamaica; and Porto Rico. East to Porto Rico; eastern Venezuela (mouth of the Orinoco River); British Guiana (Bartica); Dutch Guiana (Surinam and Maroni River); French Guiana (Cayenne); Brazil (Mixiana, Para, Chapada, Urucuia, and Pitanguy); Paraguay (Colonia Risso); Uruguay (Rocha, Montevideo, and Colonia); and Argentina (Buenos Aires and Azul). South to Argentina (Azul and Cordoba). West to Argentina (Cordoba, Tucuman, Salta, and Oran); Bolivia (Caiza); Peru (Chorillos, Cajabamba, and Tumbez); Ecuador (Guayaquil and Quito); Colombia (Cali, Novita, Medellin, Puerto Berrio, and Santa Marta); Costa Rica (San Jose); Guatemala (Los Amates and Duenas); Yucatan (Tabi); and Vera Cruz (Playa Vicente).[1]

Spring migration.—Early dates of arrival in the spring migration are: South Carolina, Charleston, March 27, and Aiken, March 30; North Carolina, Raleigh, April 4, and Weaverville, April 9; District of Columbia, Washington, March 30; Pennsylvania, State College, April 14, Sewickley, April 15, and Doylestown, April 16; New Jersey, Dead River, April 18; New York, York, April 18, Ithaca, April 20, and New York City, April 21; Connecticut, Litchfield, April 27, and New Haven, April 29; Massachusetts, Northampton, April 25, Melrose, April 26, and Fitchburg, April 28; Vermont, Randolph, April 26, Bennington, May 4, and Wells River, May 6; New Hampshire, Manchester, April 26, and Monadnock, May 11; Maine, Orono, May 3, Pittsfield, May 6, and Waterville, May 7; Quebec, Quebec, May 1, and Godbout, May 4; Mississippi, Bay St. Louis, March 17, and Biloxi, March 25; Louisiana, Hester, March 16; Arkansas, Monticello, March 24, and Tillar, March 31; Tennessee, Nashville, April 7; Kentucky, Bowling Green, April 8, and Russellville, April 9; Missouri, Jonesburg, March 19, and Monteer, April 6; Illinois, Rantoul, March 24, Danville, April 2, and Chicago, April 7; Indiana, Frankfort, March 15, Indianapolis, March 17, and Delhi, March 28; Ohio, Oberlin, March 28, Sandusky, March 31, and Scio, April 7; Michigan, Ann Arbor, April 23, Hillsdale, April 24, and Portage Lake, April 30; Ontario, Toronto, March 16, London, April 28, and Ottawa, May 2; Iowa, Hillsboro, April 10, National, April 14, and Sigourney, April 20; Wisconsin, Beloit, April 24, Milwaukee, April 25, and Madison, April 26; Minnesota, Minneapolis, April 17, Hallock, April 21, and Lanesboro, April 24; Texas, Santa Maria, March 3, Brownsville, March 17, Texas City, March 22, and Boerne, March 25; Kansas, Wichita, March 29, Emporia, April 10, and Independence, April 16; Nebraska, Neligh, April 20, Red Cloud,

---

[1] The migration dates here given probably include, in many cases, observations and records for both *solitaria* and *cinnamomea.*

April 25, and Valentine, April 27; South Dakota, Forestburg, April 16, and Huron, May 3; North Dakota, Charlson, April 27, and Bismarck, April 30; Manitoba, Aweme, April 29; Saskatchewan, Wiseton, May 13, and Osler, May 19; and Alberta, Alliance, May 2, Flagstaff, May 4, and Oonoway, May 5.

Late dates of spring departure are Colombia, La Manuelita, April 11, and eastern Santa Marta region, April 18; Costa Rica, San Jose, April 27; Yucatan, Rio Lagartoo, April 13; West Indies, San Domingo, April 27; Cuba, Isle of Pines, May 18; Bahama Islands, Nassau, May 10; Florida, St. Marks, May 10, and Pensacola, May 30; Alabama, Bayou Labatre, May 20, and Autaugaville, May 23; Georgia, Macon, May 10, and Savannah, May 17; South Carolina, Aiken, May 10, Frogmore, May 19, and Mount Pleasant, May 27; North Carolina, Weaverville, May 20, and Raleigh, May 28; District of Columbia, Washington, May 21; Maryland, Sandy Springs, May 22, and Cumberland, May 23; New Jersey, Camden, May 25, Morristown, June 7, and Bernardsville, June 11; New York, Rhinebeck, May 26, Cincinnatus, May 31, and Orient Point, June 6; Connecticut, Norwalk, May 27, and Litchfield, May 31; Rhode Island, Providence, June 3; Massachusetts, Worcester, May 30, Melrose, June 1, and New Boston, June 10; Louisiana, New Orleans, May 6, and Bains, May 12; Mississippi, Ellisville, May 17; Tennessee, Nashville, May 27, and Knoxville, June 12; Kentucky, Bowling Green, May 22; Missouri, St. Louis, May 16, and Monteer, May 20; Illinois, Chicago, May 26, Joliet, May 28, and Rantoul, May 29; Indiana, Goshen, May 24, and Holland, May 30; Ohio, Columbus, June 1, Oberlin, May 28, and Huron, May 29; Michigan, Laurium, May 26, and Detroit, May 30; Ontario, Port Perry, May 27, Toronto, June 3, and Madoc, June 7; Iowa, Sioux City, May 26, Emmetsburg, May 29, and Sioux City, May 30; Wisconsin, Madison, May 27, and La Crosse, May 29; Minnesota, Waseca, May 22, Hallock, May 25, and Minneapolis, May 31; Texas, Gainesville, May 15, Kerrville, May 20, and Hidalgo, May 23; Kansas, Lawrence, May 21, and Topeka, May 22; Nebraska, Valentine, May 20, and Lincoln, May 22; South Dakota, Huron, May 21, Vermilion, May 27, and Forestburg, May 30; North Dakota, Charlson, May 25; Manitoba, Aweme, May 26, Shell River, May 29, and Shoal Lake, June 1; and Saskatchewan, Prince Albert, June 5, and Kutanajan Lake, June 15.

Fall migration.—Early dates of arrival in the full migration are: Sashatchewan, Maple Creek, July 6; Manitoba, Margaret, July 8, and Oak Lake, July 19; South Dakota, Sioux Falls, July 1, and Forestburg, July 2; Nebraska, Valentine, July 3; Kansas, Little Blue River, July 22; Texas, Gurley, July 15, Kerrville, July 20, Brownsville, August 2; Minnesota, St. Vincent, July 2, Lanesboro,

July 4, and Minneapolis, July 15; Wisconsin, Shiocton, June 30, North Freedom, July 14, and Ladysmith, July 16; Iowa, Marshalltown, July 8, Sioux City, July 12, and Hillsboro, July 18; Ontario, Toronto, July 10, and Port Dover, July 13; Michigan, Detroit, July 7, and Charity Island, July 10; Ohio, Columbus, July 3, Wooster, July 8, and Painesville, July 20; Indiana, Sedan, July 15; Illinois, Chicago, July 3, Glen Ellyn, July 16, and Port Byron, July 21; Missouri, Monteer, July 29; Kentucky, Bowling Green, July 22; Mississippi, Biloxi, July 12, and Bay St. Louis, July 16; Louisiana, New Orleans, July 9; Massachusetts, Becket, July 8, Harvard, July 12, and Lynn, July 17; Rhode Island, Newport, July 4, and Providence, July 11; Connecticut, East Hartford, July 14, and Milford, July 28; New York, Camp Upton, July 8, Rochester, July 12, and Poland, July 15; Maryland, Calverton, July 14, and Cambridge, July 19; District of Columbia, Washington, July 15; North Carolina, Raleigh, July 14; South Carolina, Frogmore, July 24, and Charleston, July 26; Alabama, Stevenson, July 15, and Leighton, July 17; Florida, Pensacola, July 12, Bradenton, July 12, St. Marks, July 28, and Key West, July 28; Bahama Islands, Fortune Island, August 5; Cuba, Isle of Pines, August 20; Porto Rico, Comerio, July 29; and lesser Antilles, St. Croix, August 5.

Late dates of fall departure are: Keewatin, Echimamish River, September 15; Manitoba, Shoal Lake, September 17, and Aweme, October 5; North Dakota, Charlson, September 18; South Dakota, Forestburg, September 30; Nebraska, Valentine, October 9, Nebraska City, October 10, and Lincoln, October 20; Minnesota, St. Vincent, September 22, Parkers Prairies, September 30, and Lanesboro, October 4; Wisconsin, Elkhorn, October 10, Delavan, October 20, and Racine, October 30; Iowa, Marshalltown, October 5, and Hillsboro, October 20; Ontario, Toronto, October 2, St. Thomas, October 4, and Ottawa, October 31; Michigan, Detroit, October 1; Ohio, Weymouth, October 14, Austinburg, October 28, and Medina, November 1; Indiana, Indianapolis, October 15, Richmond, October 28, and Roanoke, November 15; Illinois, Chicago, October 6, La Grange, October 7, and De Kalb, October 10; Missouri, Jaspar City, October 9, and Independence, October 13; Kentucky, Bowling Green, October 11, Versailles, October 21, and Lexington, October 23; Tennessee, Knoxville, October 11, and Nashville, November 4; Quebec, Montreal, September 27; Maine, Portland, October 6, Pittsfield, October 8, and Hebron, October 20; New Hampshire, Tilton, September 29, Lancaster, October 5, and Errol, October 31; Vermont, Rutland, October 10, and West Barnet, October 17; Massachusetts, Lynn, October 28, and Boston, October 30; Rhode Island, Providence, October 13; New York, Rochester, October 10, Ithaca, October 19, and New York City, October 31; New Jersey, Montclair, October 13, Elizabeth, October 16, and Morristown, November 1; District of Columbia, Washington, October 28; Maryland, Chesapeake Beach, November 2; and South Carolina, Long Island, November 8.

Casual records.—The typical form of the solitary sandpiper has been many times taken in Western States. Among these occurrences are: New Mexico (Guadalupito, August 7, 1903); Wyoming (Arvada, August 19, 1913); Montana (Milk River, July 25, 1874, Miles City, August 14, 1900, Gold Creek, August 20, 1910, and Three Buttes, August 6, 1874). Many specimens also have been taken in British Columbia (Atlin and Okanagan Landing), where it appears to be of regular occurrence, a specimen was taken at Griffin Point, Alaska, June 1, 1914, and one at Fort Chimo, Ungava.

Two were collected on October 12, 1897, on Chatham Island, Galapagos Archipelago; one was taken on the Clyde River, Lanarkshire, Scotland; and another was obtained at Kangek, Greenland, on August 1, 1878.

Egg dates.—Alberta: 29 records, May 24 to June 24; 15 records, May 30 to June 8.

TRINGA SOLITARIA CINNAMOMEA (Brewster)

WESTERN SOLITARY SANDPIPER

HABITS

The western race of this species is larger than the eastern. In adult nuptial plumage the upper parts are much less distinctly spotted with whitish, the white bars on the tail are decidedly narrower and the outer primary is usually finely mottled, with ashy white along the border of its inner web; this last is none too constant a character and is sometimes seen in the eastern bird. The name was derived from the fact that in young birds the light spots on the back, scapulars and wing coverts are brownish cinnamon instead of white or buffy whitish.

Courtship.—The following description of the song flight of this species was originally recorded by Dr. Joseph Grinnell (1900) under the name of the undivided species, but he now evidently thinks that it should belong here:

The song flight of this species is mostly indulged in during the early morning hours. This consists of a slow circuitous flight on rapidly beating wings high over the tree tops, accompanied by the frequent repetition of a weak song somewhat resembling the call of a sparrow hawk. At the close of this song flight the bird alights, as if exhausted, and perches silently for some time at the top of the tallest spruce in the.vicinity. During the performance of the male, the female may be seen feeding around some grassy pool beneath, from all appearances entirely unmindful of the ecstatic efforts of her mate.

Nesting.—Nothing definite is known of the breeding range or nesting habits of the western solitary sandpiper. It is supposed to breed in the interior of British Columbia and Alaska. The following observations, made near Circle, Alaska, by Dr. Wilfred H. Osgood (1909) throw some light on the subject:

Within a radius of several miles from Circle one or more adults were found about almost every woodland swamp. In most cases they acted like parent birds anxious for the safety of their young. Whenever we entered certain precincts, they hovered nervously about, calling loudly, or alighted on nearby trees scolding. The first pair seen near Charlie Creek exhibited such actions on the evening of June 22, and we made a hasty search in the twilight for young birds, but found nothing. The excitement of the old birds seemed to be greatest while we were in a small grassy swamp, so the next day we made a more careful search. The old birds were even more excited than before, and it was some time before we detected that, besides the loud cries ringing all about us, a faint peeping was issuing from several points in the grass. Guided by this scarcely audible peeping, we soon found three downy young birds widely separated and squatting aimlessly in the grass. They are quite small, exactly of a size, and none shows the least indication of growing feathers; evidently they belonged to one clutch, and could not have been out of the eggs more than one or two days. The eggs of this species, like those of the European green sandpiper, have been found in the nests of other birds in trees. The small opening where the birds were found was bounded on one side by an extensive area grown with willows of relatively small size, but on the other side was only a thin line of willows and then alders, birch, poplars, and heavy spruce, in which probably such birds as olive-backed thrushes, robins, and varied thrushes nested in abundance. Therefore there was ample opportunity for the sandpipers to lay their eggs in the nests of these birds.

Plumages.—The downy young referred to above are thus described by Robert Ridgway, (1919):

General color of upper parts cinnamon drab, longitudinally varied with brownish black; forehead and crown with a broad median streak of black; a sharply defined black loral streak, extending from bill to eye; a narrow black stripe across auricular region (longitudinally), or a black postauricular spot; occiput brown centrally, black exteriorly, the black border sending from each side a forward branch; an oval patch of brownish black on median portion of rump, this bordered along each side by a stripe of pale dull vinaceous-buff, the two buffy stripes converging or almost uniting both anteriorly and posteriorly; wings cinnamon drab, margined posteriorly with dull white, the brown portion with several irregular spots or blotches of black; under parts dull white.

Subsequent plumages and molts are doubtless similar to those of the eastern race.

Winter.—As mentioned under the preceding subspecies, we know very little about the winter distribution of the two races. Dr. Frank M. Chapman (1926) says that most of his specimens from Ecuador are of this form, which he calls " a common winter resident from the coast to the tableland, arriving from the north at least as early as August 10." Dr. Alexander Wetmore (1926) says:

The specimens taken at Formosa and General Roca belong certainly to the western form, on the basis of size (male, wing, 134.3; female, wing 136.7 mm.), dorsal coloration, and the presence of mottling on the inner web of the outer primary. A female from Lazcano, Uruguay, has molted the outer primaries, but on the basis of other measurements and on the presence of some dark, buff mottling on the back seems within the limit of variation of *cinnamomea* and is identified as the same as the other two. Though the typical subspecies *solitaria* is recorded definitely from Colombia by Chapman, these findings seem to cast a doubt on its presence as far south as Argentina.

DISTRIBUTION

Range.—Western North America and South America.

Breeding range.—No unquestioned set of eggs of the western solitary sandpiper has thus far been recorded. Downy young with their parents have, however, been taken in western Alberta (Henry House) and in Alaska (Circle, Kowak River, Eagle, and Charlie Creek). There also is a strong probability of their breeding in British Columbia (Cariboo District, and Ducks).

Winter range.—As mentioned under *T. s. solitaria*, the two races of this species on their wintering grounds in South America have been distinguished only on a few occasions. It is probable that they either occupy the same winter grounds or that their ranges overlap. All specimens collected by Wetmore (1926) from Uruguay, Paraguay, and Argentina, prove to be this form, indicating that it may winter south of true *solitaria*. It also has been taken by Chapman in Ecuador (Guayaquil, Loja, and Cebollal).

Spring migration.—Early dates of spring arrival are: Texas, Samuels, April 15, and Henrietta, April 19; New Mexico, State College, May 4, and Las Vegas, May 8; Colorado, Colorado Springs, May 1, Denver, May 4, and Boulder, May 5; Montana, Terry, May 7, and Billings. May 10; Alberta, Athabaska Landing, May 5, Edmonton, May 10, and Sandy Creek, May 14; Mackenzie, Fort Simpson, May 10, and Fort Providence, May 14; Arizona, Verde Valley, April 20, and Paradise, May 9; California, Los Angeles, April 10, Gridley, April 23, and Fort Crook, May 4; Oregon, Anthony, April 16, and Malheur Lake, April 17; Washington, Tacoma, May 6; British Columbia, Okanagan Landing, May 5, and Chilliwack, May 7; Yukon, Forty-mile, May 8; and Alaska, Tocatna Forks, May 12, Nulato, May 15, and Kowak River, May 18.

Late dates of spring departure are: Colorado, Boulder, May 25, Denver, May 28, and Grand Junction, June 3; and Wyoming, Fort Saders, May 25.

Fall migration.—Early dates of fall arrival are: California, Santa Barbara, July 22; Arizona, Apache, July 29, Cave Spring, August 1, and White Mountains, August 10; Montana, Terry, June 28; Wyoming, New Castle, July 7; Colorado, Lytle, July 6, Middle Park, July 13, and El Paso County, July 23; New Mexico, Zuni Mountains, July 24; and Texas, Brownsville, July 31.

Late dates of fall departure are: Alaska, Taku River, September 15; British Columbia, Okanagan Landing, September 26; Washington, Seattle, September 11; California, Santa Barbara, September 7; Arizona, San Pedro River, October 10; Lower California, Agua Escondido, November 18; Montana, Missoula, September 4, Terry, September 5, and Bitterroot Valley, September 7; Wyoming, Yellowstone Park, September 4, and Green River, September 5; Colorado, Boulder, September 18, Florissant, October 5, and Greeley, October 25; and New Mexico, Acoma, September 27, and Glenrio, October 2.

TRINGA OCROPHUS Linnaeus

GREEN SANDPIPER

Contributed by Francis Charles Robert Jourdain

HABITS

The green sandpiper is only an accidental visitor to North America. Swainson and Richardson (1831) record it from Hudson Bay, but this is now generally acknowledged to be probably due to error. However, Dr. T. M. Brewer (1878) mentions a specimen obtained at Halifax, Nova Scotia, in 1872 or 1873 and forming part of a collection made there which was purchased by J. E. Harting from a dealer at Woolwich. The evidence is far from satisfactory and Seebohm's remarks (1884) should be consulted, but the skins in question are still in existence in the collection of the British Museum.

Courtship.—It is a most remarkable fact that though the green sandpiper is widely distributed during the breeding season over temperate Europe and is by no means a shy or retiring bird, even though it haunts the recesses of wooded marshes and wet forests, yet there is hardly anything on record about its courtship activities. Seebohm writes that the notes " are no doubt modulated into a musical trill as the male performs his amatory excursions in the air during the pairing season," but adds that he has never had the good fortune either to hear the love song or to find it described. Fortunately Prof. C. J. Patten (1906) met with a pair which frequented a moorland stream in the neighborhood of Sheffield from May 3 to June 4, 1903. He says:

They were always to be found in the same spot, and after feeding they frequently flitted on to a stone wall, where for a little while they would remain motionless. At intervals they suddenly shot up into the air for a short distance, darting down again to the same stone with astonishing speed. On the wing they displayed great activity and adroitness, the female twisting and turning to escape the addresses of the male.

Newton (1896) writes:

Yet in the breeding season, even in England, the cock bird has been seen to rise high in air and perform a variety of evolutions on the wing, all the while piping what without any violence of language may be called a song.

Doctor Hartert (1920), speaking of its habits on its breeding grounds, remarks that it may be seen shooting through the air with the speed of an arrow, and opines that this must be the love flight. With the exception of these notes and some references to the song (which are referred to under the heading of Voice), I can find nothing in the literature with regard to the actual courtship, except Hartert's statement that on the ground the male trips about, with tail outspread like a fan, calling loudly. When, however, a pair has definitely settled down in its breeding territory, both birds are exceedingly noisy and demonstrative. Wheelwright (1864) speaks of the "boisterous, noisy behavior" of this bird, and in his later work on Sweden (1865) remarks:

Now, of all our waders, this is the noisiest, and there is little trouble in finding the locality where it breeds, for the old male is always about some brook in the neighborhood, and I have before noticed that the loud, wild cry of the green sandpiper and greenshank are much alike.

Nesting.—The nesting habits of the green sandpiper have been fully described, but were practically unknown to naturalists till about 1852–1860, when quite independently Forester, Weise, and Hintz (sen.), in Germany, and H. W. Wheelwright in Sweden, published the results of their discoveries. The story is told in detail by Forest-Inspector Weise, in the *Journal für Ornithologie* for 1855 (p. 514). He had first heard of the habit of adopting old nests of other species in trees from an old ranger, but naturally discredited it. However, in 1845, the same man brought him four sandpipers' eggs from a nest in an old beech. Next spring Weise found a green sandpiper breeding in a pine about 25 or 30 feet from the ground. He climbed to the nest and found the four eggs so highly incubated that the young could be heard squeaking inside the shells. Two other nests in similar sites came to his notice subsequently, the last on May 25, 1855, when the four eggs were already chipped.

Forester, W. Hintz 1, writing in the same periodical for 1862 (p. 460) says that he had found sandpipers' nests in trees as far back as 1818, but at that time he had no correspondents who took any interest in birds' eggs and only took a clutch or two for his own collection. On April 26, 1834, he found a clutch of this species in a nest of the song thrush (*Turdus philomelus*) and from 1852 onward, as the circumstances began to be known to German naturalists, he found a long series of nests with eggs of which he gives full details. Most of these eggs were laid in old nests of song thrush (*Turdus philomelus*), but some were placed in old nests of pigeon (probably *Columba palumbus*) or squirrel's dreys, and in one case the young were found in an old nest of red-backed shrike (*Lanius collurio*). Another curious case recorded is that in which an old aspen (*Populus tremula*) was broken off and a hole which had been occupied in the previous year by a pied flycatcher, contained a brood of young green sandpipers, which had apparently only been hatched half an hour before. On the forester's approach the young birds jumped from the hole and concealed themselves among the grass. Some further details are also given in a letter from Hintz sent to the Rev. H. S. Hawkins and published in Dresser's Birds of Europe; also in the *Journal für Ornithologie* for 1864 (p. 186).

Summarizing these we find that the birds arrive on their nesting grounds in Germany from the beginning to the middle of April, choosing wooded localities in marshy districts with pools or slow-flowing streams in the neighborhood. Old nests of song thrush, blackbird, mistle thrush, red-backed shrike, and half-ruined nests of jay, woodpigeon, or squirrel are all adopted from time to time. Occasionally the eggs are laid in a hollow where dead leaves and pine needles have accumulated, and holes formerly used by starlings and flycatchers have been taken possession of. The height from the ground varies considerably, some nests may be as much as 35 or 40 feet above the ground while others are only a few feet up. The distance from the nearest water is also variable, as though most nests are within 500 yards, yet occasionally the birds have been known to nest half a mile away.

Meantime H. W. Wheelwright in Sweden had met with an exactly similar state of things, and in the *Field* newspaper of August 18, 1860, described the tree-nesting habits of this species. The editor, who was ignorant of the evidence of Weise and Hintz, openly expressed his doubts as to the accuracy of the observations, but Wheelwright stuck manfully to his facts and subsequently the editor admitted his mistake. The republication of Wheelwright's notes in Sweden in 1866 elicited further evidence from Jagmaster Lundborg, who had on one occasion taken the eggs from what appeared to be an old squirrel's drey or nest. The only important difference in the habits of the bird in the two countries appears to be that nests of the hooded crow (*Corvus c. cornix*) are freely used in Sweden and also those of the fieldfare (*Turdus pilaris*).

Like the greenshank, the green sandpiper has a great attachment to certain localities and in some cases the identical nest has been used for two consecutive seasons. In a district where the birds are not scarce, this naturally renders the discovery of the nest much more simple to the resident, and explains the success of Forester Hintz and others in discovering the eggs. Very little in the way of addition appears to be made by the sandpipers to their adopted home and the pine needles which are noted in the interior of old thrushes' nests may well have dropped from the adjacent trees in the ordinary way.

Eggs.—These are normally four in number, pyriform in shape, rather thin shelled and, as compared with those of the wood sandpiper, generally large and pale in coloring, showing more of the ground colors and fewer markings. The ground color varies from some shade of pale greenish or greenish grey to warm creamy, buffish stone color and light yellowish red. The markings are generally rather fine and in the reddish eggs are rich purplish brown, shading into very dark brown, while in the greenish eggs they are generally less reddish and more purplish in tone. Numerous fine speckles are characteristic and there are generally also some underlying shell marks of violet or ashy. The measurements of 100 eggs average 39.11 by 28.04 millimeters; the eggs showing the four extremes measure 42 by 28, 41.1 by 30.3, 34.6 by 26, and 34.8 by 25.7 millimeters.

Young.—As to the shares of the sexes in incubation, there are references to females shot from the nest and males on guard in the neighborhood, but how far this has been confirmed by dissection and how much is surmise it is not easy to say. The incubation period is also unknown. When the young are hatched their stay in the nest is very short. Besides Hintz's observation, quoted above, of recently hatched young jumping from the nest into the grass on his approach. Wheelwright also found on one occasion four very small young, apparently not a day old, at the foot of a fir, while in the nest overhead were the empty shells, still wet inside. In this case the early abandonment of the nest was not due to human interference. On another occasion Hintz found three young and a chipped egg in a squirrel's drey about 30 feet up in a birch. The young birds sprang from the nest and alighted on the ground without injuring themselves, concealing themselves at once among the grass.

Plumages.—The molts and plumages are fully described in A Practical Handbook of British Birds, edited by H. F. Witherby (1920), to which the reader is referred.

Food.—The main food of this species consists of insects, especially small coleoptera and their larvae, but larval forms of other

water insects such as the Phryganeidae are also taken and also
larvae of Diptera. Other substances recorded include wood lice,
spiders, and not infrequently the very small red worms, which are
to be met with on the edges of stagnant pools, but apparently not
common earthworms. Traces of vegetable matter are also recorded.
H. Stevenson also includes small fresh-water mollusca, and W. Farren,
algae, tender shoots of plants and on the seashore thin shelled
crustacea.

Behavior.—The green sandpiper may be met with in the British
Islands in almost every month of the year except perhaps June,
when it is decidedly rare, though only a few individuals stay with
us through the winter. As some birds have undoubtedly stayed
through the summer, breeding has been suspected on several occasions, but the evidence has always been unsatisfactory. It occurs
most frequently in spring and autumn, sometimes singly and sometimes (especially in autumn), in family parties, haunting the margins of brooks and ponds.

They are much more deliberate in their movements than the
common sandpiper and search the mud very thoroughly, boring into
it with the bill, probably in search of the small red worms on which
they feed. Without being especially shy, they have their wits about
them and frequently the piping note which they utter when well on
the wing (not just prior to rising) is the first indication of their
presence to the shooter. The striking contrast of color between
the dark greenish mantle and the snow white rump and tail coverts
render its recognition a fairly simple matter. From the wood sandpiper it can be readily distinguished if a glimpse can be caught of
the undersurface of the wing, for in the green sandpiper the axillars are very dark, looking almost black, whereas in the wood sandpiper they appear almost white with faint barrings.

Voice.—With regard to the notes, during the breeding season the
alarm is given by a loud sharp call which is variously written as *gik*,
giff, *yick*, *yeck*, etc., somewhat recalling the nuthatches call. Christo-
leit also describes a pairing song, which bears some resemblance to
that of the other sandpipers, but does not make it clear whether it is
uttered on the wing or on the ground. In forested country it is
naturally not so easy to settle a point of this kind as in open country.
The full song is written by him as: *Tittittitlwidich-luidich titlwidie
titlwidie titlwidie-titt-titt.* Probably this is the love song and forms
part of the courtship, but we still await a connected history of the
courtship of this species.

Fall.—Hintz noticed the last birds on their German breeding
grounds up to July 25, and it is about the middle of July when the
first immigrants appear in the British Isles. The great majority of

our visitors have left by November. During the period of its stay it is rarely to be met with on the seashore, but nearly always makes its way inland by means of the water courses, preferring a sheltered brookside or an inland pool to the open marshes.

Winter.—The evidence of wintering in South Africa rests entirely on some old records by Layard, unsupported by skins, but the winter quarters undoubtedly extend to Angola, British Central Africa, and Portuguese East Africa. Unlike so many waders it does not associate in large flocks, but generally is found singly or in small parties on inland waters in preference to the coast. Large numbers winter in Egypt and a good many at suitable spots in the Mediterranean Region. In Luzon (Philippine Islands) Whitehead found it common in December in Benguet, at a height of 4,000 feet, and on Rumenzon it has been met with at 6,000 feet, while in Abyssinia, Jesse describes it as common on the highlands, but did not meet with it on the coast.

DISTRIBUTION

Breeding range.—Northern Europe; but very sparingly in Norway up to Nordland; in Sweden more generally north to the Arctic Circle; Finland to 63° 10′; North Russia south of the White Sea and on the Kamin Peninsula (66° 50′). Southward it breeds in the Baltic Republics, in North Germany (Holstein?, Oldenburg?, Hanover, Mark Brandenburg, Pommern, West and East Prussia, Silesia); sparingly in Bavaria; Czechoslovakia (Bohemia), Galizia and the Carpathians; possibly occasionally in Jutland, but records from South France and North Italy can not be relied on. In Asia it breeds across the continent in the valleys of the Ob, Yenisei, Lena, etc., south to Turkestan and Transcaspia.

Winter Range.—The main winter quarters lie in southern Europe and Africa where it ranges south to Portuguese East Africa, British Central Africa, and Angola, perhaps even to the Cape (Layard) and in Asia to Iraq, India, Ceylon, the Andamans, Burma, Cochin China, China, Hainan, Formosa, and the Malay Archipelago (Philippines).

Spring Migration.—In February and March it passes north through Morocco from its African winter quarters, and in Tunisia is most abundant on spring passage in March and April, while its stay in equatorial Africa does not extend beyond March. In the marshes of Iraq it stays till mid May, the spring in North Asia being later than in West Europe. This is also the case in India, where they do not leave till about mid May. In southeast China they pass in the first half of April, usually singly. It has been noted on passage in Corsica in April (late date May 28); some winter on the Balearic Isles where it has been noted up to the end of May, while in Cyprus it is found on passage in March, April, and May (birds seen in Greece on 25th July and in South China on 11th and 24th July were either nonbreeders or extraordinarily early migrants southward). The first arrivals reach their breeding grounds in Germany about the end of March, and in the Baltic states they arrive about the end of March or early April.

Fall migration.—Leaving their breeding grounds in Central Europe about the end of July, they pass the Straits of Gibraltar about August-September and in Greece arrive in some numbers in September. In the Iraq marshes the arrival takes place during August, while in India it sometimes comes during the latter half of July, but more frequently in August. In southeastern China the first arrivals come in about the end of July or early in August, but the main body passes in September or October. In Burma it is generally distributed during the winter months, but apparently does not range down the Malay Peninsula.

Casual records.—It is a winter visitor to Japan and occurs occasionally on the Canaries, but the record from Mauritius must be regarded as doubtful, and that from Australia by R. Hall is due to confusion with *T. glareola*. Gould's record from Borneo is also doubtful and the American records can only be received with some suspicion.

Egg dates.—In Germany out of some 25 records only five fall between April 15 and 24. From May 2 to 15 there are nine records, from May 18 to 29 five records, and from June 1 to 23, six records. Probably most of these late dates are due to birds laying again which have been previously robbed. In Sweden all dates fall between May 6 and June 20 (13 records) and of these eight fall between May 6 and May 21. The second half of May is the usual time in the southern Provinces, but in the north and Finland few eggs are laid before June. In Siberia eggs may be found till the first half of July.

RHYACOPHILUS GLAREOLA (Linnaeus)

WOOD SANDPIPER

Contributed by Francis Charles Robert Jourdain

HABITS

The only record of this species within North American limits is due to Chase Littlejohn (1904), who obtained a single specimen on May 27, 1894, on Sanak Island, Alaska.

Courtship.—Our information on this point is somewhat scanty. The song flight has of course been frequently described and observed, but the actual courtship of the female can only be observed under somewhat difficult conditions and there must be a considerable element of luck in any case where it can be closely studied. All the evidence hitherto obtained goes to show that it is carried on in much the same way as that of the common sandpiper (*Tringa hypoleucos*), but the song flight forms a much more conspicuous part of the proceedings. When the male alights he has a habit of elevating his wings for a moment, until, as Seebohm says, they almost meet overhead, much as Temminck's stint also does. Apparently this forms part of the display before the hen, but the male may also be seen running by the side of the female with drooping wings. One can as a rule only get a momentary glimpse and generally at a considerable distance. The love song is, however, quite another matter. On the heaths of West Jutland one can see the males in rapid flight even from the windows of the trains, while in North Finland the loud musical *leero, leero, leero,* is one of the most familiar sounds in the wood-fringed marshes. John Hancock (1874), who by persevering search found the only nest which has ever been discovered in the British Isles, in June 1853, gives a very graphic account of it. He was on a visit to Prestwick Car, in Northumberland, at that time undrained, and as he says:

About 3 o'clock our dogs, a retriever and a setter, raised a bird about 50 yards in advance of us, which at once rose to a considerable height coursing about, rising and sinking somewhat in the manner of a snipe, and like it, while sweeping downwards with outstretched, tremulous wings, produced a peculiar drumming note, but one much shriller than that of the snipe, and almost amounting to a sort of musical whistle. From the strangeness of the actions and peculiar whistling or drumming note, I was convinced that we had met with a rare bird, and that its nest was near at hand. The birds were still in view flying about; our only chance now was to watch the bird to its nest. It was not long before one of the birds "pitched" and after allowing a little time for it to settle I went forth to raise it, but did not succeed. The bird, however, was soon in the air again flying about as before. The watching dodge was again tried and this time the bird was marked to, and raised from the nest. There lay the nest, with its four pretty eggs, on the side of a dry hillock where grew some heath and grass in the midst of a swampy spot.

One of the parents was subsequently shot by Mr. Reay to authenticate the identification, and the specimen is still extant. Seebohm (1884) also describes the song flight, but it is difficult to reconcile his account with the facts. According to him:

The note which the male utters during the pairing season is much more of a song than that of the grasshopper warbler, which it somewhat resembles; it is a monotonous *tit-it-it*, begun somewhat low and slow, as the bird is descending in the air with fluttering upraised wings, becoming louder and more rapid and reaching its climax as the bird alights on the ground or on a rail, or sometimes on the bare branch of a willow, the points of its trembling wings almost meeting over its head when its feet find support. This song is a by no means unmusical trill, and has an almost metallic ring about it.

The comparison to the trill of the grasshopper warbler seems very far fetched, and would apply far better to the persistent trilling of Temminck's stint. In fact the note reads like a paragraph drafted from filed notes jotted down when the writer was surrounded by singing stints and sandpipers; the metallic and musical song and dashing flight being that of the wood sandpiper and the monotonous trill being that of Temminck's stint. To my ear the Finnish name of the bird, " liro," exactly describes the ringing musical cadence which one hears overhead so frequently by the lake sides and marshes of Sweden and Finland. Buturlin notes the song as *peri, peri, logi, logi, logi,* and von Droste's translation is also expressive *hithitittli-a, tli-a, tli-a, tlia.* It is obvious that this bears no likeness whatever to the monotonous droning note, rising and falling slightly as the bird turns its head, of *Locustella naevia.* Occasionally the song of the wood sandpiper is uttered while the bird is perched on a bush or in treeless districts even on the ground.

Nesting.—Although often not concealed with any art, the nest of the wood sandpiper is by no means an easy one to find, as the possible area is so vast, while the sitting bird frequently remains on the eggs until almost trodden on. In consequence most nests are discovered by accident, when the bird has been flushed at one's feet, or by long and systematic beating of likely ground in the neighborhood of a singing male. The nest is, however, almost invariably on some slight eminence, a hummock in some cases as much as 2 feet high, though often smaller, and on dry ground, though there may be water within a foot or so. The actual nest is merely a hollow in the ground, lined with bents and grasses and is usually to be found on low-lying ground where willow scrub, heath mosses, and rank grasses furnish a certain amount of cover. This is the normal European site, but H. Leyborne Popham (1897), while collecting on the Yenisei in 1895, found that out of five nests discovered in that season, only one was placed on the ground, while the eggs in the other four cases were laid in the numerous old nests of fieldfares (*Turdus pilaris*) and other thrushes which were to be seen in great numbers in the trees. In 1900 Mr. Popham (1901) was able to confirm these observations, for in the forest district two more clutches were taken from old thrushes' nests, while at the edge of the tundra two nests were found on the ground. That this habit is not strictly confined to the forest districts of Asia was proved by Lieut. S. A. Davies (1895), who visited the upper waters of the River Muonio on the borders of Finland and Sweden in 1904. He obtained a clutch from an old nest of great grey shrike (*Lanius excubitor excubitor*), placed in the fork of a birch about 20 feet from the ground. A. Cnattingius also found the eggs on one occasion in Sweden in a fieldfare's nest, 8 feet from the ground. There is some evidence that in certain parts of the range this species breeds almost in colonies. Collett has described a case of this kind from the high field of southern Norway, and Forester Hintz (sen.) writes that on one marshy flat of about 60 acres in Mecklenberg from 7 to 9 pairs were breeding, and that on May 25, 1858, he received no fewer than 26 fresh and partly incubated eggs from this locality.

Eggs.—These are normally four in number, pyriform in shape and thin shelled. The ground color varies from a beautiful pale green to creamy white and exceptionally to warm buff. They are spotted and blotched, more heavily at the large end, with warm reddish brown, some eggs have most of the markings small, but others have large and almost confluent blotches. There are also a few purplish brown shell marks. The measurements of 100 eggs average 38.34 by 26.4 millimeters; the eggs showing the four extremes measure 42 by 28.1, 41.5 by 28.5, 35.5 by 25 and 37 by 24.4 millimeters.

Young.—Both sexes take part in incubation; all the birds shot by Popham from the nest in 1895 were males, but in 1900 he found that out of two killed one was a male and the other a female. Collett also notes that both sexes have incubation patches. When the young are hatched the parents display the greatest anxiety, but the male bird seems to take the greater share in brooding and guarding them. On one occasion H. J. Pearson (1904) surprised a bird with four young only about a day old in a marsh. He placed the young in his pocket after having spent half an hour in finding them, though they were fully exposed to view and all within 10 yards. The young soon began to cry out and the parent bird, which he surmised to be the male, followed him nearly a mile, often settling within 5 feet and expressing his views. He then flew back to the marsh, but actually returned and settled on a low shed near the house. Lieut. S. A. Davies (1895) having caught a brood of young, placed them on the ground in a marsh, first in one place and then in another, in order to watch them.

The male bird would run excitedly in and out of the tussocks, searching everywhere till he heard their feeble chirp. Then he would run toward them and settle down a yard or two off, quickening his note to a continuous *giff-giff-giff*. Then all the young had to tumble along laboriously (for they could hardly walk) till they reached the male bird who tucked them safely under his wings; once or twice the female bird appeared on the scene for a minute or two, when both would soar in the air like drumming snipe.

Plumages.—The molts and plumages are fully described in A Practical Handbook of British Birds, edited by H. F. Witherby (1920), to which the reader is referred.

Food.—The greater part of the food consists of insects and their larvae, but worms are also taken in some numbers and small mollusca, as well as spiders. Among insects the following classes may be mentioned: Beetles (Coleoptera), including many water beetles, *Haliplus, Hydroporus, Dytiscus, Berosus, Dryops, Helichus, Phylobius* (all recorded by Hesse), and *Gyrinus, Hydroporus, Donacia,* and *Colymbetes* (R. Gray). Of Diptera, Hesse records larva of *Stratiomys* (also recorded by Bar), and among Rhyncota, *Plea minutissima* (once by Hesse). Rey also met with Arachnida (spiders). and Jackel records small fish.

Behavior.—Many observers have called attention to the habit of perching on trees. Seebohm (1884) mentions having shot specimens from the summit of high bare trees at least 65 feet from the ground, and similar observations have been made wherever it has been met with in forested regions. Beside the love song already described, this bird has an alarm note, which Davies renders as *tchick-tchick*, or *giff-giff*, and which is generally uttered from the top of a bush or post. A. Chapman phrases this note as *chirkop, chirkop, chib, chib.*

Fall.—From July to October it appears often singly, but also at times in flocks in Great Britain. As a rule these flocks are of no great size, but on July 26, 1867, Mr. Power met with large numbers at Rainham, Kent, and when one had been shot others rose on all sides, forming one large flock, which flew round and round, keeping up a continual whistle. He estimated the number at 80–100.

Winter.—During the winter months it haunts mud banks at the mouths of rivers or marshes and streams inland in small flocks, or sometimes in pairs, feeding on worms and small insects in southern Africa. Its habit of perching on trees and bushes has also been noted when wintering in northern Africa (Tunisia). On the whole, it may be described as a fresh-water haunting species, usually avoiding the neighborhood of the sea.

DISTRIBUTION

Breeding range.—Not on the Faeroes, as stated by Ridgway, but formerly in very small numbers in Great Britain, Holland, Jutland, Scandinavia, north Germany locally. Finland, the Baltic Republics, and Russia generally; also in Asia, east across Siberia to Kamtschatka and the Commander Isles, north to about 75° on the Yenisei and 71° on the Lena. Reports of breeding in south Europe (Spain, north Italy, Pyrenees, etc.) require confirmation.

Winter range.—Africa, south to Cape Province; Asia, southern Arabia, Iraq (chiefly on passage), India and Ceylon, Burma, the Malay Peninsula, and southeast China; the Malay Archipelago

(Borneo, Sumatra, Java, Celebes, Timor, Philippines, etc.); and Australia.

Spring migration.—It leaves its winter quarters in South Africa in March, is common in the swamps of Morocco toward the end of April, fairly plentiful in Tunisia in April and also in numbers in Egypt, some remaining till May. Most have left Iraq by mid May, and the departure from India, Ceylon, and Burma also takes place in May. They pass Gibraltar from March 9 to early May; Corsica, April 12 to May 28; Cyprus, April–May (late date May 20); Corfu, April 19–May 6; while a few visit the south and east coast of Great Britain in April and May. On the lower Petchora they did not arrive till May 26.

Fall migration.—From Portugal it is recorded on August 18, Spain (early date, August 4), passes through Italy in some numbers from August to October, leaving Sweden in September and passing the eastern Pyrenees in September–October. It reaches Iraq in August, but rarely stays after October; arrives in India and Burma in August; and in South Africa in September–October, early dates, August, Transvaal (August 28) and Zambesi River.

Casual records.—Faeroes (H. C. Muller), Madeira (R. Gomez), Canaries (occasional D. A. Bannerman), Hawaiian Isles, and Sanak Island, Alaska (C. Littlejohn).

Egg dates.—In Holland, May 11 to 25 (9 dates); Jutland and Germany, May 7–25 (about 18 dates, mostly after May 20); south Sweden from mid May onward; Lapland, June 3–16 (16 dates), June 17–27 (11 dates), July 7 (one date).

CATOPTROPHORUS SEMIPALMATUS SEMIPALMATUS (Gmelin)

EASTERN WILLET

HABITS

A score of years or so ago it seemed as if this large showy wader was destined to disappear from at least the northern portion of its range on the Atlantic coast. It had entirely ceased to breed in many of its former haunts and was nearly extirpated in others. Most of the birds that we shot on migration in New England were immature birds from the West. In Wilson's (1832) time it bred "in great numbers—along the shores of New York, New Jersey, Delaware, and Maryland." Audubon (1840) wrote that "a few have been known to breed not far from New Bedford in Massachusetts," probably on some of the islands off the coast. In 1875 H. B. Bailey (1876) found it breeding "in large numbers" on Cobb Island, Va.; when we visited this locality in June, 1907, there were not over two or three pairs of willets breeding there; they have increased since then under protection. Maj. G. Ralph Meyer wrote to me in 1922 that about 15 pairs bred on Cobb Island and 5 or 6 pairs on Hog Island that year. It does not now breed in any numbers, so far as I know, north of South Carolina, except in the Nova Scotia colonies.

Although our check list does not recognize that fact, it has been known for many years that willets breed regularly in southern Nova Scotia, though during the early years of this century they came very near being extirpated. Dr. Spencer Trotter (1904) recorded the willet as " one of the most conspicuous inhabitants of the tidal marshes " near Barrington, Shelburne County. But when I visited that locality with him in July, 1907, we found only one pair. Evidently they began to increase again after that under adequate protection. Harrison F. Lewis (1920) found them breeding in Yarmouth County, and Dr. Charles W. Townsend (1920a) saw a flock of 10 on July 18 and as many as 26 on July 25, 1920, near Barrington. Later information from R. W. Tufts (1922 and 1925) shows a decided increase up to 1922, when he estimated that there were 736 willets, old and young, between Digby and Queens Counties; but in 1923 and 1924 there seemed to be no further increase.

Spring.—The northward migration of willets, which breed north of the winter range, is along the Atlantic coast, starting in March. The first migrants reach Virginia during the first or second week in April, but do not appear in Massachusetts until May, the main flight passing between the middle and last of that month. The probability of an offshore migration route is suggested by the following interesting observation made by Dr. George B. Grinnell (1916) during the last days of May, 1907:

It was in the middle of the morning of a gray, but not foggy, day, when we were off the Grand Banks of Newfoundland, that I noticed a considerable gathering of birds resting on the water in the immediate path of the ship. As we approached them I thought they looked like shore birds, and as the vessel drew quite close to them those immediately near it rose on wing and flew off to right and left, and again alighted on the water among their fellows. In the way in which they left the path of the vessel they reminded me of similar flights of waterfowl seen in Alaska. When the birds took wing they were at once recognized as willets, and there must have been somewhere near a thousand of them, not all packed together in a dense clump on the water, but more or less scattered out, in groups of forty, fifty, or a hundred, yet all fairly near one another, and suggesting a single flock. They seemed to leave the water reluctantly and gave me the impression that they were weary.

Courtship.—Very little seems to have been recorded about the courtship of the willet, but John T. Nichols has sent me the following notes:

On the shore of Wakulla County, Fla., in late March willets were evidently about to nest, March 27 they were noticed chasing one another in air, and holding the wings over the back after alighting, the black and white pattern displayed.

The following mating behavior was observed March 29 toward sunset. Out on a mud flat exposed by low water two birds were standing. One stood directly behind the other, waving its parti-colored wings over its back, and ended by mounting the back of the front bird and fluttering there. The performance was accompanied by a tern-like series of *kuk-kuk-kuk-kuk-kuk* calls.

Nesting.—The eastern willet is decidedly a coastwise bird and it is seldom seen far from the coastal marshes, beaches, and islands. Its favorite nesting places are on sandy islands overgrown with grass, tall and thick enough to conceal its nest, or on dry uplands where similar conditions may be found in close proximity to marshes or the shore. In Nova Scotia I was too late to find nests, but Mr. Lewis (1920) writes:

> I have occasionally searched for the nests or the young of the willets, but without success until June 8, 1920, when I found a nest with four eggs of this species, in an open swale in an upland pasture, about a quarter of a mile from the nearest salt marsh or salt water, at Arcadia, Yarmouth County, Nova Scotia, on the western side of the Chetogue River. The nest was near the junction of the River Road with Argyle Street, and was about 150 yards from each of those much-traveled highways, which were in full view from the nest site. Several cattle occupied the pasture at the time when the nest was found. The swale in which the nest was placed was of considerable extent and was of the kind preferred as a breeding place by Wilson's snipe; in fact, a pair of those birds were evidently nesting there. The willet's nest was a slight hollow in the damp ground, lined with a few dead rushes. It was surrounded by growing rushes, cinnamon fern, low blackberry bushes, and wild rose bushes, and was well concealed.

Mr. Tufts (1925) says that "they often nest in the open pastures or on the rough boulder-strewn uplands at a considerable distance inland," but all the nests that he found were "on low land close to the feeding grounds," near the shore. One nest was located under a tangle of wild rose bushes in a pasture in Yarmouth County.

More typical nesting conditions are to be found on the coastal islands of Virginia and South Carolina. In the Bull's Bay region of South Carolina we visited two islands, on May 22 and 23, 1915, on which willets were breeding. Most of the nests were on a sand-hill plain, back of the beach, which was overgrown with tufts of fine beach grass and with a few scattering clumps of myrtle bushes. The nests consisted of deep hollows in the sand in or under the tufts of grass, usually well concealed, and were well lined with bits of dry grass, sedges, or small sticks; the hollows measured 6 or 7 inches in diameter. A partially built nest contained only one egg, which was lying on the bare sand and was only partially surrounded by the nesting material; apparently material is added during the laying period and the nest is not completed until incubation begins. One nest was under a little dead, thorny bush, but well concealed, on a small, high spot on an open sandy reef, not far from the nests of oyster catchers and Wilson plover. Another nest, in a situation which was probably flooded at times, was built up 10 inches above the damp ground in a clump of thickly tufted sedges. H. B. Bailey (1876) says that, on Cobb Island, "the marshes are also favorite localities for breeding, and in this case the nests are more elaborate, being built up from the ground, which is wet at high tide." I think, however, that the willet prefers to nest on dry ground.

Roger Tony Peterson writes to me that, among 11 nests found by him on the South Carolina coast, "five sets of eggs on one particular strip of beach were located on the open sand with no preparation at all made for a nest." Another set was "in a very heavy, well-made nest of weeds and grass, out on the open sand, far from any grass or bushes." All were very conspicuous.

C. J. Maynard (1896) found them breeding in Florida, during the first week in May, "among the low scrub, just back of the beach ridge. The nests were placed in the midst of low bushes and were quite difficult to find." Arthur T. Wayne (1910) "found two nests on the top of a high sand hill, in wild oats (*Zizania miliacea*)" and E. A. Samuels (1883) says that it "has been known to breed in a rye field 20 miles from the seashore."

Willets which I have found breeding on the coasts of Louisiana and Texas have proved to be referable to the eastern form. On Dressing Point Island in Matagorda Bay, Tex., we found a few pairs breeding, with heavily incubated eggs, on May 8, 1923. This is a large, flat, grassy island on which we found black-crowned night herons and a few pairs of Ward herons nesting on the ground. The willets' nests were well concealed under thick tufts of luxuriant grass.

Willets on their breeding grounds are among the noisiest and most demonstrative of birds. No sooner does one land on an island where they are breeding than an outcry is started and one after another the birds arise and fly out to meet the intruder, until the whole colony is in a state of great excitement. Regardless of their own safety they circle about at short range, pouring out a steady stream of angry invectives in a great variety of loud, ringing notes. And this performance is kept up as long as the intruder is anywhere near their nests. They often alight on bushes, trees, posts, or even buildings and keep up a constant scolding.

Eggs.—The willet regularly lays four eggs; as many as six, and even seven, have been found in a nest, but these large numbers are probably the product of two females. The eggs vary in shape from ovate to ovate pyriform and they have only a slight gloss. The ground colors vary from "deep olive buff" to "olive buff," rarely "yellowish glaucous," in greenish types, and from "avellaneous" to "tilleul buff," rarely pale "Isabella color," in the buffy or brownish types; and there are numerous intermediate shades between these extremes. They are generally boldly and irregularly marked with both large and small spots and blotches, but sometimes they are quite evenly covered with small spots; rarely they are blotched around the large end only. The markings are mostly in dark browns, " burnt umber," " bister," " sepia " and " clove brown," but sometimes they are in lighter, olive browns. The underlying markings are in various shades of " brownish drab " or " drab gray." The measurements of 56 eggs average 52.5 by 38 millimeters; the eggs showing the four extremes measure **60.5** by 38, 53.5 by **40, 49** by 37, and 50 by **36** millimeters.

Young.—The period of incubation seems to be unknown. Both sexes share in the care of the young, which run soon after hatching. Arthur T. Wayne (1910) says:

The young are hatched by May 29, and the parents sometimes remove them between the thighs (as the woodcock is also known to do) to a place of safety, fully a quarter of a mile away. I observed this trait on May 29, 1899. I found a nest in an oat field, which contained one young bird just hatched and three eggs on the point of hatching. I remained near the place until the eggs were hatched, and the willets were greatly alarmed all the time. Presently I saw one of the old birds remove a young one and fly with it across three creeks and marsh land to an island a quarter of a mile away. This was repeated until all the young were removed.

Plumages.—The downy young willet is rather prettily and quite distinctively marked. There is a distinct loral stripe of brownish black, a post ocular stripe and a median frontal stripe of " warm sepia." The chin and throat are white and the rest of the head is pale buff, mixed with grayish white, heavily mottled on the crown with " warm sepia." The down of the hind neck and upper back is basally sepia with light buff tips. The rest of the upper parts are variegated with pale buff, grayish white and " warm sepia "; but in the center of the back is a well marked pattern of four broad stripes of " warm sepia " and three of light buff, converging on the rump and between the wings. The under parts are buffy white.

The young bird begins to acquire its juvenal plumage before it is half grown, beginning with the scapulars, back and wings; then comes the plumage of the breast and crown, and lastly the neck, rump and tail. In the full juvenal plumage, in July, the feathers of the crown, back, scapulars and wing coverts are " sepia "; those of the crown are tipped, those of the back and scapulars are broadly edged or notched and those of the wing coverts are still more broadly edged with " pale pinkish buff "; the greater coverts are irregularly barred, variegated or sprinkled with sepia; the rest of the wing is as in the adult; the rump is " hair brown," narrowly tipped with buffy white; the upper tail coverts are white, indistinctly barred with dusky near the tips; the central tail feathers are barred with "sepia" and "drab," tinged with "pinkish buff," these markings decreasing laterally; the chin, upper throat and belly are white; the lower throat, chest, and flanks are suffused with "pale pinkish buff," streaked on the throat and chest and barred on the flanks with "sepia." These colors soon fade until the edgings become nearly white.

A partial molt takes place mainly in September, involving the body plumage, the tail and some of the wing coverts; this produces the first winter plumage, which can be distinguished from the adult only by the retained juvenal wing coverts. This plumage is worn through the winter and I think, in most cases, through the first spring. At the next complete molt, the first postnuptial, the adult winter plumage is acquired.

Adults have a nearly complete prenuptial molt in March, April, and May, involving everything but the flight feathers of the wings, which are apparently molted later in the fall or early in the winter. I have not actually seen these feathers molting. The lighter portions of the spring plumage wear away during the breeding season, giving the birds a very black appearance above. The complete postnuptial molt begins with the body plumage in August, or even July, and by September the plain "smoke gray" winter plumage is assumed.

Food.—The favorite feeding grounds of the eastern willet are on the broad mud flats or sand flats in the bayous, bays, and estuaries on the coast; it also feeds along the muddy banks of creeks and ditches, or about the pond holes and splashes on the salt marshes. If disturbed at its feeding it rises with a loud outcry, alarming all the birds within hearing. W. J. Erichsen (1921) has noted that, although they feed at all hours of the day, the nesting birds are seldom found on their nests during the early morning hours, when there seems to be a concerted movement from the breeding grounds to their feeding places. I am inclined to think, however, that they are governed more by the tides than by the hours, as most of their feeding grounds are covered at high tide.

Their food consists of aquatic insects, marine worms, small crabs, fiddlers, small mollusks, fish fry, and small fish. Some vegetable matter is eaten, such as grasses, tender roots, seeds, and even cultivated rice.

Behavior.—The flight of the willet is said to be swift, but it has always seemed to me to be rather slow and heavy, when compared with the flight of other shore birds, though perhaps it results in better speed than it appears to do. The willet is a heavy-bodied bird and its flight is strong, direct, and protracted; it seems to fly more like a duck than the other shore birds. Occasionally it sets its wings and scales downward; and on its breeding grounds I have seen it hover on quivering wings like a poised falcon. I have not found the willet particularly shy, as compared with other large waders, though it has the reputation of being very wary. When in large flocks in open situations, it is useless to attempt to approach it; but I have often walked up to within gunshot range of single birds and have frequently had small flocks fly within range while I was standing in plain sight. On its breeding grounds it is utterly fearless and bold.

Willets often perch on bushes, trees, fences, posts, rocks, or buildings, where they can watch and scold at the intruder. Mr. Maynard (1896) has seen them " perching on the limbs of pine trees, 40 or 50 feet from the ground, and sometimes, a dozen birds would sit side by side on a single branch, presenting a novel appearance." Being partially webfooted, they can swim fairly well and probably alight on the water to rest when migrating at sea. On the ground they are rather sluggish, standing still much of the time, with heads drawn down. They indulge in the bobbing or nodding motions less frequently and more moderately than the yellowlegs do. Francis H. Allen has noted that " in bobbing, the head is drawn back and the tail lowered at the same time, the whole body turning as on a pivot, then the head is brought forward and the tail raised to its natural level."

Voice.—On its breeding grounds the willet is a very noisy bird, pouring out a great variety of notes. Its usual note is a loud, vehement *wek, wek, wek* or *kerwek, kerwek, kerwek*, varied to *piuk, piuk, piuk*. Occasionally the whistling note, *pill, will, will* or *pill-o-will-o-willet*, is heard, suggesting the note of the yellowlegs in quality, accent, and manner of delivery. Less frequently another note is heard, which sounds like *beat it, beat it*. John T. Nichols adds in his notes:

At this season one hears several variations of the *kiyuk* flight note, one of these, *ki-yi-yuk* suggesting the loudest, most ringing call of the greater yellowlegs. A loud, high-pitched *kree-uk*, which is infrequent, suggests a note of the lesser yellowlegs. Similarly *kuk-kuk-kuk-kuk-kuk* in tern-like series from two mating birds is probably homologous with the alighting and flushing notes of the yellowlegs. The ordinary loud flight note of the transient willet is a far-reaching, gull-like *kiyuk*, repeated at intervals. A less frequent call resembles the *wheu wheu wheu* of the greater yellowlegs, but is much lower pitched, not loud. It is likely to be heard from a bird lingering at a given locality.

Enemies.—Man has been the chief enemy of the willet and the main cause of the restriction of its breeding areas. When it bred abundantly in Nova Scotia and Virginia its eggs were collected in large numbers as a legitimate article of food. And the birds were shot all through the breeding season. Being a large, fat bird, it helped to fill the game bag rapidly and so was a favorite with sportsmen or market gunners. It does not come readily to decoys, but it can easily be attracted by a skillful imitation of its notes, and flocks often fly by within range of the gunner's blind. Mr. Nichols tells me that it will decoy well to the whistled imitation of the black-bellied plover's note. As it is no longer on the game-bird list, it will probably be given a chance to increase.

Some colonies have been washed out by high tides and their natural enemies, predatory animals and birds, have done considerable damage. P. B. Philipp (1910), who visited Raccoon Key, S. C., says:

The birds had been badly persecuted by fish crows and minks; broken and sucked eggs were found everywhere, and two nests were found in which the skeleton of the bird was lying on sucked eggs, the work of minks.

Field marks.—The willet, while standing on the ground, is a nondescript looking bird, almost devoid of characteristic markings, especially in the immature and winter plumages. It is about the size of the greater yellowlegs, but more heavily built, with shorter and heavier, bluish-gray legs, shorter neck, and decidedly heavier bill. Its drab colors match well into a background of sand or mud. But when it lifts its black and white wings or when flying, no bird is more easily recognized, for its color pattern is unique and conspicuous; the black wings, with their broad white band extending across the base of the tail, advertise the willet as far as they can be seen. Its notes, described above, are also quite characteristic.

Fall.—I imagine that the willets, which breed in Nova Scotia, migrate at sea to the West Indies, mainly in August. I have never seen an adult willet on the New England coast in the fall, and practically all that I have shot are referable to the western form, but it is not easy to recognize the two forms in immature plumage. Willets of some form, in immature plumage, are quite common at times in southern New England and on Long Island from the middle of July to the middle of September. The main flight comes in August. I suspect that these are practially all young western willets.

Winter.—The eastern willet spends the winter on the south Atlantic and Gulf coasts of North America, in the Bahamas and West Indies, and on the more northern coasts of South America. It is therefore resident or present the year round in much of its breeding range. It is rather rare as far north as South Carolina, but abundant in Florida and on the Gulf coasts, where the resident birds are reinforced by eastern and western willets from the North. In Florida they are occasionally seen about the ponds on the prairies or in the pine woods, but their favorite resorts are the broad mud flats in the estuaries and bayous or in the coastal marshes. In such places we often saw them in large flocks by themselves, where they were very shy and utterly unapproachable. Toward the end of March their numbers began to decrease, as the birds left for their breeding grounds.

Range.—The Atlantic and Gulf coasts of North America to northern South America; accidental in Kansas, Bermuda, and Europe.

Breeding range.—The breeding range of the willet extends north to Texas (Corpus Christi, Houston, and Galveston); Louisiana (Calcasieu, New Orleans, and Breton Island); Alabama (Grand Batture Island and Bayou Labatre); and Nova Scotia (Digby, Halifax, and Sable Island). East to Nova Scotia (Sable Island and Barrington); Massachusetts (formerly New Bedford and Nantucket); Connecticut (Madison and West Haven); New Jersey (Barnegat Inlet, Bridgeton, Beasleys Point, Sea Isle City, and Cape May); Maryland (Berlin); Virginia (Chincoteague, Hog Island, Cobb Island, and Norfolk); North Carolina (Atlantic and Beaufort); South Carolina (Waverly Mills, Sullivans Island, and Frogmore); Georgia (Savannah, Darien, and St. Simons Island); eastern Florida (Fernandina, Anastasia Island, New Smyrna, Turtle Mount, Mosquito Lagoon, Cape Canaveral, and Lake Worth); and the Bahama Islands (Great Bahama, Abaco, and Inagua.) South to the Bahama Islands (Inagua and Andros); the West Indies (Grand Cayman); western Florida (Indian Key and St. Marks); and Texas (Brownsville). West to Texas (Brownsville and Corpus Christi).

The breedings range above outlined has become greatly restricted, and while it is still reported as breeding in Nova Scotia, it is of rare occurrence at this season on the coasts of the Northern and Middle Atlantic States. Willets have been reported as nesting on Barbuda, West Indies, but the record is probably based upon non-breeding individuals which also have been noted in Cuba (Guantanamo).

Winter range.—The winter range extends north to Texas (Brownsville); Louisiana (State Game Preserve and Breton Island); Alabama (Coffee Island); and probably rarely Virginia (Cobb Island). East to rarely Virginia (Cobb Island); rarely North Carolina (Fort Macon); South Carolina (Waverly Mills and Frogmore); Georgia (Savannah and Darien); Florida (Fernandina, Mosquito Inlet, Indian River, Sebastian, and Royal Palm Hammock); the Bahama Islands (Grassy Creek and Caicos); Cuba; probably Haiti; Porto Rico (Boqueron and Anegada Island); the Lesser Antilles (Antigua, Barbados, Grenada, and Trinidad); British Guiana; and Brazil (Catejuba Island). South to Brazil (Catejuba Island and Guapore

River). West to Brazil (Guapore River); northeastern Colombia (Carthagena); probably Panama (Rio Juan Diaz); Yucatan (Merida and Cozumel Island); Tamaulipas (Matamoros); and Texas (Brownsville).

Spring migration.—Early dates of spring arrival are: New Jersey, Cape May, March 22, Long Beach, April 6, and Caldwell, April 7; Rhode Island, Rock Island, April 27; Massachusetts, Nantucket, May 2, Dennis, May 5, and Falmouth, May 11; and Nova Scotia, Yarmouth, April 22, and Wolfville, April 29.

Late dates of spring departure are: Mexico, Tampico, April 11; and Cuba, Trinidad, April 14, Siguanea, May 2, and Guantanamo, May 8.

Fall migration.—Information is lacking of the early arrival of the willet on the southern part of its winter range, but among late dates of fall departure are: Maine, Sagadahoc County, October 25; Massachusetts, Plymouth, October 4; Connecticut, Meriden, October 15; New Jersey, Salem County, October 8, and Caldwell, October 17; and Maryland, near Baltimore, about November 1.

Casual records.—The willet has been taken once in Kansas (near Hamilton, September 8, 1912); and one was obtained in Bermuda on July 3, 1848. It also has been reported on a few occasions from Europe, in all cases without complete data: France (Abbeville, also two in the Paris market); Dalmatia; and Sweden.

Egg dates.—Nova Scotia: 4 records, June 5 to 19. Virginia: 26 records, May 19 to June 16; 13 records, May 27 to June 8. South Carolina and Georgia: 53 records, March 10 to July 4; 27 records, May 9 to 22. Texas: 28 records, April 3 to June 10; 14 records, April 23 to May 24.

CATOPTROPHORUS SEMIPALMATUS INORNATUS (Brewster)

WESTERN WILLET

HABITS

When William Brewster (1887) described and named the western willet he characterized it as:

Differing from *S. semipalmata* in being larger, with a longer, slenderer bill; the dark markings above fewer, finer, and fainter, on a much paler (grayish-drab ground); those beneath duller, more confused or broken, and bordered by pinkish salmon, which often spreads over or suffuses the entire underparts, excepting the abdomen. Middle tail feathers either quite immaculate or very faintly barred.

It is a bird of the western interior; its main breeding grounds are in the Great Plains regions of the Northern States, west of the Mississippi River, and the central Provinces of Canada. Nearly all recent writers have recorded it as breeding on the coasts of Louisiana and Texas, an oft-repeated error. All the breeding birds that I have shot on the coasts of these two States, in May and June, were clearly referable to the eastern form. And I have been unable to find any specimens of *inornata* in collections that could be classed as breeding birds from these States. If the western willet breeds in Texas at all it must be on the plains or prairies of the interior. But it seems hardly likely that it would have a breeding range so widely separated from the northern range as outlined below. The eastern willet is strictly a coastwise bird and breeds, or did formerly, all along the Atlantic and Gulf coasts. On the other hand, the western willet is just as strictly a bird of the inland prairies and plains during the breeding season.

Spring.—The main migration route seems to be northward through the Mississippi Valley, chiefly in April; most of the birds are on their breeding grounds by the first of May or earlier and are laying eggs before the end of that month. Birds which winter in South Carolina and Florida probably join this route by an overland flight. There is a northward migration through the interior valleys of California to breeding grounds west of the Rocky Mountains, and probably some birds cross these mountains to the interior plains.

Nesting.—We found western willets very common about the lakes in the prairie regions of North Dakota and Saskatchewan; but owing to their habit of flying a long distance to meet the intruder and making a great fuss everywhere but near their nests, we succeeded in finding only one nest. This was on the higher portion of the open prairie, a long way from any water, near Big Stick Lake, Saskatchewan. The nest was a hollow in the ground, measuring 7 by 6 inches in diameter and 3 inches deep, lined with grasses and dry weeds. It was in plain sight in short grass; a few scattered dead weeds were standing around it, but no long grass. It contained three fresh eggs on June 14, 1906. Ernest T. Seton (Thompson, 1890) found a nest in Manitoba " which was placed in a slight hollow, shaded on one side by the skull of a buffalo and on the other by a tuft of grass," on an alkali plain.

The western willet breeds commonly in Boxelder County, Utah. Three sets of eggs in my collection, taken there on May 7, 13, and 16, 1916, by the Treganzas, came from nests described as slight depressions in short marsh grass; one was near an alkali flat, one near a water runway, and one on a partially grass-grown dike.

This bird is a rare, or very local, breeder in California. J. Van Denburgh (1919) reports five nests found on " a partially flooded mountain meadow " in Lassen County on June 1 and 6, 1918. " The nests were made of pieces of weeds rather carelessly built up on the mud. Some were found where the water was a few inches deep and some where the mud was drying."

Eggs.—The eggs of the western willet are indistinguishable from those of the eastern bird. There is a slight average difference in length, but the measurements widely overlap. The measurements of 56 eggs average 54.1 by 37.6 millimeters; the eggs showing the four extremes measure 58.1 by 39.4, 50.5 by 39.7, and 54.9 by 35 millimeters.

Plumages.—The sequence of plumages and molts is the same for both races, but juvenal western birds are somewhat paler than eastern birds, and they have less barring on the tail feathers or none at all.

Fall.—From its breeding grounds in the interior the western willet migrates in three main directions to the seacoasts, almost due east to the Atlantic coast of New York and New England, southeast and south to the south Atlantic and Gulf coasts and southwest to the California coast. Probably the birds which breed east of the Rocky Mountains take the easterly and southerly routes and those which breed west of these mountains migrate to California. Most of the willets which we get in Massachusetts in August are immature western willets; I have never seen an adult. These young birds apparently come from the Great Lakes region, where they have been recorded in Illinois and Ohio and as far north as Toronto, Ontario. John T. Nichols says in his notes:

Along the bays and marshes of the south shore of Long Island the willet is a regular late-summer migrant in small numbers varying from year to year. Southbound shore birds of other species are now following this coast to the westward, but a large majority of the willet are moving in the opposite direction; that is, from west to east. Its maximum flight seems to come in the beginning of August, and a peak of abundance for the species was reached in 1923. At Mastic on August 4, 1923, 14 willet were counted passing west to east in 3 flocks during 2½ hours' observation.

I have examined a number of specimens of these Long Island fall-migration willet, which have all been in the grey unmarked plumage of birds of the year (which I would not undertake to distinguish from adult fresh winter plumage), and remarkably uniform in size. Their bills varied scarcely at all in dimensions (slightly over 2¼ inches), being decidedly too long for the short-billed Virginia breeding bird, but much too short for the long-billed bird from the Dakotas (unless its young of the year are uniformly short-billed).

Winter.—Western willets mingle in winter with their eastern relatives on the South Atlantic and Gulf coast from Florida to Texas; they are especially abundant in Texas. They also winter abundantly from the coast of California southward. Bradford Torrey (1913) saw them, mixed with marbled godwits, near San Diego, in such numbers that he—

mistook them at first for a border of some kind of herbiage. Thousands there must have been; and when they rose at my approach they made something like a cloud; gray birds and brown birds so contrasted in color as to be discriminated beyond risk of error, even when too far away for the staring white wing patches of the willets to be longer discernible.

Mrs. Florence M. Bailey (1916) has well described their habits, as beach birds at this season, as follows:

In the flocks of brown godwits the few gray willets looked small. They fed in the same way as the godwits, though their bills were shorter and they could not probe so deep, but they ran their bills ahead of them through the wet sand, probed as far as they could reach, and then trotted back before the oncoming waves. A thoughtless one sat down just at the edge of the water line one day, its back toning in with the sand, its long legs stretched out before it; but soon after it was comfortably settled up came the foam and it had to bend forward on its tarsus, raise itself, and flee up the beach. I often saw one resting, standing on one leg, or sitting at ease with white rump showing. When stretching the black of the wings showed effectively as it does both when the birds fly up and when they alight with wings raised over the back. *Willet, willet*, they often called as they went.

DISTRIBUTION

Range.—United States and southern Canada (casually Alaska), south to northern South America.

Breeding range.—North to Oregon (Fort Klamath and Camp Harney); Montana (Bozeman); Alberta (probably Edmonton and Buffalo Lake); Saskatchewan (probably Quill Lake and Indian Head); Manitoba (Moose Mountain and Turtle Mountains); North Dakota (Cando and Larimore); Minnesota (Herman and Madison); and probably formerly Illinois (Belvidere and Glen Ellyn). East to probably formerly Illinois (Glen Ellyn). South to probably formerly Illinois (Glen Ellyn); Iowa (probably Newton and formerly Boone); Nebraska (Long Pine, Kennedy, Garden County, and Morrill County); Wyoming (probably Big Piney); Utah (Parleys Park and Salt Lake); and northern California (Beckwith). West to northern California (Beckwith, Grasshopper Valley, Alturas, and Goose Lake); and Oregon (probably Tule Lake and Fort Klamath). Non-breeding birds have been observed in summer as far south as Lower California (Mazatlan and San Quintin Bay); Colorado (Barr); Florida (Pensacola); and Alabama (Petit Bois Island).

Winter range.—North to California (Humboldt Bay); Texas (Brownsville, Corpus Christi, Rockport, and Refugio County); probably Louisiana; and Florida (Amelia Island). East to Florida (Amelia Island, Dummitts, and the Florida Keys); Tamaulipas (Tampico); probably Honduras (San Pedro); Ecuador (Bay of Santa Elena); and Peru (Tumbez). South to Peru (Tumbez); and the Galapagos Islands (Albemarle). West to the Galapagos Islands (Albemarle and Abingdon); Costa Rica (Lepanto); Guerrero (Aca-

pulco); Nyarit (San Blas); Lower California (San Quintin); and
California (San Diego, La Jolla, Morro Bay, San Francisco, Bodega
Bay, and Humboldt Bay).

Spring migration.—Early dates of arrival are: Arkansas, Osceola,
March 29; Missouri, Stotesbury, April 8, and St. Louis, April 27;
Illinois, Quincy, April 5, and Big Lake, April 29; Iowa, Cedar
Rapids, April 2, Emmetsburg, April 21, and Keokuk, April 30;
Wisconsin, Heron Lake, April 10, and Waseca, April 10; Minnesota,
Lanesboro, April 26; Kansas, Manhattan, April 28, and McPherson,
April 30; Nebraska, Niobrara, April 26, Neligh, May 1, and Valentine,
May 5; South Dakota, Pitrodie, April 25, and Forestburg, April 28;
North Dakota, Charlson, May 1, Jamestown, May 1, and Harrisburg,
May 2; Manitoba, Treesbank, April 30; Saskatchewan, Indian Head,
April 26, Wiseton, May 2, and Eastend, May 7; Colorado, Durango,
April 15, Barr, April 20, and Baca County, April 28; Utah, Great
Salt Lake, April 12; Wyoming, Cokeville, April 26, and Cheyenne,
April 30; Montana, Lewiston, May 2, and Billings, May 4; Oregon,
Narrows, April 15; and Alberta, Flagstaff, April 26, Vagreville,
April 28, and Alliance, April 29.

Late dates of spring departure are: Florida, Indian Rocks, May 6;
Alabama, Coden, May 17; Tamaulipas, Tampico, April 11; Texas,
Brownsville, April 23, and Texas City, May 13; Lower California,
Tres Marias Islands, April 8, and Cerros Island, April 18; and
Nyarit, San Blas, April 24, and Los Penas Island, May 5.

Fall migration.—Early dates of arrival in the fall are: Lower
California, San Quintin, August 8; Arizona, San Bernardino Ranch,
August 13; New Mexico, Carlsbad, August 16, and Capitan Moun-
tains, August 28; Oklahoma, Yarnaby, August 9; Texas, Padre Is-
land, August 20; and Tehuantepec, San Mateo, August 6. Western
willets also are of fairly regular occurrence in fall migration on the
Atlantic coast, specimens having been collected in Massachusetts,
Newburyport, August 5, and Boston, August 8; Connecticut, Stony
Creek, August 15, and West Haven, August 26; Rhode Island,
Quonochontaug, August 5; and New York, Amityville, August 14,
and Hempstead Bay, August 15.

Late dates of fall departure are: Oregon, Yaquina Bay, October
1; Montana, Terry, September 8; Idaho, Rupert, October 20; Nevada,
Carson River, October 13; Arizona, San Bernardino Ranch, Septem-
ber 2; Wyoming, Yellowstone Park, September 13; New Mexico,
Jicarilla Apache Reservation, September 13; Saskatchewan, Red-
berry, September 2; North Dakota, Dawson, September 17, and
Harrisburg, October 3; Nebraska, Long Pine, September 10, and
Lincoln, September 29; Iowa, Cerro Gordo County, September 2, and

Keokuk, October 27; Illinois, Chicago, September 30; and Connecticut, West Haven, September 3, and once in October.

Casual records.—In spite of its regular occurrence on the Atlantic coast, the western willet has been detected only on a few occasions in the interior States east of the Mississippi River. There appear to be several records for Ohio from April 30 (Oberlin) to November 2 (Bay Point); one for Indiana, Millers, August 14, 1897; and one for Michigan, Ann Arbor, May, 1889. One was taken July 20, 1898 at Toronto, Ontario, and four other specimens without data are presumed to be from the same locality (Fleming). Other casual occurrences are: Washington, Seattle, July 23, 1922, and Tacoma, September 6, 1913; British Columbia, Clover Point, August 18, 1898; probably Yukon, Lake Marsh, July 2, 1899; and Alaska, Lynn Canal (Hartlaub).

Egg dates.—Utah: 32 records, April 5 to May 21; 16 records, May 4 to 14. Saskatchewan and North Dakota: 19 records, May 8 to June 22; 10 records, May 23 to June 7. Washington to California: 9 records, May 8 to June 16.

HETEROSCELUS INCANUS (Gmelin)

WANDERING TATTLER

HABITS

Along the rocky and stony portions of the Pacific coast, and especially on the islands and outlying reefs, this ocean wanderer is a common and well-known bird. Here it is much at home among the surf-swept rocks, drenched in ocean spray and often enveloped in fog; it has no fear of foaming breakers, which it nimbly dodges as it seeks its bits of marine food among the kelp and barnacles on the rocks. It is, at most seasons, essentially a bird of the seashore, but is seldom seen on the sandy or muddy shores. The dark color of its upper plumage matches its surroundings and it is not easily seen among the gloomy rocks, unless its characteristic outline can be seen against the sky or water as it poses on the top of some prominent rock to watch the intruder. If he approach too near, it flies off a short distance with loud, piercing cries and alights on another rock, to bob and teeter, somewhat like our familiar spotted and solitary sandpipers. It is generally solitary and seems to be satisfied with its own society.

It is well named, as it is a famous wanderer. I am tempted to quote Dr. E. W. Nelson's (1887) well-chosen words on this subject, as follows:

Over the entire coast of the Pacific north of the equator its presence has been noted by the various naturalists whose Bohemian tastes have made their lives somewhat akin to that of this gentle wanderer. Across the broad ocean it ranges to those bits of paradise dotting the South Seas, tripping its way daintily on the beaches of the coral-enclosed islands, their feet laved by the warm waters of the tropics, and their eyes familiar with the luxuriant face of nature in its gentlest and most lovely state. The next season may find them thousands of miles to the north, under the shadow of the stupendous cliffs and grand but desolate and repellent scenes of the Aleutian Islands.

Spring.—Prof. Wells W. Cooke (1912) says that "the spring migration begins in March, bringing the birds to the coast of California by the latter part of the month. The Aleutian Islands are reached the middle of May, and the most northern part of the range by the latter part of the month." H. W. Henshaw (1902) says that "about April or May the greater number" leave the Hawaiian Islands for the north. "While most go, many remain, the latter being the immature birds and the weaklings. At all events, those that remain retain the immature or winter dress and show not the slightest inclination to breed." Henry Seebohm (1890) reports a straggler taken on the Bonin Islands on May 11, 1889. D. E. Brown's notes record one at Forrester Island, Alaska, on May 3, 1917, and several at Grays Harbor, Wash., from May 4 to 21, 1920. He says: "At low tide these birds were found, with flocks of black turnstone, on the rock jetty and at high tide among the drift logs on the upper beach."

Nesting.—The nesting habits of the wandering tattler long remained shrouded in mystery. Various observers had seen it on or near its probable breeding grounds in the interior of different parts of Alaska. Dr. Wilfred H. Osgood (1907) collected a very young bird in which "the head and neck were still downy," near the upper MacMillan River, Yukon, on September 5, 1904, and he reported a pair, which evidently had young, seen by Charles Sheldon, near Mount McKinley, July 28, 1906. Dr. Joseph Grinnell (1910) mentions a "half-grown juvenal" taken by Joseph Dixon on Montague Island, July 28, 1908.

The first nest was found in 1912 and is thus described in a letter from J. M. Jessup to Dr. Charles W. Richmond, accompanied by a specimen of the bird:

The wandering tattler was found nesting on a gravel bar near a small stream flowing into the Arctic Ocean, the exact location was about latitude 69° 10' and longitude 141° west, or about 25 miles south of the Arctic Ocean near the international boundary between Canada and Alaska. The nest was first observed by Sir Frederick Lambart of the Canadian Coast and Geodetic Survey, and was later identified by myself. Sir Frederick describes the nest as follows: "The nest was situated in the middle of an elevated gravel bar open to the sky for fully 50 feet all around. The nest was just alongside a small rock; there were no sticks or any form of nest material, it consisted merely of a semispherical hollow in dry fine and coarse gravel. Four eggs were in the nest, I should say about the size of a ptarmigan's, brownish blue and mottled very much like a sandpiper's. The young birds were noted to have come out of the eggs July 9."

Ten years later Olaus J. Murie (1924) collected a downy, young wandering tattler on Jennie Creek, a small tributary of Savage River, in the Alaska Range, on June 9, 1922. The following year he completed the record by finding a nest and collecting the first and only set of eggs ever taken. He has given us a very good account of the whole proceeding, from which I quote, as follows:

The following day, July 1, we continued up Savage River 9 miles and made permanent camp. We had been on the lookout for the birds and I had pointed out to Mr. Buhmann one in the distance, that he might have an idea for what we were looking. About noon Mr. Buhmann and my brother were riding on the wagon, while I walked ahead over the usual gravel bars, when Mr. Buhmann suddenly called out to me, " Is that one of your birds?" I turned and saw a wandering tattler flying away. The bird had been flushed by the horses. We all three walked back carefully beside the wagon and in a few moments spied the nest and eggs a short distance to the rear, not over 6 inches from the wheel track! Mr. Buhmann picked up one of the eggs, wishing, as he enthusiastically explained, to be the first one who had ever handled the egg of a wandering tattler. I explained that the eggs should not be disturbed until photographed, and it was carefully replaced in the nest. A series of exposures was made of the nest and eggs, and we moved away some distance with our outfit and prepared our lunch. In the meantime the bird returned and settled on the nest. Several photographs were then taken of the bird on the eggs, the last one at a distance of about 10 feet or less. The nest and eggs were then taken and carried to our camping ground.

All our observations indicate that this nesting site is characteristic, that the wandering tattler prefers the gravel bars of mountain streams, as typified by Savage River. These rivers are rapid and split into numerous channels, sometimes in an intricate network over the gravelly valley. This nest was found on Savage River about 5 miles above the mouth of Jennie Creek at an elevation of about 4,000 feet. It was placed on a gravel bar about 30 feet from the nearest water, and was sunk in a shallow depression in the gravel. It was well built, unusually elaborate for a shore bird. It was composed principally of fine roots carefully woven into a firm structure, including a number of twigs around the edges. Small bits of twigs and some dry leaves had been used for lining. It was so compact that I had no difficulty in picking it up and transporting it to camp. The diameter of the nest to the edges of the finely woven body was about 5 inches, but, of course, some of the twigs extended much farther.

Eggs.—The eggs taken by Mr. Murie on Savage River, Alaska, July 1, 1923, are now in the United States National Museum and are, so far as I know, the only eggs in existence. In shape they are between pyriform and subpyriform, and they have a slight gloss. The ground color is between " glaucous " and "greenish glaucous," as in some crow's eggs. They are spotted and blotched irregularly, rather heavily near the larger end and rather sparsely elsewhere, with dark browns, from "seal brown " or "bone brown" to "burnt umber " or " Verona brown "; there are some elongated splashes and some small, inconspicuous, underlying spot of various shades of "brownish drab." They measure 43.3 by 32.7, 44.5 by 31.4, 44.1 by 31.5, and 43.7 by 32.3 millimeters.

Young.—The young are able to run about soon after they are hatched and are carefully guarded by both parents. An adult, secured by Mr. Murie with the downy young, proved to be a male. "A whistled *cheep*, imitating a chick, would bring the excited bird within a few feet." Mr. Jessup writes that the mother bird was much distressed and attempted to lure him from her little one by feigning lameness.

Plumages.—Mr. Murie (1924) has described the downy young very well, as follows:

These downy young may be described as follows: Under parts dull white with a faint indication of grayish on upper breast and lower fore neck; upper parts pale gray, with a very slight suggestion of buffy on wings, rump, and tail, more evident in the fresh specimens than in the skin; upper parts narrowly, irregularly, and indistinctly barred with blackish, with dull black loral and postocular streaks and with irregular black spots on hind pileum. In a colored sketch made from freshly killed bird, tarsus and upper part of toes appear dull glaucous green; the under surface of foot olive yellow; bill dull glaucous blue.

Another bird which I have examined, as a dried skin, does not show any buffy tints. A young bird, mainly in juvenal plumage but still downy on the hind neck, chin and forehead, taken on September 5, is from "deep mouse gray" to "dark olive gray" above, with very faint whitish tips; the wing coverts have more prominent white edgings; the chest is "pallid mouse gray," and the flanks "pale mouse gray," both more or less indistinctly barred; the rest of the under parts are white. A limited postjuvenal molt of the body plumage occurs in September, producing the first winter plumage; this is much like the adult, except that the juvenal wing coverts, some of the scapulars and the mottled plumage of the breast and flanks are retained. Some young birds apparently assume a plumage which is practically adult at the first prenuptial molt in April.

Adults have a complete postnuptial molt from August to January, the wings being molted last, between October and January. I have seen birds in full nuptial plumage from April 13 to September 14 and in full winter plumage as late as April 12. In winter adults the upper parts are slightly lighter gray than in summer, the sides of the head, chest and flanks are still lighter gray and the chin and belly are white. The partial prenuptial molt occurs in April.

Food.—The usual feeding grounds of the wandering tattler are the rocky shores, where it searches for its food among the kelp-covered rocks at the water's edge, following the receding waves and nimbly dodging the incoming breakers or making short flights to avoid the surf. If over-taken and drenched it flies to a rock, shakes the water from its plumage and soon resumes its feeding. B. J. Bretherton (1896) says that on Kodiak Island:

This species seemed to habitually frequent the sand or gravel beaches in preference to rocky localities, and had regular feeding grounds to which they resorted at certain stages of the tide, returning regularly each day at the same time. Their food consists largely of decapods together with small crabs, marine worms, and minute mollusks.

Its food seems to be mainly insects, but includes small crustaceans, minute mollusks, marine worms, and other small marine animals. The contents of six stomachs, reported on by Preble and McAtee (1923) consisted of "flies (Diptera), 46.1 per cent; caddis flies 30.6 per cent; amphipods, 16 per cent; mollusks, 3.6 per cent; and beetles 1.1 per cent."

Behavior.—The movements of wandering tattlers are often suggestive of spotted sandpipers with which they are sometimes associated; they indulge in the same "tip-up" motion of the body, though less frequently; and their flight is very similar, with intermittent strokes of down-curved wings. W. Leon Dawson (1923) says:

When it alights, it sits for some time motionless in a plover like attitude, with its long bill held horizontally, invisible, in the dull light of a foggy day, unless, perchance, outlined against the surf. At other times the bird will betray its uneasiness by a jetting motion of the tail.

In his notes on the Farallones, Mr. Dawson (1911) says:

Contrary to earlier statements these tattlers do spend a considerable portion of their time upon the higher ground. The tiny bowlder-strewn meadow surrounding my earlier camp (just east of Franconia Beach) was a favorite resting place for them, and I am inclined to think the birds spent the night there, for some were invariably startled upon my first appearance mornings. Having a common affection for the tide reefs, wandering tattlers are not infrequently found in loose association with black turnstones; but when put to flight they pay no attention whatever to the fortunes of their chance shipmates nor to others of their own kind.

Dr. E. W. Nelson (1883) writes:

Their note is a loud, ringing whistle, which seems specially fitted to the bird and the haunts it occupies, and as the shrill cry reechoes from the towering cliffs and ledges at the base of which it feeds its peculiar character and intonation might lead one to fancy some genie of the rocks was uttering its cry. When the birds are approached by boat as they are feeding along the water's edge they ascend gradually, with an expression of mild curiosity, and pass from ledge to ledge until they reach a jutting point on the face of the cliff or its brow, where they stand in relief, like beautiful clear-cut statuettes, and do not utter a sound or move until they are still further alarmed, when they take flight, uttering at the same moment their loud note before mentioned.

Voice.—Doctor Nelson (1880) describes its note as "a loud, ringing *kla, kla, kla,*" and again he (1887) calls it "a loud, clear, flutelike *tu, tu, tu, tu.*" Mr. Dawson (1923) says it is "a quavering cry, somewhat like the *tew, tew, tew* of the greater yellowlegs, but more subdued." Mr. Murie (1924) writes:

> Whenever I approached the home grounds of a wandering tattler he would fly to meet me and would scold excitedly, uttering a vigorous *deedle-deedle-deedle-deedle-dee*, with variations which I failed to record minutely.

Fall.—Doctor Nelson (1887) says:

> They usually reappear on the seacoast about St. Michaels the last of July or very early in August and remain until from the 1st to 10th of September. During their presence on the coast of Norton Sound they show a decided preference for the most rugged and rock-bound parts of the shore, rarely or never occurring elsewhere. It is a frequent and regular summer bird on the rocky parts of the coast to the vicinity of Bering Straits and occurs on the islands and Siberian shore of Bering Sea.

William Palmer (1899) says that on the Pribilof Islands:

> It is the first species to return in the fall; adult birds, July 10 and afterwards. Usually in pairs on the surf-swept rocks, but sometimes seen—usually the brownish, unbarred, and less wary immature—on open sandy places, and sometimes with the turnstones on a sandy beach. They are not shy, but are seldom noticed when perched on the wet rocks, which harmonize so well with their color. Solitary birds remain quiet and unseen and will permit one to approach quite close, frequently startling us as they get up suddenly, almost under our very feet, and uttering their loud, shrill cry, flying off to another resting place.

From the Aleutian Islands and the interior of Alaska there is a southward migration to the islands in the Pacific, where it spends the winter, and a more general movement southward along the Pacific coast of North America. D. E. Brown's notes record it on the coast of Washington from August 10 to September 15. It has been recorded in California early in July, but these were perhaps summer sojourners; the return movement seems to come along between July 15 and August. H. W. Henshaw (1902) says that the return migrants begin to appear in the Hawaiian Islands "about the middle or latter part of August"; he noticed that "the first comers are adults, chiefly males, and still in nuptial dress."

Winter.—The Santa Barbara Islands, off the coast of southern California, mark the northern limit of the normal winter range of the wandering tattler, where a few may always be found in winter. Most of the birds go farther south. W. B. Alexander tells me that the wandering tattler occasionally visits Cape York, North Queensland, and there is a specimen, unquestionably of this species, in the Museum of Comparative Zoölogy in Cambridge, from Australia.

DISTRIBUTION

Range.—Western North and South America, eastern Asia, and Oceanica.

Breeding range.—The nest and eggs of the wandering tattler have actually been found only on one occasion (Savage River, Alaska [Murie]); but the evidence of young birds seems sufficient to establish additional breeding stations in Alaska (Mount McKinley and probably Montague Island); and in Yukon (Russell Mountains). They probably breed also in eastern Siberia (Plover Bay). Nonbreeding specimens have been observed or collected in summer at many localities on the Pacific coast, south to Lower California (Socorro Island, San Jose Island, and Cocos Island); and the Hawaiian Islands (Cocoanut Island).

Winter range.—The winter range of the wandering tattler extends north to the Philippine Islands (Mindanao); the Hawaiian Islands (Laysan, Kauai, and Hawaii); and probably, rarely, Oregon (Cannon Beach). East to probably, rarely Oregon (Cannon Beach); California (Santa Cruz Island, and Santa Monica); Lower California (Cedros Island, Comondu, and San Jose Island); and the Galapagos Islands (Abingdon, Indefatigable, Chatham, and Hood). South to the Galapagos Island (Hood and Albemarle); Paumotu Islands; Society Islands (Huaheine); Samoa; Fiji Islands (Ovalau); New Hebrides (Aneiteum); and northeastern Australia (Cape York). West to northeastern Australia (Cape York); and the Philippine Islands (Mindanao).

Spring migration.—Early dates of spring arrival are: Washington, Shoalwater Bay, May 1; Alaska, Forrester Island, May 7, Cape Prince of Wales, May 11, Sannak Island, May 15, Unalaska Island, May 18, and Mount McKinley, May 18; and Siberia, Copper Island, May 17.

Late dates of spring departure are: Guerrero, Acapulco, April 30; Lower California, Cedros Island, April 24, Socorro Island, May 10, Guadaloupe Island, May 18, and Clarion Island, May 20; California, San Nicholas Island, May 11, and Eureka, May 18; Washington, Neah Bay, May 20, and Flattery Rock, June 2; and British Columbia, Courtenay, May 23, and Comox, June 4.

Fall migration.—Early dates of arrival in the fall, are: British Columbia, Okanagan, July 26; Washington, Clallam Bay, July 16, and Quillayute Needles, July 17; Oregon, Seal Rocks, July 22, and Crater Lake, July 27; California, Farallon Islands, July 13, Monterey Bay, July 14, and Santa Cruz, August 1; and Lower California, Los Coronados Islands, August 6, and Cedros Island, August 14.

Late dates of fall departure are: Alaska, St. Paul Island, October 4, and Unalaska, October 16; British Columbia, Okanagan, September 20; and Washington, Seattle, September 18, and Clallam Bay, September 19.

Egg Dates.—Alaska: One record, July 1, 1925.

HETEROSCELUS BREVIPES (Vieillot)

POLYNESIAN TATTLER

HABITS

Three specimens of this Asiatic sandpiper have been taken in the Pribilof Islands; the first was secured on St. Paul Island, October 4, 1911, by M. C. Marsh; the other two were taken by G. Dallas Hanna, on the same island, September 2, 1917, and September 17, 1919. These constitute the only North American records. It is not easily distinguished in life from the wandering tattler and so may have occurred much oftener on our extreme western coasts.

Dr. Leonard Stejneger (1885), who took an adult male on Bering Island, in the Commanders, May 28, 1882, devotes considerable space to showing that this is a species distinct from *incanus;* but some recent writers have treated it as a subspecies. The principal differences are that *brevipes* is somewhat smaller, has a shorter nasal groove, and has the tarsus scutellated instead of reticulated at the back; the belly and under tail coverts are pure white in all plumages, whereas in *incanus* these parts are barred in the nuptial plumage; and the upper tail coverts, which are nearly uniform gray in *incanus*, are distinctly barred with white. The structural differences would seem to warrant specific rank.

The Polynesian tattler is supposed to breed in eastern Siberia, from Lake Baikal to Kamchatka, but, so far as I know, its nest has never been found and nothing is known about its nesting habits, eggs, or young.

Plumages.—Except for the specific characters outlined above the plumages and molts are similar to those of the wandering tattler. In the juvenal plumage the feathers of the upper parts are notched with light buff or white; the upper tail coverts are tipped and irregularly barred with the same colors; the upper breast and flanks are suffused with light gray, more or less mottled on the chest; the tail feathers and wing coverts are tipped or notched or barred with pale buff or white; they are otherwise like winter adults.

This plumage is worn until September, when the body plumage, some of the tail feathers, and some of the wing coverts are molted, to produce the first winter plumage, which can be distinguished from the adult only by the retained tail feathers and wing coverts. In some birds a partial prenuptial molt produces a plumage which is nearly adult, but in others this molt is suppressed and a molt into the adult winter plumage comes later.

Adults have a complete postnuptial molt between July and January, and a partial prenuptial molt, involving the body plumage, the tail and some of the wing coverts, scapulars, and tertials.

Behavior.—The habits, and probably the food, of the Polynesian tattler are apparently similar to those of our American bird. Doctor Hanna (1920) says:

I had an opportunity to observe this bird for a while with two wandering tattlers in view at the time. The actions of the two species were practically the same. They feed very close to the sea on rocky shores and when disturbed fly lazily, rarely more than 100 yards. The wandering tattlers on this occasion appeared perceptibly larger than the Polynesian and the notes of the two were different. The latter uttered an irregular screech not of the same intensity or pitch, whereas the former gave its usual call, a series of 6 to 10 individual notes uttered in the same pitch and rapid succession, but each of shortening duration.

Winter.—This tattler migrates southward in winter through the Kurile Islands and Japan to the Malay Archipelago, the Philippines, and Australia. W. B. Alexander (1926) says of it in North Queensland:

This was the commonest species of sandpiper on the beaches at Cairns and Yarrabah early in September, feeding in small parties. The first were noted on September 1. They are easily recognized by their gray plumage and yellow legs, though the latter are not so brightly colored as those of the two species known in America as yellowlegs.

DISTRIBUTION

Range.—Eastern Asia, Melanesia, and Australia; casual on the Pribilof Islands.

The Polynesian tattler breeds in eastern Siberia, from Lake Baikal to Kamchatka; in migration it passes through China, Japan, and the Philippine Islands to winter quarters in the Malay Archipelago and northern Australia (Queensland).

Casual records.—This species has been detected in North America on three occasions, all on St. Paul Island, of the Pribilof group, Alaska (October 4, 1911, September 2, 1917, and September 17, 1919).

PHILOMACHUS PUGNAX (Linnaeus)

RUFF

Contributed by Francis Charles Robert Jourdain

HABITS

The claim of the ruff to a place in the American list is a much stronger one than that of most of the Palaearctic species which figure in it, as it has occurred three times in Greenland, once in Canada, on many occasions in the eastern States, in Barbados, Guadeloupe, and South America.

Spring.—Apparently the ruff migrates chiefly by night and in this connection it is noticeable that the period of its greatest activity in the breeding season is during the twilight of the early morning hours. Naumann (1887) states that the first birds to arrive are the young of the preceding year, and that the adult males are the next to follow while they in turn are succeeded by the old females. Owing to the enormous development of the feathered ruff from which the species derives its names, the males are readily distinguished during the breeding season even in flight and on the ground can be recognized at almost any distance.

Courtship.—The breeding habits of the ruff are so remarkable that it is necessary to treat of them in considerable detail. When the males reach the breeding ground they are in full breeding plumage, the bare skin of the face being covered with bright yellow warts, while a disk of feathers protects the neck and two tufts project from each side of the head. The extraordinary variation in the coloring of these feather adornments renders it possible to identify individual birds, as it is rare to see two with even approximately similar coloring, and this enabled Mr. Selous (1906) to make the valuable observations which are referred to below.

Where ruffs are common, as in North Holland, one finds from time to time bare areas of ground where the grass has been worn away in patches. They are the playing grounds of the ruffs, and were known in England technically as " hills." During the daytime they are resorted to from time to time by the male birds, which may often be seen sparring with one another, but the significance of these meetings was little understood until Edmund Selous (1906) spent a fortnight in the spring of 1906 in Holland, during which he concealed himself in a hide which commanded a good view of the " hill " at close quarters, and was often on the watch before daylight. The diary of his observations was first published in the *Zoologist* for 1906 and 1907, and is too lengthy and discursive to be reproduced here, but in the following condensed account most of the essential facts have been preserved. The " hill " under observation was roughly about 10 paces by 6, with 11 distinct patches where the grass had been worn bare, besides a couple of others less plainly marked. There were other similar " hills " in the neighborhood, all much alike, placed on dry ground, in the neighborhood of marshes. They are resorted to year after year, and bear traces of excrement from previous seasons, while the grass is much worn away owing to the presence of the birds. Some of the Dutch " hills " are quite close to or actually in the way of paths, and the birds when disturbed by passers-by will return to the ground within a few minutes. Like many other Dutch birds they show much indifference to the presence of man, owing to the fact that no shooting is permitted during the breeding season. On April 14 a single male was disturbed by Selous from the " hill " at 7 a. m. and did not return, but on the next day a flock of eight or nine birds arrived and at once began to fight, but not on the " hill." It soon became evident that in order to be in place before the arrival of the birds it was necessary to get into hiding before dawn. By April 16 the " hill " was in regular use, each male resorting to the same stand and sitting there, from time to time rising and making a slight demonstration with erected tufts and ruff, sometimes followed by a slight sparring match with one of the other males, but when not engaged in fighting spending the time quite amicably side by side, in some cases almost touching. In the afternoon a similar state of things prevailed, but the proceedings were quieter and more subdued. When sparring the birds " would rush and leap high into the air against each other, rushing away and not leaping again as they came down," and this activity was generally more pronounced when a reeve appeared on the ground. The other birds on occasions of this kind also rushed about in wild excitement, suddenly pulling themselves up with the head extended forward and remaining in this position motionless, perhaps then rushing in another direction and then gradually sinking down quickly. When a reeve arrived at the " hill," where perhaps a dozen males were present, after the first wave of excitement had passed she would thread her way among the ruffs, which as she approached sank down to the ground by her side with bowed head. Her preference for one particular male was shown by halting at his side and gently nibbling with her bill the feathers at the back of his neck. If copulation followed, there was no interference on the part of the other males present, except perhaps occasionally by accident in the course of excited running to and fro.

After persistent watching it became evident that the attentions of the reeves were very unevenly distributed among the regular habitues of the " hill." There were two conspicuously handsome males—one a bird with a golden-brown ruff and the other with a blue-black one— and these two seemed to be selected far more frequently than the other ruffs. The few attempts made by males to force the compliance of the female were quite unsuccessful. Perhaps it is due to this that attempts to pair between two male birds frequently took place and, strange to relate, even between two reeves also. Selection on the part of the hen birds apparently bore no relation to the fighting powers of the male, although one serious fight, which lasted some three or four minutes, took place, during which the two birds concerned fought like demons, but finally ceased by mutual consent. The two selected birds were, however, certainly among the finest and handsomest birds on the ground. While the stations were usually occupied by the same birds day after day, there were times when over 20 birds were present, so it is probable that males from other "hills" call in at times. While it was clear that one ruff paired with several reeves, it was much more difficult to prove that the reeves paired with more than one male, owing to their general similarity of appearance, though it is probable that this was the case. The following extract from Selous (1906) gives a good description of the characteristic sparring:

Each ruff has certainly a place of its own, and the most envenomed fights appear to me to result from one bird pitching down in another's place when he flies in. The aggrieved bird instantly rushes at the intruder and there is a fight which may last for a longer or shorter time. The birds have then a perfectly frantic appearance. They kick, strike with their wings, and especially endeavor to bite or peck each other. This biting is very noticeable, the mandibles seeming to snap with rage. They leap commonly before they close and then continue to do so as a matter of course, the object seeming to be, as with other birds, to get above the adversary and strike down upon him with wings and feet and bill. Of course, when one bird is displaced by another, others are displaced also, leading to general commotion and, moreover, the mere anticipation of any fresh arrival is matter for excitement for every ruff on the ground.

Summarizing the results of Mr. Selous' observations, it becomes evident that the "hills" are the pairing grounds to which both males and females resort, but the period of the greatest activity is during the early morning from about 3.30 a. m. onward. Each male has a definite place and the choice of a mate rests entirely with the female, the males adopting an attitude of supplication, crouching low with partially spread wings, tail and beak pointing to the ground. The hen marks her preference by nibbling the back of the neck of the prostrate male with her bill, and soon afterwards coition takes place, the surrounding males remaining usually quiescent. One reeve was seen to pair with two ruffs in succession and it is probable that she is polyandrous as the ruff is certainly polygamous. There seemed to be no connection between the fighting power of the males and the preference exercised so strikingly by the females, but, on the other hand, the favored ruffs were apparently always handsome and strikingly colored birds.

Nesting.—The reeve makes her nest within a reasonable distance of the "hill," but not very close to it. Naumann (1887) says that it is never less than a hundred paces distant, and most of those which I have seen were within a quarter of a mile. In the Dutch water meadows the usual nesting site is among fine, thickly growing grass, where it is difficult to see unless one's eye is caught by a glimpse of the nest hollow. In the marshes of Lapland, where vegetation is more backward, it may be found among clumps of sedge and rushes. It is built entirely of fine grasses, and would frequently be overlooked if it were not for the sight of the bird when flushed.

Eggs.—Normally four; sets of three are quite exceptional and are probably second or third layings. They are pyriform in shape, thin shelled, and, as is frequently the case with the eggs of waders, large for the size of the bird. The ground color varies· from brownish yellow to pale olive brown as a rule, but occasionally has a greenish tinge, while varieties with a clear pale blue ground are not very scarce. The markings consist of spots and blotches of brown ranging from umber to dark sepia and ashy grey shellmarks, more numerous at the large end. White eggs have been recorded. The measurements of 143 eggs, chiefly by the writer, average 43.97 by 30.7 millimeters; the eggs showing the four extremes measure **47.5** by 30.5, 43.2 by **32.1, 39.2** by 31.6, and 42.9 by **28** millimeters.

They are usually laid in central Europe during the latter half of May and early in June, occasionally in the second week of May. In northern Europe most eggs are found during the latter half of June. Only one brood is reared in the season.

Young.—Incubation is performed by the female alone. Naumann (1887) gives the incubation period as 17 to 19 days, but this is probably too low an estimate and recently Heinroth has recorded 27 days. From observations made by Mr. W. H. St. Quinten on young hatched in captivity they leave the nest very soon after hatching, apparently directly the down is dry. The reeve is a good mother, and I have seen one when flushed from eggs on the point of hatching run from the nest, flapping her wings in a helpless way as if unable to fly. Another bird was also seen trying to distract attention by running with every feather erect, looking more like some small mammal than a bird.

Plumages.—The plumages and moults are fully described in A Practical Handbook of British Birds, edited by H. F. Witherby.

Food.—The ruff is mainly insectivorous, feeding largely on beetles (Coleoptera), chiefly the smaller species. Jäckel records specimens of the following genera: *Agonum, Bembidium, Parnus, Cyclonotum, Sitones, Pisodes, Rhinoncus, Philhydrus.* Weevils are also mentioned by Florence. Among the Orthoptera remains of grasshoppers were found by Slater. Neuroptera met with include caddis worms and cases (Phryganeidae) and larvae of *Ephemera,* Trichoptera (*Limnophilus* by Jäckel) who also records *Naucoris* (Hemiptera). It will be noted that most of the above are aquatic forms. Diptera are a staple food in the north, including larvae of Tipulidae and many small species. Of Mollusca, Slater records small fresh water bivalves, Collett worms (*Lumbrici*). In winter the food is more largely vegetable in character, though fresh water algae and seeds of *Rumex* have been recorded in summer. Rice is frequently found in birds killed in India and Mellor also found in seven cases nothing but durra grains (Sorghum) from 19 to 228 in number.

Voice.—The ruff is an extremely silent bird. One may live among them in the Dutch polders for weeks together in the spring, and never hear a sound from them, except a very low guttural or quacking note from a reeve when disturbed from a family of young. Naumann (1887) however describes a note *kack*, *kack*, *kick*, *kack*, which is probably the same as that which Slater writes as *wick*, repeated rapidly several times. Unless much persecuted it is confiding in its habits and pays little attention to the presence of men.

Enemies.—In England its extermination was primarily due to the reckless way in which the breeding stock was netted not only in autumn but also on arrival in spring on the "hilling" grounds, in order to be fattened for the table. Montagu's account of the state of things in his day has been quoted at length in many books on British birds, so that it is not necessary to repeat it here. As Pennant spoke of 40 or 50 dozen birds being taken by a single fowler in a season it is not surprising that the stock was rapidly reduced to so low a level that in spite of belated efforts to protect the birds and their eggs, it has now practically disappeared. On the continent where it is still locally common it has to contend against other avian enemies, more especially the harriers (*Circus*), but also the goshawk, peregrine, and to some extent gulls and crows.

Fall.—The distinctive plumes of the male are shed in June and in July the autumn plumage is assumed even in the extreme north. The males begin to disappear from their breeding haunts in central Europe in late July and early August, while the females are said to leave in September.

Winter.—In their winter quarters ruffs are generally sociable and are to be met with in small flocks, which show a preference to fresh water marshes rather than the sea coast. In India and the Sudan the flooded fields are a great attraction and the staple food consists of grain.

DISTRIBUTION

Breeding range.—Formerly at many places in England from Northumberland southward, lingering until recently in Norfolk. Belgium, locally in North France, Holland, Denmark, North Germany, and Bavaria (Jäckel). Hungary, Czechoslovakia, the Baltic Republics, Norway, Sweden, Finland, Russia north to Kolguev, Waigatz, and Dolgoi and south to Bessarabia and Orenburg. In Asia, Siberia north to 72° on the Yenisei and east to the Lena and Kolyma valleys, south to Dauria, Turgai and Uralsk.

Winter range.—From Europe through Africa south to Cape Province, but scarce on passage in the Atlantic Islands. Asia, south to India, Ceylon (scarce), Burma, also recorded from China and Japan, Borneo (Labuan), etc.

Spring migration.—At the Straits of Gibraltar the northward movement begins in January and does not cease till May, but it is at its height in April. Some birds winter in the Mediterranean region and these have usually gone by the middle of April. In the eastern Mediterranean the passage begins in the Ionian Isles about March 15 and in Corfu in March.

Fall migration.—The return passage through southern Spain takes place in August and September, while in Greece, where it is less noticeable, it appears to take place toward the end of September.

Casual records.—The species has been rather frequently detected on the Atlantic coast of North America and (rarely) in the interior eastern States. Among these occurrences are: Ontario, Toronto Island, spring of 1882; Nova Scotia, near Halifax, May 27, 1892; New Brunswick, Grand Manan; Maine, Scarboro, April 10, 1870, Upton, September 8, 1874, and Camden, September 14, 1900; New Hampshire, Seabrook, September 23, 1907; Massachusetts, Newburyport, May 20, 1871, Chatham, September 11, 1880, and Nantucket, July, 1901; Rhode Island, Seaconnet Point, July 30, 1900, and Point Judith, August 31, 1903; New York, two on Long Island, one of which was taken May 18, 1868, and Freeport, September 27, 1914; New Jersey, Barnegat (Elliott collection); Virginia, Four-mile Run, September 3, 1894; North Carolina, Raleigh, May 6, 1892; Ohio, Licking Reservoir, November 11, 1872, and Columbus, April 23, 1878; and Indiana, English Lake, April 12, 1905.

It also has been taken in the Lesser Antilles, Barbados, previous to 1848; Colombia, probably between the Rio Negro and the Orinoco or adjacent regions; and Alaska, St. Paul Island, September 7, 1910. It is of rare occurrence in Japan (Yezo). There is one record from Iceland (Reykjavik, September, 1820).

Egg dates.—In Holland, 4 dates between May 7 and 14; 18 dates between May 15 and 31, 8 dates between June 1 and 22. In Lapland and North Russia, 16 dates between June 8 and 27.

BARTRAMIA LONGICAUDA (Bechstein)

UPLAND PLOVER

HABITS

Let us be thankful that this gentle and lovely bird is no longer called Bartramian sandpiper. It is a sandpiper truly enough, but one that has adopted the haunts and many of the habits of the plovers. To those who love the rolling or hilly pasture lands of the east or the broad flat prairies of the middle west, it will always be known as the upland or " field plover " or " prairie dove," or, more affectionately, as " quailie." It is a characteristic bird of the prairies and wide open grassy fields, where it once abounded in enormous numbers. Excessive shooting for the market, where it was much in demand, reduced its numbers to an alarmingly low ebb. Dr. Thomas S. Roberts (1919) says that, in Minnesota,

Fifty years ago it was present all through the summer, everywhere in open country, in countless thousands. Now it is nearing extinction. Here and there an occasional breeding pair may yet be found, but they are lonely occupants of the places where their ancestors dwelt in vast numbers.

And with the disappearing prairies have gone these and other interesting birds that made the wide open places so attractive. When I visited the Quill Lake region in Saskatchewan in 1917, I found that practically all the prairies had been burned over or cultivated; the long-billed curlew had entirely disappeared, though recently abundant there, and I saw only one pair of chestnut-collared longspurs; but some of the upland plover were adapting themselves to the new conditions and were nesting in cultivated fields, much as the spotted sandpipers and the killdeer have learned to nest in grain fields and truck gardens. Perhaps such adaptation may be the salvation of a useful and attractive species. Some observers report it as already increasing in numbers.

Spring.—W. H. Hudson (1922) describes the beginning of the spring migration from the pampas of South America, as follows:

The north migration as a rule begins about the 15th of February and continues to the 15th of March, and it is at the beginning of the former month that the disquiet becomes noticeable. Now on one occasion the season of unrest began much earlier, in the month of January, increased from day to day and week to week in the most extraordinary way, and continued to about the middle of March before the birds began to fly north, the migration continuing through March. On any day in February when out riding I would see from time to time a bird spring up with its wild alarm cry and flight, and after going a little distance drop down again. Then in a minute or two another, farther away, would start up with its cry; and sitting still and watching and listening, I could see the birds rise up here and there all over the plain—rise with a cry, then settle down again; and if one rode a 100 miles to any side he would find it the same everywhere. The birds were in a continual state of agitation, of fear; and though this state began so much sooner than usual, the actual migration did not begin till a month later than the usual time.

Dr. Alexander Wetmore (1926), writing from the same general region, says:

At Tucuman, Tucuman, five were heard early in the evening of April 1 as they passed over the city traveling due north during a slow rain accompanied by heavy mist. On the night of April 5 under similar conditions an extensive flight of shore birds began at a quarter of 10 and continued until half past 11. During this period J. L. Peters, with whom I was traveling at the time, and I identified the call of the upland plover from 38 individuals. The birds were in company with yellowlegs, solitary sandpipers, and a few golden plover.

How many passed unheard in the darkness there was no way to know. The calling of these birds when in northward migration was a phenomenon of common knowledge in Tucuman during that season in the year, but all commented upon the fact that the birds seemed to have decreased greatly in abundance in recent years.

The earliest birds reach Texas and Louisiana early in March. Illustrating the abundance of this species in Texas 40 years ago, G. B. Benners (1887) says:

At the former place we found immense flocks on the prairie, and they were so tame that the flock would part in the middle and let us drive between them. We often shot enough birds while going through a flock in this way to last for several meals. When they thought we did not see them they would stand perfectly still, and being the same color as their surroundings they easily escaped detection.

From there the main migration route seems to be directly northward between the Mississippi River and the Rocky Mountains.

Fred J. Pierce writes to me:

On my rambles over the rolling country of Buchanan County, Iowa, in the early spring, I usually hear the Bartramian sandpiper and see the small speck high in the sky that I know is his form. A damp, cloudy morning seems to be the preferred time for the bird's sky circling, but it may be found frequently in the early morning, too. Cloudy days are the days which it enjoys most, it appears.

Edward S. Thomas tells me that he has seen it in Ohio as early as March 26, but that the average date of arrival is April 2. It is not recorded east of Cuba in the spring, but some birds migrate across from Yucatan to Cuba and Florida and then up the Atlantic coast. When this species bred more commonly in New England it used to arrive in April, but now it is very rare here.

Courtship.—The courtship flight song of the upland plover is well described in some notes sent to me by Fred J. Pierce, as follows:

The bird's song is very interesting, but it is given little attention in books relating to ornithology. On still wings, these large birds circle slowly about, usually so high as to be mere specks in the sky, and give their shrill, penetrating whistle, which will carry nearly a mile, depending upon the wind and the altitude of the whistler. First there are a few notes sounding like water gurgling from a large bottle, then comes the loud *whip-whee-ee-you*, long drawn out and weirdly thrilling. When I first heard this strange cry I at once thought of some species of hawk as being the author of it, and I have known others to think the same thing. It is too loud and penetrating a cry to be attributed to one of the sandpipers. I have heard the bird whistling in this manner as late as July, but I do not believe that this is a common practice. On more than one occasion I have seen the bird, after circling at such height as to be almost out of sight, close its wings and shoot to earth like a falling stone. This thrilling performance is similar to that of the prairie horned lark, which takes a head-first drop to earth when it has finished singing its contribution to the usual spring morning chorus.

Another pretty version of the courtship is given by Katharine U. Hunter (1916) thus:

It was the springtime (1916). The prolonged wail, vague and sad, of the plovers rose in our upland pasture. I watched them carry on their odd courtship; hopping toward each other, twittering, flying away, then repeating it all again, the hopping, twittering, and retreating. Ungainly, spirit-voiced birds! Once from out the black, vibrant night came the eerie, long-drawn whistle of a plover lover.

Nesting.—My first upland plover's nest was found on May 25, 1900, near the western end of Marthas Vineyard, Mass. The birds were still fairly common here in those days and there were at least three pairs of them breeding in this and adjoining pastures. The nest was on a knoll in a sheep pasture where the grass had been cropped short except for scattered tufts, where it grew from 7 to 10 inches high, offering the necessary concealment. In one of these tufts, about a foot in diameter, a hollow had been scratched, 4 or 5 inches in diameter and nearly 3 inches deep; it was lined with small bits of dried grass and held four handsome eggs.

Since then I have found several nests in Saskatchewan. These nests were all similarly located on the dry, grassy prairies, slight hollows in the ground, about 4 inches in diameter and 2 inches deep, generally well hidden in rather long, thick grass; they were lined with pieces of dry grass, and the growing grass was artfully arched over them for protection. The birds usually sat very closely; once we drove over a nest, flushing the bird under the wagon; and several times we were able to part the grass over the nest or even touch the bird before she left. She usually ran or fluttered away for a few feet and then ran about near us, with her long neck stretched up above the grass, watching us and uttering her *quip-ip-ip-ip* notes of protest.

Nests found by others have been similarly described, but Prof. W. B. Barrows (1912) says that—

in Michigan, it frequently nests in wet grounds, although the nest itself is usually placed on one of the drier spots. We have seen the birds nesting in two instances in good snipe bogs where the mud was ankle deep and dry spots few and far between.

Prof. William Rowan (1926) says that in Alberta—

the nests found were very variable in make-up and situation. One had no lining whatever and consisted of a mere scrape in the ground. This was in a hollow right in the open on a huge sandy area with but sparse vegetation, on which long-billed curlews (*Numenius americanus*) were nesting. Others were in clumps of rough brush, and this is probably typical for this locality. Another was in long grass. The most elaborate lining noted consisted of leaves, bents, and small twigs. One clutch of five was found and one of three, the latter no doubt incomplete, as the bird was not about and the eggs were fresh.

Edward R. Ford has the following observation on the selection of a nesting site:

As in the case of the larger ground-nesting birds, whose nests have little architectural pretension, the upland plover often deposits the first egg before any nest-building operations have been begun. It is probable that the physiological condition of the female urges her to seek a location generally favorable to the successful rearing of a brood; but the exact site of the nest may be in some measure accidental. It is not often that one may be fortunate enough to come upon the kind of evidence best calculated to prove a theory of animal behavior, but it happened once that we found a single egg of the upland plover, unbetrayed by the presence of the parent and hidden deep in the grass. It might have been an egg prematurely laid and, therefore, not likely to receive further parental attention. If it had been a meadow lark's egg, for example, that would have been the conclusion and the facts of experience would have borne it out. But here was the chance to test a theory and so, while not surprised, we were gratified, three days later, to flush a bird from the spot marked as the location of the single egg and to find there the full complement of four. About these the dry grass had taken hemispherical form and, with the addition of loose material and by reason of the impression made by the eggs themselves, as well as by the body of the parent, there now existed a well-defined if simple nest.

Eggs.—The upland plover lays four eggs, rarely five, and perhaps sometimes only three. These are ovate to short ovate in shape, less pointed than most shore birds' eggs; and they have only a slight gloss. In the commonest types the ground colors vary from " light pinkish cinnamon " to " pale pinkish buff"; in others they vary from " cartridge buff " or " pale olive buff " to greenish white. They are more or less evenly spotted with small spots of various shades of dark browns or reddish browns, and usually with small underlying spots, rarely large blotches, of " ecru drab " or " pale drab gray." The measurements of 66 eggs in the United States National Museum average 45 by 32.5 millimeters; the eggs showing the four extremes measure 51 by 33, 48 by 35, 41.5 by 32.5, and 48 by 29.5 millimeters.

Young.—The incubation period is said to be 17 days, but this needs confirmation. Both sexes share in the duties of incubation and care of the young. Katharine U. Hunter (1916) says:

The birds relieved each other at the nest—a true division of domestic cares: one bird would alight at a long distance, fold his wings, utter no cry, and, with head held low, walk through the grass, squatting lower and lower till finally he disappeared on the nest; then the female would retreat with the same caution, not spreading her wings till far from the eggs.

Doctor Coues (1874) describes the behavior of young birds and their parents very well, as follows:

Young birds are abroad late in June—curious little creatures, timid and weak, led about by their anxious parents, solicitous for their welfare, and ready to engage in the most unequal contests in their behalf. When half grown, but still in the down, the little creatures have a curious clumsy, top-heavy look;

their legs look disproportionately large, like those of a young colt or calf; and they may be caught with little difficulty, as they do not run very well. I once happened upon a brood, perhaps two weeks old, rambling with their mother over the prairie. She sounded the alarm, to scatter her brood, but not before I had secured one of them in my hand. I never saw a braver defense attempted than was made by this strong-hearted though powerless bird, who, after exhausting her artifices to draw me in pursuit of herself, by tumbling about as if desperately wounded, and lying panting with outstretched wings on the grass, gave up hope of saving her young in this way, and then almost attacked me, dashing close up and retreating again to renew her useless onslaught. She was evidently incited to unusual courage by the sight of her little one struggling in my hand. At this downy stage the young birds are white below, finely mottled with black, white, and rich brown above; the feet and under mandible are light colored; the upper mandible is blackish.

Although these tattlers are generally dispersed over the prairies during the summer, yet they affect particular spots by preference. Away from the river valleys, such spots are the numerous depressions of rolling prairie, often of great extent, which are moist or even watery at some seasons, and where the vegetation is most luxuriant. Here they gather almost into colonies. Riding into some such spot in July, when the young birds are being led about by their parents, some old bird more watchful than the rest, or nearest to the person approaching, gives the alarm with a loud outcry, the young scatter and hide, and all the old birds are soon on wing; hovering in the air, often at a great height, crossing each other's path, and ceaselessly vociferating their displeasure. I have often seen a dozen or twenty overhead at once, all from a little spot only a few acres in extent. Later in the season, when all the summer's broods are on wing, they make up into flocks, often of great extent, and old and young together assume the ordinary routine of their lives. They leave these northern regions early. I saw none after the forepart of September.

Plumages.—In the downy young upland plover, the crown, back, and rump are prettily variegated, marbled, or mottled, with black, "wood brown," "pinkish buff," and white, with no definite pattern. The sides of the head and the entire under parts are pale buff or buffy white, whitest on the belly and throat. A narrow, median frontal stripe and a few spots on the sides of the head are black.

The juvenal plumage is much like that of the summer adult, but it is much more buffy, especially about the head and neck, which are "cinnamon-buff" or "light ochraceous buff"; the crown is nearly solid brownish black, or with only a narrow, median, buffy line; the back and scapulars are brownish black with broad "cinnamon" edgings and with little or no definite barring on the scapulars; the lesser wing coverts are sepia with "cinnamon-buff" edgings, broader than in the adult; and the median coverts are sepia, broadly tipped, and notched with "cinnamon-buff" and with a subterminal spot or bar of dark sepia. This plumage is partially molted in August and September, producing the first winter plumage, which is like the adult, except that the juvenal flight feathers and most of the wing coverts are retained. At the first prenuptial molt young birds apparently become indistinguishable from adults.

Adults have a complete postnuptial molt, beginning with the body plumage in August and ending with the wings in December and January. Their prenuptial molt in spring involves nearly everything but the wings. The winter plumage is less buffy than the spring, more grayish above and whiter below, with paler edgings, but the color pattern is about the same.

Food.—The feeding habits of the upland plover are almost wholly beneficial. It is one of our most useful birds; living, as it does, in grass lands and cultivated fields, it destroys vast numbers of grasshoppers, locusts, and other injurious insects. W. L. McAtee (1912) writes:

From its habits the upland plover would naturally be expected to have a closer relation to agriculture than most sandpipers, and such proves to be the case. Almost half its food is made up of grasshoppers, crickets, and weevils, all of which exact heavy toll from cultivated crops. Among the weevils eaten are the cottonboll weevil; greater and lesser clover-leaf weevils; clover-root weevils; *Epicaerus imbricatus,* which is known to attack almost all garden and orchard crops; cowpea curculios; *Tanymecus confertus,* an enemy of sugar beets; *Thecesternus humeralis,* which has been known to injure grapevines; and bill bugs. *Thecesternus* alone composes 3.65 per cent of the seasonal food of the 163 stomachs examined, and bill bugs constitute 5.83 per cent. No fewer than 8 species of bill bugs were identified from the stomachs. These weevils injure, often seriously, such crops as corn, wheat, barley, and rye, as well as forage plants of many kinds. The upland plover further makes itself useful to the farmer by devouring leaf beetles, including the grapevine colaspis, southern corn leaf-beetle, and other injurious species; wireworms and their adult forms, the click beetles; white grubs and their parents, the May beetles; cutworms, army worms; cotton worms; cotton cutworms; sawfly larvae; and leather-jackets or cranefly larvae. They befriend cattle by eating horseflies and their larvae, and cattle ticks. They eat a variety of other animal forms, such as moths, ants, and other *Hymenoptera,* flies, bugs, centipedes and millipeds, spiders, snails, and earthworms. Practically 97 per cent of the food consists of animal matter, chiefly of injurious and neutral forms. The vegetable food comprises the seeds of such weed pests as buttonweed, foxtail grass, and sand spurs, and hence is also to the credit of the bird.

J. M. Bates (1907) says that, in Nebraska, " after the wheat is cut, and during migration, it frequents the wheat stubble and gorges itself with the waste grain." He has also seen it in the rye stubble in Connecticut. But this does no harm, of course.

Behavior.—When traveling the upland plover's flight is swift and strong, well sustained on its long, pointed wings; and when migrating, by day or by night, it flies at a great height. In the autumn it is wary and difficult to approach, as it jumps up at long range and flies rapidly away for a long distance. But in the spring its flight is quite different, more leisurely; it seems to drift along so high up in the sky as to be almost invisible; it might pass unnoticed, were it not for its flute like notes.   Edwin Sandys (1904) has described this very well, as follows:

This drifting flight is characteristic of the present species, and it usually ends in a diving slant earthward, which is performed without any preceptible motion of the wings.   A few feet from the ground the long, beautiful, easy descent is gently checked, and the bird alights as quietly as though it had stooped only a yard or so instead of hundreds or thousands of feet.   For a few seconds after alighting the bird is apt to keep its wings considerably elevated above its back, and the brief pose in this position is particularly attractive.   Then the airy fans are sedately furled.   This pretty trick of keeping the wings spread as if for a momentary study of how they should be correctly folded is not peculiar to this species.   Others of its near and remote kin go through the same dainty evolution, although, perhaps, without the air of studied care which is characteristic of Bartram's sandpiper.

On its breeding grounds its flight is different again; it often flies along slowly and evenly, at a low elevation, 15 or 20 feet above the ground, on quickly vibrating wings, pouring out its liquid, rolling trills or flute like notes, a delightful performance; or when flushed from its nest it flies off close to the ground with short, rapid strokes of its down-curved wings, as if using only its wing tips, suggesting the flight of the spotted sandpiper.   On a windy day it may occassionally be seen to soar or hover on quivering wings like a small falcon.

On the ground its movements are ploverlike, running swiftly and stopping suddenly.   It runs gracefully through the grass with its long neck stretched up to watch the pursuer; or, crouching down, it runs rapidly away and disappears in the grass.   It alights frequently on fences, telegraph poles, stumps, or rocks to watch the intruder and scold at him.   It is seldom seen near water, and I doubt if anyone has ever seen it swimming.   It is a gentle bird at all times and lives harmoniously with its neighbors on its breeding grounds, but it does not seem to associate with other species elsewhere.

Voice.—The voice of the upland plover is one of its greatest charms; once heard in its perfection it will never be forgotten; and it often serves to identify the species when the bird can not be seen. W. H. Hudson (1922) has referred to it very attractively, as follows:

Lying awake in bed, I would listen by the hour to that sound coming to me from the sky, mellowed and made beautiful by distance and the profound silence of the moonlit world, until it acquired a fascination for me above all sounds on earth, so that it lived ever after in me; and the image of it is as vivid in my mind at this moment as that of any bird call or cry, or any other striking sound heard yesterday or but an hour ago.   It was the sense of mystery it conveyed which so attracted and impressed me—the mystery of that delicate, frail, beautiful being, traveling in the sky, alone, day and night, crying aloud at intervals as if moved by some powerful emotion, beating the air with its wings, its beak pointing like the needle of the compass to the north, flying, speeding on its 7,000-mile flight to its nesting home in another hemisphere.

The most beautiful and striking note heard on its breeding grounds is a sweet, mellow, rolling trill, uttered as the bird flies along at a low elevation or while perched on a fence post or even on the ground; it is evidently a love note. Prof. Lynds Jones (1903) has described it very well, as follows:

> The rolling cry is not unlike the rolling call of a tree toad, but of a different quality and caliber, which makes it unmistakable. The whistle is partly double, the first part passing upward nearly half an octave, terminating abruptly there, the second part beginning where the first began and rapidly swelling through nearly or quite an octave, then gradually falling again and decreasing in volume to the close, several tones above the beginning. The first part of the whistle is usually rattling or trilled, and sometimes the trill is carried to the end, but oftener it becomes a clear whistle before the culmination and continues clear to the end. *Tre-e-e-e-e-e-e-e, tre-e-e-e-e-e-e-e-e-e-e-e-e-e-p; or tr-r-r-r-e-e-e-e-e-e-p.* Often the whistled part is never reached, but the call stops as if interrupted by some threatened danger.

The alarm note, as the bird flies away from its nest or as it runs about scolding at the intruder, is an emphatic and rapidly uttered *quip-ip-ip-ip*. It also has a rich, musical note, which sounds like *qua-a-ily*, from which one of its local names is taken. This and a modified form of its rolling trill are often heard on migration, a prolonged, mournful, mellow whistle, drifting down out of the sky, more like the whistling of the wind than a bird's voice.

Field marks.—The upland plover should be easily recognized by its size and shape; its slender, graceful form, its delicate head and neck, and its long tail are characteristic. In flight its long, pointed wings, its dark rump, and its barred, whitish, outer tail feathers are good field marks. Its manner of flight and its notes are distinctive.

Fall.—About the middle of July, or even earlier, old and young birds begin to gather into flocks, move off their breeding grounds, and start on their fall migrations. The migratory flights are made mainly during the night or early evening. At this season the birds are much wilder, the leisurely behavior of spring and summer has gone, their flight is much swifter and stronger, and it is difficult to approach the loose, detached flocks which stop to feed during the day on the hoards of grasshoppers and locusts which are then to be found in the upland pastures and dry meadows. During wet spells they do not stop, but in hot, dry weather they linger to feast on the abundant insect life and become very fat. We used to expect them in Massachusetts about the last of July, but they were most abundant in August and early September. The general movement is southward, through the interior and the Atlantic Coast States and through the West Indies to South America. The earliest birds reach Louisiana and Texas early in July and arrive in Peru and Argentina in September. The last birds leave their breeding range before the end of September.

Game.—The upland plover is, or was, a fine game bird. Over 40 years ago, in my younger shooting days, these birds were still fairly common in Massachusetts, but it was no easy job to make a fair day's bag; it meant tramping many miles over rolling, or hilly pasture lands, where the wary birds rose at long range and flew swiftly away for a long distance. One had to shoot quickly and accurately to kill his bird, and perhaps chase one for several miles before getting even a long shot at him. It was a real sporting proposition with the chances much in the bird's favor. The birds would not come to decoys, nor to the gunner's whistle and a dog was utterly useless except to retrieve birds. A thorough knowledge of the ground and of the birds' fly-ways sometimes brought results, when we could hide behind some fence or stone wall and wait for the birds to fly over. Even meager results were well worth while, for we had plenty of good exercise and the birds made delicious morsels for the table.

A more common and more successful, though less sportsmanlike, method of shooting them is thus described by Edwin Sandys (1904):

A popular method in many parts of the West is to drive to the birds in a buckboard, or other convenient rig. For a man who can shoot well in the sitting posture this is an excellent plant, as the birds almost invariably will permit a wheeled conveyance to approach within comparatively easy range. A clever driver is a valuable assistance. Such a man never heads his team directly at the birds, but drives as though he merely intended to pass them by. A good judge of distance in the open can in this way edge within comfortable range of plover which, if the driver steered straight for them, or with the gun attempted to dismount and stalk, would at once make off. I have varied the shooting from the seat by walking at the horse's shoulders. The plover do not appear to notice the extra pair of legs. This sometimes gives the prettiest kind of shooting. All one has to do is to judge when sufficiently close, then stand still with the gun at the ready, while the team moves steadily ahead. Usually the plover will take wing the moment the foot-man is uncovered; but should they not, the man can gain a few yards by briskly walking toward them. I have occasionally stalked them by keeping close to the shoulder of a steady old horse that was indifferent in the matters of smoke and loud reports.

Edward H. Forbush (1912) writes:

About 1880, when the supply of passenger pigeons began to fail, and the marketmen, looking about for some other game for the table of the epicure in spring and summer, called for plover, the destruction of the upland plover began in earnest. The price increased. In the spring migration the birds were met by a horde of market gunners, shot, packed in barrels and shipped to the cities. There are tales of special refrigerator cars sent out to the prairie regions, and parties of gunners regularly employed to follow the birds and ship plover and curlews by the carload to the Chicago market. These may not be based on facts, but we know that the birds came to market in great quantities.

Winter.—The upland plover spends our winter months on the pampas of Argentina and Patagonia, where unfortunately it is more sought for by market hunters than it is here. Mr. Hudson (1920) writes:

This species differs from its fellow-migrants of the same family from the north to Argentina in its wide and even distribution over all that portion of the pampas where the native coarse grasses which once covered the country have disappeared, an area comprising not less than 50,000 square miles. It begins to arrive as early as September, coming singly or in small parties of three or four; and, extraordinary as the fact may seem when we consider the long distance the bird travels, and the monotonous nature of the level country it uses as a "feeding area," it is probable that every bird returns to the same spot year after year; for in no other way could such a distribution be maintained, and the birds appear every summer evenly sprinkled over so immense a surface.

Doctor Wetmore (1926) says:

Formerly abundant, the upland plover is now rare in the region where it spends the period of northern winter. Its winter range on the open pampa is a region so vast that it is difficult to form a proper estimate of the actual number of individuals of the species that remain. Among epicures the species has inherited in part the name and reputation of the Eskimo curlew and is sought constantly by gunners to supply that demand. The few that survive frequent remote regions on some of the large estancias where they are secure until they leave their seclusion and begin their return flight northward. The majority of those that I noted were identified by their liquid calls, heard, as is the case in Washington, as they passed at night.

He says again (1927):

In the season of 1919–20 the upland plover was reported to have increased somewhat in abundance at Rosas in the Province of Buenos Aires, a circumstance due perhaps to protection in the United States and Canada. It can hardly be expected to regain anywhere near its former abundance, however, with increasing encroachment on its winter and summer ranges. Unfortunately, in Argentina it has replaced the Eskimo curlew as a table delicacy, and is so eagerly sought by gunners that its preservation in settled regions is doubtful. Those that remain must seek the pastures of remote estancias in order to survive.

DISTRIBUTION

Range.—North and South America; accidental in Europe.

Breeding range.—The breeding range of the upland plover extends north to Alaska (Kobuk River and Gens de Large Mountains); southern Mackenzie (probably Fort Smith); Saskatchewan (Prince Albert, Quill Lake, and Crescent Lake); Manitoba (Shoal Lake and Winnipeg); Minnesota (Clarissa, St. Cloud, Minneapolis, and Lake City); Wisconsin (Kingston and Kelley Brook); Michigan (Lovells and Zion City); Ontario (probably Plover Mills, Dunnville, and Kingston); northern New York (Canton and Potsdam); southern Quebec (Hatley); and Maine (Farmington, Plymouth, Orono, and Calais). East to Maine (Calais); Massachusetts (Salem, Marthas Vineyard, and Nantucket); probably Connecticut (South Windsor);

New York (Montauk Point); New Jersey (Princeton, Lawrenceville, and probably Tuckerton); Virginia (Wallops Island); and rarely South Carolina (Oakland). South to rarely South Carolina (Oakland); southern Indiana (Bicknell); Illinois (Olney and Odin); Missouri (Appleton and probably Stotesbury); Oklahoma (Copan and Fort Reno); probably Texas (Gainesville); Colorado (Barr and Denver); Utah (Kamas Prairies); and Oregon (Fort Klamath). West to Oregon (Fort Klamath); northern Idaho (Lapwai and Fort Sherman); British Columbia (Newgate and Osoyoos Lake); probably Alberta (Edmonton and Athabaska Landing); and Alaska (Mount McKinley and Kobuk River).

Winter range.—The main winter range of the species is confined to the southern part of South America, north to northern Argentina (Tucuman); and southern Brazil (Irisanga and probably Mattodentro). East to southern Brazil (probably Mattodentro); Uruguay (Concepcion, Sta. Elena, and Colonia); and eastern Argentina (Buenos Aires and Rio Negro). South to Argentina (Rio Negro). West to Argentina (Rio Negro, Mendoza, and Tucuman). A specimen was taken at San Angelo, Tex., January 1, 1883, but this must be considered as an accidental occurrence as the species at this season is usually found only in southern South America.

Spring migration.—Early dates of spring arrival are: Ecuador, Chaupicuz, March 30; Chiapas, Comitan, March 29; Florida, Indian Key, March 17, St. Marks, March 23, Deer Park, March 24, and Leon County, March 25; Alabama, Barachias, March 7, Coosada, March 22, and Sand Mountain, March 29; Georgia, Macon, March 18, and Savannah, March 23; South Carolina, Mount Pleasant, March 11, and Frogmore, March 24; North Carolina, Raleigh, March 28; Virginia, Alexandria, March 22; District of Columbia, Washington, March 21; Pennsylvania, Marietta, March 27, Plymouth, April 10, and Erie, April 11; New Jersey, Haddonfield, April 7, and Cape May, April 12; New York, Long Island, April 1, Watertown, April 6, and Amagansett, April 11; Connecticut, Jewett City, April 16, and Saybrook, April 22; Rhode Island, Newport, April 29; Massachusetts, Woods Hole, April 10, Salem, April 12, and Cape Cod, April 12; Vermont, Woodstock, April 17, Bennington, April 22, and Rutland, April 26; Maine, Pittsfield, April 14, Plymouth, April 25, and Portland, April 30; Louisiana, New Orleans, March 9, Hester, March 16, and Lobdell, March 19; Mississippi, Biloxi, March 10, and Rodney, March 27; Tennessee, Nashville, March 31; Kentucky, Guthrie, March 20; Missouri, St. Louis, March 17, Appleton City, March 19, and Kahoka, March 20; Illinois, Rockford, March 19, Lebanon, March 20, and Canton, March 27; Indiana, Bicknell, March 13, Vigo County, March 19, and Vincennes, April 1; Ohio, Oberlin, March 20, Berlin Center, March 23, and Columbus, March 29; Michigan, Ann Arbor, March

15, Plymouth, April 8, and Livonia, April 12; Ontario, Forest, April 16, London, April 17 and Preston, April 18; Iowa, Storm Lake, March 25 Wall Lake, March 30, and Hillsboro, March 31; Wisconsin, Delavan, March 24, Milford, April 10, and Stoughton, April 11; Minnesota, Lanesboro, April 8, North Star, April 9, and St. Cloud, April 16; Texas, Bonham, March 5, Mont Belvieu, March 8, Dallas, March 10, and Corpus Christi, March 13; Oklahoma, Copan, March 31; Kansas, Girard, March 16, Richmond, March 28, Topeka, April 1, and Onaga, April 7; Nebraska, Falls City, April 6, Badger, April 7 and Syracuse, April 9; South Dakota, Vermilion, April 9, Grand View, April 14, and Rapid City, April 15; North Dakota, Argusville, April 26, Larimore, April 26, and Marstonmoor, April 30; Manitoba, Aweme, April 26, Reaburn, April 30, Winnipeg, May 2, and Two Rivers, May 3; Saskatchewan, South qu'Appelle, April 16, Wiseton, April 25, and Indian Head, May 2; Colorado, Denver, April 18, and Colorado Springs, April 28; Wyoming, Lake Como, May 5; Montana, Billings, April 23, Columbia Falls, April 27, and Terry, May 10; Alberta, Flagstaff, May 2, Alliance, May 7, and Red Deer, May 11; and British Columbia, Osoyoos Lake, May 25.

Late dates of spring departure are: Argentina, Buenos Aires, April 3, Tucuman, April 5, and Baradero, April 13; Bolivia, Piedra Blanca, April 23; Brazil, Tonantino, May 7; Guatemala, Duenas, April 12; Mexico, Chiapas, Teopisca, May 7; Yucatan, Cancun Island, April 19; Vera Cruz, Lake Catemaco, May 5; Florida, Garden Key, May 2, Loggerhead Key, May 7, and Pensacola, May 9; Georgia, Savannah, April 28; Louisiana, Lobdell, May 15, and New Orleans, May 19; Mississippi, Biloxi, May 16; and Texas, Brownsville, April 15, Bonham, May 12, and Huntsville, May 18.

Fall migration.—Early dates of fall arrival are: New Mexico, Glenrio, July 25; Texas, San Angelo, July 4, and Lipscomb, July 10; Louisiana, New Orleans, July 5, and Abbeville, July 25; Alabama, Montgomery, July 28, and Barachias, August 22; Florida, Pensacola, August 9, and Arcadia, August 22; the Bahama Islands, Mariguana, August 5; the Lesser Antilles, Barbados, August 12, and Granada, August 24; Mexico, Jalisco, Chapata, August 27; Costa Rica, September 5; Panama, Gatun, September 1; Colombia, Cienaga, September 12; Ecuador, Carapungo, August 10, and Cerro Campania, September 24; Brazil, Matto Grosso, September 26; Paraguay, Puerto Pinasco, September 29, and Concepcion, October 3.

Late dates of fall departure are: Alberta, Red Deer River, September 22; Montana, Big Sandy, September 6; Wyoming, Little Medicine, August 15; Colorado, Fort Lyon, September 2; New Mexico, Glenrio, September 11; Manitoba, Treesbank, September 7, Margaret, September 18, and Aweme, September 28; North Dakota, Marstonmoor, September 15, and Westhope, September 24; South

Dakota, Huron, September 2, Sioux Falls, September 6, and Forestburg, September 30; Nebraska, Dewitt, September 21, Badger, September 28, and Valentine, October 5; Kansas, near Wichita, October 3, Topeka, October 13, and Onaga, October 15; Texas, Grapevine, September 25, Gainesville, September 28, and Corpus Christi, October 2; Minnesota, Lanesboro, August 22, and St. Vincent, August 31; Iowa, Emmetsburg, October 14, Newton, October 22, and Grinnell, November 2; Michigan, Livonia, September 18, and Detroit, October 20; Ohio, Lakeside, October 13, Scio, October 17, and Waverly, October 23; Illinois, La Grange, October 5, Belvidere, October 24, and Rantoul, November 29; Missouri, Monteer, September 17, and Jasper City, September 27; Kentucky, Lexington, October 11; Louisiana, New Orleans, October 7; Maine, Pittsfield, September 22; Vermont, St. Johnsbury, September 25; Massachusetts, Harvard, September 14, Taunton, September 19, and Woods Hole, September 29; Rhode Island, Block Island, September 6; Connecticut, Hartford, September 3, and Litchfield, September 6; New York, Phelps, September 14, Montauk, September 17, Orient Point, September 23, and Floral Park, October 20; New Jersey, Absalom Light, September 15; Pennsylvania, Erie, September 22, Germantown, October 2, and Bridesburg, October 18; Virginia, Alexandria, November 5; North Carolina, Weaverville, November 10; South Carolina, Mt. Pleasant, October 28; Georgia, Savannah, September 20; Alabama, Barachias, October 26; Florida, Key West, October 3; Costa Rica, San Jose, November 15; Nicaragua, Escondido River, November 26; Panama, Culebra, October 22, and Davila, November 30 and Gatun, December 8; Guiana, Cayenne, October 27; Peru, Cosnipata, October 3; and Brazil, Allianca, November 9.

Casual records.—A specimen of the upland plover taken February 8, 1923 at Deception Island, South Shetlands, must be considered accidental, as this is far south of its normal winter range (Bennett, 1926). The species has been reported as occasional in spring in Newfoundland (Macoun) and one was obtained on Sable Island in 1868 (Gilpin). There are several records for Quebec (Montreal and Godbout) from May 7 to October. Two have been taken in Bermuda (September 20, 1874, and September 18, 1875). In Porto Rico one was obtained by Stahl between 1878 and 1881 (Gundlach); F. A. Potts reports that he saw one September 10, 1921 near Central Aguirre, collected one from a flock of 15 on September 13, 1921, near Santa Isabel, and saw still another August 26, 1926 near Fortuna. On the Pacific coast south of British Columbia, it is known from a specimen taken August 8, 1896, at Tule Lake, California, and one taken at Sulphur Springs, Arizona, August 18, 1874.

There are six records for England, Warwick, October 31, 1851, Cambridge, December 12, 1854, Bigswear, January 19, 1855, Falmouth November 13, 1865, Boulmer, November 21, 1879 and the Parret River in Somersetshire (date ?); one for Denmark Tim, November 3, 1920; one for Malta, November 17, 1865; one for Holland (Meyer); one for Germany, Hessen (Naumann); and one for Italy, Liguria, October, 1859. It also was taken near Sydney, Australia, in 1865 (Gould).

Egg dates.—New England and New York: 10 records, April 28 to June 13. Pennsylvania and New Jersey: 15 records, May 6 to June 11; 8 records, May 15 to 27. Saskatchewan, Manitoba, Dakotas, and Minnesota: 86 records, May 4 to July 1; 43 records, June 1 to 15. Ohio to Iowa and Kansas: 22 records, April 30 to June 17; 11 records, May 14 to 20.

TRYNGITES SUBRUFICOLLIS (Vieillot)

BUFF-BREASTED SANDPIPER

HABITS

My acquaintance with this species is limited to a few birds seen migrating in company with golden plover on the burnt-over prairies about Quill Lake, Saskatchewan. I have never seen it elsewhere. Like the upland plover, it is a sandpiper which has associated much with plover, frequents similar haunts, and has acquired some similar habits.

Spring.—W. H. Hudson (1922) gives a striking account of the spring migration of this species in Argentina during its former abundance, from which I quote, as follows:

Now, one autumn, when most of the emigrants to the Arctic breeding grounds had already gone, I witnessed a great migration of this very species—this beautiful sandpiper with the habits of a plover. The birds appeared in flocks of about one to two or three hundred, flying low and very swiftly due north, flock succeeding flock at intervals of about 10 or 12 minutes; and this migration continued for three days, or at all events three days from the first day I saw them, at a spot about 2 miles from my home. I was amazed at their numbers, and it was a puzzle to me then, and has been one ever since, that a species thinly distributed over the immense area of the Argentine pampas and Patagonia could keep to that one line of travel over that uniform green, sealike country. For outside of that line not one bird of the kind could anywhere be seen; yet they kept so strictly to it that I sat each day for hours on my horse watching them pass, each ·flock first appearing as a faint buff-colored blur or cloud just above the southern horizon, rapidly approaching then passing me, about on a level with my horse's head, to fade out of sight in a couple of minutes in the north; soon to be succeeded by another and yet other flocks in endless succession, each appearing at the same point as the one before, following the same line, as if a line invisible to all eyes except their own had been traced across the green world for their guidance. It gave one the idea that all the birds of this species, thinly distributed over tens of thousands of square miles of country, had formed the habit of assembling previous to migration at one starting point, from which they set out in successive flocks of a medium size in a disciplined order on that marvelous journey to their Arctic breeding grounds.

Dr. Alexander Wetmore (1926) noted migrating birds at Guamini on March 3 to 8. Prof. W. W. Cooke (1912) says that " migrants appear in the interior of Brazil and in Peru during March, but there are no spring migration data for the whole distance between Peru and Texas." There is a heavy migration through Texas during April and then directly northward through the western part of the Mississippi Valley and the prairie Provinces of Canada to the Arctic tundra. The whole migration route in the spring seems to be very narrow. Prof. William Rowan (1927) writes:

This is a remarkable sandpiper from many viewpoints. Like the American golden plover and the Eskimo curlew it used to exist in millions and was slaughtered in uncountable numbers. To-day there are many widely traveled collectors who have never in their lives met with it. After extensive inquiries I can discover only one spot on the continent besides our point on which migrating buff-breasted sandpipers may be relied upon to turn up in any numbers. We, get it in hundreds every spring, and, roughly speaking, it frequents only one field. Odd birds or moving flocks may be noted elsewhere from time to time, but on the rough pasture that forms the main body of the point this species arrives with unfailing regularity within a day or two of the 18th of May. Like the golden plover, it seems to migrate by night, for at daybreak there may be hundreds in place of the few or none at all of the previous evening.

In his notes for 1924 he writes to me:

Two birds were seen May 19 and subsequently collected. On the 21st, five were seen shortly after sunrise with black-bellied plover, the first time that I have seen this association, but a large arrival took place during the day and there were scores in the evening. On the 24th they had reached numbers such as I have never before seen and numerous photographs were taken. On the 26th they must have been on the ground in many hundreds. The whole of their area, over a mile long, was crawling with them. There is no doubt that this year they outnumbered every other wader we had on the place. Even so, they never formed large flocks, and I think we never saw more than 60 get up and fly together. They dropped very suddenly in numbers after this, as though they had all cleared off together, but a few were seen each day till the 30th, when a flock of 30 constituted our last record.

Pierce Brodkorb and Frank Grasett have recorded it in northeastern Illinois as early as April 27. A. G. Lawrence's dates for Whitewater Lake, Manitoba, are from May 13 to 19. Dr. E. W. Nelson (1887) noted the first arrivals at St. Michael, Alaska, on May 31; and John Murdoch (1885) says that it arrived at Point Barrow June 6 to 8.

Courtship.—Professor Rowan (1927) has given us the most elaborate account of the nuptial display of the buff-breasted sandpiper, as follows:

As we have noted it annually, there are several distinct stages to the display, but the males do not appear to be concerned in the least with the females at any time. Nor have I ever seen a female take the slightest notice of any of the displays. Nelson comments on the fact that Murdoch frequently saw solitary males displaying, yet he was observing them on the actual breeding grounds.

Probably the most frequent performance is the raising of one wing only (either one), but this has various phases. A, the wing is spread and held steadily for a few moments with the primaries horizontal and is then closed again. B, the wing is spread with the primaries nearly perpendicular and waved round in an elipse, the bird standing still. C, the wing is spread while the bird runs round in circles. D, the wing is held aloft while the owner runs after another bird, always, so far as I have seen, another male, which instantly raises one wing also and starts zigzagging through the grass, the first bird giving chase. They may thus cover many yards before one suddenly collapses his wing and halts, the second immediately following suit. All these single-wing performances seem to be carried out in silence.

Both wings together are used for another set of actions. E, the wings are raised similarly to a bird alighting on or arising from the ground, the body horizontal. In this attitude one bird sometimes chases another. F is a double version of B, both wings being raised high and waved round and round. G, both wings are spread, undersurfaces forward, primaries horizontal, after the manner of the American eagle, the body being almost perpendicular. This may be accomplished by a rapid *tick tick tick* many times repeated. Two birds may do it simultaneously standing opposite to each other with the tips of the wings practically touching. H is the most characteristic of all and the most amusing to watch. Both wings are raised with the undersurfaces facing to the front as in G, but with the primaries perpendicular, tips practically touching each other over the bird's head. The body is held absolutely vertical and the legs stretched to capacity (I am not sure that the birds do not stand partially on tiptoe), tail cocked out horizontally behind, while the individual "*ticks*" at top speed for about a second. Each "*tick*" is accompanied with a rapid jerk of the whole body. The bird then relaxes momentarily, turns through an angle of 40 to 50 degrees, repeats the performance to a fresh audience (if there is one, for I have seen isolated birds doing this), relaxes to switch round again, and so on perhaps half a dozen times. This may also be done simultaneously by two birds, face to face, and standing so close that the wing tips appear to touch over their heads. It may then be repeated without any change of direction in the intervals. But it always seems to be done in spasms. Display is evidently infectious, particularly in fine weather, for no sooner does one start than a dozen may be at it in a moment. But it is curious to see a bird suddenly stop in its hunt for food in order to go through one of these acts and then proceed as though it never had anything else in mind, particularly if it is by itself. It seems so irrational. Occasional bickering occurs, but we have never seen serious flights or even suggestion of anything serious.

Murdoch (1885) has also observed that—

Two will occasionally meet and spar like fighting cocks for a few minutes and then rise together like towering birds, with legs hanging loose, for about 30 feet, then drifting off to leeward. A single bird will sometimes stretch himself up to his full height, spread his wings forward, and puff out his throat, making a sort of clucking noise, while one or two others stand by and apparently admire him.

Nesting.—Roderick MacFarlane found the buff-breasted sandpiper breeding commonly on the barren grounds east of Horton River and on the Arctic coast. I find the records of some 25 nests in his notes, but the data given are very meager. One nest was "near a small river, made of a few dead leaves "; another was "a depression in the ground, lined with a few withered grasses and leaves, on the slope of a gentle eminence "; a third, he said, was "precisely similar to that of the golden plover. The female made a short, low flight to a distance of about 12 yards, when the nest was approached within 9 or 10 feet."

Murdoch (1885), at Point Barrow, "collected the eggs in considerable abundance "; he says that "they were never seen on the lower marshy portions of the tundra, but always confined themselves to the high and dry banks, or what we call the black tundra." The eggs were deposited "in a shallow depression in the ground lined with a little moss," where they harmonized very well with the black and white of the ground and moss.

Eggs.—The buff-breasted sandpiper lays four eggs; one set of five is recorded. The shapes vary from ovate pyriform to pyriform, usually decidedly pointed. The prevailing ground colors are very light, from "cartridge buff " to dull white; in some darker colored eggs they are "olive-buff," "chamois," or "cream buff." They are heavily and boldly marked, chiefly at the large end, where the markings are often confluent, with longitudinal and somewhat spiral blotches and with small spots and blotches scattered over the whole egg. An occasional egg is only sparingly marked with small spots. The markings are in dark browns, "bister," "sepia," "liver brown " and "livid brown," sometimes "Saccardo's umber " or "chestnut brown." There are usually underlying blotches and spots in various shades of "brownish drab " or "drab-gray." The measurements of 62 eggs in the United States National Museum average 37 by 26 millimeters; the eggs showing the four extremes measures **40** by 27, 37.5 by **27.5, 34.5** by 25.5, and 35.5 by **25** millimeters.

Plumages.—I have never seen a downy young buff-breasted sandpiper and I doubt if any one else has. Young birds are in juvenal plumage when they migrate southward. They are like the adults, except as follows: The feathers of the mantle are sepia with an olive tinge, "dark grayish olive," narrowly edged with cream white, giving a scaled appearance, whereas in the adult these feathers are brownish black or black, with very broad edgings of "cinnamon-buff " or "pinkish buff "; the feathers of the lower back, rump and upper tail

coverts are from " hair brown " to " fuscous," tipped with " cinnamon," whereas in the adult these are brownish black, broadly edged
with " cinnamon-buff "; the inner webs of the primaries, on the
under side, are much more finely and closely sprinkled with black
than in the adult, which has larger, more widely scattered and hence
more conspicuous black spots. This last character probably per-
sists through the first year. The postjuvenal molt and the first prenuptial molt are accomplished in South America. I have seen no
specimens illustrating these.

Adults have a complete molt, apparently late in the fall or in the
winter, the wings being molted last. Doctor Wetmore (1926) shot
a male on September 21 that was still in worn breeding plumage.
Birds molting primaries have been taken in February and March.
Summer and winter plumages are very similar and the sexes are
alike, except that the female is much smaller than the male.

Food.—Professor Rowan (1927) says:

I am indebted to the Biological Survey at Washington for kindly analyzing
the contents of 17 stomachs, spring taken. Roughly, 40 per cent consisted
of Coleoptera, adults and larvae, and 50 per cent of Diptera, chiefly larvae
and pupae. Seeds of *Polygonum, Potamogeton,* and *Eleocharis* were present
to the extent of 1 per cent. The rest consisted of spider and insect remains.
I shall be glad to send a detailed list to anyone who may be interested.

Behavior.—The same observer writes:

The buff-breasted sandpiper, like Bartram's, is a plover in its ways and
habits rather than a sandpiper. Even in its coloration it differs radically
from the common sandpipers. It is extraordinarily tame and confiding at
times. When the mood seizes it, one could without difficulty wipe out every
bird of a flock, provided one killed or wounded one with the first shot. The
remainder will return again and again to a wounded bird. The noise of the
gun seems to have little more than momentary effect.

Owing to the muddy tone of their plumage, these birds are exceptionally
difficult to see on the type of ground that they so habitually frequent. One
can easily walk into a flock without knowing it till the birds get up almost
under foot. This is made the easier by their habit of " freezing." They stand
immobile on being approached, not necessarily crouching, generally the very
reverse, but without movement they readily enough escape observation. If
they start moving as one gets nearer, it is always on the run. They then
carry their necks " craned," scatter widely, and zig-zag hither and thither
rather after the manner of partridges, of which they frequently remind one.

A flock will seldom rise in unison, but the nearer birds will merely fly over
and settle on the remote side of the further ones. Even when the buff-breasts
are amongst sandpipers, such as Baird's, Semi-palmateds, etc., five times out
of ten they will remain on the spot if the others are scared up. A really large
flock is rare. We estimated the number of buff-breasts on a few acres of
grass one morning at about 2,000, and we spent several hours in trying to
photograph them. They were scattered in clumps in all directions. Although
we walked through them from one end to the other more than once, thus
tending to herd them, the largest number we were able to put up together
was about 150. This constitutes the largest flock we have ever seen. The

typical loose association is evident in the photograph. The birds merely flew round and settled again in the vicinity.

On windy days these, like other waders, become exceedingly restless and impossible to approach. They then perform the most remarkable gyrations, always but a few feet above the ground, and seldom rising and falling vertically, as do so many others. They attain great speed and keep in close formation, moving in absolute unison. As such a flock turns in the sunlight there can be no possible error as to identity, for the whole mass looks yellowish. A single bird, in favorable light, may also give one the impression of being yellow.

George H. Mackay (1892a) says of their habits in Massachusetts:

Of the few which I have seen I have remarked their extreme gentleness and desire to be in company with other birds. On one occasion I had one alight among my plover decoys on the upland (which they seem very fond of frequenting), and, not wishing to shoot it, I allowed it to remain for quite a while so I could watch it. During this time it moved about with unconcern, apparently not being aware that its supposed companions were of wood. It seemed so gentle that I determined to see how near it would permit me to approach, and it was not over 5 or 6 feet from me when it flew away, but only for a short time, however, for it returned and alighted in the course of 10 or 15 minutes. Having no desire to shoot it, I allowed it to remain until it departed not to return. All the birds that I have seen come immediately to the decoys on perceiving them, and alight without hesitation or fear. Their flight is rapid, with many turns and zigzag movements, and near the ground, constantly turning up so as to show their entire under parts.

Much of the behavior of the buff-breasted sandpiper, while on the ground, reminds one of the upland plover; it seems to prefer the grassy places rather than the open flats or shores, and often runs away to hide in the grass rather than fly; in running it lifts its feet rather high, as if accustomed to walking through grass; and it often stops and stands with its neck stretched up looking at the intruder, just as the upland plover does.

Voice.—It is not a noisy bird, and seems to have a limited vocabulary. Professor Rowan (1926) says:

The spring note of the buff-breast, on the other hand, is the most unusual and diagnostic wader note that I know. The only thing it reminds me of is the song of the short-billed marsh wren (*Cistothorus stellaris*), which produces a very excellent imitation of two stones being chipped together. The note of the buff-breast has the same quality about it; but, instead of being loud and clear, it is quiet and very short, and might be described as *tik*. This species, however, is rather silent. I call this the spring note, but perhaps it should more correctly be termed the adult note, for we have not a single good record of an adult in the autumn, wherefore I am only familiar with young at this season. Like some other waders (e. g. willet), birds of the year have a very different call or calls from spring adults. In the case of the buff-breast the note of the young is so like the pectoral's—Harold considers it shorter and less harsh—that, although distinguishable in the field, it can hardly be described adequately by itself.

Doctor Wetmore (1926) writes: "As they rise they may give a low call that resembles *chwup*, somewhat robinlike in tone; a second call note is a low trilled *pr-r-r-reet*. The species is to be confused in the field with no other shore bird."

Field marks.—Professor Rowan (1927) says, on this point:

The absence of white margins and black center to the rump, and hence the lack of contrast in this region, I have found to be the most useful diagnostic character in the field. The wing patch is also valuable. The extraordinarily rounded head seen in silhouette against the sun or in bad light at reasonable range has more than once proved useful. The note is always diagnostic.

Doctor Wetmore (1926) writes:

When in the air or on the ground they are distinctly buff in color, with a glimpse of the marbled underwing surface as they rise or pass, and a flash of the gray tail with its darker markings as they alight. On the ground in profile, they show a long neck and long legs, while the short bill is suggestive of that of a pigeon. The neck is drawn in during flight.

E. A. Doolittle (1923) observed that—

The greenish legs, finely streaked crown, buffy breast and sides of head, lack of streak through eyes, and long pointed wings reaching beyond tail were all good field marks while the bird was at rest; while lack of wing bars and rounded tail were striking when the bird took flight.

Fall.—The fall migration is much more widely extended than the spring; the main flight is directly southward through the center of North America, but it is so spread out that some birds appear on both the Atlantic and Pacific coasts. Professor Cooke (1912) says: "The main body of migrants follows the Barren Grounds to the shores of Hudson Bay, thence almost due south across the Mississippi Valley to the coast of Texas, and through Central America to northwestern South America, and diagonally across the interior of South America to Argentina." A limited flight swings eastward, south of Hudson Bay, or perhaps across it, to the eastern Provinces of Canada and New England. The species is so rare on the Atlantic coast south of Long Island as to indicate the probability of an oversea flight to the West Indies and South America. On the Pacific coast it seems to be very rare, though perhaps it has been overlooked, south of Washington, where it is probably of regular occurrence. D. E. Brown has sent me several records for Washington, the dates ranging from September 3 to 20. Major Allan Brooks (1924) says that he has noted it every year that he has been on the British Columbia coast.

In the interior the adults come along during the last three weeks in August, and the young birds all through September. In New England the dates are about the same. Here they were occasionally seen in small flocks, but now they are so rare that single birds

are more often seen in company with upland or golden plover on
the rolling uplands, or with other sandpipers on the meadows.

Winter.—It evidently spends the winter south of Argentina, for
Doctor Wetmore (1926) saw the first one on September 21 in Paraguay and the last one on November 13 near Buenos Aires; he did
not see it again until the return flight in March.   Mr. Hudson (1920)
says:

It begins to arrive, usually in small bodies, early in the month of October;
and during the summer is seldom met with in flocks of any size on the pampas,
but is usually seen on the dry, open ground associating in small numbers
with the golden plover, the whimbrel, and other northern species. I, however,
think it probable that it travels farther south than its fellow-migrants from
North America, and has its principal feeding-grounds somewhere in the interior
of Patagonia; also that its northern journey takes place later than that of
other species.

Doctor Wetmore (1927) says:

The species frequented open flats or muddy shores near lakes or channels,
where it was subject to considerable hunting, as several of those seen had been
crippled by shooting. From observations at Guamini, it appeared that the
species has some resting station in northern Patagonia, perhaps near the
mouths of the Rio Colorado and the Rio Negro, or some of the large alkaline
lakes of that region. The small numbers remaining are preserved in some
such place, but apparently the species is near extinction.

DISTRIBUTION

Range.—North and South America.

Breeding range.—The buff-breasted sandpiper is known to breed
only on the Arctic coast of northwestern North America from
Alaska (Cape Smythe, Point Barrow, and probably Cape Halkett);
east to Yukon (Herschell Island); and Mackenzie (Fort Anderson
and Bernard Harbor). It has been detected in summer and may
breed at Nulato and Fort Egbert, Alaska, and at Winter Harbor,
Franklin (Hennessey), while it also has been noted at this season in
eastern Siberia (Cape Wankarem and the south coast of the Okhotsk
Sea).

Winter range.—The winter range appears to be restricted to
southern South America. They have been noted at this season in
Uruguay (Montevideo); and Argentina (Cordoba, Missiones, Rio
Parana, Buenos Aires, and Lavalle).

Spring migration.—The spring migration of the buff-breasted
sandpiper is imperfectly known, and only a few records are available.
It has been detected at Guamini, Argentina, on March 8, at Paramba,
Ecuador, on April 22, and at Gatun, Panama, on March 29. On the
Atlantic coast of the United States it is practically unknown at this
season, old records at Frogmore, South Carolina (May 5), and Ken-

dall (April 20), and Howard (May 8), New York, constituting the meager data at hand.

The main flight is seemingly up the Mississippi Valley, but even in that region, the record is incomplete. The data available are: Louisiana, Bird Islands, May 18; Kentucky, Bowling Green, April 27; Missouri, April 15, and May 20; Illinois, Chicago, April 27; Ohio, Columbus, May 6, 1923 (only record); Iowa, Norway, April; Minnesota, Madison, May 16, and Wilder, May 21; Texas, Corpus Christi, March 17, and Gainesville, April 23; South Dakota, Sioux Falls, May 12, and Fort Sisseton, May 22; North Dakota, Jamestown, May 6, and Harrisburg, May 7; Mackenzie, Fort Chipewyan, May 24, and Fort Simpson, May 29; and Alaska, Demarcation Point, May 26.

Fall migration.—The fall record is more complete and dates of arrival and departure can be given with greater consistency. Early dates of arrival are: British Columbia, Chilliwack, July 23; Keewatin, Cape Eskimo, August 10; Manitoba, Shoal Lake, August 9; North Dakota, Grafton, August 14; South Dakota, Harding County, August 15; Nebraska, Neligh, August 12, and Waverly, August 14; Texas, Tivoli, August 3; Gainesville, August 4, and Brownsville, August 4; Minnesota, Minneapolis, August 1; Iowa, Charles City, August 1, and Sioux City, August 2; Indiana, Millers, August 30; Ohio, Lake County, August 19; Illinois, Chicago, August 16; Louisiana, Abbeville, August 4; Quebec, Godbout, August 7, and Henley Harbor, August 20; Maine, Scarboro, August 1, and Damariscane Island, August 26; New Hampshire, Rye Beach, August 25; Massachusetts, Ipswich, August 7, Cape Cod, August 16, and Nantucket, August 26; Rhode Island, Little Compton, July 22; New York, Canandaigua, July 24, Shelter Island, August 22, Syracuse, August 24, Rockaway, August 25, and Montauk Point, August 26; New Jersey, Toms River, September 8; Virginia, Wallops Island, September 5; North Carolina, Currituck, September 12; Florida, Lake Jackson, September 12; Costa Rica, San Jose, September 7; Colombia, Cienaga, August 12; Peru, Pebas, August 3, and Yquitos, September 2; and Paraguay, Puerto Pinasco, September 21.

Late dates of fall departure are: Washington, Westport, September 3, and Tacoma, September 20; California, Morro, September 14, 1923 (only record for the State); Montana, Yellowstone County, September 1; Colorado, Barr, August 25 and September 4 (only records); Manitoba, Lake Winnipeg, September 5, and Oak Lake, September 9; North Dakota, Jamestown, September 30; Nebraska, Lincoln, October 25; Kansas, Salina, October 10; Texas, Brownsville, October 7, and Corpus Christi, October 10; Wisconsin, Pittston, September 7, and Rock Prairie, September 10; Michigan, Kalamazoo

County, September 17; Ohio, Columbus, September 9, Indiana, La-
fayette, September 10; Illinois, Chicago, September 28, and Beach,
October 2; Missouri, Independence, September 15; Kentucky, Bowling Green, September 7; Quebec, Magdalen Islands, September 13,
and Port Burwell, September 28; Maine, Cape Elizabeth, September
13; Massachusetts, Nantucket, September 8, Plum Island, September
15, Monomoy Island, September 19, and Cape Cod, September 24;
Rhode Island, Middletown, September 10, Newport, September 15,
and Compton, September 23; Connecticut, New Haven, September
30; New York, Orient Point, September 8, Rockaway, September
13, and Mastic, October 6; Lesser Antilles, Barbados, October 6;
Costa Rica, San Jose, October 8; and Panama, Gatun, October 18.

Casual records.—The buff-breasted sandpiper has been recorded as
taken once at Cardenas, Cuba (Gundlach). There are fifteen or
sixteen records for the British Isles, all being for the period from
July to September, except one, taken in May, 1829, at Formby,
Lancashire. It also has been recorded from Abbeville, Picardy,
France (Dalgleish); and from the Province of Owari, Japan
(Stejneger). A record of this species from Heligoland, May 9, 1847,
is considered by Seebohn as possibly *T. subminuta.*

Egg Dates.—Arctic coasts of Canada and Alaska: 37 records, June
1 to July 18; 19 records, June 28 to July 3.

ACTITIS MACULARIA (Linnaeus)

SPOTTED SANDPIPER

HABITS

Contributed by Winsor Marrett Tyler

The spotted sandpiper is one of the successful species of birds.

The old writers, speaking of a time when the surface of the country
was very different from at present, are in accord as to the abundance
of this bird in North America. Wilson (1832) refers to it as " very
common "; Nuttall (1834) says it is " one of the most familiar and
common of all the New England marsh birds "; and Audubon (1840)
reports it " quite abundant along the margins of the Mississippi, the
Ohio, and their tributaries," and " on the island of Jestico, in the
Gulf of St. Lawrence, about 20 pairs had nests and eggs, * * *
and the air was filed with the pleasant sound of their voices."

At the present time we find the bird apparently little diminished in
numbers. In the numerous local lists published from every part of
the country the spotted sandpiper almost always has a place. Nota-
tions such as " seen daily throughout the summer " or " common along
the streams " indicate the wide distribution and abundance of the

species. Indeed it is the best known of our sandpipers, not only because of its extensive breeding range, extending from coast to coast and northward into Alaska and Labrador, but by reason of its individual and peculiar habit of flight and its characteristic notes.

Almost every inhabitant of the United States, sometime during the year, may meet this graceful little wader stepping delicately along the margin of some sandy pond, the shore of the sea, or skimming from perch to perch on the rocks bordering a mountain stream.

Poised well above the ground on its slim greenish-yellow legs it walks slowly and carefully along the shore, picking up a bit of food now on this side, now on that. It goes forward with a switching motion, head reached well forward and a little lowered. Except when creeping up within reach of an insect or when its attention is riveted on the snapping up of a bit of food the tail is almost continuously in motion up and down. At the least alarm the motion is increased to a wider arc until the posterior half of the bird's body is rapidly teetering. A little increase in alarm and the bird is off on vibrating wings held stiffly and cupped with the tips depressed, sailing along the shore away from danger. As the bird takes wing it gives, almost without exception, its whistled call, *peet-weet-weet*, a call so associated with the bird that Nuttall long ago give it the name *peet-weet*.

Spring.—The spotted sandpiper moves northward earlier than the other sandpipers. It enters the transitional zone in late April and early May, its time of arrival coinciding very closely with the chewink, another ground feeder. It returns to its breeding ground inconspicuously, never passing by in the large flocks characteristic of many sandpipers, but appears on the first day of its arrival running about on the shore of its chosen bit of water, apparently settled for the season. In this habit of not gathering into flocks it resembles its relative the solitary sandpiper.

Wright and Harper (1913) speak of a few birds, left behind after most of the species had spread over the country to the north, tarrying in the Okefinokee Swamp till late in the spring:

> The spotted sandpiper was a distinct surprise as a summer resident of the swamp Not only is this several hundred miles south of its known breeding range, but one would not expect it to find a suitable haunt in the Okefinokee. The lakes and rivers are practically shoreless; they are simply open spaces in the otherwise continuous cypress swamps. However, the logs and driftwood near the edges of Billys Lake serve as teetering stands; half a dozen were seen here on May 11, one on June 5, and still another a few days later. The species probably does not breed in this latitude.

Courtship.—The courtship of the spotted sandpiper has not been observed very minutely. Some of the few published reports on the subject show a discrepancy in details, and one, giving an instance of display by a bird proved by dissection to be a female, casts doubts on all records of courtship based on sight identification and raises the question as to the respective rôles played by the sexes in the home-life of the species.

Bradford Torrey (1885), assuming the bird to be a male, speaks of

A spotted sandpiper, whose capers I amused myself with watching, one day last June, on the shore of Saco Lake. As I caught sight of him, he was straightening himself up, with a pretty, self-conscious air, at the same time spreading his white-edged tail, and calling, *tweet, tweet, tweet*. Afterwards he got upon a log, where, with head erect and wings thrown forward and downward, he ran for a yard or two, calling as before. This trick seemed especially to please him, and was several times repeated. He ran rapidly, and with a comical prancing movement; but nothing he did was half as laughable as the behavior of his mate, who all this while dressed her feathers without once deigning to look at her spouse's performance.

Whittle (1922) describes a similar action of a bird observed in Montana on May 29:

One of the birds, judged to be a male, was seen standing on a long, inclined timber, while another, presumed to be a female, fed close by along the shore. The male first walked the length of the timber and then flew to another one, where he depressed and spread his tail, and, without teetering, stalked slowly along its entire length, with head bent low.

Lewis O. Shelley (1925) reports from New Hampshire a courtship display which differs from the two previous ones. Here again the respective sexes are assumed:

A female sandpiper came running along the brook, occasionally stopping to pick up an insect and teeter, then run on again. Behind her were two males, the first strutting along, looking much like a goose, craning his neck up, swelling out his throat drooping his wings, and spreading his tail; the second kept well to the rear, and did no strutting.

Every time the female stopped for a second, or slowed, the male would dart past her and stop, throw his head higher, and make a *fump, fump, fump*, in his throat. If that failed to attract her attention, he would again pass her and alternately spread wings and tail. This performance went on all the afternoon, until almost dusk.

This observation describes a courtship in which the behavior of the aggressive bird corresponds closely, especially in the movements of the head, with the action of the bird noted in the next quotation—a bird proved by dissection to be a female.

A. J. Van Rossem (1925) gives the following extract from Dr. Loye Miller's notebook:

Altitude, 9,000 feet; Mammoth Lakes, Inyo County, Calif.; July 4, 1923: [spotted] sandpipers are just beginning to pair, and several seen in courting flights. One especially active bird was shot and proved to be a female. She came to an imitation of the call—soared over a fallen log before alighting on it. She then ruffed out the feathers and strutted like a turkey cock, with head thrown back. The ova were the size of buckshot.

Nesting.—The breeding range of the spotted sandpiper, extending over a vast area of diversified land, ranging in altitude from sea-level to 14,000 feet, and including both arid and well-watered country, makes necessary in the bird a wide degree of adaptability in the choice of its nesting site. Few birds show a greater variation in this respect and among the places which the bird selects to lay its eggs there is but one point in common—the proximity of water.

The following quotations bring out the extreme variety of nesting sites: Mearns (1890) writing of the bird in Arizona says: " These birds were apparently breeding at a small lake, in a crater-like depression at the summit of a volcanic peak arising near the western base of the San Francisco cone, the lake being at an altitude of from 10,000 to 10,500 feet." Shick (1890) reports the bird in New Jersey as breeding " in the higher parts of the island, generally on a sandy knoll in the high, rank sedge grass," and Audubon (1840), speaks of the nests " in Labrador, where, in every instance, they were concealed under ledges of rocks extending for several feet over them, so I probably should not have observed them, had not the birds flown off as I was passing." He also speaks, quoting Nuttall, of " their eggs laid in a strawberry bed." Dwight (1893) records a nest " found in an odd situation at Tignish [Prince Edward Island]. It was under a decayed log in a boggy slope, and was carefully lined with bits of rotten wood."

In the use of material to construct or line its nest the bird shows nearly as much variation as in the choice of the nesting site and it may be stated roughly that the more northerly the latitude of the breeding ground, the bulkier is the nest. Audubon (1840) says, speaking of the nests found in Labrador:

They were more bulky and more neatly constructed than any that I have examined southward of the Gulf of St. Lawrence. * * * These nests [those in Labrador] were made of dry moss, raised to the height of from 6 to 9 inches, and well finished within with slender grasses and feathers of the eider duck.

Brewster (1925) speaks of the bird as:

Especially given to breeding on small islands in Lake Umbagog [Maine], scarce one of which is left untenanted by them at the right season or resorted to by more than a single pair. Their eggs, almost invariably four in number, are usually laid during the last week of May, in saucer-shaped hollows scraped in surface soil, and thinly lined with dry grass. * * * If the island be treeless and ledgy, the nest is likely to be on or near the most elevated or central part, and more or less well concealed by grass or other lowly vegetation. But if all the ground, not subject to inundation, be densely wooded, the spot where the bird has hidden her treasures is seldom far back from the shore, and perhaps scarce above highwater mark, usually where driftwood has accumulated, or beneath the leafy branch of some outstanding alder or Cassandra bush. In such places as these, it is by no means easy to find the nest, even when the total area to be searched is only a few rods square. The task may well seem hopeless if undertaken in the open farming country about the southern end of the Lake, for, although spotted sandpipers breed here not uncommonly, they are so widely and sparsely distributed over hilly pastures and fields of considerable extent, that it is only by the merest chance that anybody ever stumbles on a nest. The only one that I have happened upon was well hidden in a tangle of withered grass and ferns, covering a steeply sloping bank by the roadside.

In incubation as well as in courtship the male has been shown to assume duties which are usually ascribed to the female. The following quotation illustrates this fact. Van Rossem (1925) says:

On July 11, in a boggy meadow ñear the water's edge, we found a nest of four eggs which seemed nearly fresh. We often had occasion to pass this nest, but there was never more than one bird present. On July 25 the eggs had hatched and after a short search we found the downy young in the short grass. They were collected with the parent, which proved to be the male. The sides of his breast and belly were worn quite bare of feathers, showing that he had done most of if not all of the incubating. The succeeding days, we frequently passed the old nesting place, but never saw any other sandpiper in the vicinity. On July 26 Alden Miller and the writer were on the headwaters of the San Joaquin River, in Madera County [California], and while there found a nest on a grass-grown gravel bar in the river. It contained young which were just emerging from the shells. These were collected with the parent which, as in the first case, was a male. We were at this nest and in the immediate vicinity nearly an hour, but no other adult appeared.

Although as a rule the spotted sandpiper does not build near the nest of other birds of the same species, in exceptional cases many pairs nest in close proximity to each other.

L. McI. Terrill (1911), illustrating this gregarious habit, says:

A few years ago a large colony were nesting on Isle Ronde (a small island of a few acres, opposite the city of Montreal). Visiting this island on May 26, 1896, I located without difficulty 13 occupied nests. Again, on May 31, 1898, I examined upward of 25. On each occasion only a small portion of the island was examined, and I estimated that there were well over 100 pairs breeding.

Mousley (1916) points out that—

It may not be generally known that these birds if flushed whilst constructing their nest invariably desert it, at least this has been my experience on four occasions, when I have flushed both birds whilst in the act of scooping out or lining the hole. In one instance, however, they made a fresh nest within 45 feet of the old one.

Eggs.—[AUTHOR'S NOTE: The spotted sandpiper lays almost invariably 4 eggs, very rarely 5, and rarely only 3. These are ovate in shape, less pyriform than the eggs of most waders, and they have only a very slight gloss. The prevailing ground color is " cartridge buff," with some variations to " pinkish buff," or " pale olive buff." They are irregularly spotted or blotched, usually both;

sometimes they are finely and evenly sprinkled with small spots; and very rarely the markings are concentrated at the larger end. The markings are mostly in very dark browns, " seal brown," " clove brown," and " blackish brown," and rarely as light as " Mars brown " or " russet." The underlying markings are generally lacking or inconspicuous, but some handsome eggs are blotched with " lavender gray," " pallid purple drab," or " brownish drab." The measurements of 88 eggs, in the United States National Museum, average 32 by 23 millimeters; the eggs showing the four extremes measure **34** by **25, 29** by 23, and 33 by **20** millimeters.]

Young.—The young spotted sandpiper furnishes an instance of an ancestral habit springing into action almost at the moment of hatching. When no larger than the egg from which they have just stepped they run over the sand teetering their tail in the manner of their parents. My notes mention a little bird, no more than a tiny ball of fluff, which stood on my hand waving up and down the feathery plumes of its infinitesimal tail.

Wilson (1832) says: " The young, as soon as they are freed from the shell, run about constantly wagging the tail," and Nuttall (1834) speaks of " the habit of balancing or wagging the tail, in which even the young join as soon as they are fledged."

Another example of the precociousness of the fledgling sandpiper is its ability to swim while still in the down. G. M. Sutton (1925) speaks of the habit thus:

Upon several occasions within the writer's experience downy young of the spotted sandpiper, when closely pursued, have taken to the water, where they swam lightly although not very rapidly in making an escape.

Dr. C. W. Townsend (1920) cites a case in which a young bird, evidently in juvenal plumage, swam under water:

In Labrador I caught a nearly full-grown young still unable to fly and put it in a small river. It at once dove and swam under water for a distance of 3 or 4 feet, using for propulsion its wings and probably its feet, although I could not be sure of the latter point. It then rose to the surface and swam to the opposite side like a little duck and walked out on the sand, where the mother was anxiously calling.

Aretas A. Saunders also mentions in his notes a case of diving:

Young birds when away from the parent and threatened with danger often take to water and dive and swim under water, using the wings to help swim. At such times the down is covered with air bubbles, which helps keep them dry and gives them a silvery appearance. Once I pursued a young bird I wished to band, and it did this so many times that it became wet in spite of the air bubbles, and in fact was quite chilled through for a time.

More commonly the method of escaping danger adopted by the young sandpipers is to lie motionless on the beach, where a pebbly shore affords an ideal background for concealment. William Palmer (1909) brings out the success of this ruse thus:

While walking along a beach one summer a spotted sandpiper (*Actitis macularia*) and a single young were noticed some distance ahead. As I approached the place the old bird, with the startled manner characteristic of its kind at such a time, kept well ahead, but I could not find the other. Going back some distance, I waited and soon saw it again with its parent. I repeated my quest, and again failed to find the youngster. Going back once more and again seeing it rejoin the old bird, I slowly moved forward, keeping my eyes this time very intently on it, and soon picked it up from the sand, an unwilling captive.

A. A. Saunders gives in his notes a picture of the parental care of the young. The young birds are—

able to run and follow the parent when about half an hour from the egg (two instances). The parent leads them away and watches over them for a few days after hatching, after which they gradually stray away from her (?) care. At Flathead Lake [Montana] one bird hatched her young and led them down the beach, and I followed to see what would happen. When I got too near the mother (?) called *Peet! peet! peet!* in a loud, sharp call. The young immediately flattened themselves down among the pebbles so effectually I could only find one. I sat down on a log, and after waiting some 20 minutes the parent quieted down—flew to the opposite side of her young from me, turned and faced them, and began to call *tootawee, tootawee, tootawee* over and over. The young immediately responded and began a hurried run for the mother (?), calling baby *peeps* and tumbling over the pebbles in their eagerness. The parent half spread its wings as they arrived and they took shelter beneath, just as chickens do under a hen.

The period of incubation is 15 days.

Plumages.—[AUTHOR'S NOTE: The young spotted sandpiper in the natal down is quite uniformly grizzled or mottled on the upper parts, from crown to rump, with " buffy brown," " wood brown," grayish buff, and black. The forehead is grayish buff, and the entire under parts are white; a narrow black stripe extends from the bill through the eye to the nape; a black patch in the center of the crown extends as an indistinct median stripe down the nape and broadens to a black band along the back to the rump.

The juvenal plumage comes in first on the mantle and wings, then on the flanks, breast, and crown, and lastly on the neck, rump, and tail. The upper parts are "light brownish olive," more grayish on the sides of the neck and chest; the scapulars and upper tail coverts have a subterminal sepia bar and are tipped with pale buff or creamy white; the lesser and median wing coverts are conspicuously barred with pale buff and sepia; the chin, throat, and under parts are white.

During the fall, beginning late in August, or in September, some of the body plumage, tail and some tertials and wing coverts are molted, producing the first winter plumage. This postjuvenal molt is very limited and very variable; I have seen birds in juvenal plumage as late as December 3. The first winter plumage is like the adult winter, except for the retained juvenal wing coverts. It is worn until March or April. The wings are molted during the winter at any time from October to April; and during March and April the body plumage is molted, producing the first nuptial plumage. This is like the adult nuptial, but there is more gray on the sides of the neck and less spotting on the breast, sometimes very little of the latter. But the plumage is practically adult, except for a few retained juvenal wing coverts.

Adults have a complete postnuptial molt beginning with the body plumage in August, or earlier, and ending with the molt of the primaries at any time from October to April. In winter plumage the upper parts are plain "dark grayish olive," shading off lighter on the sides of the head and neck; the under parts are white, faintly washed with grayish on the throat. The partial prenuptial molt, involving only the body plumage comes in March and April and produces the spotted breast of the nuptial plumage.]

Food.—At the seacoast the spotted sandpiper searches for its food both on the beach and on the muddy borders of creeks and inlets, wading into the water, however, less frequently than most sandpipers; inland it feeds along the margins of sandy ponds, sluggish meadow streams and rushing mountain torrents; in farming country it strays into the meadows, fields, and market gardens and finds in all these situations food which it picks up from the low vegetation or from the ground.

Like some of the other sandpipers, however, and like several other birds which have the agility to do so, it easily captures flying insects even when they are on the wing. In order to come within striking distance of an insect before it flies away, the spotted sandpiper resorts to a ruse by which its approaching head and beak are concealed or made inconspicuous. As the bird walks over windrows of seaweed and such places where flies abound, it stretches its body out with the bill pointing straight in front, the whole bird lengthened into a line with the long axis parallel to the ground. In this position the head, from the flies' point of view is masked by the body as a background and the bird is enabled to come so near that it can snap up a fly, even after it has taken wing, by a straight forward movement of the head. In stalking a flying prey the spotted sandpiper creeps up to the fly, moving slowly with cat-like steps, the tail motionless, and apparently never adopts the well-known trick of the semipalmated sandpiper, the running about with the hind part of the body tilted far upward, advancing upon a fly under cover of this as a screen.

A complete list of the insects which form the spotted sandpiper's diet, could one be compiled, would doubtless be a very long one, comprising as it would both marine and land insects. The wide range of the bird's choice of food is shown by the following quotations which prove definitely that it is a very beneficial species to the agriculturalist.

E. H. Forbush (1925), speaking of the bird's habit of frequenting cultivated fields, says:

They feed largely on locusts, grasshoppers and caterpillars, such as cutworms, cabbage worms and army worms, also beetles, grubs and other pests of cultivated lands.

H. K. Job (1911) writes:

The usual food of most species of this class [shore birds] is aquatic insect life of all sorts. This is in part the diet of the spotted sandpiper. But as it is also a bird of field and pasture, its range of insect food is very wide, including grasshoppers and locusts. Probably almost anything in the insect line is grist for its hopper, and it is a most useful bird.

Austin H. Clark (1905a) furnishes the following unusual observation:

While on the island of St. Vincent, West Indies, last October, I observed a number of our shore birds feeding on the young of a small fish known as the "tri tri" (*Sicydium plumieri*), which were at that time ascending the Richmond River, near which I was staying, by thousands. The land about the lower reaches of this river was laid completely bare by the recent eruptions of the Soufrière, and in its present state proves very attractive to all the species of shore birds which visit the island during the migrations. Those observed or proved by dissection to be eating the young tri tri (which were at that time from half an inch to an inch and a quarter long) were * * * solitary sandpipers (*Helodromas solitarius*), and spotted sandpipers (*Actitis macularia*). All but the last two kept near the mouth of the river, or on the flat lands along its lower reaches; the solitary sandpiper followed the stream up into what were formerly arrowroot fields, half or three-quarters of a mile from the sea, and the spotted sandpiper was found well into the mountain forests.

W. H. Bergtold (1926) cites an instance of the bird's catching another swift-moving fish. He says that the caretakers at the Wigwam Fishing Club, Colorado, "reported the spotted sandpiper as also catching trout fry."

The following quotation adds crickets to the list of insects; H. W. Jewell (1909) writes:

While sitting on the banks of Sandy River one night I was attracted to the actions of a spotted sandpiper. There were lots of crickets on the shore of the river, and the sandpiper would catch one in its bill, run up to the water, and immerse the insect several times, then swallow it. This seemed a very interesting performance to me, and I wondered if all living insects caught are thus treated before they are eaten. The cricket is quite a large insect, and as this bird ate 10 or 12 he did not go to bed hungry that night.

Alexander Wetmore (1916), who examined the contents of nine stomachs, says: " Though mole crickets (*Scapteriscus didactylos*) were found in but two stomachs, they form 10.78 per cent of the total food." Summarizing his findings, he concludes, " From the foregoing the spotted sandpiper is a beneficial species and should not be molested."

Behavior.—Nothing is more characteristic of the spotted sandpiper than its flight. When it first starts from the shore the wings seem to vibrate like a taut wire; then, as the bird gains headway, they set and, depressed and quivering, they carry the bird slowly onward, often swaying from side to side, close to the surface of the water. As a rule, when startled, the sandpiper takes a semicircular course and alights a short distance farther up the beach, and if followed either takes another flight onward or doubles back as a kingfisher would do under similar circumstances. This scaling flight, somewhat after the manner of a meadow lark, is seen most commonly during the summer, but on infrequent occasions the sandpiper lets go his wings and carries them back with a long, free sweep and speeds through the air with the rapidity of a swallow. The transition from one kind of flight to the other is remarkable to see; with outstretched neck it drives along with regular wing beats, a long, slender, unfamiliar-looking wader.

J. T. Nichols mentions in his notes this peculiar flight; he says:

One might be familiar with the bird for years and believe it [the scaling flight] invariable. Careful attention in late summer and fall, however, will demonstrate that it is not. When, as rarely happens, the spotted sandpiper rises to some height to make a considerable aerial passage (especially over a stretch of marsh) the flight becomes regular like that of a minature yellow-legs, or swift and darting as it sometimes is with a white-rumped sandpiper for instance. It also, at times, flies low over the tops of the marsh grass in this last named manner. To identify such birds in the air is very difficult. and they will pass for some one of the other sandpipers of rather small size if one does not chance to appreciate the slenderer neck and somewhat different shape, or the more uniform color of the upper parts.

The ability to swim and dive which is so noticeable in the young of the spotted sandpiper is even more remarkably evident in the behavior of the adult bird. Of the many instances recorded in the literature, the following will illustrate this well developed proclivity.

E. H. Forbush (1912) speaks thus of the action of a wounded bird:

In September, 1876, I saw a wounded bird of this species when pursued, dive into deep water from the shore of the Charles River and fly off under water, using its wings somewhat as a bird would use them in the air. All its plumage was covered with bubbles of air, which caught the light until the bird appeared as if studded with sparkling gems as it sped away into the depths of the dark river.

Later (1925) he adds a record of the bird actually running along the bottom while entirely submerged. The spotted sandpiper—

can dive from the surface of the water or from full flight, at need. Under water it progresses by using its wings which it spreads quite widely, and in shallow water it can go to the bottom and run a short distance with head held low and tail raised like an ouzel or dipper.

G. M. Sutton (1925) describes the behavior of two birds which he startled by a close sudden approach. In the first quotation he shows that the spotted sandpiper readily dives while on the wing and continues its flight under water and in the second quotation he shows the bird's ability to rise directly into the air from beneath the water, a feat impossible for many water birds.

When the bird first flushed, its wings were fully spread, and it was headed for the open water of the lake. Upon seeing me towering above it, however, it turned its course abruptly downward, and without the slightest hesitation flew straight into the water. With wings fully outspread and legs kicking it made its way rather slowly along the sandy bottom, until it was about 8 feet out, in water over 3 feet deep. I pursued the bird, thinking at the time, strangely enough, that it was wounded. When I reached for it, it tried to go farther but apparently could not. Bubbles of air came from its mouth, and air bubbles were plainly seen clinging to the plumage of its back. At the time it was captured its mouth, eyes, and wings were all open, under water, and it remained at the bottom seemingly without difficulty. As it lay in my hands above water it seemed tired for a second or two, and then, without warning, shook itself a little, leaped into the air, and with loud, clear whistles, circled off a few inches above the water to a distant point of land.

On a subsequent occasion, May 7, 1925, Mr. Sutton—

purposely came upon a spotted sandpiper suddenly and witnessed it employ almost the identical tactics in making an effective escape. At this time, however, the bird dove into running water, swam with wings and feet rapidly moving for about 20 feet, and emerged down stream, still flying, and made off in its characteristic way, only a few inches above the water.

L. L. Jewel (1915), watching a saidpiper in Panama under most favorable circumstances was able to make out clearly the position of the feet while the bird was swimming under water. The beach where Mr. Jewel made this observation was, as he describes it:

A wide coral reef, bare at low tide, and with occasional openings or "wells" connected underneath with the sea. Some of these are of considerable size and the water in all is as clear as crystal to all depths—clear as only those who have seen such tropical "coral water" can imagine. * * *

I had however a perfect view of the bird as he "flew" the 10 feet across the pool, through the beautifully clear water which showed white pebbles distinctly on a bottom perhaps 20 feet below. The bird crossed at a unifrom depth of 18 inches to 2 feet, which he held until he brought up against the opposite wall. The head and neck were extended but not at all stretched while the legs and feet trailed behind with flexed toes, like a heron in flight. The wings seemed to be opened to only perhaps half their full extent—the primaries pointing well backward like wings are trimmed as birds cut down from some height to alight. The wing-beats were slow and even but not labored, and progress was uniform and not at all hurried.

In addition to the anomalous behavior of the spotted sandpiper in and under the water, the bird shows a further departure from the regular habits of the other shore birds in its ability and frequent tendency to perch on small supports which requires a grasping power in the feet to hold the bird in place. My notes supply an extreme instance of this habit, noting the action of an adult bird (exercised, to be sure, over the safety of its young) which alighted on a slender wire running between poles and stood crouched a little and leaning forward, but keeping its balance by securely gripping the wire.

The literature furnishes one other record of grasping a wire. L. L. Snyder (1924) reports thus:

On June 25, 1923, at Orient Bay, Lake Nipigon, Ontario, the writer observed a spotted standpiper perching on a telegraph wire. The fact that the species was perching was not surprising but the size of the perch made the observation of interest. .The bird was not in an erect position, being squatted, which probably made the feat less difficult. In this case the act was entirely voluntary and not an instance of unusual conduct due to the pressure of an emergency.

Other quotations, showing the bird acting in unsandpiper-like behavior follow. Mousley (1915) says:

On one occasion only have I seen a very excited parent bird with young alight on a cat-tail head, and very out of place and uncomfortable it seemed to be.

H. H. Cleaves (1908) says:

We were returning along a rather unused railroad when, in an area to one side, which was flooded for the most part with a number of inches of water, we noticed a spotted sandpiper flying about in circles and acting peculiarly. We had all come to the conclusion that her young were about somewhere, when she did a most peculiar thing. The wet area in question was covered with considerable underbrush, out of which grew rather tall, second-growth timber. The sandpiper alighted on the tops of some of these trees, on the small twigs, and remained balancing there for some time, fully 25 or 30 feet from the ground. This performance she repeated several times, making her appear for all the world like a perching bird.

P. A. Taverner (1919) says:

Common all along the river [Red Deer River, Alberta] and breeding everywhere. One bird on being flushed from her eggs flew into adjoining bushes and climbed about them in a most unwaderlike style while complaining at our intrusion.

J. T. Nichols points out in his notes that the foot of the spotted sandpiper is adapted to its peculiar habits; that the bird is able to grasp a small object because the front toes are nearer together than in most waders and the hind toe is more developed. He says:

> The footmarks of the spotted sandpiper on moist sand or mud are recognizable. Compared to those of related birds the toes are relatively little spreading, and the mark left by the hind toe relatively large and conspicuous.

Under the title "Spotted Sandpiper Removing its Young" J. C. Merrill (1898) describes a very remarkable performance, the only record of such behavior noted in the literature.

> A clearly observed case of the spotted sandpiper (*Actitis macularia*) removing its young by flight recently came under my notice, and I place it upon record, as such instances are rarely seen, though they are, perhaps, of tolerably frequent occurrence, as in the case of the woodcock.
>
> Last summer, in the month of July, I frequently landed on a little rocky islet near the head of the Saquenay River, shortly after it issues from Lake St. John. Each time a spotted sandpiper showed much concern for her young, which were often seen running about and were a few days old. On one of these occasions, the mother ran ahead of me to a point of rocks near which I stopped to fish. A few moments later she flew, circling in the usual manner, and as she passed in front of me and within a few feet, I saw one of the young beneath her body, apparently clasped by her thighs; its head was directed forward, somewhat outstretched, and was seen with perfect distinctness. The parent's legs were apparently hanging down as she flew, though I am not positive that what I saw were not the legs of the young. The mother was in sight for about 60 yards, flying heavily and silently, and landed on a large island, though I could not see her at the moment of alighting.

Voice.—The notes of the spotted sandpiper are mainly modified and extended from its common alarm note, the sharp, clear whistle, *peet-weet*, but as in the case of many birds, degrees of emotion may be expressed by a little change in pitch or inflection. When considerably alarmed the bird continues to repeat the *weet* note often giving a long series which trails off in diminuendo like the quacking of a duck.

J. T. Nichols (1920) describes a series of notes:

> *Hoy, hoy, weet, weet, weet, weet, weet, weet, weet* is a prolonged call frequently heard in the early part of the nesting season, in toto or in part, suggesting in that respect the songs of the cuckoos. It doubtless has value as advertisement or location notice and something the significance of a very generalized song. A series of loud *weets*, heard also at other times of year, the most far-reaching call of the species, doubtless serves as location notice.

A. A. Saunders in his notes similarly describes the "song." He says:

> I believe the long call *weet, weet, weet, weet, weet, weet, weet, peet a weet, peet a weet, peet a weet, peet a weet* serves as a song. I have seen it sung in flight, when the actions and flight of the bird were similar to those of other flight singers.

Both of these observers describe the soft crooning note used by the parent to bring together its young. Nichols says that, "a rolling note, *kerrwee, kerrwee, kerrwee,* now loud, now very low and distant, has been heard from an adult with the evident purpose of assembling her young; and Saunders speaks of a parent bird which called to its young, *tootawee, tootawee, tootawee, tootawee* over and over. The call is like the *peet a weet* in form, but lower pitched and softer."

A common note, heard during the summer on the breeding ground when the birds are undisturbed, resembles closely the whistle of the little frog, *Hyla pickeringii.* This is a far-reaching whistled note, not given in a series like the *weet, weet* call. It is a single note, apparently, repeated over and over again, not regularly, but always with an interval between each repetition.

It is clear that Nichols has this note in mind when he says, "*Pip! pip! pip!* is a note heard between adult birds in the breeding season which seems to be of polite address, or possibly impolite, as it is almost identical in form with a note of protest by old birds when nest or young are threatened."

Continuing, he describes two other notes, "the *pit-wit-wit* frequently heard from adults as a note of departure may best be considered a variation of this one [the *pip wip* of the young] as also the *peet weet weet* or *weet weet* most frequent a little later in the season as little companies of birds start out over the water for longer or shorter distances.

"An old bird, surprised near her brood and fluttering off playing wounded called *cheerp cheerp* a sort of scream as of pain and fear."

Field marks.—The spotted sandpiper is one of the prettiest, most delicate, and trim of the shore birds; in place of the browns and greys of the streaked upper parts of most waders there is a plain greenish sheen on the back, and in autumn across the breast a soft tint like a fawn. Through the glass the wings show a fine mottling, suggesting a wren. The line of white at the posterior margin of the open wing is a good diagnostic mark, and its habit of teetering makes identification certain. The only bird which resembles the spotted sandpiper at all closely is its larger relative the solitary sandpiper, but the characteristic motion of this bird is a ploverlike hitching movement or bob, as if hiccoughing, very different from the spotted sandpiper's rapid swaying up and down of the hinder part of the body.

Enemies.—The chief enemies of the spotted sandpiper are the swift-moving hawks, whose pursuit it sometimes successfully eludes by diving in the manner described above. J. E. H. Kelso (1926) records an instance of this habit. He says:

Skirting the lake shore in my sneak boat a spotted sandpiper was repeatedly disturbed, flew along in front of the boat to settle again and again on the shore.

It then made off to cross a small bay, when a pigeon hawk dashed out from some trees and made a stoop or two at the dodging sandpiper, which would certainly soon have been captured in the air if it had not suddenly alighted on the water. This for a few seconds confused the hawk, which circled just over its quarry and appeared to try to capture it with its talons. The sandpiper dove, remaining under 3 or 4 seconds. The hawk on the disappearance of its intended victim at once made off at a great pace.

W. H. Osgood (1909) describes an escape in this manner from an attack by a northern shrike.

Wilson (1832) in his most charming manner tells this delightful story:

My venerable friend, Mr. William Bartram, informs me that he saw one of these birds defend her young for a considerable time from the repeated attacks of a ground squirrel. The scene of action was on the river shore. The parent had thrown herself, with her two young behind her, between them and the land, and at every attempt of the squirrel to seize them by a circuitous sweep raised both her wings in an almost perpendicular position, assuming the most formidable appearance she was capable of, and rushed forwards on the squirrel, who, intimidated by her boldness and manner, instantly retreated; but presently returning was met, as before, in front and on flank by the daring and affectionate bird, who with her wings and whole plumage bristling up seemed swelled to twice her usual size. The young crowded together behind her, apparently sensible of their perilous situation, moving backward and forward as she advanced or retreated. This interesting scene lasted for at least 10 minutes; the strength of the poor parent began evidently to flag, and the attacks of the squirrel became more daring and frequent, when my good friend, like one of those celestial agents who in Homer's time so often decided the palm of victory, stepped forward from his retreat, drove the assailant back to his hole, and rescued the innocent from destruction.

A. A. Saunders sends the following suggestive note:

Once on Sherwoods Island, Westport, Conn., in September, I saw a bird fly ahead of me with something large and black looking dangling beneath it. The bird could hardly fly and tried to hide in the beach grass as I approached. I caught it and found that a large specimen of the common edible mussel (*Mytilus edulis*) had closed its shell on the middle toe of the bird's left foot. The toe was nearly severed just above the nail, and since I couldn't pry the mussel open, I cut through the bit of skin left and freed the bird.

Fall.—As is the case during its northward migration, the spotted sandpiper leaves its breeding ground and moves to its winter quarters inconspicuously, showing little tendency to gather into flocks. Its voice is not infrequently heard among the notes of the autumnal nocturnal migrants—an indication that the bird in a measure makes use of the safe, dark hours during its long journey southward.

Cooke (1897) says: " In the fall [in Colorado] it ranges above the pines to 14,000 feet," illustrating the tendency to wander about in autumn.

Game.—During the years, now past, when the smaller shore birds could legally be shot for food or sport the spotted sandpiper suffered less than some of the other Limicolae by reason of its more solitary habit. The gunners, waiting for several of their tiny target to come within range of a single shot, often disregarded a spotted sandpiper running alone on the shore.

Winter.—Most of the spotted sandpipers leave the United States to spend the winter on the islands to the southward, and in South America, but the species is nevertheless well represented in California during the winter, and in the Southern States on the Atlantic seaboard.

George Willett (1912) "found this species plentiful in winter around Santa Barbara Islands and on rocky shores of the mainland."

Dr. Alexander Wetmore (1916) speaking of the bird as a winter visitant of Porto Rico says:

It frequents the mangrove swamps, borders of lagoons, margins of all the streams, and occasionally the sandy beaches. During the winter season it follows inland along the small streams and occurs throughout the island.

And (1927) reporting the birds' winter status in South America says—

it is a regular migrant in South America as far as Bolivia and southern Brazil, and on March 4, 1918, several were found by Mogensen at Concepcion, Province of Tucuman, in northern Argentina. On October 25, 1920, one was taken by the writer near the mouth of the Rio Ajo on the eastern coast of the Province of Buenos Aires, the southernmost point at which the species is known.

DISTRIBUTION

Range.—North and South America; accidental in Europe.

Breeding range.—The breeding range of the spotted sandpiper extends north to Alaska (Kobuk River, Fort Yukon, and Circle); Yukon (La Pierre House); Mackenzie (Fort McPherson, Arctic Red River, Fort Anderson, Aylmer Lake, Clinton-Colden Lake, and Artillery Lake); Manitoba (Fort Du Brochet, Fort Churchill, and York Factory); Ungava (Fort Chimo); and Labrador (Okak). East of Labrador (Okak and Rigolet); eastern Quebec (Sloop Harbor and Wolf Bay); Newfoundland (Humber River and Penguin Island); Nova Scotia (Breton Island, Pictou, and Yarmouth); Maine (Thomaston); New Hampshire (Portsmouth); Massachusetts (Boston and Woods Hole); Rhode Island (Block Island); New York (Shelter Island); New Jersey (Red Bank and Five-mile Beach); Maryland (Cambridge); Virginia (Cobb Island and Richmond); North Carolina (Kona, Fort Macon, and Wilmington); and probably South Carolina (Chester and Columbia). South to probably South Carolina (Columbia); probably Georgia (Okefinokee Swamp); Alabama (Autauga County and Greensboro); Louisiana (New Orleans, Baton Rouge, and Vermilion Bay); Texas (Corsicana, Calhoun County,

Austin, Buffalo Bayou, Kerrville, Concho County, and Tom Green County); New Mexico (Las Vegas, Willis, and Espanola); Arizona (Camp Verde); and California (Santa Paula). West to California (Santa Paula, Kernville, Lime Kiln, Royal Arches, Lake Tahoe, and Eagle Lake); Oregon (Fort Klamath, Elkton, Eugene, Corvallis, Salem, Dayton, and Portland); Washington (Bellingham Bay); British Columbia (Vancouver and Skidegate); and Alaska (Lewis Point, Sitka, Idaho Inlet, Glacier Bay, Hinchinbrook Island, Port Nell Juan, Lake Clark, Mount McKinley, Nulato, and Kobuk River).

Nonbreeding individuals also have been observed in summer in the Bahama Islands; Porto Rico; Jamaica; Guadeloupe; Barbados; Grenada; St. Vincent; Dominica; Martinique; Florida (Fruitland Park, Indian Key, and Seven Oaks); Chihuahua (Pachaco); and Nyarit (Tres Marias Islands).

Winter range.—In winter, the spotted sandpiper ranges north rarely to British Columbia (Courtenay and Chilliwack); Arizona (Camp Verde and Salt River Bird Reservation); New Mexico (Carlsbad); Texas (Fort Brown); probably Louisiana (Vermilion Bay); and rarely Virginia (James River peninsula). East to rarely Virginia (James River peninsula); South Carolina (Sea Islands and Port Royal); Georgia (Savannah, Blackbeard Island, and St. Marys); Florida (Fernandina, Daytona, New Smyrna, Malabar, St. Lucie, Miami, Key Largo, and Key West); the Bahama Islands (Andros); Cuba (Santiago de Cuba); Haiti (Monte Christi); Porto Rico (Cartagena Lagoon, Mameyes, and Caguas); the Lesser Antilles (Dominica, St. Lucia, Barbados, Carriacou, and Trinidad); British Guiana (Bartica and Georgetown); French Guiana (Cayenne); and Brazil (Mixiana, Marajo, Para, and Bahia). South to Brazil (Bahia and Santa Fe); Bolivia (San Francisco); and Peru (Lima). West to Peru (Lima, Huacho, and Tumbez); Ecuador (Santa Elena, Quito, and Esmeraldas); Galapagos Islands (Albemarle); Colombia (Puerto Berrio); Panama (Panama City); Costa Rica (La Estrella de Cartago, and San Jose); Nicaragua (Escondido River); Salvador (La Libertad); Honduras (Chamelecon); Guatemala (Lake Atitlan); Oaxaca (Tehuantepec City); Lower California (San Jose del Cabo and La Paz); Sonora (Alamos); California (San Clemente Island, Santa Catalina Island, Santa Cruz Island, and Marysville); rarely Oregon (probably Klamath Lake, Elkton, and Portland); probably Washington (Seattle, Clallam Bay, and Port Angeles); and rarely British Columbia (Courtenay).

Spring migration.—Early dates of spring arrival are: North Carolina, Raleigh, April 3, Andrews, April 5, and Weaverville, April 10; Virginia, Miller, April 10, Bowers Hill, April 12, and Camp Eustis, April 14; West Virginia, Waverly, April 4, White Sulphur Springs,

April 6, and Lewisburg, April 11; District of Columbia, Washington, April 2; Maryland, Cambridge, April 13, and Sandy Spring, April 18; Delaware, Wilmington, April 27; Pennsylvania, Phillipsburg, March 27, Jeffersonville, March 31, Wallingford, April 1, Beaver, April 2, and Berwyn, April 5; New Jersey, New Brunswick, March 30, Deep Water Point Light, April 14, and Camden, April 16; New York, Rhinebeck, March 20, Locust Grove, April 2, Geneva, April 13, and Branchport, April 15; Connecticut, Canaan, April 14, Portland, April 18, and Fairfield, April 21; Rhode Island, Block Island, April 6; Massachusetts, Dorchester, April 12, Woods Hole, April 13, Holyoke, April 15, and Harvard, April 25; Vermont, Woodstock, April 23, Rutland, April 25, and St. Johnsbury, April 27; New Hampshire, Tilton, April 26, Peterboro, April 28, and Hanover, April 30; Maine, Westbrook, April 14, Ellsworth, April 16, and Portland, April 26; Quebec, Montreal, April 26, and Quebec, May 2; New Brunswick, Scotch Lake, May 2, and Blacksville, May 5; Nova Scotia, Yarmouth, May 4, and Wolfville, May 9; Arkansas, Tillar, March 17, and Monticello, March 22; Tennessee, Knoxville, April 3, and Athens, April 10; Kentucky, Bowling Green, March 29; Missouri, Marshall, March 27; Illinois, Peoria, March 20, Odin, March 24, and Rantoul, April 5; Indiana, Vigo County, March 20, Greencastle, April 1, and Vincennes, April 3; Ohio, Cleveland, March 29, Columbus, April 8, Canton, April 9, and Oberlin, April 10; Michigan, Vermontville, April 6, Ann Arbor, April 13, Battle Creek, April 14, and Grand Rapids, April 19; Ontario, Plover Mills, April 12, Guelph, April 13, and Ottawa, April 16; Iowa, Ottumwa, March 28, Elkader, March 30, and Emmetsburg, April 3; Wisconsin, Milwaukee, March 30, and Shiocton, April 13; Minnesota, Lake City, April 3, Brainerd, April 16, Lanesboro, April 18, and Minneapolis, April 19; Oklahoma, Ponca City, March 31; Kansas, Manhattan, April 5, Lawrence, April 7, Blue Rapids, April 9, and Wichita, April 15; Nebraska, Lincoln, April 18; South Dakota, Sioux Falls, April 10, Forestburg, April 15, and Pitrodie, April 23; Manitoba, Killarney, April 22, Alexander, April 24, and Aweme, April 25; Saskatchewan, Indian Head, May 3, and Eastend, May 7; Mackenzie, Fort Simpson, May 19; Colorado, Greeley, March 18, Mesa County, March 18, and Colorado Springs, April 16; Wyoming, Lake Como, May 2; Idaho, Rathdrum, May 1, and Rupert, May 3; Montana, Billings, April 1, and Columbia Falls, May 4; Alberta, Stony Plain, April 22, Carvel, April 30, and Athabaska Landing, May 6; Yukon, Dawson, May 24; and Alaska, Kuskokwim River, May 12, Craig, May 16, Nulato, May 22, and Forrester Island, May 24.

Late dates of spring departure are: Peru, Rio Perene, March 9, and La Merced, March 23; Brazil, Praia de Cajetuba, April 12, Santarem,

April 12, and Matto Grosso, April 1; Venezuela, San Bricene, April 21; Ecuador, Lake Colta, April 5, and San Pedro River, April 11; Colombia, La Concepcion, March 23; Panama, Chiriqui, April 13; Costa Rica, Guapeles, March 5; Guatemala, Puerto Barrios, April 7; Pueblo, Altisco, May 22; Yucatan, Tizimin, May 16; Tamaulipas, Victoria, April 16; Sonora, Hermosillo, April 30; Lower California, La Paz, April 16, and Gardners Laguna, April 23; Lesser Antilles, St. Croix, April 27; Porto Rico, Patillas, May 13, and Cartagena Lagoon, May 23; Haiti, April 11; Cuba, Guantanamo, May 5; Bahama Islands, Andros, April 21, Cay Lobos Light, April 25, and Abaco, April 28; and Florida, Gainesville, May 10, Daytona Beach, May 11, Palma Sola, May 22, St. Marks, May 24, and Pensacola, May 31.

Fall migration.—Early dates of fall arrival are: Florida, Palma Sola, July 7, Pensacola, July 18, Daytona Beach, July 21, and St. Marks, July 21; Porto Rico, Manati, July 9 and Bayamon, July 20; Lesser Antilles, St. Bartholomew, August 3; Lower California, Los Coronados Islands, August 6; Tehuantepec, San Mateo, August 14; British Honduras, Manatee Lagoon, August 16; Guatemala, Duenas, September 2; Nicaragua, Escondido River, July 30, and Bluefields, September 17; Costa Rica, Ujurras de Terraba, September 16; Panama, August 4; Colombia, Fundacion, August 16, Barbacoas, August 30, Cienaga, September 13, and Valle Dupar, September 25; Venezuela, Curaçao, July 27, and Macuto, August 4; Ecuador, Guainche, August 27, Guayaquil, August 28, and Portovelo, September 2; Peru, Trujillo, September 1, and Eten, September 7; and Guiana, Abary Creek, October 6, and Cayenne, October 18.

Late dates of fall departure are: Alaska, Wrangel, October 9, and Kenai River, November 14; Yukon, mouth of Moose River, October 1; Alberta, Red Deer River, September 17; Montana, Missoula, September 17, and Columbia Falls, September 22; Idaho, Priest River, Septmeber 19, and Rupert, October 2; Wyoming, Yellowstone Park, September 17; Colorado, Boulder, September 22, Denver, September 23, and Mesa County, October 7; Mackenzie, Great Slave Lake, September 16, and Point Brule, October 1; Saskatchewan, Eastend, September 10; Manitoba, Margaret, October 4, Aweme, October 7, and Killarney, October 18; South Dakota, Wall Lake, October 13, and Forestburg, October 20; Kansas, Topeka, October 11, and Lawrence, October 14; Oklahoma, Copan, October 4, and Caddo, October 16; Minnesota, St. Vincent, October 14, and Lanesboro, November 2; Wisconsin, Madison, October 4, Racine, October 6, and Burlington, October 14; Iowa, Newton, October 25, Sioux City, November 3, and Coralville, November 8; Ontario, Toronto, October 11, London, October 25, and Ottawa, October 30;

Michigan, Charity Island, September 28, Ann Arbor, October 9, and Jackson, October 27; Ohio, Huron, October 21, Sandusky, October 24, Cedar Point, October 30, and Columbus, November 7; Indiana, Albion, October 17, Elkhart, October 19, and New Harmony, October 23; Illinois, Chicago, September 29, Maxwell, October 10, and Urbana, October 18; Missouri, St. Louis, October 11, and Jaspar City, October 15; Kentucky, Bowling Green, October 13; Tennessee, Athens, October 11, and Knoxville, October 24; Nova Scotia, Pictou, October 9; New Brunswick, Scotch Lake, October 4; Quebec, Montreal, October 2, and Quebec, October 12; Maine, Portland, October 8, Kennebec County, October 15, and Orono, October 21; Massachusetts, Woods Hole, October 20, Braintree, October 22, and Boston, November 2; Rhode Island, Newport, October 3; Connecticut, Portland, October 15, Hartford, October 19, and Windsor, October 20; New York, New York City, October 13, Collins, October 15, and Highland Falls, October 15; New Jersey, Camden, October 17; Pennsylvania, Renova, October 18, and Berwyn, October 28; and Maryland, Plummer Island, October 28.

Casual records.—Spotted sandpipers have been detected twice in Argentina, Concepcion on March 4, 1918, and mouth of the Rio Ajo, October 25, 1920 (Wetmore). It also has been reported from Europe on numerous instances, among which the following cases from the British Isles, seem to be authentic: Two near Belfast, July and September, 1928; one near Whitby, March 29, 1849; one at Kingsbury Reservoir, Middlesex (date ?) ; two at Warrington, Lancashire, May, 1863; two at Eastbourne, Sussex, in October, 1866; and two at Aberdeen in August, 1867 (Dalgleish).

Egg dates.—Labrador: 7 records, June 1 to July 16. Quebec to Nova Scotia: 53 records, May 20 to July 4; 27 records, June 15 to 19. New England and New York: 41 records, May 19 to July 9; 21 records, May 30 to June 13. Ohio to Iowa: 16 records, May 14 to July 6; 8 records, May 31 to June 16. California to Washington: 13 records, June 7 to July 7; 7 records, June 15 to 28. Alaska and Mackenzie: 26 records, June 10 to July 22; 13 records, June 15 to July 7.

NUMENIUS AMERICANUS Bechstein

LONG-BILLED CURLEW

HABITS

One can not see this magnificent bird for the first time without experiencing a thrill of enthusiasm for the largest, one of the most interesting and notable of our shore birds, one that seems to embody more than any other the wild, roving spirit of the vast open prairies.

Its large size, its long, curving bill, the flash of cinnamon in its wings, and above all, its loud, clear, and prolonged whistling notes are bound to attract attention. In its former abundance this species must have been a most striking feature of the western plains, as it flew in large wedge-shaped flocks in full cry. The last of the great open prairies are rapidly disappearing; and with them are going the curlews, the marbled godwits, the upland plover, the longspurs, and a host of other birds that can not stand the encroachments of agriculture.

The long-billed curlew formerly bred over a large portion of central North America, including all of the prairie regions, at least as far east as Michigan and Illinois, and probably Ohio. But, with the settling of the country and the disappearance of the prairies, it has been gradually driven farther and farther west, and even there into a more and more restricted range. It seems to me that we can hope for its survival only on the maintenance of large, open ranges as grazing lands for cattle where it still continues to breed.

It was apparently quite common as a migrant in New England up to about the middle of the last century. The birds seen here were probably migrants from the more eastern prairies. The numerous citations given by Edward H. Forbush (1912) show its gradual decline, until now it is only a rare straggler anywhere on the Atlantic coast. In Audubon's time it was abundant in winter and as a migrant on the coasts of Florida and South Carolina. I have never seen one during my various seasons in Florida and Arthur T. Wayne (1910) says:

Since 1885 is has been supplanted by the Hudsonian curlew (*N. hudsonicus*), which is still exceedingly abundant during the spring and autumn migrations. From 1879 to 1885, *americanus* was to be found in the immediate vicinity of Charleston, but its numbers steadily diminished year after year until at the present time it is so rare that it is seldom seen; in fact I have not seen one since September 23, 1899. Audubon, in his Birds of America, states, upon the authority of Doctor Bachman, that this curlew "breeds on the islands on the coast of South Carolina, and it places its nests so close together, that it is almost impossible for a man to walk between them without injuring the eggs." It may appear hypercritical to question Doctor Bachman's statement that this species bred on the coast islands, but the eggs were not described by either Audubon or himself, and as far back as 1879 there were no eggs of *N. americanus* in the Charleston Museum, while the eggs of the "Stone Curlew" (*Catoptrophorus semipalmatus*) were well represented and were classified as eggs of the long-billed curlew, I have been unable to obtain any evidence, even from the "oldest inhabitants," that this species ever bred anywhere on the South Carolina coast.

Dr. Thomas S. Roberts (1919) says of its status in Minnesota:

As late at least as 1883 it was still breeding in southern Jackson County (J. W. Preston) and Gleason saw a single bird of this species near Euclid,

Polk County, on June 17, 1897, which at that date may be assumed to have been a breeding bird. This report of Gleason's is the very last record of the long-billed curlew in Minnesota known to the writer. It ceased to be generally abundant somewhere about 1880 and rapidly decreased in numbers, even as a migrant, until it disappeared entirely about the close of the last century.

It apparently ceased to breed in Illinois before 1880; the last published breeding record was in 1873. It probably still breeds in the interior of Texas and perhaps on the coastal prairies as well, for J. J. Carroll writes to me that on July 9 and 10, 1926, he saw 8 or 10 long-billed curlews near Matagorda Bay that acted as if they had young. It is now a very rare bird at any season east of the Mississippi River.

Spring.—The spring migration is now a general northward movement throughout the western half of the United States; there was formerly a heavy flight up the Atlantic coast as far as the Carolinas and a straggling flight farther north. The migration begins in March, but the main movement is during April and most of the birds reach their breeding grounds in April. Only one of my correspondents in Manitoba and Alberta mentions the long-billed curlew and he has seen only one in 15 years; so it must be disappearing very rapidly there.

Courtship.—The spring behavior of these curlews, or what might be called a nuptial flight is thus described by P. M. Silloway (1900):

After their arrival, the curlews inhabit the high, dry prairies, flying restlessly from one portion to another, showing a tendency to associate in pairs, though as couples, these birds are not inseparable. In the mating season, one of the pair is likely to follow the other in a few moments, when the first bird has flown far over the prairie to a more distant station. At any time the loud, prolonged whistling of these birds, either when on the ground or a-wing, will call attention to their movements, warning the disturber of their domain that his presence is known and that his actions will be watched with the closest interest.

One of the pleasing sights to the ornithologist in watching the behavior of these curlews is seen when a pair are sailing upward in company abreast of the wind, moving in perfect accord on widespread, motionless pinions curved gently downward, within several feet of each other, then fluttering downward side by side or one in advance of the other, again to sail upward, uttering the characteristic whistles.

Nesting.—The long-billed curlew is likely to nest almost anywhere on the boundless prairie, though we have found it, in Saskatchewan, showing a decided preferance for damp, grassy hollows in the prairie, or long slopes near the lakes or watercourses. The nest is a very simple affair, a slight hollow in the ground, usually thinly lined with grasses or weeds; but sometimes quite a substantial platform of grass is made and slightly hollowed. The female is often quite conspicuous, as she sits on the nest with her neck stretched out on the ground, and can sometimes be seen at a distance of 100 feet; she usually sits very closely and can sometimes be approached within 8 or 10 feet before flushing.

In some notes sent to me by A. O. Treganza, from Box Elder and Weber Counties, Utah, he says that in one "particular locality (Weber County) the birds seem to be quite gregarious, possibly due to food conditions. While there are many square miles of what seems to be similar country, they seem to have chosen a very small area in which to breed." Here he found sometimes two females sharing the same nest, resulting in sets of from five to eight eggs. In other localities, in Box Elder County, they do not seem to be at all gregarious. In one instance he found four eggs of the western willet and one of the curlew in a nest, with both the willet and curlew on guard.

P. M. Silloway (1903) has had some extensive experience with the nesting of the long-billed curlew in Fergus County, Mont. Some of his nests were on the high dry prairie a long way from any water, but most of them were in such situations as I have described above. Several of his nests were in depressions beside dried cow dung, where, perhaps, the bird was not quite so conspicuous; and chips of dried cow dung often entered into the composition of the nest. In a typical nest "the cavity was 8 inches across and 2 inches deep. The brim of the nest was elevated an inch and a half above the surroundings." He has written (1900 and 1903) some interesting accounts of his experiences in hunting for nests, and sums up the behavior of the birds as follows:

The male curlew is a most jealous guardian of the premises near the nest. When the female is sitting on her eggs, the male will denote a watchful interest in the movements of anyone who is within several hundred yards of the nest. At such times he will come flying from some quarter of the pasture, and with angry cackling will alight near the disturber, impatiently feeding and watching the movements of the one threatening the peace of his household. If the observer approaches nearer the nest the male will begin to fly at him in a straight course, turning upward abruptly with a loud whiff of wings when it seems that the disturber must certainly be struck by the determined defender of his home. The nest may still be more than a hundred yards beyond the observer. In the majority of instances it lies ahead in the line the male points in his flight. As the disturber gets nearer, the male shows more distress and flutters wildly overhead, flying at the disturber from every direction, though not from long distances as before. All the while the female is sitting unconcerned on her eggs, indifferent to the angry and distressed cackling of her spouse. Perhaps by this time a half dozen or more other males have joined in the outcry, and frequently one of these allies will try to mislead the disturber.

The female sits very closely upon her eggs, flattening herself upon them in such a manner that she resembles a dead chicken lying on the ground. When flushed from the nest she will fly low for 30 or 40 feet or flutter from the nest and run awkwardly for a short distance, feigning to be crippled. Frequently she will lower her head, with bill almost touching the ground, and run along in a shamefaced manner. Before the nest is discovered the males who are aiding to mislead the observer will sometimes act in this shamefaced way.

Eggs.—Four eggs are ordinarily laid by the long-billed curlew, occasionally five; as many as eight have been found in a nest, evidently the product of two females. The eggs vary in shape from ovate to short ovate or ovate pyriform, sometimes quite rounded; and they have a slight gloss. The prevailing ground colors are in various shades of "olive buff"; but some dark types are "ecru olive," some green types are "seafoam green" and some are as pale as buffy white. The eggs are generally quite evenly spotted, some very thickly and some very sparingly, with various shades of brown and olive, "Vandyke brown," "bister," "snuff brown," "buffy brown," and "buffy olive," with numerous underlying markings in various shades of "brownish drab" and "drab gray." A very handsome set has a rich buff ground color, between "honey yellow" and "chamois," uniformly covered with small spots of rich browns, "Sudan brown" to "russet." The measurements of 68 eggs average 65 by 45.8 millimeters; the eggs showing the four extremes measure **72** by 48, 70 by **48.5, 56** by 43.5, and 62.5 by **42** millimeters.

Young.—Incubation is said to be shared by both sexes; its exact duration does not seem to be recorded, but for the European curlew it is said to be 30 days. Both birds are certainly very solicitous in the care of the young. We were too late for eggs in Saskatchewan, but we found three broods of young. On June 1, 1905, we found two small young curlews, hardly able to walk, in a grassy hollow in the prairie; the old birds gave us a great exhibition of parental solicitude, flying about, alighting on the ground near us and making a great outcry. Their loud cries brought a third curlew which joined in the chorus of whistling cries.

When large enough to run, the young are adepts in the art of hiding; they seem to disappear entirely, even in the short grass; after hunting carefully for fully half an hour, over a limited area where we had seen one vanish, we gave it up and walked away, when we were surprised to see the youngster get up and run away from the very spot we had been hunting hardest.

Probably the mortality among young curlews is rather high, as they have many enemies. All three of the broods we found contained only two young. The parents have to work hard to preserve even this average. We saw an interesting exhibition of parental strategy one day, which probably succeeded in saving some young curlews from the jaws of a prowling coyote. The curlew was decoying the coyote away by feigning lameness, flopping along the ground a few yards ahead of him, but always managing to barely escape him. We watched them for some time until they finally disappeared over a hill, fully half a mile from where we first saw them.

Plumages.—The young curlew, when first hatched, is completely covered with long, thick, soft down. The color varies from " warm buff " on the breast and flanks, to " cream buff " on the face, upper parts and belly and to " cream color " on the throat; the crown is even paler. The markings, which are brownish black in color, consist of a broken and narrow median stripe on the forehead, irregular spotting on the posterior part of the head and large, bold, irregular spotting on the back, wings, and thighs. In older birds the bright buffs fade to paler shades.

I have seen no specimens showing the change from downy to juvenal plumage. The latter is very much like that of the winter adult, but it is somewhat more tawny, especially below, and the streaks on the neck and breast are fewer and narrower. The first winter plumage is apparently a continuation of the juvenal, subject to some wear and fading, and with very little molting. By spring young birds are practically indistinguishable from adults.

Adults have a complete postnuptial molt from August to November, most of which is accomplished in September and October, including the wings. The prenuptial molt, which involves the body plumage, most of the scapulars, many wing coverts and the tail, is prolonged through the spring, from February to June.

Food.—On their breeding grounds, and to a large extent in their winter quarters, these curlews are upland feeders, far out on the open prairies, in the damp, grassy hollows, or about the edges of prairie sloughs or ponds. But on migrations they are often seen feeding on ocean beaches or about the shores of large lakes. I have seen them on the beaches of southern California feeding at the surf line in company with marbled godwits. They were wading out into the retreating waves, picking up some small objects about an inch long or less, probably mollusks. They seemed to experience some difficulty in properly grasping the morsel with the tips of the long mandibles, but when once started right they handled it very skillfully, as the shell seemed to travel swiftly up the long bill and into the mouth. They are said to probe in the soft sand to the full extent of the long bill, but I did not see them do this.

C. W. Wickersham (1902) has described the food and the feeding habits of the long-billed curlew very well as follows:

Crawfish, small crabs, snails, periwinkles, toads, worms, larvae, grasshoppers, crickets, beetles, caterpillars when found on the ground, spiders, flies, butterflies, and berries, especially dewberries, all play minor or major parts in their diet. The worms, larvae, etc., are pulled out of the ground by the long bill, the end of which may act as a finger having separate muscles to control it, and often it is sunk into the ground as far as it will go to reach some unwilling victim. The crustaceans are taken on the beach, or, discovered beneath the surface by the probing bill, are pulled out and eaten. The berries are neatly picked off the bushes, while butterflies and other insects are taken on the wing.

Behavior.—Except on their breeding grounds, where they are concerned in the welfare of their eggs or young, long-billed curlews are exceedingly wary; when a flock is feeding, one or more birds usually stand as sentinels, and at their cry of warning the whole flock raise their wings and make off. Their flight is a bit erratic or snipelike at first, but when well under way it is strong and steady. While migrating or traveling for long distances they often fly high in the air in wedge-shaped flocks, uttering occasionally their loud, whistling notes. When alighting they drop nearly to the ground, make a graceful upward sweep, and check their speed with a flash of cinnamon wings. They walk gracefully and swiftly on land and can swim if necessary.

The night roosting habits are well described by Audubon (1840), who saw them at their best in South Carolina. He writes:

The long-billed curlew spends the day in the sea marshes, from which it returns at the approach of night to the sandy beaches of the seashores, where it rests until dawn. As the sun sinks beneath the horizon the curlews rise from their feeding grounds in small parties, seldom exceeding 15 or 20, and more usually composed of only 5 or 6 individuals. The flocks enlarge, however, as they proceed, and in the course of an hour or so the number of birds that collect in the place selected for their nightly retreat sometimes amounts to several thousands. As it was my good fortune to witness their departures and arrivals, in the company of my friend, Bachman, I will here describe them. The sun at length sunk beneath the water line that here formed the horizon, and we saw the birds making their first appearance. They were in small parties of 2, 3, or 5, and by no means shy. These seemed to be the birds which we had observed near the salt marshes as we were on our way. As the twilight became darker the number of curlews increased, and the flocks approached in quicker succession until they appeared to form a continuous procession, moving not in lines, one after another, but in an extended mass, and with considerable regularity, at a height of not more than 30 yards, the individuals being a few feet apart. Not a single note or cry was heard as they advanced. They moved for 10 or more yards with regular flappings, and then sailed for a few seconds, as is invariably the mode of flight of this species, their long bills and legs stretched out to their full extent. They flew directly toward their place of rest, called the "Bird Banks," and were seen to alight without performing any of the evolutions which they exhibit when at their feeding places, for they had not been disturbed that season. But when we followed them to the Bird Banks, which are sandy islands of small extent, the moment they saw us land the congregated flocks, probably amounting to several thousand individuals, all standing close together, rose at once, performed a few evolutions in perfect silence, and realighted as if with one accord on the extreme margins of the sand bank close to tremendous breakers. It was now dark and we left the place, although some flocks were still arriving. The next morning we returned a little before day, but again as we landed they all rose a few yards in the air, separated into numerous parties, and, dispersing in various directions, flew off toward their feeding grounds, keeping low over the water until they reached the shores, when they ascended to the height of about a hundred yards and soon disappeared.

A similar habit evidently prevails on the prairies, which Mr. Wickersham (1902) describes very well as follows:

As evening falls he becomes restless, his hunting comes to an end, his bobbing becomes more jerky and more and more repeated, until with a loud whistle he jumps forward, his long wings fly out and up and with the first unsteadiness over he joins the bunch in a long line and betakes his way with the others toward some distant marsh or pond. On, on they go; the leader whistles, the others answer, suddenly they all drop, sweep forward and up a little, and then, with wings almost meeting above them and legs held daintily down to break the shock, they all alight. For five minutes there is no movement, no sound; there are no birds to be seen where, a moment before, the graceful creatures had alighted; suddenly there is a little flutter of wings and before you know it numerous forms have run forward and bent over the water to noisily quench their thirst. For another five minutes there is as great a confusion and clamor as formerly there was order and quiet; wings are fluttering, hoarse, short cries are arising, feet are pattering up and down, the water is heavily rippling from the motion of many bills, and, in a word, all is chaos. One by one the drinkers cease, calmness is gradually restored, and, after pluming themselves, the birds draw one leg up under them, tuck their head under one wing, neatly fold the other, and sweet slumber reigns.

On its behavior with other species Mr. Silloway (1900) writes:

There is another side to the disposition of the long-billed curlew, for this spring I was once startled by an unusually piercing whistle, and looking upward I saw a curlew swooping angrily upon a ferruginous roughleg that had chanced to wander over the claimed domain of this pair of *Numenii.* Time and again the curlew swooped upon the unoffending *Archibuteo* as the latter flapped heavily along the edge of the coulee, and the cliff echoed with the shrill whistles of the angry curlew. On the other hand, the long-billed curlews are the victims of petty teasing by the longspurs which throng the prairie. I have repeatedly noticed McCown's longspur (*Rhynchophanes mccownii*) flutter up beside a curlew, sailing upward, or attempt to strike the curlew, the latter on such occasions seldom giving any attention to the petty annoyance mentioned.

E. S. Cameron (1907) says that he has seen nesting curlews make flying attacks at Swainson and marsh hawks, just as the European curlews attack the jaegers.

Voice.—Long-billed curlews are noisy birds, especially on their breeding grounds. I have recorded their ordinary notes of protest, when near their nests or young, as loud musical whistles, like *quee-hee, quee-hee, quee-hee*, sometimes prolonged into a long, rattling call, *que-he-he-he-he-he*, loud and striking. Sometimes we heard a series of somewhat guttural notes, or a melodius *coy, coy, coy*, somewhat like the autumn gather call of the bobwhite. I have heard them in Texas in the spring give rich, loud, musical notes as they flew, *wheety, wheety, wheety*, very rapidly uttered, opening the bill with each note. Our name " curlew " and the French " curlieu " are probably both derived from one of the commonest and most characteristic calls.

P. A. Taverner (1926) says:

The commonest call note is a clear *pil-will*, so nearly like that of the willet that it can not always be distinguished from it. Other notes resemble those of the upland plover. One especially delightful is a long-drawn *curl-e-e-e-u-u-u*, sparkling clear and rising in the middle about five notes, then dying gradually away, lowering in scale and volume. The entire call lasts about three seconds of time.

Field marks.—The long-billed curlew can be easily recognized by its large size, long, curved bill, and cinnamon color. It is much larger than the Hudsonian and much more cinnamon in color, especially in the wings. It is much like the marbled godwit in color, but its curved bill is easily distinguished from the straight bill of the godwit.

Fall.—I quote again from Mr. Wickersham (1902) as follows:

July is spent in raising the chicks and by the middle or latter part of August, all is ready for the flight south to Texas, Mexico, Florida, and the West Indies. Then it is that we see them in great flocks of hundreds, bobbing up and down all over the prairie, more nervous than ever; and then it is that they are least wary at times and at other times so very wary that it is impossible to approach them. They are so nervous and upset that they do not seem to know their own mind and it is at that season of the year that their antics become almost as ridiculous as they are just before the breeding season. The day comes when you stroll out to take notes on the birds that you have seen by the hundreds the day before only to find that they have disappeared; not a bird answers your call, no hoarse screaming betokens your approach; they have gone, gone far away in long V-like squadrons and, unless you follow them to their winter home in the southland, you will not see their familiar forms for many months.

The long-billed curlew is now practically unknown in any of the Eastern States, but it formerly appeared on the Atlantic coast about the middle of July and in the Southern States in early August. It is still quite common in California from the middle of July through September. The main flight goes directly south to Texas and Mexico.

Game.—Although long since removed from the game-bird list, the " sickle-bill " was a fine game bird. Its large size made it a tempting target. It decoyed readily and could be easily whistled down by imitating its notes. The cries of a wounded bird were sure to attract others, which would circle around again and again until many were killed. For these and other reasons it is well that the much-needed protection came in time to save this fine bird from certain extermination.

Dr. D. G. Elliot (1895) writes:

Once when shooting in Florida, in the vicinity of St. Augustine, a large flock of these birds passed overhead, and I brought down some by two shots from my gun. Although naturally much alarmed, the survivors immediately returned to their wounded companions, which were calling aloud as they lay upon the marsh, flying over and around them, with hanging legs, and uttering answering notes of sympathy, and approaching nearer and nearer until they were not many feet above the ground. Repeated discharges of my gun failed for a time to drive the unwounded birds from the vicinity, but as each individual fell from the ranks, the rest would swoop toward it, and with much crying seem to urge it to rise and follow them. The air was full of rapid-flying circling birds, each one screaming its best, and it was not until a considerable number had fallen that the remainder, convinced at length of the fruitlessness of their efforts, and the danger present to themselves, departed for a more secure locality.

Winter.—The long-billed curlew is still quite common in Texas and Mexico in winter. Mr. Wickersham (1902) says:

After reaching its winter home, the curlew undergoes little change of habits except in his relation to other birds. For a few days the big bunches stay together and then they begin to separate into small bunches of from 2 to 20 birds. It is rarely that a single one is seen entirely by himself but two or three feeding together and then, perhaps a mile off, two or three more and in this way scattered all over the pastures and prairies is the way we find them in Texas. They are rarely found in the brush or even in ponds or swales surrounded by the brush, but far out on the open prairie or in little mud flats on the larger swales we rarely miss them. Here they feed all day looking for almost any form of insectivorous or crustacean life.

DISTRIBUTION

Range.—North and Central America, accidental in the West Indies and Newfoundland. Failure to accurately separate the different curlews, particularly on the Atlantic seaboard, causes some uncertainty regarding their general ranges, but *americanus* is evidently now very rare east of the Mississippi River.

Breeding range.—The long-billed curlew breeds (at least formerly) north to British Columbia (150-mile House, probably Lac La Hache, and Vernon); Alberta (near Calgary, probably Flagstaff, and Walsh); Saskatchewan (Rush Lake and Quill Lake); Manitoba (Shell River, Aweme, and Pilot Mound); North Dakota (Bathgate and Argusville); and Wisconsin (Ceresco and Racine). East to Wisconsin (Racine); Illinois (formerly Chicago); Iowa (Newton and formerly Ferry); Kansas (Neosho Falls); Oklahoma (Camp Supply and Ivanhoe Lake); and Texas (Houston, Corpus Christi, and Brownsville). South to Texas (Brownsville, and Fort Davis); New Mexico (Fort Sumner, Santa Rosa, Los Pinos, and Fort Wingate); Arizona (Sulphur Springs); Utah (Fairfield, and Skull Valley); Nevada (probably Franklin Lake, Humboldt River, and Truckee Valley); and northern California (Pitt River, Butte Valley, and Eagleville). West to California (Eagleville); Oregon (Fort Klamath, Camp Harney, Haines and Dalles); Washington (Kiona,

Yakima, and Wapato Lake); and British Columbia (Okanagan, Vernon, and 150-mile houses).

Winter range.—The winter range extends north to California (San Rafael and Sacramento Valley); southern Arizona (Pima County); rarely New Mexico (Demning, Santa Rosa, and Carlsbad); Texas (Pecos, San Angelo, Clay County, and Victoria); Louisiana (Vermilion Bay); and formerly South Carolina (Charleston). East to formerly South Carolina (Charleston and Frogmore); Georgia (Savannah, Sapelo Island, and Darien); and Florida (mouth of the St. Johns River, Tarpon Springs, and Fort Myers). South to Florida (Fort Myers); and rarely Guatemala (Duenas, and Chiapan). West to rarely Guatemala (Chiapan); Oaxaca (Juchitan); Jalisco (La Barca); Durango (Rancho Santriario); Lower California (San Jose del Cabo, La Paz, Magdalena Bay, and San Quintin); and California (San Diego, Owens Lake, San Joaquin Valley, San Francisco, and San Rafael).

Spring migration.—Early dates of spring arrival are: North Carolina, Corolla, April 15, Virginia, Chesapeake, April 15, and Locustvile, April 16; District of Columbia, Washington, April 11; New York, Montauk Point, April 28; Maine, Scarboro, May 2; Missouri, Warrensburg, April 1, St. Louis, April 2, and Appleton City, April 3; Illinois, Mount Carmel, April 4, Quincy, April 10, and Canton, April 15; Indiana, Liverpool, April 2; Iowa, Mitchell, April 3, Ferry, April 13, and Coralville, April 15; Minnesota, Hallock, April 24; Oklahoma, Sentinel, April 5; Kansas, Emporia, April 9, and Manhattan, April 13; Nebraska, Valentine, March 28, Long Pine, March 29, Whitman, March 31, and Alda, April 3; South Dakota, Vermilion, April 5, and Rapid City, April 10; North Dakota, Argusville, April 8, Charlson, April 14, and Larimore, April 15; Manitoba, Aweme, April 9, Margaret, May 2, and Killarney, May 4; Saskatchewan, Eastend, April 16; Ravenscrag, April 28, Osler, May 7, and Indian Head, May 9; Colorado, Springfield, April 3, Colorado Springs, April 11, Denver, April 15, and Salida, April 29; Utah, Salt Lake County, March 28, and Camp Floyd, April 12; Wyoming, Sheridan, April 13, Cheyenne, April 15, and Jackson, April 18; Idaho, Grangeville, March 14, and Neeley, March 15; Montana, Great Falls, April 5, Terry, April 7, Corvallis, April 7, and Big Sandy, April 13; Alberta, Provost, April 22, Veteran, May 2, and Flagstaff, May 14; Oregon, Malheur Lake, March 28, Klamath Falls, March 28, Narrows, March 30, and Lawen, April 1; Washington, Prescott, March 23, and Chelan, April 6; and British Columbia, Okanagan Landing, March 29, and Osoyoos Lake, April 1.

Late dates of spring departure are: Florida, Palma Sola, May 11; North Carolina, Cape Hatteras, May 20, and Cape Lookout, May 24; Maryland, Hail Point, May 23; Missouri, Corning, May 25; Tepic, San Blas, April 28, and Los Penas Island, May 5; and Lower California, Turtle Bay, April 14, and mouth of the Colorado River, May 15.

Fall migration.—Early dates of fall arrival are: Lower California, San Quintin, July 4, and San Jose del Cabo, August 26; Sonora, Altar, September 14; New Hampshire, Rye Beach, August 12; Massachusetts, Amesbury, July 21, Plymouth, August 9, and Cape Cod, August 27; Rhode Island, Newport, July 15; New York, Orient Point, July 9, and Long Beach, July 24; Maryland, Ocean City, August 19; South Carolina, Frogmore, August 7, and Ladys Island, August 9; Florida, Tarpon Springs, July 5; and Alabama, Dauphin Island, August 21.

Late dates of fall departure are: British Columbia, Okanagan Landing, October 29; Washington, Grays Harbor, October 7; Oregon, Klamath Lake, November 19; Montana, Big Sandy, August 25, and Choteau, September 4; Idaho, Neeley, October 1; Utah, Fillmore, November 19; Wyoming, Cheyenne, August 9, and Yellowstone Park, August 22; Colorado, Denver, September 12, Yuma, September 30, and Barr, October 22; Saskatchewan, Eastend, August 6, and Quill Lake, August 11; Manitoba, Westbourne Marsh, October 8 (Nash); South Dakota, Rapid City, August 3, and Hermosa, August 15; Nebraska, Whitman, August 25, Valentine, September 1, and Long Pine, September 6; Michigan, Washtenaw County, September 12, and Ann Arbor, September 15; Ohio, Cleveland, September 15; Missouri, Jasper County, October 15; Quebec, Montreal, September 21; Massachusetts, Plum Island, September 2; Rhode Island, Jamestown, September 9; New York, Fishers Island, September 10, and Montauk Point, September 12; New Jersey, Cape May, September 14; and Virginia, Wallops Island, September 6, and Cobb Island, September 25.

Casual records.—As previously stated, the long-billed curlew is now of casual or accidental occurrence east of the Mississippi River, although it was formerly fairly. plentiful on the Atlantic coast. Macoun reports it as a rare emigrant in Newfoundland without particulars, and in the lack of subsequent confirmation it seems probable that he was misinformed. Preble (1908) records a specimen that was taken several years previous in the vicinity of Fort Simpson, Mackenzie. Several occurrences have been recorded for Alaska, among which are: Bethel, five seen May 9, 1917, by J. J. Brown (authority of A. H. Twitchell); a specimen, without date or exact locality, recorded by Macoun; St. Michael, June 19, 1874 (Turner); and upper Kuskokwim, July 23, 1898 (Hinckley). A specimen also is reported as having been taken near Spanishtown, Jamaica, in July, 1863.

Other West Indian records for this species are considered indefinite and probably refer to *N. hudsonicus.*

Egg dates.—Utah: 41 records, April 1 to May 22; 21 records, April 26 to May 9. Montana and Idaho: 24 records, April 20 to July 4; 12 records, May 16 to 29. Saskatchewan: 11 records, May 3 to July 4; 6 records, May 23 to June 10. Washington and Oregon: 7 records, May 4 to 20.

NUMENIUS ARQUATA ARQUATA (Linnaeus)

EUROPEAN CURLEW

Contributed by Francis Charles Robert Jourdain

HABITS

The European curlew is said to have occurred once on Long Island, N. Y., in 1853, and the specimen is still extant in the New York State Museum. It was originally recorded as a long-billed curlew, *Numenius longirostris,* but was identified by William Dutcher, who recorded it in the *Auk* (1892). Its claim to a place in the American list does not however rest on this ancient record, as E. Lehn Schiöler says that it has also occurred both on the west and east coasts of Greenland. The first record was that of Johan Petersen, who obtained a young male on August 23, 1913, at Angmagsalik on the east coast. Another was shot at Nanortalik in Julianehaab district in 1915 on the west side.

Spring.—Although great numbers of curlew are present throughout the winter on the mud flats and low lying coasts and estuaries of the British Isles, there is little doubt that the majority of our home-bred birds migrate southward, and this is confirmed by the fact that when the breeding birds appear on the moors, the shore haunting birds are still present in their haunts and remain for several weeks longer. The average date of the arrival of the breeding stock in the north of England is about mid February; Chapman has recorded their arrival from February 5 to March 11, and in years of heavy snowfall, such as 1886, they were unable to reach their nesting ground till March 19. In mid Derbyshire they generally arrive early in March.

Courtship.—As William Farren (1910) remarks the watchfulness of the curlew and the open nature of the country it frequents, make observation of the courtship on the ground extremely difficult.   False nests or " scrapes " are almost invariably to be found in the neighborhood of the nest, and O. R. Owen writes that in some parts of Radnorshire, where the curlew breeds commonly, it is not unusual to find two or three dozen " scrapes " in an afternoon.   The curlews arrive on the moors in flocks, which keep together for a week or so, but soon resolve themselves into pairs.   At this times, the moors reecho with their songs.   Mr. Farren describes it as follows:

The performance, with its accompanying trilling song, resembles somewhat that of the redshank.   It rises from the ground and with rapid wing beats ascends to a good height.   Often when near the summit of its flight it checks suddenly, almost throwing itself over backwards.   Recovering, it hangs poised kestrel-like in the air, and while so hovering, and also during a short temporary drop on motionless wings, it pours forth the trilling or jodelling song.   It rises again on quivering wings and again sinks as before.   This may continue for some time or it may be varied by the bird circling round on extended wings, when one is again reminded of the flight of a hawk.   More often than not the bird will stop before a circle is completed and hover again over a fresh spot. So it continues, circling, rising, and falling, and pouring forth a joyful ripple of song.   The song consists of two—or three—rising notes, rapidly repeated, high pitched, but liquid and flutelike.   I would express the curlew's song as *gur-lech, gur-lech, gur-lech, gur-lech,* pronounced rather distinctly at first and not too quickly, but quickening after the first two or three repetitions.   Toward the end the syllables must be almost run together, losing all of the first except the "g" and at no time sounding the "ch" too hard but rather as in the Scottish "loch."

Seton Gordon (1915) writes as follows:

The singer, flying along the moor a few yards above the surface of the ground, checks his flight and rises almost perpendicularly with wings rapidly beating the air.   On reaching a certain elevation he soars—glides rather—earthward in a slanting direction, and it is now that his song is uttered.   Commencing usually in a couple of long-drawn whistles, uttered in a very low key, the song quickens, the notes are sharper and clearer, and have at the middle of the performance a curious, distinctive "break," difficult to put into words.   It is at this point that the song is carried far across the moorland country, but almost at once the key is lowered, the calls become more subdued, more drawn out, until they end, as they commenced, in low, melancholy cries.   Sometimes one sees a curlew making his way across a moor and constantly fluttering up into the air.   But one imagines that there is something at fault, for time after time he utters only the first note of his song and then almost at once mounts again into the heavens. Can it be that he does not succeed in reaching the correct altitude from which all self-respecting curlew commence their appeals to their adored ones?   But perhaps the songster is not producing that bottom note satisfactorily and thus is doing his best to perfect it.   It is, I believe, only the male birds that practice these distinctive risings and dips in the air, but I can assert from personal experience the hen also makes use of the trilling, tuneful notes which most ornithologists associate only with the cock bird during the season of nesting.

Nesting.—The nesting sites are somewhat varied.   Often the eggs are laid in a slight hollow, lined with grass or sometimes sprigs of heather on moorlands among short or long heather; others will breed among the long, wiry grass of high levels or on short-cropped pasture lands. A tussock in the middle of a wet bog may be used, or, exceptionally, the nest may be in a plowed field. There is not much effort at concealment, but the sentry is generally on watch to warn the sitting bird. Occasionally I have known a bird allow approach within a few yards, and Mr. Fenwick records a case in which the sitting bird allowed itself to be stroked and even lifted from the eggs. As a rule, the bird leaves the nest long before the intruder comes anywhere near. The nest is about 5 to 5½ inches across.

Eggs.—The eggs, which are normally four, are occasionally only three or sometimes five. Of this latter number I have about a dozen records. The only recorded case of six was probably due to two hens laying together. The eggs are very large for the size of the bird, pyriform in shape and very thin shelled, and are not laid on consecutive days. In color they range from light green to olive green or olive brown, spotted or sometimes blotched with light or dark umber brown and ashy shellmarks. Exceptional varieties are pale greenish blue or whitish grey, almost unmarked. The measurements of 100 British eggs, made by the writer, average 67.6 by 47.9 millimeters; the eggs showing the four extremes measure **78.6** by **55.1, 56.2** by 44, and 61 by **43** millimeters.

Young.—Incubation is carried on by both sexes, and the period is 29½ to 30 days. In spite of their long legs the young can run soon after they are hatched, but remain in the nest longer than the young of most waders, running out and concealing themselves on the approach of danger. Both parents assist in looking after the young, and only a single brood is raised in the season.

Plumages.—The plumages and molts are fully described in A Practical Handbook of British Birds, edited by H. F. Witherby (1920).

Food.—During the winter months the main food consists of marine mollusca, such as cockles (*Cardium edule*), mussels (*Mytilus edulis*), *Mya tellina, Bythenia*, etc.; also Crustacea, especially small crabs; occasionally fishes from rock pools, such as *blennies* and Annelida (lugworms). In the breeding season land Mollusca, such as snails (*Helix aspersa, H. nemoralis*, etc.) and slugs; Amphitra (small frogs), Annelida (earthworms). Insects, including Diptera and their larvae (chiefly Tipulidae), Lepidoptera and their larvae, Orthoptera (*Acheta, Forficula*), Rhyncota (*Notonecta*, etc.), and Coleoptera (*Rhizotragus, Anisoplia, Dytiscus, Scarabicus, Aphodius, Harpalus, Zabras, Pterostichus*, etc.). Also vegetable matter, seeds of *Polygonum* and grasses, berries of crowberry (*Empetrum nigrum*) and

Vaccinium myrtillus; occasionally also blackberries. Fragments of seaweed have also been found in the stomach.

Behavior.—The curlew is not popular with the shore shooter, as he is not only exceptionally wary himself but seems to take a delight in warning other and less suspicious species. Howard Saunders says that he has seen a curlew, after shrieking wildly over the head of a sleeping seal, swoop down and apparently flick with its wing the unsuspecting animal upon which the stalker was just raising his rifle.

Although a bird of the coast and bare moorlands, it can and does perch not infrequently on trees. In North Brabant, where it breeds on the vast expanses of moorland with scattered belts of small pine trees, I have seen an excited pair perched insecurely on the tips of small trees and keeping up an unceasing succession of anxious yelping notes while their young crouched in the heather below. Although it usually wades, the curlew can on occasion take voluntarily to the water and swims well.

Enemies.—Naumann mentions the peregrine and gyrfalcon, as well as the goshawk among the enemies of this species. Saxby, J. F. Peters, and others have found remains of curlew at the feeding places of the peregrine; and Ussher also states that it is also the case in Ireland.

Fall.—Early in July the young birds are on the wing on the English moors and are already beginning to collect into packs, which leave the breeding grounds about the middle of the month and resort to the shore.

Winter.—Probably most of the birds which winter on the English coasts are migrants from northern Europe. They chiefly haunt the larger estuaries and the wide mud flats of the east coast, assembling in flocks of fifty to a hundred. When their feeding grounds are covered by the tide they will sometimes work inland, or may be seen waiting for the water to recede on some isolated clump of rock which commands a view in all directions, all facing the same way.

DISTRIBUTION

Breeding range.—The British Isles, but only locally in England in the midlands and southeast; also in the Orkneys and Shetlands; but not in the Faroes. On the Continent, France (only in Bretagne), Belgium, Holland, Germany, Denmark (Jutland), Switzerland, Austria, Carinthia, Galicia, Rumania (Dobrogea), Poland, the Baltic Republics, Sweden and Norway, Russia, and Finland south to the Perm Government. In Asia it is replaced by an eastern race (*N. arquata lineatus*), which ranges east to Japan.

Winter range.—Many winter in the British Isles, southern Europe (the Mediterranean region), and a great part of Africa. Also in small numbers to the Persian Gulf, but here it meets the eastern form.

Spring migration.—At the Straits of Gibraltar the passage takes place in March, but Irby saw a few late in April, while along the Portuguese coast they pass from March to May. In the eastern Mediterranean some leave Cyprus by the end of February, but stragglers have been seen on March 30 and April 5 and others have been seen on Crete at the end of April. In Iraq large flocks passed Feluja between mid April and May 25, flying north in the evening.

Fall migration.—Although long after the normal southward migration the advent of hard weather will bring big flocks past Heligoland flying west as late as November 19 to 20. The young birds begin to arrive there as early as mid July from Scandinavia, and on the Portuguese coast the passage lasts from late July to November and at Tangier from September through October. At the Ionian Isles and on Cyprus they arrive at the beginning of September, and the passage through Greece lasts throughout September.

Casual records.—The records for Greenland and eastern America have been mentioned. In Iceland Faber recorded the first on September 6, 1819, and since then other occurrences have taken place without exact date. To the Faroes it is only a straggler in the winter months. In the Canaries it is an occasional visitor, chiefly to the eastern isles, and has been seen there as late as June 14. It has also been recorded from the Azores, Madeira (December 7, 1893, October 25, 1896, October 28, 1896, January 30, 1897, and great numbers on April 28, 1898) and the Cape Verde Islands.

Egg dates.—British Isles, April 17 to May 31 (42 dates), April 20 to May 10 (26 dates). Holland and Germany, earliest date April 6. Scandinavia from about mid May onward, May 13 to 26 (6 dates).

NUMENIUS HUDSONICUS Latham

HUDSONIAN CURLEW

HABITS

A striking case of the survival of the fittest is seen when we compare the relative abundance of the three common species of North American curlews to-day with their status 50 years ago. Whereas, at that time the Hudsonian curlew was the rarest of the three, it is now by far the commonest. The vast flocks of Eskimo curlew, that formerly frequented the Labrador coast every summer and visited the New England coast at frequent intervals, have all disappeared. They

were tame and unsuspicious, were easily decoyed, and were therefore slaughtered in enormous numbers on their feeding grounds;
they made a long migratory flight over the ocean from Nova Scotia
to South America, where many undoubtedly perished in stormy
weather. The long-billed curlew, once so common all over the interior
prairie regions, and even on the Atlantic coast, has gradually been
driven westward and northward, until it is now occupying a comparatively restricted range. The long-billed will probably be the
next of the curlews to disappear, perhaps within the near future.
But the Hudsonian curlew, on the other hand, has held its own, and in
some sections it has apparently increased. This increase, however, is
probably more apparent than real, due to comparison with other
species which are decreasing rapidly. The reasons for its success
in the struggle for existence are not hard to find. Its breeding
grounds are in the far north, where it is never disturbed; it has no
dangerous migration route; it does not ordinarily migrate in large
flocks, which are susceptible to vicissitudes of weather and great
slaughter at the hands of gunners; but, above all, it is a shy, wary,
wily bird, quite capable of taking care of itself and well fitted to
survive. Like the crow, it is more than a match for its enemies.

The Hudsonian curlew was evidently comparatively rare in Audubon's time, for he apparently knew very little about it. Wilson seems
to have overlooked it entirely or to have confused it with the
Eskimo curlew, and Nuttall's remarks are not altogether clear on
the subject. George H. Mackay (1892b) says:

Speaking for Nantucket and Tuckernuck Islands, as far as I am aware, not
over 15 or 20 of these birds a year on an average have been shot there
during the past 17 years, and the local saying, that "it does not pay to go
after them," is true, they being too shy and too limited in number to make
it any object, either for gain or for pleasure. During these 17 years there
have never been more than 100 birds on an average living on the above
islands each year, and for the past few years I have noticed a falling off from
this number.

I am quite sure that I have seen more Hudsonian curlews on Cape
Cod during the past 10 years that I saw during the previous 20. The
species certainly has not decreased, and I am inclined to think that
it has increased. The 1927 fall flight was unusually heavy.

Spring.—From its winter range on the Pacific coast of South
America this curlew migrates through Central America to Florida
and up the Atlantic coast. It reaches Florida during the latter half
of March, the Carolinas about the middle of April, and Massachusetts
about the middle of May. During a week spent with Arthur T.
Wayne on the South Carolina coast May 18 to 25, 1915, I saw the last
part of a heavy flight of Hudsonian curlews. Mr. Wayne told me
that the first birds come early in April, but the height of the migra-

tion is between the third week in April and the second week in May, when enormous numbers (he says hundreds of thousands) may be seen every day. We saw no such numbers, but numerous flocks were seen every morning flying in to feed on fiddler crabs on the extensive marshes and flying out again at night to roost on the sand bars and islands. They flew high in the air in V-shaped flocks or in long irregular lines and their loud notes could be heard almost constantly.

Herbert K. Job (1905) saw them here in "scores of thousands"; he spent a night at each of several little low islands—mere sand bars—lying off the coast," and says:

About half past 5 or 6 o'clock, when the sun was low in the horizon or had set behind a cloud bank, the first advancing line is seen, and a string of from a dozen to 50 Hudsonian curlews come scaling over the beach, to alight on the bar, down at the other end. After a few minutes another flock is seen approaching. By half past 6 they are arriving fast, and by 7 there are two or three flocks in sight all the time, some of them containing as many as 75 birds. Meantime I am shooting at them as they pass, with my reflex camera, despite the dull light. As may be imagined, the company on the sand has become immense, covering many acres. They keep up a sort of murmuring noise, and now and then all fly up, with a perfect storm and tumult of wings and voices, soon to alight again. Even after dark they are yet arriving, as one may hear. I hazard the guess that there are often 10,000 curlews at such a roost each night. At the first glimmer of day they are off again for the marshes.

Mr. Wayne (1910) makes the following interesting suggestion:

This species supplanted the long-billed curlew between the years 1883 and 1885, for previous to these dates the former species was rare, but it gradually became more abundant each year until it established itself firmly in great numbers. The result was that the long-billed curlew was driven from its accustomed range by a smaller species in the struggle for existence. The long-billed curlews fed almost entirely upon fiddlers, and the Hudsonian curlew also subsisted upon them, and as the food supply was inadequate, one species was forced to seek other paths of migration.

The Hudsonian curlew seems to be a rare migrant everywhere in the interior; some of my correspondents do not mention it at all and others give only scattering records. But William I. Lyon writes to me that he saw a flock of about 100 on May 22, 1926, in Illinois; they were flying in V formation, uttering their characteristic four short whistles, and breaking sometimes from a V into a line. Edwin Beaupre tells me that "the foot of Amherst Island, in Lake Ontario, is a favorite crossing place for these curlews in their northward flight. May 24 is the date on which they may be looked for, passing through this locality in one large flock."

J. A. Munro (1911) records a heavy flight which occurred at Fisherman's Island, Toronto, during three days, May 24 to 26, 1910; a careful count was made of passing flocks in which over 1,000 birds were recorded. Probably the main flight from the Atlantic coast turns inland before it reaches New England and flies by way of the Great Lakes to the west side of Hudson Bay. The species is rare in New England in the spring.

Along the Pacific coast there is a heavy migration; the main flight appears in southern California about the middle of March, progresses slowly northward, reaches Alaska about the middle of May, and arrives on the breeding grounds in northern Mackenzie by the end of May. In California the main migration route is coastwise, the bulk of the flight coming in April; but John G. Tyler (1913) records them as " regular spring migrants " in the interior valleys. " Their favorite resorts are large, open fields where shallow ponds occur, and in such places they often gather in large numbers." D. E. Brown's notes record them as common, or very abundant at times, in Washington, flocks of 40 or 50 birds being not at all uncommon; his dates run from April 7 to May 14.

Nesting.—The best account of the nesting habits of this species and its behavior on its breeding grounds is given us by Dr. Joseph Grinnell (1900), who found eight nests in the Kotzebue Sound region of northern Alaska; he writes:

I found the Hudsonian curlew to be a common breeding bird over the tundras from Cape Blossom eastward into the Kowak Valley. In the vicinity of our winter camp on the Kowak, the arrival of the curlews was on May 17. From the middle to the last of June, in the Kowak delta, I became well acquainted with the Hudsonian curlew. At this season they were of course mated and most of them had eggs. They were ordinarily met with on the open stretches of tundra, of:en where these alternate with strips of timber and lakes. Where such perches are afforded, solitary birds on watch would be seen sitting on the tips of isolated dwarfed spruces or even willow bushes. As soon as an intruder entered the domains of a pair of curlew, the bird on watch would give the alarm by a loud, ringing call note, and soon both birds would fly to meet him. As long as the intruder remains in the vicinity, the pair of birds keep flying restlessly to and fro, now and then alighting on the ground and walking about, but most of the time keeping up their monotonous rolling whistle. This was the only note I heard, except earlier in the season a long, faint whistle like that of a distant locomotive, uttered by the male bird while sailing slowly, on set motionless wings over the nesting grounds. This is probably their song flight, though it is certainly very simple. The far-off whistle, however, puzzled me for some time as to its origin. I at first thought it was a steam launch on the river somewhere, until I finally connected the sound with the slow soaring of the curlew overhead.

The eggs so closely resemble the monotonous lights and shadows of the surrounding moss and grass that I have stepped directly over the nest, all the while scrutinizing every foot of the ground about me, without detecting the eggs. Sometimes from the nature of the surroundings the eggs are more conspicuous and can be seen 10 yards or more, but this is the exception. While one is at the nest, the parents fly close about one, almost deafening one with their loud penetrating cries. If anything the male bird is the most demonstrative of the two. The nest is simply a saucer-shaped depression in the top of a low hummock of moss or grass. The locality was always a wet swale or low place in the tundra, in which the clumps of grass or moss were often surrounded at their bases with water. The nests were in no way protected, the eggs always being in plain view, but the remarkable mimicry in their coloration is generally of sufficient protection.

MacFarlane collected some 13 sets of eggs on the barren grounds west of the lower Anderson River, but I find only one nest described in his notes; this he said was " a depression in the ground, lined with a few decayed leaves." Stanton Warburton, Jr. took a set of three eggs near Teller, Alaska, on July 4, 1924; he writes to me that " the nest was situated on hard, dry tundra, the eggs occupying a slight depression in light grasses; distinctive nesting material of grey lichen-light material covered the cavity. Both birds were present." A nest found by Bishop J. O. Stringer on an island in the lower Mackenzie River is described as a pile of grass, moss, and weeds.

Eggs.—The Hudsonian curlew lays almost invariably four eggs, though the set of three referred to above was heavily incubated. The eggs are hardly, if at all, distinguishable from those of the European whimbrel. They are ovate pyriform, rather pointed, in shape and show little or nó gloss. Doctor Grinnell (1900) describes them as follows:

Their ground color is very variable, from a bluish pea green through olive buff to light olive green. The markings are numerous and somewhat amassed at the larger ends of the eggs. They consist of dots, spots, and blotches of pale lavender, drab, Prout's brown, and bistre. The latter seems in every case the real pigment, and the varying depth to which it is covered with subsequent layers of shell material, seems to account for the different tints, even to the palest lavender.

In the few sets that I have seen the prevailing ground colors are dark and light shades of " olive buff," with occasionally " Isabella color " or " ecru olive." In the markings I recognized various browns, such as " bone brown," " warm sepia," " Saccardo's umber," " olive brown," and " buffy brown." The measurements of 37 eggs average 57.5 by 40.7 millimeters; the eggs showing the four extremes measure 61.9 by 41.7, 59.2 by 43.2, 52 by 38.5, and 55 by 37.2 millimeters.

Plumages.—I have never seen a downy young Hudsonian curlew, and, so far as I know, it has never been described. Young birds are in juvenal plumage when they reach us on migration. They are more easily recognized by their much shorter bills than by any plumage differences, as they look much like adults. The markings on the neck and breast are finer and closer; the feathers of the back, scapulars, tertials, and wing coverts are " warm sepia," notched with cream-white or pale buff, producing a spotted effect, most pronounced on the wing coverts and tertials (in adults these parts are more narrowly edged with buff); the rump is " sepia," with large spots of " pinkish buff," and the upper tail coverts are barred with the same colors; the under parts are more buffy than in adults and the whole effect is brighter and more variegated.

A postjuvenal body molt in late fall or early winter, which almost runs into a first prenuptial molt, produces a plumage, which can be distinguished from the adult only by the faded juvenal wing coverts and the bird becomes fully adult at the next postnuptial molt.

Adults have a complete postnuptial molt, beginning with the body molt in August and ending with the molt of the primaries in the winter; soon after the wings are molted, or from February to May they have a partial prenuptial molt, including the body plumage, the tail, and some of the scapulars and wing coverts.

Food.—Hudsonian curlews are mainly shore feeders; on the beaches and sand flats they pick up various insects, worms, small mollusks, and crustaceans, often probing for the sand fleas in the wet sand; on the mud flats they find similar animal food. I have also often seen them on the marshes, or even on high, dry pasture lands, such as are frequented by golden plover and Eskimo curlews, where they find grasshoppers, spiders, beetles, and other insects. In South Carolina we saw them at low tide on the oyster banks and on the mud banks riddled with holes of fiddler crabs, on which they were doubtless feeding. In the Magdalen Islands I have seen them on the uplands and among the sand dunes, where they were evidently eating crow berries (*Empetrum nigrum*). They are also said to eat blueberries, dewberries, and various seeds. E. W. Hadeler tells me that he once saw them feeding on the bodies of light-colored millers; the beach was lined with these moths, some dead and others alive, and the curlews did not like to leave this abundant supply of food.

Mr. Mackay (1892b) says:

They feed on fiddler crabs, grasshoppers, and the large gray sand spiders (*Lycosa*) which live in holes in the sand among the beach grass adjacent to headlands, huckleberries, which they pick from the bushes, and beetles (*Lachnosterna, Scarabaeidae*), all of which are usually mixed with coarse gravel. When a flock of these birds is on the ground where they have been feeding they become scattered, 25 or 30 birds covering 15 or 20 yards' space. At such times they do not appear to be particularly active, moving about in a rather slow, stately manner, although I have once in a while seen them run.

L. L. Jewel (1913) writes:

One of the bird surprises of my life was to see a Hudsonian curlew tiptoe and catch butterflies within 20 feet of my front door at Gatun. The clearings in and around the town seemed very attractive to these birds and they were fairly tame. Marching or advancing by rushes, always with graceful dignity, sometimes singly but more often in groups of four or five, they foraged through the shorter grass, picking up or catching on the wing their insect food. They usually kept near the water's edge or well down in dry gullies, but also fed on higher ground at times.

Behavior.—Although Hudsonian curlews may fly swiftly at times and probably make good speed when traveling they appear to me to fly rather slowly and heavily, with steady and rather moderate wing beats; they often set their wings and scale for a long distance. When migrating over land they usually fly high, in flocks, much after the manner of ducks and geese; but when migrating over water or flying to and from their roosting grounds they often fly in long lines close to the water. Their flight has been said to resemble the flight of gulls when moving in flocks, or to suggest that of herons when flying close to the water, but I could never see any such resemblance.

Dr. Charles W. Townsend (1905) says:

They walk and run rapidly, stand still, often with one foot several inches in front of the other, rest occasionally by squatting down, with tarsi flat on the ground, or standing upon one leg, with the other out behind.

William L. Dawson (1923) writes:

The curlews deploy, then, upon the dry sands of the upper beach and either potter about on listless lookout for passing insects or else squat upon the sand, tuck bill under wing, and lose themselves in dreams. There is always at least one wary fellow on guard, however, and let but the smallest appearance of motion, be it only a khaki hat, break the purity of the sky line among the attendant sand dunes, and a quaver of warning puts the scattered flock on guard. Sleepy heads are stealthily withdrawn; the birds rise slowly and begin to creep toward their leader, their neutral-colored bodies scarcely distinguishable against the background of sand; and all meanwhile scanning the horizon for the danger sign. If the alarm spreads, all run down the beach slope for a quick take-off, pass over the surf line, and then parallel the shore with moderate, firm wing strokes until a safe distance has been reached.

Voice.—John T. Nichols says in his notes:

The flight note of the Hudsonian curlew in migration resembles somewhat that of the greater yellowlegs, but is easily distinguished therefrom, being less modulated and usually lower pitched. It commonly consists of four short whistles, but is frequently prolonged, sometimes accelerated into a trill. The more prolonged calls are usually the dryer and seem characteristic of the noisiest birds, flying highest or with most uncertainty. On its northern breeding grounds (Nome, July, 1926) this species keeps up a continual vocal protest while an intruder is present. Its note then matches in form the trills which may be heard in migration but is much more musical and varied in quality. It may be described as polysyllabic, rolling, usually 10 syllabled or less; modulated and varied in tone—loud, reedy, sweet, mellow, or liquid. It is the same when the bird is in the air as when it is on the ground.

Mr. Mackay (1892*b*) says that the rolling note sounds like " that produced by a boy's lead bird whistle filled with water." They also have a soft, musical *cur-lew* note, more often heard in the spring. Dr. E. R. P. Janvrin says in his notes: " The note uttered during flight, usually just after the birds are put up and apparently an alarm note, sounds like *krek*, *krek*, *krek*, quite loud and rather metallic." E. W. Hadeler refers to this note as *pip*, *pip*, uttered five or six times in rapid succession.

John G. Tyler (1913) writes:

There are no birds with which I am acquainted that can compare with these splendid waders in the rich, musical quality of their voices. On the last day of one April I encountered a large flock of curlews in a grain field, part of which was being flooded at the time with irrigation water. The nervous lispings that at my approach threatened to break into the clamorous, screaming flight calls finally subsided, and the birds fed and waded about in the water or preened their feathers while standing storklike on one leg. Suddenly I was thrilled with a medley of subdued pipings so marvelously sweet and musical that I could hardly believe the sound came from my flock of curlews. The faintest whispering it seemed, yet the liquid melody was really far-reaching and was, as I afterwards learned, distinctly audible from a distance of a quarter of a mile when atmospheric conditions were favorable. A strange nervous unrest seemed to affect the entire group on the ground. The whistlings became louder, and the cause was suddenly revealed to me when a curlew call from overhead drew my attention to a flock of new arrivals, nine in number, that were circling preparatory to joining the company at the pond. My surprise and admiration knew no bounds when I realized the sublime heights at which these travelers through the sky had been flying. Mere specks they appeared, and yet their melodious call rang clear and distinct.

Field marks.—A large, rather pale brown bird with a long, decurved bill can easily be recognized as a curlew; the long-billed curlew is larger, has a longer bill, and is much more rufous or cinnamon colored, especially in the wings; the Eskimo curlew is, or was, smaller, with a shorter bill, though young Hudsonians have rather short bills. Mr. Nichols suggests that at close range the much barred under wing can frequently be noticed; the outer primaries look blacker and plainer than in long-billed, and a white streak near the edge of the wing, made by the primary quills, is cut off abruptly at the base by a blackish blotch.

Fall.—Like most of the northern breeding shore birds, the Hudsonian curlew moves off its breeding grounds as soon as the young are able to shift for themselves, and begins its summer wanderings, or starts on its southward migration early in July. There are two main lines of flight, down the east and west coasts of the continent, as well as a more scattering flight through the central valleys and plains. The eastward flight is from the west coast of Hudson Bay, where many birds linger through August, to the coasts of New England and southward. A few Hudsonian curlews migrate as far east as Labrador; the species has never been common there, but since the disappearance of the Eskimo curlew it has been more in evidence; Lucien M. Turner recorded it only twice in northern Ungava; a few specimens have been taken on the east coast of Labrador.

Adults appear on the coast of Massachusetts about the middle of July and the young birds about a month later; the heaviest flights come in August and September, but young birds often linger well into October; my latest date is October 20. They reach the Carolinas in July; Mr. Wayne (1910) says that he has seen them as early as July 5 and not later than October 2. They are reported as migrating over the Bermudas in August and September, but the last of the birds do not leave the West Indies until November.

Pacific coast flights occur on corresponding dates. Early in August, when the blueberries and crowberries are ripening, large flocks of this and bristle-thighed curlews come down to the Bering Sea coast of Alaska, where large numbers are brought into the markets at Nome all through August and early September. From there the migration is southward along the Pacific coast. D. E. Brown's dates for Pierce County, Wash., run from August 6 to October 2, but probably there are earlier dates. The earliest birds reach southern California about the first week in July and the latest birds linger through October. Meantime some of the birds have appeared in Peru early in August and in Chile by the middle of that month.

Game.—The Hudsonian, or " jack," curlew is a gamey bird, which will test the skill and try the patience of the most experienced sportsman. It is so shy and vigilant that it is difficult to outwit. It is almost impossible to stalk an old bird, but I have, on rare occasions, been able to creep up on a young bird. Most of my chances have been at single birds flying over, when several gunners have been spread over ground where scattered birds were feeding. Once a flock of 15 birds swung by my blind within range, but they did not alight to my decoys. Referring to the " good old days," Mr. Mackay (1892b) writes:

They were apparently as shy then as now, for even then it was considered essential in order to take them to mortise a hole in the ground for concealment in the locality which they frequented or passed over, care being taken to remove the soil taken out to some distance in a wagon in order that the place might appear perfectly natural. Stands were dug in the center of a clump of bushes, as being less noticeable. In times past, on Cape Cod, I have used a hogshead, sunken level with the marsh, from which to shoot them, but even under such conditions I never secured more than nine in one day, and that only once. The Hudsonian curlew is a very observing bird and perceives at once anything strange and out of harmony with the natural surroundings of any locality which it has been in the habit of frequenting, and in order to get a flock up to the decoys considerable care must be exercised. Single birds or pairs will, however, decoy fairly well if they have not been harassed. These birds have a way of setting their wings stationary and sailing, when headed for the decoys, at a distance of 100 yards or more, the flock separating out so that there are scarcely any two birds together, and then hanging, as it were, in the air. During this time they are most carefully listening and scanning the decoys and surroundings. A movement causes them to spring up in the air several feet, and as this is generally when aim is being taken they are apt to be missed by being undershot. In order to get them as near as possible I have frequently set my decoys only a few feet to windward of my stand, as it is customary for them, when heading for the decoys, to keep falling off to leeward of them. They are not an easy bird to kill, being strong and powerful, and as the distance is usually great at which they are shot at, owing to their vigilance, many go off wounded and are not recovered.   Should one or more be wing-broken they frequently commence falling, which causes the remainder of the flock to hover around for a short time, apparently to give encouragement to the wounded ones, and while their attention is thus absorbed they will often afford the sportsman a second shot, if he keeps concealed.   Were it not for the satisfaction of getting so shy a bird, for, as a rule, they are but indifferent eating, there would be little inducement to waste the time necessary to obtain an occasional one.   I take a few every year by getting out of my wagon into some place of concealment, when I observe a flock in the distance on the ground, and letting my companion drive around the other side and start them toward me.   Long familiarity with the ground enables me to form some idea as to what course they are likely to pursue, and I have obtained more or less in this manner.

DISTRIBUTION

Range.—North and South America; accidental in Europe.

Breeding range.—The Hudsonian curlew is known to breed only on the Arctic coast of North America from Alaska (Norton Sound, Kobuk River, Cape Blossom, and probably Camden Bay) to Mackenzie (Anderson River region).   It has, however, been noted in summer in Keewatin (Fort Churchill and near York Factory) and may possibly breed in that vicinity.

In common with several other shore birds, some individuals remain in summer far south of their breeding grounds.   At this season they have been detected from New Jersey (Great Bay), south along the Atlantic coast—Virginia (Wreck Island, Bone Island, and Wallops Island); South Carolina (Mount Pleasant); to Costa Rica (Coronado de Terraba); and the West Indies (Barbuda).

Winter range.—The winter range extends north probably to southern California (Santa Cruz Island, Santa Barbara, and Ventura County); probably rarely Louisiana; and rarely (formerly more commonly) South Carolina (Bullyard Sound and probably Charleston).   East to formerly South Carolina (probably Charleston, Sea Islands, and Frogmore); probably rarely Florida (Pine Island); probably Cuba; probably rarely Porto Rico (Gundlach); the Lesser Antilles (Barbuda); Guiana (Berbice River and Cayenne); Brazil (Praia de Cajetuba); and Chile (Island of Chiloe).   South to Chile (Island of Chiloe).   West to Chile (Island of Chiloe, Valdivia, Valparaiso, and Tarapaca); Peru (Lima, Trujillo, and Tumbez); Ecuador (Bay of Santa Elena): Galapagos Islands (Charles and Narborough Islands); Venezuela (Isla de Aves); Costa Rica; Honduras (Gulf of Fonseca); Guatemala (Chiapam); Clipperton Island; Chiapas (San Benito); Jalisco (La Barca); Sinaloa (Mazatlan);

Lower California (La Paz, San Jose Island, San Francisco Island, and Colorado River Delta); and probably southern California (Santa Cruz Island). A specimen obtained at Rockaway Beach, New York, on December 24, 1912, probably was either a crippled bird or otherwise physically deficient.

Spring migration.—Early dates of spring arrival are: North Carolina, Corolla, April 15, and Churchs Island, April 19; Virginia, Hog Island, April 1, and Cape Charles, April 13; Pennsylvania, Renovo, May 7; New Jersey, Cape May, April 12; New York, Montauk, April 28, and Shelter Island, May 9; Connecticut, Fairfield, May 6; Rhode Island, Newport, April 27, and Block Island, May 3; Massachusetts, Nantucket, April 10, and Muskeget Island, April 20; Ontario, Brighton, May 7, and Toronto, May 17; Mackenzie, Fort Anderson, May 29; northern California, Alameda, March 27, and Palo Alto, March 28; Oregon, Newport, March 14; Washington, Hoquiam, April 19, and Everett, April 26; British Columbia, Comox, May 3, and Courtenay, May 11; and Alaska, Craig, May 12, Nulato River, May 12, Hooper Bay, May 17, Kobuk River, May 17, and Fort Kenai, May 18.

Late dates of spring departure are: Chile, Concon, April 25; Oaxaca, San Mateo, May 13; Florida, Palma Sola, May 11, and St. Marks, May 19; Georgia, Savannah, May 13; South Carolina, Port Royal, May 22, and Charleston, May 23; North Carolina, Pea and Bodie Islands, May 8; Virginia, Locustville, May 27, and Alexandria, May 30; Pennsylvania, Lancaster, May 27; New Jersey, Cape May, May 23; New York, Long Beach, May 31, Canandaigua, June 1, and Branchport, June 2; Connecticut, East Haven, June 4; Massachusetts, Cape Cod, June 23, and Nantucket, June 25; Ohio, Youngstown, May 24; Ontario, Point Pelee, May 30, Beaumaris, June 4, and Brighton, June 10; Tepic, Las Penas Island, May 5; Lower California, Clima Point, April 25, and San Jose del Cabo, May 1; California, Santa Barbara, June 2; Oregon, Mercer, May 14, and Yaquima Bay, May 18; Washington, Quillayute Needles, May 30, and Dungeness Spit, June 3; and British Columbia, Courtenay, May 23.

Fall migration.—Early dates of fall arrival are: British Columbia, Courtenay, June 27; Washington, Lake Ozette, July 12, and Destruction Island, July 15; Oregon, Newport, July 10; California, Alameda, July 7, Los Angeles, July 12, and Farallon Islands, July 16; Lower California, Los Coronados Islands, August 7, and Santa Rosalia, August 15; Peru, Chimbote, August 2; Ontario, Point Pelee, July 24; Ohio, Lake County, July 14; Massachusetts, Muskeget Island, July 12, Monomoy Island, July 14, Marthas Vineyard, July 16, and Boston, July 18; Rhode Island, Block Island, July 10, and South

Auburn, July 23; Connecticut, Milford, July 20, and North Haven, July 26; New York, Rockaway, July 10, East Hampton, July 11, and Orient, July 11; New Jersey, Tuckerton Bay, July 2, Long Beach, July 9, and Cape May, July 15; Pennsylvania, Erie, August 1; Bermuda, August 14; Virginia, Chincoteague, August 1; North Carolina, Pea and Bodie Islands, July 22; South Carolina, Charleston, July 19; Georgia, Savannah, July 27; Alabama, Dauphin Island, July 27; Florida, Bradenton, July 31, and Tarpon Springs, August 3; and West Indies, Barbuda, August 12.

Late dates of fall departure are: Alaska, Craig, September 24, and St. Lazaria Island, September 30; Mackenzie, Great Bear Lake, September 30; British Columbia, Courtenay, October 5; Washington, Clallam Bay, October 9, and Point Chehalis, October 19; Ontario, Brighton, September 1; Quebec, Montreal, September 9; Nova Scotia, Wolfville, September 13; Maine, Northeast Harbor, September 5; Portland, September 9, and Dover, October 12; Massachusetts, Monomoy Island, September 28, Harvard, October 2, and Dennis, October 27; Rhode Island, Sakonnet Point, September 25, Rock Island, September 28, and Newport, October 2; Connecticut, New Haven, September 19, and North Haven, September 20; New York, Montauk Light Station, September 28, and Orient Point, September 30; New Jersey, Sandy Hook, September 13; and Virginia, Wallops Island, September 23, and Hog Island, November 10.

Casual records.—The Hudsonian curlew is of hardly more than accidental occurrence in the interior but has been noted on a few occasions. In addition to notes given under migration, mention may be made of the following records: Colorado, a specimen at Colorado Springs on September 23, 1900; New Mexico, a specimen at Fort Thorn in the spring of 1854; Texas, Brownsville, several records in spring between March 31 and May 24; Nebraska, Lincoln, October 8, 1898; Wisconsin, Milwaukee, September 9, 1903, and Cedar Grove, September 23, 1922; Iowa, Crystal Lake, Hancock County, May 25, 1895; Michigan, St. Clair Flats, May 25, 1902, Saginaw City, fall of 1896, and Forestville, April 23, 1906; and Indiana, Calumet Heights, August 3, 1902. Reports exist for other interior States but usually without satisfactory evidence.

Both Macoun and Hagerup list it as occurring in Newfoundland, but without any presentation of the evidence. In Porto Rico, Gundlach reported collecting it at Punta Arenas, and also refers to a specimen in a collection at San Juan, Stahl secured two others which were preserved in his collection, F. A. Potts obtained one May 21, 1921, near Las Mareas, and observed others from July 31 to September 24, 1921, near Central Aguirre. According to Reinhardt (1861), it has been taken on four occasions in Greenland (Godthaab,

Julianehaab, Fiskenaesset, and Jacobshavn). A specimen was recorded in 1854 by Kjärbölling from Iceland and one was taken near Seville, Spain, May 3, 1872.

Egg dates.—Alaska and Mackenzie: 11 records, May 31 to July 10; 6 records, June 14 to July 1.

NUMENIUS BOREALIS (J. R. Forster)

ESKIMO CURLEW

HABITS

The story of the Eskimo curlew is just one more pitiful tale of the slaughter of the innocents. It is a sad fact that the countless swarms of this fine bird and the passenger pigeon, which once swept across our land on migrations, are gone forever, sacrificed to the insatiable greed of man. " The Eskimo Curlew and its Disappearance," by Prof. Myron H. Swenk (1915), tells the story; it is well worth reading, but space will permit only a few quotations from it. Edward H. Forbush (1912 and 1925) also gives a very good account of the tragedy. In some of the following paragraphs the reader will find many references to its former abundance and the extent of the slaughter which exterminated it. So we shall consider here only the period of its rapid decline and some of the causes which produced it.

Professor Swenk (1915) says of its disappearance in the West:

In Texas the Eskimo curlew came in immense flocks on the prairies from 1856 to 1875, after which year the large flocks disappeared. Small flocks were seen in 1886 and 1890. The last records of the species for Texas were 1902 and 1905, one and three individuals, respectively. The species were first definitely recorded for Kansas from Russell County in 1874. In that State these curlews were abundant as late as 1878, but in 1879 their numbers were much reduced and the birds decreased rapidly. There were still a few in the Kansas markets in the early nineties. The last record is for 1902. Eastwardly in the interior the birds were always uncommon and disappeared early. The last Michigan record is in 1883. The last Ohio record is in 1878. The last Wisconsin records are April 27, 1899, and September 10, 1912, the latter specimen a male taken at Fox Lake, Dodge County, Wis. The last Indiana record is, with some doubt, April 19, 1890.

The last records of collected birds for Nebraska were made in the spring of 1911 and of 1915. On March 22, 1911, while Mr. Fred Geiger was shooting ducks near Waco, York County, two of these birds came flying by within gun range, and both were shot by him. The birds were identified by an old-time hunter, and were then brought to Lincoln, and mounted by Mr. August Eiche, in whose collection they are at present. Although no Eskimo curlews were noted in 1914, a single bird was killed about 10 miles due south of Norfolk, Nebr., on the morning of April 17, 1915. The bird was alone when taken. It came into the possession of Mr. Hoagland, who had it mounted by Allabaugh, a taxidermist of Omaha, in whose shop I saw it in May.

But this was not the last word from Nebraska, for 11 years later Professor Swenk (1926) published the following encouraging note of a sight record:

In further substantiation of the undoubtable fact that the Eskimo curlew is not yet extinct, I am now able to cite a positive instance of its occurrence in Nebraska during the present spring. On the morning of April 8, 1926, Mr. A. M. Brooking, of Hastings, an ornithologist and taxidermist who is very familiar with this species through having spent much effort in assembling several specimens of it for his extensive collection, while driving from the village of Inland to Hastings along what is known as the "north road," saw a flock of eight birds alight in a newly plowed field about 4 miles east of Hastings. He drove his car up close to the birds, and when within 40 yards of them was able to his astonishment to positively identify them as unquestionably Eskimo curlews. Mr. Brooking knows the species so well, and saw the birds so clearly, that in my opinion this sight record can be accepted without hesitation.

On the Labrador coast Eskimo curlews diminished rapidly in numbers between 1870 and 1880. Hon. F. C. Berteau, a government official in Labrador, in some notes published by W. J. Carroll (1910) says:

Up to 1889 dough-birds or Eskimo curlew were very numerous in Labrador from late in August to the end of September. They frequented the southern part of the coast only, never appearing north of Indian Harbor at the northern entrance to Hamilton Inlet. During the first 4 or 5 of the 10 years during which I was collector of customs on Labrador, they were very numerous, indeed, flying from the hills to the shore and vice versa in flocks numbering from fifty to two or three hundred. During the last years of my collectorship they gradually diminished in numbers, until in 1890 or thereabouts they entirely disappeared, and save for a few seen on one or two occasions have never returned to the coast.

The Hudson Bay Co.'s people at Cartwright annually put up large numbers of hermetically sealed tins for the use of the company's officials in London and Montreal. I have seen as many as 2,000 birds hung up in their store as the result of one day's shooting by some 25 or 30 guns. A fairly accurate idea of the plentifulness of these birds will be obtained from an account of my own experience. During the season I used to leave the cruiser at 6 a. m. and return at 9 for breakfast. I do not remember ever getting less than 30 to 40 brace during the two hours or so that I was shooting.

Dr. Henry B. Bigelow (1902), who visited the northeast coast of Labrador in 1900, heard of only about a dozen which were seen on the coast that fall, of which he saw five. Dr. Charles W. Townsend (1913) reported that seven were "shot and one other seen on the beach at West Bay, north of Cartwright, in August and September, 1912. The skins of five were saved, and sent to Cambridge, where they were seen and identified by Mr. William Brewster."

Excessive shooting of this curlew on its migrations and in its winter home in South America was doubtless one of the chief causes of its destruction. Ernest Gibson (1920) saw "some 20 or 30 * * * in the vicinity of Linconia," near Buenos Aires, on February 13, 1899; and a small flock was reported in the same locality on April 8, 1901. He evidently has seen none since then. Mr. Forbush (1925) has recently given us the latest news from Argentina in a letter from Dr. Roberto Dabbene, in which he writes that five or six were seen in the Province of Buenos Aires on February 7, 1924; one of these was captured and another solitary individual was taken at the same place on January 11, 1925; both of these specimens are in the Museo Nacional de Historia Natural, at Buenos Aires. These and the other recent records may indicate that there are a few Eskimo curlews still living; but the species is reduced to such a low ebb that it is doomed to speedy extinction, if not already gone.

One need not look far to find the cause which led to its destruction. On its breeding grounds in the far north it was undisturbed by man. And I can not believe that it was overtaken by any great catastrophe at sea which could annihilate it; it was strong of wing and could escape from or avoid severe storms; it could, like all shore birds, swim if necessary; and its migration period was so extended that no one storm could wipe it out. Several other species of shore birds make similar, long ocean flights without apparent disaster. There is no evidence of disease or failure of food supply. No, there was only one cause, slaughter by human beings, slaughter in Labrador and New England in summer and fall, slaughter in South America in winter and slaughter, worst of all, from Texas to Canada in the spring. The gentle birds ran the gauntlet all along the line and no one lifted a finger to protect them until it was too late. They were so gentle, so confiding, so full of sympathy for their fallen companions, that in closely packed ranks they fell, easy victims of the carnage.

Spring.—It was as a migrant only that we knew the Eskimo curlew. As to how it reached the United States from southern South America we know very little; but it probably followed the same route taken by its companion the golden plover. It arrived in Texas early in March and migrated northward through the prairie regions, mainly west of the Mississippi River, through central Canada and the Mackenzie region to the barren grounds on the Arctic coast. It was rare in spring east of this narrow belt, and practically unknown west of it. The flight through the United States was mainly accomplished during April and through Canada in May, arriving on its breeding grounds before the end of May.

Professor Swenk (1915) writes:

As to the abundance of these birds in Nebraska during the early years of its statehood the observations of Prof. Lawrence Bruner, who distinctly remembers the flights which occurred in the vicinity of Omaha during the years 1866–1868, when he was a boy 10 or 12 years old, are indicative. The birds would arrive about the time the later willows began to bloom (latter April), being present in force for a week or 10 days only, for by the time all of the wild plum blossoms had fallen (middle May) the birds were gone. Usually the heaviest flights occurred coincident with the beginning of corn-planting time, and enormous flocks of these birds would settle on the newly plowed fields and on the dry burnt-off prairies, where they searched industriously for insects. These flocks reminded the settlers of the flights of passenger pigeons and the curlews were given the name of "prairie pigeons." They contained thousands of individuals and would often form dense masses of birds extending for a quarter to a half mile in length and a hundred yards or more in width. When the flock would alight the birds would cover 40 or 50 acres of ground.

Dr. E. W. Nelson (1887) called this "the most abundant curlew in northern Alaska, especially along the coasts of Bering Sea and Kotzebue Sound." At Saint Michael a number were seen passing north on May 12, 1878. He says that they were "always more numerous than *hudsonicus*, and sometimes flocks of 150 or more" were seen. But Dr. Joseph Grinnell (1900) looked for it in vain about Kotzebue Sound.

Nesting.—For all that we know about the nesting habits of the Eskimo curlew, we are indebted to Roderick MacFarlane, who found this species breeding abundantly on the barren grounds east of Fort Anderson and up to the Arctic coast. He collected some 30 sets of eggs there between 1862 and 1866. He says in his notes that "this curlew never, in this quarter at least, breeds in wooded tracts, the barren grounds proper being the real habitat of the species during the season of nidification." It is "very difficult to find the nests" as the birds "get off long before our approach, while the eggs nearly resemble the grass in color." Some birds were seen to leave the nests. The nests are described as mere hollows in the ground, "lined with a few decayed leaves" and sometimes having "a thin sprinkling of hay." The birds "generally ascend in the air in a straight line after getting off the nest."

Eggs.—The normal set was evidently four eggs, but MacFarlane sent home several sets of three. The eggs are rather pointed ovate in shape and have very little gloss. Many eggs closely resemble certain types of Franklin gull's eggs. The ground colors vary from browns to olives, the latter predominating. The olive colors run from " buffy olive " or " citrine drab " to " olive buff," and the brown colors from " light brownish olive " to "buckthorn brown." Some eggs are boldly marked with heavy blotches, which are sometimes confluent about the larger end; more often they are irregularly spotted and blotched; and some eggs are sparingly marked. The markings are in dark browns, "bister," "bone brown," "buffy brown," and blackish brown, with underlying spots and blotches of various shades of "brownish drab." The measuremens of 36 eggs average 51.3 by 35.5 millimeters; the eggs showing the four extremes measure **54.5** by 36, 52 by **39.5**, **47.5** by 36, and 51 by **33** millimeters.

Plumages.—There are not enough specimens of Eskimo curlews, collected during the proper seasons, to work out the molts and plumages satisfactorily. There are no specimens of downy young or very young juvenals available. Young birds in juvenal plumage, as seen on migration, are much like adults, but the feathers of the mantle, scapulars, tertials, and wing coverts are more broadly edged, but less conspicuously notched, with " pinkish buff "; and the under parts are less extensively covered with the dusky markings.

The postnuptial molt of adults is mainly accomplished after they have left us in the fall, beginning in September; the wings are probably molted after the birds have reached their winter home. There is a prenuptial molt of the body plumage, visible during the spring migration, the new feathers, being more pinkish buff, especially on the under parts.

Food.—Professor Swenk (1915) says of its food habits in the west:

The Eskimo curlew was a bird of such food habits that it is a distinct loss to our agriculture that it should have disappeared. During the invasion of the Rocky Mountain grasshopper (*Melanoplus spretus*) it did splendid work in the destruction of grasshoppers and their eggs. Mr. Wheeler states that in the latter seventies these birds would congregate on pieces of land which had not been plowed and where the grasshopper eggs were laid, reach down into the soil with their long bills, and drag out the egg capsules, which they would then devour with their contents of eggs or young hoppers until the land had been cleared of the pests. A specimen examined by Aughey in 1874 had 31 grasshoppers in its stomach, together with a large number of small berries of some kind. The bird in its migrations often alighted on plowed ground to feed on the white grubs and cutworms turned up by the plow, or in meadow lands, probably feeding on ants in the latter situation. Richardson records finding them feeding on large ants at Fort Franklin in late May, 1849. The curlews were rarely seen near water, but were upland birds almost exclusively during the spring migration over the Great Plains region.

Doctor Coues (1874) describes its food on the Labrador coast, as follows:

Their food consists almost entirely of the crowberry (*Empetrum nigrum*), which grows on all the hillsides in astonishing profusion. It is also called the "bearberry" and "curlew berry." It is a small berry, of a deep purple color, almost black, growing upon a procumbent, running kind of heath, the foliage of which has a peculiar moss-like appearance. This is their principal and favorite food and the whole intestine, the vent, the legs, the bill, throat, and even the plumage, are more or less stained with the deep purple juice. They are also very fond of a species of small snail that adheres to the rock in immense quantities, to procure which they frequent the land-washes at low tide. Food being so abundant, and so easily obtained, they become excessively fat. In this condition they are most delicious eating, being tender, juicy, and finely flavored; but, as might be expected, they prove a very difficult job for the taxidermist.

Behavior.—Lucien M. Turner gives, in his Ungava notes, a vivid description of a large flock of Eskimo curlews, which I quote, as follows:

I saw none until the morning of the 4th of September, 1884, as we were passing out from the mouth of the Koksoak River. Here an immense flock of several hundred individuals were making their way to the south. They flew in that peculiar manner which distinguishes the curlews from all other birds in flight, a sort of wedge shape, the sides of which were constantly swaying back and forth like a cloud of smoke wafted by the lightest zepher. The aerial evolutions of the curlews when migrating are, perhaps, one of the most wonderful in the flight of birds. Long, dangling lines, either perpendicular or horizontal, the lower parts of which whirl, rise, or twist spirally, while the apex of the flock is seemingly at rest. At other times the leader plunges downward successively followed by the remainder in most graceful undulations, becoming a dense mass then separating into a thin sheet spread wide; again reforming into such a variety of positions that no description would suffice.

Mr. Mackay (1892c) says:

Of those I have observed in New England during a series of years I may say that most of their habits closely resemble those of the golden plover. In migration they fly in much the same manner, with extended and broadside and triangular lines and clusters similar to those of ducks and geese at such times. They usually fly low after landing, sweeping slowly over the ground, apparently looking it over, generally standing motionless for quite a little while after alighting, which, owing to their general color approximating so closely to the withered grass, renders it difficult at times to perceive them. I have had a flock of 50 or 60 alight within 30 yards of me, and have been unable to make out more than two or three birds. If disturbed they will frequently alight again at no great distance, if not previously harassed, and under the same conditions they can be approached at all times, for they are either very tame or very shy. They seek out and are found in the same localities selected by the golden plover with which they generally associate if any are in the vicinity, there always being a strong friendship between them. They are not so active as the plover; on the ground they appear less inclined to move about, especially after landing and during rainy weather when I have at times noticed them standing on the ground quite close together, every bird headed to the wind, with heads and necks drawn down and resting on their backs, with the rain running off their tails. At such times they could be approached on foot to within half a gunshot, showing little fear.

Doctor Coues (1874) writes:

The curlews associate in flocks of every size, from three to as many thousand, but they generally fly in so loose and straggling a manner that it is rare to kill more than half a dozen at a shot. When they wheel, however, in any of their many beautiful evolutions, they close together in a more compact body, and offer a more favorable opportunity to the gunner. Their flight is firm, direct, very swift, when necessary much protracted, and is performed with regular, rapid beats. They never sail, except when about to alight, when the wings are much incurved downward, in the manner of most waders. As their feet touch the ground, their long, pointed wings are raised over the back, until the tips almost touch, and then deliberately folded, much in the manner of the solitary sandpiper (*Rhyacophilus solitarius*).

Voice.—Professor Swenk (1915) describes the notes as follows:

The Eskimo curlew had several notes. During flight they uttered a fluttering *tr-tr-tr* note, which was given by many individuals at once, and described by Coues as a "low conversational chatter" and by Mackay as "a soft, melodious whistle, '*bee, bee.*'" Mr. W. A. Elwood describes this note as "a short, low whistle" continually repeated by many of the birds simultaneously while in flight. Mr. A. J. Leach recalls the notes as resembling quite closely the note of the bluebird when in flight, only perhaps shorter and more of a twittering whistle, and, as it was given by a large number, perhaps all, of the flock as they took wing and while flying, it was difficult to catch the individual note. This note was constantly uttered while the birds were flying and was often audible before the birds could be seen. Before alighting, as they descended and sailed, they gave a soft whistle, somewhat like the note of the upland plover, according to Professor Bruner, while as they walked over the ground when feeding they uttered a chirruping whistle, as if calling to each other.

Fall.—The adult birds must have started off their breeding grounds early in July for the first arrivals reached the coast of Labrador by the end of that month. Their course at first was east-southeast, or perhaps nearly due east, across Hudson Bay to the Labrador Peninsula, where they lingered for a week or two to feast and fatten on the abundant harvest of berries. Turner saw them as far north as the mouth of the Koksoak River, and says in his notes:

From the 10th to the 20th of August immense flocks of these birds appear on the level tracts from Davis' Inlet to the Gulf of St. Lawrence, each day adding to their number until the ground seems alive with them. They feed on the ripening berries of *Empetrum* and *Vaccinium*, becoming wonderfully fat in a few days. By the 8th of September it is asserted that none remain.

Audubon (1840) writes:

On the 29th of July, 1833, during a thick fog, the Esquimaux curlews made their first appearance in Labrador, near the harbor of Bras d'Or. They evidently came from the north, and arrived in such dense flocks as to remind me of the passenger pigeons. The weather was extremely cold as well as foggy. For more than a week we had been looking for them, as was every fisherman in the harbor, these birds being considered there, as indeed they are, great delicacies. The birds at length came, flock after flock, passed close round our vessel, and directed their course toward the sterile mountainous tracts in the neighborhood; and as soon as the sun's rays had dispersed the fogs that hung over the land, our whole party went off in search of them.

I was not long in discovering that their stay on this coast was occasioned solely by the density of the mists and the heavy gales that already gave intimation of the approaching close of the summer; for whenever the weather cleared up a little, thousands of them set off and steered in a straight course across the broad Gulf of St. Lawrence. On the contrary, when the wind was high, and the fogs thick, they flew swiftly and low over the rocky surface of the country, as if bewildered. Wherever there was a spot that seemed likely to afford a supply of food, there the curlews abounded, and were easily approached. By the 12th of August, however, they had all left the country.

The eastward flight reached as far as Newfoundland, where they were fairly numerous along the eastern and southeastern shores. There was also a migration, probably down the west coast of Hudson Bay, which reached the Atlantic coast through Ontario and the Great Lakes region. But the main flight was through Labrador, across the Gulf of St. Lawrence to Nova Scotia and then due south across the ocean to the Lesser Antilles and South America; their course in South America is not well known, but it was probably across eastern Brazil, to Uruguay, Argentina, and Patagonia, where they arrived in September.

In fair weather the 2,000-mile trip across the ocean was probably made in one continuous flight, though I believe that these birds were able to alight on and rise from the water if necessary. But if bad weather, severe southeasterly storms, thick fogs, or heavy rains occurred during their passage, they were forced to land, sometimes in enormous numbers on the coast of New England, less often on the shores farther south, or on the Bermudas; if severe westerly gales occurred they were sometimes driven far out to sea or even across the Atlantic to the British Isles. Our flights in Massachusetts could be looked for during the latter half of August and through September. On Cape Cod they used to frequent much the same localities as the golden plover, old fields and pastures, often several miles from the shore, and the drier portions of the salt marshes, where they found an abundance of grasshoppers, crickets, and other insects; on Monomoy they were often found on the low sand hills which were largely covered with gray mosses or lichens. Mr. Mackay (1892c) writes:

> Those which do visit us almost invariably land with their boon companions, the American golden plover, of whose flocks I have frequently noticed they were the leaders, and I can scarcely call to mind, as I write, an instance where any number of Eskimo curlew have landed without there being more or less golden plover present at the same time. Those birds which may come can not, if they would, remain any longer than is absolutely necessary, for they are so harassed immediately after landing that the moment there occurs a change in the weather favorable for migration they at once depart. They appear to leave the coast at Long Island, N. Y., and strike farther out to sea, and then are not seen on the Atlantic coast for another year.

Game.—The gunner's name for the Eskimo curlew was "dough-bird," not "doe-bird," for it was so fat when it reached us in the fall that its breast would often burst open when it fell to the ground, and the thick layer of fat was so soft that it felt like a ball of dough. It is no wonder that it was so popular as a game bird, for it must have made a delicious morsel for the table. It was so tame and unsuspicious and it flew in such dense flocks that it was easily killed in large numbers. On the Labrador coasts and in Newfoundland the inhabitants killed all they could and preserved them for winter use, according to Mr. Berteau (Carroll, 1910), "by parboiling them and packing them in tins and jars and covering them with melted butter or lard." Coues (1874) tells of shooting them in Labrador, as follows:

Although the curlews were in such vast numbers, I did not find them so tame as might be expected and as I had been led to suppose by previous representations. I was never able to walk openly within shooting distance of a flock, though I was told it was often done. The most successful method of obtaining them is to take such a position as they will probably fly over in passing from one feeding ground to another. They may then be shot with ease, as they rarely fly high at such times. The pertinacity with which they cling to certain feeding grounds, even when much molested, I saw strikingly illustrated on one occasion. The tide was rising and about to flood a muddy flat, of perhaps an acre in extent, where their favorite snails were in great quantities. Although six or eight gunners were stationed upon the spot, and kept up a continual round of firing upon the poor birds, they continued to fly distractedly about over our heads, notwithstanding the numbers that every moment fell. They seemed in terror lest they should lose their accustomed fare of snails that day. On another occasion, when the birds had been so harassed for several hours as to deprive them of all opportunity of feeding, great numbers of them retired to a very small island, or rather a large pile of rocks, a few hundred yards from the shore, covered with seaweed and, of course, with snails. Flock after flock alighted on it, till it was completely covered with the birds, which there, in perfect safety, obtained their morning meal.

I can remember hearing my father tell of the great shooting they used to have on "the plains" at Cohasset when I was a small boy, about 1870. As he has now gone to the happy hunting grounds I can not give the exact figures, but he saw a wagon loaded full of "dough birds" shot on the plains in one day.

The greatest killings were made on the western plains during the spring migration, which Professor Swenk (1915) describes as follows:

During such flights the slaughter of these poor birds was appalling and almost unbelievable. Hunters would drive out from Omaha and shoot the birds without mercy until they had literally slaughtered a wagonload of them, the wagons being actually filled, and often with the sideboards on at that. Sometimes when the flight was unusually heavy and the hunters were well supplied with ammunition their wagons were too quickly and easily filled, so whole loads of the birds would be dumped on the prairie, their bodies forming piles as large as a couple of tons of coal, where they would be allowed to rot while the hunters proceeded to refill their wagons with fresh victims, and thus further gratify their lust of killing. The compact flocks and tameness of the birds made this slaughter possible, and at each shot usually dozens of the birds would fall. In one specific instance a single shot from an old muzzle-loading shotgun into a flock of these curlews as they veered by the hunter brought down 28 birds at once, while for the next half mile every now and then a fatally wounded bird would drop to the ground dead. So dense were the flocks when the birds were turning in their flight that one could scarcely throw a brick or missile into it without striking a bird.

In hunting these curlew the field glass was used by the hunters to follow their flights. The fields where they were prone to gather were patroled many times during the day and carefully scanned with the glass to discover the flocks on the ground. When the birds came in they would be up quite high, perhaps from 200 or 300 yards to a quarter of a mile, and in preparing to alight they would turn and wheel, towering in the air while they whistled softly, would hover a while, and then all drop and come down, flying along over the ground for a short distance before alighting. The birds would always alight all at once and very close together, and if the day were warm they would sit down very close together on the ground, forming bunches, when they could be readily discovered with the field glass and approached close enough to get a shot.

There was no difficulty in getting quite close to the sitting birds, perhaps within 25 or 35 yards, and when at about this distance the hunters would wait for them to arise on their feet, which was the signal for the first volley of shots. The startled birds would rise and circle about the field a few times, affording ample opportunity for further murderous discharge of the guns, and sometimes would realight on the same field, when the attack would be repeated. Mr. Wheeler has killed as many as 37 birds with a pump gun at one rise. They weighed just about 1 pound each when they were fat. Sometimes the bunch would be seen with the glass alighting in a field 2 or 3 miles away, when the hunters would at once drive to that field with a horse and buggy as rapidly as they could, relocate the birds, get out, and resume the fusillade and slaughter. On rainy days the birds would fly restlessly from one field to another, moving about in this way most of the day and seeming unusually plentiful because of being so much in the air.

Winter.—There is little known about the winter habits of the Eskimo curlew except that it formerly associated with the golden plover, the upland plover, and the buff-breasted sandpiper on the pampas of Argentina and Patagonia, where it is now but a memory of the past.

DISTRIBUTION

Range.—North and South America, accidental in eastern Asia and Great Britain.

The Eskimo curlew is now nearly or quite extinct. Although formerly abundant, its occurrence in both North and South America has been so frequently confused with *Numenius hudsonicus*, that it is extremely difficult to establish its migration range. Like the golden plover, however, this species followed an elliptical route, usually passing south in the fall off the coast of the United States, the point of departure from the mainland being the coast of Labrador, Nova Scotia, or (more rarely) Long Island, New York. In spring the return trip was made up the Mississippi Valley and the prairie States at which season it was practically unknown on the Atlantic coast.

Breeding range.—The only known nests and eggs of the Eskimo curlew have been obtained in northwestern Canada, Fort Anderson, Rendezvous Lake, Franklin Bay, and Point Lake.

Winter range.—The northern limits of the winter range are not known, but probably extended rarely to Brazil (Ypanema). South to Uruguay (Montevideo); Argentina (Bahia Blanca, Buenos Aires, Concepcion, and the Chupat Valley); and Chile (Island of Chiloe, and Paposo). It also has been detected on the Falkland Islands (Abbott, 1861).

Spring migration.—Early dates of spring arrival in North America are: Texas, Gainesville, March 7, and Boerne, March 9; Arkansas, Fayetteville, March 31; Missouri, St. Louis, April 10, and Vernon County, April 16; Kansas, Emporia, April 13; Nebraska, Alda, April 2; Iowa, Burlington, April 5, and Grinnell, April 10; South Dakota, Brown County, April 16, and Mackenzie, Fort Resolution, May 26, and Fort Anderson, May 27.

A specimen of this species was taken at San Geronimo, Guatemala, in April; and one at Lake Palomas, Chihuahua, April 8, 1892. A specimen was taken at Chalmers, Ind., on April 19, 1890. In Massachusetts one was obtained at Cape Cod in May, 1873, and about 50 were reported near the mouth of the Rowley River, May 17, 1916. Spring arrivals also have been noted in Alaska, St. Michael, May 12, 1878, and Cape Lisbourne, May 25, 1886.

Late dates of spring departure are: Argentina, Concepcion, March 1; Texas, Long Point, April 23, and Fort Stockton, May 4; Missouri, Jasper County, May 1; Kansas, Lawrence, May 6; and South Dakota, Vermilion, May 3, and Harrison, May 10.

Fall migration.—Early dates of fall arrival are: Quebec, Bras d'Or, July 29, Caribou Island, August 12, and Indian Tickle, August 16; Massachusetts, Nantucket, August 18, and Edgartown, August 21; West Indies, Barbados, August 27, Carriacou, September 5, and Grenada, September 22; Brazil, Amazon River, September 4; and Argentina, Concepcion, September 9.

Late dates of fall departure are: Mackenzie, Fort Anderson, August 2; Quebec, Koksoak River, September 4, Montreal, September 7, and Magdalen Islands, September 20; New Brunswick, Tabusintac, September 8; Prince Edward Island, New London, September 1; Maine, Hog Island, September 2, and Pine Point, September 23; Massachusetts, East Orleans, September 5, Monomoy Island, September 10, and Nantucket, October 2; Connecticut, Saybrook, October 13; New York, Lockport, October 2; and West Indies, Barbados, November 4.

There are a few records in the interior for this season, among which are: Ontario, Wolf Island, October 10, 1873; Pennsylvania,

Erie, September 17, 1889; Ohio, Cincinnati, September, 1878; Michigan, Kalamazoo, October 28, 1879; Illinois, Summit, August 11, 1872; and Wisconsin, Fox Lake, September 10, 1912.

Casual records.—The Eskimo curlew has been taken or reported from several points outside its normal range, among which are: Porto Rico, once near San Juan (Gundlach); Bermuda, September, 1874; Greenland, two records (Reinhardt); Pribilof Islands, St. Paul Island, May 26, 1872; "Bering Sea," May 22, 1874; Siberia, Cape Wankarem, August 6, 1881; five records for Great Britain (Slains, Aberdeenshire, September 28, 1878; near Stonehaven, Kincardineshire, September 6, 1855; one on the Alde, Aldeburgh, Suffolk; one at Woodbridge, Suffolk; and one purchased in the flesh at Dublin, October 21, 1870); and Iceland (Kjaerbölling). The supposed occurrence of this species in southern California (San Diego region and near Tia Juana) probably refers to *N. hudsonicus*, as does also the record for the Galapagos Islands (Charles Island) and South Carolina (Charleston).

Egg dates.—Mackenzie: 28 records, June 8 to July 12; 14 records, June 18 to 25.

NUMENIUS PHAEOPUS PHAEOPUS (Linnaeus)

WHIMBREL

Contributed by Francis Charles Robert Jourdain

HABITS

The latest and best authority on the birds of Greenland, E. Lehn Schiöler, writes that in all probability the whimbrel breeds on the southern part of the west coast of Greenland, perhaps generally in the south, but more especially in the southwest. The only other American record of this species is one from south of Sable Island, Nova Scotia, on May 25, 1906.

Spring.—The whimbrel arrives on the British coasts from about mid-April to June 12, but is very frequently noted during the first days of May, from which it derives one of its local names, the "May bird." On migration it prefers to haunt the low-lying coast and the adjacent country, feeding on the mud flats and marshes. When on the wing they fly at a great height, but can be recognized by their clear seven-syllabled whistle, *tetty, tetty, tetty, tet.*

Courtship.—Practically nothing is recorded in the standard works on British ornithology on the courtship of this species, but some observations have been made both in Iceland and on the Shetlands. Reimschneider writes that in Iceland one hears its notes all through the long summer day and far into the night, a very long-drawn *kwiu,*

uttered with inflated throat and scarcely opened bill. The nuptial
song of the male is a long-drawn fluty trill, much slower and longer
than the alarm note. The bird hardly rises above the ground, but
flies with half opened bill for short distances, trilling, then makes
quick and short wing strokes and slowly descends to earth again
with extended wings, when the cry is again uttered. Bernard
Hantzsch (1905) gives a fuller description, which, however, varies
in some details. The male is perched on some hillock, from which
with wide-opened bill he utters a rolling *di-di-di*. Now he is off,
with his long feet trailing behind and head and neck outstretched.
With short and very rapid wing strokes he rises high in the clear
sky till almost out of sight, meanwhile uttering his soft fluty *du-
du-du*, sometimes for minutes together. Then follows a slightly
higher and quicker series of notes, ending with a beautiful, soft trill,
louder and faster than that of the golden plover. He then descends
spirally toward the nesting place, thence again starting on his upward flight. The female also trills, but the song flight is peculiar
to the male.

Nesting.—The breeding grounds of the whimbrel are the vast
expanses of moorland, overgrown with heather and mosses, which are
characteristic of the Arctic tundra. The actual nest is a well-defined
hollow among the heather or rough grass, scantily lined with a few
bits of ling or dry grass and moss. Some nests contain hardly any
material and are merely pressed down and hollowed by the bird.
They do not nest as a rule close together and the breeding place is
jealously guarded by the male who rises fearlessly to attack and
drive off almost any bird which approaches within a 100 yards of
the eggs. Even skuas are attacked in this way, but where they are
numerous the whimbrel stands but a poor chance of rearing young.
In the Shetlands the eggs are laid in the last days of May and early
in June, while in Iceland the normal time is at the beginning of
June and exceptionally late in May.

Eggs.—These are normally four in number, exceptionally three
only, especially in late layings, and Hantzsch (1905) records one
clutch of five. They are pyriform, and large for the size of the
birds, with thin shells. The ground color varies as a rule from pale
olive green to pale brownish buff, blotched and spotted with olive
brown or reddish brown and with ashy grey shell markings. In
some varieties the ground is a beautiful clear green and the blotches
very bold and conspicuous, while another scarce type has a bluish
grey ground with only large brownish ash blotches. The measurements of 100 eggs, by Doctor Rey and the writer, average 58.9
by 41.2 millimeters; the eggs showing the four extremes measure
65.1 by 41.7, 57 by **44**, **52** by 41.6 and 55.3 by **36** millimeters.

Young.—Both sexes have incubation patches and from Chislett's (1923) observations, confirmed also by Hantzsch, both share in the work. The only note we have as to the length of the period is that of Hantzsch (1905) who gives it as three to three and one-half weeks. In the case of a nest watched by Chislett the first two young hatched were led away by one bird while the other continued to incubate. This was on June 23 and the following day was cold with a high wind. The third chick wandered from the nest and was sometimes brooded by the incubating bird, which left the fourth egg for that purpose, but she never seemed thoroughly at ease except when covering both egg and chick. By the following morning the last chick had hatched out. Only one brood is reared in the season.

Plumages.—The plumages and molts are fully described in A Practical Handbook of British Birds edited by H. S. Witherby (1920).

Food.—This species feeds largely on earthworms, and also during the winter months on sandworms (*Arenicola*). Insects are also freely taken, chiefly beetles (Coleoptera), but also Orthoptera, especially earwigs (*Forficula*) and crickets (*Acheta*), larvae of flies (Diptera) etc. During the breeding season many small land mollusca are eaten, especially snails (*Helix ericetorum*), slugs (*Limax agrestris*), etc., and in the autumn, marine mollusca, both univalves and bivalves. Small crustacea, including small crabs, shrimps (*Crangon*) and Gammaridae are also freely taken and the berries of moorland plants such as *Empetrum nigrum* (crowberry) and *Vacinium myrtillus*.

Behavior.—The boldness of this species in defending its nest has already been referred to. It has been frequently seen to attack and drive off birds much larger and more powerful than itself, such as the raven and the larger gulls. During the winter months it appears to be less of a shore feeder than the curlew, frequently visiting the inland marshes in preference to the mud flats and shores. Chislett (1923) describes its gait as quite different to that of the curlew, its progress being much more rapid and direct. Instead of approaching the nest in a leisurely way with many detours and pauses, it walks with rapid, jerky strides, almost directly to its objective.

Enemies.—The large gulls and skuas, though often successfully driven off when approaching singly, are often successful in destroying the eggs or young where present in numbers and the enormous increase in the numbers of the great skua in the Shetlands has proved very detrimental to this species. In Iceland the Arctic fox is also an enemy to be counted with and the crow tribe (raven and hooded crow) are always ready to take advantage of any chance opportunity.

Fall.—The young are fledged according to Hantzsch (1905) within a month of hatching and about the beginning of August begin to collect into flocks which increase in size daily. In the second half of August he records great flocks of over a hundred birds which leave the island about the middle of September. The latest date on which Jönsson records them on the Westmann Isles is October 10.

Winter.—Exceptionally, small parties remain in Iceland during the winter. Thus in the winter of 1899–1900 they were noticed by many observers over Hjalteyri and the adjacent district. On the other hand, many individuals remain all the year round in their winter quarters, keeping together in small parties and evidently nonbreeding birds.

DISTRIBUTION

Breeding range.—In the British Isles, very sparingly and almost exterminated on certain islands in the Shetland group. A few pairs are said to have bred at various localities on the mainland, chiefly in the north of Scotland and perhaps also on some of the outlying isles. Breeds freely on the Faroes and Iceland and probably in southwest Greenland. On the continent and northern Scandinavia and Finland and in North Russia, south to Kanzan, Samara, Ufa, Perm, and Orenburg; also in West Siberia at least to Tara and Tobolsk, but in East Siberia replaced by *N. ph. variegatus.* Possibly also breeds in Russia in Voronezh, Kief, and the middle Urals, but proof still lacking.

Winter range.—Passes through Europe and western Asia to the coasts of Africa south to Cape Province, Madagascar, the Seychelles, Comoro Isles, Aldabra, and Mauritius. In Asia to Arabia, passing through Iraq to West India, south to Ceylon and the Islands in the Bay of Bengal.

Spring migration.—The average date of arrival of the migrating flocks at the Faroes is given as mid April, while in Iceland they arrive about the end of April or early in May; at the Westmann Isles on the south coast the earliest and latest dates are given as April 20 and May 5 by Jönsson.

Fall migration.—The departure from Iceland begins about mid September, on the Westmann Isles between September 20 and October 10 (Jönsson), while the Faroes are abandoned by September 29 (exceptionally as late as October 3).

Casual records.—It has occurred several times on Jan Meyen, once Bear Island (June 14, 1898), several times on Spitsbergen, and also on Kolguev. In the Atlantic it occurs on the Canaries, Madeira, the Azores, and the Cape Verde Islands. A specimen came on board a steamer in the vicinity of Sable Island, Nova Scotia, on May 23, 1906 (Latitude 43° north, Longitude 60° west) ; and one was obtained at Gilgo Inlet, Great South Bay, Long Island, N. Y., on September 4, 1912.

Eggs dates.—In Scotland, May 19 to June 11 (13 dates); Faroes, June 4 to 24 (34 dates), May 25 (1 date); Iceland, June 4 to 23 (22 dates).

NUMENIUS TAHITIENSIS (Gmelin)

BRISTLE-THIGHED CURLEW

HABITS

Although this species has been recognized for over 140 years, surprisingly little has been learned or published about it. It was discovered by Latham in 1785 from Tahiti, the largest of the Society Islands, hence the specific name given by Gmelin in 1788, *Scolopax tahitiensis.* But the credit is due to Peale for discovering the most peculiar character of the species, the elongated shafts of some of the flank feathers which are lacking in barbs and from which we derive the name, " bristle-thighed."

It was long supposed to be a bird of the South Pacific islands and the first birds captured in Alaska were regarded as accidental stragglers. During the last century there were only three published North American records, all for Alaska; the first specimen was taken by Bischoff on May 18, 1869, on the Kenai Peninsula, the second by Nelson on May 24, 1880, at St. Michael, and the third by Townsend on August 28, 1885, on the Kowak River. Since then it has been found to be a fairly common fall migrant in Alaska and it probably breeds somewhere in the interior of that territory.

Spring.—Dr. E. W. Nelson (1887) gives the following account of the capture of his bird:

On May 24, 1880, while I was shooting black brant, a pair of these birds settled near by on a rising stretch of land covered with large tussocks. They uttered a loud whistling call note very much like that of *hudsonicus*, but something in their general appearance led me to stalk and secure one of the birds. To my gratification it was a bristle-thighed curlew, and I made great efforts to secure the mate, which had stopped a hundred yards or so beyond. As she raised on my approach I fired at long range and the bird fell mortally hurt on a distant hillside, where it was lost amid a host of large tussocks.

Bischoff's bird was taken on May 18; and H. B. Conover (1926) collected one at Hooper Bay on May 22, 1924. These three dates, only six days apart, probably indicate the normal time of arrival of birds of this species in Alaska after their long flight over the Pacific Ocean from the Hawaiian Islands, the nearest of their winter resorts. This is a really wonderful flight and it is surprising that we have no evidence to indicate that they deviate from their direct course at all, as we have no records of any specimens from any point to the westward or to the southward of the Alaska Peninsula. The species is comparatively scarce on the Bering Sea coast of Alaska, from which we might infer that an overland flight is made from the vicinity of the Kenai Peninsula to the breeding grounds somewhere in the northern interior of Alaska.

Summer.—The breeding grounds and the nesting habits of the bristle-thighed curlew are entirely unknown, an interesting problem for some enterprising ornithologist to work out. Mr. Conover (1926) suggests that " the main breeding ground is probably above the timber line on some of the mountain ranges " of Alaska. Herbert W. Brandt says in his notes:

From the native information I was able to gather I believe that these birds may breed at the eastern end of the Askinuk Mountains, or in the Kusilvak Mountains and perhaps the mountains to the northward of Mountain Village on the Yukon River. Their early loitering appearance at Hooper Bay so shortly after nesting makes it entirely unlikely that they had traveled very far, but it seems rather strange that we did not encounter them in their spring migration and further it is apparently doubtful that they should enter the Bering Sea coast territory by following down either the Yukon or the Kuskoquim River valleys.

Dr. Charles H. Townsend shot a specimen of this curlew at Kotzebue Sound (Kobuk River) on August 25; it was a young bird which had evidently recently come from its breeding grounds. We saw none of this species about Nome in July; but after I left, Rollo H. Beck, a member of our expedition, collected quite a series of them in August. Two of his birds, now in my collection, were taken at Cape Nome on August 24, 1911. Mr. Conover (1926) writes:

By the end of July we had entered the Kashunuk Slough and traveled down it until we were about 20 miles from where it enters Hooper Bay. At this place was an Eskimo village where we stopped for a few days to have a goose drive; and it was here that we saw the bristle-thighed curlew in abundance. On July 31 a pair was seen and collected, and on August 3 one more was taken. August 4 was the big day, as several hundred of these birds were seen on the tundra feeding on blueberries. About a dozen were taken by our party, and I personally believe I saw over a hundred, while another member of the expedition, who was off in another direction, estimated that he saw three times as many. All the specimens taken were old birds.

The above facts would seem to indicate that the main breeding grounds are somewhere in the interior of extreme northern Alaska, probably on the barren grounds; that the spring migration is well inland; and that there is a heavy fall migration along the Bering Sea coast. The eggs and downy young are entirely unknown and there are not enough specimens available to work out the molts and plumages, which probably correspond to those of closely related species.

Food.—Probably the feeding habits of this curlew are not very different from those of the Hudsonian curlew, but the only food mentioned by observers consists of berries. Birds collected in Alaska were feeding on blueberries. They are said to feed on *Canthium* berries in the Hawaiian Islands; and birds shot on Midway Island by Dr. Paul Bartsch (1922) were "crammed full of *Scaevola* berries."

Behavior.—Doctor Bartsch (1922) found this bird "quite abundant on both" Midway Islands in November, "where in company with the golden plover it frequents all parts of the island excepting those covered by brush. These birds were quite tame as well as curious and when flushed would frequently fly about us, emitting their peculiar cry."

Dill and Bryan (1912) reported about 250 on Laysan Island in the spring; they say:

Just before sunset and early in the morning the bristle-thighed curlews would come up around our camp uttering their peculiar complaining notes. They roosted on the roofs of the old buildings at night, sometimes as many as 20 birds in one flock. We saw them feeding on different parts of the island but usually about the lagoon or along the beaches.

Donald R. Dickey photographed a bristle-thighed curlew on Laysan Island in the act of robbing a nest of the man-o-war bird, of which he tells me:

This was not a sporadic bit of deviltry engaged in by one perverted individual. Instead, it was characteristic of most, if not all, of the curlews present on Laysan at the time we were there. In other words, they indulged in organized banditry, working about the island in troups accompanied by numbers of turnstones and an occasional golden plover which were partners in crime with the curlew. The turnstones jammed their bills straight into the lighter-shelled eggs, but the curlew, frequently at least, got access to the contents of the larger eggs by raising them in their bills and then dropping them back on the hard sand until they broke. They can pick up and run away with an egg up to the size of a man-o-war bird's egg. In the case of the latter, the more dexterous birds seized the egg and held it endwise in the bill. It seems difficult for them to pick it up otherwise.

Dr. Alexander Wetmore has sent me the following notes on this subject:

That a bird of the shore-bird family should destroy eggs may seem almost unbelievable in view of the habits ordinary in this group, yet in work in the Hawaiian Bird Reservation in 1923 we found the bristle-thighed curlew, as well as the turnstone, making regular practice of eating the eggs of the birds nesting on these distant islands. The sooty and gray-backed terns were the greatest sufferers, as the curlew drove their long bills through the eggs with ease, or seized them in their long mandibles to carry them away and eat them at their leisure. On close observation we found that curlews attacked the eggs of all birds indiscriminately, even pulling an egg from beneath a frigate bird when the incubating bird raised on the nest for a moment, the theft being committed so adroitly that the egg seemingly was not missed. Mr. Donald Dickey in his motion pictures succeeded in filming a spirited scene in which a bristle-thighed curlew after a number of attempts accomplished the seemingly impossible feat of carrying away a frigate bird's egg held firmly between its mandibles, while a group of apparently admiring turnstones, robbers themselves but incapable of such herculean acts of banditry, scurried about in the background. On another occasion a curlew flew up to a red-footed booby's nest in a bush several feet from the ground in the temporary absence of the owner, impaled the egg, and dragged it away to be devoured. The booby was still brooding disconsolately in her empty nest two days later. On another day a curlew deliberately opened an old albatross egg found in the sand and ate eagerly from the putrid interior. As this egg had been lying unprotected from the sun for at least four months previous, its condition may be imagined, yet the bird returned avidly again and again to continue its horrid repast though I approached within 10 feet.

Voice.—Mr. Conover (1926) says:

The call and appearance of this species are entirely different from that of the Hudsonian curlew. The latter gives a very short whistling call, which is roughly as follows: *Whe-whe-whe-whe.* The former, on the other hand, has a call very similar to one of the black-bellied plover and sounds something like *wheeeu-whu.* In appearance the bristle-thigh is tawnier above and has a very reddish-brown unbarred rump, which is a very good field mark.

DISTRIBUTION

Range.—Alaska and islands in the Pacific Ocean.

Breeding range.—Unknown, but considered probable in northern or northwestern Alaska.

The bristle-thighed curlew does not seem to be abundant and consequently has been under observation at comparatively few points. Specimens have been observed or taken in summer in Alaska at Kotzebue Sound, Hooper Bay, Kobuk River, Lopp Lagoon, and Mint River. One also was taken on St. George Island, of the Pribilof group, on May 26, 1917.

Winter range.—During the winter they are found north to the Hawaiian Islands (Lisiansky, Laysan, French Frigate Shoal, Bird Island, and Hawaii); east to Hawaii, Palmyra Island, Fanning Island, Christmas Island, Marquesas Islands, Society Islands (Tahiti), and the Paumotu Archipelago (Vincennes Island); south to the Low or Paumotu Archipelago (Vincennes Island), Cook Islands (Palmerston Island), and probably New Caledonia; west to probably New Caledonia, Phoenix Islands (Canton and Phoenix Island), Gilbert Islands, the Marshall Islands (Jaluit Island), and the Hawaiian Islands (Lisiansky Island).

Migration.—Early dates of arrival for bristle-thighed curlews in Alaska are: Fort Kenai, May 18, 1869; Nome River, May 23, 1905; and Cape Mountain, May 28, 1922.

They have been detected in the Kotzebue Sound region as late as August 26, 1885.

Family CHARADRIIDAE, Plovers

VANELLUS VANELLUS (Linnaeus)

LAPWING

Contributed by Francis Charles Robert Jourdain

HABITS

The status of this bird in North America is a remarkable one. Up to 1927, with the exception of Greenland, where according to Lehn Schiöler, it is an occasional visitor, it had only been recorded on about seven occasions from the American Continent. Excluding Alaska, all the other records are from the eastern seaboard, the Bahamas and Barbados. In December, 1927, large flocks, numbering thousands, according to one reporter, were recorded from a number of places along the east coast of Newfoundland, in the middle of the country and also on the west coast. Among the birds obtained was one sent from Bonavista, Newfoundland, by Canon A. G. Bagley on December 31, which still bore the ring with which it had been marked as a nestling in May, 1926, at Ullswater, Cumberland, England, by Dr. H. J. Moon.

Spring.—In the British Isles the migratory movements are rather complicated and irregular, but many birds which have wintered in the south and near the great estuaries and marshes begin to work their way back to their breeding places inland, and to the north of Scotland which is practically deserted by them during the winter months.

Courtship.—The lapwing is a highly gregarious species and even in the height of the breeding season, when territorial jealousy on the part of the males is apparent, several pairs are generally to be found nesting within a short distance of one another. The courtship habits have been closely studied by the late S. E. Brock in Scotland, and more recently by William Farren, R. H. Brown, and J. K. Stanford, so that there is plenty of material at hand.

Even in the autumn and early winter months when the weather is open, especially after frosts, a certain amount of sexual activity is evident. Some of the males show indications of territorial defense and fighting takes place intermittently. It is not till the winter is over and the males have returned to their breeding grounds, which is generally from late February to early March, that the nesting territory is definitely parceled out among the males. The areas may vary considerably in shape and size and are not always clearly defined, but each bird shows distinct signs of jealousy at any invasion on the part of a neighbor and aerial combats take place

from time to time, though sometimes a male will desert the group of
" scrapes " which marks his territorial center and adopt a new series.
These " scrapes " form an important part in the ritual of courtship.
On the appearance of a female the male utters a grating note while
standing upright and moving wings and tail up and down rhythmi-
cally. He then drops to the ground and, as Brock describes it,
" lying far forward on his breast, shuffles the body, and scrapes ener-
getically with the feet, which may be seen in rapid motion. At short
intervals the tail is spasmodically bent downwards, the action corresponding with energetic footwork." He then rises jerking bits of
stubble over his shoulder, and in this way a little group of hollows
or " scrapes " is formed, one of which ultimately becomes the nest.
Apparently the female makes choice from several sites originally
selected by the male.

From time to time the male makes the spring flight which has been
well described by Brock.

Rising from the ground the male executes a few labored flaps, moving the
wings with exaggerated slowness, owllike; thence he quickens his pace and
rising suddenly at an abrupt angle, commences the song, the greater part of
which, however, is emitted as the bird falls again. During the utterance of the
song is a pause occurring after the penultimate note, the performer throws
himself sideways almost on his back, instantly recovering himself with a flurry
of wings. The bird now scuds rapidly over the ground at a moderate height,
making a pronounced humming sound with the motion of his sharply driven
pinions, and occasionally tilting himself from side to side, much in the manner
of a snipe when flushed.

The song is well rendered by Brock as *whey-willuchooee-willuch-
willuch-cooee*. The first syllable long and hoarse, the second and
third *willuch* uttered rapidly and staccato, then a pause, during which
the partial somersault is executed, followed by the loud and musical
final note. The Norfolk marshmen's transliteration is also good,
" Three bullocks a week, week after week.

Sometimes two rival males will rise together in the air almost perpendicularly each trying to rise above the other.

At intervals the upper bird stoops suddenly to the lower, an attack usually
avoided by an agile turn of the wing, but occasionally a distant and hollow clap
is audible, indicating an exchange of blows apparently with the wing. On at
length parting company both combatants break into full song flight, repeating
it twice or thrice ere resettling in their respective stations.

These encounters seem as a rule not to be of a very serious character and the occasional fights between rivals carried on near the
ground, in which one bird swoops repeatedly from one side or the
other at its opponent, which in turn avoids the attack by little upward
springs or swerving aside, seem to be of a more serious character.
When a hen bird approaches, the male bird runs toward her and describes a half circle round her with stiff and constrained air. Then

he makes for the nearest " scrape " and at once drops into it, working with furious energy and occasionally dropping bits of straw over his shoulder. At first the hen makes no response, but about a fortnight after the beginning of the courtship she approaches the spot where he is at work by indirect stages. The male then rises and steps forward, with his back to the hen, slowly lowering his bill to the ground and raising his tail perpendicularly, thus displaying his richly colored undertail coverts. The female now settles into the " scrape " and imitates the actions of the cock, but with less energy, the male meanwhile retaining his strange uptilted attitude and collecting nesting material which is jerked over his shoulder toward the " scrape." When at length the hen leaves the " scrape " the male reenters and sometimes the hen also repeats the process. Coition takes place a few days before the eggs are laid and immediately afterwards the hen works in the " scrape " with far more energy than before, the male often taking his place in another scrape. Both birds go through the ceremony of throwing bits of nest material over the shoulder. No serious attempt is made on the part of other males to interfere with a paired hen, and she on her part seems to avoid any strange cock bird.

Nesting.—Although it is usual for several pairs to breed in company the actual nests are usually some distance apart, and nearly always on slightly raised ground. They may be found on plowed land or on pasture and occasionally moorland, and vary somewhat in size, some being merely muddy hollows with a few bits of straw and bent, while others, especially on grass lands, are fairly substantial edifices of dead vegetable matter collected round the nesting " scrape " originally made by the male.

Eggs.—Normally four, but on rare occasions five, have been recorded, and when a bird has been robbed twice, sets of three and even two or one egg may be found late in the season. When the birds have been much persecuted as many as 20 have been laid in one season by a single female. They are pyriform in shape and lie in the nest with the points touching one another. As a rule there is not much variation, the usual ground color being stone color or brownish olive with black spots and blotches chiefly towards the large end. Some eggs have the ground almost hidden by dense black markings, and there are types in which the spots are mainly replaced by short black lines. More remarkable varieties are those in which the ground color in bluish white or some shade of greenish olive, with scanty markings of black, and the rare erythristic type in which the ground color is pale brick red or deep red brown with rich red brown markings. This wonderful variation has been recorded from Friesland as well as many parts of the British Isles.

The measurements of 100 eggs measured by the writer average 47 by 33.7 millimeters; the eggs showing the four extremes measure **58** by 32.5, 47.4 by **37.2**, **42.3** by 33 and 44.7 by **31.2** millimeters.

Young.—Incubation is performed by both sexes, but much the greater part by the hen, the male being on guard to give the alarm. Incubation begins with the third or fourth egg and the period is as a rule 24 or 25 days, but in some cases is said to extend to 27 or even 28 days. The adults are very bold and demonstrative when the eggs are chipping and will even strike sheep or dogs. The young remain in the nest until the down has been thoroughly dried and at first do not travel far afield, crouching when the parents give the alarm. They can swim readily and are led by the old birds from dry uplands toward water meadows. Directly the young are able to fly they assemble into flocks. Only one brood is reared during the season.

Plumages.—The plumages and molts are fully described in A Practical Handbook of British Birds, edited by H. F. Witherby (1920).

Ridgway (1919) says that the sexes are alike, and that he has been unable to verify the supposed differences in the wing formula of male and female. It is, however, easy to distinguish the sexes in life by the shape of the wing of the male, which is, as described by Frohawk and others, much more rounded in shape than that of the female.

Food.—This consists largely of earthworms, mollusca (including the large slugs *Arion* and *Agriolimax* as well as the smaller snails, *Helix* sp.; also during the winter months marine shell fish, *Tellina*, *Bythinia*, *Physa*, etc.) and insects. This latter family includes Coleoptera (*Otiorhynchus*, Carabidae, *Ocypusolens*, *Aphodius*, *Agriotes*, various species of *Geodephaga*, etc.), Diptera, including larvae of Tipulidae, Lepidoptera (many larvae of moths such as *Noctua segetum*, *N. exclamationes*, etc.), and Orthoptera. Vegetable matter is also eaten, but not largely. Seeds of *Ranunculus repens*, *Polygonum aviculare*, and *Spergula* have been recognized, also fragments of seaweed (Algae) in winter. Spiders and marine crustacea are also recorded.

Behavior.—The lapwing is preeminently a gregarious bird. All through the winter months it is to be met with in flocks, sometimes of great size, and even in the breeding season it is rare to find a single pair nesting out of sight and earshot of its neighbors. The curious " wobbling " flight enables the species to be recognized at great distances. Unlike some other gregarious species, such as the starling, the lapwing is not expert in the art of simultaneous maneuvers and it is a common sight to see a big flock rise together on the wing and break up at once into two bodies moving in different directions. Then gradually birds from the smaller body will gravitate toward the larger flock and after a time the two will reunite, but there is a lack of leadership and confidence in their movements which at once distinguishes them from the smartly wheeling flocks of dunlins, knots, or other gregarious waders. Sometimes a party of golden plover will associate on the wing with a flock of lapwing, but here, again, the difference is very striking.

Enemies.—Probably the rook destroys more eggs and small young than any other foe except man, but the jackdaw, hooded crow, and carrion crow are all apt to devour the eggs. I have seen a sparrow hawk drop from a tree onto a bird rising from its nest and bind onto it for a time, but the lapwing broke free after a struggle. It is not uncommon to find remains of birds on the feeding tables of the sparrow hawk near a breeding ground. The peregrine also sometimes takes lapwing, but its erratic tumbling flight renders it a difficult prey.

Fall.—Ringing has proved that some of the British-reared birds find their way to Iceland, France, and Portugal. In mild winters there are always a considerable number of flocks in our southern counties, but hard frosts or deep snow will cause them to move to the south coast or to emigrate.

Although a most useful bird from the agriculturist's point of view, the lapwing is shot freely during the autumn and winter, chiefly by shore shooters, while the demand for its eggs as delicacies has also been detrimental to its status. In Holland the earliest clutches are all taken for the market and this has had no injurious effect, as the birds lay again and are then protected strictly.

DISTRIBUTION

Breeding range.—Europe north to the Arctic Circle, the British Isles, but only exceptionally in the Faroes, and not in Iceland. In Finland to latitude 68° on the Muonio River and in Russia north to Archangel. Southward it breeds in Andalusia and in the Balkan Peninsula to Macedonia, but not in Greece or the Mediterranean Islands. Breeding in Morocco requires confirmation. It also breeds across Asia east to the Pacific, south to Transcaspia and Yarkand.

Winter range.—Many birds winter in the British Isles, but on the Continent they move to southern Europe and northern Africa, visiting the Atlantic isles occasionally (Canaries, Madeira, etc.). In Asia, Asia Minor, Palestine, Iraq, Persia, and north India, China, North Burma, and Japan.

Spring migration.—The northward movement of continental birds depends much on the weather. In mild winters they have appeared in Denmark in January and February, but the average date is about March 6. In Sweden the arrival is also irregular, from mid February to mid March, but in south Finland not till late in March. In central Europe the birds arrive as a rule on the breeding grounds early in March, and the Mediterranean passage is generally over by the beginning of that month.

Fall migration.—Migrants from the north arrive at Gibraltar about mid October, while in Malta the passage takes place in November, and in Greece at the end of October. In Iraq they arrive from October 22 onward, but chiefly in early November.

Casual records.—Greenland, occasional visitor (Julianehaab 1847; Fiskenaes 7, I, 1820, etc.) Iceland; numerous records between September and March; Labrador (Cartwright, January, 1917); Newfoundland, White Hills, November 23, 1905 and recently December, 1927); Nova Scotia (Ketch Harbor, March 17, 1897); Long Island, New York (Merrick, 2 specimens, December 26, 1883 and Meccox Bay, Waterville, autumn 1905); Bahamas (Hog Island, November, 1900); Barbados (December 24, 1886); West Alaska (small islets in Norton Sound); Madeira (Machico, December 6, 1891, December 2, 1889, December 4, 1893, January 14, 1895, March 10, 1895, December 15, 1896, and November 28, 1897); Jan Mayen (30 on April 8, 1883).

[AUTHOR'S NOTE.—The most remarkable occurrence of this species took place during the fall and winter of 1927–28. A specimen was taken on Baffin Island in October; and they appeared in large numbers in Newfoundland (Bonavista) in December, where one man was reported to have killed 60 individuals, one of which carried a band of British Bird Magazine that had been attached in Cumberland, England, in May, 1926. Capt. Donald MacMillan reported them at Anatalok Bay, Labrador, on December 22, and a specimen was obtained January 6, 1928, at North Head, Grand Manan, New Brunswick.]

C. L. Whittle (1928) has suggested the following theory, as to the possible cause of this unusual flight:

As to the cause of the movement of lapwings to Newfoundland and the route taken, it is perhaps helpful to study the Pilot Charts of the North Atlantic above referred to. During the month of December, the 16th and 17th, a well-developed cyclone of exceptional intensity had its center well to the east of Spain, with a low pressure of 28.30 inches, and with accompanying strong southeasterly winds from western Europe. These winds might easily have been instrumental in driving lapwings to Iceland, five to seven hundred miles distant, and to Greenland. Later, polar winds and a search for food may have played important parts in forcing a movement southwesterly to northern

Labrador, and then southeasterly, following the coast to Newfoundland. Here, near the shore, snowless tundras, which probably would furnish a food supply, may have existed, even in December, with the result that the recently scattered birds became gradually concentrated.][2]

Egg dates.—March 2 to 19 (9 dates); March 26 to 31 (18 dates); April 1 to 14 (60 dates); April 15 to 30 (29 dates, probably including many second layings); late date June 22. All the above from England.

EUDROMIAS MORINELLUS (Linnaeus)

DOTTEREL

Contributed by Francis Charles Robert Jourdain

HABITS

The claim of this species to a place in the American list rests on a single occurrence at King Island, Alaska, on July 23, 1897.

Spring.—The regularity of the appearance of the dotterel on migration at almost the same spots year after year and approximately about the same time in spring, has proved a great disadvantage to the species, as being very tame and unsuspicious and much sought after, not only as a delicacy for the table, but also on account of the demand for its feathers on the part of fly-fishers, it was mercilessly shot on the way to its breeding grounds in the north of England and Scotland. The usual date of arrival was about the last week of April and the beginning of May and little "trips" might be looked for annually at certain favored spots along the route northward. Exceptionally early arrivals have been recorded on March 25, April 4 and April 8, but these are quite unusual.

Courtship.—Owing no doubt partly to the inaccessible nature of its haunts and also partly to its scarcity, there is nothing on record in the literature as to the courtship of this bird. All writers are agreed that the migrants which pass through England are in small flocks or "trips" and are still unpaired. In 1922 I was on the high field of West Finmark and there was still a great deal of snow about, but here and there islands of gray rock stood out from the snow field. Here we met with dotterel in fair numbers, evidently pairing and house hunting. They shared the ground with a few snow buntings and ptarmigan, and it was obvious that already certain spots had been selected for breeding. Sometimes three birds would be seen wheeling round a bare patch of moor and rock and freely uttering their courting notes, which reminded us of those of the ring plover.

---

[2] See also A Transatlantic Passage of Lapwings, by H. F. Witherby, in British Birds, vol. 22, pp. 6–13.

We saw nothing to suggest the existence of a nuptial song flight, but further observations at this period would be of great interest.

Nesting.—In Scotland and the English lake district the breeding haunts of this species must be looked for at about 2,500 to 3,500 feet or even higher, not on the mountain tops, but on plateaus or slopes below the highest points. Here, where the only vegetation consists of a scanty growth of heather mixed with wiry grass, mosses and lichens, and occasional fragments of gray rock crop out here and there, the dotterel is at home. Few living things haunt their solitudes; a stray raven or eagle may pass over occasionally, but as a rule there is hardly a sign of life anywhere. There is some evidence that one or two "scrapes" are made by one pair of birds, but we have no information as to which of the two is responsible for making the hollow. The eggs are laid in a natural depression adapted by the bird, roughly about three and one-half inches across and fairly deep, as a rule, but generally filled with fragments of lichen or the red leaves of the cranberry, so that the eggs are not difficult to see though their coloring harmonizes with the surroundings.

Eggs.—Normally three, but frequently two only, while instances of four are comparatively rare. They are more elliptical and less pyriform than most waders' eggs and are not unlike some types of eggs of the Arctic tern, though almost always more boldly blotched. In color they range from yellowish olive to clay color, occasionally with a greenish tinge and are boldly spotted and blotched with deep blackish brown and a few ashy shell marks. The average of 100 British eggs, measured by the writer is 41.1 by 28.8 millimeters; the eggs showing the four extremes measure **46.7** by 31.3, 44.5 by **31.5, 37.5** by 29 and 41.6 by **27.4** millimeters.

The sexes are not easy to distinguish in the field, but nearly all the positive evidence from birds shot off the eggs goes to prove that the male is generally to be found incubating. H. H. Slater shot two males from eggs. H. J. Pearson and Gloger had similar experiences, and Bengt Berg, who has watched this bird at close quarters, says that only the male incubates. Many accounts have been published of the behavior of the sitting bird. When flushed from the eggs it returns by a circuitous route, cowering like a mouse, as one observer describes it, sometimes stopping to look round and sometimes doubling back on his tracks like a hunted hare, but all the time, in spite of the numerous turns and twists, gradually approaching the eggs to which at last a short direct run is made. Viewed from behind the bird is exceedingly difficult to follow with the eye in its environment, so that close watching is necessary to mark it down. When the nest has once been discovered, or if the bird is brooding young, it will show extraordinary boldness and will even allow itself to be lifted off the nest by the hand, settling down again as soon as it is removed. Bengt Berg actually succeeded in photographing a bird in the act of accepting a worm from the hand. The only information as to the length of the incubation period is Heyshams oft-quoted assertion that it rarely lasts more than 18 or 20 days. Only a single brood is reared in a season, but the hen will lay a second time about a fortnight after the first clutch has been destroyed.

Young.—In one case when Seton Gordon came across a nest with half-grown chicks, both parents showed signs of great excitement and almost complete disregard of his presence, running backward and forward and frequently uttering their soft whistle which sounded something like *twee, twee, tuur*, the first two notes pitched in a high key and the last a purring sound difficult to express in writing. On other occasions only a single old bird accompanied the young and considerable differences were apparent in their behavior, some showing signs of great anxiety when the young were approached while others were apparently almost indifferent and remained some distance off.

Plumages.—The plumages and molts are fully described in A Practical Handbook of British Birds edited by H. F. Witherby (1920).

Food.—On its breeding grounds it feeds on insects (Diptera, Coleoptera, and their larvae). Collett records *Bembridium* and *Elater* larvae; Petenyi records *Dorcadion, Silpha,* and *Pachygastra.* Earthworms are also taken, according to Saxby, Collett, and Berg. H. J. Pearson also records vegetable matter, apparently seeds of *Empetrum nigrum* or crowberry. H. B. Tristram writes that in its winter quarters in Palestine it subsists largely on small snails (*Helix*).

Behavior.—The dotterel is a quiet, unobtrusive bird, not associating much with other waders and generally met with in small parties out of the breeding season. Its general brown coloring is not striking and no doubt it is frequently overlooked. Its flight is strong, the clean-cut wings, as Gordon says, "moving with swift and powerful strokes only a few feet above the surface of the ground."

Enemies.—Naumann (1887) states that the chief enemies of the dotterel are the falcons (peregrine, hobby, and merlin) and the short-winged hawks (goshawk and sparrow hawk).

Fall.—At Heligoland Gätke (1895) observed large numbers of young birds of the year on passage on one or two occasions; on August 22, 1882, great numbers passed, although wind and rain prevailed, and on September 4 in fine weather one flight alone took five minutes to pass, an unprecedented occurrence.

Winter.—Lord Lilford found it abundant in its winter quarters on the plains of Tunisia consorting with sand grouse, lapwings, golden plover, little bustards, and cranes. He failed to get within shot on foot, but killed many from horse, donkey, or camel, though the birds would run about fearlessly within a few feet of the Arab plowmen.

DISTRIBUTION

Breeding range.—In the British Isles confined to a few localities in the North Pennine and Cumbrian Hills, and in Scotland chiefly to levels of 3,000 to 4,000 feet in the Grampians and Cairngorms, and very locally north and west. On the Continent, in northern Scandinavia, north Finland and Russia, Nova Zembla, Waigatz, and Kolguev. It is found locally in the Riesengebirge, Styria, Transylvania, etc. It is also said to breed in southeast Russia. In Asia it is found across Siberia and on the New Siberian Isles in the tundra and south to the mountain ranges of central Asia.

Winter range.—Extends to North Africa, Palestine and Syria, Iraq, Arabia, and Persia.

Spring migration.—In the western Mediterranean it is scarce on spring passage, but Brehm obtained one at Cartagena, Spain, on March 31. It is also of rare occurrence at Malta in spring and seldom recorded from Greece. At Muonioniska flocks arrive from the south about May 29 and remain for a week or two before proceeding to their breeding grounds on the tundra.

Fall migration.—The great bulk of migrants seem to pass through eastern Europe southward through Palestine, but small numbers pass the Straits of Gibraltar in August and September, and it is not uncommon on Malta in October and November (early date, August 23; late date, December 11). Whitaker notes its arrival in Tunisia in September and October.

Casual records.—Saxby records one on the Shetlands in mid-June, 1869. It is a rare visitor to the Canaries and has not been recorded there for many years. The supposed record from Spitzbergen is probably a mistaken identification, but it has occurred in Japan and on King Island, Alaska (July 23, 1897).

Egg dates.—British Isles, 8 dates between May 30, and June 15; 5 dates between June 21 and July 14; probably including some second layings. In Scandinavia, 14 dates between June 3 and 15; 33 dates between June 16 and 30; 2 dates between July 1 and 6.

SQUATAROLA SQUATAROLA (Linnaeus)

BLACK-BELLIED PLOVER

HABITS

I use the above name rather than the latest check list name, *cynosurae* because I can not see any valid reason for recognizing a North American race of this cosmopolitan species. A slight average difference in size is of little significance in a species which shows such a wide range of individual variation. Recent investigation has, I believe, convinced even Mr. Bangs that this race, which he described, has no standing. The bird which breeds in northeastern Siberia has been separated under the name *hypomelaena;* this may be a good race, though material to establish it is rather scanty in this country. Probably it is the Siberian race which breeds on the Bering Sea coast of Alaska. For life-history purposes the species, as a whole, will be considered.

The black-bellied plover is an aristocrat among shore birds, the largest and strongest of the plovers, a leader of its tribe. It is a distinguished-looking bird in its handsome spring livery of black and white; and its attitude, as it stands like a sentinel on the crest of a sand dune or on some distant mud flat, is always dignified and imposing. Its wild, plaintive, and musical whistle arouses the enthusiasm of the sportsman and serves both as a warning and as an invitation to the lesser fowl that look to it for leadership.

Its breeding range is circumpolar, but decidedly spotty; there are very few places where it breeds at all commonly. On migrations it is widely distributed over nearly all of the Northern Hemisphere. It was never as abundant in this country as the golden plover and apparently never traveled in such immense flocks; hence it was never slaughtered in such enormous numbers. Moreover, it is much wilder, more wary, and better able to take care of itself; consequently it has held its own much better and has proven more of a success in the struggle for existence.

Nevertheless, it has been considerably reduced in numbers during the past 75 years. I am inclined to think that the reduction in numbers is more apparent than real and that the birds have learned to avoid certain localities, where they were once so abundant and where they have been so persistently pursued by gunners. George H. Mackay (1892) has shown a decided decrease on Nantucket, which he attributes to such a cause. From my own 30 years' experience on Cape Cod I know that this has taken place there; I have noticed a gradual decrease in the numbers of black-bellied plover that come to Chatham and Monomoy during the fall flight, until now I often

see no more than half a dozen in a day, where formerly we used to
see them in hundreds. On the spring flight, however, they are often
very abundant there, and apparently have increased since spring
shooting was stopped; formerly they were much more abundant in
the fall than in the spring, but the reverse is now the case. This is
a striking example of the bird's sagacity. Francis N. Balch told me
that he saw at least 4,000 black-bellied plover on Monomoy on one
day during the height of the spring flight in 1927. This compares
favorably with Nuttall's much quoted statement that flocks of more
than 1,000 gathered near Boston about 100 years ago. Some of the
figures given below will show that there are still plenty of black-
bellied plover left in places where they are not too much molested.

Spring.—From the northern part of its winter range in the southern States the black-bellied plover starts on its northward migration
in April and there is a general northward movement, entirely across
the continent, all through May; the last of the migrants do not leave
the northern States until the first week in June. Arthur T. Wayne
(1910) says that, in South Carolina, "when the wind is from the
south and the tide is low in the afternoon, these birds migrate in
small flocks in a northwesterly direction," probably taking an overland route to their breeding grounds. But there is also a heavy
northward migration along the Atlantic coast, at least as far as New
Jersey, whence I believe the main flight swings inland, though there
is a well-marked spring migration in Massachusetts, mainly during
the last half of May, which seems to have increased in recent years.
During the latter part of May, 1927, I was privileged to see, through
the kindness of Dr. Harry C. Oberholser, the greatest flight of
black-bellied plover, dowitchers, and turnstones that I have ever
seen. On the coast of New Jersey, in the vicinity of Tuckerton
Bay and Little Egg Harbor, we made actual counts, or careful estimates, of all birds seen and the totals were far ahead of any he had
recorded there in recent years. Seven day's records show a total
of over 20,000 black-bellied plover; on our two best days, May 27
and 28, we recorded 6,200 and 5,600; and on our poorest day, May 25,
we counted only 238, showing that they came in waves. The black-
bellied plover were often associated in the large flocks with ruddy
turnstones; we saw one immense flock which we estimated to contain 3,500 birds of these two species. This great flock was a thrilling sight, as it swept in over the marsh like a great cloud and
alighted; twice, while we were watching, it arose like a swarm of
insects, circled about, separated into two divisions, joined again, and
alighted. We did not see it depart.

This seems to be the best place on the New Jersey coast to observe
shore birds in large numbers, where they alight to rest and feed on

the large, flat, marshy islands.   These are mud islands raised but a few feet above high water and some of them are partially flooded during spring tides; they are mainly covered with salt-marsh grasses, intersected by tidal creeks and dotted with small pond holes or bare muddy splashes.   The plover alighted on the bare spaces or in the short grass, where the large flocks seen in the distance seemed to whiten the ground.   These large flocks, with sentinels always alert, were utterably unapproachable; and even the small flocks and single birds were as shy as ever.   At low tide they resorted to the extensive mud flats to feed, though they doubtless fed on the meadows also.

On Cape Cod they frequent the same localities as in the fall; my earliest date is April 19 and my latest date for adult birds is June 29.   The spring flights here and in New Jersey are made up mainly of adult birds, mostly in full plumage, but many are mottled and there are always some " pale bellies," or young birds.

The black-bellied plover is an abundant spring migrant up the Mississippi Valley and through central Canada.   We saw it in Saskatchewan during the last week in May and first week in June.   C. G. Harold tells me that it is abundant around the prairie lakes and sloughs in Manitoba.   Prof. William Rowan (1926) calls it abundant in Manitoba; his notes mention a flock estimated at about 3,000 seen on May 23, 1925, at Beaverhill Lake.   He says:

At our lake it is one of the later arrivals in the spring, seldom appearing before the middle of May.   It stays generally in some numbers till the end of the month and may linger till the second week of June.   Flocks are usually small, anything up to 30, except when the birds are ready to start on the next lap north, when they may aggregate many hundreds if not thousands.   On May 23, 1925, we estimated the ground covered by a single flock of grey plovers, knots, and a sprinkling of goldens at about one and a half acres.   They were not scattered, but neither were they closely packed.   The grays made up about 75 per cent of the whole.   The sitting flock looked like a large patch of snow.

S. F. Rathbun has sent me the following notes from Washington which illustrates the abundance of this species on the Pacific coast:

May 12, 1927.   This morning was a dark one with a steady drizzling rain and light wind following the storm of the preceding two days.   On reaching a very wide expanse of grassy salt meadows bordering the bay we found them dotted nearly everywhere with many of the smaller sandpipers and black-bellied plover, the birds being in small and large flocks and mostly grouped around the many shallow pools with which the meadows were flecked.   It was one of the finest sights we have ever seen where shore-birds were concerned.   The beautiful black-bellied plover in full nuptial dress were scattered over a wide area, rarely as single birds, but ordinarily a number in company and not infrequently in flocks of considerable size.   One such flock consisted of 50 individuals, shortly after being joined by another of some 30 birds, the combination of so many large black-breasted birds making a striking sight.   When first alighting the birds would stand motionless, following which they would then move slowly about, although at times individuals might take wing, make several turns in the air and then alight among the others on the ground. When in its full plumage this plover is very noticeable even a long distance off, and when on the ground is always wary and alert. On alighting if it does not stand motionless, the bird will immediately move to the nearest height of land, if such there happens to be, and from such point of vantage will then scan the landscape, and should there happen to be a number in company you will always find two or three maintaining a lookout while the remainder move about rather unconcernedly.

At times associated with the many sandpipers would be a number of knots, but as a rule this latter species was found in flocks by itself with this exception, that always with a flock of knots would be one or more black-bellied plover, such acting as sentinels for the former. And this being the case, the knots would then unconcernedly feed, as they seemed to rely implicitly on the plovers' watchfulness, and we never noted this confidence misplaced. And this fact must in instances prove the salvation of those shore birds more or less unsuspicious and having this plover in company, for they seem to be governed by its actions. Sometimes, with a warning note, the sentinel would suddenly take wing and instantly was followed by the entire flock of other birds en masse, and all would then fly about perhaps for a time before once more alighting on some spot selected by the plover acting as the sentinel. At one time during our stay there were between three and four thousand of these plover on the meadows, and we were told that on the preceding day during the height of the storm this number must have been exceeded.

Courtship.—I have never seen any signs of courtships during the spring migration, though I have often looked for it; nor have I ever seen any mention of it by others. Hence I infer that it is accomplished after the birds arrive on their breeding grounds. Herbert W. Brandt says in his Alaska notes:

During courtship the male spends considerable time on the wing, speeding about like a racer; and amid the constant din of wild-fowl notes his cheery whistle *to lee, to lee,* is one of the pleasant sounds that greet the ear. But once the female is incubating her lord becomes as serious and silent as his sober black waistcoat, so that by early June it seemed as if every plover had left the country. He carries on his courtship regardless of weather, now mounting high, the next moment skimming low, with beautiful and bewildering grace, his wild whistling call meanwhile rising above the din of the storm. The advance guard of migrants of this plover arrived from the south in a " nor'-wester " on May 7, passing like phantom voyagers, and the next instant were lost in mid-air in the swirling snow.

Nesting.—Mr. Brandt has sent me the following notes on the nesting habits of the black-bellied plover in the Hooper Bay region of Alaska:

We found this jauntily attired plover the most common nesting species of the larger shore birds, frequenting the upland rolling tundra, where it preferred the ridges. It often chose for a nesting site the edge of one of the more prominent bluffs which formed the margin of the valleys, from which location the sitting bird could view the entire surrounding country. On these barren areas, where even the close-cropped moss struggles for existence, the vegetation is mottled with black and white, and as a consequence the eggs, in spite of their exposed situation, are very difficult to find. One must almost touch them to be sure that they are there, so completely do they harmonize with their background. This protective coloration is so perfect that in one case a bird deserted its nest and the eggs remained unprotected for three days, during which time jaegers, which were continuously hunting overhead and about, were, even with their sharp eyes, not able to distinguish them.

The nest is prepared by the female by scratching out in the moss a circular depression some 6 inches in diameter and about 1½ inches deep and lining it with a few white sprigs of reindeer moss. Here she lays her four large beautiful eggs, each set showing marked variation in size, shape, and markings. These eggs are distinctive, having a considerably lighter background than those of the golden plover, while the black markings are not so numerous and are more evenly distributed.

They do not nest in proximity to one another, as of the 40 or more nests observed no two were closer together than a quarter of a mile. The female is anything but a close sitter and departs from the eminence on which the nest is situated long before the intruder arrives. If the eggs are fresh, often neither bird exhibits any interest while a person is at the nest and they do not even make their appearance as long as he remains in their vicinity. As the hatching point approaches, however, the birds become more solicitous, protesting vigorously; the male develops into a miltant sentry and rushes out to meet the intruder, repeatedly whistling *lee-ah* in a scolding tone, but staying well out of gun range. He is very combative and drives away any jaeger or large gull that infringes on his area. The female often leaves her eggs to join in the attack, and even the swift-flying long-tailed jaeger can not avoid their onslaughts but beats a hasty retreat. I have seen a male plover strike a jaeger so hard that it reeled unsteadily in mid-air, but the coward made to effort to retaliate.

Roderick MacFarlane's notes contain the records of seven nests found in the vicinity of Franklin Bay, Mackenzie. The nests were all found between July 4 and 10, in 1864 and 1865. The first was on an island in the bay and was " composed of a few withered grasses, placed in a hole or depression on the side, or face, of a very gentle eminence." At least two other nests were on islands. The female was snared on one nest, but was devoured by a snowy owl, which also ate the four eggs.

The nesting habits of the grey plover, as this species is called by Europeans, are apparently similar to those of our bird. Henry J. Pearson (1896), who found seven nests on Kolguev, describes them thus:

The positions of the nests were interesting; only two were on the lower ground near the Gobista; one was a mile both from the sea and the river; all the others—also several old nests—were on the tundra not far from the edge of the bluffs which form the margin of the river basin. Grey plovers seem to prefer this position, which gives them good posts of observation and allows them to take their young easily into the marshes below to feed. We found a ready way of locating the nest of this bird was to watch a pair of Richardson's skua hunting over the tundra, for as soon as they approached the nest of the plovers, both the latter rose into the air and drove the skuas away. We never observed these birds breeding near each other, each pair appearing to take possession of about a mile of country. All the nests were slight depressions in the peat, lined with a little lichen.

If the black-bellied plover breeds in Greenland it must be very rare there, for Dr. W. Elmer Ekblaw tells me that he saw it only twice during the four years that he spent there. A flock that he saw on Sutherland Island, south of Etah, on August 17, 1914, was made up of old and young birds and the latter may have been reared there.

Eggs.—Mr. Brandt has described the eggs so much better than I can that I prefer to quote from his notes, as follows:

Of the more than 40 nests that we examined of the black-bellied plover each held four eggs when its complement was completed. Owing to the proportionate thickness compared with its length the shape of the egg is ovate pyriform inclining to subpyriform. The shell is strong, finely granular, and on every egg I have seen the lustre is uniformly dull. The ground color and markings vary so much that hardly any two sets are the same. This ground color appears to follow three different shades, which are pinkish, greenish, or brownish. These types are often quite pronounced when the eggs are fresh, but the delicate tints fade with age. The pink type ranges from "pale ochraceous salmon" to "light buff"; the green type is "pale glass green"; while the brown variety is often as dark as "cinnamon drab." The eggs are never densely spotted and are always most heavily marked about the large end, but the very tip of this end is usually bare of spots, so that, if viewed upon the long axis, a wreath of spots is observed. These spots are usually medium in size and are distinct, although in a few unusual examples the spots become confluent at the large end. The primary markings are irregularly circular and never elongated, while upon the unusual egg these jet ornaments are of thumb-nail size In rare instances the markings assume the form of short penlike scratches which mark the surface at various angles in the same manner as is occasionally found on the eggs of other members of the Charadriidae. The spots are uniformly "blackish brown" to black, but, where the pigment is spread more thinly, "deep brownish drab" or "dusky drab" tones may be noted, while here and there "hazel" to "liver brown" may be observed where the pigment is extremely thin. The underlying spots are never numerous but always present and are more prominent on some specimens than on others. They vary in tone from "pale mouse gray" to "deep violet gray," dependent upon the ground color, while one specimen with small primary spots is conspicuously beautified with "chicory blue." A series of these noble eggs is a study in black and whitish, and while the individual egg is conspicuous, yet, when resting on their mottled birthplace, it is evident that nature has most happily endowed them with protective coloration.

The measurements of 174 eggs average 52.2 by 36.5 millimeters; the eggs showing the four extremes measure **58** by 38, 55.5 by **38.2, 47.5** by 34.7 and 51.9 by **34** millimeters. The measurements of eggs from different localities do not throw much light on the relationship of the proposed subspecies; 120 eggs from Hooper Bay average 52.4 by 36.7, 14 eggs from Franklin Bay average 52 by 36, and 40 eggs from European localities average 51.6 by 35.9 millimeters.

Young.—Several observers have proven that both sexes share in the incubation. Mr. Brandt says in his notes:

The first downy young appeared on June 21 after an incubation lasting 23 days, and they were just as inconspicuous and distinctive as were the eggs whence they emerged. At that time both parents were fearless in their defense, employing all the wing-dragging and distress maneuvers known to ground-nesting birds. This was exhibited even by the male, which is rather unusual. The downy young are variegated, sulphur-yellow and black above, and harmonize well with the abundant yellowish moss of the tundra. They conceal themselves by lying with head down and with their legs drawn under their bodies and are thus very difficult to detect.

Plumages.—In natal down the young black-bellied plover resembles the young golden plover, except that the band around the neck and the under parts are purer white. The forehead, crown, and sides of the head are variegated with black, white, and bright yellows, varying from " lemon chrome " to "baryta yellow "; the back, rump, wings, and thighs are mottled with black and the above shades of yellow; the nape, a broad band around the neck and the entire under parts are pure white; the cheeks below the eyes are white bordered below by a black stripe extending from the bill to the auriculars.

In fresh juvenal plumage, as seen on the breeding grounds, the forehead and lores are mainly white; the crown and all the upper parts of the body are sepia, the feathers broadly tipped or notched with yellow, varying from " light cadmium yellow " to " light orange yellow," the spots being largest and brightest on the rump; the chin is white, but the rest of the under parts are buffy gray and pale buff, the feathers of the throat, breast, and flanks with median dusky streaks and faint dusky tips; the greater wing coverts are more narrowly edged, but more conspicuously notched than in the adult. Young birds are in juvenal plumage during migration, but the yellows have mostly faded to creamy white or white, though the rump spots are often quite yellow. A partial postjuvenal molt takes place late in the fall and in winter, involving much of the body plumage, but generally not the rump and back. Generally the molt is finished by December, but often not until January; by this time the light edgings and notches have worn away, giving the bird a very dark appearance. The first winter plumage is much like the adult winter, but it can be distinguished by the creamy or golden tips and notches of the juvenal wing coverts, by the faded yellow spots on the rump and by some old, worn scapulars and tertials.

Young birds have an incomplete and very variable first prenuptial molt, at which the sexes begin to differentiate. Young males acquire more of the adult nuptial plumage than young females; sometimes the breasts become almost wholly clear black; but in the upper parts there is generally only a sprinkling of new, adult, broadly white-tipped feathers, most of the first winter plumage being retained, with some old, worn scapulars, tertials, and tails. Young females show much less black on the breast and much more winter plumage on the back. Young birds apparently renew the primaries in February and March and the first postnuptial molt, the following summer and fall, produces the adult winter plumage.

Adults have a partial prenuptial molt between February and May, involving the body plumage, usually the tail, some of the wing coverts and tertials, but not all the scapulars, back and rump feathers. The complete postnuptial molt, begins with the acquisition of white feathers in the under body plumage in August and the body molt lasts through September, while the birds are migrating. The wings are molted later, from September to December. In winter plumage the black breast is entirely replaced by dull white, more or less marked or shaded with pale, ashy brown; and the upper parts are dull, ashy brown, the feathers tipped with white and subterminally shaded with blackish brown. No trace of the nuptial body plumage is left and adults and young look very much alike.

Food.—The main feeding grounds of the black-bellied plover along the coasts are on the broad, tidal, sand flats, and mud flats; there are many such flats about Chatham and other places on Cape Cod, where the receding tide leaves many square miles of flat mud or sand, dotted with little islands of tall marsh grass. These are favorite resorts for plover, where they may be seen away off on the edge of the water, perhaps a mile from the shore, feeding on marine worms, small mollusks, crustaceans, and marine insects. As the advancing tide drives them in onto the marshes or sand dunes, they find other food; Mr. Mackay (1892) says that "they feed also on the larvae of one of the cutworms (Noctuidae) which they obtain on the marshes. They also eat the large whitish maritime grasshopper (*Oedipoda maritima*)."

In the interior they fed, around the shores of the larger lakes and on open flats, on various forms of aquatic life. They also resort to some extent to meadows and upland pastures, where the grass is short, and to plowed fields; here they do some good by devouring grasshoppers, locusts, cutworms, grubs, beetles, and earthworms. They also eat some seeds and berries. Mr. Forbush (1912) says that Prof. Samuel Aughey found the stomachs of two of these birds "crammed with the destructive Rocky Mountain locust."

Grinnell, Bryant, and Storer (1918) mention a bird taken in California which had in its stomach "14 small snails, 1 small bivalve mollusk, and parts of 2 or more small crabs." I once watched a bird in Florida, which fed for some time on the broken remains of a dead crab.

Behavior.—Mr. Brandt, in his notes, pays the following tribute to the power of flight of this fine bird:

Only those who have met the lordly black-bellied plover on his native heath can appreciate how he seems to rule with a martial air the domains under

his control. Powerful of wing stroke, trim of form as a grayhound, and erect
of carriage, this, the largest of our common plovers, is the athlete of the
wild birds of the North. Neatly vestured in his silvery white and ebony black,
he is the fleetest racer of the air among a field of highly developed specialists.
To consider him swifter than the graceful long-tailed jaeger or the far-ranging
golden plover is indeed a startling claim, but my judgment is that the black-
bellied plover can pass through the air faster than any other feathered crea-
ture in the North. At some time in the future it will be of great interest
for some enterprising ornithologist to test out in his racing aeroplane the
various flying speeds of the northern birds. It is my prediction that the shore
birds will be found to lead the field there, and that the big black-bellied plover
will surpass them all. The Pacific godwit is a wonderful air master, darting
here and there with but the slightest effort, yet our plover seems to have only
one gear, and that high speed. This may be best appreciated during the gales
that are of such frequent occurrence in that storm-swept land. The bird can
quarter, or fly into the teeth of the wind, with such power as almost to
disregard it.

The above picture is not overdrawn, for this plover is one of our
strongest fliers. Migrating flocks fly high in great bunches or massed
formations, after the manner of many ducks. When flying short
distances or when coming in over the flats they fly low and are often
strung out in lines. Their flight seems to me to be steadier or more
duck-like than that of the smaller shore birds. The powerful, pointed
wings move very swiftly; Doctor Oberholser and I once made a number of accurate counts of the wing beats of this and several other
species in normal flight; eight counts for this plover averaged 240
beats a minute, or 4 beats a second; the slowest was 225 and the
fastest 250.

The black-bellied plover is wont to stand erect, with head held
high, in an attitude of dignified yet alert repose; it can be recognized by its bold outline almost as far as it can be seen, away out
on the shimmering sands. It is a wary sentinel for all of its smaller
companions and it is utterly useless to attempt to approach it in an
open situation. It runs swiftly along at the water's edge, stopping
frequently to look about or striking quickly at some morsel of food.
Dr. Charles W. Townsend (1905) says that they throw "the feet
well out in front as they run. Their usual stride is 3 or 4 inches,
but I have several times measured tracks that were 6 inches apart."
It is interesting to watch them bathing; they squat down in shallow
water and spend much time in splashing, fluttering the wings, and
dipping their heads; then comes the drying process, shaking the
water out of the body plumage, flapping wings and wagging tails,
followed by a long period of careful preening. Francis H. Allen
writes to me of another method of bathing, as follows:

At one time they took to bathing, one after another, and one pretty little
performance was to fly up about a foot and come splashing down into the water
with much fluttering of wings. One started this play, and another and another

took it up till half a dozen or more had gone through it. They also hopped on one foot in the water, as shore birds so often do on the beach, and, in this, one set the fashion and others followed it. This hopping altogether seems to be quite common play with various species.

Like most shore birds, they can swim quite easily, as the following note from Francis M. Weston will show:

On March 27 I was watching a small flock of black-bellied plovers feeding on a sand bar at low tide. One of the birds was separated from the others by a deep pool about 6 feet wide, and, in order to join them, entered the water and swam across the pool. While in the water, it reminded me very much of a diminutive gull—it floated high in the "stern" with the forward part of the body low in the water. The transit of the pool was made so quickly that there was no time for a detailed study of the bird's motions. Thinking that the plover was wounded and had had to swim through lack of ability to fly, I approached the flock, when all took wing and flew to another bar several hundred yards distant. An examination of the pool showed that it was more than a foot deep—far too deep for a bird of that size to wade.

Voice.—To my mind the whistle of the black-bellied plover is one of the sweetest and most fascinating of all the Limicoline voices; it is not quite as melodious as that of the piping plover, nor is it quite as startling as the loud call of the yellowlegs; but it heralds the coming of one of our finest shore birds and hence it produces a thrill. The sportsman loves to hear it and he can imitate it quite easily. John T. Nichols has contributed the following notes on it:

The flight note of this species is a clear, mellow, ringing whistle—*pe-oo-ee*. Although shortened and otherwise varied at different times, this note is the only one ordinarily heard from single individuals or small flocks. In general it may be said that the diagnostic flight or identification note of plovers is used more extensively than in yellowlegs and other species, for instance, and that they seem to have less variety of calls.

A second note heard from a flock of birds either in the air or alighted, and in chorus when such a flock is flushed, circling and hovering in uncertain manner, is a soft, mellow *quu-hu*. A dissimilar unloud *cuk cuk cuk, cuk, cuk, cuk cuk cuk cuk* which I heard from a single bird in Florida in September, alighted with decoys and running about, completes my knowledge of the calls of this plover.

The ordinary call note, referred to above, has a sweet, mellow, and plaintive quality, with a tinge of wildness, which enlivens the solitude of the ocean beaches; I should write it *pee-u-wee*, the first, loud, rich, and prolonged, the second lower and shorter, and the third higher pitched, more plaintive, and softer. Grinnell, Bryant, and Storer (1918) describe the note as "a loud, ringing *wher-rell*, far reaching and, at a distance, clear and mellow in quality." Dr. E. R. P. Janvrin tells me that he has "also heard them utter a loud note resembling that of the common tern, but no so harsh and more musical, which is apparently an alarm note."

Field marks.—The black axillars, on the under side of the wing next to the body, are very conspicuous when the bird is flying and

form the most reliable field mark in all plumages. The general outline of the bird is characteristic, with its large head, short, heavy bill,
and erect carriage. The upper parts are light colored in all plumages,
especially so in spring, the upper tail coverts are nearly white and
there is a white band in the spread wing. In the fully black-breasted
plumage the black of the under parts does not extend so far back as
on the golden plover and the crown is much whiter. The presence
of a hind toe may be detected at a short distance.

Fall.—The southward migration begins early in July and spreads
out entirely across the continent. Before the end of August the last
of the black-bellied plover have left their breeding grounds. The first
of the adults sometimes reach Massachusetts as early as the second
week in July; my earliest date is July 7; but the main flight comes
in August and most of the adults have left by the middle of September, though I have seen adults here as late as October 29. The young
birds come later; I have seen them as early as August 10, but they
usually do not come in any numbers until September, and the heaviest
flight is between September 15 and October 15; a few linger into
November. While here they mingle freely with knots, turnstones,
and red-backed sandpipers; any of the smaller sandpipers are likely
to be associated with them.

Professor Rowan (1923) gives much the same dates for Alberta
and says that the young birds are plentiful through October and
"may stay right into November, even for a week or two after the
lakes have frozen over." M. P. Skinner tells me that he has seen them
in Yellowstone Park late in September with the thermometer down
to zero. Mr. Rathbun tells me that "the black-bellied plover is a
regular and somewhat common spring and autumn migrant along
the coast of Washington and about Puget Sound." D. E. Brown's
notes from that region give dates extending from August 26 to
October 2.

Game.—It is as a game bird that the black-bellied plover or
"beetlehead," as it is called on Cape Cod, has achieved its greatest
reputation. There is no shore bird that is better known or more
eagerly sought; for it is not only a large plump bird but it is a swift
flier, and one of the wariest, most sagacious, and most difficult of the
beach birds to secure. To meet with any success in shooting this
plover the sportsman must be familiar with its habits in the locality
where he is shooting, must be well concealed in a skillfully made
blind, and must know how to imitate its notes perfectly. The old
black-bellied birds are particularly wary and will not come to the
decoys unless the surroundings are quite natural in appearance. Mr.
Mackay (1892) says:

After many unsuccessful attempts to capture them one becomes imbued with
the fact that the old birds are well calculated, under ordinary circumstances,

to avoid danger ; they succumb only to those sportsmen who have served a long apprenticeship, and who have acquired a knowledge of their habits.

John C. Cahoon (1888) a veteran gunner and collector, has described various methods used on Cape Cod, as follows:

Stands are built on the meadows and marshes by cutting bushes of about the proper height and sticking them in the grass or mud so as to form a circle of convenient size for one or more gunners. If bushes can not be found handily, dry seaweed, grass, and other materials are sometimes used. On the mud flats bunches of sedge grass afford concealment, but the most successful method is to make a bar in the sand flats and sink a box, or dig a pit in the sand. It requires considerable labor to build and keep a bar in order, also to sink a box. The bar is laid bare before any of the surrounding flats, consequently the birds, finding no other feeding place uncovered, fly to the bar. One other way in which large numbers are sometimes taken is to find out the locality on the high beaches where they roost during high tide, and digging a hole in the sand for a place of concealment. They usually come to the same spot to roost each high tide and by examining the beach these places can be easily found, by the numerous footprints in the sand. The blind should be completed soon after the tide begins to flow, as these birds leave the flats as soon as the tide commences to cover them. For the young, or " pale bellies," all that is needed is a pit dug with the sand thrown out around the top edge and a few decoys placed out the right distance from the pit. For the old " black breasts " it is necessary to have the top covered over with boards and dry sand spread on them and have an opening in the sides and front, to shoot from. It is best not to put out any decoys, as the old birds will seldom alight to decoys on the beaches, even if they are made to look very natural.

Most of my shooting has been done on the flats or beaches, from sedge grass or seaweed blinds. On the inner side of Monomoy the water is very shallow and at dead low tide the birds are away off, perhaps a mile from shore, on the edge of the water. The flats near shore are dotted with islands of sedge grass, where the gunner can easily conceal himself in the tall grass, with the decoys set out on the open mud. As the tide comes in rapidly over the shallows, preceded by an advancing line of foam, the birds begin to move, flying up to the marshes or beaches. A blind may be made on the inner side of the beach by digging a deep hole in the sand and piling up seaweed around it. In either case the blind must be in some well-established fly way between the feeding grounds and the resting places and must be well enough made to offer good concealment. The best shooting comes on the first part of the ebb and the latter part of the flood tide. The gunner must keep out of sight and be ever on the alert, for at any moment he may hear the wild, ringing cry or see single birds or small flocks dash by at high speed. They seldom alight to the decoys, though they often circle over them and are usually much scattered.

I have often found it good sport to stalk " beetleheads " on the beaches, where they rest at high tide. One kills very few birds in this way, as the chances are all in favor of the bird. Young birds are less wary than old blackbreasts and a few can sometimes be obtained by crawling up back of a sand dune and shooting them as they jump. This involves plenty of exercise, requires perseverance, and calls for quick work with the gun, and the bird generally escapes. Walter H. Rich (1907) has described this very well, as follows:

Yet let the gunner peep ever so carefully over the edge of the bank where he lies hidden and each wary feeder becomes at once a motionless statue. Had he not seen their animation a moment before he might think he had come upon a wooden congregation of decoys. While he is still they make no movement, but let him stir, either for nearer approach or to draw back from view that he may get a better position, and the instant his head goes out of sight behind the long salt grass the flock noiselessly takes wing with easy, graceful flight, alighting some hundreds of yards away to feed comfortably until the dangerous admirer, with stealthy caution and much toilsome trudging through the shifting sand dunes, once more approaches too near for safety, when the same performance again takes place. It makes little difference how the approach is managed, the result is generally the same; the gunner peers cautiously at the spot where a moment since the flock was busily feeding, and seeing them not soon discovers them 200 yards away, apparently just as ready to tease him as before.

Winter.—These plover, no longer black bellied now, spend the winter in the southern United States and from there southward to central Brazil and Peru. They winter commonly as far north as South Carolina and the southern half of California, less commonly in North Carolina, and casually farther north. I have seen them in immense flocks on the great mud flats among the Florida keys and we had them with us all winter on the beaches and sandy islands about Tampa Bay. They showed their sagacity by their confiding tameness on the protected bathing beaches and by their extreme wildness on the outer islands, where it was almost impossible to approach them within gunshot range.

The gray plover of the Eastern Hemisphere goes as far south in winter as southern Africa, Madagascar, and Australia. Charles Barrett, referring to Australia, says in his notes:

This species sometimes associates in large flocks, but more often is seen singly, or in pairs, feeding on mud flats and along the sea beaches. It is a wary bird. Arriving in spring (September) or early summer in the southern portions of the continent it becomes widely distributed, but seems to restrict itself mainly to the seashore. However, it does wander inland at times, having been recorded, for example, from the midlands of Tasmania. It leaves Australia apparently in March or April (autumn) on the northern flight to its breeding haunts.

DISTRIBUTION

Range.—Cosmopolitan.

Breeding range.—The breeding range of the black-bellied plover in North America is confined to the Arctic coast north to Alaska (Wainwright, Point Barrow, Colville River delta, Barter Island,

Collison Point, and probably Demarcation Point); northern Macken-
zie (Cape Bathurst and probably Cape Kellett); Victoria Land
(Taylor Island); and Franklin (Fury Point and Melville Peninsula).
East to Franklin (Melville Peninsula); possibly Keewatin (Cape
Fullerton); and possibly Greenland (Sutherland Island). South to
possibly Keewatin (Cape Fullerton); Mackenzie (probably Bernard
Harbor, Coleville Hills, and Franklin Bay); and Alaska (Hooper
Bay). West to Alaska (Hooper Bay and Wainwright).

In common with several other shore birds, nonbreeding specimens
of this species are frequently found during the summer months at
points far south of the breeding grounds. At this season they have
been taken or observed in Maine (Western Egg Rock); Massachusetts
(Monomoy Island, Marthas Vineyard, and Harvard); New York
(Quogue, Freeport, Rockaway, Long Beach, and Geneva); New
Jersey (Tuckerton, Great Bay, and Absecon Bay); Ohio (Bay
Point); Virginia (Cobb Island and Cape Charles region); South
Carolina (Mount Pleasant, Magnolia Beach, and White Point
Swash); Florida (Fort De Soto, Amelia Island, Key West, Fer-
nandina, and Daytona Beach); Alabama (Dauphin Island); Louisi-
ana (Breton Island); Texas (Corpus Christi); Jamaica (Port
Henderson); and the Galapagos Islands.

In the Palaearctic region it breeds from the eastern tundras of
Arctic Europe eastward throughout Arctic Asia to Kamchatka and
on Kolguev and the Siberian Islands.

Winter range.—The American winter range extends north to
Washington (Strait of Juan de Fuca, and Dungeness Spit); Texas
(Brownsville, Corpus Christi, Rockport, and Matagorda); Louisi-
ana (Breton Islands); Alabama (Dauphin Island); and Virginia
(Wallops Island). East to Virginia (Wallops Island and Sandy
Island); North Carolina (Pea Island and Southport); South
Carolina (Mount Pleasant and Port Royal); Georgia (Darien,
Cumberland, and St. Marys); Florida (Amelia Island, Fort George,
Seabreeze, Mosquito Inlet, Lake Okeechobee, Miami, and Upper
Matecumbe Key); the Bahama Islands (Abaco, Eleuthera, Watling,
Acklin, and Great Inagua); Haiti (Monte Christi); probably French
Guiana (Cayenne); and Brazil (Cajetuba and the Amazon region).
South to Brazil (Amazon region); and Peru (Callao). West to Peru
(Callao, Chimbote, and Tumbez); Ecuador (Bay of Santa Elena);
the Galapagos Islands (Albemarle); Colombia (Cartagena); prob-
ably Costa Rica (mouth of the Martina River); probably Guatemala
(Chiapam); Oaxaca (San Mateo); Lower California (San Jose del
Cabo, La Paz, and San Geronimo Island); California (Coronado,
Wilmington, Santa Cruz Island, Los Banos, San Francisco, and
mouth of Eel River); Oregon (Newport); and Washington (Point
Chehalis and Strait of Juan de Fuca).

Three specimens at Cape Cod, Massachusetts, in December, 1872, constitute the only winter record for that region.

In the eastern hemisphere it winters from the coasts of southern Europe and Asia to southern Africa, Madagascar, the Seychelles, and Australia.

Spring migration.—Early dates of spring arrival are: Pennsylvania, Neville Island, April 26; New Jersey, Atlantic City, April 27, Cape May, April 30, and Ocean City, May 5; New York, Montauk Point Light, April 30, Great South Bay, May 1, and Long Beach, May 2; Rhode Island, South Auburn, April 23, and Newport, May 9; Massachusetts, Cape Cod, April 19, Monomoy Island, April 22, and Billingsgate, April 27; Nova Scotia, Pictou, May 17; Missouri, Courtney, April 1, and Concordia, April 19; Illinois, Hennepin, April 2, and Rantoul, April 16; Indiana, Knox County, March 30; Ohio, Oberlin, April 24; Michigan, Forestville, May 2; Ontario, Toronto, May 11, and Oshawa, May 14; Iowa, Keokuk, April 22, Sioux City, May 8, and New Hampton, May 12; Wisconsin, Racine, April 14, and Leeds Center, April 17; Minnesota, Heron Lake, April 21, and Hutchinson, May 7; Nebraska, Vesta, April 21, and Lincoln, May 10; South Dakota, Pitrodie, May 1, and Vermilion, May 3; North Dakota, Rice Lake, May 5, Bathgate, May 9, and Harrisburg, May 10; Manitoba, Margaret, May 5, and Whitewater, May 20; Saskatchewan, Wiseton, May 4, and Indian Head, May 9; Mackenzie, Fort Resolution, June 2; Colorado, Denver, May 11, and Loveland, May 14; Utah, Provo, May 11; Alberta, Camrose, May 1, Sturgeon River, May 12, Tofield, May 19, Veteran, May 22, and Fort Chipewyan, May 23; British Columbia, Comox, April 23, and Courtenay, April 24; Yukon, Dawson, May 20; and Alaska, Kuiu Island, May 3, Fort Kenai, May 6, Hooper Bay, May 9, and mouth of the Yukon River, May 12.

Last dates of spring departure are: Panama, mouth of the Rio Venado, March 27; Bahama Islands, Andros, April 14; Green Cay, April 29, and Nassau, April 28; Florida, St. Marks, May 8, New Smyrna, May 14, Pensacola, May 16, Daytona Beach, May 24, and Cedar Keys, May 27; Alabama, Dauphin Island, May 19; Georgia, Savannah, May 13; South Carolina, Frogmore, May 17, and Hilton Head, May 24; North Carolina, Cape Hatteras, May 20, and Churchs Island, May 30; Virginia, Cobb Island, May 19, and Wallops Island, May 26; Maryland, Dulaneys Valley, May 13; Pennsylvania, Erie, May 19; New Jersey, Cape May County, May 23, and Elizabeth, May 30; New York, Jamaica, May 26, Lake Canandaigua, May 30, and Orient Point, May 30; Connecticut, Westport, May 28, Fairfield, May 30, and Norwalk, June 1; Rhode Island, Block Island, May

29, and South Auburn, June 5; Massachusetts, Ipswich, May 30, Dennis, June 2, and Cape Cod, June 6; Quebec, Godbout, June 9; Louisiana, Mermerton, May 2; Missouri, Concordia, May 23; Kentucky, Bowling Green, June 3; Illinois, Chicago, May 26, and Waukegan, May 27; Indiana, Indianapolis, May 30; Ohio, Oberlin, May 22, Youngstown, May 23, and Painesville, May 27; Michigan, Detroit, May 26, Jackson, May 28, and Charity Island, June 1; Ontario, Bowmanville, May 25, Toronto, May 26, Kingston, May 30; Iowa, Emmetsburg, May 25, National, May 26, and Sioux City, May 31; Wisconsin, Shiocton, May 27, and Madison, May 30; Minnesota, Waseca, May 24, Hallock, May 26, and Heron Lake, June 2; Texas, Point Isabel, June 2, and Corpus Christi, June 7; Oklahoma, Norman, May 25; Kansas, Wichita County, May 22; Nebraska, Alda, May 21; South Dakota, Vermilion, May 24, and Forestburg, June 1; North Dakota, Jamestown, May 15, Towner County, May 25, and Jerusalem, June 1; Manitoba, Margaret, May 31, and Shoal Lake, June 3; Saskatchewan, Hay Lake, June 2, and Kutanajan Lake, June 10; Colorado, Denver, May 30; Montana, Baker, May 23; Alberta, Flagstaff, June 1, and Fort Chipewyan, June 8; Yucatan, Cozumel Island, April 18; Oaxaca, San Mateo del Mar, May 15; Vera Cruz, Tampico, April 10; Lower California, San Geronimo Island, April 14, and San Quentin, May 10; California, Alameda, May 21, and Santa Barbara, May 26; Washington, "east side of mountains," May 18; and British Columbia, Masset, June 16.

Fall migration.—Early dates of fall arrival are: British Columbia, Comox, July 5; Oregon, coastal region, July 26; California, Venice, July 4; Alameda, July 22, and Santa Barbara, July 24; Alberta, Alliance, August 3; Colorado, Denver, August 21, and Barr, August 31; Saskatchewan, Kiddleston, July 7, and Last Mountain Lake, August 19; Manitoba, Oak Lake, July 31, and Shoal Lake, August 8; North Dakota, Grafton, August 23; South Dakota, Forestburg, August 11; Nebraska, Lincoln, August 7; Texas, Rockport, August 12, Tivoli, August 15, and San Angelo, August 31; Wisconsin, Lake Koshkonong, August 14; Iowa, Burlington, August 13; Ontario, Toronto, July 23, Beamsville, August 2, and Hamilton, August 9; Michigan, Little Lake, July 24, Greenville, August 10, and Charity Island, August 20; Ohio, Painesville, August 12, and Columbus, August 23; Indiana, Millers, August 8; Illinois, La Grange, August 21, and Chicago, August 24; Quebec, Godbout, July 30, and Bras d'Or, August 5; Maine, Portland, July 31; Massachusetts, Essex, July 18, Attleboro Falls, July 21, and Monomoy Island, July 7; Rhode Island, Point Judith, July 12, and South Auburn, August 13; New York, Quogue, July 1, Montauk Point Light, July 20, Orient, July 24, and Shinnecock Bay, August 5; New Jersey, Great Bay,

July 19, Stone Harbor, July 22, and Cape May, July 27; Pennsylvania, Erie, August 1, and Whites Island, August 10; Maryland, Plum Point, August 10; Virginia, Cobb Island, August 19; North Carolina, Charlotte Inlet, July 4, Cape Fear, July 7, and Carolina Beach, July 10; Georgia, Savannah, August 12; Alabama, Dauphin, and Petit Bois Islands, August 21; Florida, Key West, August 8, Daytona Beach, August 17, and Pensacola, August 28; and Lesser Antilles, Barbados, August 22, and Grenada, August 27.

Late dates of fall departure are: Alaska, Wainwright, September 13, Taku River, September 26, Kenai River, October 7, and Craig, November 14; British Columbia, Okanagan Landing, September 28, and Chilliwack, October 23; Alberta, Vermilion-Innisfrea, September 16, and Whitford Lake, October 29; Montana, Priest Butte Lakes, September 4; Colorado, Fort Collins, October 28, and Denver, November 13; Mackenzie, Great Bear Lake, September 5, and Fort Simpson, September 17; Keewatin, Swampy Lake, September 5; Manitoba, Oak Lake, October 31; North Dakota, Grafton, October 27; South Dakota, Fort Sisseton, October 25, and Sioux Falls, November 7; Nebraska, Lincoln, October 21; Kansas, Hamilton, October 13, and Lawrence, October 29; Minnesota, Minneapolis, October 28; Wisconsin, Lake Mills, October 2; Iowa, Keokuk, October 28, and Sioux City, November 3; Ontario, Point Pelee, October 18, Ottawa, November 11, and Kingston, November 16; Michigan, Detroit, November 3, Sault Ste. Marie, November 5, and Charity Island, November 21; Ohio, Youngstown, November 11, Painesville, November 29; Illinois, Chicago, November 3, and La Grange, November 6; Missouri, Independence, November 5, and Courtney, November 9; Franklin, Winter Island, August 17; Nova Scotia, Pictou, October 11, and Wolfville, November 8; Quebec, Montreal, November 1, and Tabusintoc, November 3; Massachusetts, Monomoy Island, November 14, and Boston, November 29; Connecticut, South Norwalk, November 7; New York, Orient, November 26, and Long Beach, November 26; New Jersey, Sandy Hook, October 25, and Cape May County, November 7; and Pennsylvania, Erie, November 10.

Casual records.—Two specimens of the black-bellied plover were obtained on Clipperton Island, November 19, 1901; Gundlach reported taking two at San Juan Bay, Porto Rico, Stahl had two others, while F. A. Potts saw one near Central Aguirre on September 9 and 10, 1921, and a flock of six or seven noted on several occasions near Salinas, during December, 1920; the species is of casual occurrence in Bermuda (Mangrove Bay, September 5, 1848, Sand Hills, November 5, 1874, and Warnick Camp, November 13, 1874); both Reinhardt and Hagerup record them from Greenland; and one (possibly the European form) was obtained in late October, at

Kaalualu, Hawaii (Henshaw).   Although seemingly on the regular
migration route, the only records for Arkansas are two specimens
taken at Fort Smith, September 19, 1892.

Egg dates.—Bering Sea coast of Alaska: 24 records, May 27 to
June 4; 16 records, May 29 and 30.   Arctic coasts of Alaska and
Canada: 26 records, June 10 to July 11; 13 records, June 28 to
July 5.

PLUVIALIS APRICARIA ALTIFRONS (Brehm)

EUROPEAN GOLDEN PLOVER

Contributed by Francis Charles Robert Jourdain

HABITS

The claim of the golden plover of Europe to a place in the American list rests on its occurrence not infrequently in Greenland.   The
latest authority on Greenland birds, Mr. E. Lehn Schiöler, in his
great work *Danmarks Fugle* (vol. 2), refers the Greenland birds to
the northern race of European golden plover, *Pluvialis apricarius
altifrons* (Brehm).   It is now generally agreed that there are two races
of this species, and that the black breast is more strongly developed
on the northern form, while the southern race, *P. apricarius apricarius* (Linnaeus) has only a marbling of black on the breast in
spring.   In Greenland it has occurred both on the east and west
sides, but has not been proved to breed there though suspected of
doing so.

Spring.—In the British Isles the northern golden plovers are
said by Abel Chapman to arrive in Northumberland as early as mid
February, spreading over the lower ground and remaining in packs,
while the breeding birds arrive later and are soon distributed over
the moors in pairs.   While the southern birds remain on the moorlands to breed, the northern visitors pass on to their nesting grounds
in the Faroes, Iceland, and Scandinavia.

Courtship.—Our information is, as might be expected, scanty,
owing to the inaccessible nature of its breeding ground and its retiring habits.   Abel Chapman (1889) describes the loud wild spring
call, which he renders as *tirr-pee-you*, and adds that after this has
ceased one hears only the well-known plaintive pipe of alarm and a
peculiar rippling song or warble which is wholly indescribable.
This, he says, is the joyous note of courtship and is analogous to the
drumming of the snipe, etc.   A fuller description is that of Seton
Gordon (1915) who writes as follows:

During the season of courtship and indeed up to June is heard the song of
the golden plover and this song is one of the most striking things in the habits

of moorland birds. Before commencing to sing the cock bird mounts into the air to a height of at least 100 feet and flies slowly, deliberately around the spot where his mate is listening to him below, uttering as he flies a musical whistling cry of two syllables sounding like *whee-wheeu*, the last being long drawn out. His flight during this time is quite distinctive, he no longer cleaves the air with sharp and rapid wing beats, but moves his wings with slow deliberate strokes, holding them V-shaped for an instant between the beats. Should he cease his song—even for a few moments—the normal flight is at once resumed. His cry on these occasions carries over a great stretch of moor, and I think can be heard at a greater distance even than the vibrating notes of the curlew. After some time, during which these long-drawn whistles are regularly continued, the singer shoots earthward, uttering, just as he is reaching the ground, a curious purring cry, repeated rapidly five or six times. On paper the sounds resemble *trooeu, trooeu, trooeu*. These descriptions apply strictly to the southern race, but the habits of the two forms in the breeding season are identical and the Icelandic birds perform their song flights in the same way as the Scotch birds. Hantzsch points out very justly that the golden plover is not at all quarrelsome in disposition, and though rival males may vie in song with one another they meet frequently quite amicably and the natives have long noted the toleration which the plover extends to the dunlin and which has earned for the latter the name Loa-thrall, or, as our forefathers put it, Plover's-page.

Nesting.—There is no concealment about the nest; the vast expanses of moorland or tundra are sufficient protection. Sometimes the nest hollow may be found on a tiny hillock, sometimes in wiry grass or among sparse or burnt heather. Such lining as there is is usually scanty and consists of the materials at hand, leaves, bents, or a bit of heather stem. Unoccupied scrapes may generally be found near at hand. Even where the birds are plentiful, as in some parts of Iceland, the nests are generally a considerable distance apart.

Eggs.—Normally four in number, occasionally three only, especially in late layings. Hantzsch (1905) records one instance of five in a nest, and five have also been met with in the southern race. They are pyriform and laid with the points meeting and are very beautiful. The ground varies from a pale greenish blue to very rich and warm shades of creamy brown, to almost orange, tinged brownish, heavily blotched with irregular markings of deep chocolate or blackish. The measurements of 40 eggs from Iceland average 52.3 by 35.2 millimeters; the eggs showing the four extremes measure **55.1** by 36.4, 51.6 by **38.3**, **49.2** by 33.8 and 52.3 by **33.2** millimeters.

Incubation is carried on by both sexes, as Alfred Taylor has watched the male and female change places on the eggs. This explains the rather contradictory accounts from various authors. H. H. Slater, Seebohm, and R. Collett only shot males from the nest, while Saxby, Hantzsch, and Heatherley only saw the female on the eggs. Miss F. Pitt only noted the male on the eggs during the last week of incubation, but flushed the hen once at an earlier period.

Early estimates of 16 and 20 days as the incubation period are certainly erroneous. F. Heatherley watched one nest for 24 days, but the eggs were probably laid some days earlier and in an incubator one egg hatched on the 27th day (W. Evans). Although such wary birds, it occasionally happens that a nest is placed in a hollow of the ground from which no view of the country is possible to the sitting bird. Riding at night suddenly up to a nest of this kind in Iceland, we found the incubating bird did not stir from the eggs while three men and ponies stood round, and it was not until a hand was placed within 3 inches that the bird flew off. As a rule, the melancholy piping note is the first intimation of the presence of a breeding pair and shows that they are on the alert.

Young.—The young leave the nest as soon as their down is dried and are cared for by both sexes. They grow very fast, and Hantzsch states that after 10 or 14 days they can flutter a little way, but the full flying period is about 4 weeks.

Plumages.—The plumages and molts are fully described in A Practical Handbook of British Birds, edited by H. F. Witherby (1920).

Food.—On its breeding grounds the food consists of insects, chiefly Coleoptera (*Notiophilus, Agriotes, Sitones, Curculio* and larvae); Lepidoptera (*Agrotis*); larvae and imagines of Diptera, Hymenoptera (*Formica* and *Forficula*); also Mollusca (small terrestrial species, snails and slugs); Aunclida (earthworms) and Arachnida (spiders). On migration and in winter quarters it has been recorded as eating marine mollusca (*Vitrina, Littorina, Rissoa, Lacuna*, etc., and fry of *Mytilus edulis*), also small crustacea (Isopoda) and seeds of various plants (*Glaux maritima, Carex, Polygonum*, etc.), and berries of *Rhamnus, Vaccinium, Empetrum*, etc.; also seaweeds (Algae).

Behavior.—Outside the breeding season the golden plover is a gregarious bird, nearly always to be met with in flocks of varying sizes and often associating with flocks of lapwings and feeding together. On the alarm being given, both species take to wing, but in characteristically different ways. The golden plover rise together and form a compact body, maneuvering together in any direction, while the lapwings rise gradually in an unwieldy mass, which breaks up from time to time and the component parts move in different directions. The pointed wings and more rapid strokes of the golden plover also contrast strongly with the slow, flappy, irregular flight of the lapwing. When on migration the golden plovers often adopt a loose V-shaped formation.

Enemies.—The peregrine occasionally takes toll of the flocks in the autumn and spring months, while the skua gulls, or jaegers, and in some districts the hooded crows, destroy eggs or young. The fox, no doubt, occasionally snaps up an isolated nest of eggs or young.

Fall.—About the end of October or early in November the flocks of northern golden plover arrive on the marshes of the east coast of England, sometimes in enormous numbers, but their length of stay is determined by weather conditions, to which they are very susceptible, showing extreme restlessness before the approach of stormy or windy weather and leaving the district altogether in hard winters.

Winter.—Many birds winter on the coast of the British Isles unless the weather is severe, feeding chiefly on small marine mollusca but, as a rule, avoid the mud flats, which are the favorite resort of the grey plover (*Squatarola*), except occasionally in very dry weather, feeding chiefly on the pasture lands and in the wheat fields in the daytime and leaving at dark for the higher ground.

DISTRIBUTION

Breeding range.—The northern race breeds in Iceland, the Faroes, probably a pair or two on Bear Island, northern Scandinavia, Finland, and North Russia and Siberia to the Yenisei. The southern race breeds in the mountainous parts of the British Isles, southern Scandinavia, Denmark, sparingly in Belgium, Holland, and North Germany, and in Russia south to the Perm Government.

Winter range.—It is not possible to separate the winter ranges of the two forms at present, but golden plover migrate across Europe to the Mediterranean and north Africa, occasionally visiting the Atlantic isles, and are said to have occurred in the Gabun on the west and Somaliland and Lama in East Africa; in Asia its limits are Aden, Baluchistan, and Sind.

Spring migration.—At the Straits of Gibraltar the northern migrants pass in February and March (late date March 6, L. H. Irby), but on the Portuguese coast W. C. Tait states that they leave at the end of February. In the eastern Mediterranean the passage is noted at Cyprus in early March. At Heligoland Gätke says they arrive during May and early June on their way to Scandinavia, but the Icelandic flocks arrive about mid-April as a rule.

Fall migration.—On the southward migration Gätke records the arrival of the birds of the year as early as July, but adds that the old birds only begin to arrive toward the end of October. On the west side of the Mediterranean Tait records the arrival of the earliest birds in October, but the main passage in November; and Farier also notes the passage at Tangier in October and November; while on the eastern side they reach Cyprus about the beginning of November.

Casual records.—Fischer recorded a pair on Jan Mayen on June 29, 1883, and it has occurred on the Azores, but is only a rare straggler, Madeira (recorded by Harcourt and also by Schmitz on January 13, 1896) and the Canaries, where Bannerman describes it as a rare visitor (records scanty and indefinite).

In Africa records from the Cape (J. Verreaux), Lamu, East Africa (Layard), and the Gabun (Du Chaillu) require substantiation. It is also stated to have occurred in Somaliland, but the normal winter quarters lie north of these localities. In Asia it has been shot at Gwadar, Baluchistan, in January, 1872, by W. T. Blanford, and one was obtained by Brooks near Schwan on January 27, 1878, as well as a second at Karachi on January 7, 1919, by Captain Hanna. The only other Indian record is one obtained by Reid at Lucknow. In Greenland (several records).

Egg dates.—Iceland: May 21 to June 1 (5 dates); June 2 to 29 (18 dates). North Norway, June 10 to 20 (5 dates). North Russia and Siberia, June 10 to July 1 (10 dates). Most eggs of the southern race are laid in the British Isles from May 10 onward, but exceptionally eggs have been met with from April 16 to the end of that month, and in Friesland eggs have been taken on April 19.

PLUVIALIS DOMINICA DOMINICA (Müller)

AMERICAN GOLDEN PLOVER

HABITS

The golden plover is not only one of our most beautiful shore birds in its brilliant spring plumage, but its wonderful migration excites our admiration and the comparison of its former abundance with its present scarcity furnishes a striking picture of the ruthless slaughter that has squandered our previous wealth of wild life. A few quotations will serve to illustrate the enormous flights of golden plover that swarmed over both American continents during the past century. Robert B. Roosevelt (1884) thus refers to a flock he saw near Montauk Point, Long Island, many years ago:

A gentle hollow spreads before us for several acres literally covered with the ranks of the much-desired, the matchless golden plover. As they stand in serried legions, the white mark on their heads gives a strange checkered weirdness to the phalanx; and we involuntarily pause, spellbound by the novelty of the spectacle. Our host himself, though an old hand, owns that he has never before gazed on such a sight. There they stand, with heads erect and bodies motionless, just out of gunshot. Their number is computed by our companion to be not less than 3,000, closely packed, and apparently awaiting our onset. Warily crawling to within 70 yards, we halt as we see unmistakable evidences of uneasiness and suspicion among the crowded ranks. They stoop, they run, they rise with "a sounding roar," to which the united report of our four barrels savagely responds.   Away, away with headlong speed scatters and dissolves that multitudinous host, and we hasten to secure our spoils.

Writing of conditions in Argentina about the middle of the last century, W. H. Hudson (1922) writes:

The golden plover was then one of the abundant species. After its arrival in September, the plains in the neighborhood of my home were peopled with immense flocks of this bird. Sometimes in hot summers the streams and marshes would mostly dry up, and the aquatic-bird population, the plover included, would shift their quarters to other districts. During one of these droughty seasons, when my age was 9, there was a marshy ground 2 miles from my home where a few small pools of water still remained, and to this spot the golden plover would resort every day at noon. They would appear in flocks from all quarters, flying to it like starlings in England coming in to some great roosting center on a winter evening. I would then mount my pony and gallop off joyfully to witness the spectacle. Long before coming in sight of them the noise of their voices would be audible, growing louder as I drew near. Coming to the ground, I would pull up my horse and sit gazing with astonishment and delight at the spectacle of that immense multitude of birds, covering an area of 2 or 3 acres, looking less like a vast flock than a floor of birds, in color a rich deep brown, in strong contrast to the pale gray of the dried-up ground all round them. A living, moving floor and a sounding one as well, and the sound, too, was amazing. It was like the sea, but unlike it in character since it was not deep; it was more like the wind blowing, let us say, on thousands of tight-drawn wires of varying thicknesses, vibrating them to shrill sound, a mass and tangle of 10,000 sounds. But it is indescribable and unimaginable.

Edward H. Forbush (1912) tells of two men who killed plover enough to fill a tip car two-thirds full in one day, during a big storm on Nantucket in the forties. Again he speaks of a great flight which occurred there on August 29, 1863, " when golden plover and Eskimo curlew landed on the island in such numbers as to almost darken the sun. Between seven and eight thousand of these birds were killed on the island and on Tuckernuck." He says that from 1860 on the species began to decrease, due to the demand created by the failing supply of passenger pigeons, and that in 1890 alone two Boston firms received from the West 40 barrels closely packed with curlew and plover, with 25 dozen curlew and 60 dozen plover to the barrel.

By the end of the last century this species had about reached its lowest ebb; it had become scarce where it once abounded; no more big flights occurred; and in many places it was rarely seen. But protective measures came in time to save it from extermination; the stopping of the sale of game and the removal of this species from the game-bird list were badly needed. Since the last move was made the species has shown some signs of recovery. Edwin Beaupre (1917) says that " after an absence of almost 15 years, the golden plover has apparently resumed its migratory visits to eastern Ontario." Prof. William Rowan (1923) says:

This year has been an exceptional golden-plover year. At the place referred to above, somewhere over a thousand birds were seen on the 20th of May alone, in moving flocks varying in number from 30 individuals to several hundreds. This was evidently not unique; for about the same time I got a report from quite another part of the Province that this species was unusually abundant, while from yet another quarter I got a very good description of the bird in a letter with a request that I name it for the inquirer, a careful bird observer. Her comment was that she had never seen the species before, but that it was, at the time of writing, present on the plowed fields in enormous numbers.

And John T. Nichols tells me that " of recent years there has been a distinct increase " on Long Island. If shooting conditions in its winter home could be controlled, its future would be assured.

Spring.—From its winter home on the pampas of Argentina and Uruguay the golden plover starts early on its long northward migration. Dr. Alexander Wetmore (1926) noted that—

The northward migration began with a flock of nine seen January 23, 1921, at a little fresh-water pool on the beach near La Paloma, Uruguay; when flushed these passed on to the west. Single individuals were seen near San Vicente, Uruguay, in flight toward the northwest on January 24 and 30. At Lazcano, Uruguay, birds in passage north were seen in early morning on February 7 and 8, and one was recorded February 18 at Rio Negro, Uruguay. On March 8 at Guamini, Buenos Aires, 15 came in at dusk to roost on a little mud bar in company with Hudsonian godwits. The migration seemed almost at an end then, as later I saw only four at Tunuyan, Mendoza, on March 23; and on April 5 only a few were heard calling with other shore birds in flight northward over Tucuman, Tucuman.

The exact route followed through the interior of South America is not definitely known, but it is not known to migrate along either coast of that continent. Austin H. Clark (1905) has advanced the theory that it prefers to fly with a beam wind and that it selects the route over which the prevailing winds will produce this condition. He suggests the following as the probable route:

In returning the birds would first go north (across the prevailing westerlies) until in the vicinity of Buenos Aires and the country just to the west of it, where they would encounter northeasterly winds, which would turn them inland, up the valley of the La Plata and along the plains to the east of the Andes, the course gradually becoming more northerly, and then northeasterly in the area covered by the southeast trades. They would reach the Amazon Valley in its western half, and then under the guidance of the northeast trades fly northwest toward the Isthmus of Panama and Central America. The course from here would be northwest across the trades to Texas and the Mississippi Valley. The birds follow up this valley northward and then, on reaching Canada, fly northwest across the prevailing southwesterly and westerly winds to their breeding grounds in western Arctic America.

Another theory advanced by Prof. Wells W. Cooke (1912), into which the facts seem to fit equally well, is that—

Birds follow that route between the winter and summer homes that is the shortest and at the same time furnishes an abundant food supply. The plover seeks the shortest treeless route overland, and alighting on the coast of Texas travels leisurely over the Mississippi Valley prairies, which are abundantly supplied with food, to the plains of the Saskatchewan, and thence to the Arctic coast. Not until Texas is reached can the movements of the golden plover be definitely traced, and at no place between Peru and Texas has it ever been recorded as common. In fact, the records as they stand are what they should be if the plover escapes the forested regions of northern South America and Central America by a single flight of from 2,000 to 2,500 miles from the valleys of eastern Peru to the treeless prairies of Texas.

The golden plover is practically unknown west of the Rocky Mountains in the spring; it has always been a rare straggler on the Atlantic coast at this season; and even as far east as Ohio it rarely occurs. Its main route is through the prairie regions west of the Mississippi River. I have seen what was probably the last of the migration, during the first week of May, along the coastal prairies of Texas, and have watched the late spring flight in Saskatchewan during the last week in May; probably I missed the heaviest part of the flight in both cases. On May 26 to 28, 1917, while driving about Quill Lake, Saskatchewan, I had a good chance to observe a considerable flight of these beautiful birds, all apparently in full spring plumage. The flocks appeared from the southward during the early forenoon, flying swiftly in ever-changing formations, rising to a height of 30 or 40 feet and then sweeping low close to the ground. They all seemed to follow the same course over the burnt-over prairies and the freshly plowed and harrowed lands near the shore of the lake. Occasionally a flock would stop and scatter about to feed; their black bellies and golden-spangled backs were surprisingly inconspicuous on the black ground and among the yellow stubble. They were very shy and restless, constantly on the move, and if followed up too closely they were on the wing again and soon disappeared over the northern horizon. It was almost impossible to approach them on foot when they were on the ground, though a flock would occasionally fly by within gunshot. One that I shot on the ground was 75 paces away, measured distance. Some of the flocks were accompanied by a few buff-breasted sandpipers.

Professor Rowan (1926) says that in Alberta:

The arrival of this species at our lake is precipitate, for there may be none to-day and hundreds to-morrow. The flocks would appear to arrive by night, for they are there at daybreak, when one usually takes the first walk around. They are not birds of the shore line in the spring, but like the buff-breasted sandpiper, they seem nevertheless chiefly to frequent country adjacent to some large lake. This, together with their mode of arrival, in considerable flocks and evidently at night, suggests that they have traveled a considerable distance from their last stopping place. They stay with us some days and then go in the manner in which they came, *en masse.* We have no records earlier than May 8 when the birds may first be expected, but the main contingent arrives nearer the 16th or 17th, while by the 23d or 24th they have usually all gone. Their period with us is therefore brief as compared with the majority of shore birds.

The remainder of the journey is quickly completed, for, at Point Barrow, John Murdoch (1885) says:

They are among the earlier waders to arrive, as stragglers generally appear about the 20th to the 25th of May, before there is much bare ground. In 1882 a small party in full breeding plumage, and apparently all males, arrived May 21, but no more arrived until June 11. The tundra was at this time bare only along the edge of the beach, and the ice and snow was not yet gone from the lagoons. This party remained in nearly the same place for a couple of weeks, feeding on small red worms which they found in marshy spots, and all but two of them were taken, although they were very wild.

Along through the first and second week in June they continued to arrive in small parties, and from that time on are quite plenty scattered in pairs and threes all over the tundra. They are very wild and difficult to approach, and very noisy. In addition to their ordinary well-known call note, they have in the breeding season, a loud but very melodious cry of *tud'ling!* many times repeated, uttered as the bird flies along rather high, with long slow strokes of the wings.

Nesting.—Roderick MacFarlane was very successful in finding nests of golden plover in the Anderson River region and other parts of the Arctic barren grounds. He sent a large number of eggs to Washington and I find in his notes references to over 120 nests, on which some data were given, mostly very brief. He says that "golden plover were in great abundance in the barren grounds, as well as along the Arctic coast. They seldom or never nested in the wooded country, though a few specimens were found on the open plains or commons, which occur on the borders of that tract." Some of the nests on the Arctic coast were "near the beach" or even "within a few yards of the sea water." The nests were evidently mere hollows in the open tundra, lined with dead leaves; there were no attempts at concealment, but the protective coloring of the eggs made them very difficult to find. He says that "when a nest of this plover is approached the female invariably gets off it at a quick pace, between a run and a walk, which it continues at short intervals until the intruder be attracted to a distance therefrom, when it flies away. The male generally joins its mate in this." On a few occasions, when surprised, the bird fluttered away for a short distance, but soon began to run as usual. Often the bird left the nest when the men were 100 yards away from it. Once when they had hunted in vain for an hour and a half, they retired and watched. "After a few minutes she came on at a cautious run, stopping frequently and making occasional excursions in different directions," and finally settled on the eggs.

They found that several of the party had repeatedly passed quite close to, and one had nearly trodden on the eggs. Watching the bird return to the nest, which she generally does within a few minutes, seems to be the best way of finding a nest.

Of the nests found near Point Barrow, Mr. Murdoch (1885) says:

> The nest is exceedingly hard to find, although it is not concealed at all, but is simply a depression in the bare black clayey tundra lined with a little dry moss. The only vegetation on this part of the tundra is white and grayish moss, which harmonizes so extraordinarily with the peculiar blotching of the eggs that it is almost impossible to see them unless one knows exactly where to look. A favorite nesting site is on the high banks of the gullies or small streams. No nests were ever found in the grass or in swampy ground.

W. Sprague Brooks (1915) found only one nest near Demarcation Point, Alaska, of which he says:

> I found this nest on June 25 with three eggs about one-quarter incubated. The male was on the nest. It took several days to find the nest, for the bird would leave when I was a long way off and begin running about and feeding as though it had nothing else to do. By placing a lump of tundra each day where I first saw the bird I eventually found her nest, a mere depression in some greenish moss which, with scattered bits of brown dead vegetation, harmonized extraordinarily with the eggs.
>
> When the bird saw that its nest was finally discovered it showed great distress and ran toward me until about 20 paces distant, where it stood tottering as if about to fall, with one wing raised over its back. In a short time the bird, with tail down and a wing dragging, would walk slowly from me. As I never followed, the bird would return and totter a while, repeating the same performance several times until secured for the proper identification of the eggs.

Eggs.—The golden plover's normal set is of four eggs, but Mac-Farlane collected many sets of three and one of five. These are quite uniformly ovate pyriform in shape and have only a slight gloss. The ground colors vary from " cinnamon buff " or " light pinkish cinnamon " to " light buff," " cartridge buff," or " cream color," hence more buffy or less olivaceous or grayish than in eggs of the black-bellied plover. They are boldy and profusely marked, more or less irregularly, with large and small spots and irregular blotches of very dark browns or black, " Vandyke brown," " clove brown," and brownish black. Sometimes there are a few underlying small spots of " drab gray." The measurements of 143 eggs in the United States National Museum average 47.5 by 32.5 millimeters; the eggs showing the four extremes measure **56** by 31, 50 by **34.5, 42** by 34, and 46 by **30** millimeters. Both sexes incubate. The period of incubation for the European species is said to be 27 days.

Plumages.—In the downy young golden plover the forehead, crown, back, wings, rump, and thighs are mottled with bright " wax yellow " and black, the yellow being mainly at the tips of the down.

A broad patch under the eye, extending back to the ears, and the chin, are white; a spot in front of the eye and an indistinct band above it, the hind neck and the throat are yellowish white, the hind neck being mottled with black; a broad band from the lores to the nape is pale yellow, mottled with black. The remaining under parts are grayish white.

In fresh juvenal plumage, on the breeding grounds, the crown and all the upper parts are brownish black, the feathers tipped or heavily notched with bright yellow, "light cadmium" to "buff-yellow," brightest on the rump; the wing coverts are pale sepia, notched paler yellow or white; the breast is pale drab, barred, spotted or notched with pale dusky and dull yellow, "mustard yellow" to "Naples yellow"; the belly is white, partially barred with pale dusky; and the tail feathers are sepia, indistinctly barred with darker sepia and tipped with dull yellow. By the time that young birds reach us on migration in September, the bright yellows of the upper parts have faded considerably, and the duller yellow on the breast has disappeared entirely. This plumage is not molted until after the birds leave us; late in the fall, November or later, a partial molt of the body plumage produces the first winter plumage, which can be distinguished from the adult only by the juvenal tail and some retained scapulars and tertials. What happens the next spring we have not the material to show. Most of the birds that we see here in the spring are in fully adult nuptial plumage, but I have seen quite a number of birds, some taken on their breeding grounds, that showed, more or less, old, worn, winter plumage; these may be young birds in their first nuptial plumage.

The postnuptial molt of adults begins with the body molt in August, the new pale drab and whitish feathers of the winter plumage appearing first in the black under parts; this molt continues through September while the birds are migrating. But the primaries are not molted until winter, November to February. In winter the plumage of the under parts is very pale drab, shading off to almost pure white on the chin and belly; the adult tail is irregularly barred with dusky and grayish or yellowish white; the feathers of the mantle are brownish black, narrowly edged with yellow, not notched or spotted as in spring. The prenuptial molt of the body plumage begins in March and lasts until May in some individuals; many old winter feathers are often found in breeding birds, especially in the wing coverts, scapulars, tertials and back. The beautiful nuptial plumage is too well known to need description here.

Food.—The favorite feeding grounds of the golden plover are rolling pasture lands where the grass is short or scanty, prairies, plains, plowed lands and occasionally open sand or mud flats.   Its food consists almost entirely of insects, chiefly Orthoptera which abound in the pasture lands.   It is said to feed mainly on grasshoppers, but George H. Mackay (1891), who is very familiar with it, says that he has never seen it eat any, though he has watched it through a strong glass near at hand.   He says:

I have also examined the stomachs of a good many which I have shot on Nantucket, and have never found any grasshoppers in them, nor in fact anything but crickets (which seem their principal food there), grass seeds, a little vegetable matter, like seaweed, coarse sand, and small stones.   I have also frequently shot them with the vent stained purple, probably from the berries of the *Empetrum nigrum.*

They must find abundant food in the north, for they are always very fat when they arrive here.   The large numbers of grasshoppers, locusts, crickets, and other insects that they destroy make them very beneficial birds to the farmers of the west, where they also do much good by eating the grubs, cutworms, and wireworms on freshly plowed lands, their favorite resorts in spring.   On the shores and open flats they find some small mollusks and crustaceans.   The crops of two which Lucien M. Turner collected in northern Ungava were filled with ripening berries of *Empetrum nigrum* and remains of spiders.   Hantzsch found them eating beetles and caterpillars on Baffin Island.

Behavior.—The flight of the golden plover is exceedingly swift, strong and protracted, as it must be to make such wonderful migrations.   Over the prairies the flocks sweep along in compact and ever changing formations, skimming close to the ground at times and then rising high in the air, frequently whistling as they go.   William Brewster (1925) has described their flight, as seen at Umbagog Lake, Maine, as follows:

They habitually flew faster than any of the other waders and perhaps more swiftly than any of the ducks except the hooded merganser.   Their long, pointed wings, lifting high and cutting deep at each stroke, beat rapidly and ceaselessly, yet so easily and smoothly as to indicate comparatively slight muscular effort.   If they happened to pass near at hand or overhead their flight was likely to impress one as having not only exceeding speed but irresistible momentum, also as of solid projectiles, hurtling through the air.   Seen at a distance they appear to be moving more slowly and looked not unlike passenger pigeons.

When preparing to alight the flocks often perform extensive evolutions, circling and turning, as they sweep about over the ground, as if selecting a satisfactory landing place.   When a suitable spot is chosen, they all alight in a compact bunch, raising their wings high above their backs before folding them, and soon scatter over the ground to feed.   When on the ground they are very active, running rapidly and gracefully, stopping suddenly to look around, with head held high, and then striking quickly at some morsel of food. Mr. Mackay (1891) says:

> When scattered over considerable ground, as is usual after they have been any length of time on their feeding ground, every bird apparently on its own hook, if alarmed, a note is sounded; they then rise so as to meet as soon as possible at a common center, which gained, away they go in a compact body. During the middle of the day they are fond of seeking the margins of ponds, where they sit quietly for a long time, if undisturbed. When disturbed they are almost certain to return, in a short time, to the same spot from which they have been started, that is, if they have been resting or feeding there any length of time. When suspicious, it is very difficult to approach, decoy, or call them; if not harassed, they are as a rule quite tame and gentle, and can be easily driven up to with horse and wagon.

Voice.—John T. Nichols says in his notes:

> The flight note of the golden plover in migration is a far-reaching *que-e-e-a*, with a quaver in the middle and falling at the end. Though with a thrilling plover quality it at the same time has an affinity to the killdeer's cry, being less mellow and whistled than the note of the blackbelly, which it also suggests, reversed.

Mr. Mackay (1891) says that when these birds are approaching decoys every bird seems to be whistling " a note like *coodle, coodle, coodle.*" Mr. Forbush (1912) calls its note " a plaintive *too-lee-e,*" or " a bright whistle, *queep-quee-lee-leep.*" Others have given different renderings of some of the above notes.

Field marks.—The bird with which the golden plover is most likely to be confused is the black-bellied plover, but the golden is a smaller, more slender, bird, with a generally darker appearance. When seen in flight the tone of the tail is very dark and the axillars, under the wings, are grey, whereas in the black-bellied the tail is decidedly whitish and the axillars are very conspicuously black in all plumages; furthermore the black-bellied has a conspicuous light wing bar, which is lacking in the golden. The notes of the two are quite different. When in hand the golden is seen to have no hind toe. Mr. Nichols suggests that the golden has a swifter, more buoyant flight, suggestive of the killdeer.

Fall.—Mr. Murdoch (1885) refers to the beginning of the migration as follows:

> The nesting season continues till the first or middle of July, about which time the adults begin to collect in flocks, feeding together around the ponds on the higher tundra, associated sometimes with a few knots or a struggling curlew. The old birds leave for the south about the end of July, and no more plovers are to be seen until about the middle of August, when the young, who heretofore have been keeping out of sight, scattered over the tundra, gather into flocks, and for several days are quite plenty on the dryer hills and banks, after which they depart. Stragglers may be seen up to the end of August.

The main trend of the fall migration is southeastwards, mainly west and south of Hudson Bay, but perhaps across it also, to the Atlantic coast, mostly north of New England. In favorable weather the flight is over the ocean from Nova Scotia to South America over, or to the eastward of, Bermuda, and the Lesser Antilles. Mr. Clark (1905) figures out that this is the course they would take, if they flew with a beam wind, across the prevailing winds. Of their course after landing in British Guiana, he says:

From this point their course is not accurately known; but if we apply this theory, they would follow down the northeastern tributaries of the Amazons until they came within the influence of the southeast trades, which would carry them southwest, over central Amazonia toward Peru and Boliva. Somewhat northwest of the Matto Grosso region, the birds would come under the influence of the easterly winds on the southern border of the trades, which would turn them south, and gradually (as they became more northeasterly) southeast, which would bring the plover into the prairie region of the Argentine. Here the prevailing westerlies of the pampas region would be felt, and the birds would, under their influence, continue down the eastern part of Patagonia toward Tierra del Fuego.

To add strength to his theory he says that there are specimens in the British Museum from Mount Roraima and the Maroni River, Surinam, and from Peru taken in September and October.

Some birds on the fall migration wander as far north and east as Baffin Island and northeastern Labrador. Lucien M. Turner refers in his notes to several adults which he saw and two which he collected, near the mouth of the Koksoak River, between July 24 and August 19, 1882; and I have a specimen in my collection taken near Hopedale, Labrador, a young bird. Hantzsch found this plover breeding on Baffin Island.

Edwin Beaupre (1917) writes:

In September, 1906, a great flight of plover passed over the city of Kingston, which is located on the extreme eastern end of Lake Ontario. The flight was first noticed about 8 o'clock in the evening, and to one familiar with the soft, sweet piping of the golden plover, there was no difficulty whatever in recognizing the bird. A record of the flight showed that eight flocks passed over the city, flying very low, at intervals of about 10 minutes. Toward midnight it was impossible to enumerate the flocks, the flight being continuous. This must have been the main migration for that year, and it continued until 4 o'clock in the morning, covering eight hours. Allowing a speed of 25 miles an hour—a conservative estimate—the distance between the leading flocks and the rear guard must have been approximately 200 miles. What a sublime spectacle this would have been had one the privilege of seeing it in the open light of day! The vanguard of this great aerial aggregation must have reached almost to the Atlantic seaboard, while the rear flocks were trailing their wonderful way over the eastern waters of Lake Ontario. They no doubt began their ocean journey some miles south of the coast of Nova Scotia, but not far enough to seriously affect their regular route to Argentina, in which country they escape the hardship of a Canadian winter.

The above quotation and the fact that William Brewster (1925) recorded the golden plover as visiting the Umbagog Lake region in Maine "regularly and rather plentifully not so many years ago," suggests the idea that some of the birds we used to see in New England came by an overland route. However, our big flights were probably birds that came in from the sea under stress of bad weather, either before or during easterly storms accompanied by heavy rains or thick fog. According to Mr. Mackay's (1891) records, covering a period of 32 years from 1858 to 1890, the last week in August seems to be the best time to look for a flight, though he says "it is unusual to see any but scattering birds before the 10th of September." My earliest record for adult birds is August 9; practically all the birds which come in August are adults. The young birds come in September; my latest date is October 7. The appearance of either adults or young on our coast has always been very uncertain and irregular, dependent on the necessary weather conditions coming at the proper time.

Mr. Mackay (1891) says:

While I have continually shot the young birds on Nantucket, and in other parts of Massachusetts, their arrival is a much more uncertain event than that of the older birds, there being some years when I have seen none, and others only a few. I have never known a year when they were anything like as numerous as I have seen the older birds.

During some years large flocks of golden plover pass over the Bermudas in September and October, according to Capt. Savile G. Reid (1884), "but, unless in stormy weather, they do not alight in any great numbers. Numbers appeared in September, 1874, frequenting the grassy slopes of the north shore—their favorite haunt— and even the parade grounds, during the continuance of a three day's revolving gale."

Col. H. W. Feilden (1889) writing of conditions in Barbados, the easternmost of the West Indies, says:

Stragglers arrive as early as July and the beginning of August, but the main flights come with the first heavy weather after the 27th of August, and long experience and observation proves that this date is kept year after year with wonderful accuracy. The course of all the migratory Charadriidae across Barbados in the autumn is from the northwest to southeast, and if the wind blows from southeast the birds are brought down to the island, for it appears to be a tolerably well established observation that birds prefer migrating with a "beam" wind. A shift of wind from the northeast, with squally weather to the southeast, is ardently longed for by the Barbados sportsmen toward the end of August, as this forces the migratory hosts to alight instead of passing over at a great height, as they are seen to do when the wind is from the northeast. The first arrivals of this species are invariably black-breasted birds, showing that the old birds precede the young, and the first comers are nearly all males. The young birds without black on the breast appear about the 12th of

September, and continue to pass till the end of October, sometimes stragglers are as late as November. Even in the most favorable seasons, only a fraction of the immense flights that pass over the island ever alight.

Much has been written about the Atlantic flight of the golden plover and remarkably little has been said about the southward flight in the interior, but such a flight occurs regularly, though in much smaller numbers. Professor Rowan (1926) says that in Alberta:

We have notes of hundreds going south in a single day in mid September, when the main movements occur annually. An interesting feature of the fall migration of golden plover is that it consists entirely of young birds. The earliest record we have is August 18 and the next August 24. These are rather early, September being the chief month of arrival. The fall movements are protracted, and we may have small flocks with us till toward the end of October. Another feature of the autumn migration is a change of habit. The birds, while often noted on pasture (particularly if in large flocks) more usually frequent the muds and behave like the majority of other waders. They associate freely and habitually with other species. They behave like the strays of the spring. Being birds of the year there is no doubt in their case that they are sexually undeveloped.

We have a single record of an adult bird in the fall collected by Harrold on August 22. It was noted the previous day, but not secured, and proved to be a female well advanced in its moult. There is one other reliable autumn record for an adult golden plover from the Province, seen at Sullivan Lake in July by Mr. T. E. Randall. Until we have spent the whole of July at our lake or some other suitable observation station, it will be impossible to say that adults never—except accidentally as strays—come south through the Province, but all evidence available indicates that they do not do so.

I can not wholly agree with Professor Rowan's evident belief that all the birds that migrate through the interior are young birds and that very few young birds take the Atlantic route. However, the dates given by numerous observers in the Mississippi Valley and in Texas would seem to indicate that they were nearly all referable to young birds, as they are generally late dates. The main migration route for both adults and young is evidently the Atlantic route; the species is comparatively rare in the interior, south of Canada. It is still rarer on its southward migration along the Pacific coast; the dates are mostly late, probably for young birds; D. E. Brown has sent me two records from Washington. October 7, 1917, Gray's Harbor County, and November 14, 1915, Clallam County. Apparently most of the adults take the Atlantic route; the young birds are spread out over the whole country, but are much more inclined to the eastern route.

Game.—The golden plover has been a famous game bird. It was a most desirable table bird, as it was usually very fat and its flesh had a delicious flavor on account of its clean, upland feeding habits. The uncertainty of its appearance and its enormous numbers at favorable times made its pursuit most interesting. During the years of its abundance it was slaughtered in almost incredible numbers. Audubon (1840) writes:

While at New Orleans, on the 16th of March, 1821, I was invited by some French gunners to accompany them to the neighborhood of Lake St. John to witness the passage of thousands of these birds, which were coming from the northeast and continuing their course. At the first appearance of the birds early in the morning, the gunners had assembled in parties of from 20 to 50 at different places, where they knew from experience that the plovers would pass. There stationed, at nearly equal distances from each other, they were sitting on the ground. When a flock approached, every individual whistled in imitation of the plover's call note, on which the birds descended, wheeled, and, passing within 40 or 50 yards, ran the gauntlet, as it were. Every gun went off in succession, and with such effect that I several times saw a flock of a hundred or more reduced to a miserable remnant of five or six individuals. The game was brought up after each volley by the dogs, while their masters were charging their pieces anew. This sport was continued all day, and at sunset, when I left one of these lines of gunners, they seemed as intent on killing more as they were when I arrived. A man near the place where I was seated had killed 63 dozens. I calculated the number in the field at 200, and supposing each to have shot 20 dozen, 48,000 golden plovers would have fallen that day.

John C. Cahoon (1888) describes a method of shooting golden plover employed by old gunners on Cape Cod, as follows:

Several weeks before the time for the flights to occur, they go to an old field or pasture that they know the birds usually come into and burn off the old grass and bushes for quite a space. Then a hole is dug large enough for one or two persons to sit in comfortably, with only the top of their heads above the surface. In a few weeks the grass springs up and the green patch is easily distinguished from its duller surroundings by the plover flying about, and they are sure to come to this place. The gunner, with his decoys out, sits in his pit with only the top of his head out, which is covered with a green cap. A flock, before alighting to the decoys, will usually circle about several times, often flying directly over the gunner's head only a few yards away. An experienced gunner will not shoot when they are so near and scattered, as he could kill but one or two, but will wait for them to bunch at the right distance, which they are sure to do while turning, and seize that opportunity to fire, killing many at one shot.

Mr. Mackay (1891) says: " They are extremely gregarious, and I have had the same flock return to my decoys as many as four times after some of their number had been shot each time." This remark probably refers to adult birds, which come readily to decoys or in response to skillful whistling; I have seen a single bird whistled up from so far away that it was hardly visible. Professor Rowan (1926) says that he has " found it practically impossible to whistle them within gun range." He probably refers to young birds, of which Mr. Mackay (1891) writes:

These young birds invariably appear wild and wary, much more so than the old ones. They are also very erratic in their movements and flight when with us. They usually will not pay so much attention to the decoys or call whistle as do the old birds; and I have seen them, when very shy and after being disturbed, mount up into the air and nearly turn over on their backs while flying with great velocity. It is a noteworthy fact that when a flock of these young birds is approaching no dependence can be placed on their movements. They may sometimes sweep down within a few yards of the sportsman, passing with great rapidity over his head, all scattered; or down close to the stand and then up into the air; or they may turn suddenly. My experience has taught me not to wait, as is my custom with the older birds, to get them together before shooting, but fire at them whenever and wherever I can if they are within range. The older birds rarely indulge in any similar antics.

During the days of spring shooting in the west golden plover were often shot, without decoys, by making a blind or selecting some natural hiding place within their regular fly ways, which were generally quite well established and known. It was always difficult to stalk them on foot, but where there were no fences they could be stalked successfully by a hunter on horseback or in a wagon.

Winter.—The golden plover arrive in their winter home early in September, or rarely late in August, where they remain until February or March. W. H. Hudson (1920) writing of the days when these birds were plentiful, says:

The American golden plover is abundant and well known to every one by its native name, *Chorlo*, throughout southern Argentina. Its wild, clear notes are first heard about the last week in August, and among the first comers many individuals are seen still wearing the nuptial dress. After their long journey from the Arctic regions they are lean and not worth shooting; two months later they become excessively fat, and are then much appreciated by gourmets. But although so regular in their arrival, they do not regularly visit the same localities every season; the bird may be abundant in a place one year and scarce or absent altogether the next. During the spring, from September to December, they prefer open plains with short grass and in the neighborhood of wet or marshy ground; at the end of December, when the giant thistle (*Carduus mariana*), which often covers large areas of country, has been burnt up by the sun and blown to the ground, they scatter about a great deal in flocks of from one to four or five hundred. At noon, however, they all resort to a lagoon or marshy place containing water, congregating day after day in such numbers that they blacken the ground over an area of several acres in extent, and at a distance of a quarter of a mile the din of their united voices resembles the roar of a cataract. As population increases on the pampas these stupendous gatherings are becoming more and more rare. Twenty-five years ago it was an exceptional thing for a man to possess a gun, or to use one when he had it; and if Chorlos were wanted a gaucho boy with a string a yard long with a ball of lead attached to each end could knock down as many as he liked. I have killed them in this way myself, also with the bola perdida—a ball at the end of a long string thrown at random into a cloud of birds.

Doctor Wetmore (1926) saw golden plover on migration in Paraguay during September; they "came to the open shores of lagoons with other sandpipers, but were more often seen in flocks of 30 or 40 scattered over open savannas where the grass was not too long."

He saw them also in Argentina during November and December, where they seemed " to be restricted during the resting period to the better watered grass-grown eastern pampa."

Again (1927) he says:

The golden plover in the south has been most common on open plains, but ranges to some extent on the mud flats of the coast. It is in this last area that the species may be expected to survive as the pampas become more closely occupied by man. These birds are hunted extensively and so many have been killed both in the north and south that their numbers have been greatly reduced. Though recorded in its nesting range as only fairly common at best, the region where the golden plover is found at this season is extensive, so that the number of birds in existence is still considerable. Careful watch should be kept on its abundance.

DISTRIBUTION

Range.—North and South America, accidential in Europe.

Breeding range.—The breeding range of the American golden plover has not been definitely separated from that of its western relative (*Pluvialis d. fulva*). It has, however, been found that in Alaska *fulva* is more nearly confined to the northwestern coastal regions, while *dominica* is in the interior and on the northern coast.

The breeding range may be defined as extending north to Alaska (Point Barrow, Collison Point, and Demarcation Point); Baffin Island (Kangianga, Tikerakdjuak, and Kangidli); and Franklin (Walker Bay, Bay of Mercy, Winter Harbor, Wellington Channel, and probably Igloolik). East to Baffin Island; Franklin (probably Igloolik and Winter Island); and northeastern Keewatin (Whale Point). South to Keewatin (Whale Point); Mackenzie (Casba River, Lac de Gras, Bernard Harbor, Rendezvous Lake, Fort Anderson, and Fort McPherson); and Alaska (Gens de Large Mountains, Beaver Mountains, and probably Nushagak). West to Alaska (probably Nushagak and Point Barrow).

It also has been detected in summer in Greenland (Jacobshaven and Godthaab), but there is no evidence of breeding in that region.

Winter range.—The winter range of the American golden plover extends north to rarely Chile (Arica); and rarely Brazil (Villa Maria, Matto Grosso, and Rio de Janeiro). East to rarely Brazil (Rio de Janeiro and Santa Catharina); Uruguay (Montevideo); and Argentina (La Plata, Cape San Antonio, and Bahia Blanca). South to Argentina (Bahia Blanca, Sierra de la Ventana, Carhue, and Mendoza). West to western Argentina (Mendoza); and rarely Chile (Arica). On rare occasions individuals may pass the winter season at more northern points as Nauta, Peru (Sharpe), and Old Harbor, Costa Rica (Carriker). Winter occurrences at other northern localities probably refer to crippled birds or erroneous identifications.

Migration.—The main migration route of the American golden plover is of an elliptical nature. In late summer, after the breeding season, the birds move southeast across northern Canada to the coasts of Labrador and Nova Scotia, from which points they fly, apparently without stopping, to the northeast coast of South America, passing thence through the interior to the pampas region of Argentina. The northward flight in spring is made farther west, through Ceneral America, up the Mississippi Valley to the prairie Provinces of Canada.

Individuals and small flocks are, of course, noted more or less regularly in both spring and fall, both on the Atlantic coast and in the interior, but the main route should be borne in mind when considering the following dates of arrival and departure.

Spring migration.—Early dates of arrival in the spring are: Porto Rico, Mameyes, February 16; Bermuda, March 9, 1852 (only spring record); New York, Long Island City, April 17, and Fair Haven Light, May 3; Massachusetts, Revere, March 6, and Somerville, March 20; Nova Scotia, Pictou, May 17; Quebec, Godbout, May 31; Franklin, Igloolik, June 14; Louisiana, New Orleans, March 16, Avery Island, March 28; and West Baton Rouge, April 2; Arkansas, Fayetteville, March 20; Missouri, St. Louis, March 23, Kansas City, April 11, and Kings Lake, April 12; Illinois, Mount Carmel, March 12, Lebanon, March 17, and Chicago, March 22; Indiana, Terre Haute, March 22, Greencastle, March 28, and Muncie, March 30; Ohio, Sandusky, March 26, West Liberty, April 2, and Columbus, April 4; Michigan, Pittsfield, April 20; Iowa, Scranton, March 25, Newton, March 27, and Keokuk, April 14; Wisconsin, Clinton, April 9, and Racine, April 14; Minnesota, Heron Lake, April 12, Waseca, April 21, and Wilder, April 24; Texas, Gainesville, March 7, Mont Belvieu, March 8, Boerne, March 9, and Indianola, March 15; Oklahoma, Caddo, March 11; Kansas, Richmond, March 22, Lawrence, March 29, Manhattan, April 4, and Emporia, April 18; Nebraska, Kearney, April 8; South Dakota, Fort Sisseton, April 13, Huron, April 25, and White, April 26; North Dakota, Larimore, May 2, and Grafton, May 3; Manitoba, Aweme, April 23, Treesbank, May 1, Portage la Prairie, May 8, and Margaret, May 8; Saskatchewan, Osler, May 8, and Indian Head, May 9; Mackenzie, Fort Simpson, May 15, and Fort Resolution, May 23; Alberta, Alliance, May 5, Mundare, May 12, Camrose, May 7, and Red Deer, May 9; and Alaska, Beaver Mountains, April 29, Sitka, May 5, Flat, May 11, Fort Reliance, May 13, Fairbanks, May 17, and Point Barrow, May 21.

Late dates of spring departure are: Argentina, Rio Negro, February 18, Mendoza, March 23, and Tucuman, April 5; Guatemala, Duenas, April 12; Louisiana, Avery Island, May 3, and Breton Island, May 13; Kentucky, Crab Orchard, May 10; Missouri, Hunnewell, May 18, and Boonville, May 31; Illinois, Addison, May 10, Rantoul, May 12, and Chicago, May 17; Indiana, Lebanon, May 23; and Michigan City, June 2; Ohio, Sandusky, May 19, Bay Point, May 23, and Wauseon, May 27; Iowa, Gilbert Station, May 16, Cedar Rapids, May 17, and Clear Lake, May 20; Wisconsin, Racine, May 4, and Madison, May 30; Minnesota, Hallock, May 20, Wilder, May 22, and Twin Valley, May 30; Texas, Corpus Christi, April 28, Gainesville, May 12, and Point Isabel, May 15; Kansas, Manhattan, May 4, Paola, May 7, and Lawrence, May 8; Nebraska, Valentine, May 25; South Dakota, Sioux Falls, May 23, White, May 25, and Harrison, May 27; North Dakota, Devils Lake, May 23, Jerusalem, June 1, and Larimore, June 7; Manitoba, Aweme, May 29, Margaret, June 3, and Shoal Lake, June 6; Saskatchewan, Indian Head, May 22, Winston, May 29, and Churchill River, June 2; Colorado, Denver, May 17; Alberta, Mundare, May 26, Sedgewick, May 30, and Fort Chipewyan, June 1; and British Columbia, between Shusicap Falls and Mabel Lake, May 29 (only spring record).

Fall migration.—Early dates of arrival in the fall are: British Columbia, Graham Island, July 27, Sumas Lake, August 19, and Chilliwack, August 26; Keewatin, Cape Eskimo, August 4; Manitoba, Aweme, August 6, Shoal Lake, August 21, and Margaret, August 27; North Dakota, Fort Berthold, September 16; South Dakota, White, September 12, great bend of the Missouri River, September 18, and Harrison, September 20; Nebraska, Nebraska City, August 3, and Ames, August 22; Minnesota, St. Vincent, August 29, and Hibbing, September 13; Ontario, Toronto, August 25, and Brighton, August 28; Michigan, Houghton, September 5, Charity Island, September 9, and Detroit, September 10; Ohio, Columbus, August 23, New Bremen, September 1, Youngstown, September 2, and Cleveland, September 8; Indiana, Waterloo, August 25, and Lebanon, September 29; Illinois, Rantoul, August 6, Glen Ellyn, September 10, and Chicago, September 13; Louisiana, mouth of Mermentau River, August 11; Mississippi, Bay St. Louis, September 26; Newfoundland, St. George Bay, August 17; Quebec, Gaspe Peninsula, August 29, and Montreal, August 31; Prince Edward Island, Malpeque, August 23; New Brunswick, Scotch Lake, August 21; Nova Scotia, Sable Island, August 20; Maine, Portland, August 12; Massachusetts, Ipswich, July 18, Plymouth, August 7, Nantucket, August 12, Cape Cod, August 15, and Monomoy Island, August 18; Rhode Island, Newport, August 12, and Kingston, August 19; Connecticut, Bridgeport, August 14, and

Guilford, August 27; Rhode Island, Point Judith, August 21; New York, Montauk Light Station, August 9, Long Island City, August 12, Syracuse, August 22, and Shinnecock Bay, August 29; New Jersey, Great Bay, July 19; Cuba, Guantanamo, September 30; Lesser Antilles, Barbados, July 24, Grenada, August 24, St. Croix, August 31, and Sombrero, September 2; British Guiana, Auni, August 30; and Paraguay, Puerto Pinasco, September 6. Specimens also have been detected at Bermuda as early as July 25 (Hamilton).

Late dates of departure in the autumn are: Alaska, Nome, September 14, Baranof Island, September 18, Kenai River, October 7, and St. George Island, October 18 (there is a strong possibility that all of these Alaskan records refer to the Pacific form, *Pluvialis d. fulva*); British Columbia, East Kootenay, October 13, Chilliwack, October 14, and Comox, November 4; Alberta, Edmonton, September 23, delta of the Athabaska River, October 10, and Beaverhill Lake, October 22; Montana, Terry, September 23, and St. Marys Lake, October 1; Wyoming, Rock Creek, October 25; Colorado, Newcastle, October 5; Mackenzie, Manito Islands, September 14, Lower Slave River, September 29, and Fort Liard, October 5; Saskatchewan, Indian Head, October 2, and Quill Lake, October 11; Manitoba, Aweme, October 16; South Dakota, Fort Pierre, October 21, and Fort Sisseton, October 26; Nebraska, Lincoln, November 14; Kansas, Emporia, October 22, and Lawrence, October 23; Minnesota, Madison, October 22, St. Vincent, October 26, and Lanesboro, November 2; Iowa, Bronson, November 9, and Keokuk, November 9; Ontario, Toronto, October 23, Brighton, November 3, and Ottawa, November 4; Michigan, Gibralter, October 12, Mainstee, October 17, and Detroit, November 4; Ohio, New Bremen, October 23, Painesville, October 31, and Youngstown, November 11; Indiana, English Lake, November 15; Illinois, Morgan Park, October 28, Hinsdale, November 4, and Urbana, November 8; Arkansas, Crocketts Bluff, October 22; Greenland, August 7; Franklin, Baffin Bay, September 3; Quebec, Koksoak River, September 19, Kamouraska, October 19, Montreal, November 8, and Quebec City, November 10; Nova Scotia, Sable Island, October 22, and St. Marys Bay, October 23; Maine, Lewiston, October 16, and Portland, November 15; Vermont, Wells River, October 14; Massachusetts, Monomoy Island, October 13, Plymouth, October 24, and Provincetown, November 19; Rhode Island, South Auburn, October 12, and Newport, October 24; Connecticut, West Haven, October 25, and Hartford, October 24; New York, Ithaca, October 29, Rockaway, October 30, Orient Point, November 5, and Auburn, November 8; Bahamas, Cay Lobos, October 25; Porto Rico, Anegado Lagoon, November 4; West Indies, Barbados, December 7; and Costa Rica, San Jose, December 15.

Casual records.—South of New Jersey on the Atlantic coast, this species has been recorded on a few occasions, among which are: District of Columbia, Washington, one about 1860; Virginia, Smiths Island, September 28, 1897, and Wallops Island, several occurrences between August 12 and October 3 (Warren); North Carolina, several records in spring between April 15 (Waterlily), and May 10 (Currituck), and in fall between August 29 (Martins Point), and September 29 (Churchs Island); South Carolina, Chester County, September 19, 1877, Christ Church Parish, November 27, 1912, and Charleston, November 4, 1911, and December, 1880; and Florida, Miakka, November 19, 1901, and December, 1900.

On the Pacific coast of the United States it is only casual: Washington, several records in the fall between September 9 (Port Townsend), and November 14 (Dungeness); Oregon, Netarts Bay, September 7, 1912; and California, Playa del Rey Lagoon, October 4, 1923, Santa Cruz, October 22, 1888, and possible at Coronado, January 12–20, 1908 (Torrey). Suckley reported it from the vicinity of San Francisco, and Kobbe from Menlo Park and Vallejo, but both of these records are indefinite.

The American golden plover has been obtained a few times in Great Britain, Essex, August, 1896, Perthshire, August, 1883, Leadenhall Market, fall of 1882, and Mayo County, September, 1894; while a single specimen was taken on Heligoland, December 20, 1847.

Egg Dates.—Arctic coasts of Alaska and Canada: 176 records, June 1 to July 15; 88 records, June 25 to July 2.

PLUVIALIS DOMINICA FULVA (Gmelin)

PACIFIC GOLDEN PLOVER

HABITS

The Pacific golden plover is a smaller and more brightly colored subspecies of the American golden plover. It breeds on the Arctic coast of Siberia from the Yenesei River to Bering Strait and on the Bering Sea coast of Alaska. On the coast of Alaska north of Bering Strait it intergrades with the American form, and there is some evidence that it intergrades or hybridizes with the European golden plover at the western end of its range. It is known as the Asiatic or eastern golden plover by European writers. It winters from India and China to Australia, New Zealand, the Hawaiian Islands, and many other islands in the southern Pacific Ocean.

Spring.—This plover makes even more wonderful migratory flights than its American relative, for between its winter and its summer homes it travels twice each year over thousands of miles of trackless ocean; many individuals may become lost or perish, but the majority of them seem to find their way by some marvelous sense of direction. The reader is referred to an excellent paper on the migration of this plover to and from the Hawaiian Islands by Dr. Henry W. Henshaw (1910). Of the spring migration he writes:

During the last two months of their stay in the islands both the migrating plover and turnstones get very fat, and it is probable that individuals that are not in good condition do not attempt the flight, or if they do do not survive the attempt. Toward April most plover seem to be in full breeding plumage, and I feel sure that none of the birds assuming the breeding dress remain behind unless sick or wounded. There is, however, a small contingent, both of plover and turnstones, that summer in the islands, and these appear to consist wholly of immature individuals, which, as a rule, are thin and not in good trim.

When the time to migrate comes, small parties, from a dozen or even less to flocks of 200 or more, strike boldly out to the northward, apparently without hesitancy or doubt of the result. Mr. Haswell, of Papaikou, which is on the coast about 15 miles north of Hilo, soon after daybreak during the early days of April, 1900, saw several flocks rise to a great height and, after widely circling about a few times as if to orient themselves, finally disappear in a northerly direction.

It is probable, however, that day migration is not the rule with plover and other shore birds. Apparently it is more usual for the flocks to feed by day and leave just before nightfall, as do many other birds in different parts of the world. Mr. R. C. L. Perkins states that several times he "witnessed these departures always late in the afternoon or just before dark."

How fast the birds fly or how long it takes them to make the 2,000 mile flight across the ocean to the Aleutian Islands, we do not know. If they fly at the rate of 40 miles an hour without stopping, it would take over two days. They probably can not sustain such a prolonged effort without food. Practically all shore birds are known to alight on and arise from the water at will; so the chances are that they stop to rest on the way. They probably obtain some food from floating masses of seaweed, from the refuse left by whales, or from the numerous forms of minute animal life to be found on the surface. These birds have frequently been seen migrating at sea hundreds of miles from land, and one observer has actually seen one resting on the water. Evidence that they do so is furnished by the fact that native gunners in Trinidad, according to some notes sent to me by Julian Lyder, detect the newly arrived birds by a salty taste on the feathers.

The plover leave the Hawaiian Islands during April and May. We have no data as to when they reach the Aleutian Islands, but they arrive in the Commander Islands about the middle of May, and the first arrivals were noted at Nijni Kolymsk, Siberia, on May 30. On the Pribilof Islands they have been known to arrive as early as April 18, but they usually come about the first week in May. A. H. Twitchell tells me that he has seen them at Bethel, Alaska, as early as May 8, and Herbert W. Brandt says in his notes from Hooper Bay:

When the first small flocks of this noble Asiatic visitant appeared on Point Dall on May 16 the receding snow seemed to emphasize its golden splendor. It never became really common like its larger relative, the black-bellied plover, but numerous individuals and small bands were observed which, however, proved to be transients, for they all departed by early June. They usually associated with the gaudily attired ruddy turnstone and the combined lavish color effect of these two feathered gems was lovely indeed to behold. The Eskimos claim that, when seal hunting off Point Dall, they often encountered birds of the present species flying shoreward, so perhaps many of these long-flighted migrants moved directly from the western section of the Aleutian Islands across Bering Sea to their Alaskan summer homes.

Nesting.—Mr. Brandt has sent me the following notes on the nesting habits of this plover:

The breeding realm of the aristocratic golden plover in the Hooper Bay region is confined to a narrow belt on the mountain slopes well above brush line in the Askinuk Range. Here at an altitude of from five to eight hundred feet dwells a pair nearly every half mile, or about the same relative distance apart that the black-bellied plover families maintain between themselves on the tundra below.

The only nest of the Pacific golden plover to come under my observation was found on June 27 at an altitude of 600 feet on the Bimute spur of the Askinuk Range. On this upper mountain slope amid the scattered rocky outcrops exists a grim Arctic flora of mosses and lichens which in patches is mottled black and grayish white. On one of these velvet-like spots a little top moss is removed by the birds so as to make a slight depression in which the four beautiful eggs are placed. The lining of the nest is simply a few short unarranged stems of the reindeer moss that no doubt grew on the site. The nesting cavity is 4 inches in diameter and only half an inch in depth, thus making it notable as perhaps the most meager of the limicoline abodes we found. The parti-colored eggs and their environs blend as one in coloration, so, even in that jaeger-ridden land, they enjoy unusual protective security. The male bird alone was present during my stay in the vicinity of his abiding place and failed to exhibit either the extreme timidity or the agitation so characteristic of the black-bellied plover.

Henry Seebohm (1901) gives the following account of finding a nest near the banks of the Yenesei River in Siberia:

On the top of the bank I found myself on the real tundra. Not a trace of a pine tree was visible, and the birches rarely exceeded 12 inches in height. There was less grass, more moss and lichen, and the ground was covered with patches of yellow mud or clay, in which were a few small stones, that were apparently too barren for even moss or lichen to grow upon. The tundra was hilly, with lakes, swamps, and bogs in the wide valleys and plains. As soon as I reached the flat bogs I heard the plaintive cry of a plover, and presently caught sight of two birds. The male was very conspicuous, but all my attempts to follow the female with my glass, in order to trace her to the nest, proved ineffectual; she was too nearly the color of the ground, and the herbage was too high. Feeling convinced that I was within 30 paces of the nest, I shot the male, and commenced a diligent search. The bird proved to be the Asiatic golden plover, with gray axillaries, and I determined to devote at least an hour looking for the nest. By a wonderful piece of good fortune I found it, with four eggs, in less than five minutes. It was merely a hollow in the ground upon a piece of turfy land, overgrown with moss and lichen, and was lined with broken stalks of reindeer moss. The eggs more resembled those of the golden than those of the grey plover, but were smaller than either.

Miss Maud D. Haviland (1915a) had considerable experience with this plover on the Yenesei and took some excellent photographs of it; she writes:

I first saw a few birds at Dudinka, where they were probably on migration, and afterwards the species was common all the way down to Golchika. Each pair occupied perhaps 2 furlongs of tundra. I should think that every acre of moss and lichen from the Yenesei to the Lena in summer is thus parceled out. Your progress across the tundra in July is heralded and attended by a chorus of plaintive cries. Both birds meet you a quarter of a mile from the nest and never leave you until you are at the boundaries of their own territory, and they can safely hand you over to their next neighbors for espionage. Covert, of course, there is none—but it is needless to say more. The suspiciousness and patience of the golden plover are the same all the world over; and I will not dwell upon them to those who themselves have no doubt walked vainly for half a day about the bird's breeding grounds in this country and listened to its maddening but at the same time most musical protests.

The first nest was found on July 4. It was a shallow depression, lined with dry lichen haulms on a slope of the tundra. The bird, which must, I think, either have been deaf or else exceedingly stupid, did not move until I was well over the hill and within 60 yards of her, when she jumped up and feigned a broken wing.

Eggs.—The eggs are similar to those of the American golden plover; the ground colors average paler. In three sets they run from "light buff" to "cream color"; Mr. Brandt's eggs run from "ivory yellow" to "vinaceous buff"; and in two eggs figured by Mr. Poynting (1895) the ground colors are in shades of "olive buff." Mr. Brandt says in his notes:

The eggs of this bird are no doubt subject to much variation for the two sets are very different. On one the surface markings are distinct and elongated longitudinally while on the other clutch large blotches almost cover the larger end. These spots are brownish black to black where the pigment is rich, but when occasionally it is thin, as on a few outlying edges, it becomes brick red. Pursuant to the usual rule with many of the boldly marked eggs of the shore birds the underlying spots are few and ill defined. These are in lavender tones from pale mouse gray to grayish lavender.

The measurements of 34 eggs average 48 by 33.2 millimeters; the eggs showing the four extremes measure **51.8** by 32.5, 48.5 by **34.9**, **45.2** by 32.4, and 46.4 by **31.5** millimeters.

Young.—The incubation period is probably the same as it is for the European bird, 27 days; both sexes incubate the eggs and care for the young. Thayer and Bangs (1914) write:

Mr. Koren watched the habits of the birds closely and found that the males appear to do all the incubating in the early stages, the female at that time never being near the nest. Later on, when the eggs are nearly ready to hatch, she appears again and takes her turn with the male. When the young are hatched, both parent birds are always with them. At Cape Chelakhskai, August 27, 1912, large flocks of young birds were seen ready to migrate.

Miss Haviland (1915a) says:

As soon as the young ones were able to run alone, which, roughly speaking, was about July 20, the birds left the higher ground and began to collect into flocks in the marshy places of the tundra. I am inclined to think that the young birds must need to wash and drink a great deal, as otherwise it is not easy to understand why all the waders of the tundra should leave the nesting sites so early and wander down to the sphagnum swamps. Some of the Asiatic golden plover even crossed the mud hills and came down to the banks of the river.

Plumages.—The downy young Pacific golden plover is like the American bird of the same age except that the yellow is rather brighter, about "lemon chrome," and decidedly more extensive; it predominates over the black on the crown, back, and rump; there is very little white anywhere except in the patch under the eye and on the chin, throat, and under parts. Miss Haviland (1915a), however, says:

The white tract between the homogeneous mottling of the crown and nape, and the successive black and yellow bands which lie above and behind the eye, and which in *C. apricarius* is sometimes hardly discernible, is very pronounced in *C. fulvus* and has enlarged at the expense of the colored bands below it. The nape and upper part of the body are more spotted with white, and there is little or no yellow on the cheek below the eye.

Subsequent plumages and molts are apparently similar to those of the other golden plovers. Doctor Henshaw (1910) writes:

It is of interest to note that in fall this plover migrates before it molts; in spring it molts before it migrates. The first birds to reach the archipelago in August are, as stated, adults, and while they are practically in full breeding dress they begin to molt into the winter dress almost at once. The molting season for the species is long, and many individuals, doubtless birds of the year, may be found the last of December still molting into the fall and winter dress. By the middle of February numerous individuals are already beginning to molt a second time and to assume the distinctive nuptial plumage, which, in the case of these early birds, is practically completed during the month of March, though individuals continue to moult far into April and some no doubt complete the final stages in Alaska. Doubtless the individuals to molt first in spring are the adults which arrive first, and finish the fall molt first; and doubtless, too, these are the birds first to leave Hawaii for their breeding grounds in Alaska. So protracted is the molt of the species that it is probably true that during the stay of this plover in Hawaii—from middle August till May—there is not a month when some individuals are not molting.

There is no reason for believing that the plover summering in the islands which, as before stated, are chiefly if not wholly immature birds, participate in the spring molt.   At all events the Hawaiian summer plover and turnstones that I have seen were, without exception, in the winter garb.

Food.—Lucien M. Turner (1886) says that, on their first arrival in Alaska, the plover " feed principally on berries of the *Vaccinium* and *Empetrum*, as many of these berries do not dislodge until succeeding growths push them off."   Others have noted the same habit in late summer and early fall.   Some observers on the Pribilof Islands have noted that they frequent the killing grounds and feed extensively on the blowfly maggots there.   But Preble and McAtee (1923) say that in the two stomachs that they examined " none of these larvæ were found, their food contents consisting of beetles, 72.5 per cent; flies, 22.5 per cent; Hymenoptera, 4 per cent; and seeds of crowberry (*Empetrum nigrum*), 1 per cent."

Doctor Henshaw (1910) writes:

During its stay in the islands the plover, as also the turnstone, feed chiefly in the upland pastures and clearings, up to 6,000 or 7,000 feet, and on newly plowed cane land.   Both the sugar planter and the stock raiser have much to thank the plover for, since, while the birds feed on small seeds to some extent, they live chiefly on insects, and according to Perkins, on insects of much economic importance, since they depend largely on the caterpillars of two of the most widely spread and destructive of the island " cut worms."   These insects are most abundant when the grass on the island pastures is green and luxuriant, and this usually is in winter, when rains are most copious.

Behavior.—The general behavior of the Pacific golden plover is not different from that of its commoner relatives.   My personal acquaintance with it was made on the high rolling tundra and the foot-hills back of Nome, Alaska.   Here we found it quite common during the middle of July, where it was evidently breeding or had been breeding; and we collected quite a series of adults, juvenals, and even downy young.   As we walked over the tundra, we frequently heard their rich, melodious, whistling notes, or saw a richly colored adult, in full nuptial plumage, standing like a sentinel on some little hummock or ridge.   Occasionally one would try to entice us away by running slowly through the hollows or by fluttering along the ground as if injured; but eventually it would take wing and circle back to where its young were probably hidden.

Mr. Brandt says in his notes:

The Pacific golden plover's adroit movements in approaching his nest, made to deceive the hostile eye, were interesting, and well illustrate the tactics of the members of the plover family found about Hooper Bay.   He would run rapidly without visible bodily effort, and then stop abruptly and remain motionless, not even turning his head.   His course always lay across the little ridges, never along them, and he would follow the slight depressions, but usually came to a halt on a little eminence.   When close to me, in order to get a wider range of vision, he would raise himself on the terminal joints of his toes and stretch up his neck, all with a jerky motion, the whole reminding me somewhat of the action of the burrowing owl. If agitated he ran rapidly to and fro, uttering an occasional piping note, but seldom taking wing.

Voice.—John T. Nichols describes the notes of this plover very well as follows:

I have met this western race of the golden plover only on its breeding grounds (at Nome, Alaska) where its notes are quite unlike the flight note of the eastern bird in migration, though some have almost an identical quality with that call. Running about on the ground, voicing noisy protest at the invasion of its ground, it has two unlike cries used interchangeably, *peep!* etc.; *loodlee*, etc.; the first plaintive, the second mellow. Other less frequent notes are *tudleu* and *tdlu-eep* suggesting the semipalmated plover. When the two members of a pair alight together for a moment a note of greeting suggests in form the whip-poor-will's call, *piterweeu, piterweeu, piterwit* or *peeperwip, peeperweeu, peeperwip.*

A different, striking note is associated with what seems to be nuptial display. A bird circles at moderate height waving widespread wings in slow, measured, tern-like manner, meanwhile uttering a loud, long-drawn, sweet *pee-er-wee*, and in a few minutes dives to the tundra and alights. The form of this call is rather that of the black-bellied plover though its tone is that of the golden.

Miss Haviland (1915a) describes similar notes and observes that, "roughly speaking, the alarm note of the common golden plover is monosyllabic; that of the Asiatic golden plover is dissyllabic; and that of the gray plover is distinctly trisyllabic in character."

Fall.—The plover which breed in Alaska migrate over Bering Sea, stopping on the Pribilof Islands; the first birds, probably adults, come during August; the young birds come later, mainly in September and October, with one very late date, November 5. The few available dates for the Aleutian and Commander Islands are also late, September and October, probably young birds. The first birds to reach the Hawaiian Islands are adults in breeding plumage; they arrive about the middle or latter part of August; and Doctor Henshaw (1910) says "that they are invariably in good flesh and that some are very fat. Later arrivals, however, no doubt young of the year, are comparatively poor in flesh and require considerable time to fatten." This flight to these islands is a most remarkable feat, for, even granted that they can rest and feed to some extent on the surface of the ocean, it still remains a mystery how they can find this little group of islands in the middle of such a vast expanse of ocean. Doctor Henshaw (1910) makes some suggestions which throw some light on the subject; he says:

About September the wind that prevails in the North Pacific immediately south of the Aleutians is from the northwest. It is generally believed that migrating birds prefer to fly on a beam wind. By heading southwest birds migrating to Hawaii might have the northwest abeam till about the neighborhood of latitude 30° where they would be almost sure to pick up the northeast trades. By then changing their course to southeast they would be enabled to fly with wind abeam till they sighted the islands. The Hawaiian Archipelago with the chain of low islands and sand spits to the northwest afford a reasonable chance for a successful landfall, since unitedly they stretch away in a very thin line for some 2,200 miles. Moreover the islands are close enough together so that migrants high in air would not be likely to miss them by passing between.

The birds which breed in Siberia are probably those that migrate through Mongolia and Japan and spend the winter in India, Burma, the Malay Archipelago, and Australia.

Winter.—Maj. G. Ralph Meyer has sent me the following notes on this plover in the Hawaiian Islands:

The plover are very plentiful and I see them passing over every day. They usually arrive about the middle of August and remain until the middle of March. Along about that time of the year they seem to congregate on the flats on the northeast end of the island and probably leave from there on the long flight to Alaska. During the winter they alternate between the plains of the high central plateau of the island and the lowland on both sides of the island. On the east side there is some low grassy land and they are common there. On this side they frequent tide flats during the low tides and then go up into the central plateau during the high tides. They perhaps spend some of the time in sheltered ponds on this side and wherever they can find muddy flats on which to feed.

The call note when flying is usually a whistled *too-whee*, easily imitated. They answer to the call note very readily and we use this when hunting them. We use plover decoys, placing them in the mud flats during high tide, and then at the turning of the tide the birds come from the direction of the mountains to feed. The decoys are placed on the highest part of the flats, so that the birds will have no other place to alight. We face the decoys up the wind, as the birds usually face that way when they are feeding. As they come near we call to them, merely imitating their call. They will circle around and finally decoy very nicely if they are not alarmed by any sudden movement. When circling around decoys they make a sort of chuckling noise, which I can not describe except as a chuckling whistle. Occasionally a wandering tattler will decoy and very often we get turnstones. On one occasion last year I saw a flock of about 20 to 30 birds, apparently turnstones, flying in a "V" or semicircle formation, and the leader was undoubtedly a plover. The birds were a couple of hundred feet in the air, so I could not be sure of the turnstones, but I was sure of the plover. He was leading them, for they followed him wherever he went. On a visit to Hawaii in July, 1916, I found plover on the slopes of Mauna Loa, one of the high mountains of the island. I have never seen them on this island during the summer.

W. B. Alexander tells me that this plover is—

a common visitor to Australian coasts, especially in summer, though some appear to be present at all seasons. While in Australia this species is usually found in small flocks and is partial to reedy swamps and the margins of lakes, as well as to estuaries fringed with mangroves. In fact, it evidently likes cover, though it may be met with on the open sea beach.

In his notes from Australia, Charles Barrett says:

All parts of the Commonwealth receive their quota of golden plover, and in the southern portions of the country the birds are seen about the end of October (early summer). The species is nowhere very plentiful (A. J. Campbell), but I have seen it often, singly, or in small flocks, in different localities, chiefly along the seashore and on swampy land, seeking small shellfish, etc. Sometimes it associates with the black-bellied plover (*Squatarola squatarola*). In the Capricorn Group I met with it in fair numbers on the Masthead Island beaches. Like other migrants observed among the isles, the plover were fresh arrivals, and each day their numbers increased. They were in poor condition and seemed to be exhausted after their great migratory flight. Some of the specimens taken by collectors in our party still retained some of the breeding plumage; in one example the breast was almost black.

In New South Wales I observed this species on the sand spits at the sea entrance to Wallis Lake in October, 1921. They were wary, but through field glasses we could see them busily seeking for food. In my own State, Victoria, specimens have been taken both in the summer and winter plumage. The birds frequent open grass country, as well as the seashore; in fact, they are more abundant often in country of this class than elsewhere in a district. Frequently, however, they are seen along river banks and on sea beaches, feeding in company with other species.

DISTRIBUTION

Range.—Alaska, Asia, Australia, and Oceania; casual in Europe and on the Pacific coast of North America.

Breeding range.—The Pacific golden plover breed mainly in Siberia but, as mentioned under *Pluvialis d. dominica*, they range also to western Alaska, where they apparently meet and intergrade with their eastern relatives. The breeding range may be stated as extending north to eastern Siberia (Yenisei River, Cape Chelyuskin, Liakhof Island, Nijni Kolymsk, Cape Baranof, Chaun Bay, and Cape Serdze); and Alaska (Wainwright). East to Alaska (Wainwright, probably Point Hope, probably Cape Blossom, Cape Prince of Wales, Nome, St. Michael, and Igiak Bay). South to Alaska (Igiak Bay); and Siberia (Bering Island, Kamchatka, and the Yenisei River). West to western Siberia (Yenisei River).

Winter range.—The winter range extends north to India, China, Japan, and to Hawaiian Islands (Midway, Kauai, and Maui Islands). East to the Hawaiian Islands (Maui), Polynesia, and New Zealand. South to New Zealand and Tasmania. West to Tasmania, Australia, Melanesia, Java, Borneo, and India.

Migration.—The migration of the Pacific golden plover nesting in Alaska, appears to be entirely oceanic, the flight in both directions being without intermediate stops. Nonbreeding individuals frequently remain all summer in the Hawaiian Islands and at other points in Oceania.

Spring migration.—Early dates of arrival are: China, Soochow, April 18, Shanghai, April 21, and Canton, April 30; Japan, Hakodate, May 7; Siberia, Bering Island, May 15, and Nijni Kolymsk, May 30; and Alaska, St. Michael, May 2, Bethel, May 8, Portage Bay, May 13, Hooper Bay, May 16, and Cape Prince of Wales, May 19.

Fall migration.—Late dates of fall departure are: Alaska, mouth of the Yukon River, October 12, St. Paul Island, October 25, and Attu Island, October 31; and Siberia, Bering Island, October 28.

Casual records.—This species has been reported as a casual from Algeria, Malta, Italy, Spain, Heligoland, Poland, and the British Isles (B. O. U.). In North America, specimens identified as this race, have been collected in British Colombia, Comox, November 2, 3, and 4, 1903, and Masset, August 10, 1920; Washington, Kahlotus, December 19, 1924; Idaho, Lake Chatcolet, October 1, 1923; and Maine, Scarborough, September 11, 1911.

Egg Dates.—Bering Sea coast of Alaska: 15 records, May 23 to July 1; 8 records, June 11 to 27. Siberia: 5 records, June 30 to July 5.

OXYECHUS VOCIFERUS (Linnaeus)

KILLDEER

HABITS

Contributed by Charles Wendell Townsend

It may be said of the killdeer that it is probably the most widely distributed and best known of all our shore birds. Unlike most of the group, it is not confined to the borders of lakes and of the sea but is found in meadows, pastures, and dry uplands often many miles from water. Unlike, also, the majority of our shore birds, its sojourn here is not limited to the migration periods, for it breeds and winters throughout a large portion of the United States. It is not of a retiring disposition, and it often makes its presence known by loud calls and cries, to which it owes both its common and scientific names—killdeer and *vociferus*. Its strikingly marked and handsome plumage makes it very conspicuous when it is in motion, as is nearly always the case. In all these respects it resembles the European lapwing, a resemblance to which both Wilson and Audubon called attention. Wilson (1832) says that "this restless and noisy bird is known to almost every inhabitant of the United States."

During the latter part of the last century and early in this persecution by shooting brought down the numbers of the killdeer so that in certain parts of the country where it formerly bred it became extremely rare. Thus, Forbush (1925) says:

The killdeer was once a common breeding bird in New England. Early in the present century it became so reduced in numbers that it was believed to have been practically exterminated as a breeding species. * * * Legislation protecting it perpetually has resulted in a gradual increase of the species which is now nesting locally but not uncommonly in the coastal region and river valleys of southern New England.

Other evidence of a similar nature is that of W. J. Brown (1916), who says: " Ten years ago the killdeer was a rare summer resident in the Province of Quebec. During the past five seasons the bird has become very numerous and is now a common breeder."

The killdeer is one of the most beneficial of birds; it is a delight to the eye as it runs along the field or swiftly flies and skims the ground, and its familiar calls are pleasing. Long may it flourish unharmed by man!

Spring.—The migration of the killdeer is not as marked as is that of other shore birds whose winter station is far removed from the summer breeding grounds, for it breeds in many places where it winters. As a spring migrant it is one of the earliest of shore birds; indeed, there are few land birds that precede it, coming generally in small scattered flocks, which are augmented if the birds loiter on the way. Prof. William Rowan writes of its migration at Edmonton, Alberta:

It is the first wader to come North in the spring and the last to go South in the fall. It may arrive as early as the middle of March and stay till the middle of November. These are remarkable dates for a shore bird in this country, since the lakes remain frozen as a rule till the end of April and exceptionally right into May. Even the rivers may remain solid till the middle of April.

Lynds Jones says that the killdeer, robin, and bluebird arrive about the same time in Ohio. M. P. Skinner writes of the killdeer in the Yellowstone Park that—

Usually this bird arrives on warm mornings, but on one occasion they came on a morning when the thermometer registered below zero, but a few hours later at 10 o'clock there was a sudden change and the temperature shot up above 40° F.

The killdeers migrate by day and also by night, their calls proclaiming them during the darkness.

Courtship.—The most noticeable courtship performances of the killdeer are those that take place in the air—the nuptial flight—but those that occur on the ground, although less often seen, are also spectacular.

Of the courtship in the air Dwight Isely (1912) says that in Kansas " during the first month or six weeks after their arrival killdeers seem to spend a large part of their time in courtship. The male will fly back and forth over a field giving its cry sometimes for over an hour without intermission."

Arthur T. Wayne (1910) says of the bird near Charleston: " During very cold weather the killdeer rises several hundred yards in the air, hovering on almost motionless wings and uttering its far-reaching notes. I have known a pair to remain in the heavens for fully an hour during the coldest weather." M. P. Skinner of the Yellowstone Park writes: "Although the killdeer is not a song bird I have heard some quite musical notes and even tuneful sequences from him. On the 4th of April one was heard singing while flying low in a circle over the nesting ground, and the performance was strongly suggestive of a nuptial flight song."

S. F. Rathbun of Seattle has communicated the following interesting account of his observations on the subject:

The evolutions were participated in by both birds of the pair that I watched on several occasions, and, as my knowledge goes, very early in spring prior to nesting. At this time these birds were evidently mated. As they fed about the margin of a small pond, one invariably following the other, suddenly the bird in the lead would spring into the air and mount upwards by a succession of wide, sweeping spirals, with its mate in pursuit constantly uttering its notes in a short and hurried manner. Higher and higher was the flight, but restricted over the certain àrea of the pond until both disappeared from one's vision, although the note continued to be faintly heard. As I continued to watch, the birds' cry ceased and down from the sky I first noted a speck falling, then both came into plain sight, one following the other, and then both alighted. This descent was as quickly made as if the birds fell out of the ether. After alighting the former actions were again indulged in, and shortly after the high flight was again made. These actions were repeated several times during my stay of over two hours in the vicinity.

From these reports it is evident that the courtship flight is performed in various ways, and, as Audubon (1840) says, " It skims quite low over the ground, or plays at a great height in the air, particularly during the love season, when you may see these birds performing all sorts of evolutions on the wing."

Of courtship display on the ground Theed Pearse (1924) writes:

On two occasions that I saw one getting up he ran a short distance and then went through what looked like a sexual display. Crouching on the ground and leaning toward one side with wings lowered and then opening the tail in fan shape over the back so that the cinnamon tail coverts came conspicuously into view, at the same time uttering a trilling note.

Aretas Saunders (1926) thus describes the display:

Two birds would crouch side by side but facing in opposite directions. Then they would droop the tips of the wings so that they exposed the ochraceous patch of the lower back, spread the tail, and tip the breast forward, slowly lifting the wing tips till they came way above the back, but never covered it from view. All the while they kept up a continual call, the long-trilled note *t-r-r-r-r-rrrrr*. The displaying birds would often begin the performance or end it with a little fighting.

Ira N. Gabrielson (1922) reports a case where—

the male had taken his station some distance from the female and at intervals whirled rapidly about, uttering a curious stuttering note as he did so. Every few seconds the female advanced a few steps toward the male, but when he stopped to observe the effect of this display she quickly turned her back and appeared perfectly indifferent. This was repeated several times until the female suddenly flew away.

This behavior of the female is very characteristic and common in avian, as well as in other courtship. In whirling about, the brown tail coverts must show prominently and the "stuttering note" may be another term for the "trilling note" used by other writers.

Nesting.—The killdeer nests in the open, generally in a situation that gives the bird on the nest an extended view. The nest may be close to water—river, lake, or pond more often than the sea—but it is generally in fields a few feet to several hundred yards or even a mile or two from water. Pastures, meadows, cultivated fields, and bare gravelly ground are favorite nesting places for this bird. Gravel roads and the spaces between the ties of a railroad and even a graveled roof have all been chosen by this bird for laying its eggs.

As a rule, the ground is slightly hollowed out for the eggs and a few chips of stone, wood, or weed stalks are placed in and about the hollow. Within narrow bounds there is considerable variation, and I have here set down some of the numerous nests described. Ira N. Gabrielson (1922) says:

In this region [Oregon] the favorite nesting place was at the base of a hill of corn. As usual, little or no attempt was made to build a nest—a few pebbles and bits of corn husks being the usual type. This material is seldom concentrated into a nest but is scattered over an area of 1 or more square feet, the eggs being deposited on the ground at some point within this area. * * * A rather unusual nest was found. It was placed in a small depression and carefully lined with shredded corn husks.

Harold C. Bryant (1914) reports in Merced County, Calif.—

Another nest found May 15 was unique in the fact that it was placed in a small grassy knoll surrounded by water, and that the cavity was well lined with short stems of devil grass.

J. M. Bates (1916) says of nests found in Nebraska:

The dirt is scooped out the size of my hand and is laid with thin, flat scraps of magnesian sand shale averaging an inch long. While a few dead stems lie with the stones, there is no appearance of design in their presence.

Charles R. Stockard (1905) says of the killdeer in Mississippi:

The eggs are never hidden in the grass or weeds but are placed in slight depressions on the bare ground or on short grass turf. The saucerlike depression of a nest has scattered in it bits of shells, small pebbles, short pieces of weeds or sticks, and often small bits of crayfish armor. This rubbish is never arranged so as to form a real nest, since only a few bits of it are scattered in the depression.

M. P. Skinner writes as follows of this bird nesting in the Yellowstone National Park:

All the nests I have found were on high, dry land, although never more than two or three hundred yards from water, while some were within 20 feet of it.

One nest was in a depression in the meadow grass, but not otherwise lined or showing any construction. All the other nests were on knolls or ridges, either on gravel soil or on gray formation; they were in depressions varying from a shallow saucer-shaped hollow to one that was 2 inches deep by 3 inches in diameter; and in each case the birds appear to have taken possession of a previous hollow, although possibly deepening and otherwise forming it to their purpose. All nests were unlined, although one had a few sprays of sage and phlox around the edge and another had a few shreds of dried and bleached wood scattered about.

John G. Tyler (1913), writing of the nests in Fresno district, California, says:

A typical nest throughout the cultivated sections is composed of a handful of white pebbles about the size of peas and very uniform in size, mixed with an equal number of dry shells of melon seeds of the previous year. Frequently a few dry, broken-up pieces of melon stems are used also, the whole being spread out over a space the size of a saucer, with the eggs resting in the center * * *. On the summer-fallow fields only a few dry grass blades line the place where the eggs rest, while around the ponds of the west side, the eggs generally lie half covered in the powdered alkali dust without a scrap of nest lining.

W. J. Brown (1916) speaks of finding many attempts at excavating nests in the ground not far from the real nest. He suggests they may be decoy nests. Mrs. Henry W. Nelson (1900) reports a case where the eggs were laid in the bare gravel driveway and were moved by the gardener to the edge of the turf out of the way of carriages. The bird continued to incubate. W. Lee Chambers (1901) relates the case of a killdeer's nest between the ties on a used railroad track; F. W. Aldrich, of one between double tracks of a well-used railroad, and notes of a similar case to the latter have been sent by F. A. E. Starr.

Gayle Pickwell (1925) found near Lincoln, Nebr., the nest of a killdeer in a rubbish heap of broken glass, old bottles, and other material with which the dark mottled eggs harmonized so closely in color that they were invisible until closely approached. In fact killdeers' eggs are so protectively colored for the usual surroundings that the instinct of nest concealment by furtive abandonment is exhibited by the killdeer as in the case of most shore birds.

The most unusual case of the nesting of the killdeer is that observed by Mr. Pickwell (1925) in the same locality on the gently sloping tarred and graveled roof of a race-track grandstand, some 50 feet above the ground. The eggs were laid in a slight cup-shaped depression among the crushed stones. Close observation showed that the relative position of the eggs in the nest was changed daily between 10.30 a. m. and 3 p. m., and it was not unusual to find them with their points away from the center of the nest. The young were found on the ground near the building while still but feeble walkers. In what manner the old ones transferred them from the roof was not observed.

Eggs.—[AUTHOR'S NOTE: The number of eggs in a set is almost always four, but five and three have been found. Mr. Pickwell (1925) says the roof-nesting killdeer " laid at least three clutches of eggs during the season extending from early April to the last of June, and she may have raised two broods." The eggs are ovate pyriform in shape, usually quite pointed, and they have no gloss. The ground colors vary from "light buff " or "cream color " to "cartridge buff " or "ivory yellow." They are irregularly spotted, blotched, or scrawled, often quite boldly, with blackish brown or black; some eggs have "sepia " blotches and some a few underlying spots of "pale drab gray." The measurements of 92 eggs average 36.3 by 26.6 millimeters; the eggs showing the four extremes measure **41.5** by 27, 39.5 by **28** and **33** by **25** millimeters.]

Young.—The incubation period according to the observations of J. A. Spurrell (1917) is from 24 to 25 days; according to Ira N. Gabrielson (1922) it is 25 days. J. M. Bates (1916) found it to be 26 days and Althea R. Sherman (1916) found that 28 days elapsed between the laying of the last egg and hatching.

Both sexes incubate (F. L. Burns, 1915), and both take care of the young. Robert B. Rockwell (1912) relates the following:

" Mr. [L. J.] Hersey was fortunate enough to see one set of eggs hatch. He says the parent birds carried every bit of shell away from the nest within two hours after the hatching." As soon as the moisture has dried from the down, the young are on their feet and leave the nest and the parents often lead them to the nearest water. They bob and call at an early age. Althea R. Sherman (1916) had watched a nest very closely from the beginning, but she says of the young: " So protective was their coloration, so adroit was parental management that they were not seen after leaving the nest until they had attained the size of adult house sparrows." The young often escape notice by lying motionless on the ground. At such times they may sometimes be picked up without showing signs of life.

Both parents play the usual wounded-bird act to beguile the intruder from the eggs or young. The following detailed account by Ira N. Gabrielson (1922) is worth giving here:

It is impossible to approach the nest on foot without alarming one or other of the birds, as one was always on guard some distance away. At the appearance of a person walking, the one on guard would fly in a circle about the nest, giving the alarm, at the first note of which the one on the nest ran rapidly until some distance away and then took wing to join its mate in circling about the intruder. A man ploughing corn was viewed with absolute indifference by both birds, the team often passing down the row next to the nest without disturbing the sitting bird. At an alarm, however, both birds flew about the field unless the intruder persisted in approaching the nest. In such a case one of the birds dropped to the ground near the person, invariably on the side away from the nest, and fluttered about apparently in the greatest distress. The attitude most frequently assumed was as follows: one wing was held extended over the back, the other beat wildly in the dust, the tail feathers were spread and the bird lay flat on the ground, constantly giving a wild alarm note. This performance continued until the observer came very near when the bird would rise and run along the ground in a normal manner or at most with one wing dragging slightly as long as pursuit was continued. If the observer turned back toward the nest, however, these actions were immediately repeated. When the parents had succeeded in luring the intruder about 100 yards, they seemed satisfied as they then flew away.

M. P. Skinner found that when he scared one bird from the nest, the mate was apt to steal around behind him and take its place on the nest. He says that

In addition to their broken-wing tactics, both of the killdeer at times would pretend to brood anywhere on the foundation, evidently to lead me to think that that was where their nest was. * * * On one occasion I found an adult with one young about four days old. The youngster ran under the old one and into its feathers; then the old bird squatted down, covering it. Just then I saw the other bird come running and exchange with the first parent, nestling down over the youngster.

While the broken wing tactics are used by the birds for man, dogs, and other predatory animals, in order to draw them away from the eggs or young, quite different tactics are used for browsing animals that might step on them. Thus Howard Lacey (1911) noticed that a flock of driven goats divided. "I walked up to the place expecting to find a rattlesnake, and found instead a killdeer standing over her eggs with upspread wings and scolding vigorously." Norman Criddle (1908) writes "If the danger came from a cow or horse, the tactics were changed and the birds with both wings and feathers spread out would run into the animal's face, and so by startling it drive the intruder away." This habit of scaring away a browsing animal probably accounts for the following experiences related by M. P. Skinner. The change to the broken-wing tactics appears to show great discernment and intelligence on the part of the bird.

Twice when riding near two different unsuspected nests, the birds got up with startled cries and faced me with their tails spread horizontally and quivering, although I was on horseback and towered high above them. After a few moments they made off with pretended broken wings, limping, falling down and fluttering.

Aretas A. Saunders (1926) observed a parent very zealous in the care of its young:

This brood of young was accompanied by a parent. They occupied a certain section of the shore of the pond, where the young hid beneath the rushes when danger approached, and ran over the mud flats at other times. The parent remained near, and drove all other birds from the vicinity. While shore birds and marsh birds were abundant all around the Mill Pond, at this point they kept away because of the parent killdeer. The parent was extremely belliger-ent, and I watched it attack other killdeers, yellowlegs, spotted sandpipers, soras, and song sparrows that happened to wander in the vicinity. All birds seemed glad to leave the vicinity.

Plumages.—[AUTHOR'S NOTE: The most distinctive feature of the downy young killdeer is the long, downy tail, black above and else-where barred with "pinkish buff" and black, with long, hair-like, buffy down below protruding beyond the rest of the tail; the fore-head, chin, throat, a ring around the neck and the under parts are pure white, except for a tinge of pinkish buff in the center of the forehead; a broad, black stripe above the forehead extends around the crown to the occiput; a black stripe extends from the lores, below the eyes to the occiput; there is a broad black stripe entirely around the neck, below the white; the crown, auriculars, back and inner half of the wings are grizzled "vinaceous buff" and dusky; there is a black space in the center of the back and a black band across the wing between the grizzled inner half and the white distal half.

The juvenal plumage is similar to that of the adult, but the head markings are less distinct; the feathers of the nape are tipped with "amber brown" and those of the back, scapulars, wing coverts and tertials are more or less broadly tipped or edged with the same, more broadly on the scapulars and wing coverts and more narrowly on the upper back and tertials; the intermediate white band on the breast is always more or less suffused with brownish.

The postjuvenal molt is apparently very limited and the first win-ter plumage is largely the juvenal plumage modified by wear. It is much like the adult except for the worn and faded edgings of the wing coverts, and some of the scapulars and tertials and the tail, which are retained. At the first prenuptial molt, which may take place from February to June, the plumage becomes practically adult.

Adults have a complete postnuptial molt, mainly in August and September, and a partial prenuptial molt of the body plumage in early spring. Nuptial and winter plumages are practicaly alike.]

Food.—The killdeer is man's friend. It consumes great quantities of insect pests. The most complete study of its food by examination of stomachs has been made by W. L. McAtee (1912) who sums up as follows:

" In all 97.72 per cent of the killdeer's food is composed of insects and other animal matter. The bird preys upon many of the worst crop pests and is a valuable economic factor." Of this large propor-tion he finds that beetles constitute 37.06 per cent; other insects—grasshoppers, caterpillars, ants, bugs, caddis flies, dragon flies, and two-winged flies, 39.54 per cent; other invertebrates—centipedes, spi-ders, ticks, oyster worms, earthworms, snails, crabs, crawfish, and other crustaceans, 21.12 per cent. The 2.28 per cent of vegetable matter is chiefly made up of weed seeds such as button weed, smart weed, foxtail grass, and nightshade. He found that various kinds of weevils were eaten such as those of alfalfa, cotton boll, clover, rice, white pine, etc. In a single stomach he counted 41 alfalfa weevils.

Harold C. Bryant (1914a), during an outbreak of grasshoppers in California, found that the contents of one stomach was 100 per cent grasshoppers, and he estimated that each killdeer averaged 33 grasshoppers daily. Arthur H. Howell (1906) has found that the killdeer is among the most important of the birds that eat the cotton-boll weevil. Samuel Aughey (1878) found 258 locusts and 190 other insects in the stomachs of nine birds taken in Nebraska. E. R. Kalmbach (1914) found in the stomach of a killdeer taken in a western alfalfa field 316 weevils; in another 383. C. W. Nash (1909) has found the stomachs of killdeers taken in orchards completely filled with weevils. E. R. Kalmbach (1914) has also found May beetles both in adult and grub form in the stomachs, wireworms, and insects that attack sugar cane, corn, carrots, grape vine, sweet potato, tobacco, and sugar beets. Caterpillars, he found to be a favorite article of diet, also grasshoppers and crickets, crane flies and their larvae. One stomach contained hundreds of larvae of the salt marsh mosquito. He adds:

The killdeer thus befriends man, but it does something also for the domestic animals, not only by eating horseflies and mosquitoes, as just mentioned, but also by preying on ticks, including the American fever or cattle tick, which has caused such enormous losses in some parts of the South.

Arthur T. Wayne (1910) says: "This species is very partial to fields which are being ploughed, and at this time they are always very tame, following each furrow as soon as it is turned over in order to secure the worms which are exposed." I have watched a killdeer in a ploughed field swallowing a large earthworm. Several strenuous gulps were needed before the act was accomplished.

Behavior.—The interesting behavior of this bird during courtship and in the care of the eggs and young has already been detailed under the appropriate headings. In general it may be said that the killdeer has the usual plover habits when feeding of alternately running and then of standing still, as if to listen or look, always with head up, and of dabbing suddenly at the ground for its food. Like some other species of plover, it occasionally bobs or " teeters " in a nervous manner. This varies from a slight bob of the head, which is first hitched up and then brought down, to a bob combined with a tilting up and down of the whole body on the hips. In swift running they excel, and this serves them to good purpose in the pursuit of insects.

M. P. Skinner writes: "When they get out on bare ground their speed is really astonishing. I have had them run along the road ahead of my horse for quite a distance." In plover fashion and unlike sandpipers, the killdeer in feeding does not keep in a compact flock but spreads out irregularly. John F. Ferry (1908) writes: "A curious sight was that of numbers of these birds scattered about the lawns at Leland Stanford University while the sprinklers were in operation. This recalled the robins on the lawns of the Eastern States."

Sometimes a number fairly close together may be found crouching on the sand or gravel asleep, or they may sleep standing, often on one foot. One or more are awake, however, watching, all from time to time open their eyes and look about. Notwithstanding their striking coloration, one may walk almost to a flock under these circumstances without noticing them. The " ruptive " marks about the head and neck break the continuity of the surface and the bird is not recognized as such.

The flight of the killdeer is rapid, generally close to the ground when the bird is on the lookout for food, but at other times, especially in courtship, as stated above, the flight may be at a great height. They usually fly about singly in a wavering and erratic manner, but sometimes in considerable flocks. Widely scattered birds when startled usually unite into a compact flock and fly away together. W. L. Dawson (1923) says: " I have seen flocks of 50 killdeers bunch closely and turn in silence and disappear in perfect order."

Whenever the killdeer is unmolested, as is the case now under protection, it becomes very tame, as is shown above in the account of the birds at Stanford University. N. S. Goss (1891) writes: " In Coatapec, Mexico, a pair came daily to feed and dress up their feathers beside a little run or gutter in the center of the narrow paved street opposite my room in the hotel, regardless of the people on the sidewalks, only running or dodging to avoid a person crossing or to keep out of the way of a pack of mules, etc."

Voice.—The killdeer is at times the noisiest of birds and is hated by the gunner, for its alarm cries disturb every bird within a long range. The " song " has been described under courtship. F. M. Chapman (1912) well characterizes some of its cries as " half-plaintive, half-petulant." *Kill-deé kill-deé* is the common cry from which it takes its name, for it omits the *r* at the end. But it has a great variety of other cries with which it rends the air, and I find in my notes the following: *kee-kee; eet-eet-eet; kee-ah, kee-ah; dee-dee-dee; tsee-he, tsee-he; tso-he, tso-he; ker, ker, ker*, and piercing *tee-ars*. It is, of course difficult to express these cries properly on paper, and a great variety of syllables have been recorded by different writers.

Aretas A. Saunders (1926) gives the following excellent description:

The calls are mainly of three sorts. The first is the common call heard when one approaches one or more birds, or the vicinity of a nest: *dee dee dee dee-ee kildee dee-ee*, etc., the notes usually slurred slightly upward at the end, at least the longer ones. A second call is the long trilled *t-rrrrrrrrrrrrr*, often heard when the nest or young are threatened, and when the birds are fighting or displaying. The third call is one from which the bird evidently has derived its name. It is usually indulged by birds flying about in the air in loose flocks, particularly early in the morning or toward evening. A number of observers or writers on the notes of this species seem not to have separated this call from the first one. It differs always by the fact that the notes slur downward, instead of upward, on the end. I should write it *kildeeah kildeeah kildeeah*, at least in those forms where the first note is lower in pitch than the second. It is often rendered, however, when the first note is highest in pitch, when it sounds more like *keedeeah keedeeah*.

The name *chewekee* by which it has long been known on the Carolina coast, according to Arthur T. Wayne, is probably descriptive of its cries.

Field marks.—The killdeer is a marked bird in the field, both on account of its plumage and on account of its voice. Its plover ways, its long straw-colored legs, its long tail with buff-colored upper coverts and rump and the two black bars on the breast are all good field marks. It can not be mistaken for any other bird if these points are borne in mind.

Fall.—The fall, for the same reason as the spring migration, is not as marked with the killdeer as with our other shore birds. William Rowan (1926), writing of Alberta, says: "The latest killdeers have been noted in the fall weeks after the freeze-up." Dr. Arthur P. Chadbourne (1889) recorded a memorable reverse flight of killdeer in fall on the Atlantic coast, due to the great November storm of 1888, which distributed them within a mile or two of the coast as far north as Cape Sable, Nova Scotia.

Game.—Fortunately the killdeer is now on the protected list from which it should never be removed, for it is too valuable and attractive a bird to be shot for sport. Before this protection occurred, the birds, as we have seen, were almost exterminated in some parts of the country. In other parts, luckily, they seem to have come under the protection of food prejudice. Thus W. L. Dawson (1909), writing of the birds of Washington State, says, "Fortunately for them, the flesh of the killdeer is not esteemed for food by humans, so they are allowed to gather in peace in full companies."

Enemies.—Besides man, now happily pacified, the killdeer has little to fear in the way of enemies besides a few of the larger hawks and owls. H. H. Kopman (1905) relates a curious case where he found a killdeer caught by the leg at a crayfish hole, with one toe already eaten off. He released the bird and cared for the wound. The bird was able to stand and to fly away the next morning.

Winter.—It is a pleasure to have this bird wintering throughout the southern parts of our country. R. W. Williams (1919), writing of these birds wintering in Florida, says: "They mingled freely with other shore birds on the beach, mud flats, and oyster beds." M. P. Skinner, of the birds observed at Pinehurst, says: "All through the winter, the killdeer seemed to be roughly paired. They might separate two or three hundred feet while feeding, but they always came together again soon, and any intruders were promptly chased off. The first actual mating that I saw was on January 28, 1927."

With enlightened public opinion, a knowledge of the beneficial character of this fine bird and its perpetual protection, there seems to be every prospect that the killdeer will always remain a joy to nature lovers and an aid to farmers.

DISTRIBUTION

Range.—North and Central America, casual in South America and the British Isles.

Breeding range.—The killdeer breeds north to probably Mackenzie (Fort Resolution); Alberta (Fort Chipewyan); Saskatchewan (Buffalo Lake and Churchill River); Manitoba (probably Fort Churchill); Ontario (probably Moose Factory and Ottawa); and Quebec (Montreal, Godbout, and Magdalen Islands). East to Quebec (Magdalen Islands); Maine (Bangor and Saco); New Hampshire (Portsmouth); Massachusetts (Harvard, Cape Cod, and Chatham); Connecticut (West Haven); New York (Plum Island, New York City, and Staten Island); New Jersey (Red Bank and Sea Isle City); Delaware (Lincoln); Maryland (Cambridge); North Carolina (Pea Island and Fort Macon); South Carolina (Ladys Island and formerly Frogmore); Georgia (Savannah and St. Simons Island); eastern Florida (Gainesville, Fruitland Park, Indian River, and Kissimmee); and the northern Bahama Islands (Little Abaco and New Providence). South to the northern Bahama Islands (New Providence); the west coast of Florida (Tarpon Springs, and probably James Island); Alabama (Leighton and Greensboro); Louisiana (State Game Preserve and Mermenton); Texas (Houston, Brownsville, Hidalgo, Eagle Pass, and Fort Hancock); Durango (Sestin); Chihuahua (Pachico and San Diego); and Lower California (Cape San Lucas). West to Lower California (Cape San Lucas, Victoria Mountains, San Quentin Bay, and Volcano Lake); California, Poway Valley, Escondido, Santa Monica, Santa Barbara, Santa Cruz, San Francisco, probably Cahto, and Fort Crook);

Oregon (Tule Lake, Link River, Fort Klamath, Bandon, Dayton, and
Portland) ; Washington (Yakima, Fort Steilacoom, Tacoma, and
probably Lake Chelan) ; British Columbia (Okanagan Landing and
Cariboo District) ; and probably Mackenzie (Fort Resolution).

There also is a somewhat questionable breeding record for the killdeer in Yucatan (Sisal). The breeding range in the northeastern
United States became greatly restricted when this region was extensively developed, but the birds now seem to be increasing in numbers
in this area.

Winter range.—The winter range of the killdeer extends north to
British Columbia (Chilliwack and probably Okanagan Lake) ; Utah
(Antelope Island and Provo) ; Colorado (Mesa County, Boulder, and
Denver) ; rarely Kansas (Harper and Onaga) ; rarely Iowa (Wall
Lake and Grinnell) ; Illinois (Knoxville, La Grange, and Chicago) ;
rarely Indiana (Vincennes, Bicknell, La Fayette, and Indianapolis) ;
rarely Ohio (Hillsboro, probably Oberlin and Salem) ; and rarely
Massachusetts (Marblehead). East to rarely Massachusetts (Marble-
head, Boston, and Monomoy Island) ; rarely Connecticut (Jewett
City, Meriden, and North Haven) ; rarely New York (Long Island
and New York City) ; New Jersey (Atlantic City and Five-mile
Beach) ; District of Columbia (Washington) ; Maryland (Cam-
bridge) ; Virginia (Broadwater, James River, and Back Bay) ; North
Carolina (Pea Island and Ocracoke) ; South Carolina (Waverly
Mills, Mount Pleasant, and Frogmore) ; Georgia (Savannah, Blackbeard Island, Darien, and St. Marys) ; Florida (Amelia Island, St.
Augustine, Daytona Beach, Titusville, and Upper Matecumbe Key) ;
the Bahama Islands (Nassau, Cat Island, Watling Island, and Acklin
Island) ; Haiti (Monte Christi, Sanchez, Samana, and El Valle) ; and
Porto Rico (San Juan). South to Porto Rico (San Juan, Caguas,
and Mayaguez) ; rarely Panama (Davila) ; and Costa Rica (mouth of
the Diquis, San Jose, and Miravalles). West to Costa Rica (Mira-
valles) ; Guatemala (Atitlan and Coban) ; Jalisco (Ocotlan) ; Sinaloa
(Mazatlan) ; Lower California (San Jose del Cabo, La Paz, San
Quentin, and the Colorado River delta) ; California (Escondido, Los
Angeles, San Fernando, Santa Barbara, San Francisco, and Napa) ;
Oregon (Corvallis, Rickreall, and Netarts Bay) ; Washington
(Camas, Tacoma, Dungeness Spit, and Bellingham Bay) ; and
British Columbia (Chilliwack).

The killdeer winters also in Bermuda, and is of casual occurrence at
this season in southern New Hampshire (Isle of Shoals) and in
Michigan (Plymouth).

The West Indian killdeer has been described as a distinct subspecies (*Oxyechus vociferus rubidus*), and is resident. The North
American form does, however, regularly migrate to those islands, and

it may winter there in larger numbers than is now known. Extensive collecting at this season will be necessary to decide this matter.

Spring migration.—Early dates of spring arrival are: New York, Montauk Point, February 17, New York City, February 20, Branchport, March 1, Albany, March 3, and Rochester, March 5; Connecticut, New Haven, February 24, Jewett City, March 2, Fairfield, March 3 and Carrollton, March 4; Rhode Island, Block Island, February 27, Westerly, February 28, Newport, March 4; Massachusetts, Muskeget Island, February 28, and Amherst, March 10; Vermont, Rutland, March 27; Maine, Waterville, March 11, and Farmington, March 28; Quebec, Montreal, March 25; Michigan, Petersburg, February 4, Ann Arbor, February 14, Vicksburg, February 21, and Kalamazoo, February 28; Ontario, Point Pelee, March 2, London, March 4, Hamilton, March 8, Toronto, March 20, and Ottawa, March 26; Iowa, Bentonsport, February 22, Keokuk, February 28, Iowa City, February 28, Fairfield, March 3, and National, March 5; Wisconsin, Unity, March 1, Camp Douglas, March 2, and Racine, March 3; Minnesota, Heron Lake, March 5, Jackson, March 10, Red Wing, March 12, and Lanesboro, March 13; Kansas, Harper, February 4, Wichita, February 7, Topeka, February 15, Onaga, February 22, and Independence, February 25; Nebraska, Omaha, February 19, Dunbar, February 21, and Falls City, February 23; South Dakota, Yankton, March 10, Huron, March 11, and Rapid City, March 12; North Dakota, Argusville, March 15, Fargo, March 18, and Bismarck, March 23; Manitoba, Margaret, March 23, Aweme, March 23, Pilot Mound, March 25, Treesbank, March 28, and Winnipeg, April 12; Saskatchewan, Indian Head, March 27, Eastend, March 27, Lake Johnston, March 30, April 2, and Carleton House, April 6; Wyoming, Yellowstone Park, March 12, and Laramie, March 16, Idaho, Neeley, February 1, Meridian, February 3, and Rathdrum, February 19; Montana, Wisdom, March 5, and Missoula, March 12; and Alberta, Flagstaff, April 2, Nanton, April 8, Veteran, April 10, Red Deer, April 11, and Edmonton, April 15.

Late dates of spring departure from the southern part of the winter range are not numerous, but killdeers have been observed in spring in Panama, March 3; Costa Rica, San Jose, March 15, and Porto Rico, San Juan, March 26.

Fall migration.—The arrival of these birds in that part of the winter range that is south of the breeding range, likewise has not been carefully recorded. Arrivals at this season have been reported from Porto Rico, Aguadilla, October 7; Guatemala, San Geronimo, October 29, Costa Rica, San Jose, October 15; and Nicaragua, Escondido River, November; and Panama, November 26.

Late dates of fall departure are: Alberta, Veteran, September 15, Innisfree-Mundare, September 17, and Edmonton, September 22; Montana, Missoula, December 25 (possibly winters occasionally); Idaho, Meridian, December 14, and Rupert, December 23; Saskatchewan, Eastend, October 10; Manitoba, Treesbank, October 11, Winnipeg, October 12, Aweme, October 15, and Margaret, October 15; North Dakota, Charlson, October 8, and Fargo, October 15; South Dakota, Forestburg, October 30, Sioux Falls, November 7, and Yankton, November 11; Nebraska, Nebraska City, November 10, Beatrice, November 16, and Lincoln, November 18; Kansas, Hayes, November 3, Onaga, November 8, Lawrence, November 11, and Harper, November 25; Minnesota, Correll, October 23, Hutchinson, October 25, Elk River, October 26, and St. Paul, November 26; Wisconsin, Genoa Junction, November 13, Madison, November 14, and Racine, November 16; Iowa, Emmetsburg, November 13, Grinnell, November 15, Keokuk, November 17, and Coralville, November 20; Ontario, Reaboro, November 4, Port Dover, November 8, Listowel, November 10, and Harrow, November 15; Michigan, Croswell, November 4, Sault Ste. Marie, November 5, Jackson, November 9, Livonia, November 13, and Ann Arbor, November 19; Quebec, Montreal, October 26; Maine, Phillips, October 24, and Cape Elizabeth (exceptional), December 25; New Hampshire, Hampton Beach, December 25; Vermont, Bennington, November 12; Massachusetts, Harvard, December 5, and Chatham, December 17; Connecticut, Meriden, November 22, and Hartford, November 30; and New York, Collins, November 22, Rhinebeck, November 24, Branchport, November 29, and Montauk Point, December 10.

Casual records.—The killdeer has been taken both north and south of its normal range in the Western Hemisphere, and casually in the British Isles. In Nova Scotia it was reported from Halifax Harbor on December 5, 1876, and at Meaghers Beach, on January 1 (Downs); Macoun (1909) notes it as a rare migrant in Newfoundland without further details; and a specimen in the British Museum was taken in the Hudson's Bay region. In Alaska, one was reported as seen in August, 1898, on the Kuskokwim River (Hinckley), and a specimen was collected on the Stikine Flats, May 10, 1907 (Willett).

In South America specimens have been reported from several countries but so few in number it does not appear likely that any part of that continent should be included in the regular range. Among these records are: Chile and Paraguay (specimens in the British Museum, date and exact locality of collection unknown); Peru (Tambo Valley, October 25, 1867, Callao [Cassin], Pacasmayo, June, 1877 [Taczanowski], and Arequipa [Sclater and Salvin]); Ecuador (Chaupi, in June [Salvadori and Festa], and Sical, specimen in British Museum); and Colombia (specimen from Medellin in the British Museum).

This species has been taken or observed on a few occasions in England and Scotland (Peterhead, Aberdeenshire, 1867, near Christchurch, Hanto, April, 1857, Kent, April, 1908, Hampshire, April, 1859, and the Scilly Islands, January, 1885), and in Ireland (County Dublin, January 12, 1928).

Egg dates.—California: 73 records, March 15 to July 2; 37 records, April 3 to May 13. Michigan and Wisconsin: 15 records, April 5 to July 6; 8 records, April 29 to June 13. Pennsylvania and New Jersey: 29 records, April 1 to July 17; 15 records, May 2 to 29. Florida: 11 records, May 3 to June 30; 6 records, May 22 to June 9. Texas: 11 records, March 3 to June 2; 6 records, April 3 to June 1.

CHARADRIUS SEMIPALMATUS Bonaparte

SEMIPALMATED PLOVER

HABITS

Contributed by Charles Wendell Townsend

This charming little wader, familiarly known as ring-necked plover or ringneck, is, during migrations, an abundant frequenter of our seashores as well as of the shores of lakes and rivers. But it was not as abundant in the latter part of the last century and in the beginning of this, for, as William Brewster (1925) says: "Both ringnecks and peeps began to diminish appreciably in numbers soon after 1890, and have since continued to do so, no doubt because of the ever-multiplying gunners." Fortunately the Federal law for migratory birds, passed in 1913 and extended to Canada in 1916, enforced by the enabling act in 1918, has since protected the ringneck at all times, and he has responded markedly. Flocks of several hundred are now common where flocks of 30 or 40 were becoming rare. Their confiding nature and handsome plumage make them most interesting and attractive.

Spring.—Like most of the shore birds, the semipalmated plover seems to be in a great hurry to visit the breeding grounds. While, in the region of Massachusetts he leisurely wends his way southward from about July 12 to the end of October, a period of four months, the spring flight rarely lasts little longer than a month, from May 7 to June 14. Wells W. Cooke (1912) says: "At least four-fifths of the dates on the spring migration of this species fall in May. This is true for the entire district between the winter and summer homes, and the dates indicate that the migration in the United States occurs chiefly between May 10 and June 1."

Migration occurs both by day and by night. Flock after flock may be seen on favorable days flying north along a beach, and the distinctive calls of the bird may be heard at night. I have recognized them clearly on a foggy May night when the birds were passing over the city of Boston. There are also records of the striking of lighthouses by these plover during the night.

It is evident that late migrants flying north in the spring must be late in returning, if they rear families, while those that return early in July must have been the early ones to migrate north. On July 30, 1918, I saw three semipalmated plover flying north along the shore at Ipswich. They were in full cry, and I wondered whether they were very late spring migrants or early autumn migrants temporarily turning back, or sterile birds that had no interest in the breeding grounds.

Courtship.—In the latter part of May and early in June on the southern Labrador coast I have seen this brid flying about in circles uttering its loud and rapidly repeated courtship song. The song, which is entirely unlike the call note, may be heard, and the courtship performance watched, not only in the spring but in the autumn migrations, for there is a recrudescence of the amatory instinct at this season in most birds. The song, if such it may be called, is then generally given from the ground and may be likened to a whinny or to the sound of a bouncing ball. The notes are at first slowly repeated, but the speed increases until the notes follow one another so rapidly that they nearly run together. The birds that utter this song crouch low with tails spread and slightly cocked, wings partly open, and feathers, particularly of the breast and flanks, puffed out. Sometimes one walks in this way around another, sometimes two face each other, crouched motionless and then spring at each other and up into the air like fighting cocks. Sometimes one runs after another which, on taking flight is followed by the first, but the most amusing form of this courtship is where two, thus flattened, spread, and puffed, walk slowly side by side as if they were doing a cakewalk, all the time uttering their clucking song.

H. S. Swarth communicates the following notes regarding courtship seen in northwestern British Columbia: "On as late a date as June 25 a male bird was seen going through with the mating antics, following the female about with head lowered and breast puffed out to an absurd degree, uttering frequently a low call note."

Nesting.—A mere depression in the, sand without lining or with only a few bits of shells or grass generally constitutes the nest of this species. P. B. Philipp (1925), writing of his experience in the Magdalens, says: "A nest as such is not constructed. A shallow hollow is scratched in the sand, and this is lined with bits of dead eel-grass, or a hollow is scratched in a bunch of dead seaweed."

H. S. Swarth sends the following notes of his experience with the nesting of this bird in the Atlin region of northwestern British Columbia:

A pair or two are pretty sure to be found where favorable conditions exist, but as the species requires an expanse of sandy or gravelly beach and as such beaches are not the rule about the lakes of the region, there are long stretches of shore line where the plovers are not found. They avoid rocky or stony beaches that are so favored by the spotted sandpipers.

He found his first nest, an unusual one, on the shore of Lake Atlin on June 10, and thus describes it:

The "nest" was in hard-packed gravel in a hole about 1 inch deep and with practically vertical sides. This depression was nearly filled with small chips and a very few straws. The eggs were nearly perpendicular in the nest, points down. It must have been some little labor for the bird to make this excavation, for the gravel was hard enough to retain the shape of the hole throughout the rest of the summer. I returned to the spot in September and found the cavity still sharply defined.

Audubon (1840) says of his experience in Labrador that this plover forms no nest, but makes a "cavity in the moss, in a place sheltered from the north winds and exposed to the full rays of the sun, usually near the margins of small ponds formed by the melting of the snow, and surrounded by short grass."

Eggs.—[AUTHOR'S NOTE: The semipalmated plover lays four eggs, often only three. They are ovate pyriform to subpyriform in shape, with little or no gloss. The ground colors vary from "buckthorn brown" or "clay color" to "cartridge buff," "olive buff" or "pale olive buff." They are boldly and irregularly marked with small or large spots or blotches of black, brownish black or very dark browns; some eggs are heavily blotched with "warm sepia" or "chestnut brown"; there are usually a few small underlying spots of "pale drab gray." The measurements of 100 eggs average 33 by 23.5 millimeters; the eggs showing the four extremes measure **36.2** by 24.3, 35.5 by **25.5** and **29.5** by 22 millimeters.]

Young.—The duration of incubation is not known. In the allied ringed plover of Europe the period of incubation is stated by Dr. W. H. Bergtold (1917) to be 22 and 23 days.

In the past it has generally been assumed that, with the exception in the case of the phalaropes, the female among the shore birds incubates the eggs and takes charge of the young. Joseph Dixon (1927) says: "After several seasons' experience with breeding shore birds in the north the writer has come to believe that in more of our Limicolae than is generally known it is a common practice for the males to take a leading part in domestic duties not only in incubation but also in the care and training of the downy young." With specimens in hand during the breeding season, he found incubating patches in the male semipalmated plover, and he says that "the males did a large part of the incubation and that it was the males that were the most fearless in the face of danger when caring for their young."

P. B. Philipp (1925), on the other hand, studying the nesting bird in the Magdalens, writes: "I judge that the female does most of the incubating, three birds shot off the nest being of this sex." H. S. Swarth also sustains the side of the female, for he writes: "With binoculars it is often possible to distinguish the sexes of the plovers, and it could be seen that it was the male who tired first in such efforts [shamming injury] to deflect danger from the nest. Even when he withdrew entirely, the female continued her protests until we were well out of her territory." Dr. L. B. Bishop (1900), however, reconciles both points of view, for he says: "Bare pectoral spaces showed that both sexes assisted in incubation."

The young leave the nest and run after the parents almost as soon as they are hatched. Bishop (1900) in the Yukon River region found an egg that was already pipped. He says: "I removed the young bird from the shell, and within half an hour the down was almost dry, the eyes were open, and it could hop about on its 'knees.'"

Dr. W. H. Osgood (1909) reports the following observation by N. Hollister on a downy young of this species: "Although it was perfectly able to run about as fast as the adults, it at once lay flat to the ground when approached, with head extended foreward in the sand, making it very difficult to see, so closely did it match the ground in color."

The actions of the parent incubating the eggs when a human intruder appears is well told by H. S. Swarth in a communication, as follows:

The breeding bird skulked from the nest at the first appearance of an intruder, and, after performing an unobtrusive retreat to a distant point, launched out in conspicuous protest at the trespass. The call notes served to summon the mate, and sometimes even another pair of birds, all hovering about overhead or racing close by over the sand. A liquid call note, not particularly loud, was uttered constantly, and both birds of a pair would go through the form of pretended injury, dragging themselves over the sand with drooping wings and spread tail.

In another case—

A bird was flushed, as it had been many times before, at a point 300 yards or more above the water line, and I sat down quietly to watch her from the shelter of a scrubby willow. She flew to a distance, but returned in a few minutes, to run aimlessly about over the gravel nearby. Gradually she drew away, running over and between logs and other drift, her manner changing from one of noisy protest to furtive withdrawal behind any available cover. Finally, about 20 minutes after I began to watch, she settled down on the gravel, as it developed, upon the eggs.

At Seal Island, off the southern point of Nova Scotia, I found several breeding pairs of semipalmated plover, here, probably, at its most southern breeding place. On one occasion I came upon a bird that performed the usual wounded bird act, falling on its side and fluttering its wings as if badly injured. Presently it made off, fluttering and dragging its spread tail on the ground, keeping up this method of progression for over a hundred yards, although I had stood still. I then walked in the opposite direction and found a downy young running off in company with the other parent.

On another occasion at Great Caribou Island, Labrador, one of these birds appeared greatly excited at my presence, alighting near me, bobbing nervously, and protesting in conversational tones. Then it flew away, but immediately returned and flew by several times within a few yards, apparently in great fury, but not daring to hit me.

Plumages.—[AUTHOR'S NOTE: In natal down the young semipalmated plover is darkly colored above. The entire upper parts, from forehead to rump, are mottled with "deep olive buff" and black. The auriculars and a broad band encircling the back of the head are velvety black; there is a distinct black stripe from the bill to the eye and from the lores to the auriculars. A spot under the eye, a ring around the neck, and the entire underparts are pure white.

In fresh juvenal plumage the crown, back, rump, scapulars, and wing coverts are "buffy brown," narrowly edged with creamy or buffy white, the edgings broadest on the wing coverts; the lores, cheeks, and a broad band across the chest are "buffy brown" to "sepia"; the forehead, throat, a ring around the neck, and the entire underparts are white; the tail is like the adult, but tipped with "pinkish buff." The buffy edgings mostly wear away before the partial postjuvenal molt, which occurs in late fall. The first winter plumage is like the adult winter plumage, except that some of the juvenal wing coverts are retained and the head is as in the juvenal. At the next molt, a partial prenuptial, the plumage becomes practically adult; only a few old wing coverts remain.

Adults have a partial prenuptial molt in the spring involving the body plumage, some scapulars and wing coverts, and a complete postnuptial molt from July to December; I have seen the wings molted as early as July 30 and as late as December 10. The sexes are alike in immature and winter plumage and not very different in spring, when the black markings of the female are duller or mixed with grayish brown. In both sexes in winter the black markings are replaced by grayish brown.]

Food.—The semipalmated plover is an active feeder and in this way is sometimes beneficial to man. In the stomachs of 12 birds shot on beaches I have found worms, small mollusks (*Litorina, My-telis*), various crustaceans (*Orchestia, Gammarus, Limnoria*), and insects.

W. L. McAtee (1911) says that this bird eats the larvae of the salt marsh mosquito (*Ædes sollicitans*). Samuel Aughey (1878) investigated the relation of birds to insects in Nebraska during the great invasion of Rocky Mountain migratory locusts on the western prairies and plains of the United States from 1873 to 1876. Of 11 stomachs of this species examined, he found the average number of locusts in each was 38; of other insects, 19. Junius Henderson (1927) states that this plover " on coast, feeds largely on crustaceans, mollusks, eggs of marine animals, and insects; interior, feeds on locusts and other Orthoptera, and many other insects." Audubon (1840) says: "At this period (September) they are now and then observed on plowed lands, where they appear to procure different species of seeds and insects."

Behavior.—The behavior of this bird during courtship and in the care of the eggs and young has already been described. On beaches and mud flats it is sometimes difficult to see, notwithstanding its strikingly marked plumage. As the piping plover matches the dry sand, so the semipalmated plover matches the wet sand, its favorite feeding grounds. Here one may walk almost onto them without seeing them if they stand motionless, as they often do. While sleeping on the dry sand, even with the black and white markings in plain sight, they are also difficult to see. W. V. Praeger (1891) writes as follows of a wounded bird he observed hiding in a hollow in the sand:

While admiring the perfect blending of its brown shades with the surroundings I saw in its white rings one of the commonest objects of the seashore—the empty half of a bivalve shell. The white about the base of the bill was the "hinge," the collar the outer rim, and the top of the head the cavity of the shell filled—as they usually are—with sand.

Gerald H. Thayer (1909), writing of the very similar ringed plover of Europe, speaks of the "eye-masking and 'obliterative' shadow-and-hole-picturing pattern."

Although this bird migrates and feeds both by day and night, it often happens that a flock is discovered at sunset out of reach of the tide, clustered together as if they had settled down for the night. That they spend the night there in some cases at least is shown by William Brewster (1925), who says: "I have repeatedly observed them standing motionless, singly or in clustering groups, on some mud bar to which they had thus returned, keeping them in view until it was too dark to see them longer and finding them all there the next morning."

During high tide, when their best feeding grounds are covered, these birds, like many other shore birds, are very apt to be found sleeping on the upper beach above the reach of the waves. The flock is generally huddled closely together, some standing but many squatting with their breasts resting on the sand, often in the lee of bunches of seaweeed. While some sleep with heads turned to one side and bills thrust into the feathers of the back in the usual manner of birds, others sleep with heads sunk down between the shoulders. Generally some of the flock are awake and on the lookout, while the others open their eyes from time to time.

In flight the flocks are often compact, twisting and turning as if animated by a single thought, but they also fly in loose order. On alighting they at once spread out on the sand in true plover fashion, and do not, like sandpipers, keep together and move along close to the wave line. Another plover habit which at once distinguishes them from sanderlings or other sandpipers of a similar size, is that of running about with heads up and dabbing suddenly at the ground from time to time instead of moving along with heads down diligently probing the sand. With erect figures they run about in various directions, often pausing and standing still as if in thought, occasionally jerking or bobbing their heads and necks and ever and again swiftly dabbing at some morsel of food.

The semipalmated plover associates most frequently with the least and semipalmated sandpipers, but it also flies with sanderlings and other larger waders. Sometimes these birds fly in mixed flocks, but as a rule the ringnecks keep by themselves in flight, but readily join other species on the ground.

On the seacoast the ringneck frequents the outer beaches, the shores and mud flats of estuaries and tidals pools, and the sloughs in the salt marshes. Inland it visits similar regions on the shores of lakes and rivers as well as upland fields in search of food. As I have said elsewhere (C. W. Townsend, 1905):

Like all shore birds also, the ringneck is often exceedingly fat in the autumn, and I have known the fat of the breast to split open when the bird struck the ground after being shot when flying at a height. The fat is not only everywhere under the skin, but it develops all the viscera, and the liver is often pale from fatty infiltration. How birds under these circumstances are able to fly so vigorously on their long migrations, or even to fly at all, is certainly a mystery.

Voice.—The courtship song has already been described. The common call note is a clear, rather plaintive, whistle of two notes, very distinctive and frequently emitted while the birds are on the wing. It is expressed by Hoffmann (1904) by the syllables *chee-wee;* Nichols (1920) writes it *tyoo-eep.* It is cheerful and businesslike compared with the sweet and mournful whistle of the piping plover. When calling to others as they alight, or when standing on the sand, they often emit a single note, sweet and clear, but at times harsh and rasping.

Field marks.—The semipalmated plover is easily distinguished in the field from the killdeer by its smaller size, its single neck ring, and by the absence of the rufous color on the rump. Its darker colors distinguish it from the piping plover. From the sandpipers, even at a distance on the sand, it is distinguished most readily by its plover behavior, as already described. In flying they show a faint white line on the wings which contrasts with the general brown of the upper parts. The neck ring is noticeable both in the flying and walking bird, and the orange yellow of the tarsi and base of the bill can be made out with glasses. In the young, which arrive on the Massachusetts coast about a month behind their elders in the autumn migration, the ring is gray instead of glossy black, and the tarsi are pale yellow. It may be distinguished from the Wilson's plover by the fact that that bird has a much longer bill, wholly black.

Game.—Although this little plover was formerly shot as game in the same manner as is described under the least and semipalmated sandpipers, it is now protected at all seasons. Besides its value as a destroyer of harmful insects, its greatest value is aesthetic. On the beaches of the sea and lakes its graceful flight, handsome plumage, and confiding ways are a source of great pleasure, and on this account alone it is worthy of protection for all time.

Fall.—The fall migration, as stated above, is a long and leisurely one, differing markedly in this respect from the spring migration. When a favorable spot is found, abounding in food and free from disturbances, these birds are apt to tarry there for some time. Here they grow fat and here they indulge in courtship performances as if it were the spring of the year. On beaches and marshes, where in former times gunners, hidden in blinds, were lurking to destroy them, all is now peace and quiet for these little birds, and their journey southward is undisturbed.

Of the fall migration Wells W. Cooke (1912) writes:

At one of the most southern breeding places near York Factory, Keewatin, in 1900, the most advanced young were still in the downy stage July 10 (Preble), and yet by this time the species is already in full fall migration, and the earliest individuals have appeared several hundred miles south of the breeding range. * * * Though most semipalmated plover migrate early, a few stay until freezing weather.

The adults migrate first, while the young rarely arrive on the Massachusetts coast before August 15.

Winter.—Although the majority of the species winter south of the United States, as is shown under " winter range," some are to be found at this season on the shores of the Southern and Gulf States earning their living in pursuit of their small prey.

DISTRIBUTION

Range.—North and South America.

Breeding range.—The breeding range of the semipalmated plover extends north to Alaska (Morzhovia Bay, Hooper Bay, and the Colville delta); northern Mackenzie (Mackenzie delta, Lower Anderson River, Franklin Bay, Horton River, and Bernard Harbor); Keewatin (Whale Point); Franklin (Annanostook and Kingnite Fjord); Victoria Land; Baffin Island; and western Greenland (Disco). East to western Greenland (Disco); Labrador (Port Burwell, Okak, and Tessiujaksoak); Newfoundland (Straits of Belle Isle); eastern Quebec (Upper Hamilton River, Wapitagun Island, Magdalen Islands, and Mingan Islands); and Nova Scotia (Sable Island). South to Nova Scotia (Sable Island and Yarmouth County); probably rarely New Brunswick (Grand Manan); northern Ontario (Moose Factory); Manitoba (Hayes River and Fort Churchill); southern Mackenzie (Artillery Lake); Yukon (Lake Marsh); and British Columbia (Graham Island). West to British Columbia (Graham Island); and Alaska (Berg Bay, Glacier Bay, and Morzhovia Bay).

In common with several other shore birds, nonbreeders remain throughout the summer in southern latitudes. At this season they have been taken or observed south to Venezuela (Margarita Island), Galapagos Islands, Costa Rica, the West Indies, and Jalisco (Ocotlan), while they frequently are fairly common on the coasts of the United States and at points in the interior, Ohio (Lakeside and Oberlin), and Michigan (Detroit).

Kumlien and Hollister report obtaining young not yet able to fly at Lake Koshkonong, Wis., but if their identification was correct, this record must be considered accidental. The species also has been reported in summer from eastern Siberia (East Cape), where it may breed.

Winter range.—The winter range extends north to California (rarely Palo Alto); Texas (Brownsville and Corpus Christi); Louisiana (State Game Preserve); Mississippi (Biloxi); probably Alabama (Coffee Island); South Carolina (Dewees Island); and Bermuda (Somerset). East to Bermuda (Somerset); South Carolina (Port Royal); Georgia (Savannah, Blackbeard Island, and Darien); Florida (Amelia Island, Mayport, Daytona, Mosquito Inlet, Upper Metacumbe Key, and Key West); the Bahama Islands (Abaco, New Providence, Watling Island, and Great Inagua); Haiti (Monte Cristi, and Samana); Porto Rico; the Lesser Antilles (Anegada, Sombrero Key, St. Bartholomew, Carriacou, and Trinidad); Guiana

(Abary River and Cayenne); Brazil (Island of Mixiana, Cajetuba Island, Pernambuco, Bahia, Abrolhos Island, Peranagua, and Santa Catarina); and Argentina (Puerto Deseado). South to Argentina (Puerto Deseado and Jujuy); and Chile (Calbuco). West to Chile (Calbuco, Coquimbo, and Moreno Bay); Peru (Chorillos, Ancon, Trujillo, and Payta); Ecuador (Puna Island, Guayaquil, and Santa Elena); Galapagos Islands (Albemarle and Narboro); Costa Rica; Honduras (Manatee Lagoon); Guatemala (Chiapam); Oaxaca (San Mateo); Sinaloa (Mazatlan); Lower California (La Paz); and California (San Diego, San Pedro, Saticoy, Pacific Grove, and rarely Palo Alto).

Spring migration.—Early dates of spring arrival are: Virginia, Arlington Beach, April 30; District of Columbia, Washington, May 3; Pennsylvania, Wayne, May 5, and Erie, May 8; New Jersey, Cape May, April 24, Camden, May 5, and Long Beach, May 10; New York, Long Island, April 19, Orient, May 2, Geneva, May 5, and Rochester, May 16; Connecticut, New Haven, May 1, and Fairfield, May 4; Rhode Island, Newport, April 15; Massachusetts, Rehoboth, April 21, Monomoy Island, April 28, and Dennis, May 5; Maine, Saco, May 5; Quebec, Quebec City, May 6, Montreal, May 19, Godbout, May 28, Eskimo Point, June 3, and Fort Chimo, June 11; Nova Scotia, Pictou, May 9, and Antigonish, May 15; Franklin, Winter Island, May 31; Missouri, St. Louis, April 2, and Kahoka, April 4; Illinois, Rantoul, April 9, near Chicago, April 25, and Cantine, April 26; Indiana, Denver, May 1, Terre Haute, May 5, and Bloomington, May 9; Ohio, Sandusky, April 20, Cleveland, April 21, and Oberlin, April 24; Michigan, Ann Arbor, May 5, Jackson, May 8, and Grand Rapids, May 9; Ontario, Toronto, April 21, Hamilton, April 24, Ottawa, May 9, and Guelph, May 15; Iowa, Sioux City, April 22, Ogden, April 24, and Emmetsburg, April 27; Wisconsin, Madison, May 5; Minnesota, Heron Lake, May 8, and Minneapolis, May 11; Kansas, Lawrence, April 22, Emporia, April 25, and McPherson, May 3; Nebraska, Lincoln, April 27; South Dakota, Vermilion, April 20, and Brookings, May 8; Manitoba, Brandon, April 28, and Reaburn, May 9; Saskatchewan, Lake Johnston, May 10; Mackenzie, Fort Simpson, May 16, and Fort Resolution, May 23; Alberta, Veteran, April 24, Camrose, May 6, Tofield, May 12, Peace River, May 20, and Fort Chipewyan, May 23; northern California, Eureka, April 17; Nevada, Smoky Creek, May 4; Washington, Destruction Island, April 24, and Grays Harbor, April 30; British Columbia, Ucluelet, April 28, and Çomox, May 3; Yukon, Forty-mile, May 23; and Alaska, Admiralty Island, May 8, Bethel, May 10, Bristol Bay, May 15, Coronation Island, May 15, and Hooper Bay, May 19.

Late dates of spring departure are: Brazil, Cajetuba Island, April 18; Colombia, Sabanilla, March 27; Porto Rico, Luquillo, March 5, and Vieques Island, March 30; Haiti, Samana, April 13; Bahamas, Abaco, April 28, and Green Cay, April 29; Florida, Daytona Beach, May 25, Punta Rassa, May 25, and Pensacola, May 30; Georgia, Savannah, May 13; South Carolina, Kiawah Island, June 2, and Bulls Bay, June 7; North Carolina, Pea and Bodie Islands, May 17; Cape Hatteras, May 20, and Raleigh, May 22; Virginia, Cape Charles, May 24, Smiths Island, May 25, and Wallops Island, May 30; District of Columbia, Alexander Island, May 22, and Washington, May 25; Maryland, Patapsco Marsh, May 29; Pennsylvania, State College, May 30, Wayne, June 1, and Erie, June 2; New Jersey, Cape May County, May 23, Elizabeth, May 30, and Camden, June 1; New York, Canandaigua, June 7, Geneva, June 9, Orient, June 10, and New York City, June 14; Connecticut, New Haven, June 1, and Fairfield, June 8; Massachusetts, Lynn, June 5, Harvard, June 9; and Dennis, June 10; Maine, Portland, June 3; Louisiana, Lobdell, May 18; Missouri, St. Joseph, May 13, and Corning, May 18; Illinois, Chicago, May 29, Morgan Park, May 30, and Rantoul, June 2; Indiana, Lake County, May 27; Ohio, Columbus, May 28, Oberlin, May 29, and Lakeside, June 2; Michigan, Detroit, May 30, Sault Ste. Marie, May 31; Ontario, Ottawa, May 31, Hamilton, June 3, and Toronto, June 6; Iowa, Emmetsburg, May 20, and Sioux City, May 30; Wisconsin, Shiocton, May 28, and Madison, May 30; Minnesota, Lanesboro, May 23, Hallock, May 29, and Minneapolis, June 4; Texas, Corpus Christi, May 18; Kansas, Lawrence, May 18; Nebraska, Lincoln, May 20; South Dakota, Vermilion, May 19, Dell Rapids, May 22; and Forestburg, May 27; Manitoba, Lake Winnipeg, June 7, and Shoal Lake, June 12; Lower California, San Geronimo Island, April 13, Cerros Island, April 17, and Gardeners Lagoon, April 24; California, San Diego, April 23, Alameda, May 14, Fresno, May 15, and Santa Barbara, May 22; Washington, Tacoma, May 18; and British Columbia, Indian Cove, May 29.

Fall migration.—Early dates of arrival in the fall are; British Columbia, Nootka Sound, July 23, Tahsis Canal, July 26, and Okanagan Landing, July 28; Washington, The Olympiades, July 16; California, Alameda, July 8, and Santa Barbara, July 12; Lower California, Santa Rosalia Bay, August 16, and San Jose del Cabo, August 23; Saskatchewan, Big Stick Lake, July 19, and Cochrane River, July 23; Manitoba, Red Deer River, July 22, Lake Winnepegosis, July 22, and Oak Lake, July 28; North Dakota, Kenmare, July 18; South Dakota, Forestburg, July 27, Nebraska, Lincoln, August 9; Texas, Tivoli, September 2; Minnesota, Minneapolis, July 17; Iowa, Sioux City, August 5, and Marshalltown, August 10;

Ontario, Toronto, July 22, Coldstream, July 29, and Brighton, July 31; Michigan, Charity Island, July 25, Jackson, July 25, and Detroit, July 31; Ohio, Bay Point, July 3, Oberlin, July 6, Cedar Point, July 8, and Lakeside, July 17; Indiana, Bass Lake, August 1; Illinois, Chicago, July 22, and La Grange, August 7; Missouri, St. Louis, August 20; Mississippi, Beauvoir, July 22; Louisiana, Bayou Chene, August 29; Maine, Portland, July 18, and Squirrel Island, July 31; Massachusetts, Lynn, July 18; Marthas Vineyard, July 20, and Harvard, July 26; Rhode Island, South Auburn, July 23, and Block Island, July 25; Connecticut, New Haven, July 30; New York, Long Beach, July 3, Orient, July 6, and Brockport, July 28; New Jersey, Long Beach, July 19, Brigantine Beach, July 25, and Elizabeth, July 31; North Carolina, Myrtle Sound, July 10; South Carolina, Frogmore, July 20, and Charleston, July 21; Florida, Palma Sola, July 10, Daytona Beach, July 19, and Pensacola, July 26; Bermuda, August 12; the Bahama Islands, Long Island, July 17; Cuba, Batabono, August 26; Lesser Antilles, Grenada, August 24, and Dominica, August 29; Panama, Toro Point, July 23; Brazil, Santa Catarina, August 4; and Colombia, Santa Marta region, September 13.

Late dates of fall departure are: British Columbia, Chilliwack, August 23, Atlin, August 24, and Okanagan Landing, September 3; Mackenzie, Fort Simpson, September 1, and Fort Resolution, September 1; Saskatchewan, Indian Head, September 2; Manitoba, Shoal Lake, September 14, Aweme, September 14, and Oak Lake, September 20; Nebraska, Lincoln, October 14; Minnesota, Lanesboro, September 15; Iowa, Emmetsburg, September 24, and Grinnell, October 22; Ontario, Toronto, October 26, and Point Pelee, October 29; Michigan, Portage Lake, October 25, and Detroit, October 29; Ohio, Oberlin, October 21, and Youngstown, November 2; Indiana, Hobart, September 24, and Peru, October 2; Illinois, Rantoul, October 15, and Chicago, October 28; Kentucky, Lexington, September 17; Missouri, St. Louis, September 25; Prince Edward Island, North River, October 27; Nova Scotia, Wolfville, October 22; New Brunswick, Scotch Lake, September 23; Quebec, Montreal, October 20; Maine, Lewiston, October 13; Massachusetts, Lynn, October 12, Cambridge, October 26, and Dennis, October 27; Connecticut, Fairfield, October 22, Norwalk, October 26, and New Haven, October 31; New York, East Hampton, October 22, Port Chester, October 25, and Long Beach, October 28; New Jersey, Sandy Hook, October 25; and Pennsylvania, Erie, November 2.

Casual records.—The semipalmated plover is more or less rare in the southern Rocky Mountain region where records are so few that it can be considered only as casual. Among these records are: Utah, Salt Lake City (reported by Nelson) ; Colorado, Denver, April 27,

1907, Loveland, May 6, 1890, and Grand Lake, Middle Park (Carter Collection); and Arizona, Fort Verde, September 8, 1884, Colorado River, September and October, 1865 (Coues), and Tucson, April, 1883 (Scott).

Egg dates.—Labrador and Ungava: 42 records, June 7 to July 7; 21 records, June 18 to July 1. Quebec to Nova Scotia: 33 records, June 5 to 29; 17 records, June 15 to 23. Arctic coast of Canada: 18 records, June 16 to July 20; 9 records, June 23 to July 4. Alaska and British Columbia; 19 records, May 27 to July 6; 10 records, June 1 to 9.

CHARADRIUS HIATICULA Linnaeus

RINGED PLOVER

Contributed by Francis Charles Robert Jourdain

HABITS

The ringed plover breeds both on the east and west coasts of Greenland, ranging north to Sabine and Clavering Islands and Denmark Harbor on the east side and to Inglefield Gulf on the west. It is also said to breed near Cumberland Sound in Baffin Land, but this may refer to the semipalmated plover, *Charadrius semipalmatus*, and it has occurred casually in Barbados, Chile, and southern Alaska.

The subdivision of the ringed plover into geographical races is attended with considerable difficulties owing to the presence of passing migrants on many of its breeding grounds. The Siberian form, *Charadrius hiaticula tundrae* is generally recognized, but is only distinguishable with certainty in summer plumage. Probably the Alaskan specimen belongs to this race. E. Lehn Schiöler, with fine series of carefully sexed birds before him, separates the Greenland breeding birds from the typical race under the name of *Ch. hiaticula septentrionalis*, but material with accurate data is too scarce in other collections to enable us to hazard an opinion.

Spring.—In northeast Greenland, where Manniche found this species breeding plentifully, the birds arrived about the end of May or the beginning of June, at the same time as the other waders. Icelandic birds arrive early: April 22 to 28 (Faber).

Dr. W. Elmer Ekblaw says in his notes:

The ringed plover is one of the most noticeable birds of the shorelands of northwest Greenland. Few beaches are unoccupied by these noisy little birds, and rarely is one out of sound of their shrill piping. They are quite as common about the streams and pools of the interior and along the seepage swales of the ground moraines. They come to the land as early as May 29 and stay until the last week in July. Almost invariably they are mated when they arrive and only rarely does one see more than a pair together, except where they congregate about swales or shallow pools to feed. They are sociably inclined and do not hesitate to make their nests near the Eskimo villages, probably feeling more secure from Arctic foxes when near dogs and human habitation.

Courtship.—The courtship of this species has been well described by Farren, Selous, and Stanford. The former (1910) says:

Ringed plovers may be seen in pairs skimming low over the ground, circling to a far height and descending again like a flash, almost touching the ground as they do so. They do not follow each other, but each describes similar evolutions, overlapping and crossing the other's line of flight. Their long pointed wings, showing much white, give a fictitious impression of size and as they alight on the ground after skimming a short distance with curved drooping wings they seem suddenly to vanish from sight as they touch ground; in place of the long-winged graceful flyer is a little plump-shaped gray bird, very difficult to see as it runs with short quick steps over the sand.

Edmund Selous (1901) also describes a male as advancing toward the hen a few steps at a time, and moving his legs with a rapid vibratory motion during the pauses. Stanford (1927) remarks that the courtship is by no means easy to observe even with the aid of a powerful glass.

In one party on the beach on March 20, where at least two males were contending for one female, the males ran backward and forward with short, quick steps, and when another male was near the feathers of the back and the tips of the closed wings were elevated, the tail depressed and spread out to its full extent to show the white tips of the feathers, and the whole body arched with the head and neck drawn in, the black gorget being puffed out to nearly twice its normal size. In this crouching attitude the males ran aimlessly to and fro for half an hour at a time, but making no real attempt to attack each other.

Another male—

kept running in front of the hen and sinking down on the beach every few yards exactly as if settling down on a nest. Occasionally while brooding in this way he would tilt himself forward onto his breast with the closed wing tips pointing up almost vertically over his back, the tail depressed, and the legs scratching out sand and stones behind him. The indifference displayed by the hen to this performance was as noticeable as it usually is in the case of lapwings' "rolling" on the ground. On several other occasions in April I saw cock ringed plovers settle down and appear to brood for several minutes exactly as if they were on a nest; in one case the bird kept turning round and round on one spot, and twice at least this action was followed by an attempt at coition.

The love flight often covers nearly a mile of ground, and both birds take part—crossing and recrossing with their bodies twisting from side to side and soft beats of the wings. The double note, according to Stanford, has a remarkably vibrant quality at these times and the throat appears to be swelled out.

Nesting.—Both nesting sites and the nests themselves of this species vary considerably. The commonest site is among the sand

and shingle above high-water mark on the seashore. In some cases the eggs are laid in a hollow scratched in the sand with no lining of any kind, in others small fragments of cockle shells and small stones are collected and imbedded, while other nests are more or less substantially built, from a few dead bents carelessly arranged to well-made cups in which almost any material available is utilized, such as driftwood, rabbits' droppings, stems of leaves, and shore plants, etc. On some beaches where there is no sand the eggs may be found lying on the bare pebbles, while on the north Norfolk coast they are often placed under shelter of sea heath, and nests have been met with in cornfields, several miles from the sea, or on open grassland in sewage farms inland.

Eggs.—Normally four in number, occasionally three on late layings, while instances of five are rare. In color they vary from stone color to ocherous or clay yellow sometimes with a warm tinge, spotted as a rule rather sparingly with brownish black. Occasionally varieties with large blotches of sepia are met with and white eggs have been recorded as well as bluish eggs, without markings. The shell is deep green when viewed from within. The measurements of 100 British eggs, made by the writer, averaged 35.9 by 25.9 millimeters; the eggs showing the four extremes measure **39** by 26.5, 37 by **28.5**, **32.2** by 25 and 32.7 by **24** millimeters. Eggs from Iceland and other northern localities are decidedly smaller.

Young.—Incubation is shared by both sexes which relieve one another at short intervals and the period is variously estimated at from 22 to 25 days; probably 24 or 25 days represents the average. The young are hatched within 24 hours and leave the nest as soon as the down is dry. Apparently a second brood is reared in some cases, but many of the late nests may be second or third layings.

Doctor Ekblaw writes:

The old birds were wildly agitated whenever I approached, and by the customary simulation of injury attempted to lead me away from the nest. The fledglings ran about as soon as hatched, and like all little shorebirds were quick to respond to a warning signal and sink into pebble-like immobility. The weather was so cold that the old birds did not leave the young, for when the brood was separated both parents sheltered some of the little ones.

Plumages.—The plumages and molts are fully described in **A** Practical Handbook of British Birds, edited by H. F. Witherby (1920).

Food.—Insects, including Coleoptera (*Apion, Aphodius, Haliplus, Hydroporus,* etc.), Crustacea, especially the smaller species (Gammaridae, Amphipoda, etc.), Mollusca, chiefly small marine univalves, such as Littorina, Annelida (earthworms), and vegetable matter (seeds of *Polygonum,* etc.).

Behavior.—This is an attractive and inoffensive species, sociable in its habits and met with in flocks of considerable size out of the breeding season, when their simultaneous maneuvers on the wing are a very characteristic feature of the great estuaries, the flocks appearing to change from light to dark as the upper or under surfaces are exposed. They may also be seen on the mud flats, making short runs at intervals, when the movements of the legs and feet are so rapid that the eye can not follow them.

Voice.—John T. Nichols contributes the following:

A rather clear, not very loud, low-pitched whistle, given on the ground as much as in the air, rather infrequent. This may be written *kruip* or *puik*, occasionally distinctly two syllabled and suggesting the semipalmated plover's call, but lower pitched. It was heard in late September from several birds loosely associated with a larger number of scattered dunlin on tidal sands north of Liverpool. They usually took wing in silence, and the species seems to be a rather silent one as seen here and elsewhere on British shores in September. They were very likely not traveling, and their voice therefore not comparable with that of the semipalmated on home shores. Also the note described is very likely not analogous with the full, loud-flight note of the transient semipalmated plover.

Enemies.—During the autumn and winter months the flocks are occasionally harried by a migrating merlin (*Falco columbarius aesalon*), and some clutches of eggs are annually destroyed by marauding Corvidae (crows) and Laridae (gulls). On some parts of the coast which are much exposed, great damage is done by exceptionally high tides, as many nests are built close to the high-water mark.

Fall.—In Greenland Manniche (1910) observed that the old birds left in pairs about the first week in August, as soon as the young were grown up. The young birds immediately went to the shores and estuaries, consorting with young sanderlings and turnstones and leaving for the south early in September. At the Westmann Isles in south Iceland they leave between September 20 and October 10.

Winter.—In the British Isles the wintering birds are to be met with in flocks on most of our larger estuaries. When on the wing they sometimes associate with dunlin and also occasionally with redshanks.

DISTRIBUTION

Breeding range.—In the Old World, commonly in the British Isles and sparingly in the Faroes and Iceland; also probably on Bear Island and a few pairs in Spitsbergen as well as on Waigatz, Kolguev, and Nova Zembla. On the European Continent, from the Arctic Ocean south to the Mediterranean, chiefly on the seacoasts, and only locally by lakes and rivers. In the Mediterranean it is local on some of the islands and nowhere plentiful. The north

Asiatic race has been separated, while in the New World its breeding range includes both coasts of Greenland and perhaps the east coast of Baffin Land, unless the last statement is due to confusion with the semipalmated plover.

Winter range.—Many remain in the British Isles through the winter, but birds from northern Europe migrate to the Mediterranean region and Africa, where they have been recorded as far south as Cape Province and Natal, the majority wintering south of the Sahara. The Atlantic Isles (Canaries, Madeira, and Azores) are visited on passage, and Asiatic birds have been recorded from the Indo-Malayan archipelago and even Australia, though some doubt has been cast on this.

Spring migration.—The principal passage at Gibraltar takes place in March, the latest birds leaving in April. From about mid March to mid April old birds are on passage northward and the breeding ground in Norway is reached in April, and in Sweden from late March onward.

Fall migration.—In northern Europe (Norway and Sweden) the southward movement takes place in September and at the Straits of Gibraltar the passage lasts from September to November. At Heligoland young birds begin to pass as early as the end of June and the beginning of July.

Casual records.—In Jan Mayen it apparently occurs in some numbers, but is not known to breed. Barbados, one, Chancery Lane, September 10. Gould's record of one from Port Stevens, Australia, is a somewhat questionable one. One obtained at Sultanpur, south of Delhi, November, 1878; another at Gilgit, October, 1879. (These records must refer to the Siberian race, as also probably the Chilean occurrence and that from Sitka, Alaska.)

Egg dates.—In northeast Greenland Manniche found eggs from June 17 to July 18, while in Nova Zembla the young were recently hatched at the beginning of August and eggs probably laid late in June or early in July. In the British Isles eggs have been met with in March, but most eggs are laid from the end of April onward. April 16 to 30 (5 dates), May 1 to 14 (10 dates), May 15 to 31 (21 dates), June 1 to 30 (23 dates), July 1 to 30 (7 dates).

CHARADRIUS DUBIUS CURONICUS Gmelin

LITTLE RINGED PLOVER

Contributed by Francis Charles Robert Jourdain

HABITS

The little ringed plover owes its place in the American list to a casual occurrence at Kodiak Island, Alaska. It is noteworthy that in J. F. von Brandt's paper in the Journal für Ornithologie, 1891, the Alaskan specimen is recorded as "*Charadrius alexandrinus* Pall.*" There is also a specimen in the United States National Museum (No. 39523) which is said to have been taken at San Francisco, but some doubt appertains to the latter record.

Spring.—The range of this species does not extend far to the north in western Europe and it is only a rare straggler to the British Isles. In northern Germany it appears in fair numbers on the larger rivers and at lakesides, about the middle of March, but except in southern Sweden few cross the Baltic to breed.

Courtship.—H. F. Witherby (1919) has some interesting notes on this species which was breeding in company with the Kentish plover (*Charadrius alexandrinus*) near Dunkerque, in northern France.

On April 28 the little ringed plovers were flying round after each other, with a beautiful slow, long, flap of the wings, much like the flight of a large butterfly and uttering a pleasing little song. This was evidently a "courtship" action and we found many "scoops" in the sand, but no eggs.

Liebe describes the song flight as beginning with a zigzag oblique ascent, followed by short horizontal flights at various angles over the gravelly bed where the hen is sitting, uttering meantime his musical whistle, which is answered by the bird beneath, and ending in a sharp descent in a curve toward the water's edge and thence with low, skimming flight to the hen. The little ring plover is a much more demonstrative and noisy species than the ringed plover and when its breeding haunts are approached instead of running off with a low whistle and then flying a short distance ahead, it flies round and round the intruder with loud repeated whistling notes. Naumann (1887) expresses the pairing song by the words "*duh, du dull lull lullullul*," taken in slow time and ending with a wonderful trill only to be heard on the breeding ground.

Nesting.—Continental writers lay much stress on the fact that this bird by preference always makes the nest in gravelly patches rather than in sand. This is not invariably the case, as the bird builds freely on sand banks in rivers where there is no shingle or gravel, and at times also on dry mud. It may be found nesting far inland, but nearly always in the neighborhood of water and shows a decided preference for the shores of fresh-water lakes and the larger rivers rather than the seashore.

Eggs.—The normal clutch is four, though three is not an uncommon number, and generally they are readily distinguishable from those of the other sand plovers. They are more pyriform in shape than those of the Kentish plover, and average less in size than either of the two other common European species. In color the ground color is often grayish when fresh but dries out to a yellowish stone or pale reddish ocherous, with many fine streaks and spots of dark brown and numerous small ashy streaks or spots. On the whole the markings are paler and scantier than with the Kentish plover, but in rare cases large blotches of rich brown and ash colors are found in some sets, and others show an approach to the normal type of Kentish plover. The eggs are laid in a mere hollow without lining in the gravel. The measurements of 100 eggs (68 by the writer and 32 by Rey) average 29.8 by 22.08 millimeters; the eggs showing the four extremes measure **32.8** by 23, 30.1 by **23.5**, **27.3** by 21.1, and 28.6 by **21** millimeters.

Young.—Incubation is said by Naumann (1887) to be apparently performed by both sexes, but in warm and sunny weather the eggs are left for long periods uncovered. The period is over 22 days, probably 23 or 24 (not 16 or 17 as erroneously given by Naumann). Only one brood is reared in the season as a rule, but some dates are extremely late and point to an occasional second brood.

Plumages.—The plumages and molts are fully described in A Practical Handbook of British Birds, edited by H. F. Witherby (1920).

Food.—Definite records are scanty, but it is evident that the main food consists of insects, including the smaller Coleoptera and their larvae; Diptera and larvae; Neuroptera (Phryganeidae or caddis flies and larvae). Naumann also found a small worm in one case in the stomach.

Behavior.—Witherby (1919) writes:

The little ringed plover is even more demonstrative than the Kentish and it is shyer and more difficult to mark onto its nest or young. Both species have a very plaintive alarm note which they utter constantly as they fly round the intruder, but the Kentish is less fussy and less noisy than the little ringed. When one is near the young both species go through various outcries, such as running along the ground crouching low with head stretched out, lying on the side with one wing up, the legs stretched out and the tail spread, or with the breast on the ground and both wings half spread, but the performance of the Kentish is much less abandoned than that of the little ringed.

P. W. Munn (1921) also writes:

The behavior of the birds at their nest is totally different from Kentish plovers, which are not demonstrative whilst they have eggs; but the little ringed plover flies wildly round and round, twisting and doubling and uttering its wild whistle, or else runs frantically about on the ground, whistling plaintively.

Enemies.—The eggs are occasionally taken by Corvidae, and the birds themselves sometimes fall victims to Accipitres.

DISTRIBUTION

Breeding range.—Central and southern Europe, from France, Denmark, southern Sweden, southern Finland and 64° N. in Russia, south to the Mediterranean and its islands and Africa north of the Sahara. In Asia its range extends across Siberia to the Pacific and includes also Japan. In India and the Philippines, Hainan, and Formosa it is replaced by other subspecies. It does not breed in the British Isles, but nests in Madeira and the Canaries.

Winter range.—Winters in tropical Africa, south to the Gold Coast, Fernando Po, the lower Niger, Lakes Rudolf, Albert and Victoria Nyanza, and the Red Sea coast; in Asia to Arabia and India and also to the Sunday Islands and perhaps New Guinea.

Spring migration.—In south Spain it arrives about mid March and is widely distributed in April, while in the eastern Mediterranean the passage takes place in Crete and Corfu in April. On Heligoland it is only a rare straggler.

Fall migration.—The north German breeding birds leave for the south at the end of September. Farther south the presence of immigrants from the north among the breeding birds is seldom noted.

Casual records.—In the British Isles there are about 10 well-authenticated records; April (2), August (4), and October (1 or 2). The supposed records from Iceland and the Faroes are not authenticated. Gaetke only records 2 at Heligoland in 50 years.

Egg dates.—In northern Africa eggs have been found from March onward; in Spain and the Balearic Isles, March 16 (1 date), April 15 to 30 (3 dates), May 1 to 14 (4 dates), 15 to 30 (3 dates); late dates, June 12 and July 11. In France and Germany, May 3 to 17 (7 dates), 18 to 31 (8 dates); June 1 to 15 (5 dates); late dates, July 19 and 22.

CHARADRIUS MELODUS Ord

PIPING PLOVER

HABITS

Contributed by Winsor Marrett Tyler

Wilson and Audubon were familiar with the piping plover as a common summer resident on the sandy beaches of the Atlantic coast. Audubon found it breeding as far north as the Magdelen Islands and wintering abundantly on the coast of Florida.

During the years between the time of these early writers and the present, the species has been subjected to many seasons of spring and autumn shooting which, in the closing years of the nineteenth century, brought the bird nearly to the point of extinction.

It is readily seen why persistent shooting threatened this bird's existence. Its breeding range on the coast extends for hundreds of miles in a northerly and southerly direction, but owing to the bird's very restricted nesting site it is narrowed in many places to a strip of beach only a few yards wide. Fortunately legislation intervened and removed the smaller plovers from the list of game birds, so that at the present time the piping plover is fast becoming one of our common summer residents again.

Spring.—Compared to most of the waders, the piping plover has a short and safe migration route. Moving along the coast where spring is further advanced than in the interior of the country, and having to pass over no large bodies of water on its way to its breeding ground, the bird pushes northward early in the season, often arriving in New England during the last days of March, the first of the shorebirds to reach our beaches.

Courtship.—In his notes A. C. Bent describes the courtship thus: " I saw and heard the nuptial flight and song of this bird. He flew in large circles or figure 8s low over the back beach near the marsh for several minutes, giving constantly a peculiar twittering whistling song." Another entry in his notes under date, May 20, reads: " Saw piping plover mating, two males following one female. They were running around her in crouching attitude, with wings spread and trailing and with tail spread in display, uttering whistling notes."

I once saw a male bird come up behind a crouching female and stand at full height close to her with his breast feathers puffed out and head held high, his neck stretched upward so that it was long and slim, the bird both in posture and shape resembling an upland plover. For a minute or two he stood thus while his feet beat a rapid tatoo on the sand. In this attitude of display he appeared bright colored and conspicuous in contrast to the female and the band across his breast (complete in his case) stood out sharply defined against the adjacent snowy feathers.

Nesting.—The typical nesting site of the piping plovers is the belt of sand bordering lake or ocean well above high-water mark, where the surface is becoming diversified and pebble strewn and wisps of beach grass begin to grow. Here they lay their eggs, commonly with little preparation for their reception other than a slight hollowing of the light sand, but not infrequently they collect small stones, bits of shell, or driftwood and line their nests with them or lay them near by.

The following quotations indicate differences in the appearance of the nests. In a letter to Mr. Bent, Allen H. Wood describes a very unusual nest. He says: " The nest was a hollow scooped in a mass of sand which had been piled up to a height of nearly 10 inches.

Whether the birds formed the pile or not, I do not, of course, know, but a very careful examination failed to show how else the pile could have been formed." A. C. Bent speaks in his notes of finding at Dartmouth, Mass., "three nests containing four eggs each, all on a high, sandy and pebbly beach in the heart of a tern colony. The nests were hollows in the sand, profusely lined with broken pieces of white shell and were quite conspicuous." E. W. Hadeler found on the shore of Lake Erie, at Painesville, Ohio, a paved nest. He says in his notes that there were "four eggs, almost the same color as the ground and stones, laid in a slight depression on some very small flat stones and around the nest were stones of all shapes and sizes." Philipp and Bowdish (1917) in New Brunswick " found a small colony of breeding birds, five nests, each containing four eggs, being located. The nests were on sandy beach, some in the open, others among sparse clumps of beach grass. They were slight hollows in the sand, some quite unlined, others with a well-formed rim of bits of broken shell or slate." In a letter to Mr. Bent, Edward R. Ford calls attention to some birds nesting in an unusual environment. He says:

At Dune Park, Ind., the piping plover, to the number of five or six pairs, has taken advantage of the widening of the beach (through the operations of a sand company which has removed part of the dunes) and lays its eggs at a considerable distance from the water's edge. The old ridges formed by the tramway beds, from which the rails have been, for the most part, removed; the old cinder heaps, bits of scrap iron and other odds and ends of human labor, with here and there patches of vetch and coarse grass, seem well suited to its requirements.

In common with some of its near relatives, the piping plover has the habit of making additional hollows in the sand in the vicinity of the hollow in which its eggs are laid. These hollows have been termed cock nests and have been compared to the nests which the male of some of the wrens builds while his mate is sitting.

My notes, taken on Cape Cod in the company of Charles A. Robbins in mid April, refer to this subject:

After some 10 minutes, during which time the two birds stood motionless on the sand facing the wind, they began to move about, the male taking visible interest in the female and following her as she walked away. They came to a place back of the beach where stones lay sparsely scattered on the dry sand and little bunches of beach grass and patches of Hudsonia were growing. Here the male stopped at a spot between two stones, lowered his breast to the ground and kicked out alternately with his legs scratching the sand from beneath him. Then moving off a little way he did the same in another spot while the female came to the place between the stones and continued the hollowing process which he had begun. Nearly, if not quite, in time with their rapidly moving legs, the birds uttered a series of short, high-pitched whistles, all on the same note, having the piping quality of their common call. When the scratching stopped, the notes stopped.

During perhaps a quarter of an hour the birds continued to scratch and pipe until several little hollows had been begun and abandoned. The female, however, scratched for the most part in the hollow between the stones, digging it out to a depth of an inch. Soon this phase of activity passed off and the birds began to feed.

During the hour the birds were under observation neither one made its bobbing motion.

Eggs.—[AUTHOR'S NOTE: Four eggs are the almost invariable rule with the piping plover; rarely only three are laid in second sets, and I have found one set of five. They are ovate to short ovate in shape and have no gloss. The ground colors vary from "light buff" to "cartridge buff" or buffy white. They are sparingly, but quite evenly, marked with small spots, or fine dots, of blackish brown or black, and sometimes with a few underlying spots of "pallid purplish gray." They are almost invisible on the sand or among small pebbles. The measurements of 71 eggs average 31.4 by 24.2 millimeters; the eggs showing the four extremes measure **34.4** by 25.3, 31.8 by **26.4, 29.2** by 23.8 and 30 by **23** millimeters.]

Young.—Gayle Pickwell (1925) describes in detail the hatching of an egg and ascertained that the young birds may leave the nest a few hours later. He says: "It soon refused to remain in the nest. Finally, it left, and while it was tottering insecurely away the parent bird came running up with little chuckles of solicitude."

Alexander G. Lawrence, of Winnipeg, Manitoba, says in his notes:

Careful search of the sand spit revealed a number of small white moving points, which later search proved to be baby piping plovers. While I was chasing one it tripped, fell on its back, and lay as if stunned, deceiving me so completely that I turned to get my camera to make a close-up picture of the little fellow. No sooner had I moved away than he sprang up and ran pell-mell over the sand, and the chase commenced again.

C. A. Robbins (1919) describes further the behavior of the young birds thus:

Of course it frequently happens that there is no time for concealment. Then the young birds attempt to escape by running, the tiny legs working with surprising rapidity and carrying them over the ground so swiftly and smoothly that they looked like balls of down blowing before the wind. Also, if their escape up the beach is cut off and they continue to be closely pressed, they do not hesitate to take to the water. Even those only a few hours out of the shell swim well and navigate their frail craft, if not with intelligence, at least in a direction away from the source of danger.

Plumages.—[AUTHOR'S NOTE: The downy young piping plover is sand colored above. The crown, back, wings, rump, and thighs are variegated with "cream buff," "cartridge buff," and grayish white, sprinkled or peppered with browns; on the wings the color deepens almost to "chamois." The forehead is buffy white; there is a more or less distinct V-shaped mark of dark brown in the center of the crown and a circle of small brownish tips around the edge of it. The wings and thighs are marked with brown spots. A white collar encircles the hind neck, and the entire under parts are white. The juvenal plumage appears first on the scapulars and sides of the breast, then on the remaining underparts, back, and crown; the last parts to become feathered are the throat, belly, and rump; then the wing quills appear, and lastly the tail. In fresh juvenal plumage the feathers of the crown and mantle are " drab gray " or " smoke gray," broadly tipped with " pinkish buff," giving a decidedly pinkish tone at first; but these pink tips soon fade and wear away, leaving a dull-gray crown and mantle, faintly mottled with pale tints of buffy and dusky. The black bands on the forehead and neck are entirely lacking.

The first winter plumage is acquired by a limited body molt early in the fall and by wear and fading of much of the plumage that is retained. It is like the adult winter except for the worn and faded edgings on what juvenal feathers are retained, mainly wing coverts and scapulars. A partial prenuptial molt early in the spring produces a nuptial plumage which is practically adult.

Adults have a complete molt in late summer and fall—August to October—and a partial prenuptial molt in late winter and spring, mainly in March. In winter plumage the crown and mantle are " pale ecru drab," without the pale edgings, with no black frontal band, and with a restricted brownish instead of black collar. The black frontal band and the black collar, characteristic of the nuptial plumage, are usually acquired in March; the extent of the black collar increases with age and the complete collar probably indicates an old bird.]

Food.—Arthur H. Howell (1924) says: " The food of this plover, as indicated by the contents of four stomachs secured in Alabama, consists principally of marine worms, fly larvae, and beetles." · E. H. Forbush (1925) lists the following: " Insects, crustaceans, mollusks, and other small marine animals and their eggs."

The feeding habits of the piping plover as it hunts for food along our beaches are characteristic. In marked contrast to the nervous haste of the sanderling and the rapid darting about with lightning-like thrusts of the bill of the smallest sandpipers, the behavior of the plover is leisurely, and as they pick up food from the sand the movements of the head are deliberate. Three or four may sweep down the beach together, close to the sand, but when they alight, after a moment of stillness, they separate, each bird running a little way, isolating itself from its companions (another point of difference from the sanderling, etc., which in migration tend to keep close in a flock while feeding). Generally they begin at once to hunt for food. They run a short distance, then pause and stare at the sand with neck a little outstretched, head tilted a bit to one side, perhaps looking for a movement to show where food is, for often, leaning farther forward, they pick something from the sand. As they run over the beach—a run and a pause, another run and another scrutinizing pause, often changing direction to catch up a bit of food—the birds suggest very strongly a robin feeding on a lawn and the resemblance is strengthened when the plover seizes a 3-inch-long worm and drags it from beneath the sand, pulling slowly and carefully lest it break, and swallows it whole.

Behavior.—Their actions while feeding are apparently identical with those of the semipalmated plover, and the flight of the two birds is similar if not exactly the same. Their flight is wilder than that of the sanderling, for example, which drives steadily along; they twist and turn more often and tilt from one side to the other, giving the impression of extreme swiftness and agility.

Descriptions of the action of the sitting bird when disturbed differ very little. The bird is invariably wary and steals off before the intruder comes near, leaving him in doubt as to the existence of a nest. After the eggs are hatched, however, their actions change completely, and the parents display the utmost concern for the safety of their young. In the following quotation from his notes, E. H. Forbush describes graphically this behavior, and also shows that even in the early days of the young bird's life the parents do not feed them. Mr. Forbush says:

A colony of piping plovers on the same beach had been much reduced in numbers, but the behavior of one pair showed that they had young on the beach. We saw one plover and then another fluttering along the ground like young or crippled birds. Their actions might deceive a novice, but by watching them with a glass, we soon saw that they were adult birds. They threw themselves on the ground, breast downward, and, drooping the flight feathers or primaries, raised and agitated the shorter secondaries, until the motion resembled the fluttering pinions of young or wounded birds, meantime pushing themselves along over the sand with their feet. As the wings were not spread, the long primary quills were not noticeable, and so the imitation of the struggles of a helpless bird was almost perfect. Immediately we began a careful search for the nest, looking in all the usual hiding places in or under the tufts of beach grass, but no nest could we find. As the old birds continued their plaintive cries and circled about, we extended our search, expecting to find some half-grown young flattened out somewhere on the beach. Finally, by hunting over the sand we found on the open beach, a nest exactly like that of the least tern. A few little pebbles had been grouped in a slight hollow, and there, partly beside and partly on the pebbles, lay three lovely little downy chicks and one egg. We attempted to photograph the parents, but they would not come to the young; and, as the little ones had already begun to run about, we sunk an old barrel in the beach, and put them and the egg in it, that we might know where to find them on the morrow.

The day was foggy and cold, and during the night a thunderstorm drenched the earth; but the next morning the egg had disappeared, and four lively youngsters were running around in our barrel. They were now so active, that if one were liberated it would be rather difficult to catch it, while if hidden, it would be almost impossible to find it.

We kept them there two days, until we made sure that the parents never fed them. They brooded them quite constantly, but brought no food whatever, and we made certain that the young were able and willing to find their own food within 24 hours after they were out of the shell. It was seen that unless they were liberated from the barrel they would soon starve to death.

C. A. Robbins (1919) in a study of a colony of piping plovers breeding in Massachusetts lays stress on the communal feeling that he noted in the birds. He says that the feeling—

manifests itself in a marked degree; as when, at a threat of danger, more than two adults join in driving a single brood up the beach and into the safety which the concealing color of the dry sand furnishes.

It is shown again by the number of old birds that attempt to distract attention from the same brood or even from a detached individual by feigning; creeping off with wings outstretched and fluttering, tail fanned and dragging or, if the need requires more extreme measures, collapsing utterly a short distance away as if completely exhausted.

Voice.—The piping plover's home is blue and gray and white; on one side is the long line of the horizon over a large lake or the sea, on the other the long line of the sand hills. It is a land the same the world over, wherever the sea meets the white, shifting sand. The sea slides back and forth over the hard smooth wet shining beach; above the reach of the tide is the dry, pale gray, pebbly upper beach with here and there a few strands of beach grass growing in it, and higher up are the dunes which mark on the land side the boundary of the plover's home.

Walk along the water's edge and, although the sea may be pounding on the shore and a northerly gale howling about our ears, we shall hear the plover's voice; a soft musical moan, we can not tell from where, but clear and distinct above the sound of waves and wind. The note has a ventriloquial quality and it is often our first intimation that a piping plover is near, for the soft gray of the bird's plumage matches the sandy background, whereas the note is pervasive and attracts our attention by its strangeness.

Aretas A. Saunders sends me the following summary of this plover's notes. He says:

The commonest call I have noted is the one rendered in the books as *peep-lo.* It is lower pitched than most of the shore-bird voices, a clear melodious whistle, and generally rendered *peep peep peeplo.* The *peep* is usually a tone or a tone and a half higher pitched than the *lo* and I have one record where it is three tones and a half higher. I have one or two records where the second note slurs upward, the effect like *peep-loay* and suggesting the *peeawee* of the wood pewee. Another sort of note I have several records of I do not find described in books. This is a series of short sweet notes, more rapid than the others, nine or ten notes in a series. They are either all on the same pitch, or grading slightly downward in pitch toward the end, and they are sometimes followed by the *peep-lo* notes, at least in flight.

J. T. Nichols says in his notes:

When nesting the piping plover is rather noisy. The thought of its plaintive, rather mellow whistled notes, *queep, queep, queeplo,* etc., which perhaps have an analogy with song, takes me back to the sand dunes of Cape Cod standing in the dazzling sunshine, where I first became familiar with this species a number of years ago. At other times of year piping plover are rather silent. Their whistled flight note *hee-hu,* with falling inflection at the end, is not loud or striking, and suggests that of the semipalmated plover, reversed.

Gayle Pickwell (1925) in a study of the breeding habits " on a strip of sandy beach at Capital Lake near Lincoln " [Nebraska] says:

The most interesting thing about the piping plovers was their activities when one was near the nest. As an observer approached the nest he would be met by one of the plovers dropping down out of nowhere, uttering its sharp *kee-wee, kee-wee* and striving its utmost to lead one away. It would then run briskly across the sand and disappear suddenly from sight when it stopped to crouch down and utter its long-drawn *whooaah, whooaah.*

The variety of their cries and calls was amazing.

At almost any period, while we were in the neighborhood, one of the birds could be observed flying here and there with slow, wide wing beats, uttering a rapid *kuk, kuk, kuk, kuk.* It would shortly alight and wind it up with a long-drawn, weird *whooaah whooaah* that seemed to come from nowhere in particular. The distress cries while one was near the nest were confined chiefly to a sharp *kee-ah, kee-ah.* The reason for their name of " piping " became very apparent at such times.

The *kuk* mentioned by Mr. Pickwell is seemingly analogous to a common note which the semipalmated plovers use as they carry on their harmless running flights along the beach—a sort of rattling cackle of short notes somewhat suggesting the call of the red crossbill. These utterances are evidently expressions of a heightening in the emotional state of these closely related plovers.

John A. Farley (1919) describes a mating song accompanying courting activities. He says:

I noticed a group of three, two of which chased each other around just like two robins fighting over a female. Some flew around rather low over the beach (some of them rather close to me), in apparent sexual excitement, and uttered notes while on the wing. These were different from the usual mellow, rather low notes which the birds were uttering more or less all the time while on the sand. Their notes on the wing were higher in tone and rather long drawn out, and mixed in with them were some little chuckles. The whole might be described as some sort of a mating song.

Field marks.—J. T. Nichols says in substance in his notes that the bird—

may be recognized by its exceedingly pale colors which nearly match the dry sand of the beach above high-water mark. The white in the wing shows so little contrast to the general tone of the plumage that, although in flight a pattern on the wing is visible, it is very faintly indicated. A flying sanderling sometimes appears to be about the same color, but has bolder wing pattern than the plover.

The bobbing motion characteristic of several of the plovers is a common habit of the piping plover. This is a single hitching motion by which the body is tilted up and down on the legs as a fulcrum. It is apparently identical with the bob of the semipalmated plover and is made frequently as the birds stand about on the beach.

Enemies.—The piping plover is shielded from its enemies by remarkable protective coloration which renders the bird nearly invisible as it stands motionless on the gray sand, especially when among scattered stones. The eggs, the young, and the adult bird are alike protected, so now that man is no longer its deadly enemy there is little to check the species from repopulating its breeding haunts in its former numbers.

E. Beaupre speaks in his notes of a local condition in eastern Ontario. He says: " Owing to the destructive work of crows [in eating the plover's eggs] some are obliged to lay a second clutch, and this no doubt accounts for some of the nests containing fresh eggs in June."

Fall.—The piping plover moves southward soon after its nesting activities are over, following the habit of its relatives, the Limicolae which breed during the short summer about the Arctic Circle. Early departure from its nesting ground is not imperative in the case of this southerly breeding bird, but the habit is undoubtedly of long standing and dates back to the time when the species bred close to the edge of the glacial ice field and summer passed quickly.

Winter.—W. E. D. Scott (1892), speaking of the bird in Jamaica on its winter quarters, says: " In October, 1887, piping plover were abundant among the lagoons and mangrove swamps at the Palisades; they moved about in large flocks which, when once alighted on the shell-bestrewn beaches, it was impossible to detect "

We leave the little plover covered by the helmet of invisibility.

DISTRIBUTION

Range.—Eastern North America and the West Indies.

Breeding range.—The breeding range of the piping plover extends north to Saskatchewan (Big Stick Lake and Quill Lake); Manitoba (Birch Island in Lake Manitoba and Lake Winnipeg); Michigan (Big Beaver Island and Charity Island); Ontario (Toronto and Brighton); Quebec (probably Natashquan); and probably Newfoundland (Stephenville Crossing, St. George Bay). East to probably Newfoundland (Stephenville); the Magdalen Islands; Prince Edward Island (North River); Nova Scotia (Sable Island and

Yarmouth); Massachusetts (Ipswich, Monomoy Island, and Marthas Vineyard); New York (Gardiners Island and Shelter Island); New Jersey (Barnegat Inlet, Beach Haven, Sea Isle City, and probably Cape May); Maryland (probably Ocean City); Virginia (Chincoteague Island, Cobb Island, and Cape Charles); and North Carolina (Pea Island and Beaufort). South to North Carolina (Beaufort); northern Pennsylvania (Erie); northern Ohio (Painesville, Cleveland, Oberlin, and Sandusky); northern Indiana (Millers); northern Illinois (Waukegan); southern Wisconsin (Milwaukee and Lake Koshkonong); and Nebraska (Lincoln, Dannebrog, and Doss). West to Nebraska (Goss); South Dakota (Miner County); North Dakota (Stump Lake, Minnewauken, and Kenmare); and southern Saskatchewan (Big Stick Lake).

There are many gaps in the range above outlined and the species also has been extirpated from parts of its breeding grounds.

Winter range.—Almost entirely the South Atlantic and Gulf coasts of the United States. North to southern Texas (Padre Island, Aransas River and High Island); Louisiana (Vermilion Bay); Alabama (Petit Bois Island and Dauphin Island); and Georgia (Savannah). East to Georgia (Savannah and Darien); eastern Florida (Amelia Island, Mayport, St. Augustine, Sebastian, and Miami); probably the Bahama Islands (Eleuthera and Great Inagua); and probably rarely Porto Rico. South to probably rarely Port Rico; Cuba (Matanzas and Habana); southern and western Florida (Cape Sable, Key West, Sanibel Island, Fort Myers; mouth of the Withlacoochee River, and probably Pensacola); and southern Texas (Padre Island). West to southern Texas (Padre Island). The species has been detected in winter occasionally in Bermuda.

Spring migration.—Early dates of spring arrival are: South Carolina, Frogmore, March 20; North Carolina, Pea Island, April 7; District of Columbia, Washington, March 25; Pennsylvania, Erie, April 16; New York, Shinnecock, March 24, Montauk Point, April 1, and Gardiners Island, April 7; Rhode Island, Newport, March 24; Massachusetts, Marthas Vineyard, March 18, Dennis, March 24, and Nantucket, March 26; Nova Scotia, April 24; Illinois, Colona, April 9, and De Kalb, April 18; Indiana, Waterloo, April 14, and Frankfort, April 15; Ohio, Lakeside, April 7, and Oberlin, April 15; Michigan, Port Sanilac, April 15, Ottawa Beach, April 23, and Detroit, April 26; Ontario, Point Pelee, April 10, Listowel, May 1, and Toronto, May 8; Iowa, German Center, April 10; Wisconsin, Whitewater, April 29, and Elkhorn, May 13; Minnesota, Waseca, May 11, and Heron Lake, May 11; Kansas, Lawrence, April 27, McPherson, May 3, and Topeka, May 7; Nebraska, Lincoln, April 26, Gibbon, May 4, Nebraska City, May 8, and Doss, May 11; South Dakota, Sioux Falls,

May 5, and Vermilion, May 8; North Dakota, Harrisburg, May 23, and St. Thomas, May 29; Manitoba, Shoal Lake, May 15, and Killarney, May 25; and Saskatchewan, Indian Head, May 14, Qu'Appelle, May 23, and Lake Johnston, May 23.

Late dates of spring departure are: Florida, Amelia Island, April 20, Daytona Beach, May 1, and Peninsula Point, May 11; and South Carolina, Sullivans Island, May 11, and Mount Pleasant, May 18.

Fall migration.—Early dates of arrival in the fall are: Texas, Rockport, August 12, and St. Joseph Island, August 14; Mississippi, Bay St. Louis, August 29; South Carolina, Mount Pleasant, August 2; Florida, New Smyrna, July 15, Fernandina, August 3, and Daytona, August 10; and Alabama, Dauphin Island, August 16.

Late dates of fall departure are: Manitoba, Shoal Lake, September 7; South Dakota, Forestburg, September 24; Nebraska, Bellwood, September 19, and Doss, September 24; Iowa, Grinnell, October 28; Ontario, Point Pelee, September 22, Michigan, Newbury, September 18; Ohio, Cleveland, September 24, Painesville, September 26, and Port Clinton, September 28; Indiana, La Fayette, September 18; Prince Edward Island, North River, October 20; Nova Scotia, Pictou, October 8; Vermont, Bennington, October 2; Massachusetts, Lynn, October 3, Dennis, October 12, and Boston, October 26; Rhode Island, Block Island, October 24; New York, Fair Haven Light, September 28, and Long Beach, November 7 (exceptionally late date); New Jersey, Cape May, September 13; and Pennsylvania, Erie, September 26.

Casual records.—The piping plover has been detected outside of its regular range on very few occasions. A specimen in the British Museum from the Lake of the Woods, Ontario, may indicate breeding in that locality. One was obtained at Cheyenne, Wyo., on May 30, 1892.

Egg dates.—Quebec and New Brunswick: 55 records, June 1 to 29; 28 records, June 5 to 18. New England to New Jersey: 48 records, May 22 to June 29; 24 records, May 28 to June 23. Dakotas: 13 records, May 26 to July 1; 7 records, May 28 to June 6.

CHARADRIUS NIVOSUS NIVOSUS (Cassin)

SNOWY PLOVER

HABITS

The charming little snowy plover of the Pacific coast is the counterpart of our familiar piping plover, found in similar haunts, perhaps even tamer and more confiding, but not equal to our eastern bird in melody of voice. It is a child of the sand, with which its colors blend so well that when crouched in some hollow or against some bleached piece of driftwood or half buried clam shell it seems to be just one more of the numerous, inconspicuous objects which one passes unnoticed on the beach. Its favorite haunts are the broad expanses of flat, dry sand above the ordinary wash of the tides on ocean beaches. Such places are usually strewn more or less thickly with shells, pebbles, and various bits of débris, among which the little plover, or its eggs and young, are surprisingly inconspicuous. Here it was born and has always lived; here it woos its mate and rears its little family; and hence it seldom strays except to feed along the water's edge on the ocean beach or on the bare flats along some near-by tidal creek. There are, however, a few places in the interior where the snowy plover has been found along the shores of salt or alkaline lakes. But it is mainly a bird of the ocean beaches.

Spring.—The snowy plover wanders north in the spring as far as the coast of Washington. D. E. Brown tells me that he saw it in Grays Harbor County from April 7 to 13, 1918, and from May 14 to 16, 1914, in Pacific County. But apparently no one has ever found it breeding there, although several good observers have looked for it.

Nesting.—The nesting grounds of the snowy plover have been briefly described above, but a better description is contained in the following quotation from W. Lee Chambers (1904):

The nesting ground is a white sandy cape or narrow strip of land between Ballona Swamp and the ocean about 2 miles long and 200 yards wide. This place during the fall high tides is completely flooded and deposits of small rocks and broken shells are left there. Among these the plovers place their nests. On approaching it one may be attracted by noticing the little fellows running about on the sand in front of him or occasionally flying in low, wide circles uttering a pleading whistle so characteristic of this species. This whistle I have learned is a danger signal that I am near their nests, and on looking over the ground carefully I may be able to notice fine bird tracks in the white sand or in the patches of white sand between the shells and rocks.

In going over the ground carefully where the tracks are the thickest a nest will generally be found. Sometimes the birds will build among the small rocks, where the tracks can not be seen, and here the eggs are safe, as their coloration protects them, for they look exactly like small rocks. The nests are, as a rule, found by a mark of some kind, a bone of some animal, a small dead weed, or a bit of driftwood, and are slight depressions in the sand. Some are completely lined with broken shells or fish bones with the eggs pointed toward the center, very close together and about half buried in the nest lining. A pair of birds will build several nests during the season and use only one, for I have found nests all fixed up and completely surrounded with tracks. This I noticed especially in 1901, for I found about three times as many unused nests as used ones. During this season I visited Ballona about three times a week and gave the birds careful study.

While J. Eugene Law was helping me to get acquainted with the birds of southern California, we spent a delightful day, May 29, 1914, among these birds with Mr. Chambers at Del Rey, Los Angeles County. This was once a typical nesting place of this species, a broad stretch of sand flats above an ocean beach, backed by sand dunes and bordered on the inner side by a sluggish stream meandering through a marsh and some brackish lagoons. But civilization was encroaching on the plover's paradise, for several cottages had been built on the beach and it was much frequented. Some four pairs of snowy plover still clung to their ancestral home; we found three nests with three eggs each and one empty nest, in open spaces among the houses. The nests were mostly on little mounds of sand and scattered pebbles or among low sand dunes covered with low weeds and vines. They were deep hollows in the sand, profusely lined with finely broken white and pink shells, among scattered small stones, bits of wood, or other rubbish. Amid such surroundings the eggs were not easily detected; but we could usually locate the nests by the multitude of little footprints in the sand converging toward the nest. All but one of the birds were shy and sneaked off the nests before we drew near. They watched us from a distance, running about very swiftly, whistling their soft, plaintive notes of protest. One bird was very tame; I gradually walked up very close to her and finally photographed her within 3 or 4 feet. This gentle and confiding little bird, after running about with drooping wings and spread tail, came slowly up to the nest and settled down on the eggs right in front of me, spreading out her plumage to cover her treasures. As a reward for her bravery we did not disturb her further.

Grinnell, Bryant, and Storer (1918) write that:

In the vicinity of the salt works near Alvarado, on the Alameda County shore of San Francisco Bay, L. R. Reynolds found that a great many pairs had in the summer of 1914 selected nesting sites on the dike separating the salt ponds. The workmen, in traversing the dikes with wheelbarrows, reported having broken many eggs.

Eggs.—The snowy plover ordinarily lays three eggs, but often only two. Mr. Chambers (1904) says that out of 44 sets which he collected 11 were of two eggs and 33 were of three. The two egg sets were complete, as he left them long enough to make sure. The eggs were laid about three days apart. The extended nesting season, April to July, would seem to indicate that two broods are raised, but I believe that this has not been positively proven. The eggs are short, ovate in shape, and without gloss. They are colored to match the sand—" olive buff " to " pale olive buff," or " cartridge buff." They are more or less evenly but not thickly covered with small spots, dots, or little scrawls of black and a few small inconspicuous spots of " pallid mouse gray." The measurements of 51 eggs average 30.4 by 22.3 millimeters; the eggs showing the four extremes measure **32.5** by 23.5, 30 by **24**, and **28** by **20.5** millimeters.

Young.—Apparently both sexes share the duties of incubation and care of the young, at which they prove devoted parents. When the young are approached the parents use all the artifices known to similar species to distract the attention of the intruder, fluttering along as if both wings and legs were helpless, or grovelling in the sand as if wounded. Such tactics often succeed in fooling a dog and enticing him far enough away but to human beings they are only an incentive to look carefully for the tiny balls of down that, obedient to their parents' note of warning, are crouched immovable and well-nigh invisible in some little hollow in the sand or under or against some object on the beach. And there the little one remains " frozen " until touched or until sure that he is observed; when, presto, off he goes, running at a marvelous pace on his strong little legs. We watch him for some time as he scampers away for a long distance until suddenly he vanishes; then, unless we have marked him down exactly and kept our eyes on the spot, we had better give up hope of finding him again.

Plumages.—The downy young snowy plover is quite unlike the young piping plover. The entire upper parts are pale buff, "cream buff " to " cartridge buff," mixed with grayish white. The crown, back, rump, wings, and thighs are distinctly and quite evenly spotted with black. The under parts are pure white.

In the juvenal plumage the crown, mantle, rump, cheeks, and a space in front of the wing are " drab," or " light drab," with a pinkish buff tinge on the tips of the feathers; the forehead and all under parts are white. The first winter plumage is similar, without the buffy edgings.

Adults have a complete postnuptial molt in late summer and fall, and a partial prenuptial molt in early spring. Males in nuptial plumage have the crown and nape " pinkish buff," and a broad band above the forehead, an auricular patch and a patch in front of the wing abruptly clear black. In females the crown is pale drab, like the back, and the dark markings are more restricted and more brownish. In winter the sexes are alike, similar to the spring female, but the dark markings are even duller, about the same tone as the back.

Food.—Snowy plover feed mainly on the sandy beaches, foraging on the wet sand and at the surf line, where they are expert at dodging the incoming waves and very lively, running up and down the beach as the waves advance or recede. Here they often forage in compact bunches, picking up small crustaceans, marine worms, or other minute marine organisms. Inland they feed along the muddy or alkaline shores of ponds or lakes, on various insects, such as beetles or flies. Dr. A. K. Fisher (1893) says:

This handsome little plover was observed by the writer on the shores of Owens Lake, near Keeler, May 30 to June 4, where it was common in small flocks of 5 or 10 on the alkaline flats which border the lake. Like most other birds in the vicinity, it fed extensively, if not exclusively, on a species of small fly (*Ephydra hians* Say), which was found in immense masses near the edge of the lake. Many of these swarms of flies were four or five layers deep and covered an area of 15 or 20 square feet. Some idea can be formed of the inexhaustible supply of food which this insect furnishes for birds when it is known that colonies of equal size occurred at close intervals in suitable localities all around the lake, which has a shore line of between 40 and 50 miles.

Behavior.—Grinnell, Bryant, and Storer (1918) write:

When searching for food they move about a great deal, with a distinct trot, and on occasion have been seen to hop along on one leg as Torrey has observed sanderlings to do at Santa Barbara. Their movements are rapid and their strides exceedingly long. At Netarts Bay, Oreg., Jewett says that when running fast the strides of one of these birds proved to measure 6 inches. One of the birds will start, run 3 or 4 feet, and stop suddenly, the whole performance occupying but a second or two. There is an abrupt upward tilt of the body at intervals, and with the return movement the quavering note is often uttered. In flight the birds may travel in open formation, or closely massed, and the flight may be either direct, or in zigzag course as with the small sandpipers. Both in flight, and on the ground, their chunky appearance helps to distinguish them from the small sandpipers. They are quite tame and will usually permit a close approach, preferring apparently to trot along in front of the observer, or off to one side, rather than to take wing.

Florence Merriam Bailey (1916) observes:

Besides the large waders, the godwits, willets, and surf birds, there were flocks of little sanderlings and snowy plover, looking like small chickens on the beach among the bigger birds. The snowy plover, plump, squat little fellows with head markings that suggest wide foreheads and backs that match the sand on which they love to sun themselves, when feeding on the beach would hurry back ahead of the foam, their short legs making them more in danger of getting wet than the long-legged godwits. When resting, the plump little sandy-backed fellows kept by themselves. Sometimes as I walked along above the line of the tide, bits of sand would take legs ahead of me, the brown forms that squatted in my path having been entirely overlooked. When I saw them before they got up, and stopped to talk to them, the confiding little fellows flatteringly sat still or went on fixing their feathers, looking very comfortable in the warm sand. To me they seemed the most winning and attractive of all the lovely little sandpipers. When they were surprised and ran from me they did it in a comical crouching way as if knowing their backs were sand color and trying to hide their black legs and plump white bodies. Their habit of bobbing the head is doubtless useful at times, but the motion often catches the eye when without it they would not be separated from the sand.

Voice.—Grinnell, Bryant, and Storer (1918) say: "Snowy plover are exceptionally quiet birds; but at times a low, guttural, trilling note, *cr-r-r-r* or *pe-e-e-et*, may be given, and when the vicinity of the nest is invaded the birds give utterance to relatively loud cries."

Field marks.—They also give the best recognition marks, as follows:

The snowy plover is readily distinguished from most other shore birds occurring in California by its very small size (total length, 6–7 inches). It is but slightly larger than our smallest shore bird, the least sandpiper. The chunky appearance, short, thick bill (which is shorter than the head), white collar around hind neck, uniform pale drab upper surface, pure white under surface, and conspicuous dark-brown or black patches at the sides of the breast are all useful as aids to recognition. From the killdeer, and the semipalmated and Wilson plovers, the snowy is distinguished by its lack of complete black or dark-brown breast band and by its smaller size, and from the least and western sandpipers, and from the sanderling, by its white collar around hind neck and by the dark patches at the sides of its chest; and, in spring, from the last three named birds by the absence of mixed coloration on its upper surface.

Winter.—The snowy plover is a permanent resident throughout the southern part of its range, though perhaps the same individuals may not be present all the year round. It winters as far north as San Francisco, but more abundantly from Santa Barbara southward, where its numbers are increased in winter by migrants from farther north and where flocks of 50 or more are often seen.

DISTRIBUTION

Range.—The United States (principally the western part), the West Indies, and Central and South America.

Breeding range.—The snowy plover breeds north probably to Washington (Willapa Harbor); Utah (Bear River and Farmington); southern Kansas (Comanche County); Oklahoma (Cimarron River); Mississippi (Horn Island); Florida (Pensacola, and Santa Rosa Island); and Cuba (rarely Guantanamo). East to Cuba (rarely Guantanamo). South to Cuba (rarely Guantanamo); southern Texas (Refugio County, probably San Patricio County, and Corpus Christi); probably New Mexico (Carlsbad); and Lower California* (La Paz). West to Lower California (La Paz, probably Santa Rosalia Bay, and probably San Quentin Bay); California (San Diego, probably San Nicholas Island, probably San Miguel Island, Santa Barbara, Morro, Monterey, Santa Cruz, Pescadero, San Francisco, and Eureka); probably Oregon (Netarts Bay); and probably Washington (Willapa Harbor).

Winter range.—The winter range extends north to California (Santa Cruz Islands); Texas (Brownsville, Corpus Christi, and Aransas Bay); probably coastal regions of Louisiana; Florida (Pensacola, Santa Rosa Island, Cedar Keys, Clearwater, and Fort Myers); Bahama Islands (Riley); probably Cuba (Gundlach); probably Yucatan; and Chile (Calbuco). South to Chile (Calbuco). West to Chile (Calbuco, and probably Valparaiso); Peru (Chorillos, and the valley of the Tambo); probably Guatemala (Chiapam); Lower California (La Paz, Magdalena Islands, and San Cristobal Bay); and California (San Diego, Santa Cruz Island, Santa Barbara, and Monterey Bay). They also were noted at Westport, Wash., on

December 19, 1927 (letter, J. H. Bowles), and so may winter rarely in that region.

Spring migration.—But little information is available concerning the migration of the snowy plover. Early dates of spring arrival are: Kansas, McPherson, April 14, and Douglas County, April 22; Utah, Salt Lake County, May 3; Oregon, Corvallis, March 24, and Malheur Lake, April 20; and Washington, Grays Harbor, April 7.

Fall migration.—The few available late dates of fall departure are: Washington, Point Chehalis, November 18; and northern California, San Francisco, November 1, and Alameda, December 3.

Casual records.—The snowy plover has been detected outside of its normal range on a few occasions. Among these are: Brazil (Specimen in United States National Museum); southern Chile (Coquimbo, Straits of Magellan in June [Sharpe]); Ontario, Toronto, one specimen in May, 1880, and another on July 6, 1897 (Fleming); Nebraska, two specimens at Lincoln, May 17, 1903 (Swenk); Wyoming, one taken near Cheyenne (Knight); while a specimen from Kodiak Island, Alaska, reported by Schalow (1891) as *Charadrius alexandrinus*, may be this species.

Egg dates.—California: 155 records, April 2 to July 28; 78 records, May 5 to June 14. Utah: 5 records, April 30 to June 15.

[AUTHOR'S NOTE.—The above distribution includes both North American races. Probably the birds found breeding east of the Rocky Mountains and wintering on eastern coasts will prove to be referable to *tenuirostris*, but there are not enough specimens available from these localities to outline definitely the ranges of the two races.]

CHARADRIUS NIVOSUS TENUIROSTRIS (Lawrence)

CUBAN SNOWY PLOVER

HABITS

The snowy plover which breeds on the Gulf coasts of Texas, Louisiana, and Florida, as well as in Cuba, the Bahamas, and a few places in the interior has been separated from the Pacific coast form under the above name. The difference between the two forms is not easily recognized, but the eastern bird is said to be much paler and may average a trifle smaller. The habits of the two seem to be similar. N. S. Goss (1891) found this bird breeding on the salt plains along the Cimarron River, Indian Territory, in 1886. Herbert W. Brandt sent me some notes on a nest found by him in Nueces County, Tex. Francis M. Weston writes to me that it is common and breeds near Pensacola, Fla. He says of its notes:

When on the ground the Cuban snowy plover gives a low-pitched, musical whistle, roughly indicated by the words *pe-wee-ah* or *o-wee-ah*, the accent being on the second syllable with the first and third almost inaudible at a distance of 30 feet. The flight note is a purring whistle, suggestive of the rolling note of the Carolina wren but pitched lower and not as strident.

It was apparently common during the winter in Pinellas County, Fla., frequenting the sandy islands and ocean beaches in the vicinity of Tampa Bay; but we found it difficult to separate it, in immature and winter plumages, from young piping plover, unless we were near enough to recognize its slender bill; the difference in size was not noticeable except by direct comparison. I can find nothing in its nesting habits or in its behavior in which it differs from the Pacific snowy plover. I have not seen its eggs, but presume that they are like those of the western form.

CHARADRIUS MONGOLUS MONGOLUS Pallas

MONGOLIAN PLOVER

HABITS

According to the Rev. F. C. R. Jourdain:

This species is now known to be divided into two fairly distinguishable subspecies, the typical race breeding in Mongolia, Kamchatka, and Eastern Siberia as well as on the Commander Islands, and wintering from the Philippines, Celebes, etc., to New Guinea and Australia. It is this form which has occurred in Alaska. *Charadrius mongolus atrifrons* Wagler, the western race, breeds from the Kirghis Steppes in South Russia to the Himalayas and Tibet, wintering in East Africa, Madagascar, the Seychelles, India, Malacca, and the Great Sunda Isles.

Like several other Asiatic species, it occasionally wanders across Bering Strait into extreme northwestern Alaska. Joseph Dixon (1918) throws considerable doubt over the time-honored record of specimens supposed to have been taken by Captain Moore of the plover on the Choris Peninsula in the summer of 1849; his reasoning, which seems to be sound, suggests that these specimens were probably taken on the Siberian side. However, Alfred M. Bailey (1926) collected a male of this species at Cape Prince of Wales on June 11, 1922, of which he says:

The tundra was still snow covered, only a small, sandy strip being bare along Lopp Lagoon, and there I found this little wanderer from the Siberian shore in company with yellow wagtails. A south wind had been blowing for a few days previous, which changed to the north the evening before. On these changes of winds I observed that Old World birds were likely to drift across the channel.

Harry S. Swarth has very kindly given me, in advance of publication by the California Academy of Sciences, the latest records of the occurrence of this species in Alaska. While collecting for the academy on Nunivak Island, C. G. Harrold took two specimens, a female on August 14 and a male on September 1, 1927. Two others were seen on August 14, one on September 11, and one on September 13. It looks as if this might be more than a casual straggler in Alaska.

Dr. Leonhard Stejneger (1885) writes:

The Mongolian plover is a very common resident on the Commander Islands; in fact, one of the most characteristic birds of their fauna. It is one of the brightest and handsomest shore birds, and is always gladly welcomed when making its appearance during the first half of May. I used then to watch with delight these elegant runners, wondering at the almost incredible rapidity with which they move their legs when chasing each other over the pebbly beach, or trying to escape the approaching hunter. Very soon, however, the pairs retire to the place chosen for the summer home, and, as soon as the eggs are laid, the birds become more shy and do not expose themselves as much as they did before.

Nesting.—There are three sets of eggs in the United States National Museum taken by Doctor Stejneger in the Commander Islands " during the first days of June." He says that the birds " do not fly directly from the nest but run away a distance from it before taking wing," which makes it difficult to find the nests. A nest he describes—

Was found on the islet Toporkof, on the 4th of June, 1883, and contained three eggs. They were lying, with their pointed ends inwards and downwards, in a slight hollow in the ground between the stems of four *Angelica archangelica*. Dry particles of the leaves and stems of this plant, and numerous seeds of the same, formed the nest, being evidently brought together by the bird itself. The situation of the nest was about 40 feet from the line of high water and about 14 feet above the level of the sea.

Mr. Jourdain contributes the following:

Interesting confirmation of Doctor Stejneger's observations on the breeding habits and eggs of this species have been furnished by the recent discovery of the breeding haunts of the western race by Messrs. H. Whistler (1925) and B. B. Osmaston (1927) at high altitudes in the Himalayan range. Mr. Whistler found at least five pairs breeding on the stony wastes near the Chandra Lake in Lahul, at 14,000 feet on July 10 to 11. Two clutches, each of three well-incubated eggs and one brood of three downy young were taken. Other pairs were subsequently found breeding in Spiti (13,500 ft.) and on the northern slopes of the Bara Lancha range. Mr. B. B. Osmaston found this species not uncommon in South and East Ladakh in summer, between 13,000 and 15,500 feet. It was located as breeding in Rukshu near the Tsokar and Tso Morari Lakes at about 15,000 feet and between the Indus and Shushal at 14,000 to 14,500 feet, by the Pangong Lake at 14,000 and in the upper Surun Valley at 13,000 feet.

In every case three eggs or young were found and the nest was a slight depression in the sand, among shingle (Osmaston, 1927), or in hollows among the trailing stems of a small creeping ground plant with a woodlike stem, sparingly lined with broken chips and fragments of the plant stems (Whistler 1925).

Eggs.—The nine eggs collected by Doctor Stejneger vary in shape from ovate to ovate pyriform and they show no gloss. The ground colors vary from "cinnamon buff" to "deep olive buff." They are quite evenly, but not heavily, marked with small spots of very dark browns, "warm sepia" to "bone brown," or brownish black. There is a set of three eggs, which seems to be the usual number, in the collection of Col. John E. Thayer, taken at Omsk, Siberia, on June 9, 1893. These are subpyriform in shape, without gloss. The ground colors vary from "deep olive buff" to "pale olive buff." One egg is uni formly covered with fine pen-like scrawls of "sepia" and "pale violet gray." The others are marked, chiefly in a ring near the large end, with similar scrawls and with irregular spots of brownish black or black. The measurements of 15 eggs average 35.2 by 26.2 millimeters; the eggs showing the four extremes measure **37.5** by 27, 32 by **28.8** and **30.5** by **23.2** milimeters.

Mr. Jourdain says in his notes:

The 12 eggs taken by Osmaston (1927) averaged 36.7 by 26.3, while the 6 obtained by Whistler (1925) averaged 38.4 by 26.5 millimeters, thus agreeing well on the whole with those of the eastern race, but are as a rule rather larger. The coloration is also similar, speckled with dark brown spots on a ground of creamy stone.

The parent bird slips off the nest very quietly and returns very cautiously by short runs. It is naturally very difficult to follow in the great waste of sand and shingle. When disturbed on the breeding ground the old birds behave much as other sand plovers, flying round uneasily in circles and running about swiftly, but were less noisy than common or lesser ringed plovers.

Young.—Doctor Stejneger (1885) says that the young ones are found—

about the middle of July. About this time the families retire from the beach and are now met with in the interior, where they ascend the mountains in search of tender insects. I frequently met them at an altitude of 1,000 feet or more above sea level. About the middle of September the families return to the lowlands and to the beach, soon afterwards leaving the islands.

While at Glinka, on Copper Island, in July, 1883, a young bird of this species, not yet fully feathered, was brought to me alive. Allowed to run free on the floor it immediately commenced a very animated pursuit of the rather numerous flies, which were caught with remarkable precision and rapidity and devoured with an unsatiable appetite. The little fellow did not pay any attention to the presence of several persons in the small room, but when the dog rose from his nap in the corner, the swiftfooted fly killer suddenly dropped flat on the floor, with withdrawn neck, making himself as small and flat as possible, and remained thus perfectly immovable until the dog turned his head the other way, then he ran off to the darkest corner of the room, where he remained until the former laid down in his old place. Then he started the fly hunting again; the dog rose once more, and the same performance was repeated. Within half an hour, however, he had learned that the dog did not take any notice of him whatever, and consequently he afterwards paid as little attention to the dog as to man.

Plumages.—The young bird referred to above was about half grown and largely feathered when it died, but the specimen shows a little of the natal down, mainly on the head, which is largely downy. The forehead is buffy white, the crown mostly dark " bister," and the sides of the head are mottled with buffy and " bister "; the throat is pale buff. The remiges are half grown and the new feathers of the mantle are " sepia," with " cinnamon-buff " tips; the feathers of the breast are " cinnamon buff " or " pinkish buff " and those of the belly are white.

Evidently the juvenal plumage soon fades, for a specimen taken on September 22, in full juvenal plumage, is much paler. The entire upper parts are " hair brown " or " drab," with narrow, pale, buffy edgings; the forehead and under parts are white, but the breast is suffused with " pinkish buff " and invaded on the sides with the " drab " of the upper parts.

There is not sufficient material to show the molts and plumages satisfactorily. Adults have a complete molt in August and September, at which the cinnamon of the chest, neck, and head entirely disappears.

Voice.—Doctor Stejneger (1885) says that " the call note is a clear, penetrating *drrrriit*." Mr. Jourdain adds: " The call note is described by Whistler as a soft *twip*, and the alarm note as a sort of chatter of two syllables *corr up*, not unlike the note of a frog and compared by Osmaston to that of a nightjar. It is uttered usually on the wing and also occasionally on the ground."

DISTRIBUTION

Range.—Eastern Asia and Oceanica; accidental in Alaska.

Breeding range.—This race of the Mongolian plover breeds chiefly in northeastern Siberia (Cape Serdze, Bering Island, Kamchatka, and the Commander Islands) ; probably also in Dauria and Mongolia.

Winter range.—The winter range includes the Philippine Islands, the Moluccas, New Guinea, and northern Australia.

Migration.—The species has been noted to arrive in spring at Yokohama, Japan, on April 28, and at Bering Island, on May 11. A late fall date on Bering Island is September 22.

Casual records.—On June 11, 1925, an adult male was collected at Cape Prince of Wales (Bailey). Two specimens were taken by C. G. Harrold on Nunivak Island, Alaska, in 1927, one on August 14, and one on September 1; others were seen on August 14 and September 11 and 13. These are the only North American records.

Egg dates.—Bering Island, June 4. Siberia, June 9.

PAGOLLA WILSONIA WILSONIA (Ord.)

WILSON PLOVER

HABITS

All along the Atlantic coast from New Jersey to Florida is a broken chain of sea-girt islands, with broad or steep, sandy or shelly beaches on the ocean side, backed in many places by shifting sand dunes and bordered on the inner or bay side by wide marshes of waving grass or extensive flats exposed at low tide. Here, on the broader, more open sand flats, among a scattered array of shells, pebbles, and other débris cast up by the sea, or in the flat hollows among the sand dunes, this little sand plover makes its home, within sound of the pounding surf and fanned by the ocean breezes that carve the dunes into fantastic shapes. Here, if we love to wander in these seaside solitudes, we may see this gentle bird running along the beach ahead of us, his feet twinkling so fast that we can hardly see them; he is unafraid, as he stops and turns to watch us; the black bands on his head and breast help to obliterate his form and he might be mistaken for an old seashell or bit of driftwood; but, as we draw near, he turns and runs on ahead of us, leading us thus on and on up the beach. There is an air of gentleness in his manner and an air of wildness in his note as he flies away.

Spring.—As the northern limit of the winter range extends well up to central Florida, the Wilson plover has not far to migrate. It is an early migrant. We saw it in Pinellas County, Fla., as early as February 7, where a few were present all winter. C. J. Pennock's notes record it at Charlotte Harbor on February 21 and 24, on two successive years. Arthur T. Wayne (1910) says that it arrives in South Carolina late in March; his earliest date is March 26.

Courtship.—During the month of March, when this species became common in the vicinity of Tampa Bay, Fla., I had some opportunities to watch its simple courtship display. A male shot on March 14 had sexual organs developed nearly to full breeding size and many of the birds were in pairs. In making the display the male runs around the female in a crouching, hunchbacked attitude, with the head lowered, the tail depressed and spread, and the wings drooping. The female seems indifferent at first, but finally she accepts the caresses of the male. They seem to be preoccupied in their love affairs and allow a close approach.

Nesting.—On the sandy reefs and broad ocean beaches of the outer islands about Bulls Bay, S. C., we found several nests of Wilson plover on May 22 and 23, 1915. The nests were on the higher portions of the beaches where the dry, sandy plains were sprinkled with bits of broken shells, small stones, and pieces of driftwood or other rubbish and where a few scattered weeds and grasses were the only signs of vegetation. The nests were usually placed near some such object, or partially sheltered by a few blades of grass, but some were out on the open sand or in the flat sandy hollows between the dunes; they were always beyond the reach of ordinary tides. Oyster-catchers and least terns were nesting in the same localities and not far away willets were nesting in the grassy places.

Among the Florida Keys, on May 8, 1903, we found a small colony nestings on Lake Key; there were beaches of finely broken shells surrounding a small shallow pond, more or less overgrown with small, scattered red mangroves. A colony of least terns were nesting here and a few pairs of black-necked stilts. Four nests of the plover were found, one out on the open beach among the terns' nests and the others under the shelter of little mangrove seedlings. These and all the other nests of Wilson plover that I have found were mere hollows in the sand with no apparent attempt at lining, but others have occasionally found them evidently lined with bits of broken shell. Henry Thurston (1913) found a nest "snuggled closely to the stump" of a "ripped up" palmetto; the eggs were "resting in a small hole that had been scooped out in the sand and adorned with a few twigs." He left this nest and returned later in an attempt to see the female leave the nest. As he "got within a few yards the male, unobserved before as he was facing him and was therefore practically invisible, piped several notes. Swiftly and mouse-like the female glided from her treasures, crouching low beside the stump and did not stand erect until she reached the water's edge."

The Wilson plover might almost be said to nest in colonies, although the nests are usually not close together; N. B. Moore says in his notes that they are never nearer than 20 yards apart. Oscar E. Baynard (1914) found a colony of at least 50 pairs nesting on a bank of white sand, probably half a mile long and barely a foot above high-water line. He relates an interesting experience in changing eggs from one nest to another. One of a set of three heavily incubated eggs that he had taken hatched out in his possession; as he could not find the nest from which they came, he hunted up another nest which contained fresh eggs; and following is his account of what happened:

I took these eggs and placed the young bird and my two eggs in their place, and then moved off and sat down to watch developments. In a few minutes the mother bird ran up to the nest, looked hard at the young bird, which had run off about 2 feet from the eggs, circled the nest several times, and then squatted down on the two eggs and began calling softly to the young bird. In a few minutes he crept up to the old bird. She looked him over for fully two minutes, then decided to adopt him, raked him under her out of the sun, and settled down as contentedly as if the family were really her own. Two days later I ran the boat close to the beach opposite this nest. The old bird ran off, and up jumped three young and took off up the beach after her.

Donald J. Nicholson tells me that he once found a nest " about three-quarters of the way up the side of a sand dune under the shelter of a small bunch of grass." He has also found this plover breeding on Merritts Island, Fla., " on the exposed sandy patches along the Indian River and around the water holes throughout the island "; here some of the nests were sheltered among open growths of pickerelweed or *Salicornia.*

Dr. Frank M. Chapman (1891) found this bird breeding commonly near Corpus Christi, Tex., and says: "A nest found April 25 was placed in some short grass about 50 feet from the water. It was composed of a few straws placed at the bottom of a slight depression in the sand, and contained three fresh eggs."

Eggs.—The Wilson plover ordinarily lays three eggs, often only two, and very rarely four; I have a set of four eggs in my collection, taken by Dr. Eugene E. Murphey on the coast of South Carolina. N. B. Moore says in his notes that a day often intervened between the laying of eggs, once an interval of two days occurred and in one nest the third egg was laid on the ninth day after the first. The eggs are ovate to short ovate in shape and they have no gloss. The ground colors vary from " cream buff " to " cartridge buff." They are usually thickly and quite evenly covered with small spots, small irregular blotches and scrawls of black, with a few similar, under- lying markings of pale shades of " Quaker drab." The measure- ments of 66 eggs average 35.7 by 26.2 millimeters; the eggs showing the four extremes measure **38.5** by 26, 37 by **27, 31.5** by 26, and 34 by **25** millimeters.

Young.—N. B. Moore observed that the period of incubation is 24 or 25 days. I have no data showing that the male shares in the duty of incubation, but he certainly shows considerable interest in the care of the young. The young are able to leave the nesting hollow soon after they are hatched and they are strong and swift runners, as well as adepts in the art of hiding. The female is a past master in the art of decoying an intruder away from her young. Mr. Thurston (1913) has described this strategy very well, as follows:

As I approached this strip, seemingly from nowhere there appeared a female plover, calling plaintively. Now I knew that the season of nesting had begun. She was soon joined by a male and another female that chorused with her their wishes for my departure. How she coaxed me to follow her! This I did for a time, trailing behind as she struggled along on one leg, the other crumpled under her. Tediously she kept ahead, calling—sobbing, I should have said—one of the most pathetic yet beautiful notes I have heard. Surely if ever there was a picture of parental distress it was she. Finally, as though exhausted, she sank to the sand and lay on her side gasping. The other two flew back and forth overhead, whistling plaintively, but she heeded them not, nor my approach, and lay there panting. I was sure now that she was tired by her exertion and hurried to catch her, only to learn that she was "playing possum." She allowed me to almost touch her, and fluttered off again. Evidently she was not satisfied that her nest was safe and she tried new tactics this time. With seemingly broken wings that trailed as though helpless at her sides, she started down the beach and once more I followed after, but this time increased my speed. As I had about caught up with her she gave a joyous whistle, sprang into the air, and those wounded wings carried her like a bullet around a point of wooded land and out of sight. She had accomplished her purpose, as I had hopelessly lost the place from which she started. Search as I might, and did, I could not find it.

Plumages.—The upper parts of the downy young Wilson plover are of about the same color pattern as the egg to make it equally invisible on the sand. The crown, back, rump, wings, and thighs are "cream buff," mottled with black; the forehead, sides of the head, and under parts are white; there is a broad white collar around the neck, and the outer joint of the wing is white.

The juvenal plumage, in what specimens I have seen, July 20 to 27, is much like that of the adult female in winter, but the colors are duller and the breast band is incomplete or only suggested. Perhaps earlier in the season these birds might have shown buffy edgings which had since worn away. Probably a postjuvenal molt takes place, but I have not been able to trace it. In the first winter plumage the sexes are alike; but at the first prenuptial molt, in February and March, the male assumes, partially at least, the black markings on the head and breast. At the next complete molt, the first postnuptial, the adult winter plumage is acquired.

Adults have an incomplete prenuptial molt, from January to March, involving the body plumage, and a complete postnuptial molt, from July to October. The sexes are quite unlike in nuptial plumage, the black markings on the head and breast of the male being replaced by "wood brown" in the female. In winter they are much alike, but I believe that in fully adult males there is always more or less black in the breast band.

Food.—Audubon (1840) says of these birds:

They feed fully as much by night as by day, and the large eyes of this, as of other species of the genus, seem to fit them for nocturnal searchings. Their food consists principally of small marine insects, minute shellfish, and sand worms, with which they mix particles of sand.

The stomachs of five birds taken on the coast of Alabama by Arthur H. Howell (1924) contained "crabs and shrimps, with a few mollusks and flies." One taken in Porto Rico by Stuart T. Danforth (1926) contained Dytiscid larvae and adults.

Behavior.—Audubon (1840) describes the behavior of this plover very well, as follows:

The flight of this species, is rapid, elegant, and protracted. While traveling from one sand beach or island to another, they fly low over the land or water, emitting a fine, clear, soft note. Now and then, when after the breeding season they form into flocks of 20 or 30, they perform various evolutions in the air, cutting backward and forward, as if inspecting the spot on which they wish to alight, and then suddenly descend, sometimes on the sea beach and sometimes on the more elevated sands at a little distance from it. They do not run so nimbly as the piping plovers nor are they nearly so shy. I have in fact frequently walked up so as to be within 10 yards or so of them. They seldom mix with other species, and they show a decided preference to solitary uninhabited spots.

Voice.—My field notes, written over 20 years ago, refer to Wilson plover flying about their breeding grounds, whistling their musical call notes, somewhat suggestive of the notes of the piping plover, but not so loud nor so rich in tone. Francis M. Weston writes to me that "the note of anxiety, when on the ground, is a sharp *wheet*, beween a chirp and a whistle. On the wing, it gives a low *tut-tut*, somewhat like the alarm note of the wood thrush, but pitched lower and never of more than two syllables." C. J. Pennock says, in his notes, that when they have eggs or young "they fly about close overhead, or run along the sand, calling *queet, queet, quit it, quit it*, in a high-pitched tone, frequently three or four birds joining in the vocal protest." John T. Nichols says in his notes: "The commonest note of this species on the ground and on the wing is a ternlike *quip*, sometimes double *qui-pip*. Less frequently, on the ground, it has a surprisingly human whistled *whip*."

Field marks.—The best field character of the Wilson plover is the long, heavy, wholly black bill, which is very conspicuous in all plumages; it is relatively larger and more prominent than that of the black-bellied plover. The Wilson is decidedly larger than the semipalmated or the piping plover; it is slightly lighter in color than the former and much darker than the latter. I have noticed that in flight it appears quite dark colored above, with no conspicuous white except in the lateral tail feathers.

Winter.—We recorded this species as a winter resident on the west coast of Florida as far north as Tampa Bay, but it was rare in midwinter and did not become common until March. It frequented the sand bars and sandy islands on the Gulf shore, together with other small plovers and sandpipers. It was much tamer than any of the other shore birds and less active; it was the only one of the whole tribe that could be openly approached on the unprotected beaches. It was usually seen singly, apart from the others, and never in flocks.

DISTRIBUTION

Range.—Southern United States, the West Indies, Central and South America.

Breeding range.—The Wilson plover breeds north to probably Lower California (La Paz); Texas (Brownsville, Corpus Christi, probably Rockport, probably Matagorda Island, Houston, and Galveston); Louisiana (probably Cameron Parish and the Breton Island Reservation); Mississippi (Dog Key); probably Alabama (Bayou Labatre and Dauphin Island); western Florida (Milton and probably James Island); and formerly New Jersey (Beach Haven). East to formerly New Jersey (Beach Haven, probably Great Egg Harbor, and Cape May); Virginia (Cobb Island and Cape Charles); North Carolina (Pea Island, Beaufort, and Cape Fear); South Carolina (Bulls Bay, Sullivan Island, and Frogmore); Georgia (Tybee Island, Ossabaw Island, and Blackbeard Island); the east coast of Florida (Fernandina, Amelia Island, Matanzas Inlet, Mosquito Inlet, and Coronado Beach); the Bahama Islands (New Providence, Rum Cay, and Inagua Island); and probably Porto Rico. South to probably Porto Rico; probably Jamaica (Great Salt Pond and Port Henderson); probably Cuba (Trinidad); and British Honduras (Grassy Cay). West to British Honduras (Grassy Cay); Gulf of California; and probably Lower California (La Paz).

The status of the species in the southern part of its summer range has not yet been definitely settled, and some alleged races have been described, whose breeding ranges are undoubtedly included in the summary given above.

Winter range.—The species has been detected in winter north to Lower California (San Jose Island); Sonora (Guaymas); Texas (probably rarely Brownsville and Matagorda County); probably Louisiana (Vermillion Bay); Mississippi (Hancock County); and Florida (mouth of the St. Johns River). East to Florida (mouth of the St. Johns River, St. Augustine, New Smyrna, and Key West); the Bahama Islands (Andros Islands and Watling Island); probably Santo Domingo (Samana); probably Porto Rico (Culebra Island and Vieques Island); the Lesser Antilles (Anegada); French Guiana (Cayenne and Rio Oyapok); and Brazil (Cajetuba, Bahia, and Camamu). South to Brazil (Camamu); and Peru (Tumbez). West to Peru (Tumbez); Ecuador (Puna Island); Colombia (Cartagena and Sabanilla); Honduras (Swan Islands); Guatemala (Chiapam); and Lower California (La Paz and San Jose Island).

Spring migration.—Early dates of spring arrival are Georgia, Cumberland, March 18, and Darien, March 19; South Carolina, Bulls

Point, March 10, Frogmore, March 20, and Mount Pleasant, March 26; North Carolina, Fort Macon, April 15, and Pea and Bodie Islands, April 24; and Virginia, Toms Brook, April 8.

Fall migration.—Almost nothing is known about the fall migration of this plover but Wayne (1910) says that it remains on the beaches of South Carolina " until September 22, or perhaps until October."

Casual records.—Wilson plovers have been noted or collected on several occasions outside of their normal range. Most of these have naturally been in New York and on the coast of New England. Among them are: New York, three at Far Rockaway, May 17, 1879, one at Shinnecock Bay, May 16, 1884, one at Good Ground, May 28, 1879, Orient, July 3, 1915, and Long Beach, July 1, 1872; Connecticut, taken once at Stratford, and seen at Bridgeport on July 28, 1888; Massachusetts, Gurnet Point, August 22, 1877, one at Ipswich, May 8, 1904, and about 25 reported as seen at Dennis, September 4, 1920; Nova Scotia, one at Brier Island, April 28, 1880; and one from Halifax that is preserved in the British Museum; and California, one taken at Pacific Beach, June 27, 1894, and another seen at Imperial Beach, May 11, 1918.

Egg dates.—Virginia: 22 records, May 4 to June 20; 11 records, May 27 to June 6. South Carolina and Georgia: 50 records, April 14 to June 21; 25 records, May 17 to June 10. Florida: 26 records, April 2 to July 10; 13 records, May 12 to June 11. Texas: 11 records, April 7 to June 18; 6 records, April 20 to May 19.

PODASOCYS MONTANUS (J. K. Townsend)

MOUNTAIN PLOVER

HABITS

The above name is not especially appropriate for this species. The name, Rocky Mountain plover, would have been better, for its breeding range is mainly in the Rocky Mountain plateau. It frequents elevated ground but it is not a bird of the mountains but of the dry plains. Coues (1874) says:

While most other plovers haunt the vicinity of water, to which some are almost confined, the present species is not in the least degree of aquatic habits, but, on the contrary, resorts to plains as dry and sterile as any of our country— sometimes the grassy prairies, with shore larks and titlarks, various ground sparrows, and the burrowing owl; sometimes sandy deserts, where the sage brush and the " chamizo," the prickly pear and the Spanish bayonet, grow in full luxuriance. It approaches the Pacific, but will never be found on the beach itself, with maritime birds, nor even on the adjoining mud-flats or marshes, preferring the firm, grassy fields further back from the water.

Nesting.—W. C. Bradbury (1918) has given us a very good account of the nesting habits of the mountain plover in Colorado. Of the nesting site and nest he says:

The ground is an open, rolling prairie, above the line of irrigation, and is devoted to cattle range. It is several miles from natural surface water and streams, and is covered with short-cropped buffalo or gramma grass, 2 or 3 inches high, with frequent bunches of dwarfed prickly pear, and an occasional cluster of stunted shrub or weed, rarely more than a foot in height. With the six sets secured, in no instance had the parent bird taken advantage of the slight protection offered from sight or the elements by the nearby cactus, shrubs or uneven spots of ground. In each case, she had avoided such shelter, locating in the open, generally between the small grass hummocks and not on or in them; there was no evidence of the parent birds having given more thought to nest preparation or concealment, than does any other plover. In two of the sets the eggs were all individually embedded in the baked earth to a depth of one-eighth to one-fourth of an inch, evidently having settled when the surface of the ground was reduced to soft mud by rain-water collecting in the slight depressions. As the ground dried up the eggs were fixed in a perfect mould or matrix, from which they could not roll. In fact they could hardly be disturbed at all by the sitting birds. The only nesting material was a small quantity of fine, dry rootlets and "crowns" of gramma grass, the eggs in some instances being slightly embedded in this lining. As it is also present in all other depressions on the prairie it is highly probable that here as elsewhere it was deposited about the eggs by the wind and not through the agency of the birds themselves. The protective coloration of the nest and eggs, as well as of the rear view of the birds themselves, even when in motion, is unsurpassed. In no instance, except one hereinafter noted, was the bird seen to leave the nest, nor was any nest found except in the immediate vicinity of moving birds.

H. G. Hoskin (1893) writes:

The mountain plover builds its nest on open prairie. The first egg is laid on bare ground, and as the set is finished and incubation advances the bird gradually makes a nest of dirt, pieces of hard grass, roots, etc. It takes five or six days to complete set of three eggs. I have never found more nor less than three eggs in a nest that I thought complete. Old birds will fly off the nest while a person on foot is 80 rods away, but will sit closely for man on horseback or in a buggy.

William G. Smith (1888) found three nests while traveling by wagon across the Laramie Plains in Wyoming. "They were all placed within 50 yards of the much-frequented roadway, and each time I saw the female sitting on the eggs. The old birds are very white which contrasts with the dark ground and causes them to be easily seen." The art of feigning lameness or injury, to entice the intruder away from eggs or young, seems to be very highly developed in this species. Mr. Smith speaks of one that seemed to be in a fit, as it lay on its side, within 6 feet of him, "apparently in strong convulsions." Mr. Bradbury (1918) tells of one that, "spreading her wings horizontally to their extreme width while standing, then falling flat with her neck and wings extended their full length on the ground, at times with beak open, she retreated as he approached, or followed closely as he returned toward the nest."

Eggs.—The mountain plover lays almost invariably three eggs, occasionally only two, and four eggs have been recorded. They are ovate to short ovate in shape, with no gloss. The prevailing ground colors are " deep olive buff " or " dark olive buff "; some few are " chamois " and one pink set has a " light pinkish cinnamon " ground color. They are irregularly marked, but chiefly near the larger end, with small spots and scrawls of black, which sometimes form a ring near the larger end. The measurments of 58 eggs average 37.3 by 28.3 millimeters; the eggs showing the four extremes measure 40 by 28.5, 37.5 by 29.2, 34.3 by 28.4, and 38.5 by 27 millimeters.

Young.—Apparently both sexes incubate; an incubating male has been taken. William G. Smith says in his notes:

The young are very nimble when only a few days old, and it is quite a task to catch them. They do not attempt to hide. A peculiarity of these birds is, though three eggs are generally laid, I never saw but two young with the old birds. I lived on the prairies for six years, a mile from any other habitation; I had every opportunity to observe the traits of these birds. When they are well able to run each of the old birds takes one to raise, and that method seems the rule.

Edward R. Warren's (1912) observations do not agree with the above, for he has seen a parent with three young and has seen the young attempt to hide; but he says "it was easily seen when once found, for its colors did not blend particularly well with the ground it was on."

Plumages.—In the downy young mountain plover the upper parts are " cream buff," tinged with " chamois " on the crown, wings, and rump, shading off to buffy white on the throat and under parts; the crown, sides of the neck, occiput, back, wings, rump, and thighs are conspicuously spotted with black; the forehead is unmarked. Young birds, about half grown, show the juvenal plumage coming in on the back, scapulars, crown, and sides of the breast, with the wing quills bursting their sheaths.

In full juvenal plumage, in September, the crown, back, scapulars, and wing coverts are " buffy brown," with " cinnamon-buff " edges, broadest on the wing coverts; the sides of the head are " pinkish buff " and the breast and flanks are suffused with the same color; the throat and belly are white. This plumage seems to be worn without much change, except by wear and fading, all through the first fall and winter. The upper parts are still mainly " buffy brown," but with only the faintest trace of the edgings. The spring molt apparently does not involve the wing coverts and very few scapulars, so that young birds can be recognized by these retained feathers.

Adults have a partial prenuptial molt in March and April, involving the body plumage but not the wings and tail and not all the scapulars and wing coverts. The black markings on the head are acquired and the new feathers of the mantle are broadly tipped with "pinkish buff." The complete postnuptial molt is accomplished in July and August. The winter plumage is similar to the nuptial, except that the black loral patch is lacking and the black crown patch is replaced by dull brown.

Food.—Feeding on the dry upland plains and prairies, the mountain plover's food consists almost wholly, if not entirely, of insects. Grasshoppers seem to be its principal food, but many crickets, beetles, and flies are eaten. It seems to be a wholly beneficial species. Grinnell, Bryant, and Storer (1918) quote Belding as saying "that he often found this plover in recently sown grain fields, but was never able to discover a single kernel of wheat in the stomachs of those he shot."

Behavior.—Coues (1874) writes:

They were not difficult of approach, and I had no difficulty in securing as many as I desired. On being disturbed by too near approach, they lower the head, run rapidly a few steps in a light, easy way, and then stop abruptly, drawing themselves up to their full height and looking around with timid yet unsuspicious glances. When forced to fly by persistent annoyance, they rise rapidly with quick wing beats and then proceed with alternate sailing and flapping, during the former action holding the wings decurved. They generally fly low over the ground and soon realight, taking a few mincing steps as they touch the ground; they then either squat low, in hopes of hiding, or stand on tip-toe, as it were, for a better view of what alarmed them.

Grinnell, Bryant, and Storer (1918) say:

This plover is a flocking species found in bands of from fifteen to several hun dred individuals. Often upon alighting after they have been in flight, the birds will immediately run to some distance, so that it is not always possible to follow them up easily as with other shore birds. The flocks fly low over the ground and are difficult to see, except when they wheel. As they do this the under surfaces of their wings show momentarily as silvery white flashes.

Aiken and Warren (1914) say:

The mountain plover differs greatly in habits and characteristics from its near relative the killdeer. It shows no preference for wet ground but on the contrary frequents mesas or high rolling prairie land, often remote from water. Their manner is quiet; they have no wailing cry; they run rapidly a short distance and stand silent and motionless with the head sunk low on the shoulders. Their unspotted plumage blends with the color of the dry grass and parched ground and makes them difficult to discover. But in August, when the young birds shift for themselves, they gather in flocks and repair to the vicinity of water holes and flooded fields.

William G. Smith says in his notes:

We have often foretold a hailstorm, which are very prevalent here in summer, by these birds coming near the house for protection; at these times they seem bewildered, and nothing will drive them away.

Voice.—Coues (1874) says on this subject:

Their notes are rather peculiar, as compared with those of our other plovers, and vary a good deal, according to circumstances. When the birds are feeding at their leisure, and in no way apprehensive of danger, they utter a low and rather pleasing whistle, though in a somewhat drawling or rather lisping tone; but the note changes to a louder and higher one, sometimes sounding harshly.

Field marks.—The mountain plover may be recognized as a medium sized plover, dressed in plain colors. In the spring the black markings on the head are visible at short range, but otherwise it is dull, sandy brown above and white below, without the conspicuous markings of the killdeer. In flight its axillars and the under sides of its wings are conspicuously white.

Game.—This species once figured as a game bird and many were shot and sold as game in the California markets. It was a fair-sized bird of some food value, but it was not so highly prized, as a table bird, when compared with some others. John G. Tyler (1916) writes:

Had not the Federal law intervened these birds would soon have disappeared forever, as their habits made them a very easy victim for hunters. The birds feed in loose scattered flocks, ranging over much ground, but when sufficiently disturbed all the members of a company take wing and form into a dense flock which, after beating rapidly back and forth for a few moments, usually settles again within a few yards of the intruder, a full hundred birds often occupying a space no larger than 20 feet in diameter. As they alight each bird flattens itself upon the ground where its protective coloration renders it all but invisible save for the winking of its very large eyes.

As one old resident stated, a favorite method of hunting was to drive with a horse and buggy among the scattered birds and cause them to take wing, whereupon the horse was brought to a standstill until the birds had again settled on the ground, and in nearly every case this was within easy gun range. The hunter immediately "ground sluiced" them with one barrel just as they "squatted" and fired again as the survivors took wing. My informant stated that he once killed 65 birds with two shots, and this method very rarely netted less than 30. I was informed that this plover was rated as the best table bird in this part of the State and that parties sometimes came from points as far away as San Francisco to hunt them. Verily, as my friend remarked, "they don't seem to be as plentiful as they were 25 years ago."

DISTRIBUTION

Range.—Western United States and Mexico; accidental in Florida and Massachusetts.

Breeding range.—The mountain plover breeds north to Montana (Great Falls, Fort Benton, Big Sandy, and the mouth of Milk River); and North Dakota (Stump Lake). East to North Dakota

(Stump Lake and probably Hankison); western South Dakota (Edgemont); Nebraska (probably Harrison, probably Marsland, North Platte, and Kearney); Kansas (Colby, Oakley, probably Hays, Garden City, and probably Fort Dodge); and Oklahoma (probably Camp Supply and Fort Cobb). South to Oklahoma (Fort Cobb); Texas (Washburn, Hereford, and probably Fort Davis); New Mexico (Otero County and Socorro County); and probably Arizona (Fort Whipple). West to probably Arizona (Fort Whipple); Colorado (probably Del Norte, Denver, Barr, and Loveland); Wyoming (Cheyenne, Laramie, probably Fort Bridger, and probably Dubois); Idaho (Pahsimeroi Valley); and Montana (Three Forks and Great Falls).

Winter range.—The mountain plover has the curious habit of occupying a winter range that is farther west than its summer home. North to California (probably rarely Marysville); Arizona (Santa Rosa, Buenos Ayres, and Allaires Ranch); and Texas (San Antonio). East to Texas (San Antonio, Eagle Pass, Aransas River, and Brownsville); Tamaulipas (Matamoras); and Zacatecas (Zacatecas). South to Zacatecas (Zacatecas); and Lower California (La Paz). West to Lower California (La Paz); Sonora (Santa Rosa and Hermosillo); and California (San Diego, Santa Ana, Los Angeles, Fort Tejon, Alila, Paicines, probably Stockton, and probably rarely Marysville).

Spring migration.—Sufficient data are not available to clearly define the migratory flights of the mountain plover but among early dates of spring arrival are: Oklahoma, Norman, March 15; Colorado, Loveland, March 18, Burlington, March 22, Barr, March 23, Springfield, March 29, Denver, April 6, and Colorado Springs, April 19; Wyoming, Cheyenne, April 5, Big Piney, April 12, and Fort Sanders, April 21; South Dakota, Huron, April 16; and Montana, Big Sandy, May 4, and Fort Custer, May 12.

A late date of spring departure from California is Santa Ysabel, April 3.

Fall migration.—Early dates of fall arrival in California are: Firebaugh, September 11, and Montebello, September 15.

Late dates of fall departure are Montana, Sun River, September 4, Camp Thorne, on the Yellowstone, September 13, and Big Sandy, September 18; South Dakota, Forestburg, September 20; Nebraska, Monroe Canyon, September 27; Wyoming, Efell, September 4, and Sweetwater, September 13; Colorado, Barr, October 12, and Beloit, October 15; and New Mexico, Santa Rosa, September 27, and Stinking Spring Lake, October 1.

Casual records.—The mountain plover has been detected outside of its normal range on but few occasions, three of which, curiously enough, were in Florida. A flock of six was noted on December 1, 1870, at Key West, and one specimen obtained (Maynard); R. W. Williams records several at St. James Island between July 20 and August 1, 1901; and on December 17, 1927, R. J. Longstreet secured a specimen at Daytona Beach. The only other record is one for Massachusetts, an immature male, taken at North Beach, near Chatham, on October 28, 1916, and preserved in the collections of the Boston Society of Natural History (Brooks).

The species is unknown from Canada. During the international boundary survey, Doctor Coues found mountain plover on Frenchman Creek and obtained a specimen that is now in the British Museum. This is reported as being labeled " forty-ninth parallel," but the point of collection was probably well within the present State of Montana.

Egg dates.—Colorado and Kansas: 74 records, April 30 to June 16; 37 records, May 14 to 26. Montana and Wyoming: 4 records, May 22 to July 9.

Family APHRIZIDAE. Surf birds and Turnstones

APHRIZA VIRGATA (Gmelin)

SURF BIRD

HABITS

From its summer home in the mountains of central Alaska the surf bird migrates down the Pacific coasts of North and South America as far as the Straits of Magellan. Twice each year some individuals make this long journey, while others are scattered along the coasts from southern Alaska southward. Consequently it may be found, chiefly on migrations but occasionally at other seasons, by those who seek it on the outlying rocky ledges, reefs, and promontories all along the Pacific coast. As its name implies, it is a bird of the surf line, associated in its rocky habitat with turnstones and wandering tattlers, unmindful of the flying spray. It well deserves its generic name, which is taken from two Greek words, *aphros*, meaning sea foam, and *zao*, I live.

Spring.—The spring migration is directly north along the coasts of both continents. It is difficult to trace the dates, as the winter range is so extensive. The latest recorded date for the Straits of Magellan is March 3; and the earliest date of arrival at the Kobuk River, Alaska, is May 29. The main flight along the California coast seems to come in March. Dr. Joseph Grinnell (1909) reports a flight at Admiralty Island, Alaska, on May 12, " a flock estimated to contain 300 waders, fully two-thirds of which were of this species."

Harry S. Swarth (1911) says that, at Kuiu Island, Alaska, between April 25 and May 6, "it was abundant and in large flocks, feeding in company with the numerous other waders frequenting the mud flats." H. B. Conover saw it only once at Hooper Bay, Alaska, on May 18.

Nesting.—The breeding grounds and the nesting habits of the surf bird long remained unknown. The birds vanished from the coast of Alaska about the first of June and were not seen again for six weeks or more, when they appeared again with their young. Rumors suggested that they bred in the mountains in the interior. O. J. Murie (1924) gave us the first definite information, when he discovered the breeding ground of the species in the Mount McKinley Park region of central Alaska. On July 13, 1921, he was descending a slope above timber line, "when two surf birds were flushed and circled about making an outcry." He was "presently rewarded by seeing a downy young one striding away bravely over the rough ground." The young bird was secured and one of the parents, which proved to be the male, thus establishing the first breeding record for the species.

Five years later Joseph Dixon (1927) spent considerable time in this same region and succeeded in finding, on May 28, 1926, the first nest of the surf bird. He took some excellent photographs and made a thorough study of the bird and its habits, thus completing the picture very satisfactorily. I shall quote freely from his excellent published account of it. Regarding the nesting site and the nest he writes:

One of the most striking things about the surf bird is the remarkable difference between its winter and summer habitat. Near the end of their northward migration in the spring these birds abandon the seacoast and take up their summer residence far in the interior, from 300 to 500 miles from salt water. This involves a great altitudinal shift. Instead of living at sea level as they do at other seasons, during nesting time they are to be found on barren, rocky mountains high up above timber line. During the entire summer we never found these birds below 4,000 feet elevation.

The rocky character of the surf birds' surroundings appears to remain fairly constant throughout the year. In summer the birds are to be found most frequently near the summits of the rock slides where the broken rocks are much the same as the rugged reefs they inhabit during the winter. We found in the Mount McKinley district that the summer range of the surf bird was almost identical with that of the mountain sheep and that it was useless to look for surf birds outside of "sheep" country.

When standing on a barren wind-swept ridge late in the afternoon of May 28, searching a nearby hillside with binoculars, Mr. Wright's attention was attracted to a grayish bird that was sneaking hurriedly along over the rocky ground. As he watched, the bird apparently faded out of sight some 600 feet away. Marking the point of disappearance he hurried over to the spot where the bird was last seen and, failing to find the bird, began to think he was mistaken. But, upon his taking one more step, the bird flew up suddenly right into his face, startling him mightily. As the bird flew away, the large white rump patch, together with a white patch on either wing, brought realization that this was the long-sought-for surf bird. A hasty glance at his feet revealed the nest and contents of four eggs. Another step forward and he would have placed his foot directly in the nest! To George M. Wright belongs the honor of being the first white man, of which we have any record, to lay eyes on the nest and eggs of this rare bird.

The surf bird's nest was located 1,000 feet above timber line on a rocky ridge that faced southwest and lay fair to the sun and hence was relatively free from snow. The nest site was on dry rocky ground and not on the wet tundra which was plentiful nearby. The rocky ground about the nest was clothed with a thin carpet of alpine-arctic vegetation, the tallest of which were a few creeping arctic willows less than 2 inches high. The most conspicuous plant about the nest was the white-flowered *Dryas integrifolia*. The nest was entirely out in the open with no bushes that afford the least concealment. In fact it was almost "out in the street," since the eggs were within a foot of a frequently traveled trail of the white Alaska mountain sheep (*Ovis dalli*). There was no fabricated nest such as the wandering tattler makes. Instead, the eggs were deposited in a natural erosional depression, the sides of which had been lined with a few bits of dried-up grayish-green lichens and caribou moss. The bottom of the nest was composed of the dead emarginate leaves of *Dryas integrifolia*, which only partially covered the crumbling serpentine outcrop that formed the backbone of the ridge. The nest, which was barely large enough to hold the four eggs, which were placed as close together as possible, with little ends down, measured 4 inches in diameter and an inch and a half in depth. The eggs in the nest blended so well with the reddish brown moss of the tundra that it became difficult to make them out at a distance of more than 8 or 10 feet.

The nest was found at nearly 9 o'clock in the evening. They built a crude shelter of rocks near it and kept a careful watch over it all that night and half of the next day. During this time Mr. Dixon (1927) made these observations:

When it began to rain the surf bird merely fluffed up and then spread out the feathers on his back so as completely to cover the nest. This proved an effective method, because the melting snow and the rain ran readily off the surf-bird's back and was absorbed by the moss outside the nest. We were not so well protected and were soon shivering and wet to the skin.

At 4 o'clock a female mountain sheep appeared, silently, like a ghost, out of the mist that came drifting over the mountain peaks in great white swirls. She did not see us at first, but when she was within 6 feet of and headed directly toward the surf-bird's nest she became suddenly aware of our presence and took a step or two forward. When the ewe was about to step on the nest the surf bird suddenly "exploded" right in the astonished animal's face. This unexpected movement and the sudden noise and flash of white of the bird's spread wings and tail caused the mountain sheep to jump back quickly; then she whirled around and bounded off back up the trail. This sudden movement of the surf bird at the critical moment doubtless serves to prevent sheep and caribou from trampling upon its nest and eggs. We found through repeated experiments that this was the bird's regular reaction. When we approached, whether fast or slow, the bird would stay on the nest until the last minute, and then, instead of sneaking off low to the ground like most birds do, would fly directly up into our faces. Even after we knew that the bird would do

this the psychological result on our part was the same. A person would involuntarily recoil when the bird " exploded " like a firecracker right in his face.

When first frightened off the nest by Mr. Wright the previous afternoon the
bird, which we later thought might have been the female, after "exploding,"
ran away with wings half spread and the tail spread out fanlike and dragging
on the ground. This displayed conspicuously the white rump patch. Now and
then this bird would nestle down as though covering a nest. When about
100 yards distant from the nest the bird began to wander about, pretending to
feed. It exhibited no concern whatever when Mr. Wright returned to the nest
and examined the eggs. It made no attempt to return to the nest even after
the observer had retired to a distance and waited for a period of 10 minutes,
during which interval rain began to fall.

In marked contrast with this rather indifferent attitude, the bird which
was watched on the nest for 16 hours, behaved in an entirely different manner.
This second bird, when forced off the nest, would fly directly up into the
intruder's face, and then run off to one side, a distance of 8 or 10 feet, where
it would perch on a rock, fluff out its feathers like a " sitting " hen and
utter a low plaintive call, *tee-tee-teet!* The call would often be repeated two
or three times after a slight pause of half a minute between calls. When we
started after this bird it would lead us adroitly away from the nest; but
if we stood still it would soon hustle directly back, even when we were standing only 10 feet distant. In going on to the nest the bird was very careful
not to step directly upon the eggs. It would trot up to within a foot or so of
the eggs and then sneak cautiously down to the edge of the nest. Here it
would stop, inspect the eggs, and reach out with its bill and turn the eggs
about, keeping them little ends down. Following this inspection the bird
fluffed out the feathers on its breast and sitting down gently on the edge of
the nest, slid its body forward with great care, until the eggs were completely
covered.

Eggs.—I have not yet seen these eggs, so I will quote Mr. Dixon's
(1927) excellent description of them:

The eggs of the surf bird are not easily confused with the eggs of any other
North American sandpiper or plover. In shape they are pyriform but, though
similar in form to eggs of other birds of the order Limicolae, in color they
appear more like eggs of the falcons, particularly certain eggs of the sparrow
hawk and prairie falcon.

·In the type set, which is now safely housed in the well-known Thayer
collection, there is considerable variation both in the ground color and in the
markings of the eggs. Three eggs of this set have an intensely buffy ground
color, while the fourth egg is of the same color but decidedly lighter. The
markings on the three eggs are bold, varying in color from fawn to bay. The
markings on the fourth egg are small and evenly distributed. The four
eggs may be described as follows: The first egg has a light ground color
which equals tilleul-buff. In this egg the marking consists of fine splashes,
one-half to two millimeters in length. There is but slight tendency for the
markings to form a wreath on the larger end. A few small dark brown spots
on its larger end identifies this egg, which resembles slightly certain eggs of
the yellow-billed magpie. In egg number two the ground color is rich tilleul-
buff, while the markings consist of bold bay-colored spots and splashes from
one-half to three millimeters in length. These spots are concentrated about
the larger end of the egg, where in places they are so dense as completely
to obscure the ground color. A few deep-seated lavender under-shell markings

are apparent on this egg. Egg number three is similar both in ground color and in markings to egg number two, except in egg number three the heavy bay markings form a decided wreath 21 millimeters in diameter about its larger end. Egg number four has the richest ground color of all, while its markings are fawn, but the markings are not so sharply defined as in the other eggs.

The four eggs measure 43.7 by 30.5, 41.5 by 31.5, 43.3 by 31.2, and 42.4 by 31, and they average 42.7 by 31 millimeters.

Young.—Mr. Dixon (1927) demonstrated most conclusively that the male does most, if not all, of the incubating. The bird that they had under observation for 16 hours and the only one seen near the nest proved to be the male. All of the five males collected had bare incubation patches, while none of the females had these. Mr. Murie (1924) found both parents attending the young bird which he captured; and the one shot, probably the more solicitous one, was the male. Evidence is accumulating all the time to show that with more shore birds than we realize, perhaps with all, the males perform the greater part of the domestic duties.

Plumages.—The young bird taken by Mr. Murie is still in the downy stage. The upper parts are variegated and mottled with "cinnamon buff," brownish black, "sepia," and buffy white; the forehead and sides of the head are buffy white, boldly spotted and striped with black; the crown is mainly spotted with black; the buffy tints are mainly on the upper back, wings, thighs, and rump; the under parts are grayish white, whitest on the chin and belly.

When the young birds come down to the coast of Alaska, in August, they are in full juvenal plumage. In this the crown is streaked with " fuscous " and brownish black, the feathers having white edgings; the chin and throat are white, with shaft streaks of " hair brown "; there is a broad band of " hair brown " across the breast, with white edgings, running into spots below, which are lacking on the white belly; the mantle is " hair brown," with very narrow whitish edgings, giving a scaled appearance; the scapulars also have a subterminal " fuscous " bar; the lesser and median wing coverts are broadly or conspicuously edged with grayish white.

A partial postjuvenal molt in the early fall produces a first winter plumage which is like the adult winter, except that there are fewer and smaller spots on the under parts; and the juvenal wing coverts and some scapulars are retained.

Two specimens, collected in Peru on June 30, illustrate the first nuptial plumage. These are doubtless birds which do not migrate north to breed during their first year. Apparently a nearly complete molt has taken place, as the wings and tail appear fresh, but some of the old scapulars and wing coverts are retained. The adult nuptial plumage is suggested, but all traces of cinnamon are lacking;

the feathers of the mantle are " fuscous " or " hair brown," broadly edged with grayish white and subterminally bordered with brownish black; the crown is grayish white, streaked with dusky; the scapulars are " fuscous" to brownish black, broadly tipped, notched, or spotted with pale grayish; the breast and flanks are less heavily marked than in the adult. I have not seen this plumage described elsewhere. At the next molt the adult winter plumage is assumed.

Adults have a complete postnuptial molt in August; I have seen one with primaries and secondaries molting as early as August 27. In adult winter plumage the upper parts are uniform " fuscous," with only slightly lighter (" hair brown ") edgings; the chin and throat are white, spotted with " hair brown "; there is a broad band of " hair brown " across the chest and below it the under parts are marked on the breast and flanks with hastate spots of " fuscous."

A partial prenuptial molt of the body plumage takes place in April and May, but some of the old winter feathers are generally retained. In full nuptial plumage the head and neck are grayish white, everywhere boldly streaked, or spotted, with black and slightly suffused on the crown with " pinkish cinnamon "; the feathers of the back are centrally black, broadly edged with white and tinged with " pinkish cinnamon "; but the most striking features of this plumage are the scapulars, boldly patterned with " pinkish cinnamon " and black, with narrow whitish tips; the white under parts are boldly marked, especially on the breast and flanks, with hastate, subcordate, or crescentic spots of brownish black. The cinnamon colors fade during the breeding season to pale buff and eventually to white in July birds.

Food.—On its breeding grounds in summer the surf bird feeds almost entirely on insects, mainly flies and beetles. The analysis of the stomach contents of eight birds, taken in Alaska and examined by the Biological Survey, shows the following proportions: Diptera, 55.2 per cent; Coleoptera, 36 per cent; Lepidoptera, 3.8 per cent; Hymenoptera, 3.3 per cent; Phalangidea, 1 per cent; snails, 5 per cent; and seeds, 2 per cent. Mr. Dixon (1927) says of its feeding habits:

Three days later seven surf birds were found feeding in company at midday near this same spot. This time they were foraging near the top of a very steep talus slope that lay fair to the sun. Only a few scant flowers grew amid the rocks, but insects were numerous and active. One surf bird which, when later collected, proved to be a male stood guard while the others fed. The slightest movement on my part was sufficient to cause a warning note to be given by this sentinel. When feeding, these birds ran hurriedly over the rocks, traveling as fast or faster than a man could walk. When an insect was sighted the pursuing surf bird would stretch out its neck as far and as straight as possible. Then moving stealthily forward the bird would make a final thrust and secure the insect in its bill, much in the same manner that a turkey stalks a grasshopper.

At other seasons the surf bird feeds along the water line on ocean beaches, preferring the rocky or stony shores, or reefs exposed at low tide; here it extracts the soft parts of barnacles, mussels, or other crustaceans and small mollusks, or picks up other minute forms of marine life. It also feeds to some extent at the surf line on sandy beaches or on mud flats, where it picks up similar food from the surface without probing for it. At such times the birds are quite pugnacious unless sufficiently scattered.

Behavior.—Mr. Dixon (1927) writes:

On June 18 three surf birds were seen close under the summit of a mountain. Here they occasionally ran about and picked up insects, but more often they stood still on exposed rocks and preened their feathers. One of these three birds frequently raised both wings willet fashion over its back until they almost met. These individuals were exceedingly shy and would not allow the naturalist to approach closer than 100 yards. We found that this timidity was customary during the nesting season, when the birds were encountered away from the immediate vicinity of the nest.

At 8 o'clock on the evening of June 24 I climbed to the crest of a sharp ridge of one of the lower spurs of the main Alaskan Range. As I reached the highest peak four surf birds flew in from a distance. As they circled about the peak they called, *tee, tee teet* loudly. Their flight was swift and plover-like. As they turned the white basal portions of their tails together with the white bars of their wings formed four white V's which stood out vividly in the strong glow of the evening sun. They circled the peak several times, calling loudly and evidently seeking for others of their kind. Soon there was an answering call from the ground and the four birds settled down on a rocky spur where three other surf birds were already feeding. When I crawled up to within 50 yards of them all seven birds ceased feeding and began to call loudly. After a period of several minutes they began to feed again, one remaining on guard while the others ran hither and thither chasing insects over the rocks and tundra.

Florence M. Bailey (1916) says of the behavior of surf birds on the California coast:

At high tide one day two of the surf birds were standing on the sand ridge just above the water resting from their labors, one with its back to the incoming waves staring ahead of it as if lost in reverie. On the beach one of the silent, solitary *Aphrizas* would often stand facing me, as if studying me intently, when, though I could not read its innermost thoughts, I had a good chance to note its light forehead and eye line, its white underparts, and streaked chest. Two of the droll birds were found one day engaged in an amusing performance that suggested the sparring of boys. One turned sideways to the other as if on guard, then dropped the wing on that side and spread its tail till the white rump showed. The other in turn spread its tail and they hopped over each other, doing this a number of times. They would also dip their bills menacingly, and one of them sat down several times as part of the play. As they flew off they gave their wild *key-wé-ah*.

When wanting to move down the beach one often flew close along under the green wall of the combing surf. When it alit its wings would be held out for an instant showing the clear white line down their length and the broad white base of the tail with the dusky tip. When on shore they stood around so much with their preoccupied dreamy gaze that, when one took wing and flew with swift strong wing strokes out across the surf and over the ocean, a disappearing white spot, you stood bewildered. Your idle dreamer was a child of the sea! Perhaps when it stood on the sandy beach with preoccupied gaze it was dreaming of its rocky surf-dashed home to the north, or of its rocky surf-dashed winter home to the south. How well its wild, keen, plaintive *key-ah-wee* tells the story!

Field marks.—While standing on rocks, at a distance or when the light is poor, surf birds might be mistaken for black turnstones, but they are somewhat larger. They are more stockily built and generally darker colored than other shore birds. But in flight they may be easily recognized by the broad white band in the wing, and by the white upper tail coverts and basal half of the tail; they lack the broad white patch in the center of the back and white stripes, which distinguish the turnstones.

Fall.—The birds apparently leave their breeding grounds in July and move down to the coast of Alaska; some reach Oregon before the end of July and California early in August. Apparently the adults come first. Young birds have been taken on the coast of southern Alaska as early as August 27 and have been noted at St. Michael up to the last of September. During the fall they move gradually down the coast, lingering for the winter at favorable places.

Winter.—The surf bird winters in small numbers, occasionally if not regularly, as far north as Wrangell, Alaska. Carl Lien has sent me the following notes from the coast of Washington:

Destruction Island lies 50 miles south of Cape Flattery and 3 out from the mainland. It is 35 acres in extent and surrounded by extensive reefs which are uncovered at low tide. There are numerous rocky ridges that are well above the water at high tide, these ridges forming little protected bays and harbors.

I first went to this island in December, 1910. On nice days when the sea was smooth it was my custom to row around the reefs observing the birds. I found the surf birds generally in company with Aleutian sandpipers and black turnstones. There would be a half dozen on this reef and similar bunches on neighboring reefs. Their actions were very lively, now running to a higher point on the rock as the wash from the swell came rushing up, now running down again as the water receded, feeding busily. The only thing I ever found in their stomachs was small mussels about an eighth of an inch long, occasionally up to a quarter of an inch. The following autumn they returned though I did not note the date. I saw them from time to time during the winter in the winters of 1912–13, 1913–14, 1914–15, 1915–16, 1916–17. They would arrive the last week in October or the first week in November. The flock on its first arrival would number about 200 birds. They would begin to leave the island the 1st of April and by the 1st of May there would be none left. They did not visit the high parts of the island but confined themselves to the reefs and gravel bars. They were very wary and hard to approach on foot though they would sometimes allow a boat to come within 10 yards.

Range.—Western North and South America.

Breeding range.—The breeding range of the surf bird is evidently in the higher mountains of the interior of Alaska. The nest and eggs have been found on one occasion only, in the Mount McKinley district (Dixon, 1927), but Murie (1924) found young, apparently about a week old, at the headwaters of Forty-mile River. There also seems a strong probability that the species breeds in the Selawik Range on the south side of the Kowak Valley (Grinnell, 1900), and in the region around the head of the Savage River in the Alaska Range (Murie, 1924).

Sharing a trait with other shore birds, some nonbreeders frequently remain through the summer at points far south of the breeding grounds. During this period they have been noted in California (Santa Barbara and the Farallone Islands); Oregon (Newport); and Washington (Destruction Island and Camp Mora, Clallam County).

Winter range.—In winter the surf bird is found on the Pacific coast both of North and South America. It has been detected south to the Straits of Magellan (Van Island in Trinity Channel), and at other points on the coast of Chile (Valdivia, Paposo, and Atacama); and Peru (Pisco Bay). At this season in North America it has been collected or observed in California (Monterey and probably San Francisco Bay region); Oregon (Cape Meares, Cannon Beach, and the entrance to Yaquina Bay); Washington (Jefferson County and Destruction Island); and Alaska (Wrangel and Craig). These latter records would appear to indicate that some individuals are only partially migratory.

Migration.—Because of the extensive areas that may be occupied by the species, particularly in winter, and in view of the scarcity of existing data, it is difficult to present an adequate picture of its migrations. The following dates may, however, throw some light on its movements.

Spring migration.—Early dates of arrival are Lower California, San Geronimo Island, March 15; California, San Diego, March 19; Oregon, Newport, March 21; Washington, Puget Sound, March 8; and Alaska, Admiralty Island, April 17, Forrester Island, April 20, Kuiu Island, April 25, Craig, May 9, and Kobuk River, May 29.

Late dates of spring departure are Chile, Van Island, March 3; Lower California, San Geronimo Island, April 13, Turtle Bay, April 14, and Abreojos Point, April 19; California, Los Angeles, May 1, Santa Barbara, May 4, Point Pinos, May 10, and San Nicolas Island, May 15; Oregon, Newport, May 3; and Washington, Jefferson County, April 28.

Fall migration.—Early dates of fall arrival are: Alaskan coast, Sitka, July 21, and Nushagak, August 9; British Columbia, Porcher Island, July 12, and Queen Charlotte Islands, August 2; Oregon, Newport, July 24; and California, Monterey Bay, August 3, and Point Pinos, August 5.

Late dates of fall departure are: Alaska, Craig, September 4, Sitka, September 5, and Nome, September 9; British Columbia, Comox, September 2; Oregon, Netarts Bay, November 19; and California, Berkeley, October 24.

Egg dates.—Alaska: One record, May 28, 1926.

ARENARIA INTERPRES (Linnaeus)

TURNSTONE

HABITS

The above species is cosmopolitan; it has a circumpolar breeding range, and its migrations extend over nearly all of the Northern Hemisphere and a large part of the Southern. It has been split into two, or possibly three, geographical races. In the author's opinion only two races should be recognized; the Palaearctic form, *interpres*, averages slightly larger, and is decidedly darker, the black predominating over the rufous on the upper parts; the Nearctic form, *morinella*, averages slightly smaller, is decidedly lighter, the rufous predominating on the upper parts; these two races are well marked and are generally recognized. The Pacific race has been described under the name *oahuensis*, from specimens taken on Oahu Island in the Hawaiian group. It is supposed to breed in Alaska and spend the winter in the Hawaiian and other Pacific islands. It seems to be strictly intermediate, both in size and color, between *interpres* and *morinella*. Some of the best authorities have not recognized it in nomenclature, which seems to be a wise course. For the purpose of this life history the species as a whole will be considered.

Spring.—The northward migration of the ruddy turnstone through the United States is accomplished mainly during May, but many linger along through the first week in June. I have seen turnstones in Louisiana as late as June 17 and 23, but some that I shot were immature birds, apparently 1 year old, which probably would not breed that season. Arthur T. Wayne (1910) has seen high plumaged birds in South Carolina on June 11 and 12, which were doubtless late migrants; but he says that birds in immature or winter plumage are seen in June more frequently than adults. These latter illustrate the well-established fact that many shore birds do not attain their full plumage and do not breed during their first year, but remain within their winter ranges or far south of their breeding ranges all summer.

Many observers have stated that turnstones do not migrate in large flocks in the spring, but I have seen some very large flocks on Cape Cod containing several hundred. On the coast of New Jersey during the latter part of May, 1927, we saw a wonderful flight of this and other shore birds; on the 20th we counted 3,600 turnstones, on the 26th 4,500, on the 27th 5,000, and on the 28th 7,000; many of these were in immense flocks of this species only, but more often they were associated in large flocks with black-bellied plovers; one enormous flock of the two species was estimated to contain 3,500 birds.

The main migration route is along the sea coast. Migrants have been known to reach Massachusetts as early as May 1, and my latest date is June 5; but the main flight comes during the latter half of May. Dr. W. Elmer Ekblaw tells me that it reaches its breeding grounds in northwestern Greenland during the first week in June.

There is a regular migration northward through the interior, but in much smaller numbers. Pierce Brodkorb and Frank Grasett give me dates for northeastern Illinois from April 30 to June 18. We collected specimens in Nelson County, N. Dak., on June 5, and at Lake Winnipegosis, Manitoba, on June 1 and 2; but we did not record the species at all during the two seasons spent in southwestern Saskatchewan. Prof. William Rowan tells me that it is rare in his section of Alberta. The route is evidently northward from Manitoba through the Athabaska-Mackenzie region. Samuel F. Rathbun has sent me the following notes on the former abundance of turnstones in Manitoba:

In that Province we spent the greater part of the spring and summer of 1889, and on one occasion went to Lake Manitoba driving as directly as possible across what was then an unsettled country. We clambered up one of the dunes and looked over its top, and right in front of us and up and down the beach almost as far as could be seen, were countless numbers of shore birds. On the sands nearly all of these were in constant motion, while over the surface of the lake flocks were flying to and fro. By far the greater number of the birds were turnstones and the flocks of these were always very large. I hesitate to give my estimate of the number seen, but I made many counts and forming a rough guess from these judged at the time that there must have been somewhere near eight or ten thousand of the turnstones. And I have always believed this estimate to be somewhere near correct. This was on the 30th of May and it may have been that we were fortunate to have happened to witness the height of the movement of these birds.

The ruddy turnstone is a rather uncommon migrant on the Pacific coast in April and May. Mr. Rathbun says in his notes that it—

appears to be a regular spring migrant along the ocean coast of Washington, first being seen in early May. The earlier birds seem to arrive in small numbers, to be followed by flocks of fair size, but at no time are the turnstones as common as are most of the other species of shore birds that migrate along the coast.

From its winter home in Australia the turnstone makes an early start for its long flight over the ocean; W. B. Alexander tells me that his latest record is of a pair seen April 25, 1914, on the estuary of the Lost River on the south coast of western Australia. The Pacific form of the turnstone has been named *oahuensis* from a specimen taken on the island where Honolulu is situated. The birds leave the Hawaiian Islands in May and probably make a 2,000-mile flight over the Pacific Ocean to the Commander and Aleutian Islands. Dr. Leonhard Stejneger (1885) says that they make their appearance in the Commanders " early in May (in 1883 the first ones were observed on the 7th), and the beach, especially on the north shore of Bering Island, fairly swarms with them. In June they disappear, and only a few remain during the summer." In his notes from Hooper Bay, Alaska, H. B. Conover says: " On May 15 Du Fresne shot the first bird of this species. He had found it sitting humped up on a log showing through the snow. The next day a pair was seen, and after that date they were noticed constantly. On May 28 the migration still must have been going on, as a flock of about 20 was seen mixed with 6 golden plover."

Courtship.—Doctor Ekblaw has sent me the following notes:

The ruddy turnstone is almost if not quite as common as the ringed plover along the beaches and about the gravelly moraines and terraces of northwest Greenland. It comes to the land the first week in June, frequenting the drifts of kelp along the shore when the ice foot has melted away. There they probe about the shells and seaweed, turning the long drifts over to a depth of 3 inches. Where they have worked, the shore looks as if a drove of tiny pigs had rooted about.

They begin mating as soon as they arrive, and many a bitter struggle and amorous courtship takes place among these birds during the first two weeks of June. The males outnumber the females, so the rivalry is keen. As the lowering sun of the day sinks nearest the midnight horizon the wooing antics are at the height. Frequently two males pursue the same female, seeking to win her favor, the while they are combating one another for the advantage. In giddy, reckless flight they sweep back and forth along the shore, rarely rising more than 3 feet above the beach, usually but a foot. When alighted the pursuit is just as eager, the female racing about to escape the insistent attentions of the males, the males eagerly pursuing her and struggling between themselves for supremacy. The more pugnacious usually wins out, though the other never gives up hope.

The Rev. F. C. R. Jourdain contributes the following notes on the subject:

A study of the published records of the breeding habits of the turnstone discloses the fact that practically nothing has ever been written on the courtship and song of this species. The only apparent exception is a passage by A. Trevor-Battye (1895), who says: " This lovely bird has a far more elaborate song than that of any wader I know. You really may call it a song. I put it down at the time as *chewah, chewah, chewecki, ki-ki-ki kee kee*, and he sings it *con amore* from any little mound." My first experience with the turnstone dates back to 1921, when with Mr. A. H. Paget Wilkes we found the nests of some 19 pairs in Spitsbergen. It was then late in the breeding season; every pair had incubated eggs or young, but directly one arrived within range of a breeding pair the cock would fly out to meet us and greet us with his little challenge song. As a rule attempts to describe the notes of birds by means of letters are chiefly remarkable for their discrepancies, but if Mr. Paget Wilkes's version of the "attack note" is compared with that of Mr. Trevor-Battye, the resemblance is striking, *tche-wick . . . tsche-wick, tche-wi-t-t-t-t-ck*. Obviously the two "songs" are the same, yet we heard this challenge daily from birds far advanced in incubation and even with newly hatched young. It continued as long as we remained in the neighborhood of the nest, and was sometimes repeated in a weaker form by the female. When the young were being brooded by the male and the female was on guard this challenge note was uttered by her. There is, of course, a strong element of challenge in all bird song, and the turnstone is a born fighter. No foe is too formidable to be attacked and driven off. It is most amusing to see a male chasing a bird ten times as big as himself and returning complacently to his sentry duty until the approach of another probable enemy brings him again to the attack.

There is little doubt that all the "singing" males met with by Trevor-Battye were really breeding birds defending the territories and, as they fondly imagined, driving him away. Of course the cheery little *chirrup* of the turnstone has no claim to musical excellence in spite of Trevor-Battye's exaggerated praise; no one could possibly compare it to the sweet wild notes of the curlew or even the flutelike notes of the purple sandpiper. Apparently in this species the fighting instinct has replaced the tendency to display on the wing before the female; and while many other waders utter musical notes during the love flight the turnstone reserves his for the attack.

Nesting.—Comparatively few nests of the ruddy turnstone have ever been found, as the bird nests in the far north, where few ornithologists have been. A set of three eggs in my collection, taken by Capt. Joseph Bernard on Taylor Island, Victoria Land, on August 1, 1917, possibly a second laying, was in a hollow on the tundra. Mac-Farlane found only two sets on the lower Anderson River, which were precisely similar to those of the other waders, consisting of a few withered leaves placed in a depression in the ground, each containing four eggs. Eggs collected by Rev. A. R. Hoare at Point Hope, Alaska, were laid "in depressions on mossy ridges of the tundra." Herbert W. Brandt has sent me the following notes on the nesting habits of these birds in Alaska:

At Hooper Bay the ruddy turnstone like the indigenous plovers is an open-nesting bird and it depends for concealment of its eggs upon the similarity of the shell coloration to its surroundings. Near a limpid pool in the low-rolling dunes the bird makes a shallow, circular depression in the brownish green, velvetlike moss and this it lines, haphazardly, with a few moss stems and often with small crisp leaves of low-creeping woody plants. The range of measurements of five nests is: Inside diameter, 3¾ to 4½ inches; inside depth, 1 to 1½ inches; and depth over all is 1 to 1¾ inches. The pied parents follow the habits of the open-nesting birds, for they are wild and unapproachable while breeding; so that in spite of its exposed location the nest is anything but easy to find. Incubation patches were present on both sexes and they did not employ, to lure the intruder from the nesting area, the usual wounded tactics of the other shore birds.

In the Eastern Hemisphere numerous nests have been found and considerable has been published on the subject. Henry J. Pearson (1904), during his three summers in Russian Lapland, found several nests of the turnstone. On June 13, 1899, on Little Heno Island, he found a nest with four fresh eggs on a low sand spit. "The nest was placed in a patch of dwarf sallow, 10 inches high, and near the edge of a bank, the slight depression being lined with a few dry grasses and dead leaves." Another nest was found on June 27 on Great Heno. After watching the bird in vain for a long time on "a bare stretch of peat, with scarcely a scrap of vegetation and full of puffin holes," they returned the next day and flushed the turnstone out of a puffin hole; "and there was a nest 18 inches from the mouth, containing three eggs more than half incubated; a few dead sorrel stalks had been taken in to form the nest." On June 19, 1901, on Medveji Island, a nest was found "placed under a large overhanging shelf of peat, in such a position that the bird could slip on and off in two different directions according to that from which danger was threatened. The young were formed in the four incubated eggs." He refers to two other nests found on a sand spit, which were "on the open ground with no protection beyond a few blades of grass."

W. C. Hewitson (1856) found a nest on the coast of Norway on "a flat rock, bare except where here and there grew tufts of grass, or stunted juniper clinging to its surface"; the nest "was placed against a ledge of the rock, and consisted of nothing more than the drooping leaves of the juniper bush, under a creeping branch of which the eggs, four in number, were snugly concealed."

A number of nests of the turnstone were found by the Oxford expedition to Spitsbergen, about which A. H. Paget-Wilkes (1922) has given us considerable information. He says that "in spite of the presence of large and small boulders and stones the turnstone in Spitsbergen does not lay its eggs under the shelter of this somewhat scanty cover or in the small holes or pockets in the soil, but chooses perfectly open and bare, wind-swept places for its breeding sites." Some seven nests were found on islands and one of these is described as "a very flat depression among small stones on a small ridge of dry, red mud." Other nests were scattered along the shore at intervals of about three-quarters of a mile; but in one place five or six pairs were nesting within a radius of half a mile. One nest was on a little island of hard mud, only three yards by two yards in a stream. The turnstones are very active and aggressive in defending their nests against the jaegers; these marauders are persistently harried, desperately attacked, and finally driven away.

Ralph Chislett (1925) gives an interesting account of finding the turnstone breeding on a Baltic isle, where the nests were hidden among the dense herbage. He says:

> Against the sky, not more than 30 yards away, appearing over the top of a rise in the ground, as seen from the hiding tent, was a group of chervil flower heads. One of the turnstones, on taking wing, flew directly to these flower heads and appeared to settle in the midst of them. After giving the bird time to get settled on the eggs (I hoped) I crawled out of the tent, and keeping low was within 6 yards of the chervil clump when the turnstone took wing from a point 2 yards on the other side, repeating its cry much more meaningly than hitherto. I had been prepared to find the nest under shelter of some sort, but had not expected the eggs to be so completely hidden from view as proved to be the case here. The nest lay on the seaward side of the clump. To obtain a view for the camera, a tall chervil stalk, some leaves, and grasses had to be removed. The definite scrape was lined with bits of seaweed and dry grass stems to a depth of more than 1 inch.

Eggs.—Mr. Brandt has sent me the following good description of the turnstone's eggs collected by his party in Alaska:

> The ruddy turnstone lays four eggs and these may justly claim rank as some of the handsomest of all the delightful Hooper Bay limicoline series. They are subpyriform to ovate in shape and lie points together in the shallow nest. The shell is glossy and smooth and is quite strong. The markings seldom cover more than half the area of the eggs and in consequence the ground color is prominent. The latter is quite variable, ranging from " yellowish glaucous " to " olive buff " and even " deep olive buff." The surface markings are usually bold and are most heavily concentrated on the larger end, but one striking type is known for its beautiful marbled effect as the spots which are large and clouded softly fade into the glossy ground color. These spots are irregular in outline and are often slightly elongate, twisting into a pronounced clockwise spiral. The usual color of the primary spots is " warm sepia," but in the greenish setting they are " olive brown " while in the marbled type " citrine drab " is the prevailing shade. When the underlying markings are given prominence their soft tones add to the beauty of the eggs. The colors of these partially hidden ornaments range from " pale mouse gray " to " mouse gray." The additional markings of brownish black to black are sparsely scattered over the larger part of the egg usually in the form of small spots or pen-like scratches. The vitality of the shore birds is attested by the fact that four turnstone's eggs laid in four days weigh 2½ ounces, while the parent bird herself weighs but 3½ ounces.

Most of the turnstone's eggs that I have seen are easily recognizable, though the distinctive features are more easily seen than described. The markings are usually quite evenly distributed and the egg well covered with them. The 12 eggs so well illustrated on Frank Poynting's (1895) beautiful plate, all taken from European eggs, show some variations not mentioned by Mr. Brandt. The buffy ground colors range from " dark olive buff " to " olive buff "; and the greenish ones from "water green" to "yellowish glaucous." One plain-looking egg is "dark olive buff" with faint markings of a slightly darker shade. Another is "water green" with numerous, small, almost black spots, and underlying small spots of "light mouse gray." The measurements of 100 European eggs furnished by the Rev. F. C. R. Jourdain, average 40.5 by 29.2 millimeters; the eggs showing the four extremes measure **44.5** by 30.4, 43.2 by **31.3, 36** by 28.2 and 40.5 by **26** millimeters. Mr. Brandt's 44 eggs, from Alaska, average slightly smaller, 39 by 28 millimeters; the extremes of his and all other American and Greenland eggs that I have measurements of fall within the limits given above for European eggs. Egg measurements would seem to indicate that Alaska birds should be referred to *morinella*, the smaller race.

Young.—The period of incubation does not seem to be known, but it is a well-established fact that both sexes share in this duty, as well as in the care of the young. Mr. Paget-Wilkes (1922) says:

Both sexes incubate, but when the eggs are fresh or partly incubated the hen seems to brood and the cock stands on guard. When the eggs were within a day or two of hatching or were just chipping we invariably found the cock incubating, and when the young were out we always found the cock looking after the family and the hen, with her duller plumage and weaker notes, on guard. These characteristics observed in the cases of 19 pairs should form a useful basis for further research.

On flushing the cock bird from four young in down on the Mouettes Islands I was shown an example of his tenacity and intelligence. I had taken the young birds away in my pocket and had run back to the boat across a neck of land some 300 yards broad. The cock chased me a little way and then disappeared. On reaching the sea, however, on the other side of the small peninsula, I immediately saw the cock fly around the point and make straight for me, and he stood and chattered at me until we rowed away in the boat. The hen put in no appearance at all.

Again, on one of the islands we watched a pair whose behavior puzzled us, but soon discovered that there were four young birds being looked after by the cock. The moment he was flushed the young birds scattered in all directions, and on our lying down again came back under the fatherly wing. Before I discovered that the cock incubated in the last stages I patiently watched a hen running about quite unconcernedly for almost an hour, and then suddenly jumped to the conclusion that the cock was sitting. When I got up the hen gave the alarm note and I flushed the cock from four chipping eggs.

A. L. V. Manniche (1910) writes:

The parents are very watchful against danger in the breeding time and when the young ones are small. One of them will keep a lookout from the summit of a large stone or a rock while the other is brooding or guiding the young ones. The bird on guard will discover an approaching enemy at an incredibly long distance and rush toward him uttering furious cries. Especially the skua (*Lestris longicauda*) is a detested enemy of the turnstone. Every day I could observe the hunting skuas pursued by turnstones. When one pursuer returned to its district another would appear and thus every skua was almost always accompanied by at least one turnstone. Also toward the polar fox the turnstones would betray great fear, and they would often join from afar and swoop down on the hated enemy, uttering their sharpest and most violent cries.

Toward the end of July the young ones were able to fly but were, however, generally accompanied by the old female. The young ones would often resort to the upper part of rather high rocks while the old female incessantly crying and anxiously flapping tried to divert my attention from them. When the old female had left her offspring and the country, these would immediately take to the coast and the mouths of rivers like other young waders.

Plumages.—The young turnstone in natal down is not brilliantly, yet distinctively, colored. The upper parts, including the sides of the head and neck, wings and thighs, vary from " cream buff " or " chamois " on the crown and wings to " olive buff " on the neck and flanks. The crown, back, wings, rump, and thighs are heavily spotted or broadly striped with black; the center of the crown is largely black and so are the lores; a broad space above the eyes and the forehead are " cream buff," with a black streak in the middle of the latter. There is some whitish in the center of the back and the entire under parts are pure white.

In full juvenal plumage, Alaska birds in July, the crown and mantle are dark sepia or blackish brown, the feathers of the crown edged with sandy brown, those of the back broadly edged with " pinkish buff " or " cream buff " and the wing coverts still more broadly edged with " cinnamon buff "; the tertials are edged with " cinnamon "; the feathers of the rump, the tail coverts, and the tail are tipped with a buffy wash; the under parts are similar in pattern to those of the adult, but the black patches are browner and often show buffy tips. The sexes are practically alike in juvenal and winter plumages.

The first winter plumage is acquired by a partial body molt between August and November; it can be distinguished from the adult winter plumage by the presence of some retained tertials, scapulars, and wing coverts; also it is not so uniformly dark as the adult, is more streaked with buffy and whitish edgings on the head, neck, and back, and it has less black in the gorget. The two races are distinguishable in this plumage, *interpres* being darker.

The first prenuptial molt begins in January; it is similar to that of the adult but is much less complete. I have seen a young bird in full wing molt in January and think that young birds renew their flight feathers before the first spring. The first nuptial plumage is, I believe, a nonbreeding plumage, as it is worn by birds which spend the summer far south of the breeding range. I have seen birds in this plumage, collected in Florida and Louisiana, in every month from April to August. This plumage resembles the adult nuptial, but the head is more streaked with dusky or black; and in the mantle, scapulars and wing coverts there is a mixture of new rufous feathers and both old and new blackish brown feathers. The sexes are recognizable in this plumage, the males being much brighter. A complete molt in August produces the adult winter plumage.

Adults have a complete postnuptial molt, from July to October, but mainly in August, when the wings are molted. They have a partial prenuptial molt from February to June, mainly in March and April, involving the body plumage, but not all the scapulars or wing coverts.

Food.—The turnstone is mainly a maritime species and its favorite feeding grounds are the stony and sandy beaches along the seashore and the rocky promontories and islets on the coasts. But on its inland migrations it finds its food on the shores and beaches of the larger lakes and rivers. The turnstone derives its name from its well-known and conspicuous habit of turning over, with its short, stout bill and sturdy muscles, stones, shells, clods of earth, seaweed, and other objects in search for the dainty morsels of animal food that it finds beneath them. If the object is not too large the bird stoops down and overturns it with a quick jerk of the head and neck; but against a larger obstacle it places its breast and pushes with all its strength; it is surprising to see how large a stone or clod it can move. It also has a peculiar habit of rooting like a pig in piles of seaweed or in the open sand. Windrows of seaweed and other rubbish are generally full of sand fleas and various worms and insects and their larvae, where the turnstones and other waders find an abundant feast. Frank T. Noble (1904) has described this very well, as follows:

He would select a likely spot on the loosely packed moss and go at his work with a vim and rapidity entirely different from the other species. Underneath the bits of weed, moss, and fragments of shell his sharp upturned bill would swiftly go and a perfect shower of these would soon be falling in front and beside him. Finding a morsel to his taste he would devour it in much less time than it takes to relate it, and the rooting and tossing of the bits into the air would continue. At times quite sizeable fragments of shell and pieces of moss more than an inch in length would be thrown fully 7 or 8 inches above the bird's head, and this he would keep up, with scarcely an instant's pause, for a quarter of an hour and until he had excavated a pit large enough to almost conceal his plump, mottled body. Occasionally he would turn about in his tracks, but as a rule he worked in one direction.

I have seen a similar method employed on a sand flat laid bare at low tide, where four or five turnstones were feeding, accompanied by sanderlings and peeps. The turnstones were digging holes in the wet sand, throwing out the sand for a distance of several inches, until the holes were big enough to admit the whole of a man's fist and deep enough to conceal the bird's head and neck. Meantime the sanderlings were standing close by and picking up some small objects thrown out, until driven away by savage attacks of the turnstone. On close examination I found a number of small, black snails and other minute mollusks in the sand thrown out. The stomach of one shot contained only the minute mollusks and some coarse sand.

Doctor Stejneger (1885) found turnstones feeding in large numbers on the killing grounds in the Commander Islands, " where thousands of putrified carcasses of the slain fur seals swarm with myriads of the white larvae of the flesh fly," on which they grow very fat. Francis H. Allen tells me he has seen them feeding on rocks which are bare only at low tide and covered with barnacles. One that he watched—

sometimes simply picked its food up from among the barnacles and rockweed, and sometimes it hammered away in one spot like a woodpecker before getting its morsel. The object hammered was evidently fixed. After the bird had flown, I visited the spot and found many empty barnacle shells—empty of barnacles, that is—some entirely empty and others containing small snail-like mollusks with dark-colored shells.

On the coast of South Carolina I have seen turnstones feeding on the beds of coon oysters and have watched them busily engaged in chasing the small fiddler crabs on the muddy banks of tidal creeks and on the mud lumps; they had to run very fast to catch the spry little animals and probably had to pick out the smallest ones. Mr. Wayne (1910) says: " On Capers Island it frequents live oak trees which are covered with small mussels, upon which it eagerly feeds. If some of the mussels happen to be on an inclined limb the birds walk, instead of flying, to reach them. I have seen as many as four of these, one behind the other, on a small limb out in the surf."

Mr. Manniche (1910) says that just after their arrival in Greenland the turnstones feed mainly on vegetable food; the stomach of a bird taken on May 22 contained only remains of plants. Dr. Paul Bartsch (1922), referring to his visit to Midway Island, writes: " It was a decided surprise to us to find waders in bushes feeding upon berries, and yet this was the case here. Again and again we flushed bunches of turnstones from the dense *Scaevola* thickets and watched them circle about for some time, only to realight in the tops of another clump of bushes. Specimens shot on Sand Island were filled with *Scaevola* berries."

C. J. Maynard (1896) says that they sometimes resort to marshes and feed on grasshoppers. Their main food supply evidently consists of small crustaceans, small mollusks, insects, and their larvae, all of which they consume in large quantities and in great variety. In Massachusetts it is sometimes called the " horse-foot snipe," because of its fondness for the eggs of the horse-foot crab. John T. Nichols tells me that it scratches up the eggs by " jumping in the air and striking with both its feet at once into the sand, thus making a hole about 3 inches deep and 1½ inches across."

Dr. Alexander Wetmore contributes the following interesting notes:

The greatest surprise came when on Laysan Island it was found that these and other shore birds were persistent enemies of the sooty and gray-backed terns, as they destroyed the eggs of the terns at every opportunity. For the first few days when turnstones were seen greedily eating terns' eggs I supposed that they were merely finishing eggs that had been opened by other birds, but on further observation found that these shore birds were bold marauders that drove their bills into the eggs of terns at every opportunity and were only prevented from attacking the nests of boobies and man-o-war birds by the fact that the shell of the egg in these species was so hard that they could not break it. As we moved through the great colonies of sooty terns the birds near at hand rose before us from their eggs, often communicating the alarm to neighbors so that at times clouds of birds arose to fill the air. At our heels, 15 or 20 feet behind us, came little groups of turnstones well aware that this uproar among the sharp-beaked terns meant unprotected nests, where they could attack the eggs with impunity. The turnstones ran quickly about driving their bills into the eggs without the slightest hesitation, breaking open the side widely and feeding eagerly on the contents, sometimes two or three gathering for an instant to demolish one egg and then with this one half consumed running on to attack another. The havoc wrought among the terns was so great that we forbade the sailors from approaching the colonies, and made it a rule among the naturalists to keep away except when necessity for some observation made it imperative to disturb the birds.

The densely packed colonies of aggressive sooty terns were open to attack mainly along the borders except when the birds were disturbed, but the little scattered groups of gray-backed terns (*Sterna lunata*) on the open beaches were entirely at the mercy of the turnstones, so that it seemed that the gentle terns could not hope for a successful nesting until the close of May carried the horde of their marauding persecutors away to northern homes. So bold were the shore birds that on one occasion I saw two actually push aside the feathers on the sides of the incubating tern, drag her egg from beneath her breast, and proceed to open and devour it within 6 inches of the nest. The tern remained in incubating pose, plainly troubled by such unexpected boldness but seemingly not comprehending its portent, nodding her head with that of her mate standing beside her, and finally reaching out to draw the half-empty shell of her treasure again beneath her, while the robbers, temporarily satisfied, pattered away in search of other prey. On several occasions when, in walking along the beaches above high-tide mark I flushed gray-backed terns from their nests, I saw that they carried with them as they flew away shells of broken eggs, which not understanding that they had been destroyed they had covered while the hardening albumen flowing over the outside of the shell had glued the whole to their feathers.

The Rev. F. C. R. Jourdain contributes the following notes on the food of this species:

As it is almost invariably found near the coast the food is chiefly marine in character: Mollusca, chiefly small univalves such as *Litorina* (L. Florence records 134 opercula of small molluscks); small Crustacea, especially Gammaridae; A. H. Clark records fry of a small fish (*Sicydium plumicri*) up to 1½ inches in length; insects, including Coleoptera, Diptera (*Tipulidae* and larvae of *Chironomidae*), Lepidoptera (*Argynnis charidea* and *Dasychira groenlandica* recorded by H. C. Hart and *Hymenoptera*. Also Arachnida and Acaridea (Feilden). Also some vegetable matter (seeds of *Draba alpina*, pieces of seaweed, etc.).

Behavior.—When migrating turnstones fly in large flocks by themselves or with black-bellied plovers, often in immense flocks; at such times they usually fly high. But, while sojourning on the way, they are usually in small numbers and very often seen singly. One or two birds are often associated with mixed flocks or scattered gatherings of semipalmated plover, sanderlings, or other small waders. Their flight is strong, swift, and steady, usually direct, but sometimes in a semicircle, out from the shore and back again; when not traveling they generally fly low. There is something peculiar about their flight which can be recognized at a long distance, but I can not describe it satisfactorily. They are essentially shore birds, frequenting the stony, rocky, or sandy beaches of the seashore or the larger lakes. They are not particularly shy, and sometimes very tame. When they first alight they stand and survey the landscape until sure that they are safe. They then mingle freely with the other small waders, feeding unconcernedly, and treating their companions with indifference until one comes too near. Then the turnstone shows its jealous and pugnacious disposition; it will allow no competition, in the spot where it is feeding, from another bird, even of its own species, but with lowered head, drooping wings, and hunched up back it rushes at the intruder in a threatening attitude and perhaps gives him a few jabs with its sharp bill. Many a miniature cockfight or sham battle is enacted and the turnstone is generally the aggressor, though once I saw a sanderling drive away a turnstone. It appears like a big bully that is attracted to the feast that others have found and then is unwilling to share it with them.

Turnstones can swim well and probably alight on the water to rest while making long flights over the ocean. Dr. Donald B. Mac-Millan (1918) saw "a large flock alight upon the water in Kennedy Channel." They love to bathe in shallow water, squatting down and fluttering their wings, sometimes partly rolling over; then they spend much time preening and dressing their pretty plumage. N. B. Moore says in his notes that "this species alights on the dead branches of mangroves, stumps, and stakes that stand in the water near the shore from 2 to 6 feet above it and sits in the manner of a Carolina dove."

Voice.—John T. Nichols has contributed the following on the ordinary notes of the turnstone:

The common flight note of this species is an unloud polysyllabic one, something like a cackle, which does not carry far. It is usually given by birds that are leaving the vicinity, but not so frequently heard at other times as are the flight notes of various species. This note is sometimes three syllabled, *ketakek*, or may be of a single syllable, *kek*, on taking wing. A much rarer, loud, plover-like *kik-kyu* has been heard from a turnstone when coming to decoys or flying along the edge of favorable marshes. The cackle of the turnstone is almost impossible to imitate, but they will decoy readily to a whistled imitation of the cry of their associate the black-bellied plover.

The song of the turnstone as heard on its breeding grounds few have been privileged to hear. Mr. Brandt calls it "a loud but not unpleasont note, rapidly repeated—*kye-ute-cat-tat-tah*." Mr. Jourdain has given us, under courtship, his impressions of it and those of Messrs. Trevor-Battye and Paget-Wilkes.

Field marks.—The turnstone is a conspicuous and well-marked bird, not likely to be mistaken for anything else. It is a stout, short-legged bird with a short neck and a short, straight bill. In its brilliant spring plumage the white head, black throat, red legs, and rufous back are unique field marks. But the best field marks, most conspicuous in the nuptial plumage, but present in all plumages, are the five white stripes on the upper surface, which show very plainly as the bird flies away; these are a broad central stripe on the back, separated by a black patch on the rump from the white area in the tail, a narrow stripe on the outer edge of the scapulars and a band across the wing on the secondaries and primaries. Unfortunately for observers on the Pacific coast, the black turnstone has somewhat similar white stripes, but the pattern is a little different.

Fall.—Adult turnstones begin to leave their summer homes in Greenland about the middle of July, with the knots and sanderlings, and before the end of August the last of the young birds have left. Lucien M. Turner obtained an adult from Davis Inlet on July 25; but the species apparently avoids Ungava, for the only bird he saw there was a young male taken on August 20. Probably the birds which breed in western Greenland migrate coastwise along the Labrador coast and Nova Scotia to New England. We saw the first turnstones at Cape Sable, Nova Scotia, on July 30 and 31; but my earliest record for adults in Massachusetts is on August 1; adults are common here all through August; the young birds come along late in August, and I have seen them here as late as October 12.

There is a heavy migration down the west coast of Hudson Bay. Edward A. Preble (1902) saw the first turnstones at Fort Churchill on July 30; and on August 10 to 13 he "observed many small flocks about 25 miles south of Cape Eskimo"; August 21 to 26 he saw "many flocks daily." From the Hudson Bay region the main flight seems to be southeastward through the Great Lakes region to the Atlantic coast. It seems to be very rare in the fall west of eastern

Manitoba and Ohio; and it extends as far east as the Bermudas and the West Indies.

Some of the birds which breed in Alaska migrate down the Pacific coasts of North and South America at about the same dates as the Atlantic coast birds; but large numbers pass down the Asiatic coast, through Japan and China, to islands in the Southern Hemisphere. Doctor Stejneger (1885) says that in the Commander Islands during the latter part of July large flocks return from the north.

From this time until late autumn enormous masses of them may be seen on the killing grounds, near the seal rookeries, where thousands of putrified carcasses of the slain fur seals swarm with myriads of the white larvae of the flesh fly, upon which the pretty turnstones feed and grow exceedingly fat. At sunset they retire to the beach, where they pass the night, not, however, without having performed a soldierlike drill by flying up and down the endless tundra, now in full body, now again in detached divisions, and with admirable precision turning and maneuvering as if obeying the command of a leading officer.

As to the migration on the Pribilof Islands, William Palmer (1899) writes:

On July 12, 1890, I saw probably the first bird that landed on St. Paul during the fall migration. From that date they daily increased rapidly until by the end of July they swarmed everywhere. They reach the island by way of the northeastern shore and in straggling flocks or singly fly southward through the island during the day, banking up in large numbers when the village killing ground is reached. They spread out on the slopes, resting on the rocks and little hillocks during the day. They soon find the feast awaiting them on the killing ground, and the marks of their work around nearly every seal carcass is soon noticeable. As the water disappears by soakage and evaporation in the village pond they turn up the black sand in thousands of little hillocks, each with a narrow depression made by their bill beside it. At low tide the lagoon beaches are a favorite resting and feeding place. By the end of July many become so fat that they are run down and captured by the young Aleuts. Their departure from St. Paul is quite a feature of the avifaunan exhibition. About 6 in the evening a small flock of perhaps 40 birds will rise into the air from about the village pond and uttering loud, shrill cries will fly up to near the head of the lagoon. Here making a wide sweep they return, gathering fresh recruits on their way, until the vicinity of the pond is again reached. Sweeping around in a constantly ascending course they return up the lagoon, and turning once more, screaming as they go, and adding to their numbers, they make a straight course high over the village hill and on out to sea over the reef point. This invariably took place every evening during the latter part of my stay on the island. It was always the rule that a dense fog bank hung all around the island at that time, so that even the reef point was not visible, but the birds went into the fog without the slightest hesitation. They left their landmarks behind. Several flocks averaging about a hundred birds left nearly every evening from the end of July until I left on August 10. The first arrivals on the island were always adults; the young were not noted for at least 10 days. According to Elliott they all leave the islands after the 10th of September.

Many of these birds must make the 2,000-mile flight over the ocean from the Commander or Aleutian Islands to the Hawaiian Islands.

They have repeatedly been seen in the middle of the Pacific Ocean, hundreds of miles from land. This does not seem so remarkable, now that we know that they can alight and rest on the water and rise from it easily. They must go a long time without food or find a very scanty supply of it, as it must take 40 or 50 hours to make the trip. But Dr. Henry W. Henshaw (1902) says that some of the first arrivals on these islands, which he shot about the middle of August, "were all of them plump and in fine order for the table."

Game.—The turnstone has never attained great importance as a game bird, though it was formerly counted in the list of "big birds" in the gunner's bag. It was plump and generally fat, so that it made a good table bird. It has a variety of local names, such as chicken plover, calico bird, brant bird, etc. It decoys well to almost any decoys and, although its own note is difficult to imitate, it will respond readily to the call of its favorite companion, the black-bellied plover.

Winter.—The ruddy turnstone spends the winter on the coasts of the southern States and on both coasts of South America, from South Carolina to Brazil and from southern California to Chile. The larger, Old World form, *interpres*, apparently does not winter anywhere in the Western Hemisphere, but occupies the coasts of southern Europe and Asia, much of Africa, some of the oceanic islands, and Australia. If we are to recognize the Pacific form, *oahuensis*, there is yet much to be learned about the limits of its winter and summer ranges and where it intergrades with *interpres*. The island of Oahu in the Hawaiian Islands is the type locality of *oahuensis;* and it probably has a wide range among Pacific islands.

Dr. Alexander Wetmore says in his notes:

In the remote islands of the Hawaiian bird reservation the turnstone is common during the period of northern winter, and a few sterile or injured individuals may remain through the summer. Though common along the sandy beaches and the shores of lagoons, as is usual, at times they exhibited curious habits, as on Ocean Island they ran back from the open shore beneath the thickets of beach magnolia (*Scaevola*), penetrating the entire island in cover as dense as that ordinarily chosen by woodcock. It was always a surprise when one, attracted by some sound, flew up from under the bushes and perched on a dead branch to look at me. On Midway turnstones ran about on the lawns at the cable station like robins, with so domestic and contented an air that it was at times difficult to recall that they were here merely as transients, and that soon they would be nesting in arctic tundras.

Charles Barrett writes to me from Australia, as follows:

One of our most interesting summer visitors, the turnstone frequents open beaches on the mainland generally in small flocks, and also favors reefs and coral strands among the tropical and subtropical islands. When camped, with other members of the Royal Australasian Ornithologists' Union, on Masthead Island, Capricorn Group, Queensland, in October, 1910, I observed many turnstones on the white coral-sand beach. Apparently, with waders of other species, they had recently arrived, after the long flight from their breeding grounds. They were active enough, but in poor condition. During migration, they can have little chance to obtain food, and the strain of flying thousands of miles affects even the healthiest birds. But they obtain abundance of food in their Austral haunts, and soon become plump again. Many localities in Australia are admirably suited to the turnstone's needs, and it is not a rare bird with us, indeed, on islands of the Great Barrier Reef, northeastern Queensland, it may be termed a common species.

W. B. Alexander tells me that the turnstone is "a fairly common visitor to Australian coasts. My earliest record is of a pair seen on the beach at Oyster Cay, Great Barrier Reef, North Queensland, on August 27, 1925, and my latest record a pair on the estuary of the Lost River on the south coast of Western Australia on April 25, 1914."

DISTRIBUTION

ARENARIA INTERPRES INTERPRES

Range.—Mainly in the Eastern Hemisphere.

Breeding range.—The turnstone breeds on the Arctic coasts of both hemispheres, but its exact status in North America is still somewhat indefinite. The known breeding range extends from probably Greenland (Disco Bay, Tuctoo Valley, and Bowdoin Bay); east to Iceland; Norway (Smolen Islands); Sweden; Lapland; Finland; Nova Zembla; Siberia (Balagansk, and Plover Bay); Kamchatka; probably the Commander Islands; and Alaska (St. Lawrence Island, St. Michaels, Takshagemut, Port Clarence, probably Cape Lowenstern and Point Barrow).

Winter range.—In winter the turnstone is found on the coasts of Europe and Asia north to the British Isles; Japan and Hawaii. They range south at this season to South Africa (Cape of Good Hope); Madagascar; the Mascarene Islands; Australia; New Zealand; and Chile.

Migration.—In North America, early dates of spring arrival are: Alaska, St. Michael, May 15; and Greenland, north of latitude 81° 30′, May 27. Late dates of fall departure are Greenland, north of latitude 81° 31′, September 11; and Alaska, Nushagak, September 21.

Casual record.—The turnstone can be considered only as a casual or accidental visitant anywhere in North America south of the breeding grounds. A specimen taken at Pacific Beach, California, September 8, 1904, was identified as the European race, but the record also has been questioned (Grinnell). Four specimens taken on San Geronimo Island, Lower California, March 15, 1897, were considered by Oberholser as typical of the European or Asiatic race. One was obtained at Monomoy Island, Massachusetts on September 8, 1892 (Bishop); and Wayne took a specimen on Dewees Island, South Carolina, May 30, 1918.

[AUTHOR'S NOTE.—For the author's views on the distribution of the two forms of the turnstone, see his note on the distribution of *morinella*. There is much individual variation in color, with a decided sexual difference in size, which opens the question of wrongly sexed specimens. The individual variation in size is still greater, so much so that both extremes of both forms are very close together. A large, dark female of *morinella*, wrongly sexed, might easily be recorded as *interpres*. These facts cast some doubt on North American records of *interpres*.]

Egg dates.—Norway and Sweden: 16 records, June 1 to 30; 8 records, June 7 to 13. Lapland and Finland: 14 records, May 23 to July 8; 7 records, June 8 to 18.

ARENARIA INTERPRES MORINELLA

Range.—North America; Central America; islands of the Caribbean Sea; and South America.

Breeding range.—Actual breeding records of the ruddy turnstone are not numerous, so it is difficult to accurately define its breeding range. From information available it appears that they breed east from Alaska (Hooper Bay, Colville River Delta, Collinson Point, and probably Demarcation Point); to Mackenzie (lower Anderson River, Liverpool Bay, Franklin Bay, and probably Felix Harbor); Franklin (probably Melville Island, Victoria Island, probably King Oscar Land); probably Ellesmere and Grant Lands; and northwestern Greenland. Specimens have been obtained in southern Mackenzie in June (Fort Resolution and Fort Rae), but there is not yet any evidence of their breeding in that region. Eggs also have been reported from "Hudson Bay" (Reinecke), but the record is too indefinite to stand careful scrutiny.

Nonbreeding individuals have been detected in summer as far south as Chile (Sclater); Peru (Callao); the Galapagos Islands (Baur and Adams); Venezuela (Margarita and Aruba Islands); and the West Indies (Carriacou and Jamaica). It also has been noted at this season on the Atlantic, Pacific, and Gulf coasts of the United States, as Florida (Bradentown, Passage Key, Fort De Soto, Key West, and Daytona Beach); South Carolina (Frogmore, and Mount Pleasant); North Carolina (Beaufort); Virginia (Hog Island, and Cape Charles); New York (Fair Haven Light, Long Beach, and Gardiners Island); Massachusetts (Monomoy Island, and Cape Cod); Louisiana (Chandeleur Islands, and Breton Islands); Texas (Fort Brown, and Corpus Christi); and California (Santa Cruz).

Winter range.—The winter range of *morinella* can be defined but little better as the records are frequently confused with *Arenaria i. interpres*, to which some of the following may refer. Their range at this season appears to extend north to California (rarely San Francisco Bay); Texas (Fort Brown, Point Isabel, Refugio County, and the Sabine River); probably Louisiana; probably North Carolina (Fort Macon); and Bermuda (Ireland Island). East to Bermuda (Ireland Island); South Carolina (Mount Pleasant, and Frogmore); Georgia (Savannah, Blackbeard Island, and Darien); Florida (Fernandina, St. Augustine, Daytona Beach, Mosquito Inlet, Cocoa, Fort Pierce, and Key West); the Bahama Islands (New Providence, and Great Inagua); Haiti (Monte Cristi, and Samana); Porto Rico (Mameyes, and Culebra Island); Lesser Antilles (Sombrero, St. Bartholomew, Carriacou, and Tobago); British Guiana (probably Abary River); French Guiana (probably Cayanne); and Brazil (Para, Cajetuba Island, Fernando Noronha, and Abrolhos Island). South to Brazil (Abrolhos Island); and Chile (Valdivia). West to Chile (Valdivia, Talcahuano, Paposo, and Atacama); Peru (probably Chorillos); the Galapagos Islands (Albemarle, Hood, Indefatigable and Bindloe Islands); Honduras (Swan Island); Guatemala (Chiapam); Mexico (the Valley of Mexico); Lower California (San Jose del Cabo, and Magdalena Bay); and California (rarely San Francisco Bay). Occasionally also, wintering as far north as Sanakh, Alaska (Littlejohn).

Spring migration.—Early dates of spring arrival are: Virginia, Accomac County, May 8, Chesapeake, May 10, and Locustville, May 11; New Jersey, Ocean City, May 5, Cape May, May 6, and Long Beach, May 16; New York, Fair Haven Light, May 10, Montauk Point, May 12, and Canandaigua, May 14; Connecticut, New Haven, May 18, and Norwalk, May 19; Rhode Island, Newport, May 13, and Sachuest Point, May 14; Massachusetts, Nantucket, May 1, Woods Hole, May 5, and Monomoy Island, May 6; Maine, South Harpswell, May 20, and Portland, May 22; Nova Scotia, Pictou, May 24; Franklin, Winter Island, June 10; Illinois, Northeastern, April 30, Englewood, May 22, Chicago, May 23, and Waukegan, May 24; Indiana, Starke County, May 20, and Wolfe Lake, May 23; Ohio, Lakeside, May 11, Oberlin, May 15, Huron, May 17, and Painesville, May 28; Michigan, Detroit, May 13, Kalamazoo County, May 20, and Ann Arbor, May 25; Ontario, Toronto, May 18, Kingston, May 20, Moose Factory, May 26, and Mitchells Bay, May 31; Nebraska, Lincoln, May 18; Iowa, Burlington, May 21; Minnesota, Lake And, May 20, Minneapolis, May 21, and Walker, May 24; Wisconsin, Madison, May 22; South Dakota, Coteau des Prairies, May 26, and Fort Sisseton, May 27; Manitoba, Shoal Lake, May 25; Saskatchewan, Ile a la

Crosse, May 22, and Orestwynd, May 23; Alberta, Tofield, May 15, and Fort Chipewyan, May 25; Mackenzie, Fort Simpson, May 29; California, San Nicolas Island, April 7; Oregon, Mercer, May 14; Washington, Puget Sound, May 6, Willapa Harbor, May 11, and Shoalwater Bay, May 17; and Alaska, Unalaska, May 19, and Nulato, May 23.

Late dates of spring departures are: Peru, Mathews Island, April 24; Porto Rico, Culebrita Island, April 15; Bahama Islands, Andros, April 26, and Green Cay, April 29; Florida, Punta Rassa, May 13, St. Marks, May 22, and Daytona Beach, May 24; Georgia, Savannah, May 29; South Carolina, Egg Bank, May 14, and Mount Pleasant, June 12; North Carolina, Churchs Island, May 19, and Cape Hatteras, May 20; Virginia, Wachapreague, May 24, Hog Island, May 19, and Smiths Island, May 31; Pennsylvania, Warren, May 30, and Erie, June 2; New Jersey, Camden, May 21, and Cape May County, June 3; New York, Ithaca, June 13, Montauk Point, June 9, and Orient, June 12; Connecticut, Fairfield, May 29, Westport, May 30, and Norwalk, June 1; Massachusetts, Dennis, June 2, Marthas Vineyard, June 8, and Monomoy Island, June 8; Illinois, Chicago, June 9, Northeastern, June 18; Indiana, Wolfe Lake, June 9; Ohio, Huron, June 3, Oberlin, June 5, and Lakeside, June 5; Michigan, Detroit, June 6, and Charity Island, June 15; Ontario, Toronto, June 17; North Dakota, Devils Lake, June 11; South Dakota, Vermilion, May 30; Texas, Point Isabel, May 14; Minnesota, Cass Lake, May 30; Wisconsin, De Pere, June 3; Manitoba, Dog Point, June 7, Lake Winnipeg, June 10, and Shoal Lake, June 12; Saskatchewan, Indian Head, June 2, and Churchill River, June 9; California, Santa Barbara, May 6, Farallon Islands, May 7, and San Nicolas Island, May 11; Oregon, Mercer, May 14; and Washington, Wallapa Harbor, May 16.

Fall migration.—Early dates of fall arrival are: Washington, Destruction Island, July 17; California, Monterey Bay, July 18, and Santa Barbara, July 26; Lower California, San Jose del Cabo, August 31; Oaxaca, San Mateo, August 9; Saskatchewan, Quill Lake, August 7, Bigstick Lake, August 9, and Crane Lake, August 11; Manitoba, Fort Churchill, July 30, Shoal Lake, August 7, and Oak Lake, August 8; Texas, Rockport, August 12; Ontario, Toronto, July 30, and Point Pelee, August 14; Michigan, Charity Island, August 6; Ohio, Pelee Island, July 24, Huron, August 3, and Lakeside, August 8; Indiana, Millers, August 8; Illinois, Chicago, July 20, and La Grange, August 13; Maine, Portland, July 28; Massachusetts, Marthas Vineyard July 24, Harvard, July 26, and Monomoy Island, July 27; Rhode Island, Island of Rhode Island, July 26, and Kingston, August 11; Connecticut, Meriden, August 8; New York, Montauk

Point, July 18, Orient, July 28, and Shelter Island, July 29; New Jersey, Cape May, July 16; Virginia, Cobb Island, August 1, and Locustville, August 7; North Carolina, Pea Island, August 11; Bermuda, Coopers Island, July 27; South Carolina, Mount Pleasant, July 15; Georgia, Savannah, August 18; Florida, Palmo Sola, July 26, St. Marks, July 30, Pensacola, August 1, and Daytona, August 10; Bahama Islands, Mariguana, August 5; Jamaica, Spanishtown, August 13; Lesser Antilles, Barbados, August 22, and St. Croix, September 8; Peru, Payta, September 20; and Chile, Talcahuano, September 9.

Late dates of fall departure are: Alaska, St. Michael, September 8; British Columbia, Graham Island, September 5; Washington, Simiahmoo, October 3; California, Alameda, October 15; Manitoba, Oak Lake, September 9; Wisconsin, Sheboygan, September 1; Ontario, Point Pelee, September 15, and Toronto, September 16; Michigan, Bay City, September 4, and Detroit, September 5; Ohio, Huron, October 18, Lakeside, October 21, and New Bremen, October 23; Illinois, Chicago, October 13; Franklin, Harrowby Bay, August 30, Newfoundland, September 5; Nova Scotia, La Have Ridges, September 27; New Brunswick, Grand Manan, September 4, and Tabusintoc, October 23; Quebec, Green Island, October 26; Massachusetts, North Truro, October 9, Woods Hole, October 20, and (exceptional) Dennis, November 3; Rhode Island, Point Judith, September 14, and Newport, October 8; New York, Canandaigua, September 16, Brockport, October 6, and Orient, October 7.

Casual records.—The ruddy turnstone is not now common anywhere in the Mississippi Valley and has been recorded on but few occasions in the lower part of this region and in the States west to the Rocky Mountains. Among these last are, Arkansas, reported at Osceola by Doctor Richardson (Howell); Missouri, St. Louis, September 7, 1897; Kansas, Kansas River, August 16, 1898, and Greenwood County, October 1, 1911; Colorado, Denver, April 26, 1890, and May 18, 1900, and Barr, September 9, 1907; and Wyoming, Yellowstone Park, August 30, 1922.

[AUTHOR'S NOTE.—The above is the generally accepted theory as to the distribution of the two forms of the turnstone. The author has examined a few specimens from Iceland and East Greenland and a large number from Alaska and various islands in the Pacific Ocean. The Iceland birds are nearer *interpres;* the East Greenland birds are less typical of *interpres*, with a more decided tendency toward *morinella;* no West Greenland birds have been examined and perhaps they might be nearer *morinella;* Alaska and Hawaiian Island birds, as well as those from Polynesia, are much nearer *morinella.* Apparently the range of *morinella* should be extended eastward to western Greenland, and westward to Bering Strait and to the Pacific islands. Both color and size have been taken into account in this study.]

Egg dates.—Bering Sea coast of Alaska: 10 records, May 29 to June 27. Arctic coasts of Alaska and Canada: 19 records, June 19 to August 1; 10 records, June 28 to July 21.

ARENARIA MELANOCEPHALA (Vigors)

BLACK TURNSTONE

HABITS

The black turnstone replaces to a large extent on the Pacific coast our well-known ruddy turnstone; both species are found there on migrations and in winter, but the black is the commoner on that coast, to which it is restricted. It is a characteristic bird of the barnacle-covered reefs and rocky shores, being more often seen on the outlying islands and ledges than on the mainland. There it lives at the water's edge, seeking its food within reach of the waves and often drenched with ocean spray. As it stands motionless it is almost invisible in its coat of dark brown and might easily be mistaken for a knob of rock or a bunch of seaweed; but when startled into flight its conspicuous pattern of black and white flashes out a distinctive mark of recognition.

Spring.—The black turnstone starts on its northward migration from the coast of California early in April. Much of the flight is over the ocean, as the following observation by Austin H. Clark (1910) shows:

On the first day out of San Francisco, May 4, we saw several small flocks of these birds on their way north; each succeeding day they became more abundant until on the afternoon of May 8 we saw them by thousands, in flocks of from 10 or 20 to several hundred. At one time, about 2 o'clock in the afternoon, the whole sea appeared dotted with white, so abundant were they. All the birds noticed were headed up the coast, going the same direction as we.

In the mornings these birds were comparatively rare; they began to appear about 11 o'clock, and increased in numbers until about 2, when they were very abundant; shortly after 3 there was a falling off until by half past 4 few, if any, were to be seen. This was true every day we were at sea on the voyage from San Francisco to Puget Sound. Whether they spent the night and early morning on the neighboring shores or resting on the water I am unable to say; but all we saw were on the wing; possibly there were other shore birds in these multitudes, but all which came near the ship were of this species.

Lucien M. Turner (1886) says that this is one of the earliest arrivals at St. Michael. His earliest date is May 13. "It arrives with the earlier geese, and for the first few weeks frequents the edges of the low ponds, which are the first to be freed from the ice in spring. After the sea ice has left the shores it repairs to the rocky beach and seeks its food among the stones and seaweeds." H. B. Conover says, in his notes from Hooper Bay: " The first of these birds were noted on May 16, when two were taken as they flew by a small snow-water pond on the tundra. Two days later this species was very common. Next to the western sandpiper it was probably the commonest, as well as the noisiest, wader nesting on the tundra."

Courtship.—Herbert W. Brandt, who has studied this species on its breeding grounds at Hooper Bay, Alaska, says in his notes:

The black turnstones, like many of the other shore birds during the mating season, spend considerable time chasing each other about. The female seems to say to the male, "catch me if you can," and then dashes off with such speed that the pursuer has difficulty in following her, and she usually returns to the same spot from which her zigzag flight began. Often the male will mount high into the air alone, until completely out of sight, and then will produce with his wing or tail feathers, which of the two I have not been able to determine, the same strange *zum-zum-zum* noise as made by the Wilson snipe. Before the nesting season this feather music could be heard on the flats at any time, and it deceived me at first, as I mistook it for that of the snipe. Later, however, as soon as the nesting duties began, it seemed to cease; and in this respect, the black turnstone differs from the Wilson snipe, because the feather music of the latter is continued throughout the incubation period.

Nesting.—The same observer describes the nesting habits as follows:

The fantastic shaped shore lines of the lowland brackish ponds furnish ideal homesites for the vivacious black turnstone as it usually chooses, upon which to nest, a little projecting grass-covered point or islet. Quite near the water's edge the bird will hollow a depression in the flattened dead grass and here, often upon the almost bare mud with the eternal ice strata only a few inches beneath, the hardy mother will successfully bring forth a brood. Little effort is made to build a home and the only material therein is the grass that previously grew on or about the site and is flattened down into the basin of the nest. At times there is almost no lining beneath the olive-hued eggs and they are then so besmeared that they appear to have been deliberately rolled in the mud. Occasionally, however, the bird will nest some distance away from the water on a dry site, but always the mode of construction is the same. The range of measurements of 27 nests is: diameter of basin 3½ to 4½ inches and depth 1 to 2½ inches. The undecked nests are easy to find if bordering the pools, provided their general location is known, but the birds keep up such a continual clamor that it is difficult to guess their chosen area. In favored places they breed in such close proximity to one another that they appear to colonize. In no case like the other Charadriidae did I observe these birds about the nest to feign lameness or distress. Incubation spots were found on both of the parents.

Eggs.—I can not do better than to quote Mr. Brandt's description of the eggs, as follows:

The eggs of the black turnstone, invariably four to the nest, are subpyriform to ovate pyriform in shape, and unlike the glossy egg of the ruddy turnstone, reflect but little luster. Due to the flatness of the nest, the eggs, while they usually rest points together, do not stand as erect while being brooded as eggs of the sandpipers. The texture of the surface is smooth and the eggs are not at all fragile. The eggs of the present species are unique among the eggs of the shore birds at Hooper Bay in that the ground color, the surface markings and the underlying spots are in the same category of colors which are the olive hues, but each is a different shade. The olive of the ground color is tinged with yellowish; the surface markings are much darker, favoring the browns, while the feeble underlying spots are of a shade between the two. In consequence, the spots while fairly distinctive and seldom confluent, are not prominent, the entire egg being of an olive-like cast. The common type of ground color is "light yellowish olive" to "yellowish olive," but "buffy olive" is not rare and some are even "Vetiver green." The small end is often several shades lighter than the rest of the egg, but in a large series of specimens the ground color is very similar. The surface markings are very constant in color, ranging from "light yellowish olive" to "olive." These spots are angular and fantastical and often inclined to be streaked or faintly smeared and are not at all bold. They are numerous, often almost obliterating the ground color, and are densest about the larger end. The underlying spots are very shadowy and often almost invisible and are shades of "olive gray." On the large end of every egg there are scattered additional markings of brownish black in the form of small spots and pen-like streaks. In color and style of markings the eggs of the black turnstone, when fresh, resemble a common olive type of the American crow, but even these greenish colors fade considerably in time.

The measurements of 130 eggs average 40.9 by 28.8 millimeters; the eggs showing the four extremes measure **46** by 29.5, 41 by **30.5, 38** by 28, and 40.7 by **27.8** millimeters.

Young.—Mr. Conover says, in his notes, that "both male and female take care of the young." He obtained some data which seems to show that the eggs hatch in from 21 to 22 days. A nest was found on May 31 with four fresh eggs; in the evening of June 21 this nest contained three young, already dry, and one pipped egg; the next morning the last egg had hatched. Another nest was found on May 31 with three eggs; the next day there were four eggs; at noon on June 22 the eggs had not hatched; but at 4 p. m. the next day the nest was empty and the young had disappeared from the vicinity.

Mr. Brandt says in his notes:

We enjoyed the pleasure of seeing the downy young for the first time on June 21, and were greatly interested in them, as they had not been described or figured. They are born from the egg 21 days after incubation begins, and the mottled chick, like other shore birds, leaves its nest at once. The downy young have a remarkably protective coloration, and, furthermore, are distinguishable from any of their relatives.

Dr. E. W. Nelson (1887) says that—

when the young are able to take wing in July they leave the flats, to a great extent, and frequent the seacoast, where they keep in small straggling parties searching for food along the tide line.

Plumages.—I have never seen a young black turnstone in natal down, but Mr. Conover describes it very well, as follows:

Above mottled black and "cream buff," the black strongly predominating. Line from base of bill extending over and to the center of the eye "cream buff." Distinct loral streak of black from base of bill to eye. (Some specimens also have below this loral stripe a black spot at base of lower mandible). Lower breast, abdomen and a very small area on chin clear white. Upper throat "cream buff." Neck and upper breast mixed black and "cream buff," but without distinct mottling. Bill dark horn, iris brown, legs and feet light horn with fleshy tint. Compared with absolutely identified newly hatched chicks of *A. i. morinella*, downy young of this species have a much darker appearance. On the upper parts the buffy colors are more in the form of specklings, while in *morinella* these colors are more blotch-like. *Melanocephala* also has a very distinct dark band across the chest, while in the other species this band is very faintly indicated.

In fresh juvenal plumage, in July, the head, neck, chest, back, scapulars and wing coverts are dull, blackish brown, or "sepia," with an olive gloss; the feathers of the mantle are narrowly edged with "pinkish buff"; the scapulars are more broadly edged with the same; the median wing coverts are tipped and their white edges are tinged with the same; and the tail feathers are tipped or tinged with the same color. These buffy edgings have mostly worn away or faded out to dull white before the birds migrate. Probably a partial postjuvenal molt in the fall produces a first winter plumage, which is like the adult, except that some of the juvenal wing coverts and a few scapulars are retained. A first nuptial plumage appears in a young bird, collected on March 17, which is beginning to acquire the white spots of the nuptial plumage on the head and breast, but still has some old, worn, juvenal scapulars and wing coverts. The young bird evidently acquires the adult winter plumage at the first post-nuptial molt the following summer.

Adults have a partial prenuptial molt of the body plumage in March and April and a complete postnuptial molt in August and September. The adult nuptial plumage is characterized by the white lores, the small white spots on the forehead, and the larger white spots on the sides of the head, neck and chest; otherwise it is like the winter plumage, though the latter is somewhat lighter brown on the throat and chest.

Food.—The food of the black turnstone has evidently not been carefully analyzed, but it apparently consists of small marine animals such as barnacles, slugs, small mollusks, and crustaceans, such as are eaten by surf birds and other turnstones. Grinnell, Bryant, and Storer (1918) mentioned one, taken in Alaska in May, that had been feeding on heath berries. They quote Bradford Torrey (1913), as to the method of feeding, as follows:

They were feeding in three ways. Sometimes they followed the receding breaker, gleaning from the surface, as it seemed, such edibles as it had washed in. Mostly, however, they busied themselves upon the wet sand just above the last reach of the falling tide.

Once they found a place where the shrimps or prawns were evidently more plentiful than elsewhere, and it was amusing to see how eagerly they worked, each determined to get its full share of the plunder. Thrusting their short, stout bills into the sand, they drew out their squirming prey, dropped it on the sand, picked it up and shook it, and dropped it again, till finally they had it in condition for swallowing. These manoeuvers they repeated, all in desperate competitive haste, till the beach within a circle of a few feet in circumference was thickly dotted with minute hillocks of sand, such as I should never have attributed to the work of any bird, had it not been done before my eyes. Then the supply seemed to be exhausted, and they moved on in search of another bonanza.

At other times they resorted to patches of seaweed lying here and there a little higher on the beach, turning them bottom side up, or brushing them aside, to feast on such small game as had taken shelter underneath. Their action here was like that of a dog when he buries a bone by pushing the earth over it with his nose. They lowered their heads, and with more or less effort according to circumstances accomplished their purpose. If the obstacle proved too heavy to be moved in this manner, they drew back a little and made a run at it as men do in using a battering-ram. More than once I saw them gaining the needed momentum by this means. They quarreled now and then over the business, and once two of them faced each other, bill to bill, like gamecocks—a most unusual proceeding among waders, firing off little fusilades of exclamations meanwhile. The turnstones' disagreements were of the briefest, however, slight ebullitions of temper rather than any actual belligerency.

Behavior.—S. F. Rathbun has sent me the following notes on the behavior of this species:

The tide was just turning from flood, the time being about 3 p. m. On the rocks of the jetty whose top at the edge of the beach was just above the water's surface and at times submerged by incoming waves, was a small flock of black turnstones numbering about 30. At first the birds would not allow a close approach but as we slowly neared them would take wing and, then coming together in close formation, circle in unison, rising and falling, close to the water's surface to soon return and alight on the tops of the nearly submerged rocks. It was a beautiful sight to see them in flight as then the black and white of their plumage was strongly in contrast. After a short time the birds allowed a much closer approach for on one occasion we stood within 20 feet of the flock. As the tide receded much more of the surface of the rocks became exposed, although at times the waves dashed completely over them, and whenever this occurred it forced the turnstones to take wing. Sometimes one of the birds would be caught by an incoming wave and would then emerge in flight from the water, scattering the spray in all directions. But the rapid recession of the tide soon gave plenty of ground to search for food and in this all the birds became busily engaged. Some of the birds while so doing would climb the very abrupt surface of the rocks, clinging to the moss, which adhered, while examining with their bills the crevices of the rocks and also the moss for crustaceans and minute molluscs. At times one or more would rest on the side of a rock in perfect repose and evidence that a few were paired was seen by the fact that two often persisted in remaining in company.

One thing proved somewhat amusing to us, that although during the time the birds had been feeding they were repeatedly drenched by spray from the waves striking the rocks, when they finally ceased to feed a few at odd times would drop into the shallow water at the base of the rocks to bathe by dashing it over themselves, following which they would dabble about.

Mr. Brandt says in his notes:

Among the shore birds breeding along the coast of Bering Sea there is none more interesting and fascinating than this black and white turnstone. When the mud about the edges of the ponds and tidal sloughs begins to soften, and the accumulated snow water starts to move, this bird appears enlivening the bleak, cheerless marshes with its loud-toned cries and butterfly-like appearance. In the lowland area it is the commonest shore bird, and its contrastive black and white figure is doubly conspicuous, because it resents intrusion of its haunts and sallies forth to meet the approaching stranger; whereas the rest of the shore-bird tribe found there either skulk away or exhibit indifference. As the Pacific godwit is the self-appointed guardian of the upland tundra, so the black turnstone patrols the lowlands, often to the dismay of the hunter or the irritation of the ornithologist. In spite of its chunky body and comparatively short wings, it is gifted with elegance and swiftness of flight. It does not, like the phalarope, afford an inviting target for the young native hunters, because not only does it scold on the wing, but it also moves so nervously while on the ground that it is not quiet there even for a fraction of a second. No doubt the hunting jaegers consider it the pest of the flats, for while passing through its domain, these freebooters are usually being annoyingly followed by one or more of these fiery and courageous defenders.

Mr. Turner (1886) says that—

The sea-otter hunters, both native and white, detest this bird, as it frequents the places most resorted to by marine mammals and is certain to give alarm to the otter or seal which the hunter is endeavoring to approach.

Voice.—Doctor Nelson (1887) says: " It has a habit of circling around the intruder, during the nesting season, with a fine, clear, peeping cry like the syllables *weet*, *weet too-weet*, as it moves restlessly about. When disturbed in the vicinity of its nest it also has a sharp *peet*, *weet*, *weet*, very similar to the well known note of the spotted sandpiper." Mr. Turner (1886) says that when alarmed and " taking flight they utter a rattling scream " which is quite startling.

Field marks.—When standing the black turnstone may be recognized by its uniformly dark head, neck, and chest, above a white belly; it lacks the white throat of the turnstone, and its upper parts appear all dark. But when flying it shows white patches quite similar to those of the turnstone, a patch in the center of the back, the base of the tail, a stripe in the scapulars and a broad band across the wings; there is rather more white in the wing than in the turnstone and the black tips extend along only the outer half of the wing; the surf bird has a much narrower white stripe in the wing.

Fall.—Doctor Nelson (1887) says, of the departure of these birds from Alaska: " In autumn they move gradually to the southward, until by the last of August they become rarer, and during the first half of September all have gone with the exception of an occasional straggler found along the seashore." The migration extends down the coast as far as Lower California.

Winter.—Carl Lien regards them as common winter residents on Destruction Island, off the coast of Washington. He says, in his notes that they " begin to arrive about July 26 and leave in the spring the first week in May. They confine themselves entirely to the reefs and are very sociable, keeping up a continual chatter. The Aleutian sandpiper and a surf bird or two will nearly always be found among them. About 75 or 100 birds winter here."

A. B. Howell (1917), referring to the islands off the coast of southern California, says that "this is by far the most abundant shore bird on the islands, much more so than on the mainland, occurring in flocks of as many as 30 individuals, and frequenting the rockiest shores."

DISTRIBUTION

Range.—Pacific coast of North America, casual in northeastern Siberia.

Breeding range.—So far as known, the black turnstone breeds only on the Alaskan coast, the breeding range appearing to extend from Chichagof Island on the south, north to probably Montague Island, Ugashik, Nushagak, Hooper Bay, the Yukon Valley, St. Michael, Cape Prince of Wales, and probably the Kobuk River.

At this season it also has been detected on Wrangel Island, and Herald Island (Nelson) but is not known to breed, while nonbreeders have been noted south on the coast at British Columbia, Skidegate; Oregon, Yaquina Bay; California, Farallon Islands, Monterey Bay, Point Pinos, and San Miguel Island; and Lower California, Los Coronados Islands.

Winter range.—The winter range of the black turnstone extends north nearly to the breeding grounds and but little south of the southern limit of the nonbreeders. They have been noted in winter north rarely to Alaska (Craig and Howkan). Also in southern British Columbia (Victoria); Washington (Bellingham Bay, Smith Island, Dungeness, and Clallam Bay); Oregon (Yaquina Bay and Netarts Bay); California (Eureka, Tomales Bay, San Francisco, Monterey, San Miguel Island, Santa Cruz Island, San Pedro Bay, Santa Catalina Island, San Clemente Island, and San Diego County); and lower California (San Quintin Bay, probably San Geronimo Island, Magdalena Bay, and Santa Margarita Island).

Migration.—Because of the presence of individuals throughout the year in practically the entire range of the species, migration data are not significant.

The following dates of spring arrival are, however, available: Alaska, Admiralty Island, April 17; Juneau, April 29; Forrester Island, May 6; Bethel, May 12; Craig, May 15; and Nulato, May 16. Dates of fall departure from Alaska are Nushagak, September 22; Homer, September 26; St. Lazaria Island, September 30; and Wrangel, November 4.

Casual records.—On August 15, 1912, a flock of 20 was observed at Chaun Bay, northeastern Siberia (Thayer and Bangs). A specimen in the collection of the Philadelphia Academy of Sciences was presumed to have been obtained in India, but the occurrence has been challenged (Hartert) on the basis that proof is lacking that the specimen was actually there collected. The record accordingly is eliminated for lack of evidence.

Egg dates.—Alaska: 96 records, May 28 to July 5; 48 records, May 31 to June 1.

Family HAEMATOPODIDAE Oyster catchers

HAEMATOPUS OSTRALEGUS Linnaeus

EUROPEAN OYSTER CATCHER

Contributed by Francis Charles Robert Jourdain

HABITS

This is another species whose claim to a place in the American list rests on its occurrence in Greenland, but, rather curiously, all the occurrences are recorded from the west coast and not from the east side, as might have been expected. Herbert Winge, in 1898, was able to record six specimens obtained at various localities between 1844 and 1898, as well as one reported in the autumn of 1893. As it is a breeding species in Iceland, its occurrence in Greenland from time to time may well be expected.

Courtship.—As the oyster catcher is an extremely striking bird, with its strongly contrasted plumage of black and white, red bill, and flesh-colored feet, and is also by no means scarce and very noisy, its breeding habits challenge attention, and a good deal has been recorded on the subject by Edmund Selous, Seton Gordon, William Farren, and others. It is on the whole a sociable species, and one peculiar characteristic is that in the middle of the breeding season it is not unusual to find three birds together, either resting or in flight, without any open signs of hostility. According to Selous, these associations are often composed of two males and one female, and as he observed them together not only in the early part of the pairing time but also late in the season, it would seem that, except perhaps just in the height of sexual activity, the social instinct is predominant. The following account is taken from William Farren's (1910) description of the "Piping parties":

The piping of the males depends on the presence of the female. Another male in the neighborhood hears the note, becomes interested, pipes a little, and then flies direct to where the performance is taking place. He places himself by the side of the other male and the two pipe together to the female. Generally unresponsive, the female may walk away, when she is followed by the two males, who continue their serenade. In one instance observed by Mr. Selous, the female flew down to a lower shelf of rock and the two males piped down to her from above; and when at last she flew away they, with a few single querulous notes, assumed their ordinary attitude and walked disconsolately about. The flight of the female always ended the performance.

Mr. Selous (1901), in describing the piping serenade of the male, states that when he begins he faces her, but "having once begun he seems more enthralled by his own music than by her and will turn from side to side or even right round and away from her, as though in the rhythmical sway of his piping." This remarkable song is audible a long way off and is described well by Selous as "an ear-piercing clamor." He writes it as "*kee kee kee kee kervee kervee kervee kervee kervee*," becoming fainter in its later stages and ending in a long-drawn out quavering trill. In some cases, according to Selous, the female also pipes, and one pair, presumably already mated, will chase another pair, all four piping together. He also instances a case in which an unattached male approached close to where a hen was sitting; she left the nest, and, joining her mate, the two advanced on the intruder, piping a warning, and put him to flight.

Perhaps the fullest study of the subject is contained in a paper by J. S. Huxley and F. A. Montague (1925). Here the piping is described thus:

Any number of birds, from one to seven or eight or possibly more, may take part in it. Typically, what occurs is as follows: One or more birds begin the loud characteristic piping which typically again is given in a special attitude, the head and bill directed straight downward, the bill held open and very slightly vibrated, the neck thrust forward so that the shoulders show up with rather a horsey look. Sometimes, but not always, the whole body is bobbed up and down at intervals in the way common to so many wading birds, but not very markedly. Frequently, but again not always, the performers trot rapidly round when piping, very often close side by side and usually in a serpentine course, with short quick steps. Sometimes one of the performers will suddenly turn right round through 180° in the middle of its performance; one I saw turn through the complete 360° in two spasms.

Huxley and Montague have shown that this piping performance has not only a sexual significance, but that it also plays a number of other rôles in the bird's life, as, for instance, in unilateral courtship, mutual courtship, aggression, sexual jealousy, territorial jealousy, and probably social excitement—that is, under all forms of strong emotion except fear. Details are given of observed piping by large parties, two pairs, threes (the commonest form), " twos " and "ones."

Another courtship activity recorded in the same paper is the slow-butterflylike flight with the wing beats at about half the ordinary pace carried out by a solitary bird. Coition is apparently preceded by no preliminary ceremony whatever, the initiative coming from the male, the female standing quite still and giving no visible indication of readiness to pair. For a fuller discussion on the origin and meaning of the piping ceremony the reader is referred to the paper by Huxley and Montague (1925).

Nesting.—There is considerable variation in the nesting sites of this species. Among sand dunes it is often to be met with on the summit of a dune, a mere hollow in the sand. On shingle banks it may be among pebbles, sometimes lined with small white stones or shells, obviously brought by the bird. Other nests are placed in natural recesses of rock, on grass land, when at times quite a good-sized nest is built of any wrack or rubbish available. While in many cases the nest is placed close to the shore it is frequently found in Scotland by the sides of the rivers far inland, and on the continent, in level grassy meadows in the reclaimed marshes of Holland. Exceptionally nests have been recorded from a larch wood on an island, among bracken, etc.

Eggs.—The normal number of eggs is three, but two are also commonly found, and in some districts sets of four are not at all uncommon. Exceptionally five and six eggs have been found together. As is usually the case where three eggs are normal, they are oval rather than pyriform in shape and in color are yellowish stone or ochreous, boldly marked with spots, streaks, and scrawls of blackish brown and some ashy shell marks. There are also variations with warm rufous tinge in the ground color, or very rarely with a pale bluish ground or even pure white. Some sets are boldly blotched with sepia black. The measurements of 100 British eggs, made by the writer, average 57 by 40.07 millimeters; the eggs showing the for extremes measure 70.1 by 37.4, 62.1 by 48.9, 51.6 by 40.4, and 62.6 by 35 millimeters.

Young.—Incubation is carried on by both sexes, but probably the female takes the greater share, and she has been observed to sit for three or four hours without changing. The period is estimated at 21 days (Paynter), 23 to 24 days from finding full set (W. Evans), and 24 days (Faber). Probably the latter estimates are more correct. The young when hatched remain a day or two in the nest and are attended by their parents for at least five weeks after hatching, according to J. M. Dewar (1908). R. H. Brown, however, estimates it as about 29 days.

Plumages.—The plumages and molts are fully described in A Practical Handbook of British Birds edited by H. F. Witherby (1920).

Food.—Chiefly marine mollusca; univalves, such as limpets (*Patella*), small whelks (*Buccinium*) and periwinkles (*Litorina*) and bivalves, including mussels (*Mytilus edulis*), cockles (*Cardium*), etc. Also annelida, earthworms, and sandworms; crustacea (shrimp, etc.), and insects, including Coleoptera, Diptera and their larvae (especially Tipulidae), Lepidoptera (larvae and pupae of Noctuidae); occasionally Holothurians and some vegetable matter (grass seeds, grains, etc.).

Behavior.—The feeding habits of the oyster catcher have been exhaustively studied by J. M. Dewar, who has given the results of his investigations in a paper in the Zoologist for 1908. Careful examination of the shells of mussels showed that about 78 per cent were opened by means of a stab from the bill through the dorsal border. As in their normal position this is the exposed portion this is perhaps natural, but only those which have the valves slightly opened are vulnerable and the weakest point in the shell is on the ventral border, which is rarely exposed. The best feeding time is when the scalps are first exposed by the ebb, before the mussels have closed their shells and again when the tide is rising and the shells are just beginning to open again. When the tide is up the birds rest in long lines, head to wind. The flight of the oyster catcher is peculiar and characteristic, the wings being rapidly moved within a very short arc, so that they seem to be vibrated at the tips.

Enemies.—The oyster catcher has few natural enemies, though no doubt occasionally a nest is destroyed by Corvidae (hooded crows and carrion crows or rooks).

Fall.—The Misses Rintoul and Baxter have observed a tendency to the renewal of spring display during the autumn months. The Shetland birds move southward in September and do not return until March.

Winter.—During the winter months the oyster catcher is generally to be met with in flocks, easily recognized by their striking coloration and characteristic notes. The wild ringing sound of their calls, a clear *kle-eep*, coming from hundreds of throats at once, is, as T. A. Coward remarks, as delightful as it is harmonious.

DISTRIBUTION

Breeding range.—Iceland, the Faroes, the British Isles, and the coasts of northern Europe from northwest Spain and Brittany to the Baltic, and along the Scandinavian coast to Archangel, probably also in the Black and Caspian Seas, south to Macedonia and Asia Minor. Replaced by allied forms in Asia and Japan.

Winter range.—Some winter in Iceland, many in the British Isles, but the main winter quarters lie in the Mediterranean, the Red Sea, the Persian Gulf, the African coast south to Mozambique, and India.

Spring migration.—At the Straits of Gibraltar the passage northward takes place in April and May, according to Farrer, and in Malta in April, but in the eastern Mediterranean it is apparently rather earlier, for in Greece one has been noted at the end of March, and Lindermeyer gives mid-April as the main passage date. At Corfu it has been seen on March 20. Danish birds arrive on their breeding grounds late in March or early in April, and in southern Sweden in March while in Finland not till late April.

Fall migration.—Gaetke noted many young birds on Heligoland in August and migrants have been recorded for Greece in mid-August. The autumn movement is more prolonged than the spring passage, owing to the presence of young as well as adults, so that at Malta birds have been recorded from August to November. The main passage at Tangier takes place in October.

Casual records.—Winge's Greenland records include two dated April 19, 1885, near Nanortalik, and one on June 16, 1888, north of Jakobshavn. It has also been noted on Jan Mayen (A. G. Nathorst and L. C. Masters); once north of Bear Island, July 28, 1910; and once in Spitsbergen, July, 1906 (Mathey-Dupraz).

Egg dates.—From the British Islands, April 26 to June 26 (25 dates), May 2 to 29 (14 dates), June 4 to 26 (10 dates); Holland, May 11 to 25 (25 dates); Norway, June 10 to 27 (8 dates); Faroes, May 15 to 22 (3 dates).

HAEMATOPUS PALLIATUS PALLIATUS Temminck

AMERICAN OYSTER CATCHER

HABITS

The usual impression that one gets of this large and showy wader is a fleeting glimpse of a big, black and white bird disappearing in the distance over the hot, shimmering sands of our southern beaches. It is one of the shyest and wildest of our shore birds, ever on the alert to escape from danger; I have never shot one and seldom have had half a chance to do so. Even during the breeding season when its anxiety for its eggs or young prompts it to be less wary, it flies around the intruder in wide circles, well beyond gun range, yelling its loud notes of protest. It was evidently about as shy even in the days of Audubon and Wilson, for both mentioned its wariness.

It was much commoner in those days, of course, and enjoyed a much wider distribution. Audubon (1840) records it at Portland, Me., and as breeding on the south coast of the Labrador Peninsula; it seems as if he must be mistaken about the latter locality, although it is interesting to note that the European oyster catcher breeds as far north as Russian Lapland.

The oyster catcher prefers the same broad, sandy beaches as the Wilson plover and the least tern select for their breeding grounds; and at other seasons it frequents similar resorts with all the little sand plovers and beach birds. The small plovers are protectively colored, but the oyster catcher is not only big, but is most conspicuously colored. Perhaps it needs no protection against the ordinary foes of the little fellows; and evidently its wits are sufficient protection against larger enemies. But in spite of the fact that it is well able to take care of itself, its range has been greatly restricted and its numbers very much reduced during the past 50 years. It formerly bred abundantly on Cobb Island, Virginia, but when we were there in 1907 we saw very few and found no nests or young.

H. H. Bailey (1913) says:

This large, showy bird fell an easy mark to the spring gunners, breeding as it did during the height of the spring migration of "beach birds," from May 10 to 25. Nesting among the sand dunes or flat beaches back from the ocean, over which the spring gunners tramped daily, these birds were right in the line of travel, so to speak, and were either killed or their nests broken up.

Recent records from South Carolina, where we found it common in 1915, seem to indicate that it is becoming rarer even there. And during the whole winter of 1924 and 1925, spent on the west coast of Florida, I saw only one.

Nesting.—While visiting Arthur T. Wayne on the coast of South Carolina, we found three nests of three eggs each of the oyster catcher on May 22 and 23, 1915. The first two nests were on the broad, sandy beaches of Bull's Island among numerous scattered bits of shells and pebbles. The other was on Vessel Reef in Bull's Bay, a low, flat, sand reef, with small areas of marsh grass in which willets were nesting. The oyster catchers' nests were all on the higher parts of the dry, flat, sand beaches, well above high-water mark; they were mere hollows in the sand, entirely without lining, on little mounds of sand or elevations, where the birds could have a good outlook; usually a regular pathway of footprints in the sand led up to the nest. The birds were never seen on or near the nests, but were flying about in the distance making a great outcry. The nests were easily found by following the tracks and looking for the little elevations. Several pairs of Wilson plover were nesting near them.

W. J. Erichsen (1921) "found a single egg deposited in a depression on top of a wall of oyster shells on Raccoon Key," but an unusually high tide washed the egg away. He also found a set of three eggs "in a slight depression on top of a bank of oyster shells which had been thrown up by the surf"; and he says that "where nesting sites of this character can be found, this species always selects them."

Oyster catchers' nests are usually not near together, but M. H. Burroughs has sent me some notes on some nests he found in Glynn County, Ga., that are an exception to the rule. A set of four eggs, two fresh and two partially incubated, was "on a slight mound, the nest having a few broken bits of shells in it and nearly entirely surrounded with a rim of broken bits of shells, evidently raked up by the birds." Six feet away, under a log "which had both ends resting on mounds of sand," was a set of two. There were two other nests, each about 150 feet away in different directions.

George B. Sennett (1879) found a nest on Padre Island, Tex., which was quite different; he describes it as follows:

> The nest was situated on dry mud a rod or so from the water, and was simply a slight depression, of the size of a small tea plate, lined with shells and pieces of shells; none of them were larger than an inch in diameter, and most much smaller. They were chiefly small oyster shells, and were placed more on the sides than at the bottom of the nest. No particle of grass or anything else but shells composed the nest. What was strange to me was that on the island where I found it not a shell or piece of one could be seen, and these must have been brought by the bird itself from the adjacent shell islands or oyster beds. This was the only nest found on the island.

Walter J. Hoxie (1887) claims to have seen an oyster catcher remove the eggs from a nest he was watching. Both birds were standing near the nest, when "one flew off to a distance of about 100 yards." He then observed:

> After looking carefully about for a few minutes, he gave a call, and his mate rose from her nest and joined him. They seemed to be making a lot of fuss out there, kicking up the sand, squatting down, and cackling like mad. In a few minutes, though, they seemed to get over this excitement and one bird came flying back and settled on the eggs. Now she began to act strangely, wiggling round and squatting down again, and I began to think she was going to lay another egg, when off she went and joined her mate who welcomed her coming with the most extravagant cries and gestures. But she sat down quite still and demure. I was about to rise and look for my third egg when I saw her coming back. Again she went through the same operation and her second welcome was, if possible, more exuberant than the first. Then all was quiet; one bird sat on the sand and the other stood silently by her, and though I waited some time longer they showed no sign of returning again to their eggs, and I could only conclude that they had seen me watching them and would not come back until I went away. So I arose from my uncomfortable position and went to pick up the eggs, when to my surprise the little

hollow in the sand was empty. While I was watching the curious antics of the female she had lifted the eggs between her legs and carried them off. So without giving time for her to repeat the offense I hurried to her new quarters and secured them successfully.

Eggs.—The oyster catcher lays two or three eggs, more often the latter I believe, and very rarely four. They are ovate to elongate ovate in shape and have only a very slight gloss. The ground color is usually " cartridge buff," sometimes it is " pale olive buff " and rarely " deep olive buff " or dull " chamois." They are irregularly and rather sparingly marked with spots and small blotches, occasionally a few scrawls of black, brownish black, or very dark browns, " mummy brown " or " bister," and underlying spots in various shades of " Quaker drab " or " mouse gray." The measurements of 56 eggs average 55.7 by 38.7 millimeters; the eggs showing the four extremes measure **62** by 38.9, 57.2 by **42.2**, **51.8** by 39.9, and 52 by **33.5** millimeters.

Young.—The period of incubation for the European species is from 21 to 24 days, and both sexes share in this duty, though it is mostly performed by the female. We have no data on this subject for the American species, but probably it is not much different. When the temperature is just right the eggs may be left exposed to the sun, but at night or when it is too hot or too cold they are covered by the incubating bird, whose judgment is reliable in such matters.

The young are able to run soon after they are hatched, and when they become strong on their legs they can run so fast that it is very difficult to catch them. At a note of warning from their watchful parents, they squat in the sand, or against some convenient object, and remain perfectly still, their protective coloring making them almost invisible. Both parents show their anxiety by flying around, usually at a safe distance, and yelling their loud notes of protest. Herbert K. Job (1905) once hunted thoroughly over a barren strip of sand, where he knew there was a young oyster catcher, without success; he was about to give it up and go away, when he saw a little wisp of driftweed at the water's edge on a strip of bare wet sand; and beside it the young bird was lying, flat on the sand and absolutely motionless. It did not move while he was photographing it, but as soon as it was touched off it ran as fast as it could go.

Plumages.—In the downy young oyster catcher the upper parts are grizzled with pale buff and dusky; the down is dusky basally and heavily tipped with " pinkish buff "; the crown is mostly pale buff and the hind neck and throat are mostly dusky; the back appears more mottled and has two quite distinct, broad stripes of brownish black; there is sometimes a similar broad stripe on the nape; a narrow black line runs from the bill, through the eye and to the nape; a broad black band extends from behind the wing to the tail; below this and the dusky throat the under parts are white. When very young, the bill is decidedly hooked at the extreme tips of both mandibles. In a young bird, about one-quarter grown, the primaries are bursting their sheaths and the white greater coverts are growing; the juvenal plumage is appearing on the back, scapulars and lesser wing coverts; these new feathers are " sepia," broadly tipped with " cinnamon "; the crown is " bister," faintly tipped with " cinnamon "; the white plumage is coming in on the breast.

In full juvenal plumage, when the young bird is nearly fully grown, these colors are somewhat paler; the feathers of the back, scapulars and wing coverts are " Saccardo's umber," tipped with " clay color " or " cinnamon-buff "; the crown, sides of the head, and upper chest are dark " bister," tipped with " cinnamon-buff "; the chin and throat are mottled with sepia and buffy; the upper tail coverts are white, tipped with buffy; the tail is dark " bister," tipped with " cinnamon-buff "; and the under parts are white. By the end of July the buffy tips on the mantle have nearly disappeared by wear. Early in September the post-juvenal molt begins; this involves the body plumage, but not all the scapulars and wing coverts and not the tail.

The first winter plumage is like the adult, the head and neck being " fuscous " or " Chaetura black " and the mantle " deep mouse gray." Young birds can be distinguished by a somewhat slenderer bill and by the retained and worn juvenal wing coverts, scapulars, and tail feathers. At the first prenuptial molt they become fully adult.

Adults have a partial prenuptial molt in late winter and early spring, involving the body plumage and most of the scapulars and wing coverts, and a complete postnuptial molt in late summer and fall.

Food.—Audubon (1840) says of the feeding habits of the oyster catcher:

I have seen it probe the sand to the full length of its bill, knock off limpets from the rocks on the coast of Labrador, using its weapon sideways and insinuating it between the rock and the shell like a chisel, seize the bodies of gaping oysters on what are called in the Southern States and the Floridas " raccoon oyster beds," and at other times take up a " razor handle " or solen, and lash it against the sands until the shell was broken and the contents swallowed. Now and then they seem to suck the sea urchins, driving in the mouth, and introducing their bill by the aperture, without breaking the shell; again they are seen wading up to their bodies from one place to another, seizing on shrimps and other crustacea, and even swimming for a few yards, should this be necessary to enable them to remove from one bank to another without flying. Small crabs, fiddlers, and sea worms are also caught by it, the shells of which, in a broken state, I have found in its gizzard in greater or less quantity. Frequently, while on wet sea beaches, it pats the sand to force out the insects;

and in one instance I saw an individual run from the water to the dry sand with a small flounder in its bill, which it afterwards devoured.

Wilson (1832) says that they probe in the sand " with their long, wedgelike bills in search of small shellfish. This appears evident on examining the hard sands where they usually resort, which are found thickly perforated with oblong holes, 2 to 3 inches in depth." He seemed to doubt the reports of their eating oysters, but C. J. Maynard (1896) writes:

When the outgoing tide left the tops of the oyster bars exposed, they would come flying silently in, at first singly, then in pairs, while groups of a few would follow, until, at last, they would come in flocks of a dozen or more. They would alight among the oysters and when the bivalves gaped open, as is their habit when the water first leaves them, the birds would thrust in the point of their hard, flat bills, divide the ligament with which the shells are fastened together, then, having the helpless inhabitant at their mercy, would at once devour it. They were not long in making a meal, for specimens which I shot after they had been feeding a short time were so crammed that by simply holding a bird by the legs and shaking it gently the oysters would fall from its mouth.

Behavior.—Oyster catchers are strong, swift fliers and at times are graceful and elegant in their movements. They are striking birds in flight, displaying to good advantage their conspicuous patterns of black and white and their bright red bills. Their movements on the ground are equally graceful as they walk sedately along the beach or wade out into the water until the waves lap their breasts. They can swim perfectly well and can even dive readily if necessary. Audubon (1840) describes their flight evolutions as follows:

Now wheeling with wonderful impetuosity they pass within a hundred yards of you, and suddenly checking their flight return, not low over the water as before, but high in the air. Again, they form their ranks in a broad front, and, again, as if suddenly alarmed by the report of a distant gun, they close pell-mell, and dip towards the sands or the waters. Shoot one at such a moment and you may expect to kill another; but as this is done, the wary birds, as if suddenly become aware of your intentions, form themselves into a straggling line, and before a minute has elapsed, far beyond reach, and fading on the view, are the remaining oyster catchers.

Voice.—The loud, striking notes of protest, heard as the oyster catcher flies around the intruder on its breeding grounds, are quite unlike any other bird notes; they sound like *wheep, wheep, wheeop*, and are both vehement and penetrating. John T. Nichols says in his notes: "The oyster catcher has a creeking note, *crik, crik, crik*, etc., used when the bird takes wing. A more striking cry, *cle-ar*, suggests the flight calls of the willet and the black-bellied plover."

Field marks.—A large wader, with black head and dark upper parts, with a big white patch in its long, pointed, black wings and with white under parts, can be nothing but an oyster catcher. No other bird of strong, steady flight can be mistaken for it. One is seldom near enough to recognize its long, red bill.

Winter.—The oyster catcher is resident throughout most of its range, but it retires in winter from the northern portion of its breeding range. Arthur T. Wayne (1910) says:

In the winter the oyster catcher is very gregarious and it is not unusual to see flocks containing from 20 to 75 individuals. The majority of these birds are undoubtedly migrants from points to the northward of South Carolina and not the resident breeding birds, which apparently go together in pairs or small flocks of from 4 to 6 individuals.

DISTRIBUTION

Range.—Atlantic and Gulf coasts of the United States, Central and South America. The American oyster catcher has been subdivided into several races the exact range of which it is not now possible to define. This should be borne in mind in considering the following outline, which undoubtedly includes the ranges of *H. p. durnfordi*, *H. p. prattii*, and *H. p. pitanay* (Murphy). Generally speaking, *prattii* is assumed to be confined to the Bahama Islands, *durnfordi* the South Atlantic coast of South America, and *pitanay* the Pacific coast of South America.

The species is not migratory in a strict sense, although the examples breeding at the north and south extremes of the range probably retire short distances toward the Equator when forced to do so by climatic conditions.

The range may be outlined as follows: North to Texas (Brownsville, Padre Island, Corpus Christi, and Galveston); Louisiana (Isla a Pitre); probably rarely Alabama (Petit Bois Island); and formerly southern New Jersey (Great Egg Harbor). East to formerly southern New Jersey (Great Egg Harbor, and probably Seven-mile Beach); probably rarely Maryland (Ocean City); Virginia (Hog Island, Cobb Island, and Smiths Island); North Carolina (Cape Hatteras, Ocracoke Inlet, and mouth of Cape Fear River); South Carolina (Waverly Mills, Raccoon Key, Bulls Bay, Sullivan Island, and Frogmore); Georgia (Savannah, St. Simon Island, and Cumberland); Florida (St. Johns River, Charlotte Harbor, and probably Cape Sable); the Bahama Islands (Abaco, Andros, Long, Mariguana, and Inagua Islands); probably Porto Rico (Desecheo Island); Venezuela (Aruba, Curacao, and Cumana); Brazil (Santa Catherina, Cajetuba, Rio de Janeiro, Sapetiba Bay, and Iguape); Uruguay (La Paloma and Montevideo); and Argentina (Lavalle, Cape San Antonio, Mar Chiquita, and mouth of Chubut River). South to Argentina (mouth of Chubut River) and Chile (Ancud). West to Chile (Ancud, Algarrobo, Santiago, Chanaral, and Atacama); Peru (San Nicolas Bay, Independencia Bay, Pisco Bay, Chilca, and San Lorenzo); Ecuador (Gulf of Guayaquil and Santa Elena); Panama

(Pearl Island) ; Yucatan (Cozumel Island and Merida) ; and Texas (Brownsville).

Casual records.—The American oyster-catcher has on a few occasions been directed north of its normal range. Among these occurrences are: New York, a specimen in New York Harbor, May 28, 1877, one about March 9, 1880, at Ponquogue, and one at Greenport, June 2, 1882; Massachusetts, two in August, 1899, at Chatham, one in April, 1885, at Monomoy Island, two seen September 10, 1924, at Eastham, a pair taken in 1837, at Marshfield, and one in Boston harbor, killed prior to 1814; Maine, reported by Audubon as occurring at Portland but this record is considered doubtful; New Brunswick, a specimen has been reported upon the authority of Boardman (Baird, Brewer, and Ridgway, 1884) as taken at Grand Manan. This last is considered unsatisfactory as being indefinite, while Audubon's statement that it bred in Labrador is probably an error.

Egg dates.—Virginia: 37 records, April 26 to July 9; 19 records, May 21 to June 19. South Carolina and Georgia: 25 records, March 27 to June 25; 13 records, May 5 to 23. Texas: 8 records, March 29 to May 5.

HAEMATOPUS PALLIATUS FRAZARI Brewster

FRAZAR OYSTER CATCHER

HABITS

It now seems to be generally recognized that this Lower California oyster catcher is a subspecies of *palliatus*, although William Brewster (1902) originally described it as a full species and named it in honor of the veteran collector, M. Abbott Frazar. Dr. Robert Cushman Murphy (1925) has recently reviewed this group, in which he has designated six subspecies of *palliatus*, inhabiting various parts of North and South America. To *frazari* he assigns the following limited range:

Pacific and Gulf coasts of Lower California and adjacent parts of Mexico, including the islands; formerly northward in Ventura County, Calif.; southward along the west coast of Mexico to Tepic and Jalisco, and at least occasionally to Guerrero.

Ridgway lists specimens from Sihutanejo and Acapulco, Guerrero. Contrary to former opinion, however, this race is principally confined to the zone of generally arid shores centering about the peninsula and gulf of Lower California. Its range approaches or meets that of *H. p. palliatus* on the more tropical coast farther south, probably at a point not far from the Isthmus of Tehuantepec.

He says of the characters of this race:

The subspecific characters of *frazari*, which include darker coloration of the brown upper parts than in *palliatus*, heavy mottling on the breast along the junction of white and black plumage, longer wing and tail (?), and smaller bill and feet, are given fully by Ridgway. The latter makes no mention, however, of the practical elimination of the white blotching of the primaries, a character which this oyster catcher shares with other western races. In most specimens the white spots are wholly lacking, but a few show obsolescent white or mottled markings of the conventional pattern on the eighth or ninth from the outermost quill. It is interesting to note that the mottling of the breast, which is so strongly typical of this race, appears to be carried by a genetic factor deeply rooted in the species as a whole. Scarcely any large series of *H. p. palliatus*, indeed, lacks one or more birds of this type. In its maximum expression, however, when the whole breast, sides, flanks, and under tail coverts are heavily blotched, the character is peculiar to *frazari*.

W. Leon Dawson (1923) says, in explanation of its disappearance from California:

By reason of its conspicuous coloration, as well as its excessive noisiness, the Frazar oyster catcher has suffered a fatal prominence. Its former appearances on the Channel Islands (as far north as Ventura County) were concluded by an early martyrdom, and the species is rare even in its primitive fortresses on Los Coronados Islands.

Nesting.—Being more permanently resident than even its eastern relative, the Frazar oyster catcher has no migrations, except its late summer wanderings, and remains on its breeding range throughout the year. As to the nesting habits of this bird at Scammons Lagoon, Lower California, Griffing Bancroft (1927) writes:

They climb up on the shell banks which are the back stops of the beaches and there build their nests. The shell banks are usually a yard or two above high-water mark; they are flat and quite narrow and often have fingerlike projections of 50 yards or so on the same level, running toward the east. Typically, all these higher flats are composed of nothing but shell, largely unbroken and of a size which may be judged in the accompanying illustration. Sand and small impurities have been garnered by the wind. The oyster catcher likes to build her nest where she has an unobstructed view in all directions, securing to herself the opportunity of slipping off unobtrusively at the approach of an enemy. But she is a stupid bird and is easily satisfied with a makeshift which seems to her to accomplish her purpose but in reality does not do so at all. So on some of the earthen islands we find her nesting on little mounds, from which, it is true, she can see, but to only a matter of a few feet.

In the Gulf of California the favorite site for an oyster catcher is the end of the rather long spits of cobblestones. These are so nearly level that a sitting bird has an unobstructed view for a hundred yards. There she builds a nest of fine hard material—small pebbles and bits of shell. And as she can not have broken the larger stones that were originally on the site she must have removed them. I use the analogy for Scammons. Instead of breaking the shells with her powerful bill she probably pulls them out of the way until she has a flat circle about 10 inches across. This clearing she lines as neatly as tile work, and on them deposits her eggs, one, two, or three. The breeding season seems quite long, as we found both well-developed young and fresh eggs. I have observed parents with their young long after the latter had taken wing, and so feel sure that the oyster catchers raise but one brood a year.

I have a set of two eggs in my collection, taken by W. W. Brown, jr., May 2, 1912, on San Jose Island; the nest is described as a depression, lined with pebbles, in a crevice on top of a jagged, weather-worn ledge, 40 feet above the surf. There are two sets in the Thayer collection, taken by Mr. Brown near La Paz on March 24 and 26, 1909; one nest was similarly located to mine; " it was out of reach of the surf, but the spray, no doubt, dampened it in rough weather "; the nest from which the other set was taken is described as " a depression in the sand." The eggs were laid on the bare ground, there being no lining to the nest whatever. It was 80 feet from the surf.

Eggs.—The Frazar oyster catcher lays two or three eggs, sometimes only one. These are practically indistinguishable from those of the American oyster catcher. The measurements of 27 eggs average 57.1 by 38.8 millimeters; the eggs showing the four extremes measure **60.9** by 37.8, 59.8 by **41.5**, **50.7** by 40.8, and 60.7 by **36** millimeters.

Plumages.—The plumages and molts from the downy stage to maturity are apparently the same as in the American oyster catcher. Mr. Bancroft (1927) has published some interesting notes on his observations, which suggest that either there are two color phases in these birds or that they interbreed with black oyster catchers (*bachmani*) and produce hybrids; I am inclined to accept the latter theory, but quote from Mr. Bancroft's (1927) paper, as follows:

Ninety per cent of the oyster catchers had white bellies, the rest had all their underparts black, with the exception of one, whose belly was streaked black and white. Mr. Chester Lamb wrote me that on Natividad Island there was a much larger percentage of mixed underparts than we found. That there were two phases of one bird instead of two distinct species in the lagoon was apparent to anyone watching them. There was only one case I observed of a black bird paired with another black; all the other blacks had white-bellied mates. The difference between the birds was limited to the abdomens; place a mixed series in a row with the backs up and one could not tell one bird from another. In their conduct, especially when their nests were threatened, there were no differences at all. I feel perfectly safe in saying there were no black oyster catchers (*Haematopus bachmani*) present. I have seen too many of them, from Monterey to Sitka, not to know by heart every movement they will make and every note they will utter when one trespasses on their home sites. The actions and the cries, and especially the noise, are more unusual and more uniform than those of any bird with which I am acquainted. They fly customarily in a complete half circle from the rocks on one side to those on the other, the birds keeping near each other and almost always close to the water. The noise is incessant, shrill, continuous, and loud beyond belief. The contrast with the birds in Scammons is striking. There, both the white and the black bellied are almost as silent as plover and try to win safety by a prodigious show of indifference. There is little or no excitement while we tramp around the nesting sites. When the parents find we can not be persuaded to follow them away they take up positions 50 to 100 feet from us and there remain motionless, usually as long as we are in the neighborhood. There is another great difference between *H. bachmani* and the black phase in the south. The former is decidedly darker than the latter, especially on the back, whereas true *Haematopus frazari* from both ends of the Gulf appear to be the same as those in Scammons.

We found and photographed a pair of downy young not over a few days old. These youngsters are obviously of the white and black types, respectively; we have the skins to show that there is no photographic illusion here. So we have very strong evidence that the black and the white phases do mate and do produce fertile offspring and that the young have partaken of the coloring, one of one parent and one of the other. These little birds are not mongrels, though we know from some adults that occasionally there are chicks which do inherit from both parents. Comparison shows that the white-breasted downy does not differ at all, at a cursory glance, from a baby taken on Coronado Island in the Gulf.—

Behavior.—The same observer writes:

Scammons Lagoon is a haven for oyster catchers, or appears so to such of us as are accustomed to but an occasional pair scattered along the various islands and rocky projections in the more northerly Pacific Ocean. There are at least two or three hundred oyster catchers fairly evenly distributed over the islands we visited, with an occasional pair or so on favorable mainland strands. When the tides are going down vast stretches of hard flats are exposed and become feeding grounds. The birds pursue the receding water even to the point of wading, and there they hunt the small marine life on which they live. When the tide turns they use the black levels as a lounging place until driven ashore by the sea. They are markedly indolent and slow in movement and, when undisturbed, never appear the least bit busy.

Walter E. Bryant (1890) says:

I found this oyster catcher tolerably common at Magdalena Bay and northward, and on Santa Margarita Island. They were mated in January. They were rather shy, running rapidly on the beach, and if approached, taking wing with loud, clear, whistling notes, and after flying some distance, alighting again at the water's edge. Their food was chiefly small bivalves found in the gravelly beach.

DISTRIBUTION

Range.—Pacific coast of Mexico and southern California. The Frazar oyster catcher is confined chiefly to Lower California (San Quintin Bay, Cedros Island, Natividad Island, San Roque, Ascuncion Island, Los Coronados Islands, Carmen Island, San Jose Island, La Paz, and Todos Santos); and the mainland coast of Mexico; Sonora (Quotlá); Sinaloa (Altata); Nayarit (Maria Madre Island, Maria Cleofas Island, Tres Marias, Isabela Island, and San Blas); and Guerrero (Sihutanejo, and Acapulco). The species is of casual occurrence (formerly more common) on the coast and islands of southern California (San Diego, Santa Barbara Island, San Clemente Island, and Ventura County). Breeding records for California are not satisfactory.

Egg dates.—Lower California: 39 records, March 24 to June 24; 20 records, April 22 to May 13.

HAEMATOPUS BACHMANI Audubon

BLACK OYSTER CATCHER

HABITS

At the northern end of their range, in the Aleutian Islands, I first became acquainted with these big black waders. Here we frequently saw them at various points, as we entered or left the rock-bound harbors, sitting in little groups or in pairs on the rocks or outlying ledges. They were surprisingly inconspicuous on the wet and dark colored rocks, which were often half hidden in the prevailing fogs. They seemed to fit very well into their dark and gloomy surroundings. They were not particularly shy, as they stood on the slippery rocks and nodded to us with grotesque dignity, or as they flew out around us uttering their loud and penetrating cries.

Courtship.—W. Leon Dawson (1909) writes:

Left to themselves, the birds are no Quakers, and the antics of courtship are both noisy and amusing. A certain duet, especially, consists of a series of awkward bowings and bendings in which the neck is stretched to the utmost and arched over stiffly into a pose as grotesque as one of Cruikshank's drawings, the whole to an accompaniment of amorous clucks and wails.

Nesting.—We did not succeed in finding any nests of the black oyster catcher in the Aleutian Islands, though they undoubtedly breed there. Dr. W. H. Dall (1873) found two nests in the Shumagins on June 23, 1872; there were two eggs "in one nest and one in another, if nest it could be called, being simply a depression in the gravel of the beach without even a straw to soften its asperities." Dr. Wilfred H. Osgood (1901) found a nest in the Queen Charlotte Islands, which "was merely a hollow about 2 inches deep and almost perfectly round, scooped out of a weedy turf a few feet above high-water mark. The bottom of the hollow was covered with bits of broken stone, evidently placed there by the old bird."

Referring to the rocky islands off the coast of Washington, Mr. Dawson (1909) says:

The eggs of the black oyster catcher, normally three in number, are oftenest placed in the hollow of a bare rock, lined with a pint or so of rock flakes, laboriously gathered. Occasionally bits of shell, especially the calcareous plates of the goose barnacle, are added by way of adornment. Now and then the wader emulates the gull and prepares a careful lining of grasses. One such nest with three eggs I passed repeatedly, on Carroll, languidly supposing it to be a gull's until Professor Jones exclaimed over it.

For a nesting site the upper reaches of barren reefs or shoulders are chosen, but on the smaller rocks, where the waders have exclusive rights, the eggs may be lodged on the very crest of the islet. Again, upon Destruction Island, we found eggs on a coarse beach gravel, where to the protection of color, stone-gray with black spots and blotches, was added the almost perfect assimilation of form to that of the rounded pebbles.

Eggs.—The black oyster catcher lays two or three eggs, occasionally only one and more rarely four. They are very much like the eggs of the American oyster catcher, but perhaps they will average a little more buffy. They are ovate in shape and have a very slight gloss. The ground colors vary from " cream buff " to " olive buff." They are usually quite evenly covered with small spots and scrawls of black or very dark browns, " bister " or " Dresden brown," and various shades of " Quaker drab." The measurements of 44 eggs average 56.2 by 39.5 millimeters; the eggs showing the four extremes measure **62** by 39.5, 58.1 by **42, 51** by 39.5 and 54.2 by **37.5** millimeters.

Young.—Nothing seems to be known about the period of incubation or whether both sexes share in it; both parents are interested in the care of the young and are very solicitous for their welfare. Dr. Joseph Grinnell (1910) writes:

Dixon observed two half-grown young running about on the beach; but as soon as the old birds, which were always watching, saw anyone approaching a warning note was uttered, at which the young ones promptly squatted among the rocks wherever they happened to be, even if in the edge of the water. They remained perfectly quiet and blended so nicely with their surroundings that it was difficult to locate them even when they had been previously seen from a distance. The old birds attacked and put to rout any gulls or ravens that approached the vicinity.

Prof. Harold Heath (1915) says:

The precocial fledglings very early accompanied their parents on short journeys about the cliffs, and within a week after hatching were observed pecking at limpets, although it is highly probable that for several days thereafter they depended on the old birds for the greater part of their food supply. During this time the young resemble diminutive ostriches, with thick-set legs, big feet, and fluffy plumage, which, it may be added, harmonizes to a high degree with the surroundings. Furthermore, they have the same habit of hiding the head when it is not possible to conceal the entire body beneath a stone.

Plumages.—The downy young black oyster catcher is a swarthy little fellow, clothed in short, thick, dark, grizzly down, a color pattern well suited for concealment among the dark rocks where it lives. The down of the upper parts is basally sooty black and very dark gray, but the pale buffy tips give the bird its grizzly appearance. There is an indistinct loral and postocular stripe and two broad, more distinct, parallel stripes down the back of brownish black and two blackish areas on the thighs; between the back stripes and on the rump the buff tips produce a transverse barred effect. The underparts are dull grays, darkest on the throat and breast and lightest on the belly; the sides are faintly mottled or barred.

In juvenal plumage the young bird is much like the adult, but the feathers of the wing coverts, scapulars, tertials, and back are tipped with narrow terminal bars of "cinnamon buff" and subterminal blackish bars; those of the flanks, thighs, and under tail coverts are tipped with the same color; most of these buffy tips soon wear away, and before the postjuvenal molt there are only a few spots left on the wing coverts, scapulars, and tertials, some of which are carried through the winter as evidences of immaturity. I have not seen enough material collected at the proper seasons to trace the molts of adults.

Food.—Mr. Dawson (1909) writes:

Even when visiting the mainland shore, which is not often, the bird confines its attention to the barnacle-covered rocks and high-lying mussel beds. Its food consists of marine worms and crustaceans of various sorts, barnacles, limpets, and especially mussels. Its stout, chisel-shaped beak enables it to force an entrance into the most refractory mussel shell and to sever as by a knife the strong adductor muscles, which hold the valves together. Its feet also are large and strong, and the toes are provided with an elaborate set of pectinations which enable the bird to maintain a footing upon the most slippery rocks. If the foothold on a sloping rock is anywise precarious, the bird retreats backward and uphill by means of these convenient calks.

A. B. Howell (1917) says:

Certain rocky points are selected by the birds, and to these are often brought the barnacles which they pry off the rocks. These are worked over at leisure, and at one such depot on the Coronados, which I examined there was fully a bushel of shells.

Behavior.—The flight of the black oyster catcher is strong and direct, but it seemed to me to be rather slow and heavy. Lucien M. Turner (1886) says:

The flight consists of a few rapid strokes of the wing, followed by a sail for a few yards. It is sluggish when on the wing, and flies with difficulty, and rarely long continued. When alarmed it flies over the water within a few yards of the shore, and in going from one point of rocks to another it either makes the trip in easy stages from one large rock to another, or else follows the indentations of the shore line. The bird is always on the alert, and not at all shy. It generally sees the hunter long before he suspects the presence of the bird. The bird either squats in a depression of the rocks, or stealthily creeps to the top of some huge bowlder, where it utters a piercing, whistling chatter like that of a policeman's rattle. It causes the intruder long search to discover the presence of the bird, for its color is so near that of the rocks it frequents that it is not easily detected. The note is then answered by another bird, so that in a few minutes a dozen may be chattering hideously, making the hunter wonder where all the birds came from so suddenly, as all the birds within hearing assemble on the first note of alarm.

Carl Lien says in his notes:

If occasion requires these birds are good swimmers and, if pursued when crippled, will dive deep and long. A very alert bird and always first to give alarm.

Voice.—My notes refer to the cries of this bird as loud, penetrating screams, sounding like *whee-up*, or *whee-ep*.

Doctor Dall (1873) says:

They utter, when disturbed, a peculiar, low whistle; which once heard, is likely to be remembered; and they have a habit of standing on the beach or rocks a little way apart, and whistling to one another; one calling and the other answering; and keeping it up for half an hour at a time. It is one of the most peculiar birds of the region, in its motions, having a grave, solemn and stilted gait, and bobbing its head up and down with every step.

Winter.—As the black oyster catcher is practically resident all the year round throughout most, if not all, of its range, there is not much to be said about its migrations, though there is probably some shifting of individuals. Doctor Dall (1873) refers to it as a summer visitor in the Aleutian Islands, but Mr. Turner (1886) records it as a permanent resident there.

DISTRIBUTION

Range.—Pacific coast of North America and Lower California.

Breeding range.—The breeding range of the black oyster catcher extends north to Alaska (Atka Island, Range Island, St. Paul Harbor, Montague Island, Hinchinbrook Island, Sitka, St. Lazaria Island, probably Kuiu Island, Coronation Island, Prince of Wales Island, Forrester Island, and Duke Island); south along the coast of British Columbia (Porcher Island, Skidegate, Vancouver Island, and New Westminster); Washington (Bellingham Bay, Waldron Island, Flattery Rocks, Quillayute Needles, Destruction Island, and Copalis Rock);.Oregon (Three Arch Rock, Newport, and Bandon); California (probably Prince Island, Eureka, probably the Farallon Islands, Point Pinos, San Miguel Island, Santa Cruz Island, Anacapa Island, San Clemente Island, and San Diego); and Lower California (Todos Santos, San Benito Island, Cedros Island, Natividad Island, Abreojos Point, and Los Coronados Islands).

Winter range.—In winter, the black oyster catcher is found throughout its breeding range except (normally) in Alaska and (probably) northern British Columbia. It has, however, been recorded on one occasion at this season, in Alaska, St. George Island, January 12, 1917 (Hanna).

Migration.—An early date of arrival in Alaska is Unalaska Island, April 29, while a late date of departure is St. Lazaria Island, September 30.

Egg dates.—Alaska: 14 records, June 5 to 26; 7 records, June 13 to 23. British Columbia: 13 records, May 27 to June 20; 7 records, June 6 to 12. California: 7 records, May 25 to June 10.

Family JACANIDAE Jacanas

JACANA SPINOSA GYMNOSTOMA (Wagler)

MEXICAN JACANA

HABITS

The American jacanas are now split into three species and three additional subspecies, six forms in all.   They are widely distributed throughout the American Tropics.   All are closely related and all are much alike in habits.   The above form barely comes within the range of our check list, as a rare straggler from Mexico into the valley of the lower Rio Grande near Brownsville, Tex.

I have never seen this curious bird in life, but can imagine that it must be a beautiful sight to see it tripping lightly over the floating lily pads, supported on its long toes, where it seems to be actually walking on the water; and it must produce quite a surprising thrill as it spreads its wings to fly, displaying the conspicuous yellow-green patches in its wings, which flash in the sunlight like banners of golden yellow.   It seems like a strange connecting link between the spur-winged plovers and the rails or gallinules.

It is a sedentary species of decidedly local distribution and seldom strays far from its favorite breeding haunts.   Thomas S. Gillin, who has sent me some very good notes on this bird, describes its habitat as follows:

I learned of a lake a few miles from Tampico and on my first visit to this lake on April 3, 1923, I found over a dozen birds feeding and chasing one another over the floating vegetation.   As the first sets of eggs were found on April 25 I apparently found them right in the midst of the mating season. The lake where I found them was about a half mile long and from 100 to 250 yards wide, curved and irregular in outline.   Nowhere in the lake was the water over 4 feet deep except where the alligators had their holes; in some of these spots there was always danger of getting in over one's head.   Scattered through the lake were a few stunted trees similar in appearance to our sour gum, *Nyssa sylvatica*, and in the decayed stump of one of these trees I found a nest of the black-bellied tree duck.   About one-third of the surface of the lake was open water and the remaining two-thirds was covered with a floating plant, each individual plant measuring about 12 inches across and resembling lettuce that has not headed up, though the leaves were coarser, more like cabbage leaves.   As this did not have its roots extending into the mud the entire mass of vegetation at times changed its position as the direction of the winds might change and cause the entire body of vegetation, and again only part of it, to drift to the opposite side of the lake.   The jacanas were, to all appearances, in no way inconvenienced by these free rides, though there was always the danger that the eggs might be lost by the move.   During my many visits to this lake from early April until the middle of August I always found the jacanas playing or feeding over the surface of the vegetation.   At times the green herons, little blue herons, and an occasional gallinule, least bittern, or redwing would be seen feeding on the surface of the lake.

Courtship.—He refers to the courtship, which must be a very pretty performance, as follows:

During courtship the birds raise their wings over their backs very much as the Bartramian sandpipers do and flirt their wings at each other as if they were attempting to strike one another with the sharp spurs with which their wings are armed.

Nesting.—In the above locality, Mr. Gillin found 38 nests of this jacana between April 25 and August 15, 1923, of which he says:

I sometimes surprised the birds on their nests, but as a usual thing they would leave the nest at the first alarm. The number of eggs was invariably four, though in one case I collected a set of three. The nests consisted of a few bits of green leaves of cat-tails and small pieces of the green leaves of the plants on which they nested, in all nests containing fresh eggs, though in cases where the eggs were incubated the nest material had sometimes turned brown. There was merely enough material to prevent the eggs from rolling apart or falling through into the water, though in most cases the bottom side of the eggs was laying in the water. One day while watching the lake from a blind I saw a jacana go to its eggs and stand over them apparently shading them from the hot sun; this position was maintained for five or six minutes; no attempt was made to warm the eggs by sitting on them; at the end of this shading of the eggs the birds went back to feeding near by.

The late Frank B. Armstrong distributed a large number of eggs of the jacana, taken by his collectors across the Rio Grande in Mexico, mostly near Tampico or somewhere in the State of Tamaulipas. His data describe the nests as made of floating weeds or trash on or under the leaves of lilies or other floating plants, in fresh water ponds.

Eggs.—The jacana's eggs are as unique as the bird itself, and can not be mistaken for anything else. They are ovate to short ovate, or even rounded ovate, in shape; and they are decidedly glossy. The ground colors vary from " buckthorn brown " or " Isabella color " to " chamois." They are well covered with fantastic scrawls and tangled, fine, pen-like lines of black; these markings are usually quite evenly distributed, but they are sometimes concentrated more thickly at either end or in the middle. The set almost invariably consists of four eggs, but I have records of a few sets of five and of three; Mr. Gillin's series consists of 37 sets of four and one set of three. The measurements of 50 eggs average 30.1 by 23 millimeters; the eggs showing the four extremes measure **31.8** by 23.3; 31 by **24.1**, **28.3** by 22.2, and 30.3 by **21.7** millimeters.

Young.—Mr. Gillin says in his notes:

The young run as soon as hatched, and in one case, when I came upon a nest in which the young had just hatched, they dived into the water and swam under the water for several feet before they came to the surface.

Plumages.—The young jacana in natal down is beautifully marked with rich colors. A narrow frontal line, the sides of the face and the entire underparts are white; the crown and nape are " ochraceous orange," centrally browner, with a black "crow-foot" on the occiput, and with a black line from the eye to the hind neck, which is dusky black; the central area of the back and rump is "burnt sienna," bordered on each side by a band of "ochraceous buff," below which is an indistinct dusky band; the thighs and the inner joints of the wings are "burnt sienna"; the outer joint of the wing is white; the tail and sides of the rump are jet black; and the tibia are dusky black. The bright colors become duller as the chick grows older.

In fresh juvenal plumage the crown and occiput are "warm sepia," the feathers faintly tipped with "cinnamon"; the back and sides of the neck are brownish black; the back, scapulars and wing coverts are from "sepia" to "Saccardo's umber," the feathers broadly tipped with "tawny" and with a subterminal dusky bar; a black stripe extends from the eye to the back side of the neck and a broad stripe of "cream buff" from the lores, over the eyes to the nape; the sides of the head, chin, throat, and underparts are white, suffused with "cream buff" on the breast. A partial postjuvenal body molt takes place during the fall, or else the edgings entirely wear away leaving only the plain colors of the upper parts, the juvenal wing coverts and some of the scapulars. In late winter or early spring, from January to April, a nearly, if not quite, complete prenuptial molt takes place, which produces a plumage which is practically adult, including the frontal shield. I have no data on the molts of adults. In this plumage the female is decidedly larger, is somewhat more brightly colored and has a larger frontal shield.

Food.—Mr. Gillin says in his notes:

The food of the jacanas must consist of minute insect life that they are able to find on this floating vegetation as they are very active and seem to spend practically all their time feeding, which would lead to the conclusion that their food is secured in very small morsels or else they require a great amount of food.

Behavior.—P. L. Jouy says in a letter:

When standing in reeds or sedge they frequently stretch the neck up straight on the lookout. They also have a curious habit of extending the wings and raising them up over the back until they meet. This, I suppose, is a kind of signal, the green of the primaries being conspicuous for a long distance when in this position. On wounding one of these birds I found that it was a very fair swimmer, and when I overtook it, it dived, to my astonishment, with as much confidence as a grebe, and I never saw it again.

Mr. Gillin writes:

On three different occasions I had wounded birds submerge themselves about a foot below the surface of the water for several minutes before I could locate them and secure them by hand. They clutched whatever was available with their feet and from above looked just as comfortable under water as a quail or grouse would be crouching in the leaves of a briar patch.

Voice.—Mr. Jouy says that "these birds have a noisy, cackling voice when they take flight." Mr. Gillin refers to their note as "a plaintive call of alarm."

Fall.—In September he found them "in flocks, flying around and feeding on ponds where" he "was sure that they had not bred." The records of this form in Texas and the West Indian form in Florida were probably due to such post-breeding wanderings.

DISTRIBUTION

Range.—The Mexican jacana is found in Mexico and the lower Rio Grande valley in Texas. The range extends north to Sinaloa (Mazatlan); and southern Texas (Brownsville). East to Texas (Brownsville); Tamaulipas (Alta Mira, and Tampico); Vera Cruz (Jalapa, Alvarado, Tlacotalpan, and Cosamaloapam); Tabasco (Barra de Santa Ana, San Juan Bautista, and Teapa); and Quintana Roo (Cozumel Island). South to Quintana Roo (Cozumel Island); Chiapas (Tonala); Oaxaca (Zanatepec and Santa Efigenia); and Guerrero (Acapulco). West to Guerrero (Acapulco); Michoacan (Lake Patzcuaro); Colima (Rio Coahuayana, and Manzanillo); Jalisco (Zapotlan, Ocotlan, and Guadalajara); Nayarit (Tepic, San Blas, and Santiago); and Sinaloa (Mazatlan).

In October, 1899, a specimen of jacana was killed on Pelican Bay, Lake Okeechobee, Fla. (Mearns, 1902); and H. H. Bailey (1925) reports another seen by his father in Osceola County, Fla., in March, 1911. The first of these has been tentatively referred by Ridgway (1919) to *Jacana s. violacea*, a race found in Cuba, Haiti, Jamaica, and Porto Rico.

Egg dates.—Northeastern Mexico: 68 records, April 25 to August 15; 34 records, May 28 to July 13.

REFERENCES TO PUBLICATIONS

AIKEN, CHARLES EDWARD HOWARD, and WARREN, EDWARD ROYAL.
1914—The Birds of El Paso County, Colorado.
ALEXANDER, WILFRID BACKHOUSE.
1926—Notes on a Visit to North Queensland. The Emu, vol. 25, pp. 245–260.
AUDUBON, JOHN JAMES.
1840—The Birds of America, 1840–1844.
AUGHEY, SAMUEL.
1878—Notes on the Nature of the Food of Birds of Nebraska. First Report
U. S. Entomological Commission, Appendix 2.
BAILEY, ALFRED MARSHALL.
1925–26—A Report on the Birds of Northwestern Alaska and Regions
Adjacent to Bering Strait. Part 6. The Condor, vol. 27, pp.
232–238.
BAILEY, FLORENCE MERRIAM.
1916—A Populous Shore. The Condor, vol. 18, pp. 100–110.
BAILEY, HAROLD HARRIS.
1913—The Birds of Virginia.
BAILEY, HARRY BALCH.
1876—Notes on birds found breeding on Cobb's Island, Va., between May 25
and May 29, 1875. Bulletin of the Nuttall Ornithological Club,
vol. 1, pp. 24–28.
BANCROFT, GRIFFING.
1927—Breeding Birds of Scammon's Lagoon, Lower California. The Condor,
vol. 29, pp. 29–57.
BARROWS, WALTER BRADFORD.
1912—Michigan Bird Life.
BARTSCH, PAUL.
1922—A Visit to Midway Island. The Auk, vol. 39, pp. 481–488.
BATES, JOHN MALLORY.
1907—The Bartramian Sandpiper. Bird-Lore, vol. 9, p. 84.
1916—Incubation Period of Killdeer. The Wilson Bulletin, vol. 28, pp.
150–151.
BAYNARD, OSCAR EDWARD.
1914—Photographing Birds' Nests. Bird-Lore, vol. 16, pp. 471–477.
BEAUPRÉ, EDWIN.
1917—The American Golden Plover in Eastern Ontario. The Ottawa
Naturalist, vol. 31, pp. 29–31.
BENNERS, GEORGE B.
1887—A Collecting Trip in Texas. Ornithologist and Oologist, vol. 12, pp.
49–52, 65–69, and 81–84.
BERGTOLD, WILLIAM HENRY.
1917—A Study of the Incubation Periods of Birds.
1926—Passerine Birds Eating Trout Fry. The Auk, vol. 43, p. 558.
BIGELOW, HENRY BRYANT.
1902—Birds of the Northeastern Coast of Labrador. The Auk, vol. 19,
pp. 24–31.

BISHOP, LOUIS BENNETT.
    1900—Birds of the Yukon Region. North American Fauna, No. 19.
BRADBURY, WILLIAM CHASE.
    1918—Notes on the Nesting of the Mountain Plover. The Condor, vol. 20,
        pp. 157–163.
BRETHERTON, BERNARD J.
    1896—Kadiak Island. A Contribution to the Avifauna of Alaska. The
        Oregon Naturalist, vol. 3, pp. 45–49; 61–64; 77–79; 100–102.
BREWER, THOMAS MAYO.
    1878—Changes in our North American Fauna. Bulletin of the Nuttall
        Ornithological Club, vol. 3, pp. 49–52.
BREWSTER, WILLIAM.
    1887—Three New Forms of North American Birds. The Auk, vol. 4,
        pp. 145–149.
    1902—Birds of the Cape Region of Lower California. Bulletin of the
        Museum of Comparative Zoölogy at Harvard College, vol. 41, No. 1.
    1925—The Birds of the Lake Umbagog Region of Maine. Bulletin of the
        Museum of Comparative Zoölogy at Harvard College, vol. 66,
        Part 2.
BROOKS, ALLAN [CYRIL].
    1924—Two New Sandpiper Records for California. The Condor, vol. 26,
        pp. 37–38.
BROOKS, WINTHROP SPRAGUE.
    1915—Notes on Birds from East Siberia and Arctic Alaska. Bulletin of
        the Museum of Comparative Zoölogy at Harvard College.
BROWN, WILLIAM JAMES.
    1912—Additional Notes on the Birds of Newfoundland. The Ottawa Natu-
        ralist, vol. 26, pp. 93–98.
    1916—Killdeer Plover. The Ottawa Naturalist, vol. 30, pp. 113–114.
BRYANT, HAROLD CHILD.
    1914—A Survey of the Breeding Grounds of Ducks in California in 1914.
        The Condor, vol. 16, pp. 217–239.
    1914a—Bird Destroyers of Grasshoppers in California. The Auk, vol. 31, pp.
        168–177.
BRYANT, WALTER (PIERC)E.
    1890—A Catalogue of the Birds of Lower California, Mexico. Proceedings
        California Academy of Sciences, ser. 2, vol. 2, pp. 237–320.
BURNS, FRANKLIN LORENZO.
    1915—Comparative Periods in Deposition and Incubation of Some North
        American Birds. The Wilson Bulletin, vol. 27, pp. 275–286.
CAHOON, JOHN CYRUS.
    1888—The Shore Birds of Cape Cod. Ornithologist and Oologist, vol. 13,
        pp. 121–124; 129–132; 153–156.
CAMERON, EWEN SOMERLED.
    1907—The Birds of Custer and Dawson Counties, Montana. The Auk,
        vol. 24, pp. 241–270.
CARROLL, W. J.
    1910—The Eskimo Curlew or Doughbird. Forest and Stream, vol. 74,
        p. 372.
CHADBOURNE, ARTHUR PATTERSON.
    1889—An Unusual Flight of Killdeer Plover (Aegialitis vocifera) along
        the New England Coast. The Auk, vol. 6, pp. 255–263.

CHAMBERS, WILLIE LEE.
    1901—Curious Nest of Anna's Hummingbird. The Condor, vol. 3, p. 105.
    1904—The Snowy Plover. The Condor, vol. 6, pp. 139–140.
CHAPMAN, ABEL.
    1889—Bird Life of the Borders.
CHAPMAN, FRANK MICHLER.
    1891—On the Birds Observed Near Corpus Christi, Texas, during Parts
        of March and April, 1891. Bulletin of the American Museum of
        Natural History, vol. 3, pp. 315–328.
    1912—Handbook of Birds of Eastern North America.
    1926—The Distribution of Bird Life in Ecuador.
CHISLETT, RALPH.
    1923—The Whimbrel in Shetland. British Birds, vol. 17, pp. 150–154.
    1925—Turnstones on a Baltic Islet. British Birds, vol. 19, pp. 2–9.
CLARK, AUSTIN HOBART.
    1905—The Migration of Certain Shore Birds. The Auk, vol. 22, pp. 134–
        140.
    1905a—Shore Birds Eating Small Fish. The Auk, vol. 22, pp. 208–209.
    1910—The Birds Collected and Observed During the Cruise of the United
        States Fisheries Steamer "Albatross" in the North Pacific Ocean,
        and in the Bering, Okhotsk, Japan, and Eastern Seas, from April
        to December, 1906. Proceedings of the U. S. National Museum,
        vol. 38, pp. 25–74.
CLEAVES, HOWARD HENDERSON.
    1908—Sandpiper in a Tree. The Journal of the Maine Ornithological
        Society, vol. 10, pp. 85–86.
CONOVER, HENRY BOARDMAN.
    1926—Game Birds of the Hooper Bay Region, Alaska. The Auk, vol. 43,
        pp. 162–180; 303–318.
COOKE, WELLS WOODBRIDGE.
    1897—The Birds of Colorado. The State Agricultural College, Bulletin 37,
    1912—Distribution and Migration of North American Shore Birds. United
        States Department of Agriculture, Biological Survey Bulletin No.
        35, Revised.
COUES, ELLIOTT.
    1874—Birds of the North-West.
CRIDDLE, NORMAN.
    1908—Some Bird Habits. The Ottawa Naturalist, vol. 22, pp. 153–156.
DALL, WILLIAM HEALEY.
    1873—Notes on the Avifauna of the Aleutian Islands, from Unalaska,
        Eastward.
DAVIES, SUTTON A.
    1895—In Quest of Birds on the Muonio River. Zoologist, Third Series,
        vol. 19, pp. 326–335.
DAWSON, WILLIAM LEON.
    1909—The Birds of Washington.
    1911—Another Fortnight on the Farallones. The Condor, vol. 13, pp. 171–
        183.
    1923—The Birds of California.
DEWAR, JOHN M.
    1908—Notes on the Oyster catcher. Zoologist, 1908, pp. 201–212.

DILL, HOMER R., and BRYAN, WILLIAM ALANSON.
  1912—Report of an Expedition to Laysan Island in 1911. United States
    Department of Agriculture, Biological Survey, Bulletin No. 42.
DIXON, JOSEPH.
  1918—The Nesting Grounds and Nesting Habits of the Spoon-billed Sand-
    piper. The Auk, vol. 35, pp. 387–404.
  1927—The Surf-bird's Secret. The Condor, vol. 29, pp. 3–16.
DOOLITTLE, EDWARD ARTHUR.
  1923—Occurrence of Buff-breasted Sandpiper in Lake County, Ohio. The
    Auk, vol. 40, pp. 691–692.
DUTCHER, WILLIAM.
  1892—A specimen of Numenius arquatus said to have been taken on Long
    Island, N. Y. The Auk, vol. 9, pp. 390–392.
DWIGHT, JONATHAN.
  1893—Summer Birds of Prince Edward Island. The Auk, vol. 10, pp. 1–15.
ELLIOT, DANIEL GIRAUD.
  1895—North American Shore Birds.
ERICHSEN, WALTER JEFFERSON.
  1921—Notes on the Habits of the Breeding Water Birds of Chatham
    County, Georgia. The Wilson Bulletin, vol. 33, pp. 16–28; 69–82.
EVANS, EDWARD, and STURGE, WILSON.
  1859—Notes on the Birds of Western Spitzbergen, as observed in 1855.
    The Ibis, 1859, p. 171.
FARLEY, JOHN AUSTIN.
  1919—Mating " Song " of the Piping Plover. The Auk, vol. 36, pp. 566–567.
FARREN, WILLIAM.
  1910—In the "British Bird Book," edited by F. B. Kirkman, pp. 340–356.
FEILDEN, HENRY WEMYSS.
  1889—On the Birds of Barbados. The Ibis, 1889, pp. 477–503.
FERRY, JOHN FARWELL.
  1908—Notes from the Diary of a Naturalist in Northern California. The
    Condor, vol. 10, pp. 30–44.
FISHER, ALBERT KENRICK.
  1893—The Death Valley Expedition, North American Fauna, No. 7.
FORBUSH, EDWARD HOWE.
  1912—A History of the Game Birds, Wild Fowl, and Shore Birds of Massa-
    chusetts and Adjacent States.
  1925—Birds of Massachusetts and Other New England States.
GABRIELSON, IRA NOEL.
  1922—Short Notes on the Life Histories of Various Species of Birds. The
    Wilson Bulletin, vol. 34, pp. 193–210.
GÄTKE, HEINRICH.
  1895—Heligoland as an Ornithological Observatory.
GIBSON, ERNEST.
  1920—Further Ornithological Notes from the Neighborhood of Cape San
    Antonio, Province of Buenos Aires. The Ibis, 1920, pp. 1–97.
GIRAUD, JACOB POST.
  1844—The Birds of Long Island.
GOEBEL, H.
  Numerous articles on eggs of Russian and Siberian Birds chiefly published
    in the Zeitschrift für Oologie (und Ornithologie).
GORDON, SETON PAUL.
  1915—Hill Birds of Scotland.

GOSS, NATHANIEL STICKNEY.
    1891—History of the Birds of Kansas.
GRINNELL, GEORGE BIRD.
    1916—Willets in Migration. The Auk, vol. 33, pp. 198–199.
GRINNELL, JOSEPH.
    1900—Birds of the Kotzebue Sound Region. Pacific Coast Avifauna, No. 1.
    1909—Birds and Mammals of the 1907 Alexander Expedition to South-
        eastern Alaska. University of California Publications in Zoology,
        vol. 5, pp. 171–264.
    1910—Birds of the 1908 Alexander Alaska Expedition. University of Cali-
        fornia Publications in Zoology, vol. 5, pp. 361–428.
GRINNELL, JOSEPH, BRYANT, HAROLD CHILD, and STORER, TRACY IRWIN.
    1918—The Game Birds of California.
HANCOCK, JOHN.
    1874—(In Natural History Transactions of Northumberland and Durham,
        vol. 6 (1873), published in 1874). "A Catalogue of the Birds of
        Northumberland and Durham."
HANNA, G. DALLAS.
    1920—New and Interesting Records of Pribilof Island Birds. The Condor,
        vol. 22, pp. 173–175.
HANTZSCH, BERNHARD.
    1905—Beitrag zur Kenntniss der Vogelwelt Islands.
HART, H. CHICHESTER.
    1880—Notes on the Ornithology of the British Polar Expedition, 1875–76.
        Zoologist, 1880, p. 205.
HARTERT, ERNST.
    1920—Die Vögel der Paläarktischen Fauna.
HAVILAND, MAUD DORIA.
    1915—A Summer on the Yenesei.
    1915a—Notes on the Breeding Habits of the Asiatic Golden Plover. British
        Birds, vol. 9, pp. 82–89.
HEATH, HAROLD.
    1915—Birds Observed on Forrester Island, Alaska, during the Summer of
        1913. The Condor, vol. 17, pp. 20–41.
HENDERSON, ARCHIBALD DOUGLAS.
    1923—Nesting of the Solitary Sandpiper. The Oologist, vol. 40, pp. 55–56.
HENDERSON, JUNIUS.
    1927—The Practical Value of Birds.
HENSHAW, HENRY WETHERBEE.
    1902—Birds of the Hawaiian Islands.
    1910—Migration of the Pacific Plover to and from the Hawaiian Islands.
        The Auk, vol. 27, pp. 245–262.
HEWITSON, WILLIAM CHAPMAN.
    1856—Eggs of British Birds. Third Edition.
HOFFMAN, RALPH.
    1904—A Guide to the Birds of New England and Eastern New York.
HOSKIN, H. G.
    1893—Nesting of the Mountain Plover. The Oologist, vol. 10, p. 230.
HOWELL, ALFRED BRAZIER.
    1917—Birds of the Islands off the Coast of Southern California. Pacific
        Coast Avifauna, No. 12.

HOWELL, ARTHUR HOLMES.
    1906—Birds that Eat the Cotton Boll Weevil.   United States Department of
        Agriculture.   Biological Survey Bulletin.   25.
    1924—Birds of Alabama.
HOXIE, WALTER JOHN.
    1887—An Egg Lifter.   Ornithologist and Oologist, vol. 12, p. 129.
HUDSON, WILLIAM HENRY.
    1920—Birds of La Plata.
    1922—A Hind in Richmond Park.
HUNTER, KATHARINE UPHAM.
    1916—An Upland Plover's Nest.   Bird-Lore, vol. 18, pp. 365–366.
HUXLEY, JULIAN SOREL, and MONTAGUE, F. A.
    1925—Studies on the Courtship and Sexual Life of Birds.   V. The Oyster-
        catcher.   The Ibis, 1925, pp. 868–897.
ISELY, DWIGHT.
    1912—A List of the Birds of Sedgwick County, Kansas.   The Auk, vol. 29,
        pp. 25–44.
JEWEL, LINDSEY LOUIN.
    1913—Some North American Birds in Panama.   The Auk, vol. 30, pp.
        422–429.
    1915—The Diving Instinct of Shore-birds.   The Auk, vol. 32, p. 227.
JEWELL, H. W.
    1909—Feeding Habits of the Sandpiper.   The Journal of the Maine Orni-
        thological Society, vol. 11, p. 123.
JOB, HERBERT KEIGHTLEY.
    1905—Wild Wings.
    1911—The Spotted Sandpiper.   Bird-Lore, vol. 13, pp 221–224.
JONES, LYNDS.
    1903—The Birds of Ohio (Dawson and Jones).
JOURDAIN, FRANCIS CHARLES ROBERT.
    1907—On the Eggs of some American Limicolae.   The Ibis, 1907, pp. 517–
        518.
    1912.—The Ruff, British Bird Book (Kirkman), vol. 3, pp. 448–495.
KALMBACH, EDWIN RICHARD.
    1914—Birds in Relation to the Alfalfa Weevil.   United States Department
        of Agriculture, Bulletin 107.
KELSO, JOHN EDWARD HARVEY.
    1926—Diving and Swimming Activities Displayed by the Limicolae.   The
        Auk, vol. 43, pp. 92–93.
KNIGHT, ORA WILLIS.
    1908—The Birds of Maine.
KOPMAN, HENRY HAZLITT.
    1905—A Killdeer's Mishap.   The Auk, vol. 22, pp. 209–210.
LACEY, HOWARD.
    1911—The Birds of Kerrville, Texas, and Vicinity.   The Auk, vol. 28, pp.
        200–219.
LEWIS, HARRISON FLINT.
    1920—The Willet (*Catoptrophorus semipalmatus semipalmatus*) in Nova
        Scotia.   The Auk, vol. 37, pp. 581–582.
LITTLEJOHN, CHASE.
        1904—The Capture of Totanus glareola in Alaska.   The Condor, vol.
            6, p. 138.
McATEE, WALDO LEE.
    1911—Our Vanishing Shorebirds.   Biological Survey—Circular No. 79.

McATEE, WALDO LEE, and BEAL, FOSTER ELLENBOROUGH LASCELLES.

1912—Some Common Game, Aquatic and Rapacious Birds in Relation to Man. United States Department of Agriculture, Farmers' Bulletin, 497.

MACKAY, GEORGE HENRY.

1891—The Habits of the Golden Plover (*Charadrius dominicus*) in Massachusetts. The Auk, vol. 8, pp. 17–24.

1892—Habits of the Black-bellied Plover (*Charadrius squatarola*) in Massachusetts. The Auk, vol. 9, pp. 143–152.

1892a—Tryngites subruficollis. The Auk, vol. 9, pp. 389–390.

1892b—Habits of the Hudsonian Curlew in Massachusetts. The Auk, vol. 9, pp. 345–352.

1892c—Habits of the Eskimo Curlew (*Numenius borealis*) in New England. The Auk, vol. 9, pp. 16–21.

MACMILLAN, DONALD BAXTER.

1918—Four Years in the White North.

MANNICHE, ARNER LUDVIG VALDEMAR.

1910—The Terrestrial Mammals and Birds of Northeast Greenland. Meddelelser om Grønland, vol. 45.

MAYNARD, CHARLES JOHNSON.

1896—The Birds of Eastern North America.

MEARNS, EDGAR ALEXANDER.

1890—Observations on the Avifauna of Portions of Arizona. The Auk, vol. 7, pp. 45–55.

MERRILL, JAMES CUSHING.

1898—Spotted Sandpiper Removing its Young. The Auk, vol. 15, p. 52.

MOUSLEY, HENRY.

1916—Five Years Personal Notes and Observations on the Birds of Hatley, Stansford County, Quebec, 1911–1915. The Auk, vol. 33, pp. 57–73.

MUNN, PHILIP WINCHESTER.

1921—Notes on the Birds of Alcudia, Majorca. The Ibis, 1921, pp. 672–719.

MUNRO, JAMES ALEXANDER.

1911—The Spring Migration of Birds at Fisherman's Island, Toronto, 1910. The Ottawa Naturalist, vol. 25, pp. 27–31 and 43–48.

MURDOCH, JOHN.

1885—Report of the International Polar Expedition to Point Barrow, Alaska, Part 4, Natural History.

MURIE, OLAUS JOHAN.

1924—Nesting Records of the Wandering Tattler and Surf-bird in Alaska. The Auk, vol. 41, pp. 231–237.

MURPHY, ROBERT CUSHMAN.

1925—Notes on Certain Species and Races of Oyster-catchers. American Museum Novitates, No. 194.

NAUMANN, JOHANN FRIEDRICH.

1887–1895—Naturgeschichte der Vögel Mitteleuropas. Edited by C. R. Hennicke.

NELSON, EDWARD WILLIAM.

1880—An Afternoon in the Vicinity of St. Michael's, Alaska. Bulletin of the Nuttall Ornithological Club, vol. 5, pp. 33–36.

1883—The Birds of Bering Sea and the Arctic Ocean. Cruise of the Revenue Steamer Corwin in Alaska and the N. W. Arctic Ocean in 1881.

1887—Report upon Natural History Collections made in Alaska.

NELSON, Mrs. HENRY W.

1900—A Pair of Killdeer. Bird-Lore, vol. 2, pp. 148–150.

NEWTON, ALFRED.
  1896—A Dictionary of Birds.
NICHOLS, JOHN TREADWELL.
  1920—Limicoline Voices. The Auk, vol. 37, pp. 519–540.
NOBLE, FRANK T.
  1904—Feeding Habits of the Turnstone. Journal of Maine Ornithological
      Society, vol. 6, pp. 57–59.
NUTTALL, THOMAS.
  1834—A Manual of the Ornithology of the United States and Canada.
      Water Birds.
OSGOOD, WILFRED HUDSON.
  1901—Natural History of the Queen Charlotte Islands, British Columbia.
      North American Fauna No. 21, pp. 7–38.
  1907—Probable Breeding of the Wandering Tattler in the Interior of
      Alaska. The Auk, vol. 24, p. 340.
  1909—Biological Investigations in Alaska and Yukon Territory. North
      American Fauna No. 30.
OSMASTON, BERTRAM BERESFORD.
  1927—Notes on the Birds of Kashmir. Journal of the Bombay Natural
      History Society, vol. 32, pp. 147–148.
PAGET-WILKES, ARTHUR HAMILTON.
  1922—On the Breeding Habits of the Turnstone as Observed in Spitsbergen.
      British Birds, vol. 15, pp. 172–179.
PALMER, WILLIAM.
  1899—The Avifauna of the Pribilof Islands. The Fur-Seals and Fur-Seal
      Islands of the North Pacific Ocean. Part 3, pp. 355–431.
  1909—Instinctive Stillness in Birds. The Auk, vol. 26, pp. 23–36.
PATTEN, CHARLES JOSEPH.
  1906—The Aquatic Birds of Great Britain and Ireland.
PEARSE, THEED.
  1924—Display of the Killdeer Plover. The Canadian Field Naturalist,
      vol. 38, p. 193.
PEARSON, HENRY JOHN.
  1896—Notes on Birds Observed in Russian Lapland, Kolguev, and Novaya
      Zemlya, in 1895. The Ibis, 1896, pp. 199–225.
  1904—Three Summers among the Birds of Russian Lapland.
PHILIPP, PHILLIP BERNARD.
  1910—Birds Observed in the Carolinas. The Auk, vol. 27, pp. 312–322.
  1925—Notes on Some Summer Birds of the Magdalen Islands. The Cana-
      dian Field-Naturalist, vol. 39, pp. 75–78.
PHILIPP, PHILLIP BERNARD, and BOWDISH, BEECHER SCOVILLE.
  1917—Some Summer Birds of Northern New Brunswick. The Auk, vol.
      34, pp. 265–275.
PICKWELL, GAYLE.
  1925—Some Nesting Habits of the Belted Piping Plover. The Auk, vol. 42,
      pp. 326–332.
POPHAM, HUGH LEYBORNE.
  1897—Notes on Birds Observed on the Yenisei River, Siberia, in 1895. The
      Ibis, 1897, pp. 89–108.
  1898—Further Notes on Birds Observed on the Yenisei River, Siberia. The
      Ibis, 1898, pp. 489–520.
  1901—Supplementary Notes on the Birds of the Yenisei River. The Ibis,
      1901, pp. 449–458.

POYNTING, FRANK.
    1895–96—Eggs of British Birds.
PRAEGER, WILLIAM EMILIUS.
    1891—Protective Coloration in the Genus *Aegialitis*. The Auk, vol. 8,
        p. 236.
PREBLE, EDWARD ALEXANDER.
    1902—A Biological Investigation of the Hudson Bay Region. North Ameri-
        can Fauna No. 22.
PREBLE, EDWARD ALEXANDER, and MCATEE, WALDO LEE.
    1923—A Biological Survey of Pribilof Islands, Alaska. North American
        Fauna No. 46.
RAINE, WALTER.
    1904—Discovery of the Eggs of Solitary Sandpiper. The Ottawa Natu-
        ralist, vol. 18, pp. 135–141.
REID, PHILIP SAVILE GREY.
    1884—The Birds of Bermuda. Part 4 in Contributions to the Natural
        History of the Bermudas. Bulletin United States National
        Museum No. 25.
REY, EUGENE.
    1905—Die Eier der Vögel Mitteleuropas.
RICH, WALTER HERBERT.
    1907—Feathered Game of the Northeast.
RIDGWAY, ROBERT.
    1919—The Birds of North and Middle America, vol. 8.
ROBBINS, CHARLES ALBERT.
    1919—A Colony of Cape Cod Piping Plover. The Auk, vol. 26, pp. 351–355.
ROBERTS, THOMAS SADLER.
    1919—Water Birds of Minnesota Past and Present. Biennial Report of
        the State Game and Fish Commission of Minnesota, for the
        Biennial Period Ending July 31, 1918.
ROCKWELL, ROBERT BLANCHARD.
    1912—Notes on the Wading Birds of the Barr Lake Region, Colorado. The
        Condor, vol. 14, pp. 117–181.
ROOSEVELT, ROBERT BARNWELL.
    1884—Florida and the Game Water Birds of the Atlantic Coast and the
        Lakes of the United States.
ROWAN, WILLIAM.
    1926–27—Notes on Alberta Waders included in the British List. British
        Birds, vol. 20, pp. 2–10; 34–42; 82–90; 138–145; 186–192.
    1923—Migrations of the Golden and Black-bellied Plovers in Alberta. The
        Condor, vol. 25, pp. 21–23.
SAMUELS, EDWARD AUGUSTUS.
    1883—Our Northern and Eastern Birds.
SANDYS, EDWIN.
    1904—Upland Game Birds.
SAUNDERS, ARETAS ANDREWS.
    1926—The Summer Birds of Central New York Marshes. Roosevelt Wild
        Life Bulletin, vol. 3, pp. 335–475.
SCOTT, WILLIAM EARL DODGE.
    1892—Observations on the Birds of Jamaica, West Indies. The Auk, vol.
        9, pp. 9–15.

SEEBOHM, HENRY.
    1884—History of British Birds.
    1888—The Geographical Distribution of the Family Charadriidae, or the
        Plovers, Sandpipers, Snipes, and their Allies.
    1890—On the Birds of the Bonin Islands. The Ibis, 1890, pp. 95–108.
    1901—The Birds of Siberia.
SELOUS, EDMUND.
    1901—Bird Watching.
    1906–1907—Observations on Sexual Selection in Birds. Zoologist, 1906,
        pp. 201–219, 285–294, 419–428; 1907, pp. 60–65, 161–182, 367–381.
SENNETT, GEORGE BURRITT.
    1879—Further Notes on the Ornithology of the Lower Rio Grande of Texas.
        Bulletin of the United States Geological and Geographical Survey,
        vol. 5, pp. 371–440.
SHELLEY, LEWIS O.
    1925—A Sandpiper's Wooing. Bird-Lore, vol. 27, p. 107.
SHERMAN, ALTHEA ROSINA.
    1916—" Incubation Period of Killdeer." The Wilson Bulletin, vol. 28, pp.
        195–196.
SHICK, CHARLES SAMUEL.
    1890—Birds found breeding on Seven Mile Beach, New Jersey. The Auk,
        vol. 7, pp. 326–329.
SILLOWAY, PERLEY MILTON.
    1900—Notes on the Long-billed Curlew. The Condor, vol. 2, pp. 79–82.
    1903—Birds of Fergus County, Montana. Bulletin No. 1, Fergus County
        Free High School.
SMITH, WILLIAM GILBERT.
    1888—Breeding Habits of the Mountain Plover. Ornithologist and Oologist,
        vol. 13, pp. 187–188.
SNYDER, LESTER LYNNE.
    1924—Peculiar Behavior of the Spotted Sandpiper (Actitis macularia).
        The Auk, vol. 41, pp. 341–342.
SPURRELL, J. A.
    1917—History of a Killdeer's Nest. The Wilson Bulletin, vol. 29, pp.
        101–103.
STANFORD, JOHN KEITH.
    1927—Field Notes from East Suffolk. British Birds, vol. 21, pp. 75–80.
STEJNEGER, LEONHARD.
    1885—Results of Ornithological Explorations in the Commander Islands
        and in Kamtschatka. Bulletin of the United States National
        Museum No. 29.
STOCKARD, CHARLES RUPERT.
    1905—Nesting Habits of Birds in Mississippi. The Auk, vol. 22, pp.
        146–158.
STREET, JOHN FLETCHER.
    1923—On the Nesting Grounds of the Solitary Sandpiper and the Lesser
        Yellowlegs. The Auk, vol. 40, pp. 577–583.
SUTTON, GEORGE MIKSCH.
    1925—Swimming and Diving Activities of the Spotted Sandpiper (Actitis
        macularia). The Auk, vol. 42, pp. 580–581.
SWAINSON, WILLIAM, and RICHARDSON, JOHN.
    1831—Fauna Boreali-Americana, vol. 2, Birds.

SWARTH, HARRY SCHELWALDT.
1911—Birds and Mammals of the 1909 Alexander Alaska Expedition. University of California Publications in Zoology, vol. 7, pp. 9–172.

SWENK, MYRON HARMON.
1915—The Eskimo Curlew and its Disappearance. Annual Report of the Smithsonian Institution for 1915, pp. 325–340.
1926—The Eskimo Curlew in Nebraska. The Wilson Bulletin, vol. 38, pp. 117–118.

TAVERNER, PERCY ALGERNON.
1919—The Birds of the Red Deer River, Alberta. The Auk, vol. 36, pp. 1–21.
1926—Birds of Western Canada.

TERRILL, LEWIS McIVER.
1911—Changes in the Status of Certain Birds in the Vicinity of Montreal, P. Q. The Ottawa Naturalist, vol. 25, pp. 57–63.

THAYER, GERALD HANDERSON.
1909—Concealing Coloration in the Animal Kingdom.

THAYER, JOHN ELIOT, and BANGS, OUTRAM.
1914—Notes on the Birds and Mammals of the Arctic Coast of East Siberia. Birds. Proceedings of the New England Zoological Club, vol. 5, pp. 1–66.

"THOMPSON, ERNEST EVAN," SETON, ERNEST THOMPSON.
1890—The Birds of Manitoba. Proceedings of the United States National Museum, vol. 13, pp. 457–643.

THURSTON, HENRY.
1913—Wilson's Plover. The Warbler, vol. 7, pp. 22–24.

TORREY, BRADFORD.
1885—Birds in the Bush.
1913—Field Days in California.

TOWNSEND, CHARLES WENDELL.
1905—The Birds of Essex County, Massachusetts. Memoirs of the Nuttall Ornithological Club, No. 3.
1913—Some More Labrador Notes. The Auk, vol. 30, pp. 1–10.
1920—Supplement to the Birds of Essex County, Massachusetts. Memoirs of the Nuttall Ornithological Club, No. 5.
1920a—The Willet in Nova Scotia. The Auk, vol. 37, pp. 582–583.

TREVOR-BATTYE, AUBYN.
1895—Icebound on Kolguev.
1897—The Birds of Spitsbergen, as at present determined. The Ibis, 1897, pp. 574–600.

TROTTER, SPENCER.
1904—Some Nova Scotia Birds. The Auk, vol. 21, pp. 55–64.

TUFTS, ROBIE WILFRED.
1922—Willet Census in Nova Scotia. The Canadian Field Naturalist, vol. 36, pp. 152–153.
1925.—Further Notes on the Willet in Nova Scotia. The Canadian Field Naturalist, vol. 39, pp. 116–117.

TURNER, LUCIEN McSHAN.
1886—Contributions to the Natural History of Alaska.

TYLER, JOHN GRIPPER.
1913—Some Birds of the Fresno District, California. Pacific Coast Avifauna No. 9.
1916—Migration and Field Notes from Fresno County, California. The Condor, vol. 18, pp. 167–169.

VAN DENBURGH, JOHN.
 1919—Nesting of the Western Willet in California. The Condor, vol. 21,
     pp. 39–40.
VAN ROSSEM, ADRIAAN JOSEPH.
 1925—Observations on the Spotted Sandpiper. The Auk, vol. 42, pp. 230–
     232.
WARREN, EDWARD ROYAL.
 1912—Some North-central Colorado Bird Notes. The Condor, vol. 14, pp.
     81–104.
WAYNE, ARTHUR TREZEVANT.
 1910—Birds of South Carolina. Contributions from the Charleston Mu-
     seum, No. 1.
WETMORE, ALEXANDER.
 1916—Birds of Porto Rico. United States Department of Agriculture
     Bulletin, No. 326.
 1926—Observations on the Birds of Argentina, Paraguay, Uruguay, and
     Chile. United States National Museum, Bulletin 133.
 1927—Our Migrant Shorebirds in Southern South America. United States
     Department of Agriculture. Technical Bulletin No. 26.
WHEELWRIGHT, HORACE WILLIAM.
 1864—"An Old Bushman." A Spring and Summer in Lapland.
 1865—Ten Years in Sweden.
WHISTLER, HUGH.
 1925—The Birds of Lahul, N. W. Himalaya. The Ibis, 1925, pp. 203–205.
WHITTLE, CHARLES LIVY.
 1922—Miscellaneous Bird Notes from Montana. The Condor, vol. 24, pp
     73–81.
 1928—A Lapwing Recovery in Newfoundland. Bulletin of the North-
     eastern Bird-Banding Association, vol. 4, pp. 69–70.
WICKERSHAM, CORNELIUS WENDELL.
 1902—Sickle-billed Curlew. The Auk, vol. 19, pp. 353–356.
WILLETT, GEORGE.
 1912—Birds of the Pacific Slope of Southern California. Pacific Coast
     Avifauna, No. 7.
WILLIAMS, ROBERT WHITE.
 1919—Winter Birds of Goose Creek, Florida. The Auk, vol. 36, pp. 45–46.
WILSON, ALEXANDER.
 1832—American Ornithology.
WITHERBY, HARRY FORBES.
 1919—Notes on Birds observed near Dunkerque, Nord, France. British
     Birds, vol. 12, pp. 194–205.
WITHERBY, HARRY FORBES, and OTHERS.
 1920—A Practical Handbook of British Birds.
WRIGHT, ALBERT HAZEN, and HARPER, FRANCIS.
 1913—A Biological Reconnaissance of Okefinokee Swamp: The Birds. The
     Auk, vol. 30, pp. 477–505.
YARRELL, WILLIAM.
 1871—History of British Birds. Fourth edition, 1871–85. Revised and
     enlarged by Alfred Newton and Howard Saunders.

Plates

Plates

PLATE 1. UPLAND PLOVER. Belleville, Mich., June 17, 1923, presented by Dr. Frank N. Wilson.

PLATE 2. SOLITARY SANDPIPER. *Upper:* Nesting site near Belvedere, Alberta; presented by Mr. Richard C. Harlow. *Lower:* Solitary sandpiper, Staten Island, N. Y.; presented by Mr. Howard H. Cleaves.

PLATE 3. SOLITARY SANDPIPER. *Upper:* Nesting site, Red Lodge, Alberta, May 29, 1923. *Lower:* Nest and eggs in above locality. Both photographs presented by Mr. J. Fletcher Street. Referred to on page 3.

PLATE 4. WILLET. *Upper:* Nesting site of a colony of willets. *Lower:* A nest in above colony, Bulls Island, S. C., May 22, 1915. Both photographed by the author. Referred to on page 29.

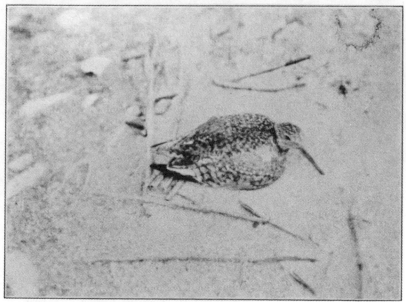

PLATE 5. WILLET. *Upper:* Nest of willet in an open situation, Bulls Island, S. C., May 23, 1915; photographed by the author. Referred to on page 30. *Lower:* Willet on its nest in a still more open situation, Sandy Point, S. C., June 7, 1927; presented by Mr. Roger T. Peterson. Referred to on page 30.

PLATE 6. WILLET. *Upper:* Willet watching the passing of a boat down a tidal creek, near Bulls Bay, S. C.; presented by Mr. Howard H. Cleaves. *Lower:* Nest of willet, Merritts Island, Fla., June 2, 1927; presented by Mr. Donald J. Nicholson.

PLATE 7. WILLET. Willet on its nest, among sand dunes, near Bulls Bay, S. C.; presented by Mr. Howard H. Cleaves. The grass pattern is well illustrated.

PLATE 8. WESTERN WILLET. Western willet on its nest, near Salt Lake City, Utah; presented by Mr. Clark Blickensderfer. Notice the protective coloration.

PLATE 9. WESTERN WILLET. Nest of western willet, near Salt Lake City, Utah; presented by Mr. Clark Blickensderfer.

PLATE 10. WANDERING TATTLER. *Upper:* Nesting site of wandering tattler, on the gravel in the foreground, upper Savage valley, Alaska, July 1, 1925. *Lower:* Nest of wandering tattler in above locality. Both photographs presented by Mr. Olaus J. Murie, by courtesy of the Biological Survey. Referred to on page 43.

PLATE 11. WANDERING TATTLER. *Upper:* Young wandering tattler, about 12 days old, Mount McKinley, Alaska, July 8, 1926; presented by Mr. Joseph Dixon. *Lower:* Wandering tattler on its nest, upper valley of Savage River, Alaska, July 1, 1925; presented by Mr. Olaus J. Murie, by courtesy of the Biological Survey. Referred to on page 43.

PLATE 12. WANDERING TATTLER. *Upper:* Male wandering tattler feeding in shallow water. *Lower:* Same bird brooding and talking to chick. Both photographs presented by Mr. Joseph Dixon and taken by him at Mount McKinley, Alaska, June 22, 1926.

PLATE 13. UPLAND PLOVER. *Upper:* Nest of upland plover, Martha's Vineyard, Mass., May 26, 1900. Referred to on page 58. *Lower:* Nest of upland plover, near Maple Creek, Saskatchewan, June 11, 1906. Referred to on page 58. Both photographs by the author.

PLATE 14. UPLAND PLOVER. Nest of upland plover, Columbus, Ohio; presented by Mr. Edward S. Thomas.

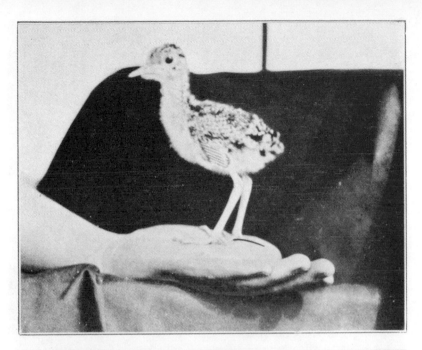

PLATE 15. *Upper:* UPLAND PLOVER. Young upland plover, Holt County, Nebr.; presented by Mr. Frank C. Pellett. *Lower:* SPOTTED SANDPIPER. Nest of spotted sandpiper, at the base of a mullein stalk, on the bank of a creek, Bear Creek, Oreg.; presented by Mr. J. E. Patterson.

PLATE 16. SPOTTED SANDPIPER. *Upper:* Nest of spotted sandpiper, Branchport, N. Y., June 24, 1914; presented by Mr. Verdi Burtch. *Lower:* Nest of spotted sandpiper, Columbus, Ohio, June, 1925; presented by Mr. Edward S. Thomas.

PLATE 17. SPOTTED SANDPIPER. *Upper:* Immature spotted sandpiper swimming. It propelled itself by wings alone while beneath the
surface and by use of the feet, like a phalarope, on the surface. Presented by Mr. Howard H. Cleaves. *Lower:* Young spotted sandpiper,
Jamestown, N. Y., June 20, 1925; presented by Mr. Roger T. Peterson.

PLATE 18. SPOTTED SANDPIPER. *Upper:* Adult spotted sandpiper in spring plumage, Staten Island, N. Y.; presented by Mr. Howard H. Cleaves and by courtesy of Collier's Weekly and Mr. Edward H. Forbush. *Lower:* Immature spotted sandpiper, Staten Island, N. Y.; presented by Mr. Cleaves.

PLATE 19. LONG-BILLED CURLEW. *Upper:* Nest of long-billed curlew, Bear River marshes, Utah, May 2, 1927. *Lower:* Adult curlew on above nest. Both photographs presented by Lieut. L. R. Wolfe.

PLATE 20. LONG-BILLED CURLEW. *Upper:* Newly hatched young and pipped eggs of long-billed curlew, near Salt Lake City, Utah; presented by Mr. Clark Blickensderfer. *Lower:* Older young, near Crane Lake, Saskatchewan, June 1, 1905; photographed by the author. Referred to on page 101.

PLATE 21. WHIMBREL. *Upper:* Whimbrel approaching its egg and chick in its nest, Shetland Islands, June 24, 1922. *Lower:* Same bird, rising to accommodate its chick. Both photographs presented by Mr. Ralph Chislett.

PLATE 22. WHIMBREL. *Upper:* Whimbrel on the nest shown below. *Lower:* Nest of whimbrel, Shetland Islands, June 11, 1923; presented by Mr. William E. Glegg.

PLATE 23. *Upper:* BRISTLE-THIGHED CURLEW. Bristle-thighed curlew, stealing an egg from a man-o-war-bird's nest, Laysan Island; presented by Mr. Donald R. Dickey, by courtesy of the National Geographic Society. *Lower:* WHIMBREL. Whimbrel settling down on its nest, Shetland Islands, June 11, 1923; presented by Mr. William E. Glegg.

PLATE 24. LAPWING. *Upper:* Nest of lapwing. *Lower:* Another nest of lapwing on a beach. Both photographs presented by Mr. C. W. Colthrup.

PLATE 25. DOTTEREL. Two views of dotterels on two different nests, near the Yenisei River, Siberia; presented by Mrs. Maud D. (Haviland) Brindley

PLATE 26. BLACK-BELLIED PLOVER. *Upper:* Immature black-bellied plover, Branchport, N. Y., October 3, 1911; presented by Mr. Verdi Burtch. *Lower:* Adult male black-bellied plover, Florida Keys, May, 1903; presented by Mr. Herbert K. Job.

PLATE 27. BLACK-BELLIED PLOVER. *Upper:* Nest and eggs of gray plover (black-bellied plover) near Yenisei River, Siberia; presented by Mrs. Maud D. (Haviland) Brindley. *Lower:* Black-bellied plover on its nest, near Point Barrow, Alaska, June 20, 1917. A photograph taken by Mr. T. L. Richardson for the author.

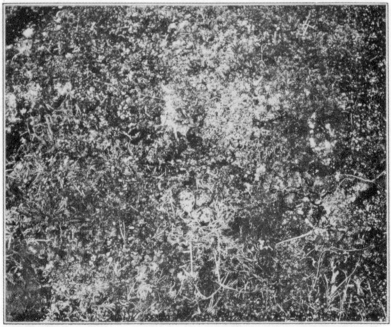

PLATE 28. AMERICAN GOLDEN PLOVER. Two nests of American golden plover, Demarcation Point, Alaska, June 23, 1914; presented by Mr. W. Sprague Brooks.

PLATE 29. PACIFIC GOLDEN PLOVER. *Upper:* Nesting site of Pacific golden plover. *Lower:* Nest and eggs of Pacific golden plover. Both photographs taken by Mr. T. L. Richardson at Unalakleet, Alaska, for the author.

PLATE 30. PACIFIC GOLDEN PLOVER. *Upper:* Pacific golden plover. *Lower:* Pacific golden plover brooding. Both photographs presented by Mrs. Maud D. (Haviland) Brindley, taken by her near the Yenisei River, Siberia.

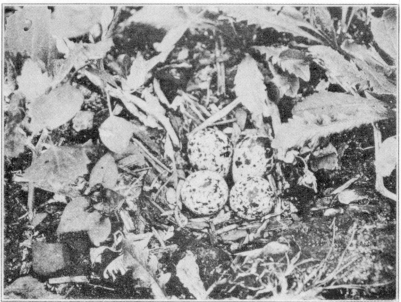

PLATE 31. KILLDEER. *Upper:* Nest and eggs of killdeer, Barr Lake, Colo.; presented by the Colorado Museum of Natural History. *Lower:* Nest and eggs of killdeer, Manitoba; presented by Herbert K. Job.

PLATE 32. KILLDEER. *Upper:* Killdeer at its nest, near Kansas City, Mo. *Lower:* Nest and eggs of the same bird. Both photographs presented by Dr. A. H. Cordier.

PLATE 33. KILLDEER. *Upper:* Downy young killdeers; photograph by H. H. Pittman. *Lower:* Nest and eggs of killdeers, Banff, Alberta; presented by Mr. Dan McCown.

PLATE 34. KILLDEER. *Upper:* Killdeer settling on its nest. *Lower:*
Young killdeer, a few days old. Both photographs presented by Mr.
Howard H. Cleaves and by courtesy of the National Geographic Society.
Taken on Staten Island, N. Y.

PLATE 35. SEMIPALMATED PLOVER. Two nests of semipalmated plover, Magdalen Islands, Quebec, June 20, 1904; photographed by the author.

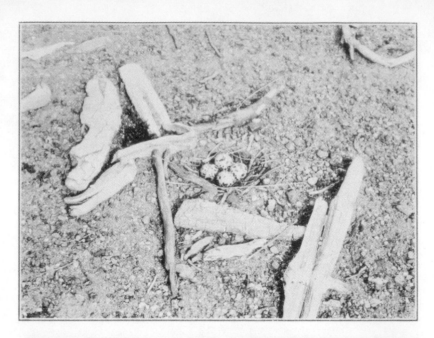

PLATE 36. SEMIPALMATED PLOVER. *Upper:* Nest and eggs of semipalmated plover, Atlin, British Columbia, June 10, 1924; presented by Mr. Harry S. Swarth. *Lower:* Semipalmated plover, Santa Barbara, Calif., May 2, 1913; presented by Mr. W. Leon Dawson.

PLATE 37. SEMIPALMATED PLOVER. Nesting site of semipalmated plover, Atlin Lake, British Columbia, June 10, 1924; presented by Mr. Harry S. Swarth.

PLATE 38. SEMIPALMATED PLOVER. *Upper:* Semipalmated plover brooding young, Magdalen Islands, June 20, 1904; presented by Mr. Herbert K. Job. *Lower:* Downy young semipalmated plover, Baffin Island, July 29, 1925; presented by Mr. J. Dewey Soper and by courtesy of the Department of Mines, Canada.

PLATE 39. RINGED PLOVER. *Upper:* Nest and eggs of ringed plover, presented by Mr. C. W. Colthrup. *Lower:* Ringed plover at its nest; presented by Mrs. Maud D. (Haviland) Brindley.

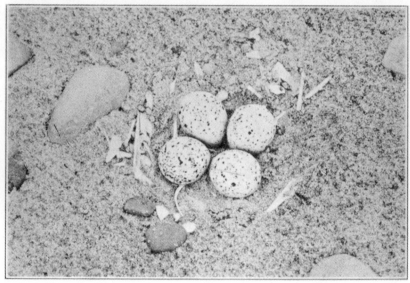

PLATE 40. PIPING PLOVER. *Upper:* Nest and five eggs of piping plover, Dartmouth, Mass., June 16, 1916; photographed by the author. *Lower:* Nest and eggs of piping plover, Bay Point, Ohio, June, 1925; presented by Mr. Edward S. Thomas.

PLATE 41. PIPING PLOVER. *Upper:* Piping plover incubating. *Lower:* Piping plover standing at its nest. Both photographs taken by the author, Chatham, Mass., June 2, 1921.

PLATE 42. PIPING PLOVER. *Upper:* Nest and eggs of piping plover,
Stump Lake, N. Dak., June 15, 1901; photographed by the author.
Lower: Piping plover chicks, about three days old, Martha's Vineyard,
Mass.; presented by Mr. Howard H. Cleaves.

PLATE 43. *Upper:* SNOWY PLOVER. Nest and eggs of snowy plover, Orange County, Calif., June 11, 1916; presented by Mr. Wright M. Pierce. *Lower:* PIPING PLOVER. Piping plover brooding young, Martha's Vineyard, Mass.; presented by Mr. Howard H. Cleaves and by courtesy of the National Geographical Society.

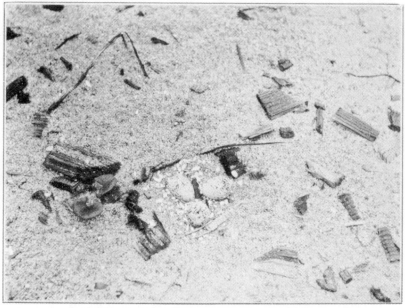

PLATE 44. SNOWY PLOVER. *Upper:* Snowy plover on its nest, Los Angeles County, Calif., May 29, 1914. *Lower:* Another nest, same locality and date. Both photographs by the author, referred to on page 248.

PLATE 45. SNOWY PLOVER. *Upper:* Downy young Cuban snowy plover, Pensacola, Fla., June 26, 1927; presented by Mr. Francis M. Weston. *Lower:* Downy young snowy plover, southern California; presented by Mr. Wright M. Pierce.

PLATE 46. WILSON PLOVER. *Upper:* Nest and eggs of Wilson plover, Bulls Island, S. C., May 22, 1915; presented by Mr. Alexander Sprunt, jr. *Lower:* Nest and eggs of Wilson plover, Chatham County, Ga., April 26, 1922; presented by Mr. W. J. Erichsen.

PLATE 47. WILSON PLOVER. *Upper:* Nest and eggs of Wilson plover, Bulls Island, S. C., May 22, 1915; photographed by the author and referred to on page 257. *Lower:* Nest and eggs of Wilson plover among pickle weed, Merritt's Island, Fla., June 20, 1926; presented by Mr. Donald J. Nicholson.

PLATE 48. WILSON PLOVER. *Upper:* Young Wilson plover, just hatched, Raccoon Key, S. C., June 7, 1927; presented by Mr. Roger Tory Peterson. *Lower:* Adult female Wilson plover, about to settle on her nest, near Bulls Bay, S. C.; presented by Mr. Howard H. Cleaves.

PLATE 49. MOUNTAIN PLOVER. *Upper:* Mountain plover at its nest. *Lower:* Nest and eggs of mountain plover. Both photographs taken in Colorado by or for Mr. William C. Bradbury, presented by the Colorado Museum of Natural History and referred to on page 264.

PLATE 50. MOUNTAIN PLOVER. *Upper:* Young mountain plover, a day or two old, June 4, 1911. *Lower:* Another, perhaps 10 days old, June 11, 1911. Both photographs taken by Mr. Edward R. Warren in Weld County, Colo., and presented by him.

PLATE 51. MOUNTAIN PLOVER. *Upper:* Adult mountain plover approaching its nest; presented by the Colorado Museum of Natural History, photographed by Mr. W. C. Bradbury, and referred to on page 264. *Lower:* Mountain plover attending its young, Weld County, Colo., June 4, 1911; presented by Mr. Edward R. Warren.

PLATE 52. SURF BIRD. *Upper:* Surf bird on its nest. *Lower:* Surf bird inspecting its eggs. Both photographs taken by Mr. Joseph Dixon in the Mount McKinley District, Alaska, May 29, 1926, presented by him and referred to on page 271.

PLATE 53. SURF BIRD. *Upper:* Male surf bird beside its nest. *Lower:* Nest and eggs of surf bird. Both photographs taken by Mr. Joseph Dixon in the Mount McKinley District, Alaska, May 29, 1926, presented by him and referred to on page 271.

PLATE 54. TURNSTONE. *Upper:* Turnstone on its nest. *Lower:* Nest and eggs of the same bird. Both photographs taken by Mr. Ralph Chislett, on a Baltic isle, off Oland, June 19, 1924, presented by him and referred to on page 283.

PLATE 55. TURNSTONE. *Left*: Male turnstone on its nest under cover. *Right*: Female turnstone. Both photographs taken by Mr. Ralph Chislett on a Baltic isle, off Oland, June 19, 1924, presented by him and referred to on page 283.

PLATE 56. TURNSTONE. *Upper:* Turnstone at its nest, Spitsbergen, 1921; presented by Mr. Seton P. Gordon and referred to on page 282. *Lower:* RUDDY TURNSTONE. Downy young ruddy turnstone, Yukon Delta, Alaska, June 19, 1914; photographed by Mr. F. Seymour Hersey for the author.

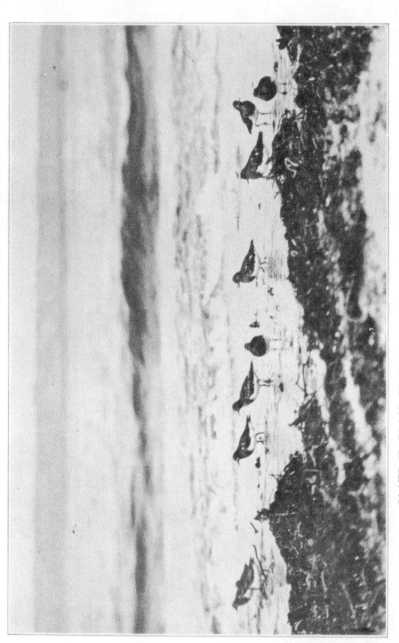

PLATE 57. BLACK TURNSTONE. Flock of black turnstones, presented by Mr. Donald R. Dickey.

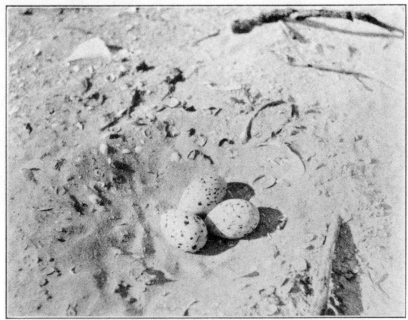

PLATE 58. AMERICAN OYSTER CATCHER. Two nests of American oyster catcher, Bulls Island, S. C., May 22, 1915; photographed by the author and referred to on page 310.

PLATE 59. AMERICAN OYSTER CATCHER. *Upper:* Immature American oyster catcher, Cape Romain, S. C., June 8, 1927; presented by Mr. Roger Tory Peterson. *Lower:* Adult American oyster catcher, Bulls Bay, S. C., May, 1904; presented by Mr. Herbert K. Job.

PLATE 60. FRAZAR OYSTER CATCHER. Two views of Frazar oyster catcher, Lower California, 1927; presented by Mr. Wright M. Pierce.

PLATE 61. FRAZAR OYSTER CATCHER. Two views of young Frazar oyster catchers, Lower California, 1926; presented by Mr. Wright M. Pierce.

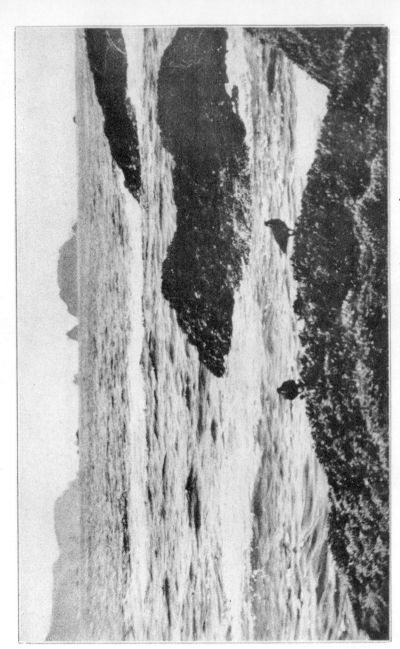

PLATE 62. BLACK OYSTER CATCHER. Black oyster catchers on a reef, coast of Washington, June 22, 1910; presented by Mr. W. Leon Dawson.

PLATE 64. BLACK OYSTER CATCHER. *Upper:* Nest and eggs of
black oyster catcher, Graham Island, British Columbia, May 26, 1927;
presented by Mr. S. J. Darcus. *Lower:* Nest, eggs and young, just
hatched, of black oyster catcher, Destruction Island, Wash., July 16,
1906; presented by Mr. W. Leon Dawson.

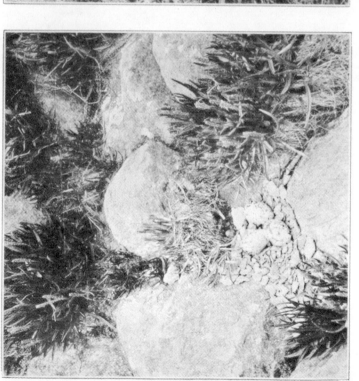

PLATE 63. BLACK OYSTER CATCHER. Nesting site and nest of black oyster catcher, Destruction Island, Wash.; presented by Mr. W. Leon Dawson.

PLATE 65. MEXICAN JACANA. Two views of Paradise Lake, near Tampico, Mexico, nesting site of Mexican jacana; presented by Mr. Thomas S. Gillin and referred to on page 324.

PLATE 66. MEXICAN JACANA. *Upper:* Nest and eggs of Mexican jacana. *Lower:* Mexican jacana at home. Both photographs taken by Mr. Thomas S. Gillin, Paradise Lake, near Tampico, Mexico; presented by him and referred to on page 325.

INDEX

A CATALOGUE OF SELECTED DOVER BOOKS
IN ALL FIELDS OF INTEREST

A CATALOGUE OF SELECTED DOVER BOOKS
IN ALL FIELDS OF INTEREST

AMERICA'S OLD MASTERS, James T. Flexner. Four men emerged unexpectedly from provincial 18th century America to leadership in European art: Benjamin West, J. S. Copley, C. R. Peale, Gilbert Stuart. Brilliant coverage of lives and contributions. Revised, 1967 edition. 69 plates. 365pp. of text.
21806-6 Paperbound $3.00

FIRST FLOWERS OF OUR WILDERNESS: AMERICAN PAINTING, THE COLONIAL PERIOD, James T. Flexner. Painters, and regional painting traditions from earliest Colonial times up to the emergence of Copley, West and Peale Sr., Foster, Gustavus Hesselius, Feke, John Smibert and many anonymous painters in the primitive manner. Engaging presentation, with 162 illustrations. xxii + 368pp.
22180-6 Paperbound $3.50

THE LIGHT OF DISTANT SKIES: AMERICAN PAINTING, 1760-1835, James T. Flexner. The great generation of early American painters goes to Europe to learn and to teach: West, Copley, Gilbert Stuart and others. Allston, Trumbull, Morse; also contemporary American painters—primitives, derivatives, academics—who remained in America. 102 illustrations. xiii + 306pp. 22179-2 Paperbound $3.00

A HISTORY OF THE RISE AND PROGRESS OF THE ARTS OF DESIGN IN THE UNITED STATES, William Dunlap. Much the richest mine of information on early American painters, sculptors, architects, engravers, miniaturists, etc. The only source of information for scores of artists, the major primary source for many others. Unabridged reprint of rare original 1834 edition, with new introduction by James T. Flexner, and 394 new illustrations. Edited by Rita Weiss. 6⅝ x 9⅝.
21695-0, 21696-9, 21697-7 Three volumes, Paperbound $13.50

EPOCHS OF CHINESE AND JAPANESE ART, Ernest F. Fenollosa. From primitive Chinese art to the 20th century, thorough history, explanation of every important art period and form, including Japanese woodcuts; main stress on China and Japan, but Tibet, Korea also included. Still unexcelled for its detailed, rich coverage of cultural background, aesthetic elements, diffusion studies, particularly of the historical period. 2nd, 1913 edition. 242 illustrations. lii + 439pp. of text.
20364-6, 20365-4 Two volumes, Paperbound $6.00

THE GENTLE ART OF MAKING ENEMIES, James A. M. Whistler. Greatest wit of his day deflates Oscar Wilde, Ruskin, Swinburne; strikes back at inane critics, exhibitions, art journalism; aesthetics of impressionist revolution in most striking form. Highly readable classic by great painter. Reproduction of edition designed by Whistler. Introduction by Alfred Werner. xxxvi + 334pp.
21875-9 Paperbound $2.50

LAST AND FIRST MEN AND STAR MAKER, TWO SCIENCE FICTION NOVELS, Olaf Stapledon. Greatest future histories in science fiction. In the first, human intelligence is the "hero," through strange paths of evolution, interplanetary invasions, incredible technologies, near extinctions and reemergences. Star Maker describes the quest of a band of star rovers for intelligence itself, through time and space: weird inhuman civilizations, crustacean minds, symbiotic worlds, etc. Complete, unabridged. v + 438pp. 21962-3 Paperbound $2.50

THREE PROPHETIC NOVELS, H. G. WELLS. Stages of a consistently planned future for mankind. *When the Sleeper Wakes,* and *A Story of the Days to Come,* anticipate *Brave New World* and *1984,* in the 21st Century; *The Time Machine,* only complete version in print, shows farther future and the end of mankind. All ؛low Wells's greatest gifts as storyteller and novelist. Edited by E. F. Bleiler. x + 335pp. (USO) 20605-X Paperbound $2.50

THE DEVIL'S DICTIONARY, Ambrose Bierce. America's own Oscar Wilde— Ambrose Bierce—offers his barbed iconoclastic wisdom in over 1,000 definitions hailed by H. L. Mencken as "some of the most gorgeous witticisms in the English language." 145pp. 20487-1 Paperbound $1.25

MAX AND MORITZ, Wilhelm Busch. Great children's classic, father of comic strip, of two bad boys, Max and Moritz. Also Ker and Plunk (Plisch und Plumm), Cat and Mouse, Deceitful Henry, Ice-Peter, The Boy and the Pipe, and five other pieces. Original German, with English translation. Edited by H. Arthur Klein; translations by various hands and H. Arthur Klein. vi + 216pp.
20181-3 Paperbound $2.00

PIGS IS PIGS AND OTHER FAVORITES, Ellis Parker Butler. The title story is one of the best humor short stories, as Mike Flannery obfuscates biology and English. Also included, That Pup of Murchison's, The Great American Pie Company, and Perkins of Portland. 14 illustrations. v + 109pp. 21532-6 Paperbound $1.25

THE PETERKIN PAPERS, Lucretia P. Hale. It takes genius to be as stupidly mad as the Peterkins, as they decide to become wise, celebrate the "Fourth," keep a cow, and otherwise strain the resources of the Lady from Philadelphia. Basic book of American humor. 153 illustrations. 219pp. 20794-3 Paperbound $1.50

PERRAULT'S FAIRY TALES, translated by A. E. Johnson and S. R. Littlewood, with 34 full-page illustrations by Gustave Doré. All the original Perrault stories— Cinderella, Sleeping Beauty, Bluebeard, Little Red Riding Hood, Puss in Boots, Tom Thumb, etc.—with their witty verse morals and the magnificent illustrations of Doré. One of the five or six great books of European fairy tales. viii + 117pp. 8⅛ x 11. 22311-6 Paperbound $2.00

OLD HUNGARIAN FAIRY TALES, Baroness Orczy. Favorites translated and adapted by author of the *Scarlet Pimpernel.* Eight fairy tales include "The Suitors of Princess Fire-Fly," "The Twin Hunchbacks," "Mr. Cuttlefish's Love Story," and "The Enchanted Cat." This little volume of magic and adventure will captivate children as it has for generations. 90 drawings by Montagu Barstow. 96pp.
(USO) 22293-4 Paperbound $1.95

PLANETS, STARS AND GALAXIES: DESCRIPTIVE ASTRONOMY FOR BEGINNERS, A. E. Fanning. Comprehensive introductory survey of astronomy: the sun, solar system, stars, galaxies, universe, cosmology; up-to-date, including quasars, radio stars, etc. Preface by Prof. Donald Menzel. 24pp. of photographs. 189pp. 5¼ x 8¼.
21680-2 Paperbound $1.75

TEACH YOURSELF CALCULUS, P. Abbott. With a good background in algebra and trig, you can teach yourself calculus with this book. Simple, straightforward introduction to functions of all kinds, integration, differentiation, series, etc. "Students who are beginning to study calculus method will derive great help from this book." Faraday House Journal. 308pp. 20683-1 Clothbound $2.50

TEACH YOURSELF TRIGONOMETRY, P. Abbott. Geometrical foundations, indices and logarithms, ratios, angles, circular measure, etc. are presented in this sound, easy-to-use text. Excellent for the beginner or as a brush up, this text carries the student through the solution of triangles. 204pp. 20682-3 Clothbound $2.50

BASIC MACHINES AND HOW THEY WORK, U. S. Bureau of Naval Personnel. Originally used in U.S. Naval training schools, this book clearly explains the operation of a progression of machines, from the simplest—lever, wheel and axle, inclined plane, wedge, screw—to the most complex—typewriter, internal combustion engine, computer mechanism. Utilizing an approach that requires only an elementary understanding of mathematics, these explanations build logically upon each other and are assisted by over 200 drawings and diagrams. Perfect as a technical school manual or as a self-teaching aid to the layman. 204 figures. Preface. Index. vii + 161pp. 6½ x 9¼. 21709-4 Paperbound $2.50

THE FRIENDLY STARS, Martha Evans Martin. Classic has taught naked-eye observation of stars, planets to hundreds of thousands, still not surpassed for charm, lucidity, adequacy. Completely updated by Professor Donald H. Menzel, Harvard Observatory. 25 illustrations. 16 x 30 chart. x + 147pp. 21099-5 Paperbound $1.50

MUSIC OF THE SPHERES: THE MATERIAL UNIVERSE FROM ATOM TO QUASAR, SIMPLY EXPLAINED, Guy Murchie. Extremely broad, brilliantly written popular account begins with the solar system and reaches to dividing line between matter and nonmatter; latest understandings presented with exceptional clarity. Volume One: Planets, stars, galaxies, cosmology, geology, celestial mechanics, latest astronomical discoveries; Volume Two: Matter, atoms, waves, radiation, relativity, chemical action, heat, nuclear energy, quantum theory, music, light, color, probability, antimatter, antigravity, and similar topics. 319 figures. 1967 (second) edition. Total of xx + 644pp. 21809-0, 21810-4 Two volumes, Paperbound $5.50

OLD-TIME SCHOOLS AND SCHOOL BOOKS, Clifton Johnson. Illustrations and rhymes from early primers, abundant quotations from early textbooks, many anecdotes of school life enliven this study of elementary schools from Puritans to middle 19th century. Introduction by Carl Withers. 234 illustrations. xxxiii + 381pp.
21031-6 Paperbound $3.50

EAST O' THE SUN AND WEST O' THE MOON, George W. Dasent. Considered the best of all translations of these Norwegian folk tales, this collection has been enjoyed by generations of children (and folklorists too). Includes True and Untrue, Why the Sea is Salt, East O' the Sun and West O' the Moon, Why the Bear is Stumpy-Tailed, Boots and the Troll, The Cock and the Hen, Rich Peter the Pedlar, and 52 more. The only edition with all 59 tales. 77 illustrations by Erik Werenskiold and Theodor Kittelsen. xv + 418pp. 22521-6 Paperbound $3.50

GOOPS AND HOW TO BE THEM, Gelett Burgess. Classic of tongue-in-cheek humor, masquerading as etiquette book. 87 verses, twice as many cartoons, show mischievous Goops as they demonstrate to children virtues of table manners, neatness, courtesy, etc. Favorite for generations. viii + 88pp. 6½ x 9¼. 22233-0 Paperbound $1.25

ALICE'S ADVENTURES UNDER GROUND, Lewis Carroll. The first version, quite different from the final *Alice in Wonderland,* printed out by Carroll himself with his own illustrations. Complete facsimile of the "million dollar" manuscript Carroll gave to Alice Liddell in 1864. Introduction by Martin Gardner. viii + 96pp. Title and dedication pages in color. 21482-6 Paperbound $1.25

THE BROWNIES, THEIR BOOK, Palmer Cox. Small as mice, cunning as foxes, exuberant and full of mischief, the Brownies go to the zoo, toy shop, seashore, circus, etc., in 24 verse adventures and 266 illustrations. Long a favorite, since their first appearance in St. Nicholas Magazine. xi + 144pp. 6⅝ x 9¼. 21265-3 Paperbound $1.75

SONGS OF CHILDHOOD, Walter De La Mare. Published (under the pseudonym Walter Ramal) when De La Mare was only 29, this charming collection has long been a favorite children's book. A facsimile of the first edition in paper, the 47 poems capture the simplicity of the nursery rhyme and the ballad, including such lyrics as I Met Eve, Tartary, The Silver Penny. vii + 106pp. 21972-0 Paperbound $1.25

THE COMPLETE NONSENSE OF EDWARD LEAR, Edward Lear. The finest 19th-century humorist-cartoonist in full: all nonsense limericks, zany alphabets, Owl and Pussycat, songs, nonsense botany, and more than 500 illustrations by Lear himself. Edited by Holbrook Jackson. xxix + 287pp. (USO) 20167-8 Paperbound $2.00

BILLY WHISKERS: THE AUTOBIOGRAPHY OF A GOAT, Frances Trego Montgomery. A favorite of children since the early 20th century, here are the escapades of that rambunctious, irresistible and mischievous goat—Billy Whiskers. Much in the spirit of *Peck's Bad Boy,* this is a book that children never tire of reading or hearing. All the original familiar illustrations by W. H. Fry are included: 6 color plates, 18 black and white drawings. 159pp. 22345-0 Paperbound $2.00

MOTHER GOOSE MELODIES. Faithful republication of the fabulously rare Munroe and Francis "copyright 1833" Boston edition—the most important Mother Goose collection, usually referred to as the "original." Familiar rhymes plus many rare ones, with wonderful old woodcut illustrations. Edited by E. F. Bleiler. 128pp. 4½ x 6⅜. 22577-1 Paperbound $1.25

THE PRINCIPLES OF PSYCHOLOGY, William James. The famous long course, complete and unabridged. Stream of thought, time perception, memory, experimental methods—-these are only some of the concerns of a work that was years ahead of its time and still valid, interesting, useful. 94 figures. Total of xviii + 1391pp.
20381-6, 20382-4 Two volumes, Paperbound $8.00

THE STRANGE STORY OF THE QUANTUM, Banesh Hoffmann. Non-mathematical but thorough explanation of work of Planck, Einstein, Bohr, Pauli, de Broglie, Schrödinger, Heisenberg, Dirac, Feynman, etc. No technical background needed. "Of books attempting such an account, this is the best," Henry Margenau, Yale. 40-page "Postscript 1959." xii + 285pp. 20518-5 Paperbound $2.00

THE RISE OF THE NEW PHYSICS, A. d'Abro. Most thorough explanation in print of central core of mathematical physics, both classical and modern; from Newton to Dirac and Heisenberg. Both history and exposition; philosophy of science, causality, explanations of higher mathematics, analytical mechanics, electromagnetism, thermodynamics, phase rule, special and general relativity, matrices. No higher mathematics needed to follow exposition, though treatment is elementary to intermediate in level. Recommended to serious student who wishes verbal understanding. 97 illustrations. xvii + 982pp. 20003-5, 20004-3 Two volumes, Paperbound $6.00

GREAT IDEAS OF OPERATIONS RESEARCH, Jagjit Singh. Easily followed non-technical explanation of mathematical tools, aims, results: statistics, linear programming, game theory, queueing theory, Monte Carlo simulation, etc. Uses only elementary mathematics. Many case studies, several analyzed in detail. Clarity, breadth make this excellent for specialist in another field who wishes background. 41 figures. x + 228pp. 21886-4 Paperbound $2.50

GREAT IDEAS OF MODERN MATHEMATICS: THEIR NATURE AND USE, Jagjit Singh. Internationally famous expositor, winner of Unesco's Kalinga Award for science popularization explains verbally such topics as differential equations, matrices, groups, sets, transformations, mathematical logic and other important modern mathematics, as well as use in physics, astrophysics, and similar fields. Superb exposition for layman, scientist in other areas. viii + 312pp.
20587-8 Paperbound $2.50

GREAT IDEAS IN INFORMATION THEORY, LANGUAGE AND CYBERNETICS, Jagjit Singh. The analog and digital computers, how they work, how they are like and unlike the human brain, the men who developed them, their future applications, computer terminology. An essential book for today, even for readers with little math. Some mathematical demonstrations included for more advanced readers. 118 figures. Tables. ix + 338pp. 21694-2 Paperbound $2.50

CHANCE, LUCK AND STATISTICS, Horace C. Levinson. Non-mathematical presentation of fundamentals of probability theory and science of statistics and their applications. Games of chance, betting odds, misuse of statistics, normal and skew distributions, birth rates, stock speculation, insurance. Enlarged edition. Formerly "The Science of Chance." xiii + 357pp. 21007-3 Paperbound $2.50

JIM WHITEWOLF: THE LIFE OF A KIOWA APACHE INDIAN, Charles S. Brant, editor. Spans transition between native life and acculturation period, 1880 on. Kiowa culture, personal life pattern, religion and the supernatural, the Ghost Dance, breakdown in the White Man's world, similar material. 1 map. xii + 144pp.
22015-X Paperbound $1.75

THE NATIVE TRIBES OF CENTRAL AUSTRALIA, Baldwin Spencer and F. J. Gillen. Basic book in anthropology, devoted to full coverage of the Arunta and Warramunga tribes; the source for knowledge about kinship systems, material and social culture, religion, etc. Still unsurpassed. 121 photographs, 89 drawings. xviii + 669pp.
21775-2 Paperbound $5.00

MALAY MAGIC, Walter W. Skeat. Classic (1900); still the definitive work on the folklore and popular religion of the Malay peninsula. Describes marriage rites, birth spirits and ceremonies, medicine, dances, games, war and weapons, etc. Extensive quotes from original sources, many magic charms translated into English. 35 illustrations. Preface by Charles Otto Blagden. xxiv + 685pp.
21760-4 Paperbound $4.00

HEAVENS ON EARTH: UTOPIAN COMMUNITIES IN AMERICA, 1680-1880, Mark Holloway. The finest nontechnical account of American utopias, from the early Woman in the Wilderness, Ephrata, Rappites to the enormous mid 19th-century efflorescence; Shakers, New Harmony, Equity Stores, Fourier's Phalanxes, Oneida, Amana, Fruitlands, etc. "Entertaining and very instructive." *Times Literary Supplement.* 15 illustrations. 246pp.
21593-8 Paperbound $2.00

LONDON LABOUR AND THE LONDON POOR, Henry Mayhew. Earliest (c. 1850) sociological study in English, describing myriad subcultures of London poor. Particularly remarkable for the thousands of pages of direct testimony taken from the lips of London prostitutes, thieves, beggars, street sellers, chimney-sweepers, street-musicians, "mudlarks," "pure-finders," rag-gatherers, "running-patterers," dock laborers, cab-men, and hundreds of others, quoted directly in this massive work. An extraordinarily vital picture of London emerges. 110 illustrations. Total of lxxvi + 1951pp. 6⅝ x 10.
21934-8, 21935-6, 21936-4, 21937-2 Four volumes, Paperbound $16.00

HISTORY OF THE LATER ROMAN EMPIRE, J. B. Bury. Eloquent, detailed reconstruction of Western and Byzantine Roman Empire by a major historian, from the death of Theodosius I (395 A.D.) to the death of Justinian (565). Extensive quotations from contemporary sources; full coverage of important Roman and foreign figures of the time. xxxiv + 965pp. 20398-0, 20399-9 Two volumes, Paperbound $7.00

AN INTELLECTUAL AND CULTURAL HISTORY OF THE WESTERN WORLD, Harry Elmer Barnes. Monumental study, tracing the development of the accomplishments that make up human culture. Every aspect of man's achievement surveyed from its origins in the Paleolithic to the present day (1964); social structures, ideas, economic systems, art, literature, technology, mathematics, the sciences, medicine, religion, jurisprudence, etc. Evaluations of the contributions of scores of great men. 1964 edition, revised and edited by scholars in the many fields represented. Total of xxix + 1381pp. 21275-0, 21276-9, 21277-7 Three volumes, Paperbound $10.50

POEMS OF ANNE BRADSTREET, edited with an introduction by Robert Hutchinson. A new selection of poems by America's first poet and perhaps the first significant woman poet in the English language. 48 poems display her development in works of considerable variety—love poems, domestic poems, religious meditations, formal elegies, "quaternions," etc. Notes, bibliography. viii + 222pp.
22160-1 Paperbound $2.00

THREE GOTHIC NOVELS: THE CASTLE OF OTRANTO BY HORACE WALPOLE; VATHEK BY WILLIAM BECKFORD; THE VAMPYRE BY JOHN POLIDORI, WITH FRAGMENT OF A NOVEL BY LORD BYRON, edited by E. F. Bleiler. The first Gothic novel, by Walpole; the finest Oriental tale in English, by Beckford; powerful Romantic supernatural story in versions by Polidori and Byron. All extremely important in history of literature; all still exciting, packed with supernatural thrills, ghosts, haunted castles, magic, etc. xl + 291pp.
21232-7 Paperbound $2.50

THE BEST TALES OF HOFFMANN, E. T. A. Hoffmann. 10 of Hoffmann's most important stories, in modern re-editings of standard translations: Nutcracker and the King of Mice, Signor Formica, Automata, The Sandman, Rath Krespel, The Golden Flowerpot, Master Martin the Cooper, The Mines of Falun, The King's Betrothed, A New Year's Eve Adventure. 7 illustrations by Hoffmann. Edited by E. F. Bleiler. xxxix + 419pp.
21793-0 Paperbound $3.00

GHOST AND HORROR STORIES OF AMBROSE BIERCE, Ambrose Bierce. 23 strikingly modern stories of the horrors latent in the human mind: The Eyes of the Panther, The Damned Thing, An Occurrence at Owl Creek Bridge, An Inhabitant of Carcosa, etc., plus the dream-essay, Visions of the Night. Edited by E. F. Bleiler. xxii + 199pp.
20767-6 Paperbound $1.50

BEST GHOST STORIES OF J. S. LEFANU, J. Sheridan LeFanu. Finest stories by Victorian master often considered greatest supernatural writer of all. Carmilla, Green Tea, The Haunted Baronet, The Familiar, and 12 others. Most never before available in the U. S. A. Edited by E. F. Bleiler. 8 illustrations from Victorian publications. xvii + 467pp.
20415-4 Paperbound $3.00

MATHEMATICAL FOUNDATIONS OF INFORMATION THEORY, A. I. Khinchin. Comprehensive introduction to work of Shannon, McMillan, Feinstein and Khinchin, placing these investigations on a rigorous mathematical basis. Covers entropy concept in probability theory, uniqueness theorem, Shannon's inequality, ergodic sources, the E property, martingale concept, noise, Feinstein's fundamental lemma, Shanon's first and second theorems. Translated by R. A. Silverman and M. D. Friedman. iii + 120pp.
60434-9 Paperbound $1.75

SEVEN SCIENCE FICTION NOVELS, H. G. Wells. The standard collection of the great novels. Complete, unabridged. *First Men in the Moon, Island of Dr. Moreau, War of the Worlds, Food of the Gods, Invisible Man, Time Machine, In the Days of the Comet.* Not only science fiction fans, but every educated person owes it to himself to read these novels. 1015pp
20264-X Clothbound $5.00

THE PHILOSOPHY OF THE UPANISHADS, Paul Deussen. Clear, detailed statement of upanishadic system of thought, generally considered among best available. History of these works, full exposition of system emergent from them, parallel concepts in the West. Translated by A. S. Geden. xiv + 429pp.
21616-0 Paperbound $3.50

LANGUAGE, TRUTH AND LOGIC, Alfred J. Ayer. Famous, remarkably clear introduction to the Vienna and Cambridge schools of Logical Positivism; function of philosophy, elimination of metaphysical thought, nature of analysis, similar topics. "Wish I had written it myself," Bertrand Russell. 2nd, 1946 edition. 160pp.
20010-8 Paperbound $1.50

THE GUIDE FOR THE PERPLEXED, Moses Maimonides. Great classic of medieval Judaism, major attempt to reconcile revealed religion (Pentateuch, commentaries) and Aristotelian philosophy. Enormously important in all Western thought. Unabridged Friedländer translation. 50-page introduction. lix + 414pp.
(USO) 20351-4 Paperbound $3.50

OCCULT AND SUPERNATURAL PHENOMENA, D. H. Rawcliffe. Full, serious study of the most persistent delusions of mankind: crystal gazing, mediumistic trance, stigmata, lycanthropy, fire walking, dowsing, telepathy, ghosts, ESP, etc., and their relation to common forms of abnormal psychology. Formerly *Illusions and Delusions of the Supernatural and the Occult.* iii + 551pp.   20503-7 Paperbound $3.50

THE EGYPTIAN BOOK OF THE DEAD: THE PAPYRUS OF ANI, E. A. Wallis Budge. Full hieroglyphic text, interlinear transliteration of sounds, word for word translation, then smooth, connected translation; Theban recension. Basic work in Ancient Egyptian civilization; now even more significant than ever for historical importance, dilation of consciousness, etc. clvi + 377pp. 6½ x 9¼.
21866-X Paperbound $3.95

PSYCHOLOGY OF MUSIC, Carl E. Seashore. Basic, thorough survey of everything known about psychology of music up to 1940's; essential reading for psychologists, musicologists. Physical acoustics; auditory apparatus; relationship of physical sound to perceived sound; role of the mind in sorting, altering, suppressing, creating sound sensations; musical learning, testing for ability, absolute pitch, other topics. Records of Caruso, Menuhin analyzed. 88 figures. xix + 408pp.
21851-1 Paperbound $3.50

THE I CHING (THE BOOK OF CHANGES), translated by James Legge. Complete translated text plus appendices by Confucius, of perhaps the most penetrating divination book ever compiled. Indispensable to all study of early Oriental civilizations. 3 plates. xxiii + 448pp.   21062-6 Paperbound $3.00

THE UPANISHADS, translated by Max Müller. Twelve classical upanishads: Chandogya, Kena, Aitareya, Kaushitaki, Isa, Katha, Mundaka, Taittiriyaka, Brhadaranyaka, Svetasvatara, Prasna, Maitriyana. 160-page introduction, analysis by Prof. Müller. Total of 670pp. 20992-X, 20993-8 Two volumes, Paperbound $6.50

THE RED FAIRY BOOK, Andrew Lang. Lang's color fairy books have long been children's favorites. This volume includes Rapunzel, Jack and the Bean-stalk and 35 other stories, familiar and unfamiliar. 4 plates, 93 illustrations x + 367pp.
21673-X Paperbound $2.50

THE BLUE FAIRY BOOK, Andrew Lang. Lang's tales come from all countries and all times. Here are 37 tales from Grimm, the Arabian Nights, Greek Mythology, and other fascinating sources. 8 plates, 130 illustrations. xi + 390pp.
21437-0 Paperbound $2.50

HOUSEHOLD STORIES BY THE BROTHERS GRIMM. Classic English-language edition of the well-known tales — Rumpelstiltskin, Snow White, Hansel and Gretel, The Twelve Brothers, Faithful John, Rapunzel, Tom Thumb (52 stories in all). Translated into simple, straightforward English by Lucy Crane. Ornamented with headpieces, vignettes, elaborate decorative initials and a dozen full-page illustrations by Walter Crane. x + 269pp.
21080-4 Paperbound $2.50

THE MERRY ADVENTURES OF ROBIN HOOD, Howard Pyle. The finest modern versions of the traditional ballads and tales about the great English outlaw. Howard Pyle's complete prose version, with every word, every illustration of the first edition. Do not confuse this facsimile of the original (1883) with modern editions that change text or illustrations. 23 plates plus many page decorations. xxii + 296pp.
22043-5 Paperbound $2.50

THE STORY OF KING ARTHUR AND HIS KNIGHTS, Howard Pyle. The finest children's version of the life of King Arthur; brilliantly retold by Pyle, with 48 of his most imaginative illustrations. xviii + 313pp. 6⅛ x 9¼.
21445-1 Paperbound $2.50

THE WONDERFUL WIZARD OF OZ, L. Frank Baum. America's finest children's book in facsimile of first edition with all Denslow illustrations in full color. The edition a child should have. Introduction by Martin Gardner. 23 color plates, scores of drawings. iv + 267pp.
20691-2 Paperbound $2.50

THE MARVELOUS LAND OF OZ, L. Frank Baum. The second Oz book, every bit as imaginative as the Wizard. The hero is a boy named Tip, but the Scarecrow and the Tin Woodman are back, as is the Oz magic. 16 color plates, 120 drawings by John R. Neill. 287pp.
20692-0 Paperbound $2.50

THE MAGICAL MONARCH OF MO, L. Frank Baum. Remarkable adventures in a land even stranger than Oz. The best of Baum's books not in the Oz series. 15 color plates and dozens of drawings by Frank Verbeck. xviii + 237pp.
21892-9 Paperbound $2.25

THE BAD CHILD'S BOOK OF BEASTS, MORE BEASTS FOR WORSE CHILDREN, A MORAL ALPHABET, Hilaire Belloc. Three complete humor classics in one volume. Be kind to the frog, and do not call him names . . . and 28 other whimsical animals. Familiar favorites and some not so well known. Illustrated by Basil Blackwell. 156pp.
(USO) 20749-8 Paperbound $1.50

A HISTORY OF COSTUME, Carl Köhler. Definitive history, based on surviving pieces of clothing primarily, and paintings, statues, etc. secondarily. Highly readable text, supplemented by 594 illustrations of costumes of the ancient Mediterranean peoples, Greece and Rome, the Teutonic prehistoric period; costumes of the Middle Ages, Renaissance, Baroque, 18th and 19th centuries. Clear, measured patterns are provided for many clothing articles. Approach is practical throughout. Enlarged by Emma von Sichart. 464pp. 21030-8 Paperbound $3.50

ORIENTAL RUGS, ANTIQUE AND MODERN, Walter A. Hawley. A complete and authoritative treatise on the Oriental rug—where they are made, by whom and how, designs and symbols, characteristics in detail of the six major groups, how to distinguish them and how to buy them. Detailed technical data is provided on periods, weaves, warps, wefts, textures, sides, ends and knots, although no technical background is required for an understanding. 11 color plates, 80 halftones, 4 maps. vi + 320pp. 6⅛ x 9⅛. 22366-3 Paperbound $5.00

TEN BOOKS ON ARCHITECTURE, Vitruvius. By any standards the most important book on architecture ever written. Early Roman discussion of aesthetics of building, construction methods, orders, sites, and every other aspect of architecture has inspired, instructed architecture for about 2,000 years. Stands behind Palladio, Michelangelo, Bramante, Wren, countless others. Definitive Morris H. Morgan translation. 68 illustrations. xii + 331pp. 20645-9 Paperbound $3.50

THE FOUR BOOKS OF ARCHITECTURE, Andrea Palladio. Translated into every major Western European language in the two centuries following its publication in 1570, this has been one of the most influential books in the history of architecture. Complete reprint of the 1738 Isaac Ware edition. New introduction by Adolf Placzek, Columbia Univ. 216 plates. xxii + 110pp. of text. 9½ x 12¾. 21308-0 Clothbound $10.00

STICKS AND STONES: A STUDY OF AMERICAN ARCHITECTURE AND CIVILIZATION, Lewis Mumford.One of the great classics of American cultural history. American architecture from the medieval-inspired earliest forms to the early 20th century; evolution of structure and style, and reciprocal influences on environment. 21 photographic illustrations. 238pp. 20202-X Paperbound $2.00

THE AMERICAN BUILDER'S COMPANION, Asher Benjamin. The most widely used early 19th century architectural style and source book, for colonial up into Greek Revival periods. Extensive development of geometry of carpentering, construction of sashes, frames, doors, stairs; plans and elevations of domestic and other buildings. Hundreds of thousands of houses were built according to this book, now invaluable to historians, architects, restorers, etc. 1827 edition. 59 plates. 114pp. 7⅞ x 10¾. 22236-5 Paperbound $3.50

DUTCH HOUSES IN THE HUDSON VALLEY BEFORE 1776, Helen Wilkinson Reynolds. The standard survey of the Dutch colonial house and outbuildings, with constructional features, decoration, and local history associated with individual homesteads. Introduction by Franklin D. Roosevelt. Map. 150 illustrations. 469pp. 6⅝ x 9¼. 21469-9 Paperbound $4.00

Two Little Savages; Being the Adventures of Two Boys Who Lived as Indians and What They Learned, Ernest Thompson Seton. Great classic of nature and boyhood provides a vast range of woodlore in most palatable form, a genuinely entertaining story. Two farm boys build a teepee in woods and live in it for a month, working out Indian solutions to living problems, star lore, birds and animals, plants, etc. 293 illustrations. vii + 286pp.

20985-7 Paperbound $2.50

Peter Piper's Practical Principles of Plain & Perfect Pronunciation. Alliterative jingles and tongue-twisters of surprising charm, that made their first appearance in America about 1830. Republished in full with the spirited woodcut illustrations from this earliest American edition. 32pp. 4½ x 6⅜.

22560-7 Paperbound $1.00

Science Experiments and Amusements for Children, Charles Vivian. 73 easy experiments, requiring only materials found at home or easily available, such as candles, coins, steel wool, etc.; illustrate basic phenomena like vacuum, simple chemical reaction, etc. All safe. Modern, well-planned. Formerly *Science Games for Children*. 102 photos, numerous drawings. 96pp. 6⅛ x 9¼.

21856-2 Paperbound $1.25

An Introduction to Chess Moves and Tactics Simply Explained, Leonard Barden. Informal intermediate introduction, quite strong in explaining reasons for moves. Covers basic material, tactics, important openings, traps, positional play in middle game, end game. Attempts to isolate patterns and recurrent configurations. Formerly *Chess*. 58 figures. 102pp. (USO) 21210-6 Paperbound $1.25

Lasker's Manual of Chess, Dr. Emanuel Lasker. Lasker was not only one of the five great World Champions, he was also one of the ablest expositors, theorists, and analysts. In many ways, his Manual, permeated with his philosophy of battle, filled with keen insights, is one of the greatest works ever written on chess. Filled with analyzed games by the great players. A single-volume library that will profit almost any chess player, beginner or master. 308 diagrams. xli x 349pp.

20640-8 Paperbound $2.75

The Master Book of Mathematical Recreations, Fred Schuh. In opinion of many the finest work ever prepared on mathematical puzzles, stunts, recreations; exhaustively thorough explanations of mathematics involved, analysis of effects, citation of puzzles and games. Mathematics involved is elementary. Translated by F. Göbel. 194 figures. xxiv + 430pp.

22134-2 Paperbound $3.00

Mathematics, Magic and Mystery, Martin Gardner. Puzzle editor for Scientific American explains mathematics behind various mystifying tricks: card tricks, stage "mind reading," coin and match tricks, counting out games, geometric dissections, etc. Probability sets, theory of numbers clearly explained. Also provides more than 400 tricks, guaranteed to work, that you can do. 135 illustrations. xii + 176pp.

20338-2 Paperbound $1.50

ALPHABETS AND ORNAMENTS, Ernst Lehner. Well-known pictorial source for decorative alphabets, script examples, cartouches, frames, decorative title pages, calligraphic initials, borders, similar material. 14th to 19th century, mostly European. Useful in almost any graphic arts designing, varied styles. 750 illustrations. 256pp. 7 x 10.   21905-4 Paperbound $4.00

PAINTING: A CREATIVE APPROACH, Norman Colquhoun. For the beginner simple guide provides an instructive approach to painting: major stumbling blocks for beginner; overcoming them, technical points; paints and pigments; oil painting; watercolor and other media and color. New section on "plastic" paints. Glossary. Formerly *Paint Your Own Pictures.* 221pp.   22000-1 Paperbound $1.75

THE ENJOYMENT AND USE OF COLOR, Walter Sargent. Explanation of the relations between colors themselves and between colors in nature and art, including hundreds of little-known facts about color values, intensities, effects of high and low illumination, complementary colors. Many practical hints for painters, references to great masters. 7 color plates, 29 illustrations. x + 274pp.
20944-X Paperbound $2.75

THE NOTEBOOKS OF LEONARDO DA VINCI, compiled and edited by Jean Paul Richter. 1566 extracts from original manuscripts reveal the full range of Leonardo's versatile genius: all his writings on painting, sculpture, architecture, anatomy, astronomy, geography, topography, physiology, mining, music, etc., in both Italian and English, with 186 plates of manuscript pages and more than 500 additional drawings. Includes studies for the Last Supper, the lost Sforza monument, and other works. Total of xlvii + 866pp. 7⅞ x 10¾.
22572-0, 22573-9 Two volumes, Paperbound $10.00

MONTGOMERY WARD CATALOGUE OF 1895. Tea gowns, yards of flannel and pillow-case lace, stereoscopes, books of gospel hymns, the New Improved Singer Sewing Machine, side saddles, milk skimmers, straight-edged razors, high-button shoes, spittoons, and on and on . . . listing some 25,000 items, practically all illustrated. Essential to the shoppers of the 1890's, it is our truest record of the spirit of the period. Unaltered reprint of Issue No. 57, Spring and Summer 1895. Introduction by Boris Emmet. Innumerable illustrations. xiii + 624pp. 8½ x 11⅝.
22377-9 Paperbound $6.95

THE CRYSTAL PALACE EXHIBITION ILLUSTRATED CATALOGUE (LONDON, 1851). One of the wonders of the modern world—the Crystal Palace Exhibition in which all the nations of the civilized world exhibited their achievements in the arts and sciences—presented in an equally important illustrated catalogue. More than 1700 items pictured with accompanying text—ceramics, textiles, cast-iron work, carpets, pianos, sleds, razors, wall-papers, billiard tables, beehives, silverware and hundreds of other artifacts—represent the focal point of Victorian culture in the Western World. Probably the largest collection of Victorian decorative art ever assembled—indispensable for antiquarians and designers. Unabridged republication of the Art-Journal Catalogue of the Great Exhibition of 1851, with all terminal essays. New introduction by John Gloag, F.S.A. xxxiv + 426pp. 9 x 12.
22503-8 Paperbound $4.50

How to Know the Wild Flowers, Mrs. William Starr Dana. This is the classical book of American wildflowers (of the Eastern and Central United States), used by hundreds of thousands. Covers over 500 species, arranged in extremely easy to use color and season groups. Full descriptions, much plant lore. This Dover edition is the fullest ever compiled, with tables of nomenclature changes. 174 full-page plates by M. Satterlee. xii + 418pp. 20332-8 Paperbound $2.75

Our Plant Friends and Foes, William Atherton DuPuy. History, economic importance, essential botanical information and peculiarities of 25 common forms of plant life are provided in this book in an entertaining and charming style. Covers food plants (potatoes, apples, beans, wheat, almonds, bananas, etc.), flowers (lily, tulip, etc.), trees (pine, oak, elm, etc.), weeds, poisonous mushrooms and vines, gourds, citrus fruits, cotton, the cactus family, and much more. 108 illustrations. xiv + 290pp. 22272-1 Paperbound $2.50

How to Know the Ferns, Frances T. Parsons. Classic survey of Eastern and Central ferns, arranged according to clear, simple identification key. Excellent introduction to greatly neglected nature area. 57 illustrations and 42 plates. xvi + 215pp. 20740-4 Paperbound $2.00

Manual of the Trees of North America, Charles S. Sargent. America's foremost dendrologist provides the definitive coverage of North American trees and tree-like shrubs. 717 species fully described and illustrated: exact distribution, down to township; full botanical description; economic importance; description of subspecies and races; habitat, growth data; similar material. Necessary to every serious student of tree-life. Nomenclature revised to present. Over 100 locating keys. 783 illustrations. lii + 934pp. 20277-1, 20278-X Two volumes, Paperbound $6.00

Our Northern Shrubs, Harriet L. Keeler. Fine non-technical reference work identifying more than 225 important shrubs of Eastern and Central United States and Canada. Full text covering botanical description, habitat, plant lore, is paralleled with 205 full-page photographs of flowering or fruiting plants. Nomenclature revised by Edward G. Voss. One of few works concerned with shrubs. 205 plates, 35 drawings. xxviii + 521pp. 21989-5 Paperbound $3.75

The Mushroom Handbook, Louis C. C. Krieger. Still the best popular handbook: full descriptions of 259 species, cross references to another 200. Extremely thorough text enables you to identify, know all about any mushroom you are likely to meet in eastern and central U. S. A.: habitat, luminescence, poisonous qualities, use, folklore, etc. 32 color plates show over 50 mushrooms, also 126 other illustrations. Finding keys. vii + 560pp. 21861-9 Paperbound $3.95

Handbook of Birds of Eastern North America, Frank M. Chapman. Still much the best single-volume guide to the birds of Eastern and Central United States. Very full coverage of 675 species, with descriptions, life habits, distribution, similar data. All descriptions keyed to two-page color chart. With this single volume the average birdwatcher needs no other books. 1931 revised edition. 195 illustrations. xxxvi + 581pp. 21489-3 Paperbound $5.00

JOHANN SEBASTIAN BACH, Philipp Spitta. One of the great classics of musicology, this definitive analysis of Bach's music (and life) has never been surpassed. Lucid, nontechnical analyses of hundreds of pieces (30 pages devoted to St. Matthew Passion, 26 to B Minor Mass). Also includes major analysis of 18th-century music. 450 musical examples. 40-page musical supplement. Total of xx + 1799pp.
(EUK) 22278-0, 22279-9 Two volumes, Clothbound $15.00

MOZART AND HIS PIANO CONCERTOS, Cuthbert Girdlestone. The only full-length study of an important area of Mozart's creativity. Provides detailed analyses of all 23 concertos, traces inspirational sources. 417 musical examples. Second edition. 509pp. (USO) 21271-8 Paperbound $3.50

THE PERFECT WAGNERITE: A COMMENTARY ON THE NIBLUNG'S RING, George Bernard Shaw. Brilliant and still relevant criticism in remarkable essays on Wagner's Ring cycle, Shaw's ideas on political and social ideology behind the plots, role of Leitmotifs, vocal requisites, etc. Prefaces. xxi + 136pp.
21707-8 Paperbound $1.50

DON GIOVANNI, W. A. Mozart. Complete libretto, modern English translation; biographies of composer and librettist; accounts of early performances and critical reaction. Lavishly illustrated. All the material you need to understand and appreciate this great work. Dover Opera Guide and Libretto Series; translated and introduced by Ellen Bleiler. 92 illustrations. 209pp.
21134-7 Paperbound $1.50

HIGH FIDELITY SYSTEMS: A LAYMAN'S GUIDE, Roy F. Allison. All the basic information you need for setting up your own audio system: high fidelity and stereo record players, tape records, F.M. Connections, adjusting tone arm, cartridge, checking needle alignment, positioning speakers, phasing speakers, adjusting hums, trouble-shooting, maintenance, and similar topics. Enlarged 1965 edition. More than 50 charts, diagrams, photos. iv + 91pp. 21514-8 Paperbound $1.25

REPRODUCTION OF SOUND, Edgar Villchur. Thorough coverage for laymen of high fidelity systems, reproducing systems in general, needles, amplifiers, preamps, loudspeakers, feedback, explaining physical background. "A rare talent for making technicalities vividly comprehensible," R. Darrell, *High Fidelity*. 69 figures. iv + 92pp. 21515-6 Paperbound $1.00

HEAR ME TALKIN' TO YA: THE STORY OF JAZZ AS TOLD BY THE MEN WHO MADE IT, Nat Shapiro and Nat Hentoff. Louis Armstrong, Fats Waller, Jo Jones, Clarence Williams, Billy Holiday, Duke Ellington, Jelly Roll Morton and dozens of other jazz greats tell how it was in Chicago's South Side, New Orleans, depression Harlem and the modern West Coast as jazz was born and grew. xvi + 429pp.
21726-4 Paperbound $2.50

FABLES OF AESOP, translated by Sir Roger L'Estrange. A reproduction of the very rare 1931 Paris edition; a selection of the most interesting fables, together with 50 imaginative drawings by Alexander Calder. v + 128pp. 6½x9¼.
21780-9 Paperbound $1.25

VISUAL ILLUSIONS: THEIR CAUSES, CHARACTERISTICS, AND APPLICATIONS, Matthew Luckiesh. Thorough description and discussion of optical illusion, geometric and perspective, particularly; size and shape distortions, illusions of color, of motion; natural illusions; use of illusion in art and magic, industry, etc. Most useful today with op art, also for classical art. Scores of effects illustrated. Introduction by William H. Ittleson. 100 illustrations. xxi + 252pp.
21530-X Paperbound $2.00

A HANDBOOK OF ANATOMY FOR ART STUDENTS, Arthur Thomson. Thorough, virtually exhaustive coverage of skeletal structure, musculature, etc. Full text, supplemented by anatomical diagrams and drawings and by photographs of undraped figures. Unique in its comparison of male and female forms, pointing out differences of contour, texture, form. 211 figures, 40 drawings, 86 photographs. xx + 459pp. 5⅜ x 8⅜.
21163-0 Paperbound $3.50

150 MASTERPIECES OF DRAWING, Selected by Anthony Toney. Full page reproductions of drawings from the early 16th to the end of the 18th century, all beautifully reproduced: Rembrandt, Michelangelo, Dürer, Fragonard, Urs, Graf, Wouwerman, many others. First-rate browsing book, model book for artists. xviii + 150pp. 8⅜ x 11¼.
21032-4 Paperbound $2.50

THE LATER WORK OF AUBREY BEARDSLEY, Aubrey Beardsley. Exotic, erotic, ironic masterpieces in full maturity: Comedy Ballet, Venus and Tannhauser, Pierrot, Lysistrata, Rape of the Lock, Savoy material, Ali Baba, Volpone, etc. This material revolutionized the art world, and is still powerful, fresh, brilliant. With *The Early Work,* all Beardsley's finest work. 174 plates, 2 in color. xiv + 176pp. 8⅛ x 11.
21817-1 Paperbound $3.00

DRAWINGS OF REMBRANDT, Rembrandt van Rijn. Complete reproduction of fabulously rare edition by Lippmann and Hofstede de Groot, completely reedited, updated, improved by Prof. Seymour Slive, Fogg Museum. Portraits, Biblical sketches, landscapes, Oriental types, nudes, episodes from classical mythology—All Rembrandt's fertile genius. Also selection of drawings by his pupils and followers. "Stunning volumes," *Saturday Review.* 550 illustrations. lxxviii + 552pp. 9⅛ x 12¼.
21485-0, 21486-9 Two volumes, Paperbound $10.00

THE DISASTERS OF WAR, Francisco Goya. One of the masterpieces of Western civilization—83 etchings that record Goya's shattering, bitter reaction to the Napoleonic war that swept through Spain after the insurrection of 1808 and to war in general. Reprint of the first edition, with three additional plates from Boston's Museum of Fine Arts. All plates facsimile size. Introduction by Philip Hofer, Fogg Museum. v + 97pp. 9⅜ x 8¼.
21872-4 Paperbound $2.00

GRAPHIC WORKS OF ODILON REDON. Largest collection of Redon's graphic works ever assembled: 172 lithographs, 28 etchings and engravings, 9 drawings. These include some of his most famous works. All the plates from *Odilon Redon: oeuvre graphique complet,* plus additional plates. New introduction and caption translations by Alfred Werner. 209 illustrations. xxvii + 209pp. 9⅛ x 12¼.
21966-8 Paperbound $4.00

THE ARCHITECTURE OF COUNTRY HOUSES, Andrew J. Downing. Together with Vaux's *Villas and Cottages* this is the basic book for Hudson River Gothic architecture of the middle Victorian period. Full, sound discussions of general aspects of housing, architecture, style, decoration, furnishing, together with scores of detailed house plans, illustrations of specific buildings, accompanied by full text. Perhaps the most influential single American architectural book. 1850 edition. Introduction by J. Stewart Johnson. 321 figures, 34 architectural designs. xvi + 560pp.
22003-6 Paperbound $4.00

LOST EXAMPLES OF COLONIAL ARCHITECTURE, John Mead Howells. Full-page photographs of buildings that have disappeared or been so altered as to be denatured, including many designed by major early American architects. 245 plates. xvii + 248pp. 7⅞ x 10¾. 21143-6 Paperbound $3.50

DOMESTIC ARCHITECTURE OF THE AMERICAN COLONIES AND OF THE EARLY REPUBLIC, Fiske Kimball. Foremost architect and restorer of Williamsburg and Monticello covers nearly 200 homes between 1620-1825. Architectural details, construction, style features, special fixtures, floor plans, etc. Generally considered finest work in its area. 219 illustrations of houses, doorways, windows, capital mantels. xx + 314pp. 7⅞ x 10¾. 21743-4 Paperbound $4.00

EARLY AMERICAN ROOMS: 1650-1858, edited by Russell Hawes Kettell. Tour of 12 rooms, each representative of a different era in American history and each furnished, decorated, designed and occupied in the style of the era. 72 plans and elevations, 8-page color section, etc., show fabrics, wall papers, arrangements, etc. Full descriptive text. xvii + 200pp. of text. 8⅜ x 11¼.
21633-0 Paperbound $5.00

THE FITZWILLIAM VIRGINAL BOOK, edited by J. Fuller Maitland and W. B. Squire. Full modern printing of famous early 17th-century ms. volume of 300 works by Morley, Byrd, Bull, Gibbons, etc. For piano or other modern keyboard instrument; easy to read format. xxxvi + 938pp. 8⅜ x 11.
21068-5, 21069-3 Two volumes, Paperbound $10.00

KEYBOARD MUSIC, Johann Sebastian Bach. Bach Gesellschaft edition. A rich selection of Bach's masterpieces for the harpsichord: the six English Suites, six French Suites, the six Partitas (Clavierübung part I), the Goldberg Variations (Clavierübung part IV), the fifteen Two-Part Inventions and the fifteen Three-Part Sinfonias. Clearly reproduced on large sheets with ample margins; eminently playable. vi + 312pp. 8⅛ x 11. 22360-4 Paperbound $5.00

THE MUSIC OF BACH: AN INTRODUCTION, Charles Sanford Terry. A fine, nontechnical introduction to Bach's music, both instrumental and vocal. Covers organ music, chamber music, passion music, other types. Analyzes themes, developments, innovations. x + 114pp. 21075-8 Paperbound $1.25

BEETHOVEN AND HIS NINE SYMPHONIES, Sir George Grove. Noted British musicologist provides best history, analysis, commentary on symphonies. Very thorough, rigorously accurate; necessary to both advanced student and amateur music lover. 436 musical passages. vii + 407 pp. 20334-4 Paperbound $2.75

DESIGN BY ACCIDENT; A BOOK OF "ACCIDENTAL EFFECTS" FOR ARTISTS AND DESIGNERS, James F. O'Brien. Create your own unique, striking, imaginative effects by "controlled accident" interaction of materials: paints and lacquers, oil and water based paints, splatter, crackling materials, shatter, similar items. Everything you do will be different; first book on this limitless art, so useful to both fine artist and commercial artist. Full instructions. 192 plates showing "accidents," 8 in color. viii + 215pp. 8⅜ x 11¼. 21942-9 Paperbound $3.50

THE BOOK OF SIGNS, Rudolf Koch. Famed German type designer draws 493 beautiful symbols: religious, mystical, alchemical, imperial, property marks, runes, etc. Remarkable fusion of traditional and modern. Good for suggestions of timelessness, smartness, modernity. Text. vi + 104pp. 6⅛ x 9¼. 20162-7 Paperbound $1.25

HISTORY OF INDIAN AND INDONESIAN ART, Ananda K. Coomaraswamy. An unabridged republication of one of the finest books by a great scholar in Eastern art. Rich in descriptive material, history, social backgrounds; Sunga reliefs, Rajput paintings, Gupta temples, Burmese frescoes, textiles, jewelry, sculpture, etc. 400 photos. viii + 423pp. 6⅜ x 9¾. 21436-2 Paperbound $4.00

PRIMITIVE ART, Franz Boas. America's foremost anthropologist surveys textiles, ceramics, woodcarving, basketry, metalwork, etc.; patterns, technology, creation of symbols, style origins. All areas of world, but very full on Northwest Coast Indians. More than 350 illustrations of baskets, boxes, totem poles, weapons, etc. 378 pp. 20025-6 Paperbound $3.00

THE GENTLEMAN AND CABINET MAKER'S DIRECTOR, Thomas Chippendale. Full reprint (third edition, 1762) of most influential furniture book of all time, by master cabinetmaker. 200 plates, illustrating chairs, sofas, mirrors, tables, cabinets, plus 24 photographs of surviving pieces. Biographical introduction by N. Bienenstock. vi + 249pp. 9⅞ x 12¾. 21601-2 Paperbound $4.00

AMERICAN ANTIQUE FURNITURE, Edgar G. Miller, Jr. The basic coverage of all American furniture before 1840. Individual chapters cover type of furniture—clocks, tables, sideboards, etc.—chronologically, with inexhaustible wealth of data. More than 2100 photographs, all identified, commented on. Essential to all early American collectors. Introduction by H. E. Keyes. vi + 1106pp. 7⅞ x 10¾. 21599-7, 21600-4 Two volumes, Paperbound $11.00

PENNSYLVANIA DUTCH AMERICAN FOLK ART, Henry J. Kauffman. 279 photos, 28 drawings of tulipware, Fraktur script, painted tinware, toys, flowered furniture, quilts, samplers, hex signs, house interiors, etc. Full descriptive text. Excellent for tourist, rewarding for designer, collector. Map. 146pp. 7⅞ x 10¾. 21205-X Paperbound $2.50

EARLY NEW ENGLAND GRAVESTONE RUBBINGS, Edmund V. Gillon, Jr. 43 photographs, 226 carefully reproduced rubbings show heavily symbolic, sometimes macabre early gravestones, up to early 19th century. Remarkable early American primitive art, occasionally strikingly beautiful; always powerful. Text. xxvi + 207pp. 8⅜ x 11¼. 21380-3 Paperbound $3.50

AGAINST THE GRAIN (A REBOURS), Joris K. Huysmans. Filled with weird images, evidences of a bizarre imagination, exotic experiments with hallucinatory drugs, rich tastes and smells and the diversions of its sybarite hero Duc Jean des Esseintes, this classic novel pushed 19th-century literary decadence to its limits. Full unabridged edition. Do not confuse this with abridged editions generally sold. Introduction by Havelock Ellis. xlix + 206pp. 22190-3 Paperbound $2.00

VARIORUM SHAKESPEARE: HAMLET. Edited by Horace H. Furness; a landmark of American scholarship. Exhaustive footnotes and appendices treat all doubtful words and phrases, as well as suggested critical emendations throughout the play's history. First volume contains editor's own text, collated with all Quartos and Folios. Second volume contains full first Quarto, translations of Shakespeare's sources (Belleforest, and Saxo Grammaticus), Der Bestrafte Brudermord, and many essays on critical and historical points of interest by major authorities of past and present. Includes details of staging and costuming over the years. By far the best edition available for serious students of Shakespeare. Total of xx + 905pp. 21004-9, 21005-7, 2 volumes, Paperbound $7.00

A LIFE OF WILLIAM SHAKESPEARE, Sir Sidney Lee. This is the standard life of Shakespeare, summarizing everything known about Shakespeare and his plays. Incredibly rich in material, broad in coverage, clear and judicious, it has served thousands as the best introduction to Shakespeare. 1931 edition. 9 plates. xxix + 792pp. (USO) 21967-4 Paperbound $3.75

MASTERS OF THE DRAMA, John Gassner. Most comprehensive history of the drama in print, covering every tradition from Greeks to modern Europe and America, including India, Far East, etc. Covers more than 800 dramatists, 2000 plays, with biographical material, plot summaries, theatre history, criticism, etc. "Best of its kind in English," *New Republic.* 77 illustrations. xxii + 890pp. 20100-7 Clothbound $8.50

THE EVOLUTION OF THE ENGLISH LANGUAGE, George McKnight. The growth of English, from the 14th century to the present. Unusual, non-technical account presents basic information in very interesting form: sound shifts, change in grammar and syntax, vocabulary growth, similar topics. Abundantly illustrated with quotations. Formerly *Modern English in the Making.* xii + 590pp. 21932-1 Paperbound $3.50

AN ETYMOLOGICAL DICTIONARY OF MODERN ENGLISH, Ernest Weekley. Fullest, richest work of its sort, by foremost British lexicographer. Detailed word histories, including many colloquial and archaic words; extensive quotations. Do not confuse this with the Concise Etymological Dictionary, which is much abridged. Total of xxvii + 830pp. 6½ x 9¼. 21873-2, 21874-0 Two volumes, Paperbound $6.00

FLATLAND: A ROMANCE OF MANY DIMENSIONS, E. A. Abbott. Classic of science-fiction explores ramifications of life in a two-dimensional world, and what happens when a three-dimensional being intrudes. Amusing reading, but also useful as introduction to thought about hyperspace. Introduction by Banesh Hoffmann. 16 illustrations. xx + 103pp. 20001-9 Paperbound $1.00

AMERICAN FOOD AND GAME FISHES, David S. Jordan and Barton W. Evermann. Definitive source of information, detailed and accurate enough to enable the sportsman and nature lover to identify conclusively some 1,000 species and sub-species of North American fish, sought for food or sport. Coverage of range, physiology, habits, life history, food value. Best methods of capture, interest to the angler, advice on bait, fly-fishing, etc. 338 drawings and photographs. 1 + 574pp. 6⅝ x 9⅜.

22383-1 Paperbound $4.50

THE FROG BOOK, Mary C. Dickerson. Complete with extensive finding keys, over 300 photographs, and an introduction to the general biology of frogs and toads, this is the classic non-technical study of Northeastern and Central species. 58 species; 290 photographs and 16 color plates. xvii + 253pp.

21973-9 Paperbound $4.00

THE MOTH BOOK: A GUIDE TO THE MOTHS OF NORTH AMERICA, William J. Holland. Classical study, eagerly sought after and used for the past 60 years. Clear identification manual to more than 2,000 different moths, largest manual in existence. General information about moths, capturing, mounting, classifying, etc., followed by species by species descriptions. 263 illustrations plus 48 color plates show almost every species, full size. 1968 edition, preface, nomenclature changes by A. E. Brower. xxiv + 479pp. of text. 6½ x 9¼.

21948-8 Paperbound $5.00

THE SEA-BEACH AT EBB-TIDE, Augusta Foote Arnold. Interested amateur can identify hundreds of marine plants and animals on coasts of North America; marine algae; seaweeds; squids; hermit crabs; horse shoe crabs; shrimps; corals; sea anemones; etc. Species descriptions cover: structure; food; reproductive cycle; size; shape; color; habitat; etc. Over 600 drawings. 85 plates. xii + 490pp.

21949-6 Paperbound $3.50

COMMON BIRD SONGS, Donald J. Borror. 33⅓ 12-inch record presents songs of 60 important birds of the eastern United States. A thorough, serious record which provides several examples for each bird, showing different types of song, individual variations, etc. Inestimable identification aid for birdwatcher. 32-page booklet gives text about birds and songs, with illustration for each bird.

21829-5 Record, book, album. Monaural. $2.75

FADS AND FALLACIES IN THE NAME OF SCIENCE, Martin Gardner. Fair, witty appraisal of cranks and quacks of science: Atlantis, Lemuria, hollow earth, flat earth, Velikovsky, orgone energy, Dianetics, flying saucers, Bridey Murphy, food fads, medical fads, perpetual motion, etc. Formerly "In the Name of Science." x + 363pp.

20394-8 Paperbound $2.00

HOAXES, Curtis D. MacDougall. Exhaustive, unbelievably rich account of great hoaxes: Locke's moon hoax, Shakespearean forgeries, sea serpents, Loch Ness monster, Cardiff giant, John Wilkes Booth's mummy, Disumbrationist school of art, dozens more; also journalism, psychology of hoaxing. 54 illustrations. xi + 338pp.

20465-0 Paperbound $2.75

MATHEMATICAL PUZZLES FOR BEGINNERS AND ENTHUSIASTS, Geoffrey Mott-Smith. 189 puzzles from easy to difficult—involving arithmetic, logic, algebra, properties of digits, probability, etc.—for enjoyment and mental stimulus. Explanation of mathematical principles behind the puzzles. 135 illustrations. viii + 248pp.
20198-8 Paperbound $1.75

PAPER FOLDING FOR BEGINNERS, William D. Murray and Francis J. Rigney. Easiest book on the market, clearest instructions on making interesting, beautiful origami. Sail boats, cups, roosters, frogs that move legs, bonbon boxes, standing birds, etc. 40 projects; more than 275 diagrams and photographs. 94pp.
20713-7 Paperbound $1.00

TRICKS AND GAMES ON THE POOL TABLE, Fred Herrmann. 79 tricks and games—some solitaires, some for two or more players, some competitive games—to entertain you between formal games. Mystifying shots and throws, unusual caroms, tricks involving such props as cork, coins, a hat, etc. Formerly *Fun on the Pool Table*. 77 figures. 95pp.
21814-7 Paperbound $1.00

HAND SHADOWS TO BE THROWN UPON THE WALL: A SERIES OF NOVEL AND AMUSING FIGURES FORMED BY THE HAND, Henry Bursill. Delightful picturebook from great-grandfather's day shows how to make 18 different hand shadows: a bird that flies, duck that quacks, dog that wags his tail, camel, goose, deer, boy, turtle, etc. Only book of its sort. vi + 33pp. 6½ x 9¼. 21779-5 Paperbound $1.00

WHITTLING AND WOODCARVING, E. J. Tangerman. 18th printing of best book on market. "If you can cut a potato you can carve" toys and puzzles, chains, chessmen, caricatures, masks, frames, woodcut blocks, surface patterns, much more. Information on tools, woods, techniques. Also goes into serious wood sculpture from Middle Ages to present, East and West. 464 photos, figures. x + 293pp.
20965-2 Paperbound $2.00

HISTORY OF PHILOSOPHY, Julián Marias. Possibly the clearest, most easily followed, best planned, most useful one-volume history of philosophy on the market; neither skimpy nor overfull. Full details on system of every major philosopher and dozens of less important thinkers from pre-Socratics up to Existentialism and later. Strong on many European figures usually omitted. Has gone through dozens of editions in Europe. 1966 edition, translated by Stanley Appelbaum and Clarence Strowbridge. xviii + 505pp. 21739-6 Paperbound $3.00

YOGA: A SCIENTIFIC EVALUATION, Kovoor T. Behanan. Scientific but non-technical study of physiological results of yoga exercises; done under auspices of Yale U. Relations to Indian thought, to psychoanalysis, etc. 16 photos. xxiii + 270pp.
20505-3 Paperbound $2.50

Prices subject to change without notice.
Available at your book dealer or write for free catalogue to Dept. GI, Dover Publications, Inc., 180 Varick St., N. Y., N. Y. 10014. Dover publishes more than 150 books each year on science, elementary and advanced mathematics, biology, music, art, literary history, social sciences and other areas.